DRAGON AGE
ORIGINS

PRIMA Official Game Guide

Written by

Mike Searle

Prima Games
An Imprint of Random House, Inc.

3000 Lava Ridge Court, Suite 100
Roseville, CA 95661
www.primagames.com

Product Manager: Todd Manning
Associate Product Manager: Sean Scheuble
Copyeditor: Asha Johnson
Design & Layout: Bryan Neff & Jody Seltzer
Manufacturing: Suzanne Goodwin & Stephanie Sanchez
eProduction: Cody Zimmer

ISBN: 978-0-7615-6142-2
Library of Congress Catalog Card Number: 2008943353
Printed in the United States of America

09 10 11 12 GG 10 9 8 7 6 5 4 3 2 1

Special Thanks

Prima would like to thank Mark Darrah, Mike Laidlaw, Matt Atwood, Chris Corfe, Erik Einsiedel, Kevin Loh, Adriana Lopez, Fernando Melo, and the entire BioWare *Dragon Age: Origins* development team for all of their tireless support and assistance in making this guide (and such a fantastic game!). Prima would also like to thank Paul "Sedd" Giacomotto, Brandon "Wasup" Olafsson, and Asha "Copyeditor Extraordinaire" Johnson for all of their support throughout the project.

About the Author

Mike Searle remembers playing the simple yet addictive *Missile Command*, and the days of Atari *Adventure*, where your square hero could end up in a hollow dragon stomach. His desire to play computer games into the wee hours of the morning really took hold when his parents made him play outside, instead of on the console, so the first chance he got, he bought a PC to play the *Ultima* series, *Doom*, and countless others. Mike started working with Prima Games in 2002 and has written more than 30 strategy guides, including *Lord of the Rings Online: Shadows of Angmar*, *Jurassic Park: Operation Genesis*, *Dark Messiah: Might and Magic*, *Pirates of the Burning Sea*, and several guides in the Tom Clancy's *Ghost Recon* and *Splinter Cell* series. He can't wait for thought technology, so game controls can catch up with his brain and stop all that needless in-game dying. At least, that's what he keeps telling himself about his FPS kill ratio.

We want to hear from you! E-mail comments and feedback to msearle@primagames.com.

Dragon Age Origins

PRIMA Official Game Guide

Contents

primagames.com

How to Use This Guide

Throw out your notions of unicorns and esteemed elves: *Dragon Age™: Origins* is about to enlighten you with a new take on dark fantasy. Every sight and sound, companion and creature, immerses you in the magical world of Ferelden, where you choose the honorable, harrowing, and epic path of the Grey Warden on a nearly impossible task of ending the teeming and terrible Blight. With a game so massive, you need a guide bulging with advice, stats, maps, and expert tips to master your adventuring experience, and it's all here...

Basics

Learn how to navigate the world of Ferelden and explore important game terms such as experience points, leveling, races, classes, skills, talents, and more. Suit up for combat with some fundamental strategy and tips.

Character Generation

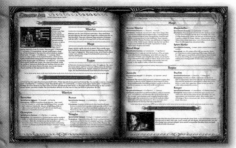

Which race and class do you want to play? Unlike other games, your choice affects your origin story and how you interact with certain characters throughout Ferelden. Your choices regarding race, class, specializations, attributes, and origin story will make a big impact on the events in your individual game experience.

Classes

A Grey Warden can train in the talents of a warrior or rogue, or tap into the spells of a mage. All three can decimate darkspawn; it's just about whether you want to have fun smashing hurlocks with sword and shield, slashing out of the shadows with twin daggers, or torching possessed corpses with fireballs. Master all three with our special leveling class guides that include specs on a tank, melee DPS, ranged DPS, healer, mage DPS, scout, and more.

The Party

Chaotic free-for-alls will see you to an early grave. We show you the dos and don'ts of party combat, and the best engagement strategies for solo creatures, big mobs, boss fights, and ambushes. Comb through this chapter and you'll master group dynamics, threat, combat roles, engagement strategies, and tactics, among many other things.

Companions

Get into the minds of your trusted companions, from what specialization they can teach you to what gifts will get them into bed with you. Find out how to unlock them all for your party and how to make each the ultimate combatant.

Companions covered include: Alistair (warrior), Dog (Mabari pet, war dog), Leliana (rogue), Loghain Mac Tir (warrior after the Landsmeet only), Morrigan (mage), Oghren (warrior), Shale (golem available via downloadable content), Sten (warrior), Wynne (mage), and Zevran Arainai (rogue).

Supporting Cast

Will Queen Anora rule? Can First Enchanter Irving survive the perils befallen the Circle Tower? Should Lord Harrowmont be trusted? Ferelden isn't just about you and your companions; hundreds of lively NPCs interact with you and shape this age's future. Take a peek in this chapter at the most important faces around the land.

How to Use This Guide

Basics ~ Character Generation ~ Classes ~ The Party ~ Companions ~ Supporting Cast ~ Equipment ~ Bestiary ~ Walkthroughs ~ Side Quests ~ Random Encounters ~ Achievements/Trophies

Equipment

You may walk naked through flames to touch the Urn of Sacred Ashes, the holiest of artifacts in Ferelden, but your birthday suit won't get you far anywhere else. Gear up with complete specs on all weapons, armor, accessories, gifts, runes, crafting and usable items, and more.

The Bestiary

In the dankest tombs you'll slice through the rotting flesh of walking corpses, or tame a dragon on the loftiest mountaintop. Monsters thrive in Ferelden and threaten the kingdom, and it's not just the darkspawn invasion you have to worry about. From abominations to hurlocks to werewolves, uncover all the secrets of these nasty denizens in our complete Bestiary chapter.

Walkthroughs

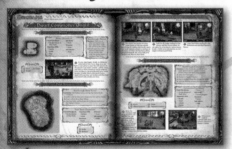

Everything you wanted to know about your Grey Warden quests is here, including super-detailed maps, runthroughs of every major encounter, boss strategies, treasure locations, and even where to find Denerim's hidden assassins' guild.

Side Quests

To score some extra loot or uncover more of Ferelden's secrets, seek out the side quests spread across the land from Denerim to Orzammar, many hosted by special organizations such as the Mages' Collective, Blackstone Irregulars, and Chanter's Board. This chapter preps you on quest locations, destinations, rewards, and a quick walkthrough of how to complete each quest.

Random Encounters

Traveling across the countryside isn't always a stroll in the park. You may encounter a stray demon, hurlock, or werewolf. Our handy random encounter runthrough lists all the encounters, triggers, important plot points, and strategy tips on how to come out on top.

Achievements & Trophies

Who doesn't have fun collecting titles? Get the scoop on the storyline unlocks, plus what you have to do to achieve combat titles (inflict 250 damage in a single hit, yet?), and other fun feats such as romancing companions, mastering spell blocks, setting traps, and exploring every area of the game.

primagames.com

Dragon Age: Origins

Basics

Welcome to the world of *Dragon Age: Origins*! Our job is to keep you alive and to maximize your playing experience, so with that in mind, we're going to run through the basics in this chapter. Master the essential concepts and ground rules first, then add layers of strategy and tactics to your favorite class and Ferelden will be safe from darkspawn until the last Grey Warden takes his final breath.

NOTE

Stop! We know you're anxious to dive right into tips and hints on gameplay, but you should really read your *Dragon Age: Origins* manual first. The manual provides a great introduction to the basics. Come back here when you understand the game controls, user interface, menu options, etc. We won't go anywhere.

Key Terms

Here are some of the key terms that the game and this guide will use while discussing various play styles and tactics. Familiarize yourself with these so you're up on the lingo.

AoE: "Area of Effect." A talent or spell that affects a radius, not just a single target. AoE spells and attacks damage multiple targets at once and can help greatly against large groups of enemies. Keep in mind that you may hit multiple targets, but you also may draw additional threat and possibly nullify existing effects on the targeted enemies.

NOTE

Depending on your game's difficulty setting, AoE spells and attacks from your party may or may not cause friendly fire damage to your party. We assume friendly fire damage as a factor in our guide's strategy.

Armor Stat: Reduces damage done to a character from physical attacks. A weapon's armor penetration score directly counteracts the opponent's armor rating.

Attack Stat: Increases the likelihood of successfully landing physical attacks.

Buff: A talent or spell that delivers a positive effect for a prolonged time.

Camp: To remain in one spot in order to kill a specific NPC or monster, or trigger a certain event.

Cold Resistance: Measures resistance or vulnerability to cold-based attacks against the character. Cold damage is reduced (if green) or increased (if red) by this percentage.

Constitution: Constitution represents health and resilience. Higher constitution directly increases the amount of damage a character can take before falling on the battlefield.

Crit: Short for "critical chance" or "critical strike chance."

Cunning: Cunning determines how well a character learns and reasons. Most skills, such as Herbalism or Combat Tactics, require a quick mind to master—and an observant eye can more easily find weaknesses in enemy armor. Rogues benefit most from this statistic, as many of their class talents and special attacks rely on subtlety or reading the target, not raw strength.

Damage Stat: The equipped weapon's potential damage against an unarmored opponent, adjusted for the speed of the weapon.

Debuff: A skill or ability that delivers a negative effect for a prolonged time.

Defense Stat: Increases the chance of dodging or parrying physical attacks.

Dexterity: Dexterity is the measure of agility, reflexes, and balance. Higher dexterity improves a character's chances to hit, makes the character more likely to dodge incoming blows, and contributes to the damage dealt by piercing weapons such as bows or crossbows. Archery and dual-weapon fighting styles demand high dexterity to master, making this attribute a favorite for rogues.

DLC: Abbreviation for "downloadable content."

DoT: "Damage over time." Talents or spells that deal initial damage and then additional damage every few seconds for a set amount of time.

DPS: "Damage per second." A stat that factors in the speed and power of a weapon to gauge its average damage every second. DPS is also used as a generic reference to damage and dealing damage.

DPSer: A character whose primary role in the group is to deal damage.

Electrical Resistance: Measures resistance or vulnerability to electricity-based attacks against the character. Electrical damage is reduced (if green) or increased (if red) by this percentage.

Fatigue: Wearing armor causes fatigue, which is a percentage increase of the basic mana or stamina cost to activate a spell or talent.

Follower: A companion who travels with you on your quests. There can only be four people in your party at one time: the main (player) character, and up to three followers. The rest stay back at party camp and level as you level.

Fire Resistance: Measures resistance or vulnerability to fire-based attacks against the character. Fire damage is reduced (if green) or increased (if red) by this percentage.

Health: How much damage a character can sustain without falling in battle. A character whose health is completely depleted may sustain an injury.

Key Terms - Experience and Leveling

Basics ~ Character Generation ~ Classes ~ The Party ~ Companions ~ Supporting Cast ~ Equipment ~ Bestiary ~ Walkthroughs ~ Side Quests ~ Random Encounters ~ Achievements/Trophies

Injuries: When one of your party members has fallen in combat, he or she may sustain a serious injury. These injuries cause penalties that can only be cured with an injury kit or certain high-level spells.

Loot: Another term for treasure or rewards.

Magic: In the general sense, it's energies beyond the material world. In a stat sense, magic is the measure of a character's natural affinity for the arcane. This attribute is crucial for mages, because it directly increases a character's spellpower score, which determines the potency of all spells. The magic attribute also determines how effective potions, poultices, and salves are for all classes.

Mana: Magical energy consumed when casting spells.

Mental Resistance: Measures the character's ability to resist mental effects such as a sleep spell.

Mob: A group of enemies.

Nature Resistance: Measures resistance or vulnerability to nature-based attacks against the character (like poisoning). Nature damage is reduced (if green) or increased (if red) by this percentage.

NPC: "Non-player Character." Any character in the game not in your party.

Party: A group of characters who adventure together, limited to four. You can always return to party camp to recruit other followers.

PC: Abbreviation for "Player Character."

Physical Resistance: Measures the character's ability to resist physical effects such as being knocked down.

Pull: To draw an enemy toward you, usually to avoid engaging other enemies as well.

Root: To freeze an enemy in place with a special talent or spell.

Spawn Point: A spot where the game generates a mob.

Spirit Resistance: Measures resistance or vulnerability to spirit-based attacks against the character. Spirit damage is reduced (if green) or increased (if red) by this percentage.

Stamina: Physical energy consumed when using talents or skills.

Strength: Strength measures a character's physical prowess, and directly affects the damage a character deals in physical combat. It also contributes to the accuracy of melee attacks. High strength is essential for warriors, in particular if they wish to wield two-handed weapons, and is nearly as critical for rogues.

Tank: A character who draws threat well and holds a mob's attention. An "off-tank" is a secondary character who holds the attention of the second strongest mob. Warriors generally tank the best, especially due to their "Weapon and Shield" talent tree.

Taunt: To enrage a mob so that it focuses its threat and attention on you.

Threat: Sometimes referred to as "aggro" or "aggression" of a mob. The game ranks threat based on your actions, generally revolving around the amount of damage or healing you do. The more threat you generate, the greater the chance that a monster will attack you.

Willpower: Willpower represents a character's determination and mental fortitude. With high willpower, mages can cast more spells thanks to a deeper mana pool. For warriors and rogues, willpower grants more stamina for combat techniques and special attacks.

Wipe: A term for the death of everyone in the party.

XP: Stands for "experience points." Experience marks your progress as you level up in your class.

Experience and Leveling

Everyone loves to level. The thrill of watching your warrior, mage, or rogue gain levels and earn new skills comes second only to slaying darkspawn in a heroic last stand. Your followers also gain experience (XP) at roughly the same rate that you do. Don't worry about the followers you leave back at camp; they progress at the same rate as the rest of your party. If you leave Morrigan home at level 8, travel around on a few adventures, and return at level 12, she won't still be stuck at level 8. She will most likely be level 12, or close to it.

Each class gains levels at the same rate and gains the same points to spend, although each class will spend those points very differently.

For every level you gain, you gain three attribute points and one talent point. Mages and warriors get one skill point every three levels, while rogues get a skill point every two levels. You gain specialization points at levels 7 and 14. Points are precious, so spend them wisely. Don't be caught with a level 20 warrior who has only the first couple of abilities in many chains. His or her contribution to the party will be limited and you don't get a second chance at spending these points.

primagames.com

Level Chart

Character Level	XP Required to Gain a Level	Total Current XP	Character Level	XP Required to Gain a Level	Total Current XP
1	2,000	0	11	7,000	49500
2	2,500	4,500	12	7,500	57,000
3	3,000	7,500	13	8,000	65,000
4	3,500	11,000	14	8,500	73,500
5	4,000	15,000	15	9,000	82,500
6	4,500	19,500	16	9,500	92,000
7	5,000	24,500	17	10,000	102,000
8	5,500	30,000	18	10,500	112,500
9	6,000	36,000	19	11,000	123,500
10	6,500	42,500	20	11,500	135,000

Your Health

Obviously, staying alive is your first priority whenever you're out adventuring. Those with high constitution scores will have more health, and thus take a lot more hits before perishing. Warriors generally want high health to stay on their feet, despite being the punching bags for enemies. Rogues may have high health, depending on how much they like to mix it up in combat. Mages usually concentrate on less-physical attributes and may be more fragile in the midst of swinging swords and smashing clubs.

Your best ally against loss of health is a healer. A simple Heal spell can do wonders, and Group Heal keeps everyone up in a fight. Health poultices serve the same purpose. Judge how much damage you've taken and use the appropriate level poultice: lesser if your health is still above 50 percent, regular if your health dips below 50 percent, and greater when you're knocking on death's door.

If you do drop in battle, you won't lose the game unless all your party members fall as well. In a fight where you fall, but your allies manage to win the day, you will climb back to your feet after the battle. Check this character for wounds. A persistent injury penalizes you according to the following chart:

Injuries

Injury Name	Penalty To	Injury Name	Penalty To
Bleeding	Health Regeneration	Deafened	Defense
Broken Bone	Dexterity	Gaping Wound	Maximum Health
Concussion	Magic	Head Trauma	Willpower
Coughing Blood	Fatigue	Open Wound	Nature Resistance
Cracked Skull	Cunning	Torn Jugular	Constitution
Crushed Arm	Damage	Wrenched Limb	Attack Speed
Damaged Eye	Attack		

Your Health - Races and Classes

Basics ~ Character Generation ~ Classes ~ The Party ~ Companions ~ Supporting Cast ~ Equipment ~ Bestiary ~ Walkthroughs ~ Side Quests ~ Random Encounters ~ Achievements/Trophies

Races and Classes

During character creation, you will choose a race and class (see the Character Generation chapter for complete details). Not only do race and class give different bonuses to different stats, but they also determine which of the six origin stories you play through at the start of the game. Here are brief descriptions of the three races and three classes.

Races

Human: The most numerous, yet the most divided of all the races. Only four times have they ever united under a single cause, the last being centuries ago. Religion and the Chantry play a large part in human society. It distinguishes them culturally from elves and dwarves more than anything else. Humans can be warriors, rogues, or mages.

Elf: Once enslaved by humans, most elves have all but lost their culture, scrounging an impoverished living in the slums of human cities. Only the nomadic Dalish tribes still cling to their traditions, living by the bow and the rule of their old gods as they roam the ancient forests, welcome nowhere else. Elves can be warriors, rogues, or mages.

Dwarf: Rigidly bound by caste and tradition, the dwarves have been waging a losing war for generations, trying to protect the last stronghold of their once-vast underground empire from the darkspawn. Dwarves are very tough and have a high resistance to all forms of magic, thus preventing them from becoming mages.

Classes

Warrior: Warriors are powerful fighters, focusing on melee and ranged weapons to deal with their foes. They can withstand and deliver a great deal of punishment, and have a strong understanding of tactics and strategy.

Mage: As dangerous as it is potent, magic is a curse for those lacking the will to wield it. Malevolent spirits that wish to enter the world of the living are drawn to mages like beacons, putting the mage and everyone nearby in constant danger. Because of this, mages lead lives of isolation, locked away from the world they threaten.

Rogue: Rogues are skilled adventurers who come from all walks of life. All rogues possess some skill in picking locks and spotting traps, making them valuable assets to any party. Tactically, they are not ideal front-line fighters, but if rogues can circle around behind their target, they can backstab to devastating effect.

primagames.com

Skills, Talents, and Specializations

Besides attributes, your skills, talents or spells, and specializations define who you are and how effective you'll be in combat. Each level you will get more powerful as you add points in these areas. For more specifics on skills, talents, and specializations, see the Classes chapter.

Skills

All three classes share the same skill tree, which includes the following: Coercion, Stealing, Trap-Making, Survival, Herbalism, Poison-Making, Combat Training, and Combat Tactics. Whether you want to focus on persuading others, detecting enemies, crafting health potions, or learning combat tricks, among other things, you gain skill points every three levels (or one every two levels if you're a rogue) to explore the skill tree. Because you will probably be able to fill out only two skills, put some serious thought into which ones you want to master.

Talents and Spells

Talents are specific to warriors and rogues; mages learn spells. They are the bread and butter abilities of your class, and you will rely on them more than anything else in combat. You can't take everything, so choose talents/spells that fit into your play style. For example, a warrior can dual-wield weapons, fight with weapon and shield, rely on a two-handed weapon, or strike at range with bow and arrows. All talents don't complement each other; choose a path and stick with it to unlock the better talents/spells at higher levels.

Talents require stamina to use, while spells cost mana. While stamina and mana do regenerate, leaving certain talents/spells activated will not allow a character to fully regenerate their stamina or mana. This could prevent the character from using other talents/spells when starting a new encounter, so always keep an eye on your stamina/mana levels before and during a battle.

Specializations

You unlock your first specialization at level 7 and your second at level 14. Specialization gives special bonuses to your attributes and opens up a new chain of talents unique to the specialization. They are very powerful abilities in the right situation. Specializations for a warrior include berserker, templar, champion, and reaver. Mage specializations include spirit healer, shapeshifter, arcane warrior, and blood mage. Rogue specializations are ranger, bard, duelist, and assassin.

Items

Gear can be just as important as your abilities. The proper items can vault you from normal soldier to tweaked-out death-dealer. Concentrate on grabbing items that beef up your PC's main stats, and leave the other items to help out your followers' classes. A mage, for example, might want a little extra magic and willpower from an item, but doesn't care about strength.

Combat

Parties work the best when you know the strengths, and limitations, of each class and plan your battle strategies accordingly. Each class falls into one of these general categories: tank (warrior), DPS (rogue, mage, warrior), and healer (mage). As the name implies, a tank's job is to draw fire and take as much damage as possible to protect everyone else. This job is executed right at the front lines of a battle and generally never shifts from that location. Tanks have talents that force enemies to attack them for a short time and high damage potential to keep the threat on them instead of their companions. Warriors make the best tanks.

Skills, Talents, and Specializations - Combat

Basics ~ Character Generation ~ Classes ~ The Party ~ Companions ~ Supporting Cast ~ Equipment ~ Bestiary ~ Walkthroughs ~ Side Quests ~ Random Encounters ~ Achievements/Trophies

The second category, DPS (damage per second), is divided into two subcategories: ranged and melee. Ranged DPS characters do lots of damage, and as a result, generate large amounts of threat and will die very quickly when their ranged advantage is lost and there's no tank protection nearby. Ideally a ranged DPS character should stay in the back of a battle and let the tanks and melee DPS protect them. On the other hand, a melee DPS character is usually more durable and can try to let the tanks take the hits while they kill off enemies directly. Rogues make great DPS characters, as do mages focusing on damage and area-effect spells. Though you generally need your warrior to be a tank, a warrior studying the art of two-handed weapons can deal major DPS.

The third category, the healer, is a key support role in any group. Your job as a healer is to keep everyone alive. For a healer to be successful, they need to stay as far away from the enemies as possible and avoid getting hit. A healer that can do this, while keeping his fellow companions healthy, is one of the most effective members of a group. Just watch your mana and always keep lyrium potions available in case you need to gain extra mana for a crucial healing spell. Mages concentrating on Creation magic prove to be strong healers.

Mobs

Mobs are the monsters and people you fight to complete quests and gain experience. There are two types of mobs: normal and ranked. Normal mobs have a white name above their heads. One of your party members is generally more than a match for a normal monster. Ranked creatures have different colored names. Opponents with yellow names are more challenging and aggressive than average. Orange names represent extremely powerful enemies capable of threatening a full party of adventurers by themselves.

Threat

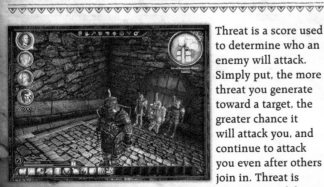

Threat is a score used to determine who an enemy will attack. Simply put, the more threat you generate toward a target, the greater chance it will attack you, and continue to attack you even after others join in. Threat is commonly generated by damage, so the more DPS you deliver, the greater the chance you'll attract attention. Luckily, there

are some threat-reduction talents in the game that allow you to shed the threat temporarily (or possibly completely if you don't jump back into the fight).

Tanks are the ones most concerned with threat. They generate the most threat with special talents (sometimes known as "taunts") that automatically attract an enemy's attention and lock it on the tank. It's generally good form to allow your tank to build up threat by leaving him alone for the first few seconds of the combat as he launches a few damaging attacks. If you have an off-tank, he should be ready to grab threat on any target that breaks free of the main tank or any extra monsters that show up unannounced.

When monsters in *Dragon Age: Origins* perceive a character, they evaluate a base level of threat. That base level is influenced by the class of armor the character is wearing at the moment of perception. Robes generate extremely low levels of threat, while massive armors generate the most. Outfit your party accordingly. You can control the initial flow of threat by distributing gear based on each companion's role. An off-tank, for example, can avoid catching most of the damage by wearing heavy or medium armor, while the main tank wears massive.

TIP

Some specific creatures target casters. Rogues and shrieks are the key monsters with this behavior, and they may beeline for a healer at the start of a fight.

A DPS specialist has a relatively simple task: Don't out-damage the tank so much that you gain threat. It might take some practice in the group, but you'll eventually learn how many talents you can launch, and how frequently, to maximize your damage without surpassing the tank's ability to hold threat. The biggest mistake to avoid as a DPSer is to start attacking too soon in the fight; allow the tank a few seconds to build up threat before you dive in.

Tactics

All characters have tactic slots that can be programmed with automatic behavior based on a certain set of circumstances. You may want to slot an action that says to use a health poultice if your health drops below 50 percent, or an action that dictates you defend the healer whenever they are attacked by an enemy. You can always pause combat and manually choose your characters' action; however, at some point in every fight, your characters will act on their own, and tactics allow them to function effectively based on the skill sets of their fellow party members. For more on tactics, see the "Tactics" section of the Party chapter.

primagames.com

The Map

Of course, you can't really get anywhere unless you understand the map. The map will be used for so many things, but the most useful aspect is to view plot helpers. Unless the option is turned off on the Options menu, plot helper arrows display on the map at various key quest points, especially where you have to go for the next leg of your journey. On the map, a yellow dot represents a party member, and a yellow dot with a circle around it represents the PC. A blue dot signifies an ally, and a red dot equals an enemy. Plot givers show up as white exclamation points, and key locations display as white Xs. A vendor or store looks like a house, and map exit points appear as white-rimmed black circles.

The Codex

The codex is the parchment icon on your Journal screen and is the repository of important knowledge uncovered in the game. It falls into 10 categories: creatures, items, magic and religion, culture and history, characters, books and songs, notes, spell combinations, control, and quest-related. As you unlock a codex entry, a scroll appears in the appropriate category and you can read volumes on the various topics. Check it regularly for information, especially if you need a clue to a puzzling mystery on your current quest.

Decisions, Decisions

You may be a warrior who can slice through steel, a mage who melts rock with fiery blasts, or a rogue who slips through deadly traps like an alley cat through trash on a midnight stroll, but all your hack-and-slashing and dungeon finesse means little if you don't pay attention to the storyline. At almost every turn in *Dragon Age: Origins*, you will be tested with dilemmas that tempt and torture your moral fiber. Will you help a friend escape a terrible predicament placed on him by your respected peers? Can you choose to save one race and damn another? Shall you choose personal renown or ultimate sacrifice? Immerse yourself in the tales of Ferelden and you shall be rewarded.

Now if you're anxious to enter this magical land, it's time to take that crucial first step on the path to glory: character creation.

The Map - Gender and Race

Basics ~ Character Generation ~ Classes ~ The Party ~ Companions ~ Supporting Cast ~ Equipment ~ Bestiary ~ Walkthroughs ~ Side Quests ~ Random Encounters ~ Achievements/Trophies

Character Generation

Entering the world of Ferelden is unlike any experience you've had before in a role-playing game. There are six distinct origin stories to play through at the start of the game, separately determined by your race/class combination and your background choice. Sure, it's important to pick your race and class based on the bonuses to your attributes and the talents/spells you'll eventually learn, but it's more important to select a race/class/background that fits your play style. Do you want to bust heads in the middle of countless darkspawn? A warrior is the class for you. Love to sling powerful spells? Mage sounds like a good bet. Hungry for extra treasure and the protection of shadowy corners? A rogue fits your needs. Of course, you can make several characters if you like, though you want to be happy in your adventures with them.

Gender and Race

First you choose your gender, male or female; it's cosmetic and has only small bearings on the story regarding romantic encounters. Next, select one of three races: human, elf, or dwarf. Humans and elves have access to all three classes. Dwarves do not have access to the mage class. Humans gain versatility across the board: +1 strength, +1 dexterity, +1 magic, and +1 cunning. Elf bonuses tend toward the mage class: +2 magic, +2 willpower. Dwarves give fighting bonuses: +1 strength, +1 dexterity, +2 constitution. Due to their natural magic resistance (and reason a dwarf cannot be a mage), a dwarf character gains a 10 percent chance to resist hostile magic. If you enjoy maximizing your character's stats from the start, pick a race whose bonuses complement your career choice.

NOTE

Your race selection has a major impact on your origin story. Elves and dwarves have access to two unique origin stories; humans have access to one unique origin story, and they share the mage origin story with the elves. Race also affects how certain NPCs interact with you in the game.

Warrior

Attributes	Human	Elf	Dwarf	Class Bonuses	Human Bonuses	Elf Bonuses	Dwarf Bonuses
Strength	15	14	15	4	1	—	1
Dexterity	14	13	14	3	1	—	1
Willpower	10	12	10	—	—	2	—
Magic	11	12	10	—	1	2	—
Cunning	11	10	10	—	1	—	—
Constitution	13	13	15	3	—	—	2

Mage

Attributes	Human	Elf	Dwarf	Class Bonuses	Human Bonuses	Elf Bonuses	Dwarf Bonuses
Strength	11	10	—	—	1	—	1
Dexterity	11	10	—	—	1	—	1
Willpower	14	16	—	4	—	2	—
Magic	16	17	—	5	1	2	—
Cunning	12	11	—	1	1	—	—
Constitution	10	10	—	—	—	—	2

Rogue

Attributes	Human	Elf	Dwarf	Class Bonuses	Human Bonuses	Elf Bonuses	Dwarf Bonuses
Strength	11	10	11	—	1	—	1
Dexterity	15	14	15	4	1	—	1
Willpower	12	14	12	2	—	2	—
Magic	11	12	10	—	1	2	—
Cunning	15	14	14	4	1	—	—
Constitution	10	10	12	—	—	—	2

primagames.com

Class

As previously mentioned, choose your class for the whole game experience, not simply for the small attribute bonuses during character creation. However, it's good to know what you're getting when you launch a career. Warriors gain +4 strength, +3 dexterity, +3 constitution. As you would expect, these are all nice bonuses to the stats that aid you most in combat. Mages gain +5 magic, +4 willpower, +1 cunning. These bonuses scale in favor of the mental faculties, which proves highly useful when casting spells and storing larger amounts of mana. Rogues gain +4 dexterity, +2 willpower, +4 cunning. With nimble hands and tongue, the rogue particularly needs the attribute bonuses to dexterity and cunning. Here is a brief rundown on the three classes; for more, turn to the Classes chapter and flip to the appropriate class section.

Warrior

Warriors use the best weapons and armor. They need them, because they are the ones who charge into combat and take on foes face first. They can withstand large amounts of damage, and can inflict even more damage back on their adversaries.

Mage

Mages tap into spells instead of talents. These spells range from healing to devastating AoE blasts to defensive buffs for the mage's companions. They tend to stay out of hand-to-hand combat and cast their magic from behind the protection of warriors and rogues.

Rogue

In between warriors and mages in terms of toughness, the rogue has many talents (and we're not just talking about the abilities you unlock level by level!). Rogues can learn to pick locks, spot traps, and deal lethal backstabs from behind enemy targets.

Specializations

Each class has four specializations associated with it. These specializations grant stat bonuses too. For example, a warrior champion gains +2 willpower, +1 cunning; a mage shapeshifter gains +2 constitution, +1 armor; and a rogue duelist gains +2 dexterity, +1 damage. However, because you don't open your first specialization until level 7, it shouldn't hold much bearing on stat considerations. Rather, you may consider the specialization abilities on what sort of character you'd like to play down the line. For more information on specializations, their abilities, and the methods to obtain them, see the appropriate class sections of the Classes chapter.

Warrior

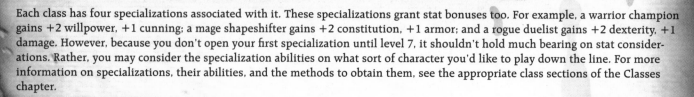

Berserker

Specialization bonuses: +2 strength, +10 health

Description: The first berserkers were dwarves. They would sacrifice finesse for a dark rage that increased their strength and resilience. Eventually, dwarves taught these skills to others, and now berserkers can be found among all races. They are renowned as terrifying adversaries.

Champion

Specialization bonuses: +2 willpower, +1 cunning

Description: The champion is a veteran warrior and a confident leader in battle. Possessing skill at arms impressive enough to inspire allies, the champion can also intimidate and demoralize foes. These are the heroes you find commanding an army, or plunging headlong into danger, somehow making it look easy.

Reaver

Specialization bonuses: +1 constitution, +5 physical resistance

Description: Demonic spirits teach more than blood magic. Reavers terrorize their enemies, feast upon the souls of their slain opponents to heal their own flesh, and can unleash a blood frenzy that makes them more powerful as they come nearer to their own deaths.

Templar

Specialization bonuses: +2 magic, +3 mental resistance

Description: Mages who refuse the Circle's control become apostates and live in fear of a templar's powers—the ability to dispel and resist magic. As servants of the Chantry, the templars have been the most effective means of controlling the spread and use of arcane power for centuries.

Class - Appearance and Voice

Basics ~ **Character Generation** ~ Classes ~ The Party ~ Companions ~ Supporting Cast ~ Equipment ~ Bestiary ~ Walkthroughs ~ Side Quests ~ Random Encounters ~ Achievements/Trophies

Mage

Arcane Warrior

Specialization bonuses: +1 dexterity, +5 attack

Description: Among the ancient elves, there were mages who trained their magical arts to augment their martial prowess. They channeled magical power through their weapons and bodies, becoming terrors on the battlefield. Most consider these skills lost forever, but they may still linger in forgotten corners of the world. Arcane warriors may learn to use their magic score to satisfy the strength requirement to equip higher-level weapons and armor.

Blood Mage

Specialization bonuses: +2 constitution, +2 spellpower

Description: Every mage can feel the dark lure of blood magic. Originally learned from demons, these dark rites tap into the power of blood, converting life into mana and giving the mage command over the minds of others. Such power comes with a price, though; a blood mage must sacrifice his own health, or the health of allies, to fuel these abilities.

Shapeshifter

Specialization bonuses: +2 constitution, +1 armor

Description: Rumors speak of barbarians who hold secrets of transforming the body into the form of animals. The Circle of Magi denies such rumors, but this rare art survives in the forgotten corners of Thedas. Mastery of their bodies allows shapeshifters some protection, even in human form, making them durable opponents and staunch allies.

Spirit Healer

Specialization bonuses: +2 magic, minor combat health regeneration

Description: Not all entities of the Fade are demonic. Many are benevolent entities consisting of life energy, which can be called upon to mend flesh and heal disease. Spirit healers focus on channeling the energies granted by these spirits, making them indispensable members of a party of adventurers.

Rogue

Assassin

Specialization bonuses: +2 dexterity, +2.5 percent critical chance

Description: The assassin finds any notion of fairness a quaint ideal that has no place in combat. Poisons are their weapon of choice, as are crippling strikes that inflict persistent wounds on their foes. As killers, assassins are a marvel of stealth and efficiency.

Bard

Specialization bonuses: +2 willpower, +1 cunning

Description: Bards follow an Orlesian tradition, acting as assassins, spies, and saboteurs, and following other secretive pursuits in the constant, and sometimes petty, struggles between nobles. Having taken the minstrel's art to new levels, bards are skilled performers and master manipulators. They can inspire their allies or dishearten their foes through song and tale.

Duelist

Specialization bonuses: +2 dexterity, +1 damage/hit

Description: Duelists are deadly combatants who prefer to fight in light armors and strike with light, but precise attacks. Experienced duelists have preternatural reflexes that allow them to evade their opponents' clumsy blows, as well as strike with remarkable precision.

Ranger

Specialization bonuses: +1 constitution, +5 nature resistance

Description: Rangers have an affinity for open country and wilderness, but as independent scouts and militia, they are opportunists, not stewards of nature. They exploit every advantage of their environment, and can lure wild beasts to attack their foes.

Appearance and Voice

You can skip this step if you want to go with the preset look, or you can customize facial features such as skin, hair, eyes, nose, mouth, jaw and cheeks, and neck and ears. You can also change your portrait and pick from several voice profiles that affect how you speak (mostly in battle situations).

Attributes

After you choose your race and class, the next screen allows you to spend five points on attributes. See the appropriate sections in the Classes chapter for details on the best paths for leveling your character. The following sections run down how each attribute most affects your character:

Strength

- Increases damage from all weapons except crossbows, bows, and staves
- Increases attack score in melee combat by 0.5 for each point purchased
- Prerequisite for most weapon talents and higher-level armor and weapons
- Contributes to physical resistance and intimidation

Dexterity

- Increases attack score in melee combat by 0.5 for each point purchased
- Increases attack score in ranged combat by 1 for each point purchased
- Increases defense by 1 for each point purchased
- Increases damage from piercing weapons (bows and crossbows)
- Prerequisite for some weapon talents
- Contributes to physical resistance

Willpower

- Increases mana or stamina by 5 for each point purchased
- Contributes to mental resistance

Magic

- Increases spellpower by 1 for each point purchased
- Increases effectiveness of potions, poultices, and salves
- Prerequisite for higher-level staves and many spells
- Contributes to mental resistance

Cunning

- Increases effectiveness of rogue talents
- Prerequisite for many skills
- Contributes to armor penetration, mental resistance, and persuasion

Constitution

- Increases health by 5 for each point purchased
- Contributes to physical resistance

Some important concepts, though, apply to all characters. First, as tempting as it is to spread out your attribute points and stay decent at everything, it's a better idea to focus on your key stats and raise them first. Look at your talents/spells and see what attribute thresholds you need to unlock them. Make sure you get those attributes up before you throw points anywhere else.

Second, familiarize yourself with all stats and don't discount anything. For example, all classes need stamina (energy for physical actions) or mana (energy for magical actions). Willpower raises stamina or mana, which means even a warrior needs to build up willpower to some degree. Again, concentrate on your core attributes first, but when you find a point or two free, it might be a good idea to throw it to willpower as a warrior or rogue, or maybe constitution as a mage—you get the idea.

Third, some of the "secondary" stats take a bit of research to understand, and they may have some bearing on your class choice. Resistances reduce specific types of damage and effects. For example, physical resistance helps prevent you from being knocked down. Armor protects a character from physical attacks when you get hit, while your defense score increases the chance of dodging or parrying those attacks completely. Your attack score indicates the chance of landing physical attacks. Your damage score shows your equipped weapon's potential damage against an unarmored opponent, adjusted for the speed of the weapon. For example, let's say you have a rogue with damage scores on two weapons: 12.7 and 7.9. The rogue will deal 12.7 damage with his main hand and 7.9 damage with his off-hand to an unarmored opponent. Critical chance increases your ability to deal maximum damage on a success. Don't forget about your fatigue stat, especially if you play a warrior with all that heavy armor. Fatigue causes an increase in the basic stamina or mana cost to activate a spell or talent. For example, a fatigue rating of 8.5 means that your stamina/mana cost for all abilities goes up by 8.5 percent.

Attributes – Origin Stories

Basics ~ **Character Generation** ~ Classes ~ The Party ~ Companions ~ Supporting Cast ~ Equipment ~ Bestiary ~ Walkthroughs ~ Side Quests ~ Random Encounters ~ Achievements/Trophies

Origin Stories

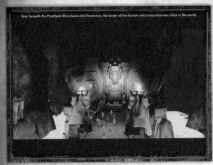

Deep beneath the Frostback Mountains sits Orzammar, the larger of two known remaining dwarven cities in the world.

Dragon Age: Origins immerses you in an epic story that will sweep you from one end of Ferelden to the other. Unlike other games where you concentrate on your character's stats and class abilities, in *Dragon Age: Origins*, the story has a huge impact on your game experience. Many of you will put story above all else, and that's fine. If so, you can work backward on your character generation and choose the origin story you would like to play first and select the correct race and class for that origin. Read through these six backgrounds to see which is the best origin story for you.

Dwarf Commoner

Deep beneath the Frostback Mountains sits Orzammar, largest and proudest of the two remaining dwarven cities. Once the seat of an underground empire, Orzammar now stands alone, cut off from the world by the darkspawn, still clinging to the memory of its former glory. Below the vast statues and gilded halls where the noble families play at politics, the lower castes live in their shadows, scurrying to serve like their ancestors before them. Below that...is you. You are casteless, the dirty secret staining Orzammar's perfect society, forced, along with your sister, to sell your services to the crime lord, Beraht. To the rest of Orzammar, you are proof that the casteless deserve their fate; but you know that you do what you must—the same as everyone—just to survive.

Dwarf Noble

Deep beneath the Frostback Mountains sits Orzammar, the larger of two known remaining dwarven cities. Orzammar was once the seat of a major empire connected by tunnels, called Deep Roads, which stretched thousands of miles. The city now stands alone, cut off from the rest of the dwarven ancestral lands by the darkspawn incursion. Secure in Orzammar's impregnable construction, the dwarven noble houses continue their centuries-old power struggles. Assassination and blackmail are commonplace, but the appearance of honor is paramount. You are the second child of King Endrin of House Aeducan—the ninth Aeducan ruler elected by the Noble Assembly. You grew up in a world rife with political intrigue and have struggled against brothers and cousins for honor and prestige. Today, a feast celebrates your first military commission, the opening move toward real power in the ever-changing game of dwarven politics.

City Elf

Denerim is the largest city and capital of Ferelden. Long ago, the elves lived as slaves to humans, and although they have been free for many generations now, they are far from equals. Here they live in a walled-off community known as the Alienage, working as servants and laborers when they can. Despite these hardships, Denerim's elves are a strong people who take pride in their close community. This is the only world you've ever known...until now.

Dalish Elf

You were born amid the Dalish elves: noble wanderers who refuse to join the society of humans who subjugated their homeland so long ago. The Dalish travel the land in tightly knit clans, struggling to maintain their half-forgotten lore in a human world that fears and despises them. You spend your time hunting with your clan-mate Tamlen in the forests, and as is sometimes the case, your quarry is not always the local wildlife...

Human Noble

For generations, your family, the Couslands, has stewarded the lands of Highever, earning the loyalty of your people with justice and temperance. When your country was occupied by the Orlesian Empire, your father and grandfather served the embattled kings of your land. Today, your elder brother takes up House Cousland's banner in service to the Crown—not against the men of Orlais, but against the bestial darkspawn rising in the south.

Magi

On a cliff overlooking the dark waters of Lake Calenhad stands the tower fortress that is home to the Circle of Magi. This tower is the only place in Ferelden where mages may study their art among others of their kind. Within the high stone walls, the Circle practices its magic and trains apprentices in the proper use of their powers. But the Circle Tower is as much a prison as a refuge; the ever-vigilant templars of the Chantry watch over all mages, constantly alert for any sign of corruption. This gilded cage is the only world you know. Found to be sensitive to magic at a young age, you were torn from your family and grafted here as an apprentice. Now, that apprenticeship is nearly over and all that remains is the final test: the Harrowing.

primagames.com

The Classes

Grey Wardens come from all backgrounds in life, hone many skills, and walk the path of adventure as one of the three classes: warrior, mage, or rogue. As a warrior, you brave the heart of the enemy vanguard with solid steel in hand and sturdy shield to guard your side. You punish foes with great two-handed weapons or a spray of arrow volleys. A mage draws mana from the Fade and bombards enemies with freezing blasts or blistering infernos. Their command of ranged attacks and unparalleled healing powers triumphs on the battlefield. Hiding in the shadows, a rogue slays the unwary from behind and detects dungeon traps with a discerning eye. His thieving hands collect more coin than a covetous merchant. The possibilities are nearly endless no matter which class you choose.

Leveling

Each level you gain three attribute points and one talent point. Attribute points can be spent on raising your core stats, while talent points can purchase new talents (for warriors and rogues) or new spells (for mages). Mages and warriors get one skill point every three levels, while rogues get a skill point every two levels. You gain specialization points at levels 7 and 14. Using this information, spend your points wisely. Don't be caught with a level 20 warrior who has only the first couple of abilities in many chains. His contribution to the party will be limited, and you don't get a second chance at spending these points.

Experience Gain

Level	XP Required to Gain a Level	Total Current XP
1	2,000	0
2	2,500	4,500
3	3,000	7,500
4	3,500	11,000
5	4,000	15,000
6	4,500	19,500
7	5,000	24,500
8	5,500	30,000
9	6,000	36,000
10	6,500	42,500

Level	XP Required to Gain a Level	Total Current XP
11	7,000	49,500
12	7,500	57,000
13	8,000	65,000
14	8,500	73,500
15	9,000	82,500
16	9,500	92,000
17	10,000	102,000
18	10,500	112,500
19	11,000	123,500
20	11,500	135,000

Skills

All characters have the same set of skills from which to choose (not to be confused with talents/spells, which are unique for each class). Skills range from Coercion, which influences how well you can change NPCs' points of view, to Combat Tactics, which gives you more options in battles. For the most part, your cunning score and level affect how far you can advance in a skill. Raise your cunning to 16 to access all of Coercion, Stealing, Survival, and Combat Tactics. Gaining level 10 opens up all of Trap-Making, Herbalism, and Poison-Making. Combat Training has no restrictions on it.

When you purchase a skill for the first time, you start at its basic effect, and with each upgrade your ability grows and more options open up. For example, a basic

Leveling - Skills

Basics ~ Character Generation ~ **Classes** ~ The Party ~ Companions ~ Supporting Cast ~ Equipment ~ Bestiary ~ Walkthroughs ~ Side Quests ~ Random Encounters ~ Achievements/Trophies

herbalist can create lesser potions, while an improved herbalist can craft normal lyrium and health potions, and so on up the ladder to expert and master Herbalism. With only one skill point available every three levels (or every two if you're a rogue), make your skill choices count. At most you will max out two skills during the game, or you may master one skill and dabble in two others. To aid in choosing the best skill for you, here are some pointers on the various skills.

NOTE

For a list of all crafting items, ingredients, and recipes, see the "Crafting" section of the Items chapter.

Coercion

You can access more game areas and information, bargain for better rewards or terms, and talk your way out of many difficult situations with this skill. While all classes can intimidate effectively (given a high Coercion skill and some fearsome party members), warriors can use their strength score (instead of cunning) to gain a bit of an edge in their intimidations. For the origin stories, you will likely gain the most use out of this skill. When in doubt, put your points into Coercion.

Stealing

You are quick enough to pilfer small items from others, whether friendly or hostile, as long as they aren't too alert. Of course, you may have to pay the price later on. For example, if you steal from the Dalish elves in the Dalish camp, even if you don't get caught in the act, they may hunt you down elsewhere later on and try to make you pay for your crimes.

Trap-Making

Learning how to make traps and lures seems like a good rogue talent, but this can be very useful for mages as well. If you're not all that strong in melee range, use traps and lure to draw in enemies and deal some preliminary damage while you cast a barrage of spells from afar. Even a warrior can throw a trap around once in a while to root extra enemies.

Survival

The more you advance this skill, the better chance you have to detect creatures on your mini-map before they surprise you. This skill can save you from more than a few ambushes. In addition, you get a bonus to nature resistance, which protects against poison attacks of all sorts as well as spells such as Stonefist, Walking Bomb, and Virulent Walking Bomb.

Herbalism

Gain the ability to make your own potions, poultices, and salves with this skill. These are invaluable items, and you'll always want at least five in any difficult fight. In addition, if you plan on concentrating your mage in the Spirit school (healing and such), this can be a nice complement. Even if your mage is concentrated on dealing damage or shapeshifting, you can use this skill to make up for your lack of healing spells.

Poison-Making

The ability to create poison works best for rogues, or warriors who want a boost to damage. You need at least one point in Poison-Making to use poisons and bombs. If you already have a character crafting health and mana potions, it never hurts to increase your offensive potential as well, even with just one level in this skill.

Combat Training

The more points you spend here, the better your warrior or rogue performs in combat. It's essential for any melee-based character. Warriors and rogues gain access to new weapon talents, stamina regeneration, attack bonuses, and armor upgrades. Mages can take more damage before it interrupts spellcasting.

Combat Tactics

Spending points in this skill gives you more tactics slots for your character. If you make all the decisions yourself, it's not that important; if you allow the characters to act on their own in combat, it's a big deal to get more tactics slots to better customize your combat strategies.

NPC Crafters

Not every skill has to come from you or your party; some NPCs around the world can craft items for you. You might not have the hands of a blacksmith, for example, but if you gather drake scales and speak to the proprietors of Wade's Emporium in the Denerim Market District, they will craft you some superior armor. Look for help wherever you go.

NOTE

See the Side Quests and Random Encounters chapters for details on side quests that lead to special items.

Choosing Skills

You should choose skills that appeal to your play style, and vary it from character to character. A rogue may enjoy Stealing, while Herbalism is a natural fit for a mage because it benefits from a high magic score. That doesn't mean a rogue shouldn't learn Herbalism or a mage learn Stealing. Always have fun with your choices, and remember that between the four characters in your party, you can play with most, if not all, of the game's skills.

However, some skills influence the game directly more than others. Coercion is the most important. It can give you options in dialogue to avoid fights or open up new areas of play that you might not have received without the art of persuasion. Survival points out enemies on the mini-map, which helps you set up your party for fights and avoid deadly ambushes. Herbalism creates super-useful health poultices and lyrium potions. Unless you want to spend tons of coin on these essential accessories, invest in Herbalism to make your own at a fraction of the price. Without a doubt, Combat Training is vital to warriors and rogues who want access to top-tier weapon talents.

Warrior Combat Skills

A high-level warrior primarily concerned about combat and dialogue options with eight points to spend on skills might lean toward this configuration:

- Combat Training +4
- Coercion +3
- Survival +1

Mage Healing and Persuasion Skills

A high-level mage primarily concerned about dialogue options and healing and with eight points to spend on skills might lean toward this configuration:

- Coercion +4
- Herbalism +4

Rogue Combat Skills

A high-level rogue primarily concerned about combat and Poison-Making with ten points to spend on skills might lean toward this configuration:

- Combat Training +4
- Poison-Making +4
- Stealing +1
- Coercion +1

The biggest choice of your early career comes next: Do you play a warrior, mage, or rogue? All experiences are rewarding, but each is unique in the origin story you play through, the talents/spells you gain, and your ability to affect combat and influence the storyline. Which type of Grey Warden will you be?

Skills ~ The Warrior

Basics ~ Character Generation ~ **Classes** ~ The Party ~ Companions ~ Supporting Cast ~ Equipment ~ Bestiary ~ Walkthroughs ~ Side Quests ~ Random Encounters ~ Achievements/Trophies

The Warrior

You are sword and shield, retribution and resilience, the cornerstone of a party's defenses. A warrior charges into the heat of battle to engage the enemy first, simultaneously damaging foes while protecting fellow party members from harm. When danger surrounds you, a warrior heeds the call to battle despite cut, gash, or threat of an early grave. Without a warrior, the party cannot survive long against sterner threats.

If you like to jump straight into battle and be the first to draw blood, the warrior class is for you. Superb weapons and armor are at your disposal, and melee damage comes as naturally to you as forging to a blacksmith. You will be the toughest party member, and you may have to save those less armored than yourself from time to time, but it's all part of the responsibility of the hero with the biggest muscles.

To deal with darkspawn and other deadly perils, the warrior has access to better weapons and armor than the mage or the rogue. You may be fortunate enough to find these fine weapons and pieces of armor in shops, or you may discover them as loot hidden in dungeon treasure chests; regardless, the warrior has the best selection of combat goods. The warrior uses them well in battle too. Whether in hand-to-hand melee or at longer bow range, the enemy cannot escape the warrior's severe punishment. Swords slice through mail, while arrows plunge into flesh.

As part of their natural training and skill sets, warriors have a strong understanding of battle tactics and strategy. You will have a wide array of talents to deal massive combat damage to single targets and groups of foes. A warrior's talents are broken down by how you plan to use your weapons. If you plan to use gear in both hands, a warrior can pursue Dual Weapons or Weapon and Shield. Alternately, the warrior can concentrate on larger Two-Handed Weapons to savage an opponent, or learn the ways of Archery to harass enemies at range. Some of the warrior's general talents increase health and stamina, reduce armor penalties, draw hostilities away from allies, grant damage bonuses, improve critical hit percentages, and make you the meanest combatant on the battlefield.

Warrior specializations crank up your battle effectiveness. As a berserker, a warrior's rage fuels his strikes, adding damage to the blows at the expense of other qualities such as stamina. A templar, on the other hand, hunts enemy mages and beats them down with mana drains and more damage. A champion inspires those around him with party-influencing abilities. Finally, a reaver revels in the dark side as he sucks life back into himself from the pain of others.

primagames.com

Strengths and Weaknesses

The strength of a warrior is in his arms and armor. A warrior can deal major damage to adversaries, especially in melee where he can land pounding blows and critical strikes with excellent hand-to-hand weapons. Return blows from enemies will either glance off a warrior's superior armor or the warrior's defenses will limit the extent of the damage. The warrior's natural bonuses aid in the cause too. His +4 strength bonus augments your most important attribute, and a +3 bonus to constitution raises health and makes you that much more difficult to kill.

Advantages

- Stat Bonuses to Strength, Dexterity, and Constitution
- Top Weapons, Best Armor
- Superior Melee Damage
- High Survivability
- Enhanced Combat Talents and Tactics

The warrior may be a wrecking ball in combat, but he does have limitations. Most importantly, a warrior needs to close on his target to be at his best. Where a mage can hurl spells from the back, or a rogue can hide and surprise with a backstab, most warriors must get close to his enemy at some point to do maximum damage. It's possible to deal some damage with a good ranged weapon, but the majority of warrior talents trigger off hand-to-hand combat. While you close on the enemy, it's likely you'll take some ranged damage and may take heaps of damage from magic attacks, which warriors will be vulnerable to early on. Your armor may reduce damage, but the damage will come, and most warriors do not have healing to regain health. Stock up on healing potions and stay near your party healer in case your health suddenly drops.

Disadvantages

- Limited Healing
- Must Close on Enemies to Be Most Effective
- Generally Weak Against Magic Attacks

If you like a brash, in-your-face play style and really love to hack and slash monsters, the warrior's advantages far outweigh his disadvantages. Nothing beats a 10-on-1 battle where the warrior walks away with just a scratch and the enemies...well, they just don't walk away at all.

Attributes

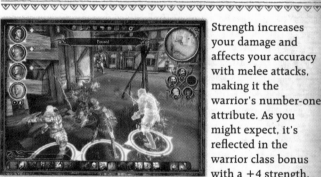

Strength increases your damage and affects your accuracy with melee attacks, making it the warrior's number-one attribute. As you might expect, it's reflected in the warrior class bonus with a +4 strength. Many talents will require high strength scores, and more powerful weapons and armor require a higher strength stat. When you level up, you may consider spending two points on strength for every one point you spend somewhere else, especially early in your warrior career to unlock talents quicker (you may even decide to put all three points per level in strength to unlock talents earlier).

Next, a warrior should stock up on constitution. You can always use more health, which constitution directly increases, and constitution also boosts resilience to keep you fighting on the battlefield longer. The warrior's starting bonus of +3 constitution gives you a good jump, and you should consider throwing points to constitution if you don't have any other attribute you want to improve immediately.

Warrior Attribute Bonuses

+4 Strength

+3 Dexterity

+3 Constitution

Dexterity can do a lot for a warrior. It affects your chance to hit, increases your chance to dodge enemy blows, and augments damage from piercing weapons like arrows and daggers. Archery and dual weapon–specced warriors should load up on dexterity, even forgoing strength early if you need to unlock certain ranged or dual-weapon talents. The warrior's +3 dexterity bonus pushes you to above-average dexterity from the start, and you should continue spending points if you plan on a healthy balance of offense and defense.

The Warrior

Basics ~ Character Generation ~ **Classes** ~ The Party ~ Companions ~ Supporting Cast ~ Equipment ~ Bestiary ~ Walkthroughs ~ Side Quests ~ Random Encounters ~ Achievements/Trophies

TIP

Gear bonuses can amplify your attribute's strengths or offset any shortcomings. A ring, for example, that bulks up constitution could provide some extra health without costing any precious attribute points.

At first glance, you might dismiss willpower as a stat for mages. But read the fine print. Willpower increases stamina, so if your warrior loves to perform daring maneuvers that drain a lot of stamina—and who doesn't!—you'll have to throw points to this attribute once in a while. At lower levels, you won't have the extra points to boost willpower, but when you hit the teens, start looking to expand your stamina pool.

Magic shouldn't be a priority at all; however, it does increase the effect of potions and salves, and because most warriors rely on potions to buff health in a fight, magic is not entirely useless.

Cunning can be neglected, unless you plan to use Coercion and wish to persuade many of the NPCs with your tongue. However, because you can also intimidate many of those same NPCs with your strength score, cunning is a luxury stat that you should only bump up once all your main attributes are in great shape.

During character creation, feel free to choose a race based on the corresponding origin story you would like to play through as a warrior. It's much more important to enjoy the origin story for your character than it is to worry about a point here or there in your attributes. However, if maximizing your warrior stats appeals to you, choose a dwarf or human. A dwarven warrior gives you a starting 15 strength, 14 dexterity, and 15 constitution. You can't beat that for your main attributes. For a more well-rounded approach, try the human warrior with 15 strength, 14 dexterity, and 13 constitution (with a couple of points spread to magic and cunning). The elven warrior isn't as solid out of the gates as his natural race bonus applies to willpower and magic, so an elf's main warrior attributes aren't as high.

Warrior Starting Attributes

Attribute	Human	Elf	Dwarf
Strength	15	14	15
Dexterity	14	13	14
Willpower	10	12	10
Magic	11	12	10
Cunning	11	10	10
Constitution	13	13	15

Once you choose your warrior's race, you begin with five extra points to add to your attributes. That's almost two "level ups" worth of attribute growth, so spend it wisely. If you want a powerful and damaging warrior, apply all five points to strength. If you want a more defensive juggernaut, spend three points on constitution and two points on dexterity. In most cases, though, it's probably best to stick with the standard warrior advice—strength first, then constitution—and spend three points on strength and two points on constitution.

Skills

All warriors need to pick up the Combat Training skill as soon as they can. Combat Training opens up the higher tier weapon talents, which you can't live without. Spend your first skill point here to vault up to at least Improved Combat (even better, a Human Noble warrior can spend a point to gain Expert Combat Training). Other skills can be helpful, such as Trap-Making if you want to add a little AoE damage to your repertoire; however, they aren't essential like Combat Training.

NOTE

Beyond your starting skills, you're likely to obtain 7–9 skill points throughout the game. Pick your two or three favorite skills and stick with them. If you spread your points too thin, you'll end up doing a bunch of things—but not well.

After you finish off your Combat Training, think about Coercion. It's an incredibly useful skill in dialogue; it gives you story options that you won't get access to otherwise. Cunning opens up the Coercion skills, and more cunning will increase your Persuade skill, but in most situations you can use your Intimidate skill in lieu of Persuade. Intimidate works off your strength stat, which fits perfectly with a warrior loading up on strength.

Warrior Skill Recommendations

Assuming you spend 8 skill points by career's end, here's a good spread to consider. Note that many other combinations could work better for you, so experiment!

- Combat Training +4
- Coercion +3
- Survival +1

Survival can be a good skill to have because the more you advance it, the better chance you have to detect creatures on your mini-map before they surprise you. You can save yourself from more than a few ambushes with this skill. Don't forget about the bonus to nature resistance too.

If you aren't directly playing your warrior companions (see the Companions chapter for more details) and want one of them to run around on their own, investing in Combat Tactics for extra tactic slots might be a good investment too. The more tactic slots you open, the more you can shape how your companions behave in battle. Inevitably, even if you plan on controlling your warrior during fights, there will be moments when you don't program your warrior's every move (or something more important is going on) and tactics come into play. One or two points should be good, or max it out if you want the character to go on autopilot.

primagames.com

Talents

Warriors will shine in combat, amid talons scraping at flesh and blood spurting in faces. Like the other classes, the warrior offers more than a single way to play. You can choose the tank role, focusing on defense and holding your team together, or the melee DPS role, concentrating on pounding out as much damage as your two hands can manage. If you want to affect combat from the perimeter, the ranged fighter can be a gem; he may not have the same firepower as a mage, but a warrior archer has many tools and the tough skin to back them up.

You start with one point in different talents, depending on what race you choose. The Dwarf Noble and Human Noble begin with Shield Bash (ideal for tanks). The Dwarf Commoner and City Elf start with Dual-Weapon Sweep (useful in many melee situations, and a great start if you want to wield two weapons). The Dalish Elf begins with Pinning Shot (essential for a ranged warrior going into the Archery talents). In addition, you'll receive one point for every level you gain. Working with this, if you get to level 20 by the end of the game, you'll have 22 total points to spend. It might seem like a lot, but you really have to plan what talent chains you want, because you'll cap only three or four regular chains if you decide to specialize.

NOTE

It's possible to have six warrior companions in the game: Alistair, Dog, Loghain (after the Landsmeet), Oghren, Sten, and Shale (available from downloadable content). Develop each differently to have access to a wider arsenal.

All warriors should familiarize themselves with the cooldown component of each talent. The worst situation is to have plenty of stamina and no available talents to use. Branch out into different chains to avoid the cooldown problem. For example, if you develop the Weapon and Shield school primarily for defense, having a talent or two in Two-Handed can help with extra damage and keeping your options open.

Your talents drain stamina from your pool. Watch how much stamina you're using in a fight and act accordingly. If you run short without a healer's Restoration spell to replenish you, it could cost your party a victory. Gauge what you have to do to help the team. There's little sense running off a series of moves that drains three quarters of your stamina on the first opponent when there are three more to go. Save your stamina. You never know when the next fight will start, or how long the current fight will go if you have unexpected ambushers, and you'll be grateful you didn't waste stamina.

Warrior Weapon Sets

Take advantage of your warrior's second set of weapons. Gear your first equipment set for your primary focus, and your secondary set as backup. For example, arm yourself with an excellent two-handed weapon if your focus is in the Two-Handed school, and a crossbow in the second set for a little ranged damage. If you want to broaden your fighting style, pair your main style with one other style. Use a few Archery talents paired with any of the other schools and you have a well-prepared warrior ready for ranged and melee combat. Use Dual Weapons with Weapon and Shield when you want to shift focus from defending and attacking to becoming a whirlwind of attacks. Use Two-Handed with Dual Weapons when you want to go from that whirlwind of attacks to being able to take on giant foes.

Remember, though, as you level up, you'll gain access to specializations, so you'll want to spend points in those talent chains too. Usually by level 20, you'd have enough talent points to max out your Warrior talent school, all but one weapon type talent chain, and all but one in a specialization talent chain. Also remember that the secondary set of weapons (and accompanying talents for them) are meant to be a backup, so avoid splitting your talent points evenly between both styles or you'll be be decent at both but excel at neither.

Warrior School

You have two choices: one for basic defense and one for basic offense. The chain that starts with Powerful leans toward defense (though both chains give you offensive and defensive options). Powerful adds extra health and reduces fatigue, which means all of your abilities cost less. Even if you don't want to spec in the Warrior school at all, think about spending an extra point in Powerful because it's a great early ability. The sustained ability Threaten is a must for tanks who get into the thick of things and need to keep threat on themselves. Bravery is all-around good, with its bonuses to damage, resistances, and critical hit chance. Death Blow restores stamina for each foe a warrior fells in battle.

The Precise Striking chain centers around increasing your attacking skills. You sacrifice attack speed with Precise Striking, but you gain a bonus to your attack chance and critical hit chance. Taunt works as another excellent threat-magnet for tanks who want to suck in everything around them. It can also work with an off-tank to help them control enemies when they need to play the tank role. Disengage reduces threat and allows the warrior to shed enemies when the pressure gets too great; this is another excellent ability for off-tanks who only want to hold a foe for a little while. Perfect Striking gains you a massive attack bonus for a short time.

The Warrior

Basics ~ Character Generation ~ **Classes** ~ The Party ~ Companions ~ Supporting Cast ~ Equipment ~ Bestiary ~ Walkthroughs ~ Side Quests ~ Random Encounters ~ Achievements/Trophies

Dual Weapon School

For those warriors who prefer dexterity, Dual Weapons gives you more offense without relying on strength. You deal damage with two weapons simultaneously; alas, the drawback is that your defense suffers. The focus of your passive abilities is on your second hand: you want to deal as close to normal damage as possible and score close to the same number of critical hits as your main hand.

You gain a bonus to attack and defense with Dual-Weapon Finesse. Dual-Weapon Expert gives a bonus to critical chance and lets you cause bleeding lacerations on your opponent, inflicting damage over time. You may wield full-sized weapons in your off-hand while reducing the stamina cost of all dual weapon talents with Dual-Weapon Mastery.

Increase your attack damage with Dual Striking in the second chain. Score a two-hit combo with a possibility of stunning your opponent and scoring a critical hit with Riposte. Cripple gives you a chance to score a critical hit and inflict your opponent with penalties to movement speed, attack, and defense. Punisher is a three-hit combo that can score a critical hit, knock an opponent down, and cause penalties to movement and attack speed.

Dual-Weapon Sweep deals significant damage with each sweep. Flurry is a three-hit combo, while Momentum increases your attack speed with every hit. Whirlwind is a flurry of constant attacks: the signature of a Dual Weapon expert.

This talent chain can also be a deadly combination with the Warrior talent school. Draw enemies in and knock them down, stun them, cause damage over time, and inflict penalties to movement speed, attack, and defense. Powerful and Bravery give you bonuses to attack, defense, and resistances while Death Blow restores stamina with each kill, making you a whirlwind of death...if you don't get hammered by arrows or spells from opponents.

Archery School

Another school for warriors who build up dexterity, Archery gives ample special effects for a ranged combat enthusiast. Melee Archer lets you fire while being attacked (eliminating some of the pain of being an archer). Master Archer gives you bonuses to activated abilities and eliminates the penalty to attack speed when wearing heavy armor. Aim reduces attack speed but gives bonuses to attack, damage, armor penetration, and critical chance. Defensive Fire gives you a boost to defense but slows your attack speed.

In the second chain, Pinning Shot is a necessity because it impales the victim's leg and either pins it in place or slows its movement speed. Crippling Shot deals normal damage to an enemy and gives it penalties to attack and defense, and Critical Shot delivers maximum damage upon impact. The deadly Arrow of Slaying usually scores a critical hit, often dropping weakened enemies.

Rapid Shot increases attack speed, but you lose the ability to score critical hits. Shattering Shot deals normal damage and opens up an enemy's armor. If a warrior finds open armor, its wearer will be in sore shape. Suppressing Fire is like Rapid Shot, but its foes now take penalties to their attack rating. Scattershot stuns a foe and then shatters, dealing damage to other enemies around it.

When you have room to breathe, Pinning Shot and Crippling Shot turn enemies into sitting ducks for mage attacks, deadly rogues, or more of your carefully aimed arrows. Shattering Shot is excellent against heavily armed foes. Rapid Shot, Suppressing Fire, and Scattershot hack away at the collective hit points of enemy ranks.

TIP

A good combo against a heavily armed foe is Shattering Shot, Crippling Shot, Aim/Rapid Shot, and Arrow of Slaying. Mix in another Shattering Shot if the first armor penalty runs out.

Don't think an archer just scores a hit or two before having to engage an opponent in melee. You can kill a couple enemies in a few hits while pinning others in place and continuing to fire while other attackers swarm you. This turns you into a deadly sniper that enemies need to deal with or suffer the consequences. If the enemy swarms you, switch to Defensive Fire while you have the passive ability Melee Archer. You can fire off arrows while being attacked and still have decent defense.

Weapon and Shield School

Your standard warrior tank usually dips into the Weapon and Shield school a lot. In the offensive chain, Shield Bash deals normal damage and has a chance to knock an enemy down. Shield Pummel is a two-hit combo that can stun an enemy. Overpower is a three-hit shield combo that might deal a critical hit with the third strike. Assault is a four-hit combo that diminishes in power with each strike. Use any of these with Shield Defense, Shield Wall, or Shield Cover to get in some good, solid hits while bolstering your defenses. Use any of these with Threaten or Taunt in the Warrior talent school to pull enemies in and knock them back on their collective back sides.

primagames.com

Shield Wall or Shield Defense used with Taunt or Threaten from the Warrior talent school makes a great combination because you lure enemies in and beef up your defenses while resisting knockdown effects and shrugging off missiles. The Shield Block passive ability eliminates your enemies' flanking advantage on your shield side, while the Shield Tactics passive ability eliminates your enemies' flanking advantage altogether. This comes in very handy because hordes of enemies swarm your characters in many battles. When they flank you, they score bonuses to attacks and critical hits. Shield Cover and Shield Defense help you shrug off missile attacks. This is very useful, for example, when hurlocks are swarming you while genlock archers are slamming you with arrows.

The many passive abilities in this talent chain give bonuses to the sustained and activated abilities, so they get stronger the more you progress in Weapon and Shield training. Now, if only there were 300 more of these guys in your army at the end of the game...

Two-Handed School

In this talent school, you get to deal massive damage, but you're slower moving and you don't have as much in the way of defense. The Stunning Blows passive ability adds a chance to stun your target each time you strike. Shattering Blows gives you attack bonuses against golems and other heavily armored foes. Destroyer means that every attack you deal has a chance to sunder an opponent's armor. Two-Handed Strength reduces your attack and defense penalty in Powerful Swings.

Indomitable gives you a bonus to attack while making you immune to stun or knockdown effects. If you're in a swarm of larger enemies, use Indomitable to protect against getting stunned or knocked down, but careful with this because it uses a nice chunk of your stamina. The Powerful Swings sustained ability gives you a nice bonus to damage but reduces your attack and defense.

Pommel Strike knocks an opponent to the ground. Critical Strike is a massive hit that scores a critical hit and sometimes kills a foe outright. Sunder Arms targets an enemy's weapon, giving a penalty to attack, while Sunder Armor targets the armor, giving a penalty to armor and dealing normal damage to the unlucky victim. Mighty Blow can deal a critical hit and reduce the opponent's movement, and Two-Handed Sweep hits enemies in a wide arc, dealing normal damage and knocking them down.

TIP

Try Sunder Arms, Sunder Armor, normal attack, Mighty Blow, and Critical Strike. For some foes, you might not even need Mighty Blow.

Warrior Talents

Chain	Name	Prerequisite	Description	Cost (mana /stamina)	Upkeep (mana /stamina)	Fatigue (% mana/stamina)	Ranged	Cooldown (sec.)	Area of Effect Radius (ft.)
			Warrior School						
Chain 1	Powerful	Strength 10	Through training and hard work, the warrior has gained greater health and reduced the fatigue penalty for wearing armor.	0	0	0	No	0	0
	Threaten	Strength 14, Level 4	The warrior adopts a challenging posture that increases enemy hostility with each melee attack, drawing them away from other allies while this mode is active.	0	35	2	No	15	0
	Bravery	Strength 20, Level 8	The warrior's unwavering courage grants bonuses to damage, physical resistance, and mental resistance, as well as a bonus to critical chance that increases proportionally to the number of enemies above two that the warrior is engaging.	0	0	0	No	0	0
	Death Blow	Strength 25, Level 12	Each time the warrior fells an enemy, the end of the battle seems closer at hand, restoring a portion of the warrior's stamina.	0	0	0	No	0	0
Chain 2	Precise Striking	Dexterity 10	The warrior tries to make each attack count, sacrificing attack speed for a bonus to attack as well as an increased chance to score critical hits for as long as this mode is active.	0	40	5	No	15	0
	Taunt	Strength 14, Level 4	A mocking bellow catches the attention of nearby foes, increasing their hostility toward the warrior. Frightening Appearance increases the effect.	40	0	0	No	20	10
	Disengage	Dexterity 18, Level 8	A relaxed position makes the warrior seem less threatening, reducing the hostility of nearby enemies, who may seek other targets instead.	10	0	0	No	10	10
	Perfect Striking	Strength 22, Level 12	The warrior focuses on precision, gaining a massive attack bonus for a moderate time.	60	0	0	No	30	0

The Warrior

Basics ~ Character Generation ~ Classes ~ The Party ~ Companions ~ Supporting Cast ~ Equipment ~ Bestiary ~ Walkthroughs ~ Side Quests ~ Random Encounters ~ Achievements/Trophies

Chain	Name	Prerequisite	Description	Cost (mana/stamina)	Upkeep (mana/stamina)	Fatigue (% mana/stamina)	Ranged	Cooldown (sec.)	Area of Effect Radius (ft.)
			Dual Weapon School						
Chain 1	Dual Striking	Dexterity 12	When in this mode, the character strikes with both weapons simultaneously. Attacks cause more damage, but the character cannot inflict regular critical hits or backstabs.	0	50	5	No	10	0
Chain 1	Riposte	Dexterity 16	The character strikes at a target once, dealing normal damage, as well as stunning the opponent unless it passes a physical resistance check. The character then strikes with the other weapon, generating a critical hit if the target was stunned.	40	0	0	No	20	0
Chain 1	Cripple	Dexterity 22	The character strikes low at a target, gaining a momentary attack bonus and hitting critically if the attack connects, while crippling the target with penalties to movement speed, attack, and defense unless it passes a physical resistance check.	35	0	0	No	30	0
Chain 1	Punisher	Dexterity 28	The character makes three blows against a target, dealing normal damage for the first two strikes and generating a critical hit for the final blow, if it connects. The target may also suffer penalties to attack and defense, or be knocked to the ground.	50	0	0	No	40	0
Chain 2	Dual-Weapon Sweep	Dexterity 12	The character sweeps both weapons in a broad forward arc, striking nearby enemies with one or both weapons and inflicting significantly more damage than normal.	20	0	0	No	15	2
Chain 2	Flurry	Dexterity 18	The character lashes out with a flurry of three blows, dealing normal combat damage with each hit.	40	0	0	No	20	0
Chain 2	Momentum	Dexterity 24	The character has learned to carry one attack through to the next, increasing attack speed substantially. This mode consumes stamina quickly, however.	0	60	5	No	30	0
Chain 2	Whirlwind	Dexterity 30	The character flies into a whirling dance of death, striking out at surrounding enemies with both weapons. Each hit deals normal combat damage.	40	0	0	No	40	2
Chain 3	Dual-Weapon Training	Dexterity 12	The character has become more proficient fighting with two weapons, and now deals closer to normal damage bonus with the off-hand weapon.	0	0	0	No	0	0
Chain 3	Dual-Weapon Finesse	Dexterity 16	The character is extremely skilled at wielding a weapon in each hand, gaining bonuses to attack and defense.	0	0	0	No	0	0
Chain 3	Dual-Weapon Expert	Dexterity 26	The character has significant experience with two-weapon fighting, gaining a bonus to critical chance, as well as a possibility with each hit to inflict bleeding lacerations that continue to damage a target for a time.	0	0	0	No	0	0
Chain 3	Dual-Weapon Mastery	Dexterity 36	Only a chosen few truly master the complicated art of fighting with two weapons. The character is now among that elite company, able to wield full-sized weapons in both hands. Stamina costs for all dual-weapon talents are also reduced.	0	0	0	No	0	0
			Archery School						
Chain 1	Melee Archer	Dexterity 12	Experience fighting in tight quarters has taught the archer to fire without interruption, even when being attacked.	0	0	0	No	0	0
Chain 1	Aim	Dexterity 16	The archer carefully places each shot for maximum effect while in this mode. This decreases rate of fire but grants bonuses to attack, damage, armor penetration, and critical chance. Master Archer further increases these bonuses.	0	35	5	No	10	0
Chain 1	Defensive Fire	Dexterity 22	While active, the archer changes stance, receiving a bonus to defense but slowing the rate of fire. With the Master Archer talent, the defense bonus increases.	0	40	5	No	15	0
Chain 1	Master Archer	Dexterity 28	Deadly with both bows and crossbows, master archers receive additional benefits when using Aim, Defensive Fire, Crippling Shot, Critical Shot, Arrow of Slaying, Rapid Shot, and Shattering Shot. This talent also eliminates the penalty to attack speed when wearing heavy armor, although massive armor still carries the penalty.	0	0	0	No	0	0
Chain 2	Pinning Shot	Dexterity 12	A shot to the target's legs disables the foe, pinning the target in place unless it passes a physical resistance check, and slowing movement speed otherwise.	20	0	0	Yes	15	0
Chain 2	Crippling Shot	Dexterity 16	A carefully aimed shot hampers the target's ability to fight by reducing attack and defense if it hits, although the shot inflicts only normal damage. The Master Archer talent adds an attack bonus while firing the Crippling Shot.	25	0	0	Yes	10	0
Chain 2	Critical Shot	Dexterity 21	Finding a chink in the target's defenses, the archer fires an arrow that, if aimed correctly, automatically scores a critical hit and gains a bonus to armor penetration. The Master Archer talent increases the armor penetration bonus.	40	0	0	Yes	10	0
Chain 2	Arrow of Slaying	Dexterity 30	The archer generates an automatic critical hit if this shot finds its target, although high-level targets may be able to ignore the effect. The archer suffers reduced stamina regeneration for a time. Master Archer adds an extra attack bonus.	80	0	0	Yes	60	0
Chain 3	Rapid Shot	Dexterity 12	Speed wins out over power while this mode is active, as the archer fires more rapidly but without any chance of inflicting regular critical hits. Master Archer increases the rate of fire further still.	0	35	5	No	30	0
Chain 3	Shattering Shot	Dexterity 16	The archer fires a shot designed to open up a weak spot in the target's armor. The shot deals normal damage if it hits and imposes an armor penalty on the target. Master Archer increases the target's armor penalty.	25	0	0	Yes	15	0
Chain 3	Suppressing Fire	Dexterity 24	When this mode is active, the archer's shots hamper foes. Each arrow deals regular damage and also encumbers the target with a temporary penalty to attack. This penalty can be applied multiple times.	0	60	5	No	10	0
Chain 3	Scattershot	Dexterity 27	The archer fires a single arrow that automatically hits, stunning the target and dealing normal damage. The arrow then shatters, hitting all nearby enemies with the same effect.	50	0	0	Yes	40	0

Chain	Name	Prerequisite	Description	Cost (mana /stamina)	Upkeep (mana /stamina)	Fatigue (% mana/stamina)	Ranged	Cooldown (sec.)	Area of Effect Radius (ft.)
			Weapons and Shield School						
Chain 1	Shield Bash	Strength 11	The character shield-bashes a target, dealing normal damage as well as knocking the target off its feet unless it passes a physical resistance check. Shield Mastery doubles the strength bonus for this attack.	25	0	0	No	20	0
Chain 1	Shield Pummel	Strength 15	The character follows up an attack with two hits from the shield, dealing normal damage with each attack. If the target fails a physical resistance check, it is stunned. Shield Mastery doubles the character's strength bonus for each strike.	30	0	0	No	20	0
Chain 1	Overpower	Strength 25	The character lashes out with the shield three times. The first two hits inflict normal damage. The last strike is a critical hit if it connects, knocking the target down unless it passes a physical resistance check. Shield Mastery increases the damage.	30	0	0	No	20	0
Chain 1	Assault	Strength 32	The character quickly strikes a target four times, but dealing reduced damage with each hit. If the character has Shield Mastery, the damage from each hit increases.	40	0	0	No	20	0
Chain 2	Shield Block	Dexterity 10	Practice fighting with a shield improves the character's guard. Enemies can no longer flank the character on the shield-carrying side.	0	0	0	No	0	0
Chain 2	Shield Cover	Dexterity 16	While in this mode, the warrior's shield provides a greater chance of deflecting missile attacks. Shield Mastery increases this bonus further.	0	20	5	No	15	0
Chain 2	Shield Tactics	Dexterity 20	The character is proficient enough with a shield to defend from all angles, so that attackers no longer benefit from flanking strikes.	0	0	0	No	0	0
Chain 2	Shield Mastery	Dexterity 26	The character has mastered the use of the shield for both offense and defense, and receives additional benefits when using Shield Bash, Shield Pummel, Assault, Overpower, Shield Defense, Shield Wall, and Shield Cover.	0	0	0	No	0	0
Chain 3	Shield Defense	Strength 11	While this mode is active, the character drops into a defensive stance that favors the shield, gaining a bonus to defense and an increased chance to shrug off missile attacks, but taking a penalty to attack. With Shield Balance, the attack penalty is reduced. With Shield Expertise, the defense bonus increases. With Shield Mastery, the defense bonus increases further.	0	35	5	No	5	0
Chain 3	Shield Balance	Strength 14	The character has learned to compensate for the weight of a shield in combat and no longer suffers an attack penalty while using Shield Defense.	0	0	0	No	0	0
Chain 3	Shield Wall	Strength 20	In this mode, the character's shield becomes nearly a fortress, adding a significant bonus to armor and a greater likelihood of shrugging off missile attacks, but at the cost of reduced damage. Shield Expertise makes the character immune to direct knockdown attacks while in this mode, and Shield Mastery gives a bonus to defense.	0	55	5	No	15	0
Chain 3	Shield Expertise	Strength 26	The character's experience using a shield in combat has made certain abilities more efficient, increasing the defense bonus for Shield Defense and making the character immune to direct knockdown attacks while using Shield Wall.	0	0	0	No	0	0
			Two-Handed School						
Chain 1	Mighty Blow	Strength 15	The character puts extra weight and effort behind a single strike, gaining a bonus to attack. If it hits, the blow deals critical damage and imposes a penalty to movement speed unless the target passes a physical resistance check.	40	0	0	No	20	0
Chain 1	Powerful Swings	Strength 21	While in this mode, the character puts extra muscle behind each swing, gaining a bonus to damage but suffering penalties to attack and defense. Two-Handed Strength reduces the penalties to attack and defense.	0	30	5	No	10	0
Chain 1	Two-Handed Strength	Strength 28	The character has learned to wield two-handed weapons more effectively, reducing the penalties to attack and defense from Powerful Swings.	0	0	0	No	0	0
Chain 1	Two-Handed Sweep	Strength 36, Level 10	The character swings a two-handed weapon through enemies in a vicious arc, dealing normal damage to those it hits and knocking them down unless they pass a physical resistance check.	40	0	0	No	20	3
Chain 2	Pommel Strike	Strength 12	Instead of going for the fatal attack an enemy expects, the player strikes out with a weapon's blunt end, knocking the opponent to the ground unless it passes a physical resistance check.	20	0	0	No	10	0
Chain 2	Indomitable	Strength 20	Through sheer force of will, the character remains in control on the battlefield, gaining a slight increase to attack damage while being immune to stun or knock down effects for the duration of this mode.	0	60	5	No	30	0
Chain 2	Stunning Blows	Strength 28	The character's fondness for massive two-handed weapons means that each attack offers a chance to stun the opponent due to the sheer weight behind the blow.	0	0	0	No	0	0
Chain 2	Critical Strike	Strength 34	The character makes a single massive swing at the target, gaining a bonus to attack. If the strike connects, it is an automatic critical hit, possibly killing the opponent outright if its health is low enough.	40	0	0	No	60	0

The Warrior

Basics ~ Character Generation ~ **Classes** ~ The Party ~ Companions ~ Supporting Cast ~ Equipment ~ Bestiary ~ Walkthroughs ~ Side Quests ~ Random Encounters ~ Achievements/Trophies

Chain	Name	Prerequisite	Description	Cost (mana /stamina)	Upkeep (mana /stamina)	Fatigue (% mana/stamina)	Ranged	Cooldown (sec.)	Area of Effect Radius (ft.)
			Two-Handed School (continued)						
Chain 3	Sunder Arms	Strength 18	The character attempts to hinder a target's ability to fight back, rather than going directly for a killing blow. Unless the target passes a physical resistance check, it suffers a penalty to attack for a short time.	25	0	0	No	10	0
	Shattering Blows	Strength 23	The character is as adept at destruction as at death and gains a large damage bonus against golems and other constructs.	0	0	0	No	0	0
	Sunder Armor	Strength 28, Level 10	The character aims a destructive blow at the target's armor or natural defenses. The attack deals normal damage, but also damages the armor unless the target passes a physical resistance check.	40	0	0	No	20	0
	Destroyer	Strength 40, Level 14	Few can stand against the savage blows of a destroyer. Every attack sunders the target's armor, reducing its effectiveness for a short time. The effects of multiple blows are not cumulative.	0	0	0	No	0	0
			Power of Blood School (downloadable content only)						
Chain 1	Blood Thirst	None	The warrior's own tainted blood spills in sacrifice, increasing movement speed, attack speed, and critical hit chance. For as long as the mode is active, however, the warrior suffers greater damage and continuously diminishing health.	30	30	5	No	5	0
	Blood Fury	None	The warrior sprays tainted blood in order to knock back nearby enemies, which they may resist by passing a physical resistance check. The gush of blood, however, results in a loss of personal health.	30 & 40*	0	0	No	10	5

* Stamina and Health

▲▲▲▲▲▲▲▲▲▲▲▲▲▲▲▲▲▲▲▲▲▲▲▲▲▲▲

Specializations

▼▼▼▼▼▼▼▼▼▼▼▼▼▼▼▼▼▼▼▼▼▼▼

Each class can learn two out of the four possible specializations throughout the course of the game. Your first specialization can be learned at level 7; your second at level 14. Most companions can teach a specialization, though your approval rating must be high enough for the companion to want to teach you. Oghren, for example, can teach the warrior's berserker specialization. Specializations are difficult to achieve, but very rewarding if you gain one. As long as the specific abilities fit with your play style and character breakdown, a specialization is generally worth spending points in over regular talents.

Definitely experiment with specializations. A tank could, for example, specialize in templar to take out spellcasters even if he can't get to them directly. However, here are some suggested play style fits for the four specializations:

Berserker
- **Primary:** DPS (max out damage at the expense of stamina)
- **Secondary:** Knockout punch (use Final Blow to finish off a foe but exhausts you in a long fight)

Champion
- **Primary:** Party buffer (increase attack and defense bonuses for everyone)
- **Secondary:** Enemy control (use Superiority to knock enemy groups off their feet)

Reaver
- **Primary:** AoE DPS (radiate spirit damage and fear)
- **Secondary:** Health resilient (absorb health from nearby corpses)

Templar
- **Primary:** Mage killer (pound enemy mages with abilities)
- **Secondary:** Dispel magic (clean area of spell effects)

Warrior Specializations

Specialization	Talent Name	Prerequisite Level	Description	Cost (mana /stamina)	Upkeep (mana /stamina)	Fatigue (% mana/stamina)	Ranged	Cooldown (sec.)	Area of Effect Radius (ft.)
Learned From: Oghren (Companion), Gorim (Denerim Market)									
Berserker	Berserk	7	The stench of blood and death drives the berserker into a willing fury, providing a bonus to damage. Rages incur a penalty to stamina regeneration, however, which Constraint reduces. Resilience adds a bonus to health regeneration in this mode.	0	20	5	No	30	0
Berserker	Resilience	8	Rages no longer wear so heavily on the berserker's body. The stamina regeneration penalty applied by Berserk is reduced, and the berserker gains a bonus to nature resistance.	0	0	0	No	0	0
Berserker	Constraint	10	The berserker has learned to retain control during rages, reducing Berserk's penalty to stamina regeneration.	0	0	0	No	0	0
Berserker	Final Blow	12	All the berserker's stamina goes into a single swing. If the blow connects, the attack inflicts extra damage proportional to the amount of stamina lost.	0	0	0	No	60	0
Learned From: Arl Eamon (at the end of the "Urn of Sacred Ashes" quest line)									
Champion	War Cry	7	The champion lets out a fearsome cry that gives nearby enemies a penalty to attack. With Superiority, nearby enemies are also knocked down unless they pass a physical resistance check.	25	0	0	No	20	10
Champion	Rally	12	The champion's presence inspires nearby allies, giving them bonuses to attack and defense while this mode is active. When coupled with Motivate, the attack bonus increases.	0	50	5	No	30	10
Champion	Motivate	14	The champion inspires allies to attack with renewed vigor. The Rally talent now increases attack, in addition to its defense bonus.	40	30	0	No	0	0
Champion	Superiority	16	The champion is so fearsome that War Cry now knocks nearby opponents off their feet unless they pass a physical resistance check.	60	0	0	No	0	0
Learned From: Kolgrim (Wyrmling Lair)									
Reaver	Devour	7	The reaver revels in death, absorbing the lingering energy of all nearby corpses, each of which partially restores the reaver's own health.	25	0	0	No	30	5
Reaver	Frightening Appearance	12	This talent focuses the reaver's unsettling countenance into a weapon, making a target cower in fear unless it passes a mental resistance check. Frightening Appearance also increases the effectiveness of Taunt and Threaten.	25	0	0	No	20	0
Reaver	Aura of Pain	14	Radiating an aura of psychic pain, the reaver takes constant spirit damage while this mode is active, as do all enemies nearby.	0	60	5	No	45	4
Reaver	Blood Frenzy	16	Driven by pain, the reaver gains larger bonuses to damage whenever health decreases. Because this mode also incurs a penalty to health regeneration, the reaver flirts with death the longer the frenzy persists.	0	60	5	No	60	0
Learned From: Alistair (Companion), Bodahn's Wares (Party Camp)									
Templar	Righteous Strike	7	Templars are enforcers specifically chosen to control mages and slay abominations. Each of the templar's melee hits against an enemy spellcaster drains its mana.	0	0	0	No	0	0
Templar	Cleanse Area	9	The templar purges the area of magic, removing all dispellable effects from those nearby. Friendly fire possible.	40	0	0	No	30	10
Templar	Mental Fortress	12	The templar has learned to focus on duty, gaining a large bonus to mental resistance.	0	0	0	No	0	0
Templar	Holy Smite	15	The templar strikes out with righteous fire, inflicting spirit damage on the target and other nearby enemies. If the target is a spellcaster, it must pass a mental resistance check or else loses mana and takes additional spirit damage proportional to the mana lost. All affected enemies are stunned or knocked back unless they pass physical resistance checks.	75	0	0	Yes	40	5

The Warrior

Basics ~ Character Generation ~ **Classes** ~ The Party ~ Companions ~ Supporting Cast ~ Equipment ~ Bestiary ~ Walkthroughs ~ Side Quests ~ Random Encounters ~ Achievements/Trophies

Gear

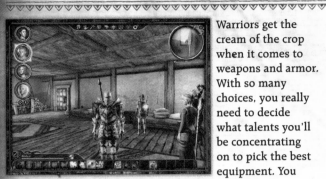

Warriors get the cream of the crop when it comes to weapons and armor. With so many choices, you really need to decide what talents you'll be concentrating on to pick the best equipment. You don't, for instance, want an awesome two-handed sword if you're training in Weapon and Shields. Any weapon that grants you strength (or dexterity for warriors in Archery and Dual Weapon) should be considered. Bonuses to damage, attack, and criticals can be great too. If you want more defense, bulk up your armor rating, but it's always a fine line between great armor rating and too much fatigue. Armor doesn't do a lot of good if you can't use any of your talents. You can always look for armor with a bonus to armor rating (no fatigue penalty), or even armor that grants constitution bonus or healing bonus.

There's more warrior gear than you could ever hope to equip in a single play. The general rule of thumb is to wait for loot that serves as an upgrade and snatch it up. If you have extra coin to buy a nice gear upgrade, feel free to spend away, though most of the low-level equipment will be easily replaced by future loot, and the high-level equipment is very expensive (generally bought during the Landsmeet for a run at the archdemon).

With so much good gear, here are some beauties to shoot for based on beginning (1–5), intermediate (6–10), advanced (11–15), and expert levels (16–20):

	Lvl 1-5	Lvl 6-10	Lvl 11-15	Lvl 16-20
Armor	Heavy Chainmail	Dwarven Heavy Armor	Armor of Diligence	Evon the Great's Mail, Wade's Superior Dragonbone Plate Armor
Helm	Commander's Helm	Knight Commander's Helm	Juggernaut Helm	Corruption
Boots	Heavy Chainmail Boots	Effort's Boots	Wade's Dragonbone Plate Boots	Wade's Superior Dragonbone Plate Boots, Juggernaut Plate Boots
Gloves	Heavy Plate Gloves	Gloves of the Legion	Wade's Superior Dragonbone Plate Gloves	Juggernaut Plate Gloves
Shield	Aeducan Shield	Redcliffe Elite Shield	Eamon's Shield	Duncan's Shield
Two Handed	Balanced Greatsword	Asala (Sten only)	The Summer Sword	Chasind Great Maul
One Handed	Borrowed Longsword	Saw Sword	Imperial Edge	King Maric's Blade

Party Responsibilities

Are you the party's tank or a damage-dealer? If you're the tank, your primary responsibility is holding threat and making sure that none of your companions die. That generally means stocking up on defensive talents and gear. If you're melee or ranged DPS, you can concentrate on offense and how much damage you can deal to enemy combatants. All non-tank warriors need to be aware of threat and avoid pulling too much at once. Learn to time your attacks so you don't create too much threat on yourself, yet deal significant damage to the enemy.

If your warrior is the main PC, the other three companions should fill in talents around you for a well-balanced party. If you're building up a companion warrior, look to fill in where the party is lacking. Not dealing enough damage? Crank up the offense. Tank having trouble holding all the enemies? Invest in some off-tank talents, such as Taunt, to grab enemies when needed. In the final party configuration, your PC should play whatever role you have the most fun with while the other three companions add the components necessary to maximize your combat efficiency.

The warrior ranks highest of the three classes in access to weapons and armor. Your talents and gear allow you to defensively tank for the group, deal huge amounts of single-target damage, and chip in with AoE every once and a while. There's no tougher adventurer in the land, so if you want to get right in the face of a raging hurlock or slash through spider ichor, step into the boots of a warrior.

Model Characters

With the game's best weapon talent trees, you can create dozens of warriors who each wield something a little different in combat. Don't feel constrained to play according to the following warrior models to the letter; take bits and pieces that appeal to your play style and add your own spin. However, these are basic models for a tank, melee DPS warrior, or ranged DPS warrior. Each shows you how to choose your talents up to level 20, what talent chains are effective, how specializations fit in, and sample combat strategies for that model.

Tank Model

Level	Talent
0	Shield Bash (Dwarf Noble or Human Noble)
1	Powerful, Shield Defense
2	Shield Balance
3	Shield Wall
4	Threaten
5	Shield Block
6	Shield Cover
7	War Cry (Champion)—First Specialization Available at This Level
8	Bravery
9	Shield Tactics
10	Shield Pummel
11	Overpower
12	Shield Mastery
13	Death Blow
14	Rally (Champion)—Second Specialization Available at This Level
15	Motivate (Champion)
16	Superiority (Champion)
17	Shield Expertise
18	Assault
19	Pinning Shot
20	Crippling Shot

Overview: A tank protects his companions and deals significant damage to boot. He generally concentrates in the Warrior school and the Weapon and Shield school.

Leveling: Choose a Dwarf Noble or Human Noble if you can. They come with the built-in Shield Bash talent, which puts you one talent into the Weapon and Shield school and exactly where you want to be. Sink your initial five points into strength and spend your skill point on Expert Combat Training, both of which satisfy your early talent prerequisites.

At level 1, pick up Powerful and Shield Defense. Level 2 gives you Shield Balance. At level 3, choose Shield Wall. Level 4 is an automatic choice: Threaten. In three levels, you now have the core of your tanking defense ready to go. Shield Defense is a great all-purpose protection stance; Shield Wall defends even better, but at the cost of reduced damage, which may not matter much if you have enough damage-dealers in the party. Shield Balance reduces the penalty to battle with a shield in your off-hand—another crucial talent for a Weapon and Shield warrior. Threaten should stay on in almost any fight to draw most of the threat to you.

TIP

If you want a more offensive-minded tank, simply switch some of the earlier defensive talents, such as Shield Block and Shield Cover, and load up on Shield Pummel, Overpower, and Assault.

When you reach levels 5 and 6, add Shield Block and Shield Cover to the mix. You could go with more offense here, but in this model we're concentrating on building the best defensive juggernaut we can to hold the line for your party. Stick with defense first, offense second. Make sure that you have 16 dexterity at this point to pick up Shield Cover.

You want the champion specialization by level 7 if at all possible. You can gain the champion specialization by completing the "Arl of Redcliffe" and "Urn of Sacred Ashes" quests and freeing Arl Eamon from his illness. If you can't get it by level 7, add it as soon as you can. The first champion talent, War Cry, hits all nearby enemies with an attack penalty, and it really shines when you gain Superiority at level 16.

At level 8, invest in Bravery. It gives bonuses to damage, physical resistance, mental resistance, and critical chance. In other words, it helps all facets of combat. Continue to add points to dexterity and strength as you level so you're prepared to meet the prerequisites of more advanced talents.

With 20 dexterity at level 9, you can finally gain Shield Tactics. This may be the most important talent a good tank needs, because it prevents enemies from scoring flanking bonuses against your warrior. No matter where your tank stands now, which is usually in the middle of an enemy swarm, it's just like he's facing the enemy head on.

Next switch to offense for two levels. At level 10, pick up Shield Pummel, and at level 11, purchase Overpower. Shield Pummel is a two-hit combo that can stun an opponent; Overpower is a three-hit combo that can knock a target down. Your strength and dexterity scores need to be in the mid-20s to open up your new talents.

Another milestone comes at level 12 with Shield Mastery. The majority of your offensive and defensive abilities gain bonuses with Shield Mastery. At level 13, you cap out the Warrior school when you gain Death Blow. Now, whenever your warrior slays an enemy, stamina gets restored. With enough killing, you can continuously operate your talents.

For levels 14 through 16, study all the rest of your champion talents. Rally and Motivate enhance the entire party's offense and defense, but Superiority is the coup de grace. Now when you trigger War Cry, it has a chance to knock down all enemies around you and give you a great advantage in battle.

At levels 17 and 18, fill out the rest of your Weapon and Shield chains. If you lean toward defense, learn Shield Expertise first; if you lean toward offense, get the four-hit combo Assault (requires 32 strength).

Your final two points could be spent on almost anything. You could pick up Precise Striking and Taunt in the Warrior school to give yourself another method of drawing threat. You could experiment with Two-Handed or Dual Weapon. Instead, we'll add a ranged component with Pinning Shot at level 19 and Crippling Shot at level 20. If you can't reach them on foot, pull out the bow and give them a reason to come to you.

Talent Choices: A tank concentrates on the defensive gems in the Warrior school, such as Powerful, Threaten, and Bravery. Other than that, a tank maxes out the Weapon and Shield school to take advantage of all its defensive components, with a little offense thrown in for good measure. No matter the enemy configuration, your tank should have an answer for it.

Specialization: The champion's War Cry hampers enemy attacks. Rally and Motivate increase offense and defense for your party. Superiority knocks enemies off their feet if they fail a physical resistance check.

Battle Tactics: Meet the enemy head on and intercept any attack on your companions. Unless you have Shield Tactics, you don't want to let yourself get surrounded where you fall prey to flanking bonuses. Instead, choose a tactical location that shields you from some enemy attacks while protecting your party's flanks. Use Threaten or Taunt to pull the threat toward you and away from companions.

Study your situation and choose the correct defense accordingly. For strict defense, go with Shield Wall, which boosts armor and prevents you from getting knocked down (a huge headache for your party if you don't have an off-tank ready to jump in). If you want more offense, go with the standard Shield Defense instead. If you're unsure on how the battle will go, always opt for more defense.

Once your defensive position is secure, think about dealing damage back to the monsters nearest you (or any ones who seem like they want to break free of your grasp). You can use Overpower and Assault to inflict serious harm. Save Shield Bash and Shield Pummel when you want to stun or knock down a target, especially if your health is low or an enemy is on another companion.

Melee DPS Model

Level	Talent
0	Shield Bash (Dwarf or Human Noble)
1	Pommel Strike, Powerful
2	Mighty Blow
3	Indomitable
4	Stunning Blows
5	Powerful Swings
6	Critical Strike
7	Berserk (Berserker)—*First Specialization Available at This Level*
8	Resilience (Berserker)
9	Two-Handed Strength
10	Constraint (Berserker)
11	Two-Handed Sweep
12	Final Blow (Berserker)
13	Sunder Arms
14	Shattering Blows—*Second Specialization Available at This Level*
15	Sunder Armor
16	Destroyer
17	Precise Striking
18	Taunt
19	Disengage
20	Perfect Striking

Overview: Concentrate on dealing combat damage as quickly as you can without pulling too much threat.

Leveling: Begin with a Dwarf or Human Noble to start with the Shield Bash talent (always a handy backup). Because most of what a melee DPSer loves to do is deal hand-to-hand damage, you only have to worry about strength. Spend all five of your initial character creation points on strength. Up through level 6, all your attribute points should be spent on strength, and all your skill points should go toward Combat Training. To maximize your DPS role, you need to achieve 34 strength and Master Combat Training by level 6. After that, you can pretty much spend your attribute and skill points freely.

At level 1, select Pommel Strike and Powerful with your first two talent points. Pommel Strike gives you a knockdown attack, and Powerful enhances your health and reduces fatigue; useful defensive abilities, but the offense will come in bunches soon.

At level 2, Mighty Blow begins a run to some major offense by level 6. Mighty Blow gives a bonus to attack and, if the blow connects, scores a critical hit on the target. Indomitable at level 3 serves as a stepping stone talent to reach the better offensive top-tier talents; you may use Indomitable against creatures such as golems who you know will knock you down, but otherwise all your efforts go toward offense and you can leave it off. At level 4, make sure you have 28 strength and Expert Combat Training to select Stunning Blows. It's a passive talent that can make a world of difference: all your blows have a chance to stun the enemy. At level 5, Powerful Swings increases your damage; however, it gives a penalty to attack and defense until you gain Two-Handed Strength at level 9.

If you've maxed out your strength and skills properly, you can pick up Critical Strike at level 6. Critical Strike promises an automatic critical hit and massive damage to a single target. Use it in any one-on-one fight or when you have lots of stamina in a longer fight.

At level 7, dip into the berserker specialization. One way to get this one is to work on the Orzammar quests early in the game; Oghren joins you on the "Paragon of Her Kind" quest and will teach you the specialization if you befriend him. These quests can be tough at lower levels, however, so you can also purchase the specialization from Gorim at the Denerim Market. Berserk increases damage for each of your strokes, though your stamina will suffer a bit. Resilience at the next level helps offset Berserk's stamina penalty, as does Constraint at level 10. Speaking of offsetting penalties, Two-Handed Strength, at level 9, minimizes the penalties from Powerful Swings.

At level 11, Two-Handed Sweep gives you an option against multiple foes. You deal normal damage, but can knock them off their feet. Berserker's Final Blow at level 12 hits an opponent with a massive blow inflicting damage proportional to all of your stamina (which is expended in the process).

For the next four levels, invest in the Sunder chain: Sunder Arms, Shattering Blows, Sunder Armor, and Destroyer (requires 30 strength). If you like, feel free to buy part of this chain earlier for extra damage penetration, but you will lose out on some AoE and suffer penalties while using talents such as Powerful Swings. The chain can dramatically alter a battle against heavily armored foes, or massive foes such as golems.

Your final four levels pick up the offensive Warrior chain: Precise Striking, Taunt, Disengage, and Perfect Striking. Taunt lets you off-tank if necessary, while Disengage is a nice option to reduce threat and shed enemies if the onslaught becomes too much.

Talent Choices: In this version of a DPS warrior, your combat skills revolve around a two-handed weapon that, though slower, generally deals the most DPS of any weapon. Most of your talents maximize damage potential, with a few that give you AoE or stunning capabilities. It's possible to branch out into Archery and Dual Weapon, but you don't want to spread yourself too thin or you won't max out your two-hander's damage.

Specialization: Berserker is a big plus as soon as you can achieve it. The extra damage from the specialization is exactly what you want in a DPS melee class. The stamina penalty can be rough; however, two of your talents minimize the penalty, and the last talent, Final Blow, will win you some battles.

Battle Tactics: Be patient. You can deal a huge amount of damage, which means if you attack too swiftly, you may pull the threat off your tank. You won't be much use to the group with four enemies stomping on your shredded corpse. Wait for the tank to set up, then attack from the flank or rear and cut through enemy after enemy. It's fine to go all out on an enemy and even pull it off the tank so long as it dies almost immediately.

Watch the battle and see where you're most needed. If you have off-tank skills, pick up any stragglers that go for the healer or other non-tank companions. The quicker the enemies drop, the less damage the party receives, so bounce from weakest enemy to weakest enemy as you help the tank chop away at the numbers. Save your big special effects (stuns, critical strikes, etc.) for bosses or tough enemies that just won't go down with the normal party tactics. If the tank looks to be in trouble, pull out all the stops and dive into the main enemy line.

Ranged DPS Model

Level	Talent
0	Pinning Shot (Dalish Elf)
1	Crippling Shot, Rapid Shot
2	Shattering Shot
3	Critical Shot
4	Suppressing Fire
5	Melee Archer
6	Scattershot
7	Arrow of Slaying—*First Specialization Available at This Level*
8	Righteous Strike (Templar)
9	Cleanse Area (Templar)
10	Aim
11	Defensive Fire
12	Master Archer
13	Mental Fortress (Templar)
14	Dual Striking—*Second Specialization Available at This Level*
15	Holy Smite (Templar)
16	Riposte
17	Cripple
18	Punisher
19	Dual-Weapon Training
20	Dual-Weapon Finesse

The Warrior

Basics ~ Character Generation ~ **Classes** ~ The Party ~ Companions ~ Supporting Cast ~ Equipment ~ Bestiary ~ Walkthroughs ~ Side Quests ~ Random Encounters ~ Achievements/Trophies

Overview: Much like an offensive mage, a ranged DPS warrior concentrates weapons and talents on enemies at a distance. He focuses on the Archery school, and may dip into some talents, such as Dual Weapon, when melee becomes imminent.

TIP

Your draw speed with bows is normally slowed down if you wear heavy or massive armor. However, if you take the Master Archer talent, the penalty on heavy armor is removed, thus you can draw at full speed in everything but massive.

Leveling: Begin as a Dalish Elf and you start with the Pinning Shot talent. As you'll be working with a bow and dual weapons, load up on dexterity. Your goal is to have 27 dexterity and Master Combat Training by level 6.

With your first two talent points at level 1, choose Crippling Shot and Rapid Shot. You now can hamper someone's attack and defense with Crippling Shot or reload much faster with Rapid Shot. Shattering Shot at level 2 imposes an even greater penalty to a foe's defense as it reduces armor value.

If you have 21 dexterity and Expert Combat Training at level 3, select Critical Shot. If you hit, Critical Shot inflicts critical damage and a bonus to armor penetration. Follow that up with Suppressing Fire at the next level to further encumber targets with attack penalties.

At level 5, slip in Melee Archer. It's an all-around useful ability: it prevents attacks from interrupting your firing.

You reach your first pinnacle at level 6 with Scattershot. This awesome talent automatically stuns your target and deals normal damage, then splinters off and does the same to all nearby enemies. Use this effectively against enemy spellcasters or large enemy groups to impede flanking attempts.

If you can reach 30 dexterity by level 7, you gain Arrow of Slaying. This scores an automatic critical hit against all but high-level opponents, and it's another offensive threat you can deliver.

At level 8, search out the templar specialization. Ask Alistair if you're friendly, or you can pick up the training manual at the party camp vendor. The first talent, Righteous Strike, lets you drain mana with any successful melee strike against an enemy spellcaster. You may have to get close to use this talent, but it's generally worth it against spellcasters, and it opens the door for the better templar talents later, such as Cleanse Area at the next level. This removes all magic effects on your party, which is great when you have negative debuffs on the group, but watch that you don't strip the good buffs in the process.

The next three levels, 10–12, fill out the rest of the Melee Archer chain: Aim, Defensive Fire, Master Archer. Use Aim for more offense and Defensive Fire when you fear return fire. Master Archer improves almost every Archery talent.

At level 13, Mental Fortress gives you a huge upgrade to your mental resistance. At level 14, you branch into melee combat with Dual Striking. Now that your ranged abilities are maxed out, select Holy Smite at level 15 (which decimates enemy spellcasters by dealing damage and draining mana), then spend the rest of your points beefing up your melee combat.

Riposte at level 16 gives you a stunning attack, which can help tremendously by getting you out of tight melee spot and allowing you to move to a new location and return to your ranged attacks. Level 17's Cripple can also hamper enemy movement while you escape. Level 18's Punisher may knock the enemy down, but it's more about dealing big melee damage when you are absolutely engaged in hand-to-hand fighting.

Because you've devoted a few talents to fighting with two melee weapons, your final two talents help offset the dual-weapon penalties: Dual-Weapon Training and Dual-Weapon Finesse. By this point, you'll destroy them at range, and should they limp into melee range, you're not half-bad nose-to-nose either.

Talent Choices: The Archery school and all its ranged surprises are your bread and butter. Dual Weapons provide some support talents in case an enemy gets close enough to melee.

Specialization: Templar enhances your skill in taking down enemy spellcasters. Righteous Strike can be fantastic once you reach higher levels and can tap into your Dual Weapon talents. Cleanse Area and Mental Fortress bulk up your defensive abilities. Holy Smite gives you another powerful ranged attack that will destroy an enemy spellcaster in a single energy burst.

Battle Tactics: Once the battle begins, stand your ground. Let the tank and other melee DPSers embrace the enemy. You want to nuke them from afar. Unlike a mage who stays in the rear, however, the ranged DPS warrior can enter melee with his better armor, weapons, and Dual Weapon talents at higher levels.

Survey the battlefield and pick your targets wisely. Concentrate fire on the tank's target to bring it down quicker, or look for injured foes that you can drop with an arrow or two. If you see an enemy spellcaster in the enemy's rear, make it your priority. You don't want it getting off damaging spells. Same goes for enemy archers. If your melee companions can't reach them, it's your job to stop them from pelting the team with damage.

On offense, your rotation goes something like this: Aim, Pinning Shot (against moving targets), Critical Shot (against near-dead targets), Arrow of Slaying. On defense, go Defensive Fire, Crippling Shot, Suppressing Fire, and Scattershot (especially against enemy spellcaster or enemies charging at you).

As a ranged DPS warrior, you have much of the offense of a DPS mage, yet you can still wear most of the better armor and use high quality weapons. Keep on the go to avoid enemy melee encounters and let your arrows serve as warnings to any new darkspawn that stumble across the field of arrow-strewn corpses.

The Mage

You are channeler and healer, death-dealer and life-giver, the spellpower behind the party's muscle. A mage stays in the rear, choosing targets carefully and always thinking ahead to the next damage spell or heal. A mage can conjure fire, encase allies in impenetrable force fields, or drain the very life from a victim. Tapping into any of the four magic schools (Primal, Creation, Spirit, Entropy), the DPS mage supplies firepower, especially against large enemy groups, the healer supports benevolent spells that can turn the tide in a close contest, or the hybrid mage balances both offense and defense in one versatile package.

Though the mage doesn't have the same kind of access to weapons and armor as a warrior or rogue (unless the mage specializes in arcane warrior), consider his spell arrays his artillery. The Primal school gives the mage the power of the elements: fire, earth, cold, electricity. By the third spell in any of these chains, the mage can cast devastating AoE attacks that destroy large enemy groups. In the Creation school, healing and buffs take precedent. The power to regenerate health, mana, and stamina fuels your party to greater glory. Your last two schools, Spirit and Entropy, grant mind-bogglingly cool abilities that stretch beyond pure damage or healing. With nearly 70 spells to choose from, no two mages need be the same.

Mage specializations offer the greatest possibilities to transform your class into something outside the normal class boundaries. An arcane warrior trades magic score for strength, ditches staff and robe for weapons and armor usually restricted to warriors, and can enter melee as a hand-to-hand brawler. A blood mage taps into the life force flowing in most creatures' veins, and uses that dark magic to control minds, damage enemies, convert blood to mana, and heal from the pain of others. A shapeshifter can change into a combat-oriented spider, bear, and insect swarm, or master them all for potent alternate fighting forms. Finally, a spirit healer is the ultimate savior, able to heal the entire party at once, cure injuries, and even bring the dead back to life.

If you like to sling spells from tactical positions and play around with the fantastical, the mage class is for you. World-class spells are at your fingertips, and you will rule the battlefield from afar. No other class can touch you when it comes to obliterating hordes of monsters at once. Just remember that if those monsters get up, you'd better have enough mana to knock them back down.

The Mage

Basics ~ Character Generation ~ **Classes** ~ The Party ~ Companions ~ Supporting Cast ~ Equipment ~ Bestiary ~ Walkthroughs ~ Side Quests ~ Random Encounters ~ Achievements/Trophies

Strengths and Weaknesses

Think of the mage as a cannoneer or a field medic, depending on your play style and spell spec. If you lean toward a DPS mage, your spells can do tremendous damage to single targets (possibly killing them with a single spell) or major damage to a large enemy group. You can even contribute damage over time to opponents with such spells as Fireball and Walking Bomb. If you become a healer, your spells will keep you and your allies alive, even in battles that may seem lost at the start. Either of those skills sets would earn you a place on the team, but you also have crowd control spells (Grease, Earthquake, Cone of Cold, etc.) that keep enemies from swarming the party, and party buffs (the Heroic chain, Spellbloom, etc.) that aid your allies with additional abilities.

Advantages

- Stat Bonuses to Magic, Willpower, and Cunning
- Great Ranged and AoE Damage
- Healing
- Crowd Control Spells
- Party Buffs

With all those great spells a hand gesture away, mages pay the price with armor and weapons: they can use only robes, cowls, staves, and the less powerful armor and weapons. Mages aren't built for hand-to-hand melee, unless they devote several spells to melee offense/defense or seek out the arcane warrior specialization, and spellcasters can't go toe-to-toe with foes like warriors and rogues can. Even worse, mages' damage spells, especially AoE spells that strike multiple targets, generate significant threat and will pull monsters to you. You need a capable tank to regain the threat or you will find yourself bloodied on the ground.

Disadvantages

- Limited Armor and Weapon Choices
- Generally Weak in Melee
- Damage Spells Can Generate Significant Threat

You may not be the party member who jumps into the thick of melee, but you can be the tactician who stands in the back and surveys the whole battlefield. If you like to blow up lots of things at once, or, on the flip side, choose your targets wisely to pick them off one by one, the mage's spells have you covered. You will have the firepower to bolster your party from competent fighters to veritable forces of nature.

Attributes

Spells are your livelihood as a mage, thus your magic score is essential. Magic directly increases your character's spellpower score, which determines the potency of all spells. The prerequisite for the various schools of magic begins at 18 magic, but goes as high as 36 magic, so put most of your points here to unlock crucial spells. Magic also determines how effective potions, poultices, and salves are for characters; your mage will gain bigger benefits from lyrium potions and health poultices because of your affinity for magic.

Mage Attribute Bonuses

+5 Magic
+4 Willpower
+1 Cunning

Willpower works in conjunction with magic. The more points you throw into willpower, the larger your mana pool and the more spells you can cast. If you have a party member with good Herbalism, you may be able to stock up on lyrium potions to offset a lower willpower score, but you definitely need to spend as many points here as you can afford. If you have a good tank who holds threat well, and you don't get hit much by monsters in melee, sink all your extra points into growing your mana pool.

 **TIP**

Gear bonuses can amplify your attribute's strengths or offset any shortcomings. A ring, for example, that bulks up constitution could provide some extra health without costing any of your precious attribute points.

After magic and willpower, your attributes will go more according to your play style. In general, you may want to add a little constitution. Every mage, even if they don't plan on beating mobs over the head with a staff, needs health and resilience. The more you have, the longer you'll stay in a fight, and if your tank fails to hold a creature's threat and it comes gunning for you, that extra constitution and health bonus will make a difference.

primagames.com

Cunning contributes to learning skills, and it's huge if you take Coercion and want to persuade NPCs. If you don't invest in Coercion, then feel free to spend these points in constitution and dexterity.

Dexterity has limited use for most mages. It can be helpful to dodge incoming blows, and an arcane warrior mage may want some points in dexterity for accuracy while wielding melee weapons. If you do spend points, spend only a few.

Because you shouldn't be engaging foes physically, strength means very little. There's always something better to spend points on, so leave this attribute alone. If you're worried about combat damage, it's probably best to spend the points on constitution instead.

During character creation, feel free to choose a race based on overall story possibilities. It's much more important to enjoy the origin story for your character than it is to worry about a point here or there in your attributes. However, if maximizing your mage stats appeals to you, choose an elf. An elven mage gives you a starting 17 magic and 16 willpower. A human mage offers one fewer point in magic and two fewer points in willpower. Most of your points are socked away in magic and willpower, so later in your character's evolution you'll need to spread out the points to other attributes. Dwarves cannot be mages; if you want to play a dwarf, you won't be casting spells.

Mage Starting Attributes

Attribute	Human	Elf
Strength	11	10
Dexterity	11	10
Willpower	14	16
Magic	16	17
Cunning	12	11
Constitution	10	10

Once you choose your mage's race, you begin with five extra points to add to your attributes. That's almost two "level ups" worth of attribute growth, so spend it wisely. Most builds require you to spend all, or most, of your points in magic out of the gate. It's important to unlock spells early, and because magic is the main prerequisite for spells, you must reach the 25–30 magic range to gain the better spells. If you don't care about reaching the upper echelon spells soon, then think about a 3/2 split between magic and willpower, or a 2/2/1 split among magic, willpower, and constitution.

Skills

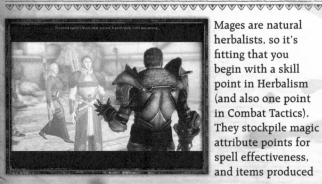

Mages are natural herbalists, so it's fitting that you begin with a skill point in Herbalism (and also one point in Combat Tactics). They stockpile magic attribute points for spell effectiveness, and items produced by Herbalism rely on magic for effectiveness. It's a perfect union. At least one party member must be skilled in Herbalism per party. Otherwise, you lose out on essential healing and mana potions, and won't have the same staying power in fights as a fully stocked party. Unless one of your companions (say, Wynne) supports Herbalism, you should strongly consider it as your top skill.

NOTE

Beyond your starting skills, you're likely to obtain 7–9 skill points throughout the game. Pick your two or three favorite skills and stick with them. If you spread your points too thin, you'll end up doing a bunch of things—but not well.

Because mages gravitate toward magic, Herbalism ranks high, but Coercion is usually the best skill to take. As with any other class, Coercion grants you access to story possibilities that aren't available through brute force. Spend all your skill points here first if you don't plan on becoming a herbalist.

The more points you spend in Combat Training, the more damage you can take before the damage interrupts your spellcasting. If you're a mage who expects to get hit often in combat, or you don't want to blow a key spell because of mob interference, then stock up on Combat Training. Two points is enough to withstand disruption from all but the most damaging attacks.

Mage Skill Recommendations

Assuming you spend 8 skill points by career's end, here's a good spread to consider. Note that many other combinations could work better for you, so experiment!

- Herbalism +4
- Coercion +4

Survival can be a good skill to have because the more you advance it, the better chance you have to detect creatures on your mini-map before they surprise you. You can save yourself from more than a few ambushes with this skill. Don't forget about the bonus to nature resistance too.

For companion mages, who you might not always control directly, consider spending skill points in Combat Tactics. The more tactic slots you open, the more you can shape how your companion behaves in battle. Inevitably, even if you plan on controlling your mage during fights, there will be moments when you don't program your mage's every move (or something more important is going on) and tactics come into play. One or two points should be good, or max it out if you want the character to go on autopilot.

None of the other skills really fit the mage profile, except perhaps Trap-Making. At first it seems solely a rogue skill, but if your mage isn't strong in ranged damage (a healer, for example), you may want Trap-Making to use traps to lure enemies in. Traps deal decent damage up front while you cast a spell barrage from afar.

The Mage

Basics ~ Character Generation ~ **Classes** ~ The Party ~ Companions ~ Supporting Cast ~ Equipment ~ Bestiary ~ Walkthroughs ~ Side Quests ~ Random Encounters ~ Achievements/Trophies

Spells

Mages have access to a vast arsenal of spells, many more than you could attain in the course of the game. Rather than focusing on one school, pick the type of mage you'd like to be (DPS, healer, or blend) then round out your mage with a selection of spells that could deal with an array of situations. For example, you'll want a few spells for AoE, direct attacks on single targets, buffs, etc. Notice how the stronger spells are at the end of individual chains. With that in mind, develop individual chains rather than focusing on an entire school.

You start with one point in the Mage spell school and two more points to spend wherever you like. In addition, you receive one point for every level you gain, and you gain one talent bonus point when you survive the Joining and a second bonus point at the end of the Landsmeet when you become commander of your army. Working with this, if you get to level 20 by the end of the game, you'll have 24 total points to spend. It might seem like a lot, but you really have to plan what spell chains you want, because you'll cap only three or four regular chains if you decide to specialize.

NOTE

It's possible to have three mages in the game: Wynne, Morrigan, and you. Develop each differently to have access to a wider arsenal of magic.

All mages need to familiarize themselves with the cooldown component of each spell. The worst situation is to have plenty of mana and no available spells to cast. Branch out into different spells to avoid the cooldown problem. Yes, you may love to cast Lightning on a target, but you need a follow-up damage spell or two to use while Lightning reloads. You also want to branch out into different chains so that your spell rotation cycles through separate damage types. For example, if you develop the Fire chain as your sole damage source and run into rage demons, who are resistant to fire, you won't do too well. But if you have Winter's Grasp or Cone of Cold in your arsenal, you can contribute massive damage.

Even DPS mages should carry a Heal spell. It's always a luxury to have a mage who can serve the same function as a health poultice, only on a continuous basis with sometimes greater effect. In the same regard, don't under-value your defensive spells. Your main priority may be to deal damage as a DPS mage, but at some point you will need to protect yourself. Spells such as Arcane Shield and Force Field minimize damage that would otherwise kill you in an encounter.

Your spells draw mana from your pool. Watch how much mana you're using in a fight and cast accordingly. If you run short without ample lyrium potions to replenish, you could cost your party a victory. Gauge what you have to do to help the team. There's no sense casting a huge Chain Lightning spell on a group of enemies that go down with one or two swings, just as you may want to hold back on that Petrify spell if the tank has the situation under control. Save your mana. You never know when the next fight will start, and you'll be grateful you didn't waste mana.

Spell Combos

- Earthquake + Grease + Fireball + Walking Bomb should stymie most groups before they can do too much harm to your party.

- A fire spell on Grease works great at lower levels or when you don't have all kinds of time.

- Glyph of Paralysis + Glyph of Repulsion causes an explosive effect that paralyzes those nearby.

- Blizzard + Inferno + Tempest becomes Storm of the Century (spectacular electrical storm).

- Cast Blizzard on a burning Grease slick to extinguish it.

- Send a tank to draw all kinds of threat from a mob away from the party. Cast Force Field on the tank for immunity from all damage and then follow with Inferno to engulf the entire area. The enemies burn while fighting a tank that can't die.

- Drain Life and Mana Drain are twice as effective on a target with a Vulnerability Hex.

- Cast Spell Might on yourself and then cast Animate Dead on a skeleton. This skeleton is much more powerful than the ordinary skeletons you can animate.

- Cast Sleep on a target and then cast Horror on it. This inflicts massive spirit damage on the target, often killing many lesser foes outright. Those who survive emerge in a state of fear.

- Immobilize a target with Cone of Cold or Petrify. When the target is in that vulnerable state, a critical hit from any weapon, a hit from the Stonefist spell, or the effects of the Crushing Prison spell will shatter it. (Bosses and lieutenants are highly resistant to this.)

- Cast a Death Hex on a target and then cast a Death Cloud in its area. If the target is touched by the Death Cloud, it sustains massive spirit damage.

CAUTION

Friendly fire is very possible. Many spells have an area of effect much larger than just one target. The higher the spell in the chain, the more damage your party members can take if they're caught in the affected area, so be careful.

primagames.com

Mage School

Arcane Bolt is a basic all-around damage spell with a long range, decent damage, and minor cost. Arcane Shield is a sustained ability that helps divert attacks and bolsters your mage's defense. Staff Focus increases the power of your basic staff attack, and Arcane Mastery grants a permanent bonus to spellpower, augmenting all your spells. Almost any mage build wants Arcane Mastery as soon as it becomes available at level 10. On the attack, cast your powerful spells, then follow them up with Arcane Bolt. When you're being swarmed, use your Arcane Shield, then let your other characters take the threat while you move back and come at your enemies with another wave of spells.

Primal School

Your main offensive spells find their home in the Primal school. Mostly focused on activated abilities, both in direct attacks and AoE attacks, Primal taps fire, earth, cold, and electricity for your staple damage attacks. The first spell in each chain gives you a decent damage spell (except for the Earth chain, which gives you Stonefist second), and the third spell grants you a powerful AoE blast. Monsters will be affected differently based on their resistances and vulnerabilities, and each chain has its own special effects: fire causes damage over time; earth gives you defense and one-shot kill with Petrify; cold hampers enemy movement; electricity forks to adjacent targets.

Creation School

Your primary school as a healer, Creation focuses on restoring health, replenishing mana, enhancing the party, and warding an area with glyphs. The healing chain is the most important; you'll want Heal right out of the gate and Regeneration as soon as you can reach the 23 magic prerequisite. The Spell Wisp chain can work for any mage as well: Spell Wisp increases spellpower, Grease traps enemies in a flammable AoE, Spellbloom regenerates mana, and Stinging Swarm is like an AoE damage spell as it bounces from target to target, except it doesn't create tons of threat focused on a single creature each time. The Heroic chain is for mages who want to buff the party, sacrificing offense for utility. The Glyph chain gives the mage some crowd control with paralysis, warding, repulsion, and neutralization effects.

Spirit School

Two of the chains can be unexpected powerhouses if used well. The Walking Bomb chain poisons a single target, or explodes a host of similar monsters with Virulent Walking Bomb, plus the chain provides mana regeneration and additional melee support through Animate Dead. The Mind Blast chain splits between great defensive and great offensive abilities. Mind Blast stuns all nearby enemies (great for when the mage gets swarmed), Force Field nullifies all damage to a target for a short time (the ultimate threat negation), Telekinetic Weapons beefs up armor penetration for your whole squad, and Crushing Prison completely shuts down a target, rooting the enemy in place and causing enough damage to kill weaker targets. The Spell Shield chain is a must for defensive mages, especially Dispel Magic to remove devastating hexes and Anti-Magic Ward to cancel enemy spellcasting on one of your allies. Finally, the Mana chain centers around disrupting enemy spellcasters' mana, and replenishing your own in the process. If your party doesn't have a templar, think about spending a few points in this chain's abilities.

Entropy School

The Entropy chains slide into the dark side of magic. The Drain/Death chain may be the most useful; the first two abilities net you health, while Curse of Mortality is lethal against healing mobs and Death Cloud is lethal to everything. The Weakness chain strips offense, defense, and movement from enemies, or it outright paralyzes them. The upgrades (Miasma and Mass Paralysis) do it even better, affecting whole groups. The Fear chain begins with Disorient, which inflicts combat penalties, works toward Horror, which causes the targets to cower in fear, and then knocks out enemies with Sleep. Combo Sleep with Waking Nightmare and hostile targets become randomly stunned, attack other enemies, or become the caster's ally for the duration of the spell. The last chain of hexes grants four different effects: vulnerability to resistances, AoE resistance penalties, inaccuracy, and bad luck (all normal hits become critical strikes).

The Mage

Basics ~ Character Generation ~ **Classes** ~ The Party ~ Companions ~ Supporting Cast ~ Equipment ~ Bestiary ~ Walkthroughs ~ Side Quests ~ Random Encounters ~ Achievements/Trophies

Mage Spells

Chain	Name	Prerequisite	Description	Cost (mana /stamina)	Upkeep (mana /stamina)	Fatigue (% mana/stamina)	Ranged	Cooldown (sec.)	Area of Effect Radius (ft.)
Mage School									
Chain 1	Arcane Bolt	None	The caster fires a sphere of magical energy at an enemy, dealing moderate spirit damage.	15	0	0	Yes	6	0
	Arcane Shield	Level 3	The caster generates protective sheath that helps divert incoming attacks, gaining a bonus to defense while this mode is active.	0	30	5	No	10	0
	Staff Focus	Level 7	The character has specialized in direct attacks using a mage staff, gaining a permanent bonus to damage from basic attacks.	0	0	0	No	0	0
	Arcane Mastery	Level 10	The mage has gained a keen familiarity with the arcane arts, granting a permanent bonus to spellpower.	0	0	0	No	0	0
Primal School									
Chain 1	Flame Blast	None	The caster's hands erupt with a cone of flame, inflicting fire damage on all targets in the area for a short time. Friendly fire possible.	20	0	0	Yes	10	35
	Flaming Weapons	Magic 18	While this spell is active, the caster enchants the party's melee weapons with flame so that they deal additional fire damage with each successful attack.	0	50	5	Yes	10	0
	Fireball	Magic 27	The caster's hands erupt with an explosive ball of flame, inflicting lingering fire damage on all targets in the area as well as knocking them off their feet unless they pass a physical resistance check. Friendly fire possible.	40	0	0	Yes	10	7
	Inferno	Magic 34	The caster summons a huge column of swirling flame. All targets in the area take constant fire damage as they burn. Friendly fire possible.	70	0	0	Yes	60	10
Chain 2	Lightning	Magic 18	The caster fires a bolt of lightning at a target, dealing electricity damage. Friendly fire possible.	20	0	0	Yes	10	0
	Shock	None	The caster's hands erupt with a cone of lightning, damaging all targets in the area. Friendly fire possible.	40	0	0	Yes	15	35
	Tempest	Magic 28	The caster unleashes a fierce lightning storm that deals constant electricity damage to anyone in the targeted area. Friendly fire possible.	50	0	0	Yes	40	10
	Chain Lightning	Magic 33	The caster's hands erupt with a bolt of lightning that inflicts electricity damage on a target, then forks, sending smaller bolts jumping to those nearby, which fork again. Each fork does less damage than the previous. Friendly fire possible.	60	0	0	Yes	60	0
Chain 3	Rock Armor	None	The caster's skin becomes as hard as stone, granting a bonus to armor for as long as this mode is active.	0	40	5	No	10	0
	Stonefist	Magic 18	The caster hurls a stone projectile that knocks down the target and inflicts nature damage, possibly shattering those that have been petrified or frozen solid. Friendly fire possible.	30	0	0	Yes	15	0
	Earthquake	Magic 25	The caster disrupts the earth, causing a violent quake that knocks everyone in the targeted area to the ground unless they pass a physical resistance check every few seconds. Friendly fire possible.	40	0	0	Yes	40	10
	Petrify	Magic 30	The caster draws from knowledge of the elements to turn the target into stone unless it passes a physical resistance check. While petrified, the target is immobile and vulnerable to shattering from a critical hit. Creatures already made of stone are immune.	40	0	0	Yes	40	0
Chain 4	Winter's Grasp	None	The caster envelops the target in frost, freezing lower-level targets solid. Those that resist suffer a penalty to movement speed.	20	0	0	Yes	8	0
	Frost Weapons	Magic 18	While this mode is active, the caster enchants the party's weapons with frost so that they deal additional cold damage with each melee attack.	0	50	5	Yes	10	0
	Cone of Cold	Magic 25	The caster's hands erupt with a cone of frost, freezing targets solid unless they pass a physical resistance check, and slowing their movement otherwise. Targets frozen solid by Cone of Cold can be shattered with a critical hit. Friendly fire possible.	40	0	0	Yes	10	35
	Blizzard	Magic 34	An ice storm deals continuous cold damage to everyone in the targeted area and slows their movement speed while granting bonuses to defense and fire resistance. Targets can fall or be frozen solid unless they pass a physical resistance check. Friendly fire possible.	70	0	0	Yes	60	10
Creation School									
Chain 1	Glyph of Paralysis	None	The caster inscribes a glyph on the ground that paralyzes the first enemy who crosses its bounds, unless the opponent passes a physical resistance check. A single caster can maintain a limited number of Glyphs of Paralysis at once.	25	0	0	Yes	40	2.5
	Glyph of Warding	Magic 18	The caster inscribes a glyph on the ground that bestows nearby allies with bonuses to defense and mental resistance as well as a bonus against missile attacks.	40	0	0	Yes	30	2.5
	Glyph of Repulsion	Magic 25	The caster inscribes a glyph on the ground that knocks back enemies unless they pass a physical resistance check.	35	0	0	Yes	30	2.5
	Glyph of Neutralization	Magic 33	The caster inscribes a glyph on the ground that neutralizes all magic, dispels all effects, drains all mana, and prevents spellcasting or mana regeneration within its bounds.	60	0	0	Yes	60	2.5

Chain	Name	Prerequisite	Description	Cost (mana /stamina)	Upkeep (mana /stamina)	Fatigue (% mana/stamina)	Ranged	Cooldown (sec.)	Area of Effect Radius (ft.)
			Creation School (continued)						
Chain 2	Heal	None	The caster causes flesh to knit miraculously, instantly healing an ally by a moderate amount.	20	0	0	Yes	5	0
	Rejuvenate	Magic 18	The caster channels regenerative energy to the selected ally, granting them a short term boost to mana or stamina regeneration.	25	0	0	Yes	45	0
	Regeneration	Magic 23	The caster infuses an ally with beneficial energy, greatly accelerating health regeneration for a short time.	25	0	0	Yes	5	0
	Mass Rejuvenation	Magic 28	The caster channels a stream of rejuvenating energy to all members of the party, significantly increasing mana and stamina regeneration for a short duration.	45	0	0	No	90	0
Chain 3	Heroic Offense	None	The caster enhances an ally's aptitude in battle, granting a bonus to attack.	20	0	0	Yes	5	0
	Heroic Aura	Magic 15	The caster sheathes an ally in an aura that completely shrugs off most missile attacks for a moderate duration.	30	0	0	Yes	5	0
	Heroic Defense	Magic 20	The caster shields an ally with magic, granting bonuses to defense, cold resistance, electricity resistance, fire resistance, nature resistance, and spirit resistance, although at a penalty to fatigue, meaning that the ally's talents or spells will cost more to activate.	40	0	0	Yes	10	0
	Haste	Magic 30	While this mode is active, the caster imbues the party with speed, allowing them to move and attack significantly faster, although the spell also imposes a small penalty to attack and drains mana rapidly while in combat.	0	60	10	Yes	30	0
Chain 4	Spell Wisp	None	The caster summons a wisp that grants a small bonus to spellpower for as long as this mode is active.	0	30	5	No	5	0
	Grease	Magic 20	The caster summons a grease slick that slows anyone who walks on it, as well as causing them to slip unless they pass a physical resistance check. If the grease is set on fire, it burns intensely for a time. Friendly fire possible.	25	0	0	Yes	20	7.5
	Spellbloom	Magic 23	The caster creates an energizing bloom of magic that grants anyone nearby, friend or foe, a bonus to mana regeneration.	25	0	0	Yes	30	10
	Stinging Swarm	Magic 33	A swarm of biting insects descend on the target, dealing a large amount of damage over a short time. If the targeted creature dies before the swarm dissipates, the insects will jump to another nearby enemy.	50	0	0	Yes	30	0
			Spirit School						
Chain 1	Mana Drain	None	The caster creates a parasitic bond with a spellcasting target, absorbing a small amount of mana from it.	0	0	0	Yes	10	0
	Mana Cleanse	Magic 18	The caster sacrifices personal mana to nullify the mana of enemies in the area.	40	0	0	Yes	20	10
	Spell Might	Magic 25	While in this mode, the caster overflows with magical energy, making spells more powerful, but expending mana rapidly and suffering a penalty to mana regeneration.	0	60	5	No	10	0
	Mana Clash	Magic 33	The caster expels a large amount of mana in direct opposition to enemy spellcasters, who are completely drained of mana and suffer spirit damage proportional to the amount of mana they lost.	50	0	0	Yes	40	10
Chain 2	Mind Blast	None	The caster projects a wave of telekinetic force that stuns enemies caught in the sphere.	20	0	0	No	30	5
	Force Field	Magic 18	The caster erects a telekinetic barrier around a target, who becomes completely immune to damage for the duration of the spell but cannot move. Friendly fire possible.	40	0	0	Yes	30	0
	Telekinetic Weapons	Magic 23	While this mode is active, the caster enchants the party's melee weapons with telekinetic energy that increases armor penetration. The bonus to armor penetration is based on the caster's spellpower and provides greater damage against heavily armored foes.	0	50	5	Yes	5	0
	Crushing Prison	Magic 30	The caster encloses a target in a collapsing cage of telekinetic force, inflicting spirit damage for the duration and possibly shattering those that have been petrified or frozen solid.	60	0	0	Yes	60	0
Chain 3	Spell Shield	None	While this ability is active, any hostile spell targeted at the caster has a 75% chance of being absorbed into the Fade, draining mana instead. Once all mana has been depleted, the shield collapses.	0	45	5	No	10	0
	Dispel Magic	Magic 18	The caster removes all dispellable effects from the target. Friendly fire possible.	25	0	0	Yes	2	0
	Anti-Magic Ward	Magic 25	The caster wards an ally against all spells and spell effects, beneficial or hostile, for a short time.	40	0	0	Yes	30	0
	Anti-Magic Burst	Magic 33	This burst of energy eliminates all dispellable magical effects in the area. Friendly fire possible.	40	0	0	Yes	30	7

The Mage

Basics ~ Character Generation ~ **Classes** ~ The Party ~ Companions ~ Supporting Cast ~ Equipment ~ Bestiary ~ Walkthroughs ~ Side Quests ~ Random Encounters ~ Achievements/Trophies

Chain	Name	Prerequisite	Description	Cost (mana /stamina)	Upkeep (mana /stamina)	Fatigue (% mana/stamina)	Ranged	Cooldown (sec.)	Area of Effec. Radius (ft.)
			Spirit School (continued)						
Chain 4	Walking Bomb	None	The caster magically injects a target with corrosive poison that inflicts continual nature damage. If the target dies while the effect is still active, it explodes, damaging all targets nearby. Although this spell is related to Virulent Walking Bomb, the magic behind the two does not interact; a target cannot be infected with both. Friendly fire possible.	30	0	0	Yes	20	0
	Death Syphon	Magic 20	While this mode is active, the caster draws in nearby entropic energy, draining residual power from any dead enemy nearby to restore the caster's mana.	0	45	5	No	10	5
	Virulent Walking Bomb	Magic 25	The caster magically injects a target with corrosive poison that inflicts continual nature damage. If the target dies while the effect is still active, it explodes, damaging nearby targets and possibly infecting them in turn. Although this spell is related to Walking Bomb, the magic behind the two does not interact; a target cannot be infected with both. Friendly fire possible.	40	0	0	Yes	40	0
	Animate Dead	Magic 33	The caster summons a skeleton minion from the corpse of a fallen enemy to fight alongside the party for a short time, although, as a puppet of the caster, it will not use any talents or spells without specific instruction.	0	80	10	No	60	0
			Entropy School						
Chain 1	Disorient	None	The caster engages in subtle mental manipulation that disorients the target for a short time, making the target a less effective combatant by inflicting penalties to attack and defense.	20	0	0	Yes	10	0
	Horror	Magic 18	The caster forces a target to cower in fear, unable to move, unless it passes a mental resistance check. Targets already asleep when the spell is cast cannot resist its effect and take massive spirit damage.	40	0	0	Yes	20	0
	Sleep	Magic 30	All hostile targets in the targeted area fall asleep unless they pass a mental resistance check, although they wake when hit. Sleeping enemies cannot resist the Horror spell, which will inflict additional damage.	35	0	0	Yes	50	10
	Waking Nightmare	Magic 32	Hostile targets are trapped in a waking nightmare unless they pass a mental resistance check. They are randomly stunned, attack other enemies, or become the caster's ally for the duration of the effect. Enemies that are already asleep cannot resist.	40	0	0	Yes	40	5
Chain 2	Drain Life	None	The caster creates a sinister bond with the target, draining its life energy in order to heal the caster.	20	0	0	Yes	10	0
	Death Magic	Magic 20	While active, the caster draws in nearby entropic energy, draining residual life-force from any dead enemy nearby to heal the caster.	0	45	5	No	10	5
	Curse of Mortality	Magic 25	The caster curses a target with the inevitability of true death. While cursed, the target cannot heal or regenerate health and takes continuous spirit damage.	40	0	0	Yes	60	0
	Death Cloud	Magic 34	The caster summons a cloud of leeching entropic energy that deals continuous spirit damage to all who enter. Friendly fire possible.	50	0	0	Yes	60	10
Chain 3	Vulnerability Hex	None	The target suffers a hex that inflicts penalties to cold resistance, electricity resistance, fire resistance, nature resistance, and spirit resistance.	20	0	0	Yes	20	0
	Affliction Hex	Magic 20	A contagious hex inflicts penalties to cold resistance, electricity resistance, fire resistance, nature resistance, and spirit resistance on the target and all other enemies nearby.	40	0	0	Yes	20	10
	Misdirection Hex	Magic 28	The target suffers a frustrating hex of inaccuracy. All hits become misses, while critical hits become normal hits.	45	0	0	Yes	40	0
	Death Hex	Magic 36	The target suffers a hex of lethal bad luck. Every normal hit it suffers becomes a critical hit.	60	0	0	Yes	60	0
Chain 4	Weakness	None	The caster drains a target of energy, inflicting penalties to attack and defense, as well as reducing its movement speed unless it passes a physical resistance check.	20	0	0	Yes	10	0
	Paralyze	Magic 18	The caster saps a target's energy, paralyzing it for a time unless it passes a physical resistance check, in which case its movement speed is reduced instead.	35	0	0	Yes	30	0
	Miasma	Magic 25	While this mode is active, the caster radiates an aura of weakness, hindering nearby enemies with penalties to attack and defense. Unless the opponents pass a physical resistance check, they also suffer a penalty to movement speed.	0	60	5	No	30	0
	Mass Paralysis	Magic 35	All hostile targets in the area are paralyzed for a short time unless they pass a physical resistance check, in which case their movement speed is reduced instead.	70	0	0	Yes	50	8
			Power of Blood School (downloadable content only)						
Chain 1	Dark Sustenance	None	A self-inflicted wound lets the mage draw from the power of tainted blood, rapidly regenerating a significant amount of mana but taking a small hit to health.	40*	0	0	No	60	0
	Bloody Grasp	None	The mage's own tainted blood becomes a weapon, sapping the caster's health slightly but inflicting spirit damage on the target. Darkspawn targets suffer additional damage for a short period.	15	0	0	Yes	10	0

* Health (gains 100 mana as a result)

Specializations

Each class has two specializations (out of four) that they can learn during the game. Your first specialization can be learned at level 7; your second at level 14. Most companions can teach a specialization, though your approval rating must be high enough for the companion to want to teach you. Morrigan, for example, can teach the mage's shapeshift specialization. Specializations are difficult to achieve, but very rewarding if you gain one. As long as the specific abilities fit with your play style and character breakdown, a specialization is generally worth spending points in over regular spells.

You should definitely experiment with specializations. A pure healer could, for example, specialize in shapeshifter to add some offense to the mix and some defense if they generate too much threat. Here are some suggested play style fits for the four specializations:

Arcane Warrior

- **Primary:** Melee/ranged mage (standard ranged spells with arcane warrior abilities for melee component)
- **Secondary:** Mana powerhouse (use Fade Shroud to regenerate mana faster) or tanking capability

Blood Mage

- **Primary:** Enemy control (use Blood Control to possess enemies to fight for you)
- **Secondary:** Health resilient (use Blood Sacrifice to heal self along with standard healing spells)

Shapeshifter

- **Primary:** DPS mage (shapeshifter melee attacks complement ranged spells)
- **Secondary:** Health resilient (use Flying Swarm to avoid health damage)

Spirit Healer

- **Primary:** Main party healer (Group Heal essential for party survival)
- **Secondary:** Savior (return dead comrades to life with Revival)

Mage Specializations

Specialization	Talent Name	Prerequisite Level	Description	Cost (mana/stamina)	Upkeep (mana/stamina)	Fatigue (% mana/stamina)	Ranged	Cooldown (sec.)	Area of Effect Radius (ft.)
Learned From: The Presence in Brecilian Ruins ("Nature of the Beast" quest line)									
Arcane Warrior	Combat Magic	7	While this mode is active, the arcane warrior channels magic inward, trading increased fatigue for an attack bonus and the ability to use spellpower to determine combat damage. Aura of Might and Fade Shroud improve the effects. Additionally, regardless of whether the mode is active, an arcane warrior who has learned this spell may use the magic attribute to satisfy the strength requirement to equip higher-level weapons or armor.	0	50	50	No	10	0
	Aura of Might	12	The arcane warrior's prowess with Combat Magic grows, granting additional bonuses to attack, defense, and damage while in that mode.	0	0	0	No	0	0
	Shimmering Shield	14	The arcane warrior is surrounded by a shimmering shield of energy that blocks most damage and grants large bonuses to armor and all resistances. When active, however, the Shimmering Shield consumes mana rapidly.	0	40	5	No	30	0
	Fade Shroud	16	The arcane warrior now only partly exists in the physical realm while Combat Magic is active. Spanning the gap between the real world and the Fade grants a bonus to mana regeneration and a chance to avoid attacks.	0	0	0	No	0	0
Learned From: Desire Demon in Fade ("Arl of Redcliffe" quest line)									
Blood Mage	Blood Magic	7	For as long as this mode is active, the blood mage sacrifices health to power spells instead of expending mana, but effects that heal the blood mage are much less effective than normal.	0	0	5	No	10	0
	Blood Sacrifice	12	The blood mage sucks the life-force from an ally, healing the caster but potentially killing the ally. This healing is not affected by the healing penalty of Blood Magic.	0	0	0	Yes	15	0
	Blood Wound	14	The blood of all hostile targets in the area boils within their veins, inflicting severe damage. Targets stand twitching, unable to move unless they pass a physical resistance check. Creatures without blood are immune.	40	0	0	Yes	20	10
	Blood Control	16	The blood mage forcibly controls the target's blood, making the target an ally of the caster unless it passes a mental resistance check. If the target resists, it instead takes great damage from the manipulation of its blood. Creatures without blood are immune.	40	0	0	Yes	40	0

The Mage

Basics ~ Character Generation ~ **Classes** ~ The Party ~ Companions ~ Supporting Cast ~ Equipment ~ Bestiary ~ Walkthroughs ~ Side Quests ~ Random Encounters ~ Achievements/Trophies

Specialization	Talent Name	Prerequisite Level	Description	Cost (mana/stamina)	Upkeep (mana/stamina)	Fatigue (% mana/stamina)	Ranged	Cooldown (sec.)	Area of Effect Radius (ft.)
			Learned From: Morrigan (Companion), Varathorn (Dalish Camp)						
Shapeshifter	Spider Shape	7	The shapeshifter can transform into a giant spider, gaining a large bonus to nature resistance as well as the spider's Web and Poison Spit abilities. The caster's spellpower determines how powerful the form is. With Master Shapeshifter, the mage becomes a corrupted spider, growing still stronger and gaining the Overwhelm ability.	0	50	5	No	90	0
	Bear Shape	8	The shapeshifter can transform into a bear, gaining large bonuses to nature resistance and armor as well as the bear's Slam and Rage abilities. The caster's spellpower further enhances this bear's statistics and abilities. With Master Shapeshifter, this form transforms the caster into a powerful bereskarn and gains the Overwhelm ability.	0	60	5	No	90	0
	Flying Swarm	10	The shapeshifter's body explodes into a swarm of stinging insects that inflict nature damage on nearby foes, with the damage increasing based on the caster's spellpower and proximity. While in this form, the caster gains Divide the Storm, and any damage the shapeshifter suffers is drawn from mana instead of health, but the caster regenerates no mana. The swirling cloud of insects is immune to normal missiles and has a very good chance of evading physical attacks but is extremely vulnerable to fire. With Master Shapeshifter, the character gains health whenever the swarm inflicts damage.	0	30	5	No	60	0
	Master Shapeshifter	12	Mastery of the shifter's ways alters the forms of Bear Shape and Spider Shape, allowing the caster to become a bereskarn and a corrupted spider, both considerably more powerful than their base forms. In those forms, the shapeshifter also gains Overwhelm. Additionally, the Flying Swarm shape drains health from foes whenever the main swarm inflicts damage.	0	0	0	No	0	0
			Learned From: Wynne (Companion), Wonders of Thedas (Denerim, after Landsmeet starts)						
Spirit Healer	Group Heal	7	The caster bathes allies in benevolent energy, instantly healing them by a moderate amount.	40	0	0	Yes	20	0
	Revival	8	The caster revives fallen party members in an area, raising them from unconsciousness and restoring some health.	60	0	0	Yes	120	2
	Lifeward	12	The caster places a protective ward on an ally that automatically restores health when the ally falls close to death.	55	0	0	Yes	30	0
	Cleansing Aura	14	While this mode is active, waves of healing and cleansing energy emanate from the caster, restoring health to all nearby allies every few seconds and curing the injuries of allies very close to the caster.	0	60	5	No	30	10

Gear

Mages might not get the pick of the litter for equipment, but the gear they do receive should pump up their main abilities if you shop correctly. Don't worry about defense too much; concentrate on bumping up your magic and willpower scores, or gaining spellpower points to enhance all spells, or adding mana boosts. The goal of all mages is to avoid drawing too much threat, and if you're achieving that goal, armor won't be too much of a factor. If you're worried about taking damage, invest in constitution to increase health and ward you against melee and ranged

attacks. The same goes with weapons: don't pick a staff based on DPS; pick one that increases your main attributes. Also, think about your spell preferences. If you invest in fire spells, for example, a ring that generates extra fire damage is a huge boon.

There's more mage gear than you could ever hope to equip in a single play. The general rule of thumb is to wait for loot that serves as an upgrade and snatch it up. If you have extra coin to buy a nice gear upgrade, feel free to spend away, though most of the low-level equipment will be easily replaced by future loot, and the high-level equipment is very expensive (generally bought during the Landsmeet for a run at the archdemon).

With so much good gear, here are some beauties to shoot for based on beginning (1–5), intermediate (6–10), advanced (11–15), and expert levels (16–20):

	Lvl 1-5	Lvl 6-10	Lvl 11-15	Lvl 16-20
Armor	Apprentice Robes	First Enchanter Robes	Tevinter Mage Robes, Robes of Possession (Morrigan)	Reaper's Vestments Robe
Helm	Apprentice Cowl	Enchanter Cowl	First Enchanter's Cowl	Libertarian's Cowl
Boots	Fade Striders	Enchanter's Footing	Imperial Weavers	Magus War Boots
Gloves	Leather Gloves	Polar Gauntlets	Cinderfel Gauntlets	Elementalist's Grasp
Ring	Thorn	Key to the City	Ring of Ages	Lifegiver
Staff	Pyromancer's Brand	Blackened Heartwood Staff	Malign Staff	Staff of the Magister Lord

Party Responsibilities

Ask yourself two questions when playing a mage: "Are you primarily a damage-dealer or a healer?" and "Are you the only mage in the party?" If you want to perform the damage role, you will naturally concentrate on ways to harm your opponent. If you want to play the role of healer, regeneration and rejuvenation spells are in order. If you're the only mage in the party, you must take some healing spells as part of your repertoire.

Another important question: "What need do you fulfill best?" Perhaps, you may look at your other three companions and fill in the void that they lack. For example, if you have a warrior concentrating on two-handed weapons, a backstabbing rogue, and your sword-and-shield tank, DPS would seem to be covered while healing/party buffs are lacking. On the flip side, if you have a spirit healer such as Wynne in the group, you can stretch out to damage spells and maybe supplement her talents with a heal or two.

In the end, though, you should choose the role that you want your mage to be and work the team around that. If you want to play DPS, go for it and make sure you have Wynne involved. If you want to play the healer, drop Wynne and pick up Morrigan or another DPS-driven companion. If you want to play a little DPS and a little healing, you might be able to swing it as a single mage, or you may need help from one of the companion mages; it all depends on your combat style and tactics.

One thing all mages should strive for is to remain in the background and avoid threat whenever possible. You aren't built for melee combat (unless you spec an arcane warrior properly), and if you draw threat, you will die quickly. Don't pull targets away from your tank, except, possibly, if they are near death and easy kills.

The mage ranks highest of the three classes in versatility. You can deal damage, heal, control large enemy groups, buff your party, and more. Save your mana for the right reactions at the correct times and you'll excel in this class. So long as you remember not to lead the battle charge, your magic will work wonders in fights.

Model Characters

With 64 spells to choose from and four specializations, you can make myriad mages. Don't feel constrained to play according to the following mage models to the letter; take bits and pieces that appeal to your play style and add your own spin. However, these are basic models for a DPS mage, healer, or blend mage who balances offense and defense. Each shows you how to choose your spells up to level 20, what spell chains are effective, how specializations fit in, and sample combat strategies for that model.

DPS Mage Model

Level	Spell
0	Arcane Bolt
1	Flame Blast, Heal
2	Flaming Weapons
3	Fireball
4	Spell Wisp
5	Grease
6	Walking Bomb
7	Death Syphon—*First Specialization Available at This Level*
8	Arcane Shield
9	Staff Focus
10	Arcane Mastery
11	Virulent Walking Bomb
12	Inferno
13	Lightning
14	Spider Shape (Shapeshifter)—*Second Specialization Available at This Level*
15	Bear Shape (Shapeshifter)
16	Flying Swarm (Shapeshifter)
17	Master Shapeshifter
18	Animate Dead
19	Shock
20	Tempest

The Mage

Overview: A DPS mage deals heavy damage from medium to long range. He generally concentrates in the Primal and Spirit schools.

Leveling: What does a DPS mage do best? Damage. Naturally, then, you should start off with a Primal chain. In this case, we'll choose the Fire chain, mostly because Fireball is such a great AoE damage spell. You could, of course, start with any of the Primal chains. (The Earth chain, however, may prove a little troublesome at level 1; it's the only Primal chain that doesn't start out with a damage spell.) Note that to hit Fireball at level 3, you need to spend your five character creation points in magic to bring you up to 21, then spend the three attribute points you earn at level 2 and three on magic as well to raise the score to 27 (elf mages begin with one extra magic point than humans, so you can spend that one point in willpower if you like).

At level 1, invest in Flame Blast to start the Fire chain and give you an additional attack to Arcane Bolt (all mages start with this basic attack). Pick up Heal as well. Yes, it's a defensive spell, but every mage should carry it to save allies or themselves in a pinch. Take Flaming Weapons at level 2 for some melee support. Once you hit level 3 and learn Fireball, you can roast enemy groups from a great distance. You have fine weapons already, so long as you don't run into fire-resistant mobs.

At levels 4 and 5, choose Spell Wisp and the second spell in that chain, Grease. Spell Wisp increases spellpower, which augments all your damage spells, and Grease causes enemies to slip if they miss a physical resistance check (crowd control) and the slick surface can be set on fire for extra damage, making it a perfect combo for your fire-based spells.

Start your second damage chain with Walking Bomb at level 6. This gives you a separate source of poison damage (and sets you up for another lethal AoE attack at level 11). The follow-up to Walking Bomb, Death Syphon at level 7, restores mana; always handy in longer battles.

Levels 8, 9, and 10 fill out the standard Mage school. Arcane Shield helps divert incoming attacks, giving you some more defense. The overlooked Staff Focus powers up your basic staff attack, which you always use as back-up damage when your mana runs low. The real reason for running these spells in a row here is to ensure that you pick up Arcane Mastery at its earliest availability: level 10. Because Arcane Mastery grants a permanent bonus to spellpower, it makes all your DPS stronger no matter what spell you choose.

At levels 11 and 12, you maximize your two damage chains. Virulent Walking Bomb functions similar to Walking Bomb with one big difference: when targets explode, they have a chance to infect other enemies and start a chain reaction of explosions. Inferno, the top of the Fire chain, engulfs an entire area in continuous flame and will decimate enemies if they can't escape to the cooler perimeter. Note that you need 34 magic to access Inferno.

Branch out into a third damage chain, Lightning, at level 13. Two separate damage sources are usually enough, but if you rotate three, you should always have a damage spell available as long as your mana lasts.

At level 14 we try out the shapeshifter specialization with Spider Shape. With a DPS mage who really wants to hammer out lots of damage, it's best to go with your core damage spells early and slip into a specialization at level 14. The shapeshifter specialization lets you deal melee DPS, which is fantastic for when your mana runs low or if you find yourself under direct melee attack. To gain all the creature abilities from shapeshifter, we'll invest four points in a row to the specialization, though you could spread them out through level 20 if you like.

At levels 18 through 20, you should fill in with whatever tickles your fancy. At level 18, we pick up Animate Dead to finish off the Walking Bomb chain and gain some combat allies in the process. For levels 19 and 20, we crank up the damage in the Lightning chain with Shock and Tempest. By level 20, you have three separate damage chain nearly maxed out, some good support spells, and an entire specialization at your disposal.

Spell Choices: Fire spells serve as your primary AoE if you have the space to deal damage to your foe without catching the party in friendly fire. The Spell Wisp chain gives you extra spellpower and a crowd control spell in Grease. The Walking Bomb chain focuses on another cycle that can serve as either single-target damage or AoE damage. The Lightning chain gives you a third damage alternative, the effect of bouncing from one target to the next, and another option to avoid cooldown problems.

Specialization: Shapeshifter provides melee DPS so you can conserve on mana and defend yourself if under direct attack. Spider Shape has an effective Web snare, Bear Shape offers a good Overwhelm ability, and Flying Swarm turns into an AoE attack that also protects you from physical damage (all damage comes off your mana instead). Master Shapeshifter improves all forms, and you can hold your own against less powerful mobs.

Battle Tactics: Your standard tactic is to deal steady damage to enemies without pulling so much threat that the enemies escape your tank's hold and charge toward you. With that in mind, you may have to delay a few seconds at the start of the fight, or during the fight, depending on the enemy position and your tank's ability to lock down the threat.

Your general spell cycle will be Fireball (if you won't hit your party with friendly fire), Walking Bomb, Arcane Bolt, and Lightning (if you've reached level 13 or higher). A neat trick inside dungeons is to open a door and hurl a Fireball at enemies on the far side of the room. The explosion consumes the room and the walls prevent the burst from burning your party; just cast it well away from the door.

Similarly, you can use your higher damage spells, such as Tempest, to hurt enemies you can't even see. Target the spell around a corner or inside another room (if the door is open) and let it rip. Enemies inside will take tons of damage or come running out into your well-positioned party's ambush.

An important part of your job may be to contain rather than destroy. Think of Grease whenever you see a large group ready to flank your party, or if something unexpected happens, such as your tank getting stunned and losing threat. Grease will delay most of the enemies, and you can always follow up with a Flame Blast to ignite the oil and cause great pain to the enemy.

If you're playing pure DPS, you should have another mage, a healer, in your party too. They can do the heavy lifting when it comes to healing and keep the party alive. However, don't ignore the supplemental healer role. In tough fights, throw a Heal into your rotation. If your primary healer is having trouble, you may even heal after every other damage spell. As soon as that Heal spell becomes active, glance at everyone's health bars and kick it off if wounds are piling up. Yes, you are a master DPSer, but if you are the only one standing, it won't do you much good.

Healer Model

Level	Spell
0	Arcane Bolt
1	Heal, Rejuvenate
2	Regeneration
3	Winter's Grasp
4	Spell Shield
5	Dispel Magic
6	Arcane Shield
7	Group Heal (Spirit Healer)—First Specialization Available at This Level
8	Revival (Spirit Healer)
9	Staff Focus
10	Arcane Mastery
11	Mass Rejuvenation
12	Lifeward (Spirit Healer)
13	Frost Weapons
14	Cleansing Aura (Spirit Healer)—Second Specialization Available at This Level
15	Cone of Cold
16	Blizzard
17	Vulnerability Hex
18	Affliction Hex
19	Misdirection Hex
20	Death Hex

Overview: A healer focuses on health regeneration and rejuvenation. These mages generally concentrate in the Creation school.

Leveling: A healer should concentrate in the Creation school, at least until they reach Regeneration and have two solid heals. Note that to hit Regeneration at level 2, you need to spend your five character creation points in magic to bring

you up to 21, then spend two more attribute points at level 2 to raise the score to 23 (elf mages begin with one extra magic point than humans, so you can spend that one point in willpower if you like).

At level 1, pick up Heal and Rejuvenate. Heal will be your staple health spell; Rejuvenate helps to restore stamina for warriors and mana for mages. If you increase your magic attribute correctly, you can net Regeneration at level 2. It's crucial to have at least two healing spells; otherwise, while Heal is on cooldown, a party member could become gravely wounded and you'll have no healing to help him.

Every healer should have a form of damage as well. In addition to your standard Arcane Bolt, we'll pick up Winter's Grasp at level 3. The Cold chain has the built-in effect of freezing a target in place, which serves to slow down foes and help out on defense; this defensive component complements your healing role.

Next, branch out into the Spirit school for levels 4 and 5. Spell Shield comes first as a potential defense against hostile spells, but it's really a prerequisite for Dispel Magic. This is always handy to remove enemy effects on party members, Dispel Magic proves critical to remove Curse of Mortality, which prevents healing and will kill party members if you don't eliminate it fast.

At level 6, pick up Arcane Shield. Much like Spell Shield, it's extra defense that may come into play in certain fights, but it's mostly a prerequisite to ramp up to Arcane Mastery later.

No matter what you have to do, you want to gain the spirit healer specialization as soon as you hit level 7. The first spell in the chain, Group Heal, is *the* most important spell as a healer. The ability to heal all your party members at once will turn the tide in many battles. At level 8, the spirit healer ability Revival may tip the battle scales in your favor when one of your companions drops and you can bring them back from the brink of death.

At levels 9 and 10, you fill out your basic Mage school. Choose Staff Focus at level 9 and Arcane Mastery at level 10. Arcane Mastery will augment all your healing spells, which is a very good thing for your party's health.

Mass Rejuvenation comes in big in long battles where everyone needs a boost to stamina and mana. At level 11, this fills out your main Heal chain.

At level 12, grab Lifeward from spirit healer. It's another healing spell that works when a companion's near death: a nice luxury to throw on a tank, or someone else that you can't heal immediately.

Frost Weapons at level 13 inches you up in the Cold chain and lets you boost your party's offense if it looks to be a light fight that won't require much healing.

Cleansing Aura finishes off the spirit healer specialization at level 14. It's an AoE healing effect, which also cures injuries (and saves on buying injury kits!).

At levels 15 and 16, fill out your Cold chain with Cone of Cold and Blizzard. You won't blast an area too much with Blizzard unless your party is desperate for damage, but you will fire off a Cone of Cold once in a while. Cone of Cold also freezes targets in place, and if your enemies aren't attacking, you don't have to spend mana healing.

The Mage

Basics ~ Character Generation ~ **Classes** ~ The Party ~ Companions ~ Supporting Cast ~ Equipment ~ Bestiary ~ Walkthroughs ~ Side Quests ~ Random Encounters ~ Achievements/Trophies

Your final four slots can go to any spell chain you like. We'll go with the Hex chain: Vulnerability at level 17 up to Death at level 20. The hexes can reduce attack percentages against your party (as well as enemy defenses), which plays to your strength as the group's main defender.

Spell Choices: Your Heal chain will be the most active as you cycle back and forth between Heal and Regeneration throughout all future battles. The Cold chain gives you offense and defense, because foes may be frozen in place after you hit them with Winter's Grasp or Cone of Cold. Dispel Magic comes out automatically as soon as one of your companions falters to a lingering negative spell effect. At higher levels, your Hex chain supplements your main strategy with spells that reduce the effectiveness of the enemy against your party.

Specialization: Spirit healer is paramount at level 7. Seek it out as soon as you unlock the specialization potential. Group Heal proves super effective, healing everyone at once. Revival brings a companion back into the fight who would have been useless otherwise. Lifeward prevents an overwhelming amount of damage from finishing off an ally, while Cleansing Aura generates continuous health to all around you.

Battle Tactics: All good healers know to stay out of the heat of battle and focus not on spilling enemy blood, but on staunching the blood on your companions' tunics. Stay out of the main confrontation so as not to draw the attention of your foes. Don't waste mana on offense except in dire circumstances where you need to kill something before it kills you, or possibly minor fights where the outcome is never in doubt. Before you leave one encounter for the next, make sure your mana has topped back off.

Learn your allies' armor and health reserves. If you misjudge someone's threshold for damage, they may end up dead before you can heal them. With some practice, you will know when to fire off a Heal to bring a companion back to full health without wasting healing that goes above their max health rating.

Cycle through Heal and Regeneration, throwing in any other healing you have for longer fights. Preventive healing is a good idea; it keeps your companions' health high and avoids the problem of direly needing a heal that's unavailable on cooldown.

Once you gain Group Heal, master it. It's great to use when multiple party members are taking damage: you cast an economical heal that saves several people at once. You can counteract big bursts of damage that wound your team, such as traps or an unexpected Chain Lightning from an enemy spellcaster. Should multiple party members start taking damage over time—such as from a dragon's firebreathing—Group Heal helps boost everyone's health at once and keep the party out of immediate danger.

Heal as often as seems feasible. Unlike a DPS mage, you can't afford to heal conservatively to avoid threat if companions are at risk. Be sure to stock up on lyrium potions to replenish mana. If a DPS mage comes up dry, you might rely on the warrior to belt out the extra damage; if your healer gets stuck on empty, you had better win the fight in a matter of seconds or someone might not make it.

Blend Model

Level	Spell
0	Arcane Bolt
1	Heal, Rock Armor
2	Stonefist
3	Earthquake
4	Mind Blast
5	Force Field
6	Arcane Shield
7	Combat Magic (Arcane Warrior)—*First Specialization Available at This Level*
8	Petrify
9	Staff Focus
10	Arcane Mastery
11	Telekinetic Weapons
12	Aura of Might (Arcane Warrior)
13	Crushing Prison
14	Shimmering Shield (Arcane Warrior)—*Second Specialization Available at This Level*
15	Lightning
16	Fade Shroud (Arcane Warrior)
17	Heroic Offense
18	Heroic Aura
19	Heroic Defense
20	Haste

Overview: A blend mage has the most versatility, splits talents between offense and defense, and may pull spells from all schools.

Leveling: At level 1, choose two defensive spells: Heal and Rock Armor. As with all mages, Heal serves as health rejuvenation whenever someone needs a boost. Rock Armor gives you an armor bonus, which you'll need because a blend mage draws more threat and enters melee more than the average mage. Note that to hit Earthquake at level 3, you need to spend your five character creation points in magic to bring you up to 21, then spend the three attribute points you earn at levels 2 and 3 on magic as well to raise the score to 27 (elf mages begin with one extra magic point than humans, so you can spend that one point in willpower if you like).

At levels 2 and 3, you'll take two offensive spells: Stonefist and Earthquake. Stonefist is a great offensive spell that pummels a single enemy with damage and can knock it off its feet. Earthquake will be your staple AoE attack. Note that you could take any main damage chain here (fire, cold, or electricity).

primagames.com

Next, enter the Mind Blast chain at level 4. Mind Blast can play out hugely when surrounded by large groups. Stun them to prevent a swarm on you, or to give your companions more time to get into position and wield their best attacks. Perhaps the best defensive spell in the game, Force Field at level 5 nullifies all damage against you or a targeted ally for a short duration. You can almost stack Force Fields one after the other and keep a target alive against ridiculous damage—the only drawback is the target of the Force Field can't react in any way while defended.

At level 6, pick up Arcane Shield as added defense and the second step toward Arcane Mastery at level 10.

With this blend build, we want the arcane warrior specialization at level 7. Learn Combat Magic and suddenly you can equip high-level armor and weapons. You might not be a tank, but you're no slouch in combat any longer.

Levels 8 and 9 boost your offense again. Petrify can be a single-target kill spell if they fail a physical resistance check. (Follow up Petrify with Stone Fist for shattering results!) Staff Focus increases the damage done with your basic staff attack.

Arcane Mastery at level 10 improves spellpower and thus increases the effectiveness of all spells.

At level 11, Telekinetic Weapons enhances your companions' weapons, and even your melee weapon if you wade into melee as an arcane warrior. The level 12 Aura of Might bolsters your attack, defense, and damage. Note that you need reach 34 magic to access Aura of Might.

Your best offensive spell comes at level 13: Crushing Prison. Break this out against single foes and encase them in a prison that roots them to the spot and deals continuous spirit damage.

At level 14, Shimmering Shield continues your arcane warrior abilities. The shield sucks up damage and cranks up resistances; it's great for melee fighting, but it drains mana quickly, so don't count on casting many spells in conjunction with your defense.

Pick up Lightning at level 15. It's another damage spell that gives you a new source of damage and single-foe targeting.

Finish off the arcane warrior specialization at level 16 with Fade Shroud. While Combat Magic is active, Fade Shroud increases mana regeneration and gives a chance to avoid attacks.

At level 17 start the Heroic chain and complete it at level 20. The first three (Heroic Offense, Heroic Aura, Heroic Defense) grant bonuses to the respective categories. The fourth, Haste, shines for an arcane warrior, speeding up the melee damage you can do at the expense of mana. If you've maximized your character, though, you won't have to rely on damage spells as much as a DPS mage.

Spell Choices: The Earth chain gives you lots of offensive options: single-target stun with Stonefist, AoE with Earthquake, and single-target kill with Petrify. Mind Blast and Force Field offer excellent defense, all on the way to your best offensive spell in Crushing Prison. Lightning adds an extra damage dimension to your spell rotation, and the Heroic chain can add extra offense or defense just when you need it. Haste gives a melee edge to your entire team, even if it doesn't last a super long time.

Specialization: Arcane warrior drives this blend build. Rather than drops spells constantly, the arcane warrior mixes ranged DPS with defensive spells and hand-to-hand combat. Combat Magic gives the mage access to armor and weapons only the warrior class would normally have. Aura of Might bolsters stats across the board. Shimmering Shield can keep you alive in a melee fight, but will cut you off from spells as your mana drains away. On the opposite extreme, Fade Shroud will replenish your mana and help you avoid damage once you level high enough to unlock it.

Battle Tactics: Unlike your standard mage who stays in the rear, this blend mage isn't afraid to enter melee after he specializes in arcane warrior at level 7. Suddenly, the lowly mage can wear excellent armor and wield weapons normally above his pay grade. The specialization is worth it just for that benefit alone, and it gets better for a brawler mage when you add the next three talents.

On the spell end, your offensive rotation will usually go Earthquake (if you can avoid friendly fire), Arcane Bolt, Stonefist (targeting any enemy heading directly for you), and Petrify or Crushing Prison for the kill (or against the strongest opponent). You can pick and choose the correct spell for the situation if you forgo pure spellcasting and slip into arcane warrior mode.

Your defensive spell rotation generally goes Rock Armor, Mind Blast (when enemies close), Heal (whenever necessary), and Force Field for all-out defense. You can do lots of tricks with Force Field. You can, of course, save someone from certain death with a handy Force Field. You can send a tank in against a difficult foe, let him pile on threat, then throw up a Force Field; the enemy will most likely stay on the tank while you deal with the surrounding enemies. Even better still, you can take on bosses yourself. Cast a major spell, such as Earthquake or Fireball, on the enemy and follow up with a few damage spells to get him mad and fixated on you. As soon as the return damage heads your way, throw up a Force Field. While you're trapped in the Force Field, have a second mage cast Rejuvenate on you to replenish your lost mana (or quaff a lyrium potion as soon as you emerge from the Force Field). You can deal a ton of damage over a long time, while barely taking a nick.

As a blend mage, you can tap into anything, dabbling here and there. The idea is to learn a balance of offense and defense to jump into any situation with an answer in hand. To some degree, all good mages are blends.

The Mage - The Rogue

Basics ~ Character Generation ~ Classes ~ The Party ~ Companions ~ Supporting Cast ~ Equipment ~ Bestiary ~ Walkthroughs ~ Side Quests ~ Random Encounters ~ Achievements/Trophies

The Rogue

You are flashing daggers and a snarl out of the shadows, savagery and subtlety, the jack-of-all trades for the party. A rogue slips into battle unseen and lethal, able to deal deadly damage from behind and escape harm when enemies take notice. When combat is over, the rogue is the only one who can penetrate locked doors and claim extra treasure from almost every dungeon.

The rogue sits between the warrior and the mage in terms of gear access. They can gain almost any suit of armor or weapon that a warrior gets; however, to do that would cost a ton of attribute points in strength and forgo points in dexterity and cunning that enhance most rogue talents. They certainly have higher DPS weapons and sturdier armor than mages.

Talents for a rogue fall into three main categories: Rogue, Dual Weapon, and Archery. The Rogue talents increase damage from backstabs and critical hits, teach you how to evade the enemy's mightiest blows, enable you to lockpick doors and chests, deactivate traps, and hide invisibly in the shadows through stealth. Dual Weapons gives the rogue a weapon in each hand for double the fun, and once they erase the penalties for wielding two weapons, rogues deal tremendous melee damage. If you don't want to go with melee, the rogue can lean toward Archery, where a single shot can stun multiple targets or split a hurlock skull in two.

Rogue specializations delve into a wide array of abilities. Assassin and duelist give the melee DPSer more combat talents, with assassin concentrating on pure damage-dealing and duelist aiding defense as well. Bard is all about crowd control and party buffs. You can stun a single target or hold an entire group fixated on your song, or you can boost all your companions' stats. Finally, ranger allows you to summon animal allies into a fight, adding a pet wolf, bear, or spider to your side.

If you like to play it a bit sinister and secret, yet go ruthlessly offensive once you dive into combat, the rogue class is for you. Outside of combat, your lockpicking and stealth abilities prove useful in innumerable situations. You will be the party's favorite companion just for the extra loot you find.

Strengths and Weaknesses

When an enemy has locked onto a tank and the rogue is free to backstab, you can deal out massive single target damage and kill things very quickly. A rogue should get into backstab position whenever possible.

Out of combat, you can gain extra experience and loot from opening locked doors and chests. Enemies sometimes defend their lair with traps; the rogue not only detects them but disarms them to avoid the brutal consequences from one misstep. Stealth aids a rogue in almost any situation; in combat, you can slip into the perfect position unseen by enemies, and out of combat, you can recon areas or bypass enemies with high enough skill. And rogues get a skill point every two levels, rather than every three.

Advantages

- Single-target DPS
- Lockpicking
- Trap Detection and Disarmament
- Stealth
- Access to More Skill Points

Rogue defense is rather weak, because it's difficult, if not impossible, to wear heavier armor. Being hit by several mobs or a large boss will take you out pretty fast. This makes using AoE attacks difficult because they usually pull threat and get you killed fast unless your party includes an excellent tank. To be most effective, a rogue needs to be behind his target, which isn't always easy to do and may get you into a combat hotspot. You also don't have much defense against magic, other than going into stealth mode and trying to sneak up on enemy casters.

Disadvantages

- Limited Defense
- Must Get Behind Targets to be Most Effective
- Generally Weak Against Magic Attacks

Attributes

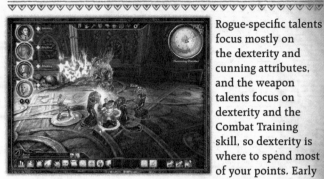

Rogue-specific talents focus mostly on the dexterity and cunning attributes, and the weapon talents focus on dexterity and the Combat Training skill, so dexterity is where to spend most of your points. Early on, devote as many points as you need into dexterity to unlock the talents you wish to obtain; you can always fill in the other attributes later after you have your core talents well underway.

As for the other attributes, spend the required points in dexterity and spread the remainder of the points among cunning (requirement for many other rogue abilities), constitution (for resilience), willpower (for higher stamina), and strength (for power and armor requirements). Don't leave magic too far behind because spending points here will make potions more effective. Make sure to build strength to at least 20 so the character can use Tier 7 armor, and dexterity to at least 36 if you plan on getting Dual-Weapon Mastery.

Rogue Attribute Bonuses

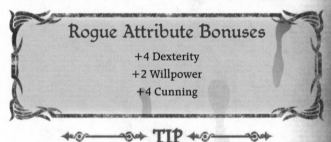

+4 Dexterity
+2 Willpower
+4 Cunning

TIP

Gear bonuses can amplify your attribute's strengths or offset any shortcomings. A ring, for example, that bulks up constitution could provide some extra health without costing any of your precious attribute points.

During character creation, feel free to choose a race based on the corresponding origin story you would like to play through as a rogue. It's much more important to enjoy the origin story for your character than it is to worry about a point here or there in your attributes. However, if maximizing your rogue stats appeals to you, choose a dwarf or human. A human rogue gives you a starting 15 dexterity and 15 cunning. Dwarves are only one point behind in cunning. The elven rogue is the third choice, because elves start with only 14 dexterity and 14 cunning.

The Rogue

Basics ~ Character Generation ~ Classes ~ The Party ~ Companions ~ Supporting Cast ~ Equipment ~ Bestiary ~ Walkthroughs ~ Side Quests ~ Random Encounters ~ Achievements/Trophies

Rogue Starting Attributes

Attribute	Human	Elf	Dwarf
Strength	11	10	11
Dexterity	15	14	15
Willpower	12	14	12
Magic	11	12	10
Cunning	15	14	14
Constitution	10	10	12

Once you choose your rogue's race, you begin with five extra points to add to your attributes. That's almost two "level ups" worth of attribute growth, so spend it wisely. If you want a combat-oriented rogue, focus on dexterity and a little strength. If you want a rogue who concentrates on lockpicking and stealth, spend three points on cunning and two points on dexterity.

Skills

All rogues need to pick up Combat Training as soon as they can. Combat Training opens up the higher tier weapon talents, which you can't live without. Spend your first skill point here to vault up to at least Improved Combat Training. You need to reach Expert Combat Training by level 6 and Expert Combat Training by level 9 if you want to focus on combat talents.

Poison-Making can help improve your damage totals, so it's probably the second best rogue skill. Buy beyond the first rank to access stronger poisons and different special effects. You could also go the Trap-Making route and branch out a little more into AoE damage.

If you want more options during dialogue, especially to sway people's opinions or avoid certain fights, invest in Coercion. It's an incredibly useful skill in dialogue; it gives you story options that you won't get otherwise. Cunning opens up the Coercion skills, which fits in with many rogue talents.

Don't forget about Stealing. It focuses on a high cunning score, something rogues should have. Use the Stealing skill to grab gear not normally dropped by foes.

NOTE

Beyond your starting skills, you're likely to obtain 8–10 skill points throughout the game. Pick your two or three favorite skills and stick with them. If you spread your points too thin, you'll end up doing a bunch of things—but not well.

Rogue Skill Recommendations

Assuming you spend at least 10 skill points by career's end, here's a good spread to consider. Note that many other combinations could work better for you, so experiment!

- Combat Training +4
- Coercion +1
- Poison-Making +4
- Stealing +1

If you aren't directly playing your rogue companions and want one of them to run around independently, invest in Combat Tactics for extra tactics slots. The more tactic slots you open, the more you can shape how your companion behaves in battle. Inevitably, even if you plan on controlling your rogue during fights, there will be moments when you don't program your rogue's every move (or something more important is going on) and tactics come into play. One or two points should be good, or max it out if you want the character to go on autopilot.

Talents

Rogues have many areas to spend their points, but not enough points to develop them all (never mind the specializations). So what do you choose? Rogue-specific active and passive talents? Lockpicking and disarming traps? Stealth? The Dual Weapon talent school? The Archer talent school? A specialization or two? If you decide to let your focus slide on the weapon talent chains, you can still use dual weapons and bows, but you won't be nearly as efficient at it. You will be a master at stealth, lockpicking and disarming traps, and your other rogue-specific talents. In addition, you can spend fewer of your skill points on Combat Training and more on Poison-Making, Herbalism, Survival, Coercion, and Stealing. If you choose to focus on one of the weapon talent chains, some of your rogue-specific talents will suffer.

So what kind of rogue do you want to be? Does passing up locked treasure and rooms drive you nuts? Do you love being able to stealth through places and situations? Would you prefer to have a deadly combat rogue? Whatever you choose, make sure it complements the rest of your party. For example, a rogue who is adept in lockpicking, stealth, and rogue-specific talents should be paired with a solid melee rogue or warrior (someone who can take the threat and deal the damage). It also wouldn't hurt to have a good ranged attacker in this party too. You won't be the best one-on-one melee opponent, but you'll be able to:

- Drop your threat
- Evade many incoming attacks
- Stun opponents
- Move deftly in combat
- Gain bonuses to critical chance on all attacks
- Backstab stunned and paralyzed foes

- Deliver penalties to your foes' armor, movement speed, and defense

It's not the most sportsmanlike character, but you'll have a solid advantage in many situations. In addition to your below-the-belt style of dealing with things, you can steal, sneak, and pick your way into many interesting places and treasure chests.

NOTE

It's possible to have three rogues in the game: Leliana, Zevran, and you. Develop each differently to have access to a wider talent arsenal.

All rogues should familiarize themselves with the cooldown component of each talent. The worst situation is to have plenty of stamina and no available talents to use. Branch out into different chains to avoid the cooldown problem.

Your talents drain stamina from your pool. Watch how much stamina you're using in a fight and act accordingly. If you run short without a mage's Restoration spell to replenish you, it could cost your party a victory. Gauge what you have to do to help the team. There's little sense running off a series of moves that drains three quarters of your stamina on the first opponent when there are three more to go. Save your stamina. You never know when the next fight will start, or how long the current fight will go if you have unexpected ambushers, and you'll be grateful you didn't waste stamina.

Full-Sized Weapons vs. Daggers

When you play a dual-wielding rogue, one of the first questions to come to mind is what weapon combination deals the most damage in combat. Obviously, the weapons themselves make the biggest impact on the decision: a high DPS weapon with great bonuses will beat out anything.

The only way you can wield two full-sized weapons is by having the Dual Weapon Mastery ability, which also reduces stamina costs for all other dual-weapon abilities. Because two full-sized weapons do more damage than two daggers, your damage-dealing capabilities are enhanced, but you have to spend lots of points in strength to access those weapons, which means fewer points to spend on your core talent needs. Even with the higher damage output, let's not forget about armor penetration and critical chance. Daggers are higher in both. It comes down to the type of enemy or situation you're facing. If you're facing heavily armored foes, the armor penetration and critical chance you get with the Coup de Grace auto backstab, Lethality, Combat Movement, and Evasion rogue abilities are a better choice than a rogue wielding two full-sized weapons coming at the target head on. This is why so many of the rogue abilities require and complement dexterity—not strength and brute force. Because you're building up dexterity for most rogue talents, that's probably the approach you want to take; otherwise, play a warrior. Keep in mind: There is no one dominant strategy for any class versus all enemies and challenges.

Rogue School

In your first chain, Dirty Fighting stuns a target for a short duration. Combat Movement is a passive ability that allows rogues move more swiftly in combat, allowing them a greater chance to flank or get behind their foes (for backstabs and such). Considering that it's sometimes difficult to get directly behind foes in the flow of combat, this one really comes in handy. Coup de Grace is a passive ability that allows your rogue to automatically backstab stunned or paralyzed foes (combos with Dirty Fighting or Dual Strike, warrior's Shield Pummel and Stunning Blows, mage's Mind Blast, to name a few). Feign Death is like the warrior's Disengage: it greatly reduces your threat, making enemies seek other targets.

The second chain holds Below the Belt, an attack that deals normal damage and gives the target penalties to defense and movement speed. Deadly Strike gives you a bonus to armor penetration. Use this on heavily armored foes. Lethality is a passive ability that gains the rogue a bonus on critical chance for all attacks. In addition, if the rogue's cunning score is higher than his strength score, the cunning score affects the attack damage in place of the strength score. If your rogue is high on cunning and low on strength, this is an excellent ability to have. So with this passive ability in the background, use Dirty Fighting to stun a heavily armored foe, sneak around behind it for an automatic backstab and critical hit (courtesy of Coup de Grace), and then use Deadly Strike to get in another attack with a bonus to armor penetration. Pair this with Mark of Death, Exploit Weakness, Lacerate, and Feast of the Fallen in the assassin specialty talents, and you'll mark this guy's weak spots for other party members, gain a bonus to your backstab with Coup de Grace, deal damage over time with your Lacerate passive ability, and restore some stamina when your target falls to the ground.

If you've had enough offense, Evasion is a passive ability that gives the rogue a 20 percent chance to dodge physical attacks, including attacks used to stun or knock down the rogue. The Deft Hands chain improves your ability to pick locks and disarm traps; it's a must for rogues who aren't just into combat. Finally, the more you develop the Stealth chain, the more you can do while stealthed (use potions and other items such as traps and lures, and use stealth while in combat).

The Rogue

Basics ~ Character Generation ~ **Classes** ~ The Party ~ Companions ~ Supporting Cast ~ Equipment ~ Bestiary ~ Walkthroughs ~ Side Quests ~ Random Encounters ~ Achievements/Trophies

Dual Weapon School

The Dual Weapon talent school focuses more on activated abilities and attacks. In addition, you get to deal damage with two weapons simultaneously.

You don't need the Dual Weapon talent school to be able to wield two weapons, but it's a good school to develop to be more proficient at melee. The focus of your passive abilities is on your second hand—you strive to deal similar damage and a similar rate of critical hits as your main hand. You gain a bonus to attack and defense with Dual-Weapon Finesse. You gain a bonus to critical chance and gain the ability to cause bleeding lacerations on your opponent, inflicting damage over time with Dual-Weapon Expert. You can wield full-sized weapons in your off hand while reducing the stamina cost of all Dual Weapon talents with Dual-Weapon Mastery.

Increase your attack damage with Dual Striking, but be careful because it eliminates your ability to critical hit or backstab. Next, you can score a two-hit combo with a possibility of stunning your opponent and scoring a critical hit with Riposte. Cripple gives you a chance to score a critical hit and inflict your opponent with penalties to movement speed, attack, and defense. Punisher is a three-hit combo that has a chance to score a critical hit, knock an opponent down, and cause penalties to movement and attack speed.

Dual-Weapon Sweep deals significant damage with each sweep, Flurry is a three-hit combo, Momentum increases your attack speed with every hit, and Whirlwind is a flurry of constant attacks: the signature of a Dual Weapon expert.

Archery School

Another school for rogues who build up dexterity, Archery gives ample special effects for a ranged combat enthusiast. Melee Archer lets you fire while being attacked (eliminating some of the pain of being an archer). Master Archer gives you bonuses to activated abilities and eliminates the penalty to attack speed when wearing heavy armor. Aim reduces attack speed but gives bonuses to attack, damage, armor penetration, and critical chance. Defensive Fire gives you a boost to defense but slows your attack speed.

In the second chain, Pinning Shot is a necessity because it impales the victim's leg and either pins it in place or slows its movement speed. Crippling Shot deals normal damage to an enemy and gives it penalties to attack and defense, and Critical Shot delivers maximum damage upon impact. The deadly Arrow of Slaying usually scores a critical hit, often dropping weakened enemies.

Rapid Shot increases attack speed, but you lose the ability to score critical hits. Shattering Shot deals normal damage and opens up an enemy's armor. If a warrior finds that one, it'll be in sore shape. Suppressing Fire is like Rapid Shot, but its foes now take penalties to their attack rating. Scattershot stuns a foe and then shatters, dealing damage to other enemies around it.

When you have room to breathe, Pinning Shot and Crippling Shot turn enemies into sitting ducks for mage attacks, deadly warriors, or more of your carefully aimed arrows. Shattering Shot is excellent against heavily armed foes. Rapid Shot, Suppressing Fire, and Scattershot hack away at the collective hit points of enemy ranks.

TIP

A good combo against a heavily armed foe is Shattering Shot, Crippling Shot, Aim/Rapid Shot, and Arrow of Slaying. Mix in another Shattering Shot if the first armor penalty runs out.

Don't think an archer just scores a hit or two before having to engage an opponent in melee. You can kill off a couple enemies in a few hits while pinning others in place and continuing to fire while other attackers swarm you. This you turns you into a deadly sniper that enemies need to deal with or suffer the consequences. Should the enemy swarm you, switch to Defensive Fire while you have the passive ability Melee Archer. You can fire off arrows while being attacked and still have decent defense.

Rogue Talents

Chain	Name	Prerequisite	Description	Cost (mana /stamina)	Upkeep (mana /stamina)	Fatigue (% mana/stamina)	Ranged	Cooldown (sec.)	Area of Effect Radius (ft.)
			Rogue School						
Chain 1	Dirty Fighting	Dexterity 10	The rogue incapacitates a target, who takes no damage from the attack but is stunned for a short time.	25	0	0	No	25	0
	Combat Movement	Dexterity 14, Level 4	The quick-stepping rogue can more easily outmaneuver opponents, granting a wider flanking angle that makes backstabs easier to achieve.	0	0	0	No	0	0
	Coup de Grace	Dexterity 18, Level 8	When a target is incapacitated, the opportunistic rogue strikes where it hurts the most, inflicting automatic backstabs against stunned or paralyzed targets.	0	0	0	No	0	0
	Feign Death	Dexterity 22, Level 12	The rogue collapses at enemies' feet, making them lose interest and seek other targets until the rogue gives up the ruse.	0	40	5	No	300	0
Chain 2	Below the Belt	Dexterity 10	The rogue delivers a swift and unsportsmanlike kick to the target, dealing normal combat damage as well as imposing penalties to defense and movement speed unless the target passes a physical resistance check.	25	0	0	No	15	0
	Deadly Strike	Dexterity 14, Level 4	The rogue makes a swift strike at a vulnerable area on the target, dealing normal damage but gaining a bonus to armor penetration.	25	0	0	No	15	0
	Lethality	Dexterity 23, Level 8	The rogue has a keen eye for weak spots and thus gains a bonus to critical chance for all attacks. Additionally, if the rogue's cunning score is greater than strength, sharpness of mind lets the character use the cunning modifier to affect attack damage in place of the strength modifier.	0	0	0	No	0	0
	Evasion	Dexterity 35, Level 12	The rogue gains an almost preternatural ability to sense and avoid danger. This talent grants a one-in-five chance of evading physical attacks, including being stunned or knocked down.	0	0	0	No	0	0
Chain 3	Deft Hands	Cunning 10	All rogues have some understanding of opening locks and spotting traps, but particularly dexterous hands and a steady grip give the character a bonus when picking locks or disarming traps. The character's cunning score also contributes to these skills.	0	0	0	No	0	0
	Improved Tools	Cunning 14, Level 4	The rogue has taken to carrying a full set of implements designed to defeat trickier locks and spring traps without harm. These tools add a further bonus when lockpicking or disarming traps, which the character's cunning score also affects.	0	0	0	No	0	0
	Mechanical Expertise	Cunning 18, Level 8	Through practice and research, the rogue has come to possess an encyclopedic knowledge of devices designed to prevent entry. Knowing the right technique for the job lends the rogue yet another bonus when dealing with locks or traps. The character's cunning score also contributes to these skills.	0	0	0	No	0	0
	Device Mastery	Cunning 22, Level 12	Practice makes perfect, and only the most intricate locks or elaborate traps give the rogue pause at this level of mastery. A further bonus applies when lockpicking or disarming traps. The character's cunning score also contributes to these skills.	0	0	0	No	0	0
Chain 4	Stealth	Cunning 10	The rogue has learned to fade from view, although perceptive enemies may not be fooled. Taking any action beyond movement, including engaging in combat or using items, will still attract attention. If the rogue initiates combat while still stealthed, the first strike is an automatic critical hit or backstab.	0	0	5	No	10	0
	Stealthy Item Use	Cunning 14, Level 4	The rogue has learned how to use items while sneaking.	0	0	0	No	0	0
	Combat Stealth	Cunning 18, Level 8	The rogue is stealthy enough to try sneaking during combat, although at a significant penalty.	0	0	0	No	0	0
	Master Stealth	Cunning 22, Level 12	The rogue has mastered the art of stealth, gaining significant bonuses on all stealth checks.	0	0	0	No	0	0
			Dual Weapon School						
Chain 1	Dual Striking	Dexterity 12	When in this mode, the character strikes with both weapons simultaneously. Attacks cause more damage, but the character cannot inflict regular critical hits or backstabs.	0	50	5	No	10	0
	Riposte	Dexterity 16	The character strikes at a target once, dealing normal damage, as well as stunning the opponent unless it passes a physical resistance check. The character then strikes with the other weapon, generating a critical hit if the target was stunned.	40	0	0	No	20	0
	Cripple	Dexterity 22	The character strikes low at a target, gaining a momentary attack bonus and hitting critically if the attack connects, while crippling the target with penalties to movement speed, attack, and defense unless it passes a physical resistance check.	35	0	0	No	30	0
	Punisher	Dexterity 28	The character makes three blows against a target, dealing normal damage for the first two strikes and generating a critical hit for the final blow, if it connects. The target may also suffer penalties to attack and defense, or be knocked to the ground.	50	0	0	No	40	0

The Rogue

Basics ~ Character Generation ~ Classes ~ The Party ~ Companions ~ Supporting Cast ~ Equipment ~ Bestiary ~ Walkthroughs ~ Side Quests ~ Random Encounters ~ Achievements/Trophies

Chain	Name	Prerequisite	Description	Cost (mana /stamina)	Upkeep (mana /stamina)	Fatigue (% mana/stamina)	Ranged	Cooldown (sec.)	Area of Effect Radius (ft.)
			Dual Weapon School (continued)						
Chain 2	Dual-Weapon Sweep	Dexterity 12	The character sweeps both weapons in a broad forward arc, striking nearby enemies with one or both weapons and inflicting significantly more damage than normal.	20	0	0	No	15	2
	Flurry	Dexterity 18	The character lashes out with a flurry of three blows, dealing normal combat damage with each hit.	40	0	0	No	20	0
	Momentum	Dexterity 24	The character has learned to carry one attack through to the next, increasing attack speed substantially. This mode consumes stamina quickly, however.	0	60	5	No	30	0
	Whirlwind	Dexterity 30	The character flies into a whirling dance of death, striking out at surrounding enemies with both weapons. Each hit deals normal combat damage.	40	0	0	No	40	2
Chain 3	Dual-Weapon Training	Dexterity 12	The character has become more proficient fighting with two weapons, and now deals closer to normal damage bonus with the off-hand weapon.	0	0	0	No	0	0
	Dual-Weapon Finesse	Dexterity 16	The character is extremely skilled at wielding a weapon in each hand, gaining bonuses to attack and defense.	0	0	0	No	0	0
	Dual-Weapon Expert	Dexterity 26, Level 9	The character has significant experience with two-weapon fighting, gaining a bonus to critical chance, as well as a possibility with each hit to inflict bleeding lacerations that continue to damage a target for a time.	0	0	0	No	0	0
	Dual-Weapon Mastery	Dexterity 36, Level 12	Only a chosen few truly master the complicated art of fighting with two weapons. The character is now among that elite company, able to wield full-sized weapons in both hands. Stamina costs for all dual-weapon talents are also reduced.	0	0	0	No	0	0
			Archery School						
Chain 1	Melee Archer	Dexterity 12	Experience fighting in tight quarters has taught the archer to fire without interruption, even when being attacked.	0	0	0	No	0	0
	Aim	Dexterity 16	The archer carefully places each shot for maximum effect while in this mode. This decreases rate of fire but grants bonuses to attack, damage, armor penetration, and critical chance. Master Archer further increases these bonuses.	0	35	5	No	10	0
	Defensive Fire	Dexterity 22	While active, the archer changes stance, receiving a bonus to defense but slowing the rate of fire. With the Master Archer talent, the defense bonus increases.	0	40	5	No	15	0
	Master Archer	Dexterity 28	Deadly with both bows and crossbows, master archers receive additional benefits when using Aim, Defensive Fire, Crippling Shot, Critical Shot, Arrow of Slaying, Rapid Shot, and Shattering Shot. This talent also eliminates the penalty to attack speed when wearing heavy armor, although massive armor still carries the penalty.	0	0	0	No	0	0
Chain 2	Pinning Shot	Dexterity 12	A shot to the target's legs disables the foe, pinning the target in place unless it passes a physical resistance check, and slowing movement speed otherwise.	20	0	0	Yes	15	0
	Crippling Shot	Dexterity 16	A carefully aimed shot hampers the target's ability to fight by reducing attack and defense if it hits, although the shot inflicts only normal damage. The Master Archer talent adds an attack bonus while firing the Crippling Shot.	25	0	0	Yes	10	0
	Critical Shot	Dexterity 21	Finding a chink in the target's defenses, the archer fires an arrow that, if aimed correctly, automatically scores a critical hit and gains a bonus to armor penetration. The Master Archer talent increases the armor penetration bonus.	40	0	0	Yes	10	0
	Arrow of Slaying	Dexterity 30	The archer generates an automatic critical hit if this shot finds its target, although high-level targets may be able to ignore the effect. The archer suffers reduced stamina regeneration for a time. Master Archer adds an extra attack bonus.	80	0	0	Yes	60	0
Chain 3	Rapid Shot	Dexterity 12	Speed wins out over power while this mode is active, as the archer fires more rapidly but without any chance of inflicting regular critical hits. Master Archer increases the rate of fire further still.	0	35	5	No	30	0
	Shattering Shot	Dexterity 16	The archer fires a shot designed to open up a weak spot in the target's armor. The shot deals normal damage if it hits and imposes an armor penalty on the target. Master Archer increases the target's armor penalty.	25	0	0	Yes	15	0
	Suppressing Fire	Dexterity 24	When this mode is active, the archer's shots hamper foes. Each arrow deals regular damage and also encumbers the target with a temporary penalty to attack. This penalty can be applied multiple times.	0	60	5	No	10	0
	Scattershot	Dexterity 27	The archer fires a single arrow that automatically hits, stunning the target and dealing normal damage. The arrow then shatters, hitting all nearby enemies with the same effect.	50	0	0	Yes	40	0
			Power of Blood School (downloadable content only)						
Chain 1	Dark Passage	None	Tapping the power of tainted blood makes the rogue more nimble, able to move more quickly while using Stealth and more likely to dodge a physical attack.	0	0	0	No	0	0
	The Tainted Blade	None	The rogue's blood gushes forth, coating the edges of weapons with a deadly taint. The character gains a bonus to damage determined by the cunning attribute, but suffers continuously depleting health in return.	40	40	5	No	5	0

Specializations

Each class has two specializations (out of four) that they can learn during the game. Your first specialization can be learned at level 7; your second at level 14. Most companions can teach a specialization, though your approval rating must be high enough for the companion to want to teach you. Leliana, for example, can teach the rogue's bard specialization. Specializations are difficult to achieve, but very rewarding if you gain one. As long as the specific abilities fit with your play style and character breakdown, a specialization is generally worth spending points in over regular talents.

Definitely experiment with specializations. A DPS rogue could, for example, specialize in ranger to add an extra "companion" to a fight for more support. Here are some suggested play style fits for the four specializations:

Assassin
- **Primary:** DPS (all-out offense to max out damage)
- **Secondary:** Stamina replenishment (use Feast of the Fallen to recoup lost stamina)

Bard
- **Primary:** Enemy control (Captivating Song can corral whole crowds)
- **Secondary:** Party buffer (replenish party mana/stamina or augment offense/defense)

Duelist
- **Primary:** Balanced DPS (excellent offense with a touch of defense)
- **Secondary:** Crit-happy (reach Pinpoint Strike for multiple critical successes in a row)

Ranger
- **Primary:** Pet lover (summon beasties for party support)
- **Secondary:** Off-tank (summoned creatures tank for you)

Rogue Specializations

Specialization	Talent Name	Prerequisite Level	Description	Cost (mana /stamina)	Upkeep (mana /stamina)	Fatigue (% mana/stamina)	Ranged	Cooldown (sec.)	Area of Effect Radius (ft.)
			Learned From: Zevran (Companion), Alarith's Store (Denerim, after Landsmeet starts)						
Assassin	Mark of Death	7	The assassin marks a target, revealing weaknesses that others can exploit. All attacks against a marked target deal additional damage.	40	0	0	Yes	60	0
	Exploit Weakness	12	A keen eye and a killer instinct help the assassin exploit a target's weak points. During a successful backstab attack, the assassin gains additional damage based on cunning.	0	0	0	No	0	0
	Lacerate	14	Whenever a backstab deals enough damage, the assassin's foe is riddled with bleeding wounds that inflict additional damage for a short time.	30	60	0	No	60	0
	Feast of the Fallen	16	The assassin thrives on the moment of death. Stamina is partially restored whenever the assassin fells an opponent with a backstab.	0	0	0	No	0	0
			Learned From: Leliana (Companion), Alimar (Orzammar)						
Bard	Song of Valor	7	The bard sings an ancient tale of valorous heroes, granting the party bonuses to mana or stamina regeneration at a rate affected by the bard's cunning. The bard can only sing one song at a time.	0	50	5	No	30	10
	Distraction	8	The bard's performance, replete with dizzying flourishes, is designed to distract and confuse. The target forgets who it was fighting and becomes disoriented unless it passes a mental resistance check.	40	0	0	Yes	30	0
	Song of Courage	10	The bard launches into an epic song of the party's exploits, granting them bonuses to attack, damage, and critical chance. The size of the bonuses are affected by the bard's cunning. The bard can only sing one song at a time.	0	50	5	No	30	10
	Captivating Song	12	The bard begins an entrancing song that stuns hostile targets nearby unless they pass a mental resistance check every few seconds. Continuing the song does not drain stamina, but the bard cannot move or take any other action while singing.	0	60	5	No	30	4

Specialization	Talent Name	Prerequisite Level	Description	Cost (mana /stamina)	Upkeep (mana /stamina)	Fatigue (% mana/stamina)	Ranged	Cooldown (sec.)	Area of Effect: Radius (ft.)
			Learned From: Isabela (The Pearl in Denerim)						
Duelist	Dueling	7	The duelist focuses on proper form, gaining a bonus to attack while the mode is active. Keen Defense adds a bonus to defense while in this mode.	0	30	5	No	5	0
Duelist	Upset Balance	12	The duelist executes a quick move that throws the opponent off balance, imposing penalties to movement speed and defense unless the target passes a physical resistance check.	25	0	0	No	15	0
Duelist	Keen Defense	14	The duelist has an uncanny knack for simply not being there when the enemy attacks, receiving a bonus to defense.	0	0	0	No	0	0
Duelist	Pinpoint Strike	16	The duelist has learned to strike the vitals of an enemy with pinpoint accuracy and from any angle. For a moderate duration, all successful attacks generate automatic critical hits.	60	0	0	No	180	0
			Learned From: Bodahn's Wares (Party Camp)						
Ranger	Summon Wolf	7	The ranger calls a great forest wolf to fight alongside the party.	0	50	5	No	60	0
Ranger	Summon Bear	8	The ranger calls a powerful bear to fight alongside the party.	0	50	5	No	90	0
Ranger	Summon Spider	10	The ranger calls a large spider to fight alongside the party.	0	50	5	No	120	0
Ranger	Master Ranger	12	The ranger has learned to summon stronger companion animals. Animals summoned by a Master Ranger are significantly more powerful in combat than their normal counterparts.	0	0	0	No	0	0

Gear

Daggers are a natural weapon for a rogue to use, given their high speed, armor penetration, and critical chance. Other one-handed weapons work well too, but you won't be able to dual wield them until you reach Dual-Weapon Mastery at 36 dexterity. And definitely dual wield, even if it's not something you planned to spec in, because another weapon never hurts.

Carry a bow in the backup weapon slot and make good use of it. You need to build dexterity anyway for the Dual Weapon school, so you might as well use it to complement a bow, right?

There's more rogue gear than you could ever hope to equip in a single play. The general rule of thumb is to wait for loot that serves as an upgrade and snatch it up. If you have extra coin to buy a nice gear upgrade, feel free to spend away, though most of the low-level equipment will be easily replaced by future loot, and the high-level equipment is very expensive (generally bought during the Landsmeet for a run at the archdemon).

With so much good gear, here are some beauties to shoot for based on beginning (1–5), intermediate (6–10), advanced (11–15), and expert levels (16–20):

	Lvl 1-5	Lvl 6-10	Lvl 11-15	Lvl 16-20
Armor	Studded Leather Armor (any type)	Studded Leather Armor (any type)	Shadow of the Empire (Drakescale)	The Felon's Coat (Drakescale)
Helm	Studded Leather (any type)	Studded Helmet (any type), Studded Leather Helm (any type)	Qunari Thickened Cap (Reinforced)	Conspirator's Foil, The Long Sight (Drakeskin)
Boots	Studded Leather Boots (any type)	Dalish Boots (any type)	Deygan's Boots (Reinforced)	Bard's Dancing Shoes (Drakescale), Wade's Superior Drakeskin Boots
Gloves	Studded Leather Gloves (any type)	Dalish Gloves (Leather)	Backhands (Hardened)	Red Jenny Seekers (Drakescale)
Offhand	Noble's Dagger	Enchanted Dagger (Grey Iron), Falon'Din's Reach (Dragonthorn)	Beastman's Dagger (Red Steel)	The Rose's Thorn (Dragonbone), Crow Dagger (any type but Dragonbone with 3 rune slots is best)
Main Hand	Borrowed Longsword	Saw Sword	Imperial Edge	King Maric's Blade
Bow	Darkspawn Longbow	Spear Thrower	Far Song	Marjolaine's Recurve

Party Responsibilities

Are you the party's damage-dealer or scout? If you're DPS-focused, your primary responsibility is dealing melee or ranged damage. That generally means stocking up on offensive talents and gear. If you're picking a lot of locks and stealthing around, spread more points to the non-combat talents; think balance over cutthroat combat expertise. All rogues need to be aware of threat and avoid pulling too much at once. Learn to time your attacks so you don't draw too much threat but still deal significant damage to the enemy.

If your rogue is the main PC, the other three companions should fill in talents around you for a well-balanced party. If you're building up a companion rogue, look to fill in where the party is lacking. Not dealing enough damage? Crank up the offense. Want to avoid more traps and earn more treasure? Make sure you build up those nimble-fingered talents. In the final party configuration, your PC should play whatever role you have the most fun with while the other three companions add the components necessary to maximize your combat efficiency.

The rogue ranks very well in terms of armor, weapons, and all-purpose talents. Those talents and gear enable you to surprise your foes with killer damage, slip in and out of combat for great defense, and deal with non-combat dungeon obstacles (traps, locks) that other companions cannot. From whirlwind flair in a sea of armor to steady precision with lockpick tools, the rogue covers everything that warriors and mages can't—all with a wink and smile.

Model Characters

With the game's best weapon talent trees, you can create dozens of rogues who each wield something a little different in combat. Don't feel constrained to play according to the following rogue models to the letter; take bits and pieces that appeal to your play style and add your own spin. However, these are basic models for a melee DPS rogue, ranged DPS rogue, and scout rogue. Each shows you how to choose your talents up to level 20, what talent chains are effective, how specializations fit in, and sample combat strategies for that model.

Melee DPS Model

Level	Talent
0	Dirty Fighting
1	Below the Belt, Dual-Weapon Training
2	Dual Striking
3	Dual-Weapon Finesse
4	Combat Movement
5	Deadly Strike
6	Riposte
7	Mark of Death (Assassin)—*First Specialization Available at This Level*
8	Lethality
9	Dual-Weapon Expert
10	Coup de Grace
11	Cripple
12	Dual-Weapon Mastery
13	Punisher
14	Exploit Weakness (Assassin)—*Second Specialization Available at This Level*
15	Lacerate (Assassin)
16	Feast of the Fallen (Assassin)
17	Evasion
18	Feign Death
19	Dual-Weapon Sweep
20	Flurry

The Rogue

Basics ~ Character Generation ~ **Classes** ~ The Party ~ Companions ~ Supporting Cast ~ Equipment ~ Bestiary ~ Walkthroughs ~ Side Quests ~ Random Encounters ~ Achievements/Trophies

Overview: The name of the game is to deal damage quickly. Generally, Dual Weapon talents combined with the backstabbing Rogue talents work best.

Leveling: If you choose a Human Noble or Dwarf Noble, you gain the first Combat Training skill and can spend your skill point on Improved Combat Training. You begin with Dirty Fighting talent, an excellent starting skill and always useful. You can stun, then move behind the enemy to get in a couple of backstabs. This skill helps tremendously when you are forced to fight face-to-face, or for helping out a healer or teammate about to die.

At level 1, Below the Belt gives you a decent attack that can slow down enemies so they can't escape or can't pursue. Dual-Weapon Training starts the first Dual Weapon chain, which will be your primary focus. Continue your Dual Weapon basics for the next two levels with Dual Striking and Dual-Weapon Finesse. Make sure you take Improved Combat Training by this point.

Next, Combat Movement presents a wider flanking area to produce backstabs easier. In the bigger fights with bodies all bunched together, it's difficult to get directly behind a target in time, so this helps a lot. At level 5, pick up Deadly Strike as a precursor to Lethality and extra armor penetration. At level 6, pick up Riposte to add another stun to your arsenal. With Coup de Grace, you prevent damage to your party while hacking away for criticals.

You gain your specialization at level 7. You could go with duelist, but assassin concentrates on damage, and that's your priority. Mark of Death increases all damage against a single target. It's perfect against bosses and tougher foes that require that special touch.

The passive talent Lethality at level 8 increases your critical chance and converts cunning to strength for damage purposes. Dual-Weapon Expert adds even more critical chance at level 9. You need 26 dexterity and Expert Combat Training by this point.

Coup de Grace and Cripple, at levels 10 and 11, pile on the damage with more chances for backstabs and critical hits. At levels 12 and 13, top off your two Dual Weapon chains with Dual-Weapon Mastery and Punisher. You can deal with huge threats now, wield full-sized weapons in both hands, use more talents because your stamina costs are reduced, and punish an opponent with three crushing blows. You must have 36 dexterity and Master Combat Training by now.

Complete your assassin specialization with levels 14 through 16. Exploit Weaknesses increases your damage potential by finding holes in your enemy's defenses, Lacerate gives you a damage-over-time effect, and Feast of the Fallen replenishes your stamina with every kill.

Now that you've nearly maxed out your offense, add a little defense with Evasion at level 17 and Feign Death at level 18. You can always gain these defensive talents earlier if you find yourself hit a lot in combat. With a good party, though, you probably want to favor the offense.

You can finish up your talents with virtually anything you want. Here we'll add Dual-Weapon Sweep and Flurry for multiple-target damage, which could improve your damage output tremendously.

Talent Choices: Melee DPS tends toward Dual Weapon talents as a natural fit. You can dabble in the cunning Rogue talents, but to maximize your offensive potential, stick with most, if not all, of the dexterity Rogue talents.

Specialization: Assassin is all about enough damage to kill targets before they kill you. It's possible to go with the duelist specialization as well, if you want a little defense mixed in with your offense, but for all-out DPS, assassin slays the competition.

Battle Tactics: Wait a few seconds for the tank and other companions to engage the enemy. Angle into the fight from the side or rear, and always position yourself for a backstab attempt. In general, you want to help the tank eliminate his prime adversary, but if you see targets of opportunity with half health or less, make quick work of them.

Based on the position and number of foes, select your attacks appropriately. Tank's target putting up a fight? Hit from behind with Coup de Grace and Punisher. Enemy turning its attention on you? Stun it with Dirty Fighting or Riposte, or slow it down with Cripple so you can escape. Boss lumbering into view? Hit it with Mark of Death so everyone piles on extra damage.

Ranged DPS Model

Level	Talent
0	Dirty Fighting
1	Pinning Shot, Rapid Shot
2	Below the Belt
3	Crippling Shot
4	Shattering Shot
5	Deadly Strike
6	Critical Shot
7	Suppressing Fire—*First Specialization Available at This Level*
8	Lethality
9	Scattershot
10	Arrow of Slaying
11	Melee Archer
12	Aim
13	Defensive Fire
14	Master Archer—*Second Specialization Available at This Level*
15	Dueling (Duelist)
16	Upset Balance (Duelist)
17	Keen Defense (Duelist)
18	Pinpoint Strike (Duelist)
19	Deft Hands
20	Stealth

Overview: Much like an offensive mage, a ranged DPS rogue concentrates weapons and talents on enemies at a distance. He focuses on the Archery school, and may dip into some talents,

such as the duelist specialization, when melee becomes imminent.

Leveling: You begin with Dirty Fighting. It's not ideal for range, but very helpful when an enemy closes on you and you need a quick stun to get your distance again. As you'll be working with a bow, load up on dexterity. Your goal is to have 27 dexterity and Master Combat Training by level 9.

With your first two talent points at level 1, choose Pinning Shot and Rapid Shot. You now can hamper someone's movement with Pinning Shot or reload much faster with Rapid Shot. Below the Belt at level 2 gives you another melee talent, which also helps you avoid prolonged face-to-face encounters.

At level 3, gain the Improved Combat Training skill and start working on the next tier of talents. Crippling Shot hampers a foe's offense and defense, while Shattering Shot and Deadly Strike put holes in enemy's armor.

If you have 21 dexterity and Expert Combat Training at level 6, select Critical Shot. If you hit, Critical Shot inflicts critical damage and a bonus to armor penetration. Follow that up with Suppressing Fire at the next level to further encumber targets with attack penalties.

At level 8, purchase Lethality. It's an all-around excellent ability: it increases the critical chance for all attacks and possibly replaces cunning for strength when considering damage bonuses.

You reach your first pinnacle at level 9 with Scattershot. This awesome talent automatically stuns your target and deals normal damage, then splinters off and does the same to all nearby enemies. Use this effectively against enemy spellcasters or large enemy groups to impede flanking attempts.

If you can reach 30 dexterity by level 10, you gain Arrow of Slaying. This scores an automatic critical hit against all but high-level opponents.

Beginning at level 11, concentrate on the Melee Archer chain. Melee Archer prevents attacks from interrupting your firing, while Aim and Defensive Fire provide offensive and defensive oriented bonuses, respectively. At level 14 you finish the chain with Master Archer. You can fire arrows while taking damage, gain bonuses to offense and damage, slow the rate of fire to gain bonuses to defense, and bulk up almost all your Archery talents with Master Archer. This skill also allows the rogue to wear heavy armor without attack speed penalties.

Now it's time for some melee talents in case enemies get close. At level 15, seek out Isabela at the Pearl to learn the duelist specialization. Dueling and Pinpoint Strike ratchet up your offense while Upset Balance and Keen Defense ensure you won't go down so easily with swords and claws flying.

To fill out through level 20, dip into the cunning Rogue talents, with one point for locking picking and one for stealth. If you aren't pure ranged DPS, you'll want these talents earlier; however, choosing them at higher levels still gives you options for the final quests in the game.

Talent Choices: The Archery school and all its ranged surprises are your go-to talents. Duelist provides some melee talents in case an enemy gets close enough to grab you.

Specialization: The Dueling sustained ability gives a bonus to attack while active. Upset Balance can slow an enemy's movement speed and hinder its defense. The passive Keen Defense does just that: add a permanent bonus to defense. Your top melee talent, Pinpoint Strike, converts all hits into critical strikes for a moderate duration.

Battle Tactics: Once the battle begins, stand your ground. Let the tank and other melee DPSers embrace the enemy. You want to nuke them from afar. Unlike a mage who stays in the rear, however, the ranged DPS rogue can enter melee with his better armor, weapons, and duelist talents at higher levels.

Survey the battlefield and pick your targets wisely. Concentrate fire on the tank's target to bring it down quicker, or look for injured foes that you can drop with an arrow or two. If you see an enemy spellcaster in the enemy's rear, make it your priority. You don't want it getting off damaging spells. Same goes for enemy archers. If your melee companions can't reach them, it's your job to stop them from pelting the team with damage.

On offense, your rotation goes something like this: Aim, Pinning Shot (against moving targets), Critical Shot (against near-dead targets), and Arrow of Slaying. On defense, go Defensive Fire, Crippling Shot, Suppressing Fire, and Scattershot (especially against enemy spellcasters or enemies charging at you).

As a ranged DPS rogue, you have much of the offense of a DPS mage, yet you still can wear most of the better armor and use high-quality weapons. Keep on the go to avoid enemy melee encounters and let your companions wade through the blood and limbs.

Scout Model

Level	Talent
0	Dirty Fighting
1	Deft Hands, Stealth
2	Dual-Weapon Training
3	Combat Movement
4	Improved Tools
5	Dual-Weapon Finesse
6	Dual Striking
7	Song of Valor (Bard)—*First Specialization Available at This Level*
8	Mechanical Expertise

Level	Talent
9	Dual-Weapon Expert
10	Distraction (Bard)
11	Song of Courage (Bard)
12	Device Mastery
13	Captivating Song (Bard)
14	Dual-Weapon Mastery—*Second Specialization Available at This Level*
15	Riposte
16	Coup de Grace
17	Feign Death
18	Cripple
19	Punisher
20	Stealthy Item Use

Overview: A master thief slinks through the shadows and opens locked doors with a flick of the wrist. A scout rogue can DPS well, but knows more than a thing or two about the business of treasure and traps.

Leveling: With your two points from the start, choose your key noncombat talents, Deft Hands (for lockpicking and trap detection) and Stealth (for hiding invisibly). The Deft Hands chain is your priority; you want to be able to open locked doors and chests, and it will take up to Device Mastery at level 12 to open anything that comes your way.

At levels 2 and 3, begin on your offense with Dual-Weapon Training and Combat Movement. The following level, pick up Improved Tools to further enhance your lockpicking and trap detection. With this build, you should increase cunning and dexterity to unlock all the necessary talents.

For the next two levels, continue your offense with Dual-Weapon Finesse at level 5 and Dual Striking at level 6. The big penalties to your off-hand weapon will be gone, and you now can attack with a two-hit combo.

At level 7, ask Leliana to train you in the bard specialization. Song of Valor provides regeneration to mana and stamina, which always proves useful after a long battle. At level 8, you gain the third lockpicking rank with Mechanical Expertise. You will need 18 cunning.

To become a Dual-Weapon Expert at level 9, make sure you have 26 dexterity and Expert Combat Training. Your critical chance increases, and you may inflict lacerations that cause enemies to bleed more damage over time.

At levels 10 and 11, continue down the bard path. Distraction is a single-target stun, while Song of Courage improves the party's attack, damage, and critical chance scores.

If you have 22 cunning by level 12, welcome to the ultimate lockpicking and trap detection talent: Device Mastery. You will never fail to open a locked door or chest (unless it requires a special key), or to detect a trap and disarm it.

You cap out two more key talent chains at levels 13 and 14. First, the bard's Captivating Song is the rogue's finest crowd control talent if you have the stamina to use it properly. At level 14, Dual-Weapon Mastery finishes off your expertise with two weapons, including wielding full-sized weapons if you like.

For level 15 and on, you can fill out talents as desired. Here we went with Riposte and Coup de Grace next for more stunning and backstabbing. Feign Death and Cripple, at levels 17 and 18, give you options to remove yourself from combat if you have too much threat on you. Level 19's Punisher gives you a powerful finishing move, and the final talent, Stealthy Item Use, improves your stealth to the second rank.

Talent Choices: The Rogue cunning abilities come in the most handy, supported by its dexterity talents and some Dual Weapon conditioning.

Specialization: The bard specialization may not produce extra damage, but it gives the rogue phenomenal control over enemies with the stuns Distraction and Captivating Song. The group buffs Song of Valor and Song of Courage raise the stats of the entire party. If you aren't worried about pure combat, the bard specialization is the best option for helping out the entire party.

Battle Tactics: You don't have as much DPS as your other companions, so let the tank and other melee specialists roam out into the enemy crowds. You can slip into stealth and pick your best spot to enter combat. At higher levels, once you've stacked up a few Dual Weapon talents, you should hold your own against lesser enemy groups or a stronger one-on-one fight.

Your chief role will be crowd control. Once you have the bard's Captivating Song at level 13, charge out just behind the tank or other DPSers. Activate Captivating Song once the enemy throng presses in. You won't be able to move, but all enemies within a moderate radius will be stunned unless they pass a mental resistance check every few seconds. Most mobs are susceptible to mental attacks, so the song is very effective. With the song active, you lose stamina over time, and when you hit zero, all enemies break loose. Build up your willpower if you plan on using Captivating Song a lot. By pinning enemies in place, you prevent incoming damage and allow your fellow companions ample free shots on the dazed enemies.

The Party

The name of the game should give you a clue that monstrous beasts are in store for you. From dungeon depths to snowy mountaintops, your four-person party will battle anything from devastating dragons to drooling darkspawn. Unless you want to end up as chew toys for ogres, hone up on the basics and learn expert party dynamics.

Buddy Basics

You begin your adventuring career on your own. As the story unfolds, you meet companions who join your party and become your allies in battle. A companion could be a fellow Grey Warden like Alistair, or the unlikeliest of allies, Zevran, an Antivan Crow sent to assassinate you. It's up to you to decide which companions you travel with, because you can have only three companions at once. The rest remain behind at party camp, a place easily reached from the world map that serves as haven for you and your companions, fully equipped with a dwarven merchant to buy excess goods and sell you wares at a discount. Each time you leave party camp, you can pick three new companions to accompany you, and in certain non-hostile regions, you can use the Party Configuration button on your top menu to immediately switch companions. For more on each companion, flip to the Companions chapter.

Group Dynamics

Each of the three classes has a distinct role in the party. In general, class roles fall into categories that take best advantage of class talents. However, be prepared to improvise at any given moment. For example, if you're a rogue bard intent on keeping a second monster away from the party and you see the first enemy about to defeat your tank, you may want to switch to offense and help out with the first enemy.

The party's main tank responsibilities fall on the shoulders of a warrior. His superior defense and ability to hold the mob's threat safeguard the group in the heat of battle. If the tank falls, it generally spells doom for the rest of the party as the enemies split and attack the more vulnerable companions. The warrior's primary job is to the hold the line and keep the enemy's attention on him at all times so that others can do their thing.

Every party needs a healer, and the mage provides the health-pumping spells to excel at that. The mage's single and party heals keep companions alive. When not healing, the mage can augment the party with stat-enhancing buffs. A mage can also concentrate almost completely on DPS, stacking up on single-target and AoE damage spells to obliterate whole enemy groups.

A rogue acts as the scout for the fellowship. He slips into the shadows with stealth and recons the area for enemy positions, traps, treasure locations, and quest objectives. When going up against enemies, a rogue can hide until the opportune moment to dart in for a backstab. In the heat of battle, the rogue adds extra DPS to the fight with superior Dual Weapon talents and bonuses to critical hit chances.

As you adventure with the same team, you gain experience, loot, and better skills. Develop your team as a whole and not just individuals. For example, you don't need four party members with Herbalism. One person who's mastered Herbalism can supply all the potions, leaving the others free to spread out their points to other valuable skills. It's fine to have two party members with Poison-Making so they can both enhance their weapon DPS, but also try out Trap-Making, and leave crucial skill points open for your PC to put into Coercion and possibly Survival. After a successful quest run, distribute your gear to the most appropriate characters. Don't always give the best items to your PC (though he or she should certainly get great loot whenever possible). It's much better to hand the top-notch armor to your tank than your rogue PC, and it makes little sense to give an accessory with magic bonus to your melee DPS character.

Buddy Basics - Combat Roles

Basics ~ Character Generation ~ Classes ~ **The Party** ~ Companions ~ Supporting Cast ~ Equipment ~ Bestiary ~ Walkthroughs ~ Side Quests ~ Random Encounters ~ Achievements/Trophies

Dealing with Threat

If anyone in your party does manage to pull threat, always make sure to run to the tank to have it picked up. Attempting to run away only increases the time it takes to get the mob pulled off, likely resulting in the character's death or even the whole party's. Monitor the threat from critical hits. If you land a couple of high critical strikes in a row, disengage for a second then reengage. Critical strikes increase your threat, so consider this when monitoring your threat output.

If you have an off-tank in a party, don't use the off-tank's threat-generating abilities unless a difficult enemy breaks from the main tank or the main tank dies. Pulling off of the main tank will interrupt his threat generation, and your healer may not have enough mana, or time, to heal both.

If the main tank loses threat, everyone in the party must disengage until the main tank has regained threat. Use any threat-reducing abilities, such as the rogue's Feign Death, if you have them. Once the main tank picks the enemies back up, wait a few seconds for the tank to build threat, then reengage.

Healing

The party's healer will save or damn a group when an encounter gets hot and heavy. As a healer, you have to know when to launch your Group Heal, when to throw around a Heal or Regeneration, and when to avoid healing. In general, save your big heal to counteract large spike damage (unexpected damage that crits through a party members' defense for a significant amount of health), or if you desperately need to float a party member's health back up to a manageable level. Those levels will depend on the enemy's damage and how much backup healing and mana you have at your disposal, but you shouldn't panic unless a party member's health is consistently dropping below the one-third mark. Even then, the healer's main responsibility is to the tank, then himself. Keep the tank alive, even if it means losing a DPSer in the fight. If the tank falls, the whole party will most likely perish. A good rule of thumb is to never switch off the main tank unless another companion's health is dropping rapidly. If you have to heal elsewhere, switch to the party member that needs help, throw a single Heal or Regeneration, and return to the main tank immediately.

TIP

Don't always burn your healer's mana. You may need to pop a healing potion from time to time and save the healer's magic for tougher stretches of the fight. If it looks like a companion is going to die despite the heals, use your best health poultice to help you climb back up to full.

A healer definitely must learn when *not* to heal. Obviously, you must conserve your mana so you don't run out at a crucial time, but you must also look at the big picture. You only have so many heals you can throw around, and the majority will be directed at the tank. You don't want to let anyone drop, but if you find yourself limited, you may have to skip a heal or two that you would have normally cast and let everyone's health bars get much closer to zero. Unless you are cruising through an encounter, you should never heal a non-party member, such as a blue-circled ally or one of the ranger's summoned animals. These allies are expendable, and the ranger's pets can always be re-summoned.

Combat Roles

Each companion's role in a party will be different based on their spells, talents, and what you expect them to accomplish during the fight. As you level, choose the talents and spells that best fit your party configuration, and gear up appropriately. The following general strategies should work well for a tank, healer, mage DPS, general melee DPS, and general ranged DPS.

Tank

A tank doesn't muck around with fancy spells or dainty arrows; he charges at a foe and hacks at it with his weapon of choice. It's the tank's job to engage all enemies and direct their attention on him. Taunt abilities, such as Threaten and Taunt (of course!), increase threat against a target and force that target to become more hostile toward the tank; you can never get a foe mad enough as a tank, so load up the threat and keep those enemies foaming at the mouth! Also, keep aware of the ever-changing battlefield, because it only takes one stray mob to veer toward one of your fellow DPSers (even worse, a healer) to turn an otherwise controlled fight into a free-for-all. Make sure you rope in all the enemies so others are free to aid the party as they should. Because all the damage is focused on you, carry a lot of health poultices and the best gear you can scrounge up. Good gear will mitigate damage, making the healer's job easier and allowing you to go longer in fights, especially boss fights and ones where you handle several foes at once.

Healer

Harnessing great magical powers, a mage healer's primary role is that of savior in a group. They can deal some damage to enemies, but their focus is keeping the party members, and primarily the tank, alive. In any group setting, everyone staying alive is important but if the tank dies, everyone dies. So keeping the tank alive is critical. Secondary to that is keeping oneself alive. Many a healer has fallen in battle when they failed to tend to their own wounds. The healer may also apply buffs (bonuses) to their party that help them do more damage or defend better. One skill a healer needs to master is where to stand and when to move. Most of their magic requires them to remain motionless, yet on some fights, the party can be spread out so the healer needs to move to get within range. The healer has to balance running around and leaving enough time to heal everyone who needs it, while keeping the tank alive. Anyone can stand in one spot and heal. A truly skilled healer can move, heal, and buff with ease. Remember to watch your mana, and if you have to make tough choices, keep the tank alive first and yourself second. A dead healer is no use to the party.

Mage DPS

Some mages incinerate their enemies from afar, others freeze them solid or crumble the earth down around them. The end result is always the same: mass destruction. Their damage makes them extremely valuable in a party, but they also need to control their power, allowing the tank enough time to build up threat before they unleash their destruction. DPS mages do so much damage in such a spectacular way that they often attract unwanted attention. If an opponent gets too close, the mage, wearing only basic robes, could be done for. Mage spells also have decent range. If a mage stands far from the tank and draws the monster's threat, it becomes harder for fellow companions to save the mage. So the mage needs to stand in the right spot and learn the right spell timing. It often is not about how fast one can cast, but knowing when to cast.

Melee DPS

The rogue DPS character, or the non-tank warrior DPSer, relies on cunning and savagery to take down his target as quickly as possible. Melee DPSers are not built for long one-on-one fights like a tank, nor can they usually handle large groups of foes; however, they are excellent damage-dealers who offer support DPS in a party. After the tank engages and holds threat, a rogue DPSer can prowl unseen behind the enemy, then unleash crippling backstab blows to stagger the opponent. A warrior DPSer can dish out damage on the tank's target, then grab threat on a stray creature if it breaks from the pack. Because melee DPS characters have the talents to deal huge damage very quickly (especially critical strikes), they must be extremely careful not to pull threat away from the party's tank. This usually means holding back and not running through the best regimen of combos, except on boss fights or with one creature left standing. You may also choose to slow down your combos so you don't trigger them as quickly. Depending on your skill choices, a melee DPSer can add even more support damage through Poison-Making, Trap-Making, or certain usable items. A competent and poised melee DPSer can be the difference in your party between a long, drawn-out fight that teeters on the edge of failure and a quick, efficient boss execution.

Combat Roles - Configurations and Engagement

Basics ~ Character Generation ~ Classes ~ **The Party** ~ Companions ~ Supporting Cast ~ Equipment ~ Bestiary ~ Walkthroughs ~ Side Quests ~ Random Encounters ~ Achievements/Trophies

Ranged DPS

Lightly armored but fast, the ranged DPS character adds similar firepower to the party as a mage DPS character. They can close and deal melee damage, but they are at their best when firing a barrage of arrows from afar.

In addition to dealing out damage, the ranged DPSer can snare (slow down movement), stun opponents, and set up defensive fire. Because ranged DPSers have few ways to eliminate the threat they generate, they need to remain focused on when to attack and how hard to attack any given opponent. It is critical to their survival and group success that the monster stays focused on the tank. Make sure to bring health poultices to heal yourself and avoid getting the attention of the mobs.

NOTE

See the Classes chapter for how to spec each of the classes to exactly what you need to satisfy your party's demands.

Configurations and Engagement

The ideal party depends on a number of factors: nature of the encounter, size of the enemy group, play style, and more. Here are four configurations that serve in many all-purpose situations.

Balanced

- Warrior (Tank)
- Mage (Healing)
- Rogue (Scouting, DPS)
- Mage or Warrior (DPS)

Blitzkrieg

- Warrior (Tank)
- Warrior (Off-Tank)
- Mage (Healing)
- Rogue (DPS)

Control

- Warrior (Tank)
- Mage (Healing)
- Rogue (DPS)
- Mage (Crowd Control)

Unbalanced

- Warrior (Tank)
- Warrior (DPS, Off-Tank)
- Warrior (Ranged)
- Mage (Healer)

A balanced party contains a warrior as the tank, mage as the healer, rogue as the scout, and mage or warrior as support. This configuration spreads the talents around and prepares the group for any challenge. Some abilities overlap, which helps in cases where a companion may be overwhelmed at a critical time, or has already fallen in battle.

The "blitzkrieg" configuration emphasizes speed and damage over healing or defense. You carry at least two tanks on the team, a combat-oriented rogue for more damage and some light healing with a mage who also has offensive spells at his fingertips. This type of party plans to rip through one enemy group before a second can engage them; they don't have the defenses for prolonged fighting, so it's got to be swift or not at all.

Engagement 1: Enemy Group

The tank waits for the enemy front line and engages the toughest creature, or the center of an enemy swarm. His job is to hold threat from as many creatures as possible and deal damage as he can. The two DPS characters swing out and attack from the flank (or rear in the case of a rogue). Their jobs are to deal as much damage as possible, without drawing too much threat. The healer holds position in the rear and casts heals as needed to keep the party intact. In general, each companion should target the enemies the tank has and pick off the weakest ones first to reduce the enemy numbers against you.

A party that concentrates on control stands behind healing and crowd control abilities. You still need a warrior tank, and you need a dedicated healer, which falls to a spirit healer mage. The rogue lays down a lot of DPS, but must be flexible enough to off-tank once in a while or throw out some crowd control (such as a bard's Captivating Song). A second mage brings offense to the table, of course, but also spells like Grease and Crushing Prison that can slow or stop extra enemies from engaging. This particular party may enter long fights, battling for continued periods of time with solid healing and abilities that dictate when enemies confront them.

Engagement 1: Enemy Group
(continued)

An unbalanced party may not share abilities optimally, but it can be a lot of fun nevertheless. The idea is to overbalance with a single class or strategy and pursue it to the max. You can generally get away with any combination, so long as you have a mage healer in the mix (parties without a healer won't do well unless you have unlimited health poultices at your disposal, and that gets very expensive). In this example, we have three warriors, fully armed and armored, who can charge into melee if there aren't any ranged threats, or engage and leave one warrior back to shoot down targets at range and act as bodyguard for the healer in the rear. A three-warrior group dishes out tremendous damage and has serious defensive resilience, even if it lacks the finesse of a rogue's touch or the all-out AoE firepower of a DPS mage.

We all know that the perfect combination of party members doesn't automatically means success. You have to apply your skills and react quickly to the challenges that will inevitably assault you during quests. Smart parties will identify which mobs they can handle and which they can't, and as long as you dodge or control the adds that wander in your direction, your team will thrive in style.

Engagement 2: Boss Fight

The tank waits for the boss to approach, or charges in if the boss has ranged attacks. His job is to keep the boss's attention focused on him and deal damage as he can. The two DPS characters swing out and attack from the flank (or rear in the case of a rogue). Their jobs are to deal as much damage as possible, without drawing too much threat. The healer holds position in the rear and casts heals as needed to keep the party intact, mainly healing the tank who will likely take big damage spikes

Engagement 2: Boss Fight
(continued)

from the boss. In general, each companion should go all-out with their best talents/spells as long as they don't pull the boss off the tank. Note that this strategy works the same for a single enemy of any kind; it will just fall that much faster if it's not a boss.

Let's take a look at a sample fight with a tank (warrior), healer (mage) and two DPSers (rogue, mage DPS). You've cleared a path to the boss, and now it's time to take the ugly mug down. Before you launch the first attack, make sure all characters have the proper gear, usable items, and talents ready to go.

As the tank readies his weapon, the healer throws a precautionary Regeneration on him, which serves as a little extra health at the start of the battle and absorbs a few shots. Only then does the tank charge in and hit the boss with Taunt, or whack him a few time to activate Threaten, to draw the monster's attention for the first few seconds.

The mage DPSer holds his ground. He will out-damage the tank if he rains down destruction alongside the tank. The rogue circles behind the boss to get into backstab position (but not close enough for the boss to strike him with an AoE attacks). The tank rolls into his offensive routine, smacking the boss with his best chain of attacks.

After three or four tank attacks land on the boss, it's the DPSers' turn. The mage begins his offensive rotation of spells, while the rogue darts in and backstabs the boss. The rogue continues assaulting the boss unless he fears the tank will lose control or the boss will start pounding him with AoE.

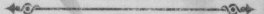

TIP

A safe rule of thumb is to let the tank attack twice for every one of the DPSer's attacks, unless you need to race and finish off the boss very quickly.

If this were a full group instead of a single enemy, the roles would stay the same, except the party would generally concentrate damage on the weakest foe to reduce the numbers quicker. If there was a dangerous foe on the battlefield—for example, a genlock emissary casting spells—the tank may have to charge that foe with DPS following, unless the ranged DPSers can take it out.

Configurations and Engagement - Tactics

Basics ~ Character Generation ~ Classes ~ **The Party** ~ Companions ~ Supporting Cast ~ Equipment ~ Bestiary ~ Walkthroughs ~ Side Quests ~ Random Encounters ~ Achievements/Trophies

Engagement 3: Strategic Retreat

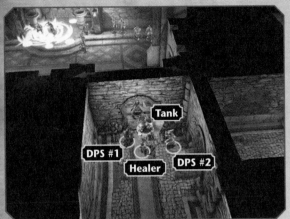

Given time, all companions retreat to defensive positions in a doorway, corridor, or even a corner. If there isn't time, the tank holds the line with as many creatures as possible, while the group positions itself away from the swarm. If the tank can slowly retreat near the party, he should do so; otherwise, all other companion to use single-target ranged attacks. The tanks's job is still to hold threat from as many creatures as possible and deal damage as he can. The two DPS characters use ranged attacks, or may be forced to do the best they can head-to-head in melee with creatures.

Engagement 3: Strategic Retreat
(continued)

The healer holds position in the rear and casts heals as needed to keep the party intact. In general, each companion should target the enemies the tank has and pick off the weakest ones first to reduce the enemy numbers against you.

With the tank dealing steady damage, the mage and rogue supporting with lots of damage but not enough to draw threat away from the tank, and the healer concentrating Heals and Regenerations on the tank to keep him healthy, the party will take down the boss after a short fight. If the boss throws around a lot of AoE, or brings in enemy allies to the fight, the healer should launch a Group Heal whenever it's active to raise everyone's health.

It's important for every member of the group to keep the self buffs, group buffs, and debuffs up at all times! If it's about to drop, refresh it and continue your DPS on the boss. Group buffs/debuffs can have a dramatic effect over the course of a battle. Remember: Damage-reducing and damage-mitigating buffs can translate directly into heals and mana saved for your healer over the course of a fight.

In the end, though, a team effort, where the player knows the roles of each of his or her characters, will bring victory to a party of four even against dozens of enemies.

Tactics

Tactics are not just about figuring out the correct movement and attack procedure in a battle. In *Dragon Age: Origins* the Tactics screen is a tool used to customize your party's actions and reactions based on the current combat situation. You unlock more tactic slots for each companion by leveling up and spending skill points on Combat Tactics. The more tactic slots your companion has, the more "programming" you can do to have them behave appropriately in various predicaments when you aren't directly controlling them, or when you don't want to pause the game and would like your party to continue in real-time.

TIP

Even if you plan to always control your characters, there will be times in long battles where you can't manage them all at once, and tactics will kick into action. Set them anyway!

In the Tactics menu, each character has base preset options and behavior patterns from which to choose. First, set these to the appropriate play style for each character. For example, you should probably set your tank with a "defender" preset and a "defensive" or "default" behavior mode. A ranged DPSer might have an "archer" preset and "ranged" behavior mode.

After the base preset and behavior mode is selected, each character has a number of customizable slots, which really open up your combat options. The first tactic slot will be the first priority and so on down the slots in descending priority order. You can choose options that affect your self, ally, enemy, individual party member, or controlled party member. Tactics can trigger actions based on status (rooted, slowed, grabbing, movement impaired), health percentages, mana or stamina levels, armor type, type of attack, surrounded by enemies, and more. Once conditions are met, you can deactivate and activate whatever combination of talent/spells you desire. For example, you can set one slot to check if you are surrounded by at least two enemies and then activate Captivating Song, or set your final slot to always switch to your melee weapon if all spell options are exhausted. Remember to save your new preset as a Custom save for future use.

primagames.com

Basic Tactics

Choose the following options for the basic tactic combos. Experiment with various conditions to get exactly what you want on the battlefield.

- **Attack:** Enemy, condition (such as nearest or magic-using), Attack (or activate a specific talent/spell)
- **Defense:** Self, condition (such as low health or being attacked), Use Ability or Use Mode (any defensive talent or spell)
- **Aid Ally:** Ally, condition (such as low health or being attacked), Use Ability or Use Mode (any defensive talent or spell)
- **Use Potion (or any item):** Self, condition (such as Health < 50%), Use health poultice (most powerful or least powerful)

Let's take a look at how you could program a balanced party of warrior (tank), mage (healer), rogue (DPS and crowd control), and mage (ranged DPS):

Warrior (Tank)

Preset: Defender
Behavior: Defensive
1. **Self:** Any (Activate: Threaten)
2. **Self:** Being attacked by a ranged attack (Activate: Shield Cover)
3. **Self:** Surrounded by at least two enemies (War Cry)
4. **Enemy:** Health >= 75% (Shield Bash)
5. **Enemy:** Health >= 50% (Overpower)
6. **Enemy:** Nearest Visible Mage (Holy Smite)

1. The warrior activates Threaten at the start of each battle to direct all future threat at himself.
2. If enemies are attacking at range, the warrior activates Shield Cover (instead of standard Shield Defense).
3. This warrior is a champion. When surrounded by more than a single enemy, he triggers War Cry. If he also has Superiority, this combination may knock enemies off their feet in addition to buffing companions.
4. Against a healthy opponent, the warrior first tries Shield Bash to stun the enemy.
5. Against a moderately healthy opponent, the warrior tries Overpower second to chip away at health.
6. This warrior is also a templar. Whenever he spots an enemy mage, he casts Holy Smite to smack the spellcaster with spirit damage and drain the caster's mana.

Mage (Healer)

Preset: Healer
Behavior: Defensive
1. **Self:** Being attacked by a melee or ranged attack (Activate: Rock Armor)
2. **Self:** Mana or Stamina < 50% (Group Heal)
3. **Self:** Mana or Stamina < 25% (Use Lyrium Potion)
4. **Self:** Health < 75% (Heal)
5. **Self:** Health < 75% (Regenerate)
6. **Ally:** Health < 75% (Heal)
7. **Ally:** Health < 75% (Regenerate)
8. **Ally:** Mana or Stamina < 25% (Rejuvenate)
9. **Enemy:** Target using ranged or magic attack (Earthquake)
10. **Enemy:** Target of Alistair (Switch to ranged weapon)

1. If an enemy targets the healer, she will activate Rock Armor for protection.
2. This is a timer effect. You don't want to cast Group Heal early in the fight or it will be mostly useless. Once the healer's mana drops below 50 percent, the tactics will check to cast Group Heal. As soon as its available for the rest of the battle (unless the healer gains mana above 50 percent), Group Heal goes off.
3. Once the healer's mana drops below 25 percent, the healer quaffs a lyrium potion to replenish mana.
4. The healer checks for damage on herself. If health is below 75 percent, she casts Heal on herself.
5. If Heal isn't available due to cooldown, or the healer's health is still below 75 percent, she casts Regenerate on herself.
6. The healer checks for damage on an ally. If health is below 75 percent, she casts Heal on the ally.
7. If Heal isn't available due to cooldown, or the ally's health is still below 75 percent, she casts Regenerate on the ally.
8. If an ally's mana or stamina drops below 25%, the healer casts Rejuvenate to replenish mana or stamina.

Tactics

Basics ~ Character Generation ~ Classes ~ **The Party** ~ Companions ~ Supporting Cast ~ Equipment ~ Bestiary ~ Walkthroughs ~ Side Quests ~ Random Encounters ~ Achievements/Trophies

9. If all healing options are clear, the healer switches into offensive mode and casts Earthquake (or your favorite AoE spell) at a ranged or magic-wielding enemy. Avoid casting on melee targets or else you may catch your party members in the AoE. To counteract this problem, you can switch to a single-target spell such as Stonefist.

10. If mana is exhausted, or there are no ranged enemy targets, the healer uses her staff to fire at the tank's enemy.

Rogue (DPS)

Preset: Scrapper

Behavior: Default

1. **Self:** Any (Venom)
2. **Self:** Any (Dueling)
3. **Enemy:** Target of Alistair (Pinpoint Strike)
4. **Enemy:** Target rank is elite or higher (Upset Balance)
5. **Self:** Being attacked by a melee attack (Dirty Fighting)
6. **Enemy:** Target of Alistair (Attack)

1. The rogue coats his weapon with poison at the start of the fight for extra DPS.

2. The rogue is a duelist. He activates Dueling for added bonuses.

3. Once he is in position, the rogue will attack the tank's target with a series of critical blows.

4. If the enemy is ranked above the normal foe, the rogue will try to stun the foe with Upset Balance.

5. If an enemy attacks the rogue in melee, he'll stun it with Dirty Fighting.

6. When he's out of special options, the rogue will always attack the tank's target.

Mage (DPS)

Preset: Damager

Behavior: Ranged

1. **Self:** Surrounded by at least two enemies (Mind Blast)
2. **Enemy:** Target between medium and long range (Fireball)
3. **Enemy:** Target rank is elite or higher (Crushing Prison)
4. **Enemy:** Target rank is elite or higher (Paralyze)
5. **Enemy:** Target using magic attack (Mana Drain)
6. **Enemy:** Nearest visible (Lightning)
7. **Enemy:** Nearest visible (Arcane Bolt)

1. If surrounded by more than a single enemy, the mage defends himself by stunning enemies with Mind Blast.

2. The mage casts a medium- or long-range Fireball at the enemy.

3. If a foe is ranked higher than normal level, the mage attempts to root it with Crushing Prison.

4. If a foe is ranked higher than normal level, and Crushing Prison failed, is on cooldown, or there is a second opponent who fulfills the conditions, the mage attempts to root it with Paralyze.

5. If the mage spots an enemy spellcaster, he will sap its mana with Mana Drain.

6. Otherwise, the mage will chose the nearest target and blast away with Lightning (or your favorite single-target spell).

7. If Lightning is on cooldown, the mage will hit the nearest target with Arcane Bolt (or another single-target spell).

primagames.com

Companions

In Ferelden, you can only trust a few adventurers with your life, and even with the ones who volunteer to stand with you against the Blight cannot all be trusted. Companions are your allies in battle, the NPCs who team with your PC and who you control on your quests. Choose companions based on your PC's needs. If you play a mage, you will definitely need a warrior like Alistair, possibly a rogue like Leliana, and maybe another warrior like Sten or another mage like Wynne for healing if you concentrate on DPS.

You run into only a handful of companions on your travels, as they are scattered from Ostagar to Orzammar. Know them well, for they are as vital as your own flesh and blood.

Grey Warden Companions

Companion	Class	Location
Alistair	Warrior	Ostagar
Dog (Mabari)	War Dog	Ostagar or Human Noble Origin
Leliana	Rogue	Lothering
Loghain Mac Tir	Warrior	Landsmeet
Morrigan	Mage	Korcari Wilds
Oghren	Warrior	Orzammar
Shale	Warrior	Downloadable Content
Sten	Warrior	Lothering
Wynne	Mage	Circle Tower
Zevran Arainai	Rogue	Random Encounter

Understanding Companions

Companions aren't simple NPCs who point you toward the next quest; they think, have opinions, fall in and out of favor with your decisions, and level along with you. Without companions, you would be a one-person party.

To grasp the intricacies of companion interaction, read through the following pages and familiarize yourself with what works and what doesn't work for your current party make-up. After companion basics, each companion receives a dedicated section with everything you need to know about your favorite ally. The Supporting Cast chapter details other famous characters of the land; consider it a list of the important NPCs and relevant game info to aid you on your quests.

Approval Ratings

Your approval ranges from -100 to 100, with all companions beginning at zero when you first meet them. The higher the approval rating, the more the companion enjoys your company and will be willing to follow your lead. A low approval rating equals a disgruntled companion, and one who might walk out on the group at any moment. In most cases, the approval rating caps at 74 unless you are either "friendly" or in a romance with a companion. You can warm up to companions by talking with them every chance you get and exploring all their dialogue options; you get a friendly rating with a companion by doing each NPC's personal quest.

Approval Chart

Your approval rating with companions ranges from -100 to 100. However, you can only get to max positive approval if you are either "friendly" or having a romance with the companion. You can get "friendly" if you do each companion's personal quest.

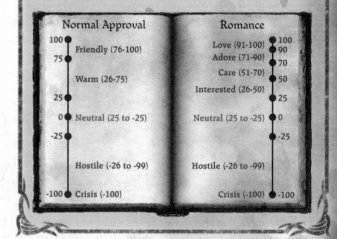

Normal Approval	Romance
100 —	Love (91-100) — 100
Friendly (76-100)	Adore (71-90) — 90
75 —	— 70
	Care (51-70)
Warm (26-75)	— 50
	Interested (26-50) — 25
25 —	
0 — Neutral (25 to -25)	Neutral (25 to -25) — 0
-25 —	— -25
Hostile (-26 to -99)	Hostile (-26 to -99)
-100 — Crisis (-100)	Crisis (-100) — -100

Understanding Companions

Basics ~ Character Generation ~ Classes ~ The Party ~ **Companions** ~ Supporting Cast ~ Equipment ~ Bestiary ~ Walkthroughs ~ Side Quests ~ Random Encounters ~ Achievements/Trophies

Gifts

You can give some specific items from your inventory to companions to increase approval. All gifts can be given to all companions, but each companion prefers a specific type of gift that gives a higher approval rating if you match companion and gift appropriately. Dialogue can also be initiated based on gifts being given, and is a component of the romance dialogues with some of the party members. See the Items chapter for the complete listing of all gifts and matching companions.

Companion Gifts

Whenever you hand a gift to a companion (drag it from the inventory to the appropriate companion picture on the left), the item disappears from party inventory permanently. An item thus given provides a bonus to that character's approval rating (from +1 to +10) based on the following rules:

- Base approval bonus: +5
- If companion likes the gift: +5
- For every gift given before: -1
- If the companion's approval is negative at the moment of gifting: half the value of the bonus
- Minimum approval bonus: +1

Only certain items labeled as "gift" can be given for approval rating boosts. Giving the wrong gift to the wrong companion will raise the companion's approval by only half of what it would. Certain gifts that are "plot" are given back to the player if they are given to the wrong character. When you donate gifts to companions, listen for the audio clue and watch for the rising heart that displays the approval bump number. Because there are limited gifts in the game, don't just give them away randomly; it's always better to hear a "Wow!" than a "Thanks, I guess."

Companion Quests

Most companions have a personal quest that you can help them undertake. Some are more involved than others. For example, you have to slay a dragon in Morrigan's personal quest, but only knock on a door with Alistair for his. Complete all your companions' quest if you can, because this will solidify your friendship with them. See the individual companion sections for how to unlock each one.

Romance

You can romance four of the companions in the game: Alistair (female PC only), Leliana (male or female PC), Morrigan (male PC), and Zevran (male or female PC). Some companions are easier than others to heat things up with. Alistair and Zevran, for example, are more likely than the women to be interested in what you have to say if you're of the preferred gender. If you can advance the romance far enough, sleeping with them is possible, though only once and it will happen at party camp. See the individual companion sections for tips on how to seduce a partner.

CAUTION

You can try to two-time by starting a romance with a second character while romancing another. However, the older romantic interest will eventually confront you about it, and then you'll have to decide on one relationship or the other. Once you are cut off from a romantic partner, you are cut off for good and will lose your friendly status.

Plot Abilities

Companions can be inspired by your leadership. If you increase a companion's approval rating high enough, they will gain one of several bonuses to their primary attribute. For example, a warm Wynne will gain "Inspired: Minor Willpower" and a warm Alistair will gain "Inspired: Minor Constitution." There are four levels for the plot abilities—minor, moderate, major, and massive—and each upgrades the bonus the companion gets to an attribute, so keep pumping up the approval rating of the companions you prefer to travel with, and they'll become better party members. Plot abilities can degrade, though, if you lose sufficient approval with a companion.

Crisis Moments

When talking to the companions, or if you make decisions in the game that are contrary to a companion's goals, the companion will definitely not approve. If they disapprove, you lose approval rating and they will certainly have words with you.

When you are in a romance, the companion may break up with you. If you aren't in a romance, or if it continues after the romance is over, they will reach a "crisis" point where they say they have to leave. You still have a chance to talk them out of it, and if you're successful, they will stay. But if they reach crisis for a second time it's over. The companion will leave for good. See the individual companion sections for the crisis moments and how to avoid them.

Alistair

Alistair at a Glance

A listair is the newest Grey Warden (besides the player). He's been sent to guide you and the other Grey Warden candidates through the Joining process. Over time, the player will find out that Alistair was a templar before he was a Grey Warden, a ward of Arl Eamon of Redcliffe before that, and eventually, it will be revealed that he was the illegitimate child of King Maric and a serving girl, and thus is theoretically heir to the throne. You meet Alistair in Ostagar after Duncan brings you to King's Camp. Alistair remains in your party until the end of the Landsmeet; you cannot ask him to leave, nor will he take offense and leave, even if your approval rating plummets. He's a fellow Grey Warden and will stick with you as long as his heart can bear it.

Combat Advice

Alistair will most likely be your party's tank. If your main PC happens to be a tank, and you want to switch Alistair to DPS, immediately alter his talent choices out of Weapons and Shield and into Two-Handed or Dual Weapon. Otherwise, concentrate most of your early talent points on the Warrior school (Threaten, Taunt) and Weapons and Shield to make sure he can hold threat and absorb lots of damage from enemy attacks. In melee, Overpower and Assault should be staple offensive talents for Alistair, while Shield Tactics is crucial to avoid flanking damage.

If Alistair is your tank, he will charge smaller enemy groups, unless you have an ambush staged. Give him a few moments to build up threat, and he should always bash the most dangerous target so that target doesn't go in search of someone else. Don't stress over damage output with Alistair; his job is to hold the enemies and suck up damage while the party's DPS-oriented members chop them down. Load Alistair with the best medium or heavy armor available (possibly even better than the armor you give the PC). He should wield a fine blade (main hand only; his off hand should hold a shield) to inflict good damage and further increase threat against his targets. In his secondary weapon slot, give Alistair a crossbow for long-range combat. Your healer will usually target Alistair for heals, but just in case, you should always keep a good supply of health poultices for emergencies.

~ Starting Attributes ~

Strength 20	Dexterity 17
Willpower 16	Magic 14
Cunning 11	Constitution 13

~ Class ~
Warrior

Main Tank: Because you meet with Alistair earliest in the game, and he's already fully vested in the Weapon and Shield school, which is ideal for tanking, you can groom your fellow Grey Warden to lead the team into battle. Stay with the tanking talents in Weapon and Shield as your priority, and you will probably keep Alistair in your active party the entire adventure.

~ Starting Talents ~

Templar: Righteous Strike

Warrior: Powerful

Weapon and Shield: Shield Bash, Shield Pummel, Shield Block, Shield Cover

~ Location ~
Ostagar, King's Camp

~ Unlock Condition ~

When you arrive at Ostagar, Duncan asks you to seek out Alistair, a fellow Grey Warden. Once you talk to Alistair, he joins your party and will stay with you for the duration if you choose.

Romance

Romantically speaking, Alistair prefers women to men. However, that doesn't stop Zevran from hitting on him. Alistair is demure and inexperienced, and will likely shy away the first time you proposition him, but he'll eventually join you in your tent when he adores the player sufficiently. Alistair wants to feel that he is special to the player, that he is necessary; he responds well to flirting, to talk of love, and to perhaps a bit of bossiness on the player's part. ("Just follow my lead, Alistair.") He responds very badly to being mocked, particularly in intimate moments. Alistair's approval increases are generally very small because there are so many ways to gain them.

To romance him as a female PC, get Alistair to tell you about his past as a templar. Mention how handsome he is, or tell him you like him for who he is, or any one of many choices. He's not that hard. After he's interested, ask him to join you in your tent at camp. If he's interested, and you're very gentle, he will say yes.

TIP

When he becomes very close to the player, he will offer the player a rose as an expression of his affections. The player may accept it or not.

At the Pearl in Denerim, there is a duelist named Isabela who is acquainted with Zevran. If you are in a romance with Alistair and bring him to the Pearl, and you have hardened Alistair's personality, he will join you in a threesome if that's something you're into.

Crisis Moment

Certain game choices will force a companion to reconsider you as their ally. For Alistair, at the end of the Landsmeet you have a choice to mete out justice to Loghain or allow him to join your group to defeat the archdemon. If you let him join your group, Alistair will be appalled and leave the party for good. The only way to keep Alistair is to punish Loghain for his crimes.

Alistair

Basics ~ Character Generation ~ Classes ~ The Party ~ **Companions** ~ Supporting Cast ~ Equipment ~ Bestiary ~ Walkthroughs ~ Side Quests ~ Random Encounters ~ Achievements/Trophies

Dialogue Choices

As with any companion, Alistair has dialogue choices whenever you interact with him, and sometimes he will pull you aside to speak with you about a topic. However, at important points in the game, you should know about plot-specific and camp-specific dialogue that could change the game for your companion.

Plot-Specific Dialogue

- Alistair has dialogue in the Fade and dialogue for the "Captured" quest in Denerim.
- He has dialogue to discuss Anora and the player's preference for how he should handle the throne.
- He has Arl Eamon–related dialogue (see the Camp-Specific Dialogue section).
- Alistair can be convinced to sleep with Morrigan during the final battle to save the lives of the Grey Wardens while killing the archdemon. If you are still in love with/care about/are friends with him, be sure to reiterate this, or ask for his trust; remind him that it will save your life. Ask him, "What if there were a way to avoid dying tomorrow?" It will be easiest if you lie to him. Don't tell him there's a child involved, but try not to play on his distrust of Morrigan too much; avoid the questions as much as possible. Ask him to trust you, or tell him that you believe it's the right thing to do. This is slightly easier if he is changed during his personal quest to meet his sister.

Camp-Specific Dialogue

Alistair will initiate conversation in camp a number of times:

- After cutscenes about the dragon (dreams the player is having), he'll tell you how Grey Wardens feel and how they see the darkspawn and the archdemon in their dreams. At one point, darkspawn will attack after one of these dreams.
- Alistair will ask to talk about what happened at Redcliffe with Connor and Isolde. If you killed Connor or Isolde, he will be upset and you will lose 20 approval points.
- If Alistair is in love with you and you have yet to ask him to sleep with you, he will initiate the conversation, and ask you to have sex with him. It's very sweet and romantic. You can, of course, turn him down at this point.
- Alistair's crisis mode will be initiated in camp. He won't leave you, but he will want to talk about it.
- All sex-related dialogue with Alistair is in camp, naturally, except the threesome with Isabela (see the Romance section).

Personal Quest

From the beginning in Ostagar, keep talking to Alistair whenever he has anything new to say. Ask him about the Joining after going through it, ask him about the Grey Wardens, etc. Eventually, he talk about his sister Goldanna if you adhere to the following steps:

- He'll reveal he has a sister if his approval rating is warm or higher, and he has told you the truth about his family background.
- In Denerim at her house, he'll recognize the door (it's the door next to Wade's Emporium in the market district).
- Go in and talk to his sister, Goldanna. She is rude and heartless, asking for money and offering none of the familial affection for which Alistair was hoping. Afterward, you can calm Alistair down, or harden him up.
- If you calm him down, he'll continue to be a nice guy. It will become much harder to convince him to become king at the Landsmeet, either with or without Anora or yourself at his side.
- If you want to harden him, select the dialogue option, ""Everyone is out for themselves. You should learn that." When you talk to Alistair next, so long as you don't say, "That's not what I meant. Don't do that!" Alistair will be changed. This will make it easier to convince Alistair to take the position as king, with or without Anora or yourself as queen. It will also make it easier to engage in a threesome with Isabela (see the Romance section).

Gifts

Alistair's Mother's Amulet and Duncan's Shield will each initiate a specific conversation with Alistair, in which it is possible to gain further approval. Duncan's Shield will also be transformed into a real object and equipped on Alistair's person, once given. The part of the Market Warehouse that holds the shield will not open up until after the Landsmeet plot begins; it is part of a Denerim side quest.

Gift	Found In	Location
Alistair's Mother's Amulet	Desk	Castle Redcliffe: Main Floor
Black Runestone	Chest	Aeducan Thaig
Duncan's Shield	Armor Stand	Market Warehouse
Onyx Demon Statuette	Pile of Bones	East Brecilian Forest
Small Carved Statuette	Crate	Lothering
Stone Dragon Statuette	Chest	Castle Redcliffe: Upper Floor
Stone Warrior Statuette	Pile of Dragon Filth	Caverns (Haven)
White Runestone	Abomination	Third Floor of Circle Tower

Highlights

- Alistair may teach the templar talents if he warms up to the PC.
- Alistair is sweet, funny, and cute, and has an excellent voice. He likes a bit of teasing, and occasionally doesn't mind being ordered about. Unless hardened, he is very uncomfortable with the idea of being in command, and will surrender to your will even though he is the senior Grey Warden.
- Alistair loved Duncan like a father; say nice things about him to gain his approval.
- Isolde may not have been kind to Alistair, but that doesn't mean he wants her or her son dead. Killing either Connor or Isolde in the Arl Eamon plot will mean a large decrease in his approval rating, no matter how much they might deserve it. You can, however, make a deal with the demon inside of Connor to become a blood mage and avoid the approval penalty (see the "Arl of Redcliffe" walkthrough).
- Alistair is fairly religious and poisoning Andraste's ashes will not go over well with him (see the "Urn of Sacred Ashes" section of the walkthrough).
- Alternately, sparing Loghain's life at the end of the Landsmeet will not go over well. King or no, Alistair will leave the party forever if you let Loghain live as a Grey Warden.
- He's the illegitimate son of King Maric! If you romance him (and you are a human), you could potentially be queen!

Leliana

Leliana at a Glance

~ Starting Attributes ~

Strength **18**

Dexterity **22**

Willpower **18**

Magic **14**

Cunning **19**

Constitution **10**

~ Class ~

Rogue

Lockpick Extraordinaire: Build up Leliana's lockpick skills to open locked chests and doors. Once you get up to Device Mastery at level 12, she will be invaluable for entering areas you wouldn't have had access to without her nimble fingers. She can shoot a bow better than anyone else in the group.

~ Starting Talents ~

Bard: Song of Valor

Rogue: Dirty Fighting, Below the Belt, Deft Hands, Improved Tools

Archery: Pinning Shot, Crippling Shot, Rapid Shot, Shattering Shot

~ Location ~

Lothering

~ Unlock Condition ~

When you enter Dane's Refuge in Lothering, Leliana will join up with you after you smack around some mercenaries causing a ruckus.

A lay sister of the Chantry who can beat the stuffing out of trained mercenaries would be notable enough, but one who also claims to have been sent to fight the darkspawn by the Maker Himself is...unusual to say the least. There's more to Leliana than had even been apparent at Lothering, however. She spent much of her life as a bard in Orlais: a minstrel, assassin, and spy employed by the nobles of Val Royeaux in their elaborate games of intrigue.

Combat Advice

Arm Leliana with a pair of daggers and let her Dual Weapon talents kick in. At higher levels, you can equip her with rune-slotted daggers and load up on damage bonuses to really shred through targets. She has the basics to be a quality archer from the start, and you can pour more talent points into Archery if you want to develop her as a ranged expert. However, concentrate most of your talents in the Rogue school and the bard specialty. The Rogue talents can improve her backstab, which is really where she shines against enemies, and the bard talents help with crowd control. Once you reach Captivating Song, Leliana can single-handedly lock down a handful of foes, which is an exceptional ability when swarmed by several difficult assailants.

In combat, let the other companions lead and Leliana will gladly follow. She can either shoot at range with her bow, or wait a few seconds for the field to set and then maneuver in for flank attack or backstab tries from the enemy's rear. You want her to move quickly, so don't overload her with armor; top-notch leather is probably her best option or else the fatigue penalty gets too harsh and she won't get off as many abilities.

Personal Quest

Similar to Alistair and his personal quest with his sister Goldanna, you can "change" Leliana to be a tougher, sterner person by encouraging her to stay an assassin when the dialogue opportunity arises. If you tell Leliana that she is a natural killer and shouldn't fight it, she will "change" her demeanor and become more accepting of events such as you sleeping with Isabela. Changing her also affects her clothing at the end of the game: normal Leliana will appear in Chantry robes, while changed Leliana will appear in leather.

To embark on Leliana's main personal quest, you must do the following, in order:

- Talk to her in camp and eventually ask her, "What would someone like you be doing in Lothering's Chantry?" She will bring up being a minstrel.
- Get Leliana's approval rating to warm (approval 25+).
- Talk to Leliana in camp about how minstrels are sometimes spies.
- Leave the camp and come back to the camp. Talk to Leliana again (must still be warm approval). She'll talk about how she lied about Orlais.
- The next random encounter should be Leliana's assassin's encounter. The last human male surrenders when you beat him, and he'll talk about who sent him. You can decide to kill him or not, then leave the encounter and Leliana will talk. She will tell you all about a former love interest, Marjolaine.

Dialogue Choices

As with any companion, Leliana has dialogue choices whenever you interact with her, and sometimes she will initiate a topic. However, at important points in the game, you should know about plot-specific and camp-specific dialogue that could change the game for your companion. Listen to all her stories to know more about her (and to increase your approval rating). If your approval gets high enough, she will even sing a whole song just for you.

Crisis Moment

Certain game choices will force a companion to reconsider you as their ally. At the end of the "Urn of Sacred Ashes" quest, you have the option of destroying the ashes. If you choose to do this, Leliana will turn against you (as will Wynne if she is in the party).

Leliana

Basics ~ Character Generation ~ Classes ~ The Party ~ **Companions** ~ Supporting Cast ~ Equipment ~ Bestiary ~ Walkthroughs ~ Side Quests ~ Random Encounters ~ Achievements/Trophies

Romance

Leliana may be difficult to start a relationship with; however, she will with either a male or a female (male is easier). If you are male, when you talk to Leliana initially about her time in the cloister, you just have to talk to her in camp. You don't even have to be at warm. Follow these dialogue choices:

- "I'd like to talk."
- "What was someone like you doing in Lothering's Chantry?"
- "You know, a beautiful charming woman like yourself."
- "Those initiates can't have been more lovely than you."
- Romance will be started.

If your approval is 50+ with Leliana and you are female, you can talk to her in camp she'll say (only once), "I...have I ever told you I really like the way you wear your hair?" Respond with the following dialogue choices:

- "My hair? Thank-you."
- "Dear Maker!"
- "Well we are friends aren't we?"
- "And do you enjoy the company of other women?"
- "I think I might giggle and maybe look coy?"
- Romance will be started.

If you finish the Marjolaine personal quest, talk to Leliana. She'll say something like, "I know that look—you have something on your mind don't you?" Respond with the following dialogue choices:

- "We need to talk."
- "Are you feeling better?"
- "Er, I think I see what you mean."
- "She was special to you wasn't she?"
- "I'm sorry it ended so badly."
- "Everyone changes unfortunately."
- "I can only hope to one day be as special as she was to you."
- Romance will be started.

If you're looking to seduce Leliana, you have to be in a romance with her and she has to be in love with you, which means you have to have your approval at 100. Talk to her in camp. If she gives you the line, "It has been some time since I left Lothering. When I stepped out of the cloister I had no idea where my path would lead." Keep being nice and eventually she'll invite you to her tent. This only happens once.

Gifts

Leliana enjoys higher-priced religious jewelry or a random critter. Some personal dialogue will open up with Leliana if you give her Andraste's Grace or the nug, which can be acquired from a young dwarf in Orzammar's Dust Town, but only after Leliana mentions that she finds "those little bunny pigs adorable." Take advantage of these gifts because you want her approval high if you plan on starting a romance.

Gift	Found In	Location
Andraste's Grace	Flower	Redcliffe Village (near mill), West Brecilian Forest, or Elven Alienage (near giant tree)
Bronze Symbol of Andraste	Chest	Lothering Chantry
Chantry Amulet	Templar Corpse	Senior Mage Quarters in Circle Tower
Etched Silver Symbol	Ruck	Ortan Thaig
Golden Symbol of Andraste	Legnar's Store	Orzammar Commons
Nug	Nug Wrangler	Orzammar Commons
Silver Sword of Mercy	Dwarven Vendor	Random Encounter
Steel Symbol of Andraste	Chest	Brother Genitivi's Home in Denerim Market

Highlights

- Leliana may teach the bard talents if she warms up to you.
- Leliana is very religious and chooses the morally proper path in most cases.
- Despite her religious upbringing, Leliana is not all that she seems. Complete her personal quest to discover the truth.
- Leliana doesn't enter relationships lightly. She must have an approval of 100 to be in love with you and consider inviting you to her tent.

primagames.com

Morrigan

Morrigan at a Glance

Her mother claims to be Flemeth. If that's true, the Morrigan might well be a very powerful witch, for the tales of the daughters of Flemeth tell of twisted, monstrous women who can kill a man with fear. She was made to accompany the surviving Grey Wardens; the payment, Flemeth said, for saving their lives at the Tower of Ishal. Morrigan is the offensive-minded companion mage.

~ Starting Attributes ~

Strength 14	Dexterity 15
Willpower 21	Magic 26
Cunning 12	Constitution 12

~ Class ~

Mage

DPS Mage: Increase Morrigan's spells in Primal and her shapeshifter specialization to deal more damage in combat.

~ Starting Talents ~

Shapeshifter: Spider Shape

Primal: Winter's Grasp

Spirit: Mind Blast

Entropy: Vulnerability Hex, Disorient, Horror, Drain Life, Death Magic

~ Location ~

Korcari Wilds

~ Unlock Condition ~

When you seek out the Ancient Treaties in the Korcari Wilds, Morrigan will find you. After the battle at the Tower of Ishal, Morrigan will join your party.

Combat Advice

Morrigan's early spells open up possibility for future combat dominance. Start out with the Cold chain and get to Cone of Cold and Blizzard as soon as you can. After Mind Blast, increase your defense tenfold with Force Field, then inch up to gain Crushing Prison for a powerful single-target root/damage spell. Build on her Entropy spells also and pick up Sleep, Waking Nightmare, and Death Cloud. Don't forget, you can get Bear Shape at level 8, Flying Swarm at level 10, and Master Shapeshifter at level 12.

Most mages must stay in the rear to be effective. Not necessarily with Morrigan. Use her ranged spells early, until your mana is low or the enemy engages in melee, then switch to one of your specialization forms and deal effective melee damage. Your spells are more powerful, but it's a nice luxury to be able to adapt to the ever-changing combat dynamics.

Dialogue Choices

As with any companion, Morrigan has dialogue choices whenever you interact with her, and sometimes she will initiate a topic. However, at important points in the game, you should know about plot-specific and camp-specific dialogue that could change the game for your companion. Listen to all her tales to know more about her (and to increase your approval rating), but be careful, Morrigan is quick to disapprove if you don't agree with her cynical and judgmental views.

Personal Quest

To embark on Morrigan's personal quest, you must do the following, in order:

- Retrieve the Black Grimoire from Irving's room in the "Broken Circle" quest. Give the book to Morrigan.
- Become warm with Morrigan.
- Finish "Broken Circle" quest line.
- Go back to camp and she'll disclose how she's learned about her past, and how you have to kill Flemeth. Accept.
- Leave Morrigan at camp and do not include her in the party. Return to Flemeth's Hut.
- Talk to Flemeth. Tell her you are here to kill her.
- She'll transform in a dragon. Kill her. (Have fun!)
- Flemeth will have a key on her. Grab the key and open the door to her hut. Open the chest in her hut and grab the grimoire and Morrigan's best magical robes there. The robes are significantly better version of what she starts the game in.
- Go back to the camp and talk to Morrigan. Give her the grimoire.
- She'll have a long talk with you. Now you are friendly with Morrigan.

Crisis Moment

Morrigan doesn't have any one big event, but she can get cross often with you in dialogue. Be careful to say what she wants to hear or you'll lose approval quickly.

Morrigan

Basics ~ Character Generation ~ Classes ~ The Party ~ **Companions** ~ Supporting Cast ~ Equipment ~ Bestiary ~ Walkthroughs ~ Side Quests ~ Random Encounters ~ Achievements/Trophies

Romance

Morrigan only likes men. Don't even try to court her if you're female. Begin by asking her questions about her upbringing and her powers. To make her friendly when she's ready, talk to her in camp and she'll say, "Tis a curious thing. I do not know how to describe it." She'll only say this line once, so make sure to say the right things. Choose:

- "What? Is something wrong?"
- "Why would I do that?"
- "Because I need you here."
- "I was hoping to be more than friends."

To take it further and get romance started, start a conversation in camp after getting the Circle Tower grimoire and she will say, "I have a thought." Respond with:

- "Oh? What's on your mind?"
- "And? What's in it for me?"
- "My tent does get rather cold..."

After killing Flemeth and returning to Morrigan, she'll talk to you after you give her Flemeth's Grimoire. During the conversation say:

- "Flemeth is dead, you are free."
- "Yes, but I intend to keep it for myself."
- "What? That's it? Just a thank you?"
- "What was that last bit again?"

To get Morrigan to invite you back to her tent, you have to be at care approval rating (50+ approval and romance active). Morrigan will *not* sleep with you if she's in love with you (90+ approval). She's into flings, and it only happens once.

Gifts

Morrigan's critical eye is not reserved solely for others. Knowing or not, she has a simple fondness for jewelry and is very particular about her appearance.

Gift	Found In	Location
Black Grimoire	Irving's Quarters	Circle Tower
Flemeth's Grimoire	Chest	Flemeth's Hut
Gold Amulet	Garin	Orzammar Commons
Golden Demon Pendant	Corpse	Urn of Sacred Ashes Room
Golden Mirror	Garin	Orzammar Commons
Golden Rope Necklace	Barlin	Dane's Refuge in Lothering
Locket	Locked Chest	Village Store in Haven
Silver Brooch	Varathorn	Dalish Camp
Silver Chain	Vanity	Senior Mage Quarters in Circle Tower
Silver Medallion	Dragon Hoard	Upper Level of Elven Ruins
Tribal Necklace	Barrel	Top Floor of Tower of Ishal

Highlights

- Morrigan may teach the shapeshifter specialization if she warms up to you.

- Listen to her banter with Alistair on party walks. It's quite amusing.

- Morrigan's mother, Flemeth, and Morrigan play a crucial part in the beginning and end of your journey. Don't cause her to leave too early.

- A loner, Morrigan stands away from the others in the corner of camp. Seek her out by her own little camp area if you want to chat.

primagames.com

Oghren

Oghren at a Glance

~ Starting Attributes ~

Strength **38**	Dexterity **17**
Willpower **21**	Magic **14**
Cunning **16**	Constitution **18**

~ Class ~

Warrior

DPSer or Off-Tank: In a pinch, Oghren could tank a fight in place of Alistair or the PC. If you do that, however, you negate his specialization: berserker. The berserker talents increase damage, which fits into a DPS role, and the only way a stamina-deprived berserker can hold threat well is to out-damage everyone else.

~ Starting Talents ~

Berserker: Berserk, Resilience, Constraint

Warrior: Powerful, Threaten, Bravery, Death Blow

Two-Handed: Pommel Strike, Indomitable, Stunning Blows, Sunder Arms, Shattering Blows, Sunder Armor, Mighty Blow, Powerful Swings, Two-Handed Strength, Two-Handed Sweep

~ Location ~

Orzammar

~ Unlock Condition ~

When you meet Oghren at the entrance to the Deep Roads, he will volunteer to join you and track down his lost wife, Branka.

You meet Oghren in Orzammar. In the first encounter, he is arguing with a dwarven nobleman about finding Branka; when the player is given permission to go into the deeps to find Branka, he asks to join you, citing particular knowledge of both Branka (his ex-wife) and the Deep Roads. Regardless of how the plot ends, the rough-and-tumble warrior will remain with your party after the "Paragon of Her Kind" quest line is completed if the PC wishes it.

Combat Advice

Fill out Oghren's berserker specialty and Two-Handed school as soon as you get the chance. Odds are you can capitalize on some of the top-tier talents quickly, which will seriously increase his damage potential and make him an excellent DPS addition to your party. As with rogues, Oghren should allow the tank to control enemy mobs and then attack from the rear or flank. Because Oghren is so durable, he doesn't have to watch his spacing as much as a rogue, and he can off-tank easily if you need him to grab a creature that the tank can't hold threat on. His skills are best used with heavy or massive armor, either sword and shield or two-handed weapons, with a crossbow for ranged attacks.

Berserk ramps up Oghren's damage and a well-placed Mighty Blow can hammer an adversary. Sunder Armor rips through a heavily defensive melee attacker, while Pommel Strike and Stunning Blows can knock an enemy out of combat for several seconds. Two-Handed Sweep is great at striking multiple foes, as long as you don't steal threat away from the tank, and at the end of a fight, Final Blow deals massive damage but drains the rest of Oghren's stamina.

Personal Quest

If you speak to Oghren about his past, he will tell you about a woman he was once involved with, who has since moved to the surface. Her name is Felsi, and although he is unclear about where she has moved, you can discover her working at the Spoiled Princess at the Lake Calenhad Docks. If you want to help Oghren reconnect with his past love, follow these steps:

- Talk to Oghren about Felsi to start the quest (with a high Persuade score, you can get him to tell you what actually went wrong between Felsi and him in the first place). Go to the Spoiled Princess at the Lake Calenhad Docks.

- If Oghren is in the party, he will see her and initiate conversation with you.

- If he isn't, you may talk to Felsi about Oghren. You can pick up some hints to give to Oghren on how to woo her.

- Oghren will eventually declare his desire to talk to her, then start the conversation. You can either help him with whispered hints and talking him up to Felsi, or try to sabotage his efforts with insults.

- Oghren will talk to you after talking to Felsi. If he has gotten his mojo back, Oghren will now be eligible to be friendly with you.

- If you chose to torpedo Oghren's chances with Felsi, she will turn him down when he goes to talk to her. Not helping Oghren will have the same effect as actively attempting to hurt his chances, as he needs to get into her good books. Needless to say, this will result in an approval drop.

Dialogue Choices

As with any companion, Oghren has dialogue choices whenever you interact with him, and sometimes he will pull you aside to speak with you about a topic. However, at important points in the game, you should know about plot-specific and camp-specific dialogue that could change the game for your companion.

Plot-Specific Dialogue

- Oghren has plot-specific dialogue in the Fade in the "Broken Circle" quest line.
- He has dialogue in the "Captured" plot in Denerim.
- He's very keen on killing the dragon if you take him to the "Urn of the Sacred Ashes" quest.

Camp-Specific Dialogue

Some of his camp dialogues will only trigger after specific plots have been completed ("Nature of the Beast," "Paragon of Her Kind," "Landsmeet"), but they don't relate specifically to that plot. It just has to occur later in the game.

- He's very depressed the first few times you talk to him in camp; if you ask him what's wrong, and he is starting to warm to you, he will first talk about how he felt about Branka.
- You can ask him how he likes the surface.
- You can ask him if he's homesick.
- You can ask him if he misses Orzammar.
- You can ask him what it's like to be a warrior in Orzammar.
- When he talks about being "war buddies," he'll challenge you to drink with him. It takes a high constitution check to pass this, but he'll still be amused if you fall over.

Gifts

Oghren loves to drink, and his gifts reflect that. Other companions might like a sip of wine from a tavern, but Oghren likes vintage alcohol to get stinking drunk.

Gift	Found In	Location
Alley King's Flagon	Legnar's Store	Orzammar Commons
Chasind Sack Mead	Dusty Scrolls	Ruined Temple
Garblog's Backcountry Reserve	Dog	Random chance he'll fetch it
Golden Scythe 4-90 Black	Crate	Lothering
Legacy White Shear	Sarcophagus	Lower Ruins
Sun Blonde Vint-1	Vanity	Templar Quarters in Circle Tower

Crisis Moment

Through dialogue choices, you can make Oghren so angry that he will try to leave, if his approval has dropped low enough. When this occurs, you can try to convince him to stay, you can engage him in combat (Oghren will surrender before the end of the combat, and you can choose to kill him, threaten him back into line, or send him away), or you can just let him go. This can happen twice.

Highlights

- Oghren will teach the berserker specialization if he feels warm enough to the PC.
- Oghren will fall over drunk halfway through conversations quite often.
- Oghren burps, drinks, spits, and swears a lot. A drinking game could be made.
- Oghren likes to be appreciated, to be told he's better than he thinks he is, and to be flirted with a bit (if the player is a woman).
- If you take Oghren into the "Broken Circle," you get a bar fight in the Fade!

primagames.com

Shale

Shale at a Glance

Crafted by the ancient dwarves as their first line of defense against the darkspawn, the dread sentinels known as golems dwindled in number after the art of their creation was lost. Shale, one of the few golems remaining, was found in the Deep Roads, reactivated and brought to the surface, and may prove to be the Grey Wardens' most effective weapon against the onslaught of the Blight.

NOTE

Shale is a companion available only through special *Dragon Age: Origins* downloadable content.

~ Starting Attributes ~

Shale's starting attributes scale depending on what level you get the golem at.

~ Class ~

Warrior

Main Tank or DPS: The burly Shale can step in for other tanks such as Alistair if you prefer stone to steel. As a warrior, Shale has full access to the standard Warrior school talents, but doesn't know any of the weapon talents, which means it'll be without Weapon and Shield. Instead, Shale comes with its own set of 16 individual talents that can help the golem play defense as a tank or crush opponents with DPS.

~ Available Talents ~

Warrior: Powerful, Threaten, Bravery, Death Blow, Precise Striking, Taunt, Disengage, Perfect Striking

Shale: Pulverizing Blows, Slam, Quake, Killing Blow; Stoneheart, Bellow, Stone Roar, Regenerating Burst; Rock Mastery, Hurl Rock, Earthen Grasp, Rock Barrage; Stone Aura, Inner Reserves, Renewed Assault, Supernatural Resilience

~ Location ~

Village of Honnleath

~ Unlock Condition ~

After you leave Lothering, journey to Sulcher's Pass and get the golem control rod from Felix. Travel to the Village of Honnleath and follow the clues to discovering Shale's activation phrase.

New Golem Talents

Shale serves dual purposes: the party's main tank or a heavy melee damage-dealer. If you want Shale to take over as your main tank, concentrate on the Stoneheart chain first. Stoneheart activates Shale's defensive talents and increases the golem's threat. Bellow increases Shale's threat and has a chance to stun nearby enemies if they fail a mental resistance check. Stone Roar gains a health regeneration bonus for Shale and attracts the attention of a single targeted enemy, who will veer toward Shale immediately (great for pulling foes off allies). Regenerating Burst damages and possibly stuns nearby enemies, plus it increases stamina regeneration and threat generation.

The Stone Aura chain supports a Shale tank strategy. Stone Aura imbues nearby party members with bonuses to attack, defense, and health regeneration. It provides excellent party buffs; however, the sustained ability paralyzes Shale and imposes a personal penalty to defense as well as draining stamina. Inner Reserves beefs up Shale's armor, and party members within Stone Aura receive additional bonuses to armor, health regeneration, stamina regeneration, and spellpower. Renewed Assault further increases Shale's armor and ability to resist hostile spells, and party members within the aura gain bonuses to attack, stamina regeneration, critical chance, and armor penetration. Plus, enemies within the aura suffer penalties to movement speed, attack, and defense. Supernatural Resilience gives more bonuses to armor and the ability to resist hostile spells. Party members within the aura gain additional bonuses to health regeneration, spellpower, damage, and to resist hostile spells.

If you'd rather have Shale deal damage than suck up damage, first concentrate on the golem's Pulverizing Blows chain. Pulverizing Blows activates Shale's offensive talents, taking a penalty to defense in exchange for a bonus to damage. Slam swings at a nearby enemy and, if it connects, automatically generates a critical hit and knocks the target back. Quake hits nearby enemies with an AoE that damages and knocks them back. Killing Blow smashes a target with a critical hit (if it connects) and extra damage equal to Shale's remaining stamina, which drains away after the blow.

Shale's final chain beginning with Rock Mastery supports a DPS orientation and gives Shale more ranged options. Rock Mastery activates the golem's ranged talents and gains a large bonus against incoming ranged attacks, though at a penalty to defense, armor, and melee critical chance. Nearby party members also gain bonuses to ranged critical chance and ranged attack speed. Hurl Rock throws a stone projectile at a targeted area and all enemies near the point of impact take physical damage and may be knocked down. Earthen Grasp immobilizes enemies unless they pass a physical resistance check. Rock Barrage throws multiple rocks into the air, which rain down on a targeted area and inflict movement penalties and knock down anyone within if they fail a physical resistance check.

NOTE

Each of Shale's four golem-specific tactical roles are separate modes. When Shale is in Stoneheart mode, for example, only Bellow, Stone Roar, and Regenerating Burst are available. When Shale is in Stone Aura mode, only talents in the Stone Aura chain are available, and so on for each mode. Shale's warrior talents are not affected by these modes, however, and are always available.

Shale

Basics ~ Character Generation ~ Classes ~ The Party ~ **Companions** ~ Supporting Cast ~ Equipment ~ Bestiary ~ Walkthroughs ~ Side Quests ~ Random Encounters ~ Achievements/Trophies

Personal Quest

After you free Shale from imprisonment in the Village of Honnleath, take the golem with you when you attempt the "Paragon of Her Kind" quest in Orzammar's Deep Roads. After the encounter with Caridin in the Anvil of the Void, if you sided with Caridin over Branka or if you can Persuade Shale to stay with you after you sided with Branka, Shale will tell you about a secret Thaig, forgotten in the Deep Roads until now. For complete details on Cadash Thaig, see the "Stone Prisoner" section of the Walkthrough chapter.

Gear

Shale doesn't put on sword, shield, and armor like other warriors. Golems rely on crystals to power up their offense and defense. Shale has two equipment slots, one for offense and one for defense. A Large Flawless Fire Crystal, for example, fits into the defensive slot and gives Shale the following abilities: 16.2 armor, 26.4% fatigue, +2 strength, +6 defense, +40% fire resistance, and +8 stamina regeneration in combat.

Crisis Moment

Reluctant as Shale is to join your party at the start, the golem will leave only if its approval rating drops too low or if you choose the mad Branka over the tormented Caridin at the end of the "Paragon of Her Kind" quest line. If you choose to fight with Branka against Caridin and Shale is in your party at the time, the golem will rebel and attack you while defending Caridin. If Shale is not in your party when you choose Branka, the golem will confront you when you return to the party camp. Unless you convince Shale to stay, the golem will leave your group permanently.

Highlights

- You can only find Shale in a special downloadable quest that takes you into the midst of a darkspawn horde and through the tunnels of a secret mage laboratory.
- Shale can be a dynamo in combat, either as a huge tank or a brawling DPSer.
- Golems don't use regular equipment. Instead, you plug magic crystals into them to power them up.
- With 16 new golem-only talents, Shale can aid in melee damage, defense, ranged combat, and party buffing.
- Shale may have some anger management issues, but the golem's dry wit can leave you in stitches. Well, so can its fists if you aren't careful.

Shale's Crystals

As a stone golem, Shale doesn't use weapons and armor as the other companions; golems rely on special crystals to power up their abilities. Shale has 50 equipable crystals in the game, and you can gain them from several sources: loot drops throughout the world (PC version only); items found in the Village of Honnleath, Wilhelm's Cellar, and Cadash Thaig; and available for purchase from Garin's Gem Store in Orzammar Commons. (Each time you enter the Orzammar Commons, a random set of six crystals will generate in Garin's store inventory.)

Crystals come in two sizes: large and small. Large crystals act as armor and appear on Shale's shoulders and feet. Small crystals act as weapons and appear on Shale's fists. Each crystal comes in one of five elemental types: fire (orange), ice (white), electrical (purple), natural (green), and spirit (blue). If you match a large and small crystal of the same elemental type on Shale, the golem receives a special item set bonus. There are also five degrees of crystal quality: chipped (lowest quality), flawed, clear, flawless, brilliant (highest quality).

As with other characters' equipment, Shale's crystals dynamically scale based on the golem's level.

Gifts

There's definitely something remarkable about the objects Shale values in life. Find any of nine "remarkable" gemstones and Shale might just crack a smile on that stony golem visage.

Gift	Found In	Location
Remarkable Amethyst	Alimar's Emporium	Orzammar's Dust Town
Remarkable Diamond*	Garin's Gem Store	Orzammar Commons
Remarkable Emerald	Figor's Store	Orzammar Commons
Remarkable Garnet	Wonders of Thedas Store	Denerim Market District
Remarkable Greenstone	Cellars	Village of Honnleath
Remarkable Malachite	Shaperate Store	Circle Tower
Remarkable Ruby	Alarith's Store	Denerim's Elven Alienage
Remarkable Sapphire	Legnar's Store	Orzammar Commons
Remarkable Topaz	Faryn's Store	Frostback Mountains

* Console version only.

primagames.com

Wynne

Wynne at a Glance

Wynne's talent became apparent early on, particularly her skill at healing magic. She was well-liked by all her mentors and recognized as an exceptionally gifted student. Even the templars who watched her could not deny that she represented the best the Circle had to offer. She was an intelligent young woman who possessed a quiet confidence and maturity beyond her years. She spent many years mentoring apprentices within the Circle, and her peers thought so highly of her that she was asked to be First Enchanter Irving's successor, but she refused, saying that she had no desire to work in the upper echelons. When word reached the Circle Tower of King Cailan's call to arms, Wynne volunteered to go to Ostagar. Many events later she would join the party after saving the Circle Tower.

Combat Advice

Ramp to the top-tier spirit healer spells as soon as you can pick them up. Mass Rejuvenation is a great party boost when you have a free spell point. Paralyze in the Entropy school provides excellent defense for those occasions when a creature locks onto her, and Earthquake and Petrify fill out the chain beginning with Rock Armor and deliver serious offensive muscle.

Unless you have an easy fight, or one where Wynne has no choice but to add to the DPS for a shot at winning, she should concentrate on healing. Save your mana for your healing spells unless absolutely necessary. Spot heal companions as wounds appear. If someone is getting hammered, such as the tank in a large fight, Heal and Regenerate back to back. If several companions get injured at once (by enemy AoE) or combat slowly chips away at everyone's health, fire off a Group Heal to boost everyone's health across the board. Later, you can add Lifeward to the rotation for companions knocking on death's door. If they pass over that unfortunate threshold, bust out a Revival and raise them right back into the fight.

~ Starting Attributes ~

Strength **14**	Dexterity **14**
Willpower **24**	Magic **29**
Cunning **15**	Constitution **11**

~ Class ~
Mage

Party Healer: No one is better at keeping the party alive than Wynne. Her Creation spells do a fine job of maintaining single companion's health levels, but her spirit healer specialization takes things to a new level with group healing.

~ Starting Talents ~

Mage: Arcane Bolt

Spirit Healer: Group Heal

Primal: Rock Armor, Stonefist

Creation: Heal, Rejuvenate, Regeneration, Heroic Offense, Heroic Aura

~ Location ~
Circle Tower

~ Unlock Condition ~
You meet Wynne on the first level of the Circle Tower. She joins your party as soon as you get locked in the tower, and will join the party permanently after you save the tower in the "Broken Circle" quest.

Vessel of the Spirit

Wynne gains a special plot ability after completing her personal quest: Vessel of the Spirit. She disorients nearby enemies with a release of energy, restoring some health and mana and earning bonuses to spellpower and mana regeneration. However, once she deactivates the ability, she is stunned and suffers penalties to movement, attack, and defense. Exact specifics include:

- Sustained Ability
- Range: Personal
- Upkeep: 60
- Fatigue: 15%
- Cooldown: 300 seconds

Get this ability early, even if it means letting Wynne "die" to trigger the personal quest chain. Thereafter, when Wynne's mana drops low in a long fight, move in close to an enemy group and activate Vessel of the Spirit. You may stun some of the enemies, but more important, you can gain back mana and earn mana regeneration. The effect usually lasts long enough that you can finish out the fight with renewed vigor before the penalty sets in.

Wynne

Dialogue Choices

As with any companion, Wynne has dialogue choices whenever you interact with her, and sometimes she will pull you aside to speak with you about a topic. Wynne is definitely not afraid to voice her opinion about morally outrageous situations; listen to what she has to say or her approval rating will plummet fast. Speak with her often in camp to gain her favor and learn about her history.

Personal Quest

Wynne's personal quest is tricky, because it requires you to first raise her approval level and then trigger a random encounter. Follow these steps:

- Talk to Wynne about her past. And get her to warm.
- You'll have a random encounter where Wynne collapses at the end of it. When she does, go back to the camp and talk to her about it.
- Later there will be another encounter where Wynne will release her inner spirit finally giving her a new spirit form (see the Vessel of the Spirit sidebar).
- (Bonus) Ask Wynne about her time at the Circle Tower and she'll eventually talk about her old apprentice Anerin.
- (Bonus) Go to the Brecilian Forest, and you should find Anerin. Talk to him with Wynne in the party, and he will give Wynne an amulet that will strengthen her Vessel of the Spirit ability.

Gifts

For Wynne, the printed word is a window to true understanding. A scholar by heart, she feels that what a people commit to the page is sacred by definition, and she enjoys collecting books, scrolls, and other pieces of history.

Gift	Found In	Location
Discovering Dragon's Blood: Potions, Tinctures, and Spicy Sauces*	Bookshelf	Ruined Temple
Fancy Scroll	Sarcophagus	Lower Ruins
Tattered Notebook	Dog	Random chance he'll fetch it
The Guerrins of Ferelden: A Genealogical History*	Bookshelf	Upper Level of Castle Redcliffe
The Rose of Orlais	Pile of Books	Senior Mage Quarters of Circle Tower
The Search for the True Prophet	Locked Chest	Shaperate in Orzammar

* Name shortened on console version.

Highlights

- You can meet Wynne in Ostagar before the darkspawn invade. She'll give you bits of wisdom, but she won't join your party until you see her again at the Circle Tower.
- Bar none, Wynne is the best healer in the game. Unless you spec one of your other mages with some healing spells, Wynne should be a staple member of your party.
- Unlock Wynne's special ability, Vessel of the Spirit, through dialogue in camp and then a series of random encounters. Once she has the ability, trigger it whenever your mana drops low in a long fight.
- In matters of faith and virtue, Wynne always makes the most admirable choice. To keep her approval rating high, never choose an action that strays from the straight and narrow.

Crisis Moment

In the "Urn of Sacred Ashes" quest, Wynne will turn against you if you decide to destroy the ashes, just as Leliana will. You will have to fight them and kill them if they are in the party. During the "Broken Circle" quest, on the fourth floor of the tower, Cullen will suggest that killing all the mages in the tower is the only way to fix things. If you side with Cullen, Wynne will leave the party for good and fight you to the death. Later, if you reveal that you are a blood mage (or accepted the blood mage specialization from the desire demon in the Fade), Wynne will also turn against you.

primagames.com

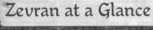

Zevran

Zevran at a Glance

You meet Zevran at a random encounter after having finished at least one major world plot. Your party is accosted by a traveler who begs for help from bandits. When you follow her to the camp, you get attacked by a group of assassins led by Zevran. You must talk to Zevran after he has been defeated, and he will explain that he is an assassin hired by Loghain to kill all the remaining Grey Wardens, but that he is willing to work for you instead—in exchange for his life, of course.

Combat Advice

Zevran contributes best when you sneak up on opponents and surprise them. Before you enter line of sight with a mob, Zevran should go into stealth mode and slink around to the mob's rear where he can use Combat Movement to ensure a backstab and Exploit Weakness to deliver extra damage based on his cunning score. If he can't reach the enemy's rear, stay hidden and wait for adversaries to move and expose their vulnerable backs. Never engage head on; Zevran can always at least strike from a flanking position.

Focus on Zevran's dexterity and willpower as he levels. He will probably be an accomplished poisoner. He will take best to light armor, dual weapons, and archery with shortbows or longbows. Fill out Zevran's assassin specialization as soon as they open up (especially up to level 14's Lacerate). Concentrate on the Dual Weapon school whenever you don't have an assassin point to spend. Dual-Weapon Finesse should be a priority to avoid the standard penalties associated with fighting two-handed; the goal, of course, is to reach Dual-Weapon Mastery. Whirlwind provides damage against multiple foes at once, while Riposte gives Zevran a stun attack for those targets that just won't go down.

~ Starting Attributes ~

Strength **19**	Dexterity **33**
Willpower **19**	Magic **14**
Cunning **15**	Constitution **10**

~ Class ~

Rogue

DPSer: With the assassin specialization, Zevran works well with a tank when he can get behind a target and rip it to shreds.

~ Starting Talents ~

Assassin: Mark of Death

Rogue: Dirty Fighting, Below the Belt, Deadly Strike, Lethality, Stealth, Stealth Item Use, Combat Stealth

Dual Weapon: Dual-Weapon Training, Dual-Weapon Sweep, Flurry, Momentum

~ Location ~

Random Encounter

~ Unlock Condition ~

After you complete at least one major world quest line, you will eventually meet Zevran in a random encounter.

Gifts

Antivan Leather Boots and Dalish Gloves will each initiate a specific conversation with Zevran, in which it is possible to gain further approval. They will be transformed into real objects and equipped on Zevran's person, once given. The chest that holds the Dalish Gloves appears only after you kill the shade in the West Brecilian Forest.

Gift	Found In	Location
Antivan Leather Boots	Iron Chest	Village Store (Haven)
Dalish Gloves	Chest	West Brecilian Forest
Medium Gold Bar	Treasure Pile	Arl of Denerim's Estate—Interior
Medium Silver Bar	Chest	Anvil of the Void
Small Gold Bar	Charmed Templar	Templar's Quarters in Circle Tower
Small Silver Bar	Inscribed Chest	Haven Chantry

Crisis Moments

Unlike most of the other companions, you can lose Zevran easily if you aren't careful. He did try to kill you once, remember? Here are the three main ways to lose Zevran from the group:

- During the first random encounter, Zevran can be killed before you ever talk to him, or at any time during the first conversation before he is recruited. Shame on you.
- Based on poor approval rating, you can make Zevran so angry that he will try to leave. You can try to convince him to stay, or you can engage him in combat (thereby killing him), or you can just let him go. This can happen twice; the second time there is no more convincing.

Just before the Landsmeet, Zevran's old friend Taliesin will ambush you in a back alley random encounter with a number of Antivan Crows. If Zevran likes you a lot, he'll stay and fight them, though your dialogue choices in this encounter can cause him to leave even if he likes you enough to stay. If he really doesn't like you, he'll join them to fight against you. If he's somewhere in between, he'll leave during the fight but stay in the party afterward.

Zevran

Basics ~ Character Generation ~ Classes ~ The Party ~ **Companions** ~ Supporting Cast ~ Equipment ~ Bestiary ~ Walkthroughs ~ Side Quests ~ Random Encounters ~ Achievements/Trophies

Dialogue Choices

As with any companion, Zevran has dialogue choices whenever you interact with him, and sometimes he will pull you aside to speak with you about a topic. However, at important points in the game, you should know about plot-specific and camp-specific dialogue that could change the game for your companion.

Plot-Specific Dialogue

- Zevran has specific dialogue in the Fade in "Broken Circle" and in the "Captured" quest in Denerim.
- If you ask him what he thinks of the Dalish, he will tell you about his Dalish mother. If you have killed all the elves in favor of the werewolves, he will be displeased with you.
- He will ask you about your plans to be queen or king, after the Landsmeet, if you are a Human Noble. Ask about Antiva (to get the Boots quest).
- Ask about the Dalish (to get the Gloves quest, which is only available after entering the Dalish camp and talking to Mithra).

Camp-Specific Dialogue

Zevran has no camp-initiated dialogue, but it is a good time to talk to him in general.

- Ask him about the Crows.
- Ask about being an assassin.
- Ask about his adventures until he's not willing to talk about a particular mission.
- You will get to a point where he's not willing to talk about his adventures for a while. Eventually, he will again.
- He should talk about his last mission before Ferelden when he's friendly, in love, or adore.
- If you are in a romance with Zevran (at adore level) and have not initiated sex with him, he will do so at camp. All sex-related dialogue, of course, is at camp.
- If you have rescued him from the Crows and have reached friendly (or love), he will thank you at camp.

Romance

Zevran is unabashedly bisexual, and will hit on you regardless of gender. You can cut him off quickly, or engage him in a light flirtation that will lead to romance almost as soon as you wish.

Zevran responds well to sympathy in the early stages of his conversation and blatant flirtation and sexual innuendo. He also likes to feel needed, but also appreciates the occasional sassy bossiness. ("I decided I wanted to torture you, first" or "Fine. Get in my tent. No more questions." generates an increase, where "Quiet! You'll answer when spoken to!" generates a decrease.) He doesn't like to feel caged in: offering him his freedom, reluctantly, will go over well (but don't go too far— he might take you up on it). Talking about love or commitment before he talks to you about it might not be the best way to deal with him.

It's possible to anger him, but you really have to work at it, and a medium Persuade skill and a plea to his better nature (I need you) or his greed (don't you want to stay for the treasure) will generally be enough to convince him to stay.

TIP

When he becomes very close to you, he will offer you an earring as an expression of his affections.

At the Pearl in Denerim, there is a duelist named Isabela who is acquainted with Zevran. If you are in a romance with him and bring him to the Pearl, he will join you in a threesome with her. If you have Leliana in your party, and she has changed to a more hardened personality, and she is in a romance with you, she will also join you in a foursome. This is very hard to achieve, as Leliana is more jealous/insecure than the other romance characters, and will object to your romances with others much earlier than anyone else. If any of your other romances are at adore level, you'll need to talk to her only when she initiates, and then after the Marjolaine quest encounter (in order to harden her), and then go straight to the Pearl.

However, once Zevran falls too far in love with you (after you free him from the Crows by killing Taliesin), he will be unwilling to sleep with you any longer, until he sorts through his feelings. If you ask him about it, he will tell you how he feels, and depending on how you respond, will decide to stay with you in a romance or not. But as long as you don't reject him outright, he'll stay.

If you decide to become king consort to Anora or queen consort to Alistair (only on the Human Noble path), Zevran will be happy to remain your lover on the side.

Highlights

- Zevran will teach the assassin specialization if he feels warm enough to the PC.
- He has many excellent stories about his life as an assassin; you can ask him about these at almost any time.
- Zevran will hit on almost all the other companions unabashedly in banter. Take him everywhere for fun.

primagames.com

Dog

Dog at a Glance

You gain your Mabari war dog in one of two ways: 1) a small side quest in the Human Noble origin story; or 2) talk to the Kennel Master in Ostagar and complete the "Mabari Hound" side quest. If you choose to ignore these side quests, you won't have the dog in your party for the rest of the game. When the Mabari war dog first joins the party, you can name him whatever you like (for purposes of the guide we'll call him "Dog"). There may be better warriors to take in your party, but he is a tough combatant, and you don't have to worry about approval rating with him: Dog is always 100 percent loyal.

TIP

Ask Dog to fetch things in every area of the game. Sometimes he'll bring back some strange things…

Combat Advice

Even though his Dog talents are few, they can pack a punch in combat. Don't underestimate them, especially because they have no attribute or level restrictions. Dread Howl delays nearby enemies with an AoE stun; Combat Training boosts critical chance, attack, and armor; and Overwhelm puts targets on the ground and deals a series of hits. Shred is vicious, dealing an automatic critical strike on a successful hit and bleed damage over time. When you reach Nemesis, Dog gains bonuses to health and health regeneration; he can now absorb a ton of damage. Dog should follow your party tank's lead and deal DPS to the mobs. Attack from the side or rear for maximum effectiveness, and, as you may expect from a dog, he makes the perfect bodyguard to protect weaker party members.

Alas, because other warriors have so many more talents and so many more equipment slots, Dog can be outstripped in the long run by veteran warriors. Early in your career, though, he's very useful as a second warrior.

Equipment

Dog's only equipment is kaddis (battle tattoos) and a dog collar. There are many different types to be found in stores and loot across the game, each offering different increases to his abilities and defenses.

~ Starting Attributes ~

Strength	Dexterity
21	20
Willpower	Magic
13	10
Cunning	Constitution
10	18

~ Class ~
Warrior

DPSer: Dog may be limited with gear and abilities, so other warriors, such as Alistair, will make better tanks, but he can deal decent damage with those canine teeth.

~ Starting Talents ~
Dog: Growl, Dread Howl, Fortitude, Charge

~ Location ~
Castle Cousland or Ostagar

~ Unlock Condition ~
Side quests in the Human Noble origin story or Ostagar unlock your Mabari friend.

Dialogue Choices

The only plot-specific dialogue Dog has outside of the Human Noble origin is in the Fade. Other companions can have conversations with Dog if you talk to him in camp, but he doesn't have any self-initiated dialogues in camp.

Highlights

- Dog gets a health boost if you ask him to clean up your gore.
- Dog will bring you random objects if you ask him if he sees something interesting; some of them can be used as gifts to other companions. Once he brings you a child. Once he brings you cake. Have fun with it.
- Because he has been "imprinted" on you, Dog will always love you 100 percent, no matter what. Thus, gifts are unnecessary, but he'll be grateful nonetheless.
- If you pet Dog, sometimes he'll roll around in the dirt. It's adorable.
- Dog gets different reactions from different companions. Be sure to start conversations with Dog in camp from time to time for some surprises.

Gifts

Simply put: Dog loves bones. You can give other companions a small approval bump with one of the game's bones—and yes, Dog doesn't need to be any more loyal than he is—but can you really do that to the poor beast?

Gift	Found In	Location
Beef Bone	Sacks / Chest	Ostagar / Templar's Quarters in Circle Tower
Lamb Bone	Chest	Castle Redcliffe: Main Floor
Large Bone	Corpse	Village Store (Haven)
Ox Bone	Rubble	West Brecilian Forest
Veal Bone	Chest	Run-down Apartments (Denerim Alienage)

Dog - Loghain Mac Tir

Basics ~ Character Generation ~ Classes ~ The Party ~ Companions ~ Supporting Cast ~ Equipment ~ Bestiary ~ Walkthroughs ~ Side Quests ~ Random Encounters ~ Achievements/Trophies

Loghain Mac Tir

During the battle at Ostagar, he fled the field, leaving King Cailan and the Grey Wardens to die. His actions sparked a civil war. Loghain's supporters found themselves fighting their neighbors who blamed Loghain for the death of the king, as well as those who simply wished to take advantage of the power vacuum. He was defeated in single combat at the Landsmeet, and sentenced to undertake the Joining ritual. He survived, and rejoined the fight for Ferelden as a Grey Warden.

➤◆➤ NOTE ➤◆➤

The only chance to have Loghain as a companion is to spare his life after the Landsmeet and force him to do the Joining and become a Grey Warden. If you do this, Alistair will leave the party forever.

Combat Advice

Loghain will most likely be your party's tank after Alistair leaves the group. Concentrate most of your talent points on filling out the Weapon and Shield school and picking up Death Blow from the Warrior school. You want to make sure he can hold threat and absorb lots of damage from enemy attacks. In melee, Overpower and Assault should be staple offensive talents for Loghain, while the War Cry/Superiority combo will flatten enemy groups.

If Loghain is your tank, he will charge smaller enemy groups, unless you have an ambush staged. Give him a few moments to build up threat, and he should always bash the most dangerous target so that target doesn't go in search of someone else. Don't stress over damage output with Loghain; his job is to hold the enemy and suck up damage while the party's DPS-oriented members chop down the enemy. Load Loghain with the best heavy or massive armor available (possibly even better than the armor you give the PC), and he should wield a fine blade (main hand only; his off hand should hold a shield) to inflict good damage and further increase threat against his targets. In his secondary weapon slot, give Loghain a crossbow for long-range combat. Your healer will usually target Loghain for heals, but just in case, Loghain should always stock 5–10 health poultices for emergencies.

Dialogue Choices

You and Loghain probably won't be too chatty leading up to the battle against the archdemon. Talk to him at camp only if you want to gain some approval.

Gifts

Loghain loves maps. If you find anything historical, give it to Loghain for a bump up in approval.

Gift	Found In	Location
Ancient Map of the Imperium	Wonders of Thedas Store	Denerim Market District
Botanist's Map of Thedas	Chest on Main Floor (after the Landsmeet)	Castle Redcliffe
Current Map of Ferelden	Alarith's Store	Elven Alienage in Denerim
Map of the Anderfels	Gorim	Denerim Market District
Map of Occupied Ferelden	Chest in the Upper Floor Guest Room	Redcliffe Castle

Highlights

- Although he was once your sworn enemy, desperate times call for desperate measures. With the Joining, Loghain becomes a Grey Warden.
- If you can warm up to Loghain, he may teach you the champion specialization.
- He's Queen Anora's father, and you get on the queen's good side by keeping her father alive after the Landsmeet.
- Loghain may be obnoxious, but he's no slouch in combat. Let him carry the lion's share of melee duties.

Loghain at a Glance

~ Starting Attributes ~

Strength **28**	Dexterity **23**
Willpower **32**	Magic **14**
Cunning **18**	Constitution **24**

~ Class ~

Warrior

Tank: As a replacement for Alistair, Loghain can do just fine with his Weapon and Shield talents, plus his champion specialization.

~ Starting Talents ~

Champion: War Cry, Rally, Motivate, Superiority

Warrior: Powerful, Threaten, Bravery, Precise Striking, Taunt, Disengage, Perfect Striking

Weapon and Shield: Shield Bash, Shield Pummel, Overpower, Assault, Shield Block, Shield Cover, Shield Tactics, Shield Mastery

~ Location ~

Royal Palace in Denerim

~ Unlock Condition ~

You must first defeat Loghain in combat after the Landsmeet, then invite him to join the Grey Wardens.

primagames.com

Sten

He was sent with a small group of qunari soldiers to investigate the Blight and report back. Near Lake Calenhad, they were ambushed by darkspawn. They fought off the attack, but only Sten survived. Farmers found him dying and took him in, but when he awoke, alone and unarmed, he panicked, killing the entire family. Realizing he had sacrificed his honor, Sten waited for the villagers to come, and surrendered, expecting death. Instead, your party arrived and offered him penance for his sins. His sword and his honor restored, Sten chose to continue with you and take the battle to the archdemon.

Sten at a Glance

~ Starting Attributes ~

Strength	Dexterity
28	16

Willpower	Magic
15	11

Cunning	Constitution
10	13

~ Class ~
Warrior

DPSer or Off-Tank: Sten enjoys grabbing a two-hander and cleaving skulls. The more damage, the better. In a pinch, Sten can tank a fight in place of Alistair or the PC, simply by dealing enough damage to hold the threat.

~ Starting Talents ~

Warrior: Powerful, Threaten, Precise Striking, Taunt

Two-Handed: Pommel Strike, Indomitable, Sunder Arms, Mighty Blow, Powerful Swings

~ Location ~
Lothering

~ Unlock Condition ~

Release Sten from his cage in Lothering before the town gets invaded by darkspawn (see the "Lothering" section of the Walkthrough chapter for complete details).

Combat Advice

Fill out Sten's Two-Handed school as soon as you get the chance. Capitalize on some of the top-tier talents quickly, which will seriously increase his damage potential and make him an excellent DPS addition to your party. As with rogues, Sten should allow the tank to control enemy mobs and then attack from the rear or flank. Because Sten is so durable, he doesn't have to watch his spacing as much as a rogue, and he can off-tank if you need him to grab a creature that the tank can't hold threat on. His skills are best used with heavy or massive armor and two-handed weapons, with a crossbow for ranged attacks.

Dialogue Choices

As with any companion, Sten has dialogue choices whenever you interact with him, and sometimes he will pull you aside to speak with you about a topic. He's not a big talker but will interject if you aren't on a straight path toward the archdemon.

Gifts

Sten has an eye for paintings, an appreciation that might seem out of character, but is actually an extension of qunari discipline. He respects an artist for careful composition, a skill that is as much about where the brush stroke stops as where it begins.

Gift	Found In	Location
Painting of a Rebel Queen	Dwarven Merchant	Random Encounter
Portrait of a Goosegirl	Faryn	Frostback Mountains
Silver Framed Still-Life	Chest	Upper Level of Castle Redcliffe
Sten's Sword	Scavenger near Lake Calenhad Docks, then Faryn in Frostback Mountains	Dwyn in Redcliffe Village (kill him, pay him, or convince him to give it to you)
Totem	Chest	Caridin's Cross
Water-stained Portrait	Charred Corpse	Senior Mage Quarters in Circle Tower

Crisis Moment

If you travel to the Urn of Sacred Ashes, Sten will question your commitment to destroying the archdemon. If you are a bit too lippy with him, he'll challenge you for control of the party. If you beat him, he'll want to leave.

Personal Quest

To complete Sten's personal quest, you must do the following, in order:

- Talk to Sten about his past. He should tell you about losing his sword.
- Start the quest for his sword at the beginning of Lake Calenhad. Near the entrance is a scavenger.
- You'll find Faryn at the Mountain Pass, just before the entrance to Orzammar. Ask him about the sword and bring Sten along.
- Find Dwyn in Redcliffe Village. Bring Sten along again to bully him into giving you the sword.
- Grab the sword from the chest in the back of Dwyn's room and gift it to Sten.

Highlights

- Sten will not survive the darkspawn incursion against Lothering unless you free him from his prison before leaving town.
- His no-nonsense attitude lets you know where he stands, but Sten won't be happy unless you stick with killing darkspawn.
- Sten complements Alistair if you journey with two warriors. Alistair gains the one-handed weapons; Sten uses the better two-handers.
- Sten cares nothing about romance. You can't seduce him as a female player.

Sten - Bann Teagan Guerrin

Basics ~ Character Generation ~ Classes ~ The Party ~ Companions ~ **Supporting Cast** ~ Equipment ~ Bestiary ~ Walkthroughs ~ Side Quests ~ Random Encounters ~ Achievements/Trophies

Supporting Cast

NOTE

Companions aren't the only important characters you'll encounter in Ferelden. The following supporting cast includes some of your staunchest allies and most treacherous enemies. For NPCs that appear in combat, we present the NPC's class, rank, and abilities to match the same helpful statistics you find with the enemies in the Bestiary chapter.

Arl Eamon Guerrin

As the maternal uncle of King Cailan, Arl Eamon is one of the king's most trusted advisors. Redcliffe, while not a large or especially wealthy part of Ferelden, is a critical strategic location. The fortress guards the western pass that leads to Orlais, as well as the major trade route with Orzammar. He's a well-respected man, though not the most charismatic. King Cailan once said of him, "My Uncle Eamon is a man everyone thinks well of—when they remember to think of him at all." He doesn't appear in combat until the final battle.

- Class = Warrior
- Rank = Lieutenant
- Special Abilities = Champion (Weapon and Shield)

Arlessa Isolde

The arling of Redcliffe was a source of constant trouble for Emperor Reville during the occupation; it was rumored that because each new report sent the emperor into a fit of violent rage, his court had taken to poisoning messengers before they could deliver their accounts. Isolde's family was the tenth to be given the difficult task of governing Redcliffe, and because most of the previous arls had either been murdered by their banns or beheaded by the emperor, they did not approach the job with a great deal of enthusiasm. Isolde met Eamon, not realizing he was the rightful heir to her father's domain, and quickly became smitten with him for being part of the resistance—nevermind that it was her family he was resisting. Perhaps a bit too romantic for her own good, she insisted upon staying behind.

Arl Rendon Howe

The arling of Amaranthine winds along the sinuous northeastern coast of Ferelden. The Waking Sea is known for its temper, and the storms that sweep in from the warmer northern waters are sudden and brutal. These are the lands of Rendon Howe. He was born during the occupation, and like many of the nobles at the time, he joined Prince Maric's rebels. He fought alongside young Bryce Cousland, future teyrn of Highever, and Leonas Bryland, future arl of South Reach, at the bloody battle of White River. It was the most catastrophic defeat of the entire occupation, from which only 50 rebel soldiers escaped alive. Although he was decorated for valor by King Maric, Howe's abrasive manners have earned him almost universal dislike among his peers. He appears in combat at the Arl of Denerim's Estate in the "Landsmeet" quest.

- Class = Rogue
- Rank = Boss
- Special Abilities = Assassin (Dual Wield)

Bann Teagan Guerrin

Younger brother to Arl Eamon of Redcliffe, and uncle to King Cailan, Teagan holds the bannorn of Rainesfere, a tiny province of Redcliffe's squeezed between the Frostback Mountains and Lake Calenhad. Bann Teagan avoids the Denerim court except to go hunting with his nephew, and rarely makes himself heard at the Landsmeet, preferring to leave politics to his brother.

- Class = Warrior
- Rank = Lieutenant
- Special Abilities = Champion (Weapon and Shield)

Beraht

Beraht is the crime lord in Orzammar's Dust Town, and his mercenary thugs earn him as much respect as their fists can collect on a daily basis. If you start the game as a Dwarf Commoner, you reluctantly serve under his iron boot.

- Class = Warrior
- Rank = Lieutenant
- Special Abilities = Weapon and Shield

Bhelen Aeducan

Third of King Endrin's children, Bhelen has always been considered the last and least of his family. Not the heir, nor the favorite, and not as accomplished as either sibling, Bhelen's most notable trait is his ability to stay out of trouble.

- Class = Warrior
- Rank = Boss
- Special Abilities = Weapon and Shield

Branka

Lost in the Deep Roads for two years, the Paragon smith Branka has been hunting for an ancient artifact, the Anvil of the Void, to return its power to the dwarven empire. Prince Bhelen and Lord Harrowmont both hope that Branka is found to lend her support to their bid for the throne.

- Class = Warrior
- Rank = Boss
- Special Abilities = Weapon and Shield

Brother Ferdinand Genitivi

Brother Genitivi is one of the Chantry's best-known scholars, primarily on the basis of the stories he has published (which many of his contemporaries dismiss as fanciful) of his travels across the length and breadth of Thedas.

Caladrius

A Tevinter slave trader with a smooth wit and tongue, Caladrius leads the extraction of elf slaves from the Elven Alienage. You meet him as you try to uncover evidence against Loghain during the "Landsmeet" quest.

- Class = Mage
- Rank = Boss
- Special Abilities = Blood Mage

Connor Guerrin

While most of the banns and arls of Ferelden cart their children with them to the Landsmeet in the interest of eventually marrying them off, Connor has spent his entire life at Redcliffe. And it's hardly surprising: the child possessed the gift of magic. By law, he should have been taken to the Circle of Magi at the first sign, abdicating his claim to Redcliffe. Instead, the boy was kept out of public view and his magic hushed up...with disastrous results. All mages are beacons that attract the attention of Fade spirits. Because of this, they are trained and tested by the Circle to ensure that they can withstand attacks from malevolent Fade creatures that seek entry into the waking world. Untrained, Connor drew the attention of a powerful demon that tore the Veil asunder.

Beraht - Isabela

Basics ~ Character Generation ~ Classes ~ The Party ~ Companions ~ Supporting Cast ~ Equipment ~ Bestiary ~ Walkthroughs ~ Side Quests ~ Random Encounters ~ Achievements/Trophies

Duncan

Like many others, Duncan gave up his family name when he joined the ranks of the Wardens in a symbolic gesture of cutting ties. He might say this was a convenience in his case, however. His mother was from the Anderfels, his father from Tevinter, and his childhood was spent in the Free Marches and Orlais. His people were everywhere and his homeland was nowhere. He was given the almost impossible task of leading the Wardens in Ferelden—a kingdom that had thrown the order out 200 years earlier. Facing local suspicion and hostility, he set about finding recruits.

- Class = Warrior
- Special Abilities = Dual Wield

First Enchanter Irving

There is no higher office in a Circle Tower than that of first enchanter. The one who holds this title must not only be an able administrator, but also a mentor, leader, and surrogate parent to all the mages of the tower. Irving has proven himself to be all these things and more. Apprentices and mages alike know that few matters escape his watchful eyes. He can soothe templars angered by childish magical pranks while he lauds the pranksters at the same time.

- Class = Mage
- Rank = Boss (in the "Broken Circle" if you fight him, or Lieutenant in the "Final Onslaught" if he's on your side).
- Special Abilities = Spellcaster

Flemeth

Ages ago, legend says Bann Conobar took to wife a beautiful young woman who harbored a secret talent for magic: Flemeth of Highever. And for a time they lived happily, until the arrival of a young poet, Osen, who captured the lady's heart with his verse. They turned to the Chasind tribes

Flemeth (continued)

for help and hid from Conobar's wrath in the Wilds, until word came to them that Conobar lay dying. His last wish was to see Flemeth's face one final time. The lovers returned, but it was a trap. Conobar killed Osen and imprisoned Flemeth in the highest tower of the castle. In grief and rage, Flemeth worked a spell to summon a spirit into this world to wreak vengeance upon her husband. Vengeance she received, but not as she planned. The spirit possessed her, turning Flemeth into an abomination. A twisted, maddened creature, she slaughtered Conobar and all his men, and fled back into the Wilds.

- Class = Mage
- Rank = Normal
- Special Abilities = Spellcaster

Guardian (Urn of Sacred Ashes)

The Guardian of the Urn is a ghostly human figure who is dedicated to protecting it and has done so for millennia. The guardian hints that he is one of the original disciples of Andraste, who brought the ashes to the mountain. The magic in the ashes and in the mountain itself has kept him alive for a very long time, and has turned him into something beyond human. He is duty made flesh. Nothing else matters to him. Don't attack him and he won't attack you. The Guardian greets you at the entrance to the Gauntlet as you near the Urn of Sacred Ashes. Listen to his wisdom and it may help you through the Gauntlet's challenges.

- Class = Warrior
- Rank = Boss
- Special Abilities = Two-Handed

Isabela

The rogue Isabela earns a little pocket coin by cheating patrons in the Pearl at games of "chance." She's confident in her abilities, and you first meet her taking on several thugs at once and beating them handily. She will teach you the duelist specialization if you can outwit her at her own game.

- Class = Rogue
- Rank = Boss
- Special Abilities = Duelist

Keeper Zathrian

It is said that elves lived in Ferelden long before any others set foot there, and though most of their knowledge has been lost, it falls to the keeper of each clan to preserve what they have. Zathrian is an old, severe elf with little love for outsiders, but his clan is facing a more trying enemy than most. Long ago, in retribution for an attack against his clan, he unleashed a terrible curse: He summoned a spirit into this world, and set it upon the humans who had wronged him. The spirit did not simply slaughter Zathrian's enemies; it transformed them into monstrous beasts. In time, however, the werewolves he had created regained their minds, and they sought out the one responsible for their suffering, turning the curse upon Zathrian's own people.

- Class = Mage
- Rank = Lieutenant
- Special Abilities = Blood Mage

King Cailan Theirin

Son of the legendary King Maric Theirin, Cailan was the first Ferelden king born into a land free from foreign rule in two generations. Since his father's death, he's held the throne alongside his queen, Anora.

- Class = Warrior
- Special Abilities = Two-Handed

King Endrin Aeducan

Endrin of House Aeducan traces his ancestry back to the Paragon Aeducan, the greatest warrior of Orzammar's history, who beat back the darkspawn hordes in the First Blight. The second son of King Ansgar Aeducan, he became heir after his elder brother died in a Proving. The most respected

King Endrin Aeducan (continued)

king in four generations, he restored contact with Kal Sharok, the only other remaining city of the once-vast Dwarven Empire, which had been lost during the First Blight.

Knight-Commander Greagoir

Grim and taciturn, Greagoir has been knight-commander of the templar forces stationed at the Circle Tower for so many years that hardly anyone except the first enchanter recalls that he is not simply part of the tower itself.

- Class = Warrior
- Rank = Boss (if you fight him in the "Broken Circle," or Lieutenant if he's fighting on your side in the "Final Onslaught")
- Special Abilities = Templar (Weapon and Shield)

Kolgrim

Kolgrim is the leader of a mysterious cult based in the twisted village of Haven. Brother Genitivi's research on the Urn of Sacred Ashes has lead him and many fated knights to the clutches of Kolgrim and his followers.

- Class = Warrior
- Rank = Boss
- Special Abilities = Two-Handed

Keeper Zathrian - Ser Cauthrien

Basics ~ Character Generation ~ Classes ~ The Party ~ Companions ~ Supporting Cast ~ Equipment ~ Bestiary ~ Walkthroughs ~ Side Quests ~ Random Encounters ~ Achievements/Trophies

Loghain Mac Tir

A master tactician who has led many armies to victory in Ferelden, Loghain betrays King Cailan and the Grey Wardens at the battle of Ostagar. From that moment on, he is your sworn enemy and sets all his resources to seeing you dead and gone.

- Class = Warrior
- Rank = Boss
- Special Abilities = Champion

NOTE

See the Companions chapter for more details on how to get Loghain to join your party.

Lord Pyral Harrowmont

House Harrowmont is one of the oldest noble houses, as old as Orzammar itself. Endrin's most trusted advisor, Harrowmont is well-known for being an able administrator, and the author of many compromises in the ever-warring Assembly.

- Class = Warrior
- Rank = Boss
- Special Abilities = Weapon and Shield

Marjolaine

Marjolaine can only be revealed by embarking on Leliana's personal quest. She is an elite bard who will see you all dead as she tries to strike at Leliana.

- Class = Rogue
- Rank = Elite Boss
- Special Abilities = Bard

Queen Anora

The only child of the war hero Loghain Mac Tir, Anora has never been one to stay quietly in the background. It is common knowledge that in the five years Anora and Cailan held the throne together, she was the one wielding the power. She is held in much higher esteem than her husband by the people of Ferelden, nobility and commoners alike, and commands the respect even of foreign nations, having once inspired Empress Celene of Orlais to declare, "Anora of Ferelden is a solitary rose among brambles."

Ser Cauthrien

Cauthrien came to Loghain's service the hard way—she belonged to a poor family and was out working on the farm when she saw a man on horseback being attacked by several bandits. She rushed to his assistance, and found out belatedly that the man she "saved" was none other than the great hero Loghain. Though she was hardly more than a child, he took her in, offering her a position with his soldiers, and she climbed the ranks through sheer determination. Becoming the commander of Maric's Shield, Loghain's elite soldiers, was the proudest moment of her life.

- Class = Warrior
- Rank = Boss
- Special Abilities = Two-Handed

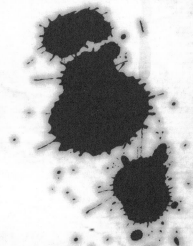

Taliesin

Between the Tevinter Imperium, Rivain, and the Free Marches sits the nation of Antiva. Although it possesses few resources of its own, Antiva's location makes it a center for trade in the north, and the capital, Antiva City, is the wealthiest in the world. Antiva has virtually no army—the monarchy is too weak to support one. Most Antivans would be hard-pressed even to name the current king. The true power lies in the hands of a dozen merchant princes, each with a personal army, and each locked in a constant struggle for power against all the others. Anyone would think, then, that Antiva would be a ripe target for invasion by one of her neighbors, but even the qunari leave Antiva alone for one very good reason: the House of Crows. The most efficient, most feared, and most expensive guild of assassins in the world calls Antiva home, and the guild's reputation alone defends the borders. Taliesin, an old partner of Zevran's from the Antivan Crows, returns to either kill or save Zevran just before the Landsmeet.

- Class = Rogue
- Rank = Lieutenant
- Special Abilities = Assassin (Dual Wield)

Trian

The oldest brother of the Aeducan heirs, Trian has a gruff manner that would turn allies away from him if not for his strength of arms. When it is time for his father, King Endrin Aeducan, to step down from the throne, Trian is in line for the crown.

- Class = Warrior
- Rank = Lieutenant
- Special Abilities = Warrior Archer

Valendrian

Every alienage has a hahren, an elder. It falls to the hahren to arrange marriages for those without family, to negotiate with the guards when there's trouble, and to act as a sort of mayor and surrogate uncle to the people of the alienage. The title, like so many things, is a holdover from the time of Arlathan, for hahrens are not necessarily the oldest person in their community, or even all that old. Tradition gives the role to the oldest soul, the wisest, cleverest, and the most level-headed. Valendrian has been hahren of the Denerim Alienage since he was in his 30s.

Vaughan

In the City Elf origin story, you have plans for marriage. But before you can be joined in matrimony, the ceremony is interrupted by a noble lord, Vaughan, the son of the arl of Denerim. Vaughan and his mercenary friends kidnap all the women in the wedding party and take them back to his estate to await his pleasure. He pays for his crimes and eventually ends up in a Denerim cell.

- Class = Rogue
- Rank = Lieutenant
- Special Abilities = Duelist

Weylon

The real Weylon died unbeknownst to his master, Brother Genitivi in Denerim. This imposter works to cover up Genitivi's strange disappearance, and it's up to the PC and his companions to track Brother Genitivi down to find the Urn of Sacred Ashes—even if it means going through Weylon.

- Class = Mage
- Rank = Lieutenant
- Special Abilities = Blood Mage

Taliesin - Vendor Shopping

Basics ~ Character Generation ~ Classes ~ The Party ~ Companions ~ Supporting Cast ~ Equipment ~ Bestiary ~ Walkthroughs ~ Side Quests ~ Random Encounters ~ Achievements/Trophies

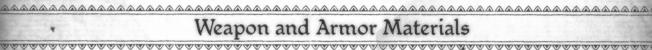

Equipment

Everyone loves decking a character out in the fanciest armor or most vicious sword. Each upgrade is another step on the path toward adventuring godhood. After all, you can't be the ultimate veteran without the best gear that merchants and monsters have to offer.

All adventurers need good weapons, helmets, gloves, chest pieces, boots, and various accessories. Magical or otherwise, these items bulk up your defense, improve attribute scores, and possibly give you special powers. Whatever you don't fit in your character equipment slots goes into your party inventory, which you can draw from with any character.

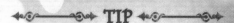
TIP

Companions back at party camp can hold onto items as well. If you don't have enough space in your inventory to store everything, load up your extra companions.

Weapon and Armor Materials

When purchasing weapons and armor from vendors or upgrading from monster drops or treasure finds, pay close attention to the items' material types. The game breaks items down into seven different tiers in several different materials. For example, tier 1 iron won't provide as much damage or damage reduction as the tier 4 veridium. In general, a higher tier means a better item, if you have the requirements to use it. However, some items may hold special bonuses that override the tier system. If, for example, you're a warrior and find a tier 5 weapon with bonuses to cunning, you may want to hold on to your old tier 3 weapon with its strength bonus.

Most of your equipment comes from vendors, monsters, or treasure; however, you can also find very special items as you unlock codex entries and complete side quests. You can find the full set of the durable Legion of the Dead armor, for example, in the Dead Trenches during Orzammar's "The Dead Caste" side quest. Check your codex "Items" and "Quest-Related" entries any time they update for clues on where to find these treasured items.

	Material Type	Damage Modifier	Armor Modifier
Metals	Iron (Tier 1)	1	1
	Grey Iron (Tier 2)	1.1	1.2
	Steel (Tier 3)	1.2	1.4
	Veridium (Tier 4)	1.3	1.6
	Red Steel (Tier 5)	1.4	1.8
	Silverite (Tier 6)	1.5	2.1
	Dragonbone (Tier 7)	1.6	2.5
Woods	Elm (Tier 1)	1	1
	Ash (Tier 2)	1.1	1
	Yew (Tier 3)	1.2	1.33
	Whitewood (Tier 4)	1.3	1.66
	Ironbark (Tier 5)	1.4	2
	Sylvanwood (Tier 6)	1.5	2.33
	Dragonthorn (Tier 7)	1.6	2.66
Leathers	Rough Hide (Tier 1)	1	1
	Cured Hide (Tier 2)	1.1	1.33
	Leather (Tier 3)	1.2	1.66
	Hardened Leather (Tier 4)	1.3	2
	Reinforced Leather (Tier 5)	1.4	2.33
	Inscribed Leather (Tier 6)	1.5	2.66
	Drakeskin (Tier 7)	1.6	3

Vendor Shopping

In every major city and village, merchant vendors sell their goods to anyone who will flash a coin at them. Some specialize in armor, while others dabble in the elements of crafting. Some places like the Denerim Market District are home to many vendors, and you can find just about anything, legal or otherwise, in Ferelden's capital city.

Backpacks

As soon as you can afford a backpack, go out and buy one. Each backpack increases your inventory capacity by 10 slots. It's well worth the investment to gain extra holding space on those long dungeon treks. You can find backpacks on the following vendors:

- Circle Tower (Quartermaster)
- Dalish Camp (Varathorn's Goods)
- Denerim Market (Gorim after the Landsmeet)
- Ostagar (Quartermaster)
- Party Camp (Bodahn's Wares)

Manuals

A manual trains you in a class specialization, a rare and valuable thing. You can find manuals on the following vendors:

- Dalish Camp, Varathorn (Manual: Shapeshifter)
- Denerim Market, Gorim after the Landsmeet (Manual: Berserker)
- Denerim Market, Wonders of Thedas after the Landsmeet (Manual: Spirit Healer)
- Elven Alienage, Alarith's Store after the Landsmeet (Manual: Assassin)
- Orzammar, Alimar (Manual: Bard)
- Party Camp, Bodahn's Wares (Manual: Ranger)
- Party Camp, Bodahn's Wares (Manual: Templar)

primagames.com

Tomes

Tomes grant you extra points to spend on talents, skills, and attributes. You can find tomes on the following vendors:

- Circle Tower, Quartermaster (Tome of Arcane Technique)
- Dalish Camp, Varathorn (Tome of Skill and Sundry)
- Dalish Camp, Varathorn (Tome of the Mortal Vessel)
- Denerim, Wonders of Thedas after the Landsmeet (Tome of Arcane Technique)
- Elven Alienage, Alarith's Store (Tome of Skill and Sundry)
- Haven, Shop Keeper (Greater Tome of the Mortal Vessel)
- Orzammar Commons, Garin (Tome of Physical Technique)
- Orzammar Commons, Legnar (Tome of the Mortal Vessel)
- Party Camp, Bodahn's Wares (Tome of Arcane Technique)
- Party Camp, Bodahn's Wares (Tome of Physical Technique)
- Random Encounter, Dwarven Merchant (Tome of Skill and Sundry)

Grandmaster Runes

Once you level up a bit and have some gold weighing down your pockets, you'll want to invest in top-notch runes to empower your better weapons. Look for the best. the grandmaster runes, at the following vendors:

- Deep Roads, Ruck's Store (Grandmaster Cold Iron Rune)
- Denerim Market, Cesar after the Landsmeet (Grandmaster Dweomer Rune)
- Denerim Market, Gorim, after the Landsmeet (Grandmaster Silverite Rune)
- Denerim Market, Wonders of Thedas after the Landsmeet (Grandmaster Flame Rune)
- Denerim Market, Wonders of Thedas after the Landsmeet (Grandmaster Paralyze Rune)
- Frostback Mountains, Faryn (Grandmaster Silverite Rune)
- Party Camp, Bodahn's Wares (Grandmaster Frost Rune)
- Party Camp, Bodahn's Wares (Grandmaster Lightning Rune)
- Party Camp, Bodahn's Wares (Grandmaster Slow Rune)
- Redcliffe, Owen (Grandmaster Hale Rune)

Merchant Vendor Lists

Until you can craft items for yourself with Herbalism, Poison-Making, and Trap-Making, vendors will be your primary source for health poultices, lyrium potions, and any poisons or traps you may use in your adventuring. Even after you start crafting, you will visit vendors often to fill up on the components necessary for your crafts. Note which vendors service your needs the best, because you'll return to them often. While shopping, you will spot high-priced magic items in almost every shop; build up your gold to purchase these choice items for your end-game campaign. Also keep in mind that vendors' stores can change later in the game (many after the Landsmeet); stock that was once dull may hold a new surprise or two. Any time that you want to unload items and sell for profit, take a quick glance at the merchandise in case something new, or suddenly relevant, catches your eye.

TIP

Sell most of your extra inventory at Bodahn's Wares in your party camp. Vendors keep the items you sell to them, and you never know when you'll want to buy back that main-hand mace or hunk of garnet later in the game. If it's at Bodahn's, you definitely know where to find it.

The following merchant vendor lists show you all saleable items organized by location. If you happen to be passing through Orzammar, just look up the shops and note anything that you need to stock up on. If a vendor lists "second store" next to it, that means the vendor opens up a new shopping inventory at some point later in the game (usually following the Landsmeet announcement). So gather up some coin and get shopping already!

Merchant Name	Item Name	Item Quantity
Circle Tower		
Quartermaster	Andruil's Blessing	1
Quartermaster	Backpack	1
Quartermaster	Chainmail	1
Quartermaster	Chainmail Gloves	1
Quartermaster	Concentrator Agent	3
Quartermaster	Corrupter Agent	4
Quartermaster	Crossbow	1
Quartermaster	Dagger	1
Quartermaster	Demonic Ichor	1
Quartermaster	Double-Baked Mabari Crunch	2
Quartermaster	Expert Dweomer Rune	1
Quartermaster	Explosive Bolt	20
Quartermaster	Fire Arrow	50
Quartermaster	Fire Bolt	50
Quartermaster	Fire Bomb	2
Quartermaster	Fire Bomb Recipe	1
Quartermaster	Fire Crystal	4
Quartermaster	Flaming Coating Recipe	1
Quartermaster	Glamour Charm	2
Quartermaster	Greater Health Poultice	1
Quartermaster	Greater Lyrium Potion	1
Quartermaster	Greater Spirit Balm	1

Vendor Shopping

Merchant Name	Item Name	Item Quantity
Circle Tower (continued)		
Quartermaster	Greatsword	1
Quartermaster	Health Poultice	3
Quartermaster	Heavy Chainmail Boots	1
Quartermaster	Heavy Wooden Shield	1
Quartermaster	Incense of Awareness Recipe	1
Quartermaster	Injury Kit	2
Quartermaster	Injury Kit Recipe	1
Quartermaster	Lesser Elixir of Grounding	1
Quartermaster	Lesser Ice Salve	1
Quartermaster	Lesser Spirit Balm Recipe	1
Quartermaster	Lesser Warmth Balm	1
Quartermaster	Lesser Warmth Balm Recipe	1
Quartermaster	Liberator's Mace	1
Quartermaster	Longsword	1
Quartermaster	Lyrium Dust	1
Quartermaster	Lyrium Potion	2
Quartermaster	Lyrium Potion Recipe	1
Quartermaster	Mace	1
Quartermaster	Magic Staff	1
Quartermaster	Maul	1
Quartermaster	Metal Shard	3
Quartermaster	Pocketed Searing Gloves	1
Quartermaster	Polar Gauntlets	1
Quartermaster	Reinforced Magus Cowl	1
Quartermaster	Scale Armor	1
Quartermaster	Soldier's Helm	1
Quartermaster	Soulrot Bomb	1
Quartermaster	Spiral Band	1
Quartermaster	Spirit Shard	3
Quartermaster	Splintmail Boots	1
Quartermaster	Splintmail Gloves	1
Quartermaster	Staff of the Magister Lord	1
Quartermaster	Swift Salve	1
Quartermaster	Thorn	1
Quartermaster	Tome of Arcane Technique	1
Quartermaster	Toxin Extract	2
Quartermaster	Trap Trigger	4
Quartermaster	Wooden Kite Shield	1
Dalish Camp		
Varathorn's Goods	Acid Flask	2
Varathorn's Goods	Acid Flask Recipe	1
Varathorn's Goods	Acidic Coating	1
Varathorn's Goods	Acidic Coating Recipe	1
Varathorn's Goods	Acidic Trap	2
Varathorn's Goods	Acidic Trap Plans	1
Varathorn's Goods	Adder's Kiss	1
Varathorn's Goods	Chasind Robes	1
Varathorn's Goods	Clan Shield	1
Varathorn's Goods	Concentrated Venom	2
Varathorn's Goods	Concentrator Agent	2
Varathorn's Goods	Corrupter Agent	2
Varathorn's Goods	Dalish Armor	1
Varathorn's Goods	Dalish Boots	1
Varathorn's Goods	Dalish Gloves	1
Varathorn's Goods	Dalish Longbow	1
Varathorn's Goods	Dal'Thanaan	1
Varathorn's Goods	Dal'Thanu	1
Varathorn's Goods	Dar'Misaan	1

Merchant Name	Item Name	Item Quantity
Dalish Camp (continued)		
Varathorn's Goods	Dar'Misu	1
Varathorn's Goods	Deathroot	1
Varathorn's Goods	Deathroot Extract	2
Varathorn's Goods	Distillation Agent	3
Varathorn's Goods	Elf-Flight Arrow	40
Varathorn's Goods	Elfroot	1
Varathorn's Goods	Elfrope	1
Varathorn's Goods	Fire Arrow	40
Varathorn's Goods	Greater Health Poultice	2
Varathorn's Goods	Greater Health Poultice Recipe	1
Varathorn's Goods	Greater Nature Salve	1
Varathorn's Goods	Health Poultice	3
Varathorn's Goods	Health Poultice Recipe	1
Varathorn's Goods	Ice Arrow	40
Varathorn's Goods	Injury Kit	2
Varathorn's Goods	Large Grease Trap Plans	1
Varathorn's Goods	Leather Helm	1
Varathorn's Goods	Lesser Lyrium Potion	4
Varathorn's Goods	Lesser Nature Salve	3
Varathorn's Goods	Lesser Nature Salve Recipe	1
Varathorn's Goods	Lesser Spirit Balm	1
Varathorn's Goods	Lesser Spirit Balm Recipe	1
Varathorn's Goods	Lifestone	5
Varathorn's Goods	Lyrium Potion	2
Varathorn's Goods	Mabari Crunch	3
Varathorn's Goods	Manual: Shapeshifter	1
Varathorn's Goods	Rock Salve	1
Varathorn's Goods	Scout's Bow	1
Varathorn's Goods	Silver Brooch	1
Varathorn's Goods	Small Grease Trap Plans	1
Varathorn's Goods	Spirit Shard	3
Varathorn's Goods	Swift Salve	1
Varathorn's Goods	Toxin Extract	1
Varathorn's Goods (second store)	Acid Flask	4
Varathorn's Goods (second store)	Acid Flask Recipe	1
Varathorn's Goods (second store)	Acidic Coating	3
Varathorn's Goods (second store)	Acidic Coating Recipe	1
Varathorn's Goods (second store)	Acidic Grease Trap	2
Varathorn's Goods (second store)	Acidic Grease Trap Plans	1
Varathorn's Goods (second store)	Acidic Trap	2
Varathorn's Goods (second store)	Acidic Trap Plans	1
Varathorn's Goods (second store)	Adder's Kiss	1
Varathorn's Goods (second store)	Armsman's Tensioner	1
Varathorn's Goods (second store)	Backpack	1
Varathorn's Goods (second store)	Concentrator Agent	2
Varathorn's Goods (second store)	Corrupter Agent	4
Varathorn's Goods (second store)	Dalish Armor	1
Varathorn's Goods (second store)	Dalish Boots	1
Varathorn's Goods (second store)	Dalish Gloves	1
Varathorn's Goods (second store)	Dalish Longbow	1
Varathorn's Goods (second store)	Dalish Shield	1
Varathorn's Goods (second store)	Dal'Thanaan	1
Varathorn's Goods (second store)	Dal'Thanu	1
Varathorn's Goods (second store)	Dar'Misaan	1
Varathorn's Goods (second store)	Dar'Misu	1
Varathorn's Goods (second store)	Deathroot	1
Varathorn's Goods (second store)	Distillation Agent	3
Varathorn's Goods (second store)	Double-Baked Mabari Crunch	3

Merchant Name	Item Name	Item Quantity
Dalish Camp (continued)		
Varathorn's Goods (second store)	Elf-Flight Arrow	40
Varathorn's Goods (second store)	Elfroot	1
Varathorn's Goods (second store)	Fire Arrow	40
Varathorn's Goods (second store)	Greater Health Poultice	3
Varathorn's Goods (second store)	Greater Health Poultice Recipe	1
Varathorn's Goods (second store)	Greater Injury Kit	1
Varathorn's Goods (second store)	Greater Lyrium Potion	2
Varathorn's Goods (second store)	Greater Nature Salve	2
Varathorn's Goods (second store)	Greater Nature Salve Recipe	1
Varathorn's Goods (second store)	Greater Spirit Balm	1
Varathorn's Goods (second store)	Greater Spirit Balm Recipe	1
Varathorn's Goods (second store)	Health Poultice	3
Varathorn's Goods (second store)	Health Poultice Recipe	1
Varathorn's Goods (second store)	Ice Arrow	40
Varathorn's Goods (second store)	Incense of Awareness	2
Varathorn's Goods (second store)	Injury Kit	3
Varathorn's Goods (second store)	Large Grease Trap Plans	1
Varathorn's Goods (second store)	Leather Helm	1
Varathorn's Goods (second store)	Lesser Nature Salve Recipe	1
Varathorn's Goods (second store)	Lesser Spirit Balm Recipe	1
Varathorn's Goods (second store)	Lifestone	6
Varathorn's Goods (second store)	Lyrium Potion	3
Varathorn's Goods (second store)	Magebane	2
Varathorn's Goods (second store)	Manual: Shapeshifter	1
Varathorn's Goods (second store)	Potent Health Poultice	1
Varathorn's Goods (second store)	Potent Health Poultice Recipe	1
Varathorn's Goods (second store)	Scout's Bow	1
Varathorn's Goods (second store)	Small Grease Trap Plans	1
Varathorn's Goods (second store)	Soldier's Bane	2
Varathorn's Goods (second store)	Soulrot Bomb	2
Varathorn's Goods (second store)	Soulrot Bomb Recipe	1
Varathorn's Goods (second store)	Soulrot Coating	2
Varathorn's Goods (second store)	Soulrot Coating Recipe	1
Varathorn's Goods (second store)	Soulrot Trap Plans	1
Varathorn's Goods (second store)	Spirit Shard	4
Varathorn's Goods (second store)	Swift Salve	1
Varathorn's Goods (second store)	The Dark Moon	1
Varathorn's Goods (second store)	Tome of Skill and Sundry	1
Varathorn's Goods (second store)	Tome of the Mortal Vessel	1
Varathorn's Goods (second store)	Toxin Extract	1
Dalish Elf Origin		
Ilen's Wares	Acid Flask	1
Ilen's Wares	Clan Shield	1
Ilen's Wares	Dalish Armor	1
Ilen's Wares	Dalish Boots	1
Ilen's Wares	Dalish Gloves	1
Ilen's Wares	Dalish Longbow	1
Ilen's Wares	Dal'Thanu	1
Ilen's Wares	Dar'Misaan	1
Ilen's Wares	Dar'Misu	1
Ilen's Wares	Deathroot	2
Ilen's Wares	Deathroot Extract	1
Ilen's Wares	Elf-Flight Arrow	20
Ilen's Wares	Elfroot	4
Ilen's Wares	Flask	5
Ilen's Wares	Leather Helm	1
Ilen's Wares	Lesser Health Poultice	3

Merchant Name	Item Name	Item Quantity
Dalish Elf Origin (continued)		
Ilen's Wares	Lesser Injury Kit	3
Ilen's Wares	Lesser Nature Salve	1
Ilen's Wares	Metal Shard	2
Ilen's Wares	Scout's Bow	1
Ilen's Wares	Small Caltrop Trap	1
Ilen's Wares	Spring Trap	2
Ilen's Wares	Swift Salve	1
Ilen's Wares	Toxin Extract	2
Ilen's Wares	Trap Trigger	3
Ilen's Wares	Venom	1
Deep Roads		
Ruck's Store	Armor of the Divine Will	1
Ruck's Store	Deep Mushroom	1
Ruck's Store	Destructionist's Belt	1
Ruck's Store	Dwarven Heavy Boots	1
Ruck's Store	Dwarven Large Round Shield	1
Ruck's Store	Dwarven Longsword	1
Ruck's Store	Dwarven Mace	1
Ruck's Store	Dwarven Waraxe	1
Ruck's Store	Etched Silver Symbol	1
Ruck's Store	Fire Crystal	3
Ruck's Store	Frostrock	5
Ruck's Store	Frozen Lightning	6
Ruck's Store	Grandmaster Cold Iron Rune	1
Ruck's Store	Heavy Dwarven Helmet	1
Ruck's Store	Lifestone	1
Ruck's Store	Shield of the Legion	1
Denerim Market District		
Cesar	Ash Warrior Axe	1
Cesar	Barbarian Helmet	1
Cesar	Barbarian Mace	1
Cesar	Clan Shield	1
Cesar	Concentrated Crow Poison Recipe	1
Cesar	Concentrator Agent	2
Cesar	Corrupter Agent	4
Cesar	Crow Dagger	1
Cesar	Crow Shield	1
Cesar	Deathroot	4
Cesar	Demonic Ichor	3
Cesar	Demonic Poison Recipe	1
Cesar	Enchanter's Staff	1
Cesar	Fire Arrow	40
Cesar	Ice Arrow	40
Cesar	Magebane Poison Recipe	1
Cesar	Orlesian Bow	1
Cesar	Qunari Infantry Helm	1
Cesar	Saw Sword	1
Cesar	Soldier's Bane Recipe	1
Cesar	Tevinter Shield	1
Cesar	Toxin Extract	3
Cesar (second store)	Antivan Crossbow	1
Cesar (second store)	Antivan Longbow	1
Cesar (second store)	Arrow of Filth	40
Cesar (second store)	Barbarian Axe	1
Cesar (second store)	Concentrated Crow Poison Recipe	1

Vendor Shopping

Basics ~ Character Generation ~ Classes ~ The Party ~ Companions ~ Supporting Cast ~ **Equipment** ~ Bestiary ~ Walkthroughs ~ Side Quests ~ Random Encounters ~ Achievements/Trophies

Merchant Name	Item Name	Item Quantity
Denerim Market District (continued)		
Cesar (second store)	Concentrated Demonic Poison Recipe	1
Cesar (second store)	Concentrated Magebane Recipe	1
Cesar (second store)	Concentrated Soldier's Bane Recipe	1
Cesar (second store)	Concentrator Agent	4
Cesar (second store)	Corrupter Agent	5
Cesar (second store)	Dar'Misu	1
Cesar (second store)	Deathroot	7
Cesar (second store)	Demonic Ichor	4
Cesar (second store)	Demonic Poison Recipe	1
Cesar (second store)	Dwarven Waraxe	1
Cesar (second store)	Executioner's Helm	1
Cesar (second store)	Explosive Bolt	20
Cesar (second store)	Fire Arrow	40
Cesar (second store)	Fire Bolt	40
Cesar (second store)	First Enchanter Robes	1
Cesar (second store)	Grandmaster Dweomer Rune	1
Cesar (second store)	Heavy Maul	1
Cesar (second store)	Ice Arrow	40
Cesar (second store)	Ice Bolt	40
Cesar (second store)	Knight-Commander's Helm	1
Cesar (second store)	Knockback Bolt	20
Cesar (second store)	Magebane Poison Recipe	1
Cesar (second store)	Magic Staff	1
Cesar (second store)	Orlesian Bow	1
Cesar (second store)	Quiet Death Recipe	1
Cesar (second store)	Qunari Commander Helm	1
Cesar (second store)	Qunari Sword	1
Cesar (second store)	Saw Sword	1
Cesar (second store)	Soldier's Bane Recipe	1
Cesar (second store)	Toxin Extract	8
Gnawed Noble Tavern (after Landsmeet)	Concentrator Agent	1
Gnawed Noble Tavern (after Landsmeet)	Deep Mushroom	1
Gnawed Noble Tavern (after Landsmeet)	Distillation Agent	1
Gnawed Noble Tavern (after Landsmeet)	Elfroot	7
Gnawed Noble Tavern (after Landsmeet)	Flask	1
Gnawed Noble Tavern (after Landsmeet)	Greater Health Poultice Recipe	1
Gnawed Noble Tavern (after Landsmeet)	Health Poultice	2
Gnawed Noble Tavern (after Landsmeet)	Health Poultice Recipe	1
Gnawed Noble Tavern (after Landsmeet)	Injury Kit Recipe	1
Gnawed Noble Tavern (after Landsmeet)	Lesser Health Poultice	3
Gnawed Noble Tavern (after Landsmeet)	Lesser Injury Kit	5
Gnawed Noble Tavern (after Landsmeet)	Lesser Injury Kit Recipe	1
Gnawed Noble Tavern (after Landsmeet)	Mabari Crunch	4
Gorim	Crossbow	1
Gorim	Dagger	1
Gorim	Dwarven Armor	1
Gorim	Dwarven Armored Boots	1
Gorim	Dwarven Armored Gloves	1
Gorim	Dwarven Heavy Armor	1
Gorim	Dwarven Heavy Boots	1
Gorim	Dwarven Heavy Gloves	1
Gorim	Dwarven Helmet	1
Gorim	Dwarven Large Round Shield	1
Gorim	Dwarven Longsword	1
Gorim	Dwarven Mace	1
Gorim	Dwarven Waraxe	1

Merchant Name	Item Name	Item Quantity
Denerim Market District (continued)		
Gorim	Gorim's Shield	1
Gorim	Gorim's Sword	1
Gorim	Heavy Dwarven Helmet	1
Gorim	Manual: Berserker	1
Gorim	Metal Shard	5
Gorim (second store)	Axe	1
Gorim (second store)	Backpack	1
Gorim (second store)	Camenae's Barbute	1
Gorim (second store)	Chasind Great Maul	1
Gorim (second store)	Crossbow	1
Gorim (second store)	Dagger	1
Gorim (second store)	Diamond Maul	1
Gorim (second store)	Dwarven Armor	1
Gorim (second store)	Dwarven Armored Boots	1
Gorim (second store)	Dwarven Armored Gloves	1
Gorim (second store)	Dwarven Heavy Armor	1
Gorim (second store)	Dwarven Heavy Boots	1
Gorim (second store)	Dwarven Heavy Gloves	1
Gorim (second store)	Dwarven Helmet	1
Gorim (second store)	Dwarven Large Round Shield	1
Gorim (second store)	Dwarven Longsword	1
Gorim (second store)	Dwarven Mace	1
Gorim (second store)	Dwarven Massive Armor	1
Gorim (second store)	Dwarven Massive Armored Boots	1
Gorim (second store)	Dwarven Massive Armored Gloves	1
Gorim (second store)	Fire Bolt	40
Gorim (second store)	Grandmaster Silverite Rune	1
Gorim (second store)	Heavy Dwarven Helmet	1
Gorim (second store)	Heavy Metal Shield	1
Gorim (second store)	Ice Bolt	40
Gorim (second store)	Katriel's Grasp	1
Gorim (second store)	Manual: Berserker	1
Gorim (second store)	Metal Shard	8
Gorim (second store)	Meteor Sword	1
Gorim (second store)	Rock-Knocker	1
Gorim (second store)	Sword Belt	1
Gorim (second store)	Thorval's Luck	1
Wade's Armor	Chainmail	1
Wade's Armor	Chainmail Gloves	1
Wade's Armor	Heavy Chainmail	1
Wade's Armor	Heavy Chainmail Boots	1
Wade's Armor	Heavy Chainmail Gloves	1
Wade's Armor	Helmet	1
Wade's Armor	Leather Armor	1
Wade's Armor	Leather Boots	1
Wade's Armor	Leather Gloves	1
Wade's Armor	Leather Helm	1
Wade's Armor	Metal Shard	4
Wade's Armor	Scale Armor	1
Wade's Armor	Scale Boots	1
Wade's Armor	Soldier's Helm	1
Wade's Armor	Splintmail Boots	1
Wade's Armor	Splintmail Gloves	1
Wade's Armor (second store)	Evon the Great's Mail	1
Wade's Armor (second store)	Heavy Chainmail	1
Wade's Armor (second store)	Heavy Chainmail Boots	1

primagames.com

Merchant Name	Item Name	Item Quantity
Denerim Market District (continued)		
Wade's Armor (second store)	Heavy Chainmail Gloves	1
Wade's Armor (second store)	Heavy Plate Armor	1
Wade's Armor (second store)	Heavy Plate Boots	1
Wade's Armor (second store)	Heavy Plate Gloves	1
Wade's Armor (second store)	Kaddis of the Mountain-Father	1
Wade's Armor (second store)	Soldier's Heavy Helm	1
Wade's Armor (second store)	Soldier's Heavy Helm	6
Wade's Armor (second store)	Soldier's Helm	1
Wade's Armor (second store)	Studded Leather Armor	1
Wade's Armor (second store)	Studded Leather Boots	1
Wade's Armor (second store)	Studded Leather Gloves	1
Wade's Armor (second store)	Studded Leather Helm	1
Wade's Armor (second store)	The Felon's Coat	1
Wonders of Thedas (after Landsmeet)	Ancient Map of the Imperium	1
Wonders of Thedas (after Landsmeet)	Apprentice Cowl	1
Wonders of Thedas (after Landsmeet)	Apprentice's Amulet	1
Wonders of Thedas (after Landsmeet)	Archivist's Sash	1
Wonders of Thedas (after Landsmeet)	Demonic Ichor	3
Wonders of Thedas (after Landsmeet)	Enchanter Cowl	1
Wonders of Thedas (after Landsmeet)	Expert Flame Rune	1
Wonders of Thedas (after Landsmeet)	Expert Hale Rune	1
Wonders of Thedas (after Landsmeet)	Expert Paralyze Rune	1
Wonders of Thedas (after Landsmeet)	Fire Crystal	6
Wonders of Thedas (after Landsmeet)	Flask	8
Wonders of Thedas (after Landsmeet)	Frostrock	5
Wonders of Thedas (after Landsmeet)	Glamour Charm	6
Wonders of Thedas (after Landsmeet)	Grandmaster Flame Rune	1
Wonders of Thedas (after Landsmeet)	Grandmaster Paralyze Rune	1
Wonders of Thedas (after Landsmeet)	Greater Ice Salve Recipe	1
Wonders of Thedas (after Landsmeet)	Greater Lyrium Potion	2
Wonders of Thedas (after Landsmeet)	Greater Lyrium Potion Recipe	1
Wonders of Thedas (after Landsmeet)	Greater Warmth Balm Recipe	1
Wonders of Thedas (after Landsmeet)	Hearthstone Pendant	1
Wonders of Thedas (after Landsmeet)	Incense of Awareness	2
Wonders of Thedas (after Landsmeet)	Journeyman Cold Iron Rune	1
Wonders of Thedas (after Landsmeet)	Journeyman Frost Rune	1
Wonders of Thedas (after Landsmeet)	Lend of the Lion	1
Wonders of Thedas (after Landsmeet)	Lesser Lyrium Potion	5
Wonders of Thedas (after Landsmeet)	Lightning Rod	1
Wonders of Thedas (after Landsmeet)	Lyrium Dust	10
Wonders of Thedas (after Landsmeet)	Lyrium Potion	4
Wonders of Thedas (after Landsmeet)	Mabari Dog Chain	1
Wonders of Thedas (after Landsmeet)	Magic Staff	1
Wonders of Thedas (after Landsmeet)	Manual: Spirit Healer	1
Wonders of Thedas (after Landsmeet)	Master Cold Iron Rune	1
Wonders of Thedas (after Landsmeet)	Master Dweomer Rune	1
Wonders of Thedas (after Landsmeet)	Master Hale Rune	1
Wonders of Thedas (after Landsmeet)	Overpowering Lure Trap Plans	1
Wonders of Thedas (after Landsmeet)	Potent Lyrium Potion Recipe	1
Wonders of Thedas (after Landsmeet)	Reaper's Vestments	1
Wonders of Thedas (after Landsmeet)	Ring of Ages	1
Wonders of Thedas (after Landsmeet)	Robe of the Witch	1
Wonders of Thedas (after Landsmeet)	Shock Bomb Recipe	1
Wonders of Thedas (after Landsmeet)	Shock Coating Recipe	1
Wonders of Thedas (after Landsmeet)	Spirit Shard	4
Wonders of Thedas (after Landsmeet)	Swift Salve Recipe	1
Wonders of Thedas (after Landsmeet)	Tevinter Mage Robes	1

Merchant Name	Item Name	Item Quantity
Denerim Market District (continued)		
Wonders of Thedas (after Landsmeet)	Tevinter Robe	1
Wonders of Thedas (after Landsmeet)	Tome of Arcane Technique	1
Wonders of Thedas (after Landsmeet)	Torch of Embers	1
Wonders of Thedas (after Landsmeet)	Twitch	1
Wonders of Thedas (after Landsmeet)	Wintersbreath	1
Dwarf Commoner Origin: Orzammar Commons		
Merchant	Crossbow	1
Merchant	Dagger	1
Merchant	Duster Leather Armor	1
Merchant	Duster Leather Boots	1
Merchant	Duster Leather Gloves	1
Merchant	Dwarven Longsword	1
Merchant	Dwarven Mace	1
Merchant	Dwarven Waraxe	1
Merchant	Leather Helm	1
Merchant	Shortbow	1
Merchant	Small Metal Round Shield	1
Olinda's	Deathroot	1
Olinda's	Deep Mushroom	4
Olinda's	Elfroot	3
Olinda's	Fire Bomb	1
Olinda's	Flask	5
Olinda's	Lesser Health Poultice	3
Olinda's	Lesser Injury Kit	3
Olinda's	Lesser Warmth Balm	1
Olinda's	Metal Shard	2
Olinda's	Rock Salve	1
Olinda's	Small Claw Trap	1
Olinda's	Spring Trap	2
Olinda's	Toxin Extract	2
Olinda's	Trap Trigger	6
Olinda's	Venom	2
Olinda's	Wine	1
Merchant	Amethyst	1
Merchant	Diamond	1
Merchant	Dwarven Armor	1
Merchant	Dwarven Armored Boots	1
Merchant	Dwarven Armored Gloves	1
Merchant	Dwarven Helmet	1
Merchant	Dwarven Large Round Shield	1
Merchant	Emerald	1
Merchant	Fluorspar	1
Merchant	Garnet	1
Merchant	Glamour Charm	1
Merchant	Greenstone	1
Merchant	Malachite	1
Merchant	Metal Shard	4
Merchant	Noble Clothing	1
Merchant	Noble Clothing	1
Merchant	Noble Clothing	1
Merchant	Noble Clothing	1
Merchant	Noble Clothing	1
Merchant	Noble Clothing	1
Merchant	Noble Clothing	1
Merchant	Noble Clothing	1
Merchant	Quartz	1
Merchant	Ruby	1

Vendor Shopping

Basics ~ Character Generation ~ Classes ~ The Party ~ Companions ~ Supporting Cast ~ **Equipment** ~ Bestiary ~ Walkthroughs ~ Side Quests ~ Random Encounters ~ Achievements/Trophies

Merchant Name	Item Name	Item Quantity
Dwarf Commoner Origin: Orzammar Commons (continued)		
Merchant	Sapphire	1
Merchant	Small Metal Round Shield	1
Merchant	Topaz	1
Elven Alienage		
Alarith's Store (after Landsmeet)	Choking Powder Cloud Trap Plans	1
Alarith's Store (after Landsmeet)	Current Map of Ferelden	1
Alarith's Store (after Landsmeet)	Deathroot	2
Alarith's Store (after Landsmeet)	Double-Baked Mabari Crunch	2
Alarith's Store (after Landsmeet)	Fire Crystal	2
Alarith's Store (after Landsmeet)	Flaming Coating Recipe	1
Alarith's Store (after Landsmeet)	Freezing Coating	1
Alarith's Store (after Landsmeet)	Freezing Coating Recipe	1
Alarith's Store (after Landsmeet)	Glamour Charm	1
Alarith's Store (after Landsmeet)	Greater Health Poultice	1
Alarith's Store (after Landsmeet)	Greater Injury Kit Recipe	1
Alarith's Store (after Landsmeet)	Greater Nature Salve	1
Alarith's Store (after Landsmeet)	Greater Warmth Balm	1
Alarith's Store (after Landsmeet)	Health Poultice	3
Alarith's Store (after Landsmeet)	Injury Kit	2
Alarith's Store (after Landsmeet)	Lesser Health Poultice	4
Alarith's Store (after Landsmeet)	Lesser Injury Kit	3
Alarith's Store (after Landsmeet)	Lesser Nature Salve	2
Alarith's Store (after Landsmeet)	Lesser Nature Salve Recipe	1
Alarith's Store (after Landsmeet)	Lesser Warmth Balm	2
Alarith's Store (after Landsmeet)	Lesser Warmth Balm Recipe	1
Alarith's Store (after Landsmeet)	Mabari Crunch	4
Alarith's Store (after Landsmeet)	Manual: Assassin	1
Alarith's Store (after Landsmeet)	Mild Choking Powder Trap	2
Alarith's Store (after Landsmeet)	Mild Sleeping Gas Trap	2
Alarith's Store (after Landsmeet)	Rock Salve	1
Alarith's Store (after Landsmeet)	Rock Salve Recipe	1
Alarith's Store (after Landsmeet)	Senior Enchanter's Robes	1
Alarith's Store (after Landsmeet)	Sleeping Gas Cloud Trap Plans	1
Alarith's Store (after Landsmeet)	Staff of the Ephemeral Order	1
Alarith's Store (after Landsmeet)	Swordsman's Girdle	1
Alarith's Store (after Landsmeet)	Tome of Skill and Sundry	1
Alarith's Store (after Landsmeet)	Trap Trigger	10
Alarith's Store (after Landsmeet)	Warpaint of the Waking Sea	1
Frostback Mountains		
Faryn	Arrow of Filth	20
Faryn	Chasind Crusher	1
Faryn	Chevalier's Gloves	1
Faryn	Concentrated Deathroot Extract Recipe	1
Faryn	Concentrator Agent	3
Faryn	Dagger	1
Faryn	Dalish Longbow	1
Faryn	Dal'Thanaan	1
Faryn	Darkspawn Crossbow	1
Faryn	Demonic Ichor	2
Faryn	Dwarven Longsword	1
Faryn	Dwarven Smith's Belt	1
Faryn	Elfroot	5
Faryn	Explosive Bolt	20
Faryn	Fleshrot Recipe	1
Faryn	Frostrock	4
Faryn	Glamour Charm	3

Merchant Name	Item Name	Item Quantity
Frostback Mountains (continued)		
Faryn	Grandmaster Silverite Rune	1
Faryn	Greater Lyrium Potion Recipe	1
Faryn	Heavy Chainmail	1
Faryn	Knight Commander's Plate	1
Faryn	Large Grease Trap Plans	1
Faryn	Lesser Ice Salve Recipe	1
Faryn	Lord's Hunting Jabot	1
Faryn	Magic Staff	1
Faryn	Portrait of a Goosegirl	1
Faryn	Qunari Infantry Helm	1
Faryn	Qunari Sword	1
Faryn	Scale Boots	1
Faryn	Small Grease Trap Plans	1
Faryn	Soulrot Trap Plans	1
Faryn	Spirit Shard	2
Faryn	Studded Leather Boots	1
Faryn	Sureshot Bolt	20
Faryn	Swift Salve Recipe	1
Faryn	Tevinter Shield	1
Faryn	Throwback Harness	1
Faryn	Toxin Extract	3
Haven		
New Shop Keeper	Acid Flask Recipe	1
New Shop Keeper	Acidic Coating Recipe	1
New Shop Keeper	Andraste's Arrows	10
New Shop Keeper	Apprentice's Amulet	1
New Shop Keeper	Axe	1
New Shop Keeper	Choking Powder Trap	1
New Shop Keeper	Choking Powder Trap Plans	1
New Shop Keeper	Concentrated Magebane	1
New Shop Keeper	Concentrated Soldier's Bane	1
New Shop Keeper	Dagger	1
New Shop Keeper	Freeze Bomb	2
New Shop Keeper	Greater Elixir of Grounding	1
New Shop Keeper	Greater Elixir of Grounding Recipe	1
New Shop Keeper	Greater Health Poultice	2
New Shop Keeper	Greater Ice Salve	1
New Shop Keeper	Greater Tome of the Mortal Vessel	1
New Shop Keeper	Health Poultice	3
New Shop Keeper	Ice Arrow	40
New Shop Keeper	Incense of Awareness	1
New Shop Keeper	Injury Kit	2
New Shop Keeper	Interesting Lure Trap Plans	1
New Shop Keeper	Kaddis of the King's Hounds	1
New Shop Keeper	Large Wooden Round Shield	1
New Shop Keeper	Lesser Elixir of Grounding	2
New Shop Keeper	Lesser Elixir of Grounding Recipe	1
New Shop Keeper	Lesser Ice Salve	2
New Shop Keeper	Lesser Ice Salve Recipe	1
New Shop Keeper	Lesser Injury Kit	3
New Shop Keeper	Longbow	1
New Shop Keeper	Longsword	1
New Shop Keeper	Lyrium Potion	3
New Shop Keeper	Lyrium Potion Recipe	1
New Shop Keeper	Mace	1
New Shop Keeper	Magebane	2

primagames.com

Merchant Name	Item Name	Item Quantity
Haven (continued)		
New Shop Keeper	Magebane Poison Recipe	1
New Shop Keeper	Mild Choking Powder Trap Plans	1
New Shop Keeper	Mild Lure Plans	1
New Shop Keeper	Shock Bomb	2
New Shop Keeper	Shock Coating	1
New Shop Keeper	Shock Trap	2
New Shop Keeper	Shortbow	1
New Shop Keeper	Small Shield	1
New Shop Keeper	Soldier's Bane	2
New Shop Keeper	Soldier's Bane Recipe	1
New Shop Keeper	Studded Leather Armor	1
New Shop Keeper	Studded Leather Boots	1
New Shop Keeper	Studded Leather Gloves	1
New Shop Keeper	Studded Leather Helm	1
New Shop Keeper	Swift Salve	1
New Shop Keeper	Wooden Kite Shield	1
Shop Keeper	Acid Flask Recipe	1
Shop Keeper	Acidic Coating Recipe	1
Shop Keeper	Andraste's Arrows	10
Shop Keeper	Axe	1
Shop Keeper	Dagger	1
Shop Keeper	Greater Elixir of Grounding	1
Shop Keeper	Health Poultice	2
Shop Keeper	Ice Arrow	40
Shop Keeper	Large Wooden Round Shield	1
Shop Keeper	Lesser Elixir of Grounding	2
Shop Keeper	Lesser Elixir of Grounding Recipe	1
Shop Keeper	Lesser Health Poultice	3
Shop Keeper	Lesser Ice Salve	2
Shop Keeper	Lesser Injury Kit	2
Shop Keeper	Lesser Lyrium Potion	3
Shop Keeper	Longsword	1
Shop Keeper	Lyrium Potion Recipe	1
Shop Keeper	Mace	1
Shop Keeper	Magebane	1
Shop Keeper	Mild Choking Powder Trap	2
Shop Keeper	Mild Choking Powder Trap Plans	1
Shop Keeper	Mild Lure Plans	1
Shop Keeper	Shock Bomb	2
Shop Keeper	Shock Trap	1
Shop Keeper	Shortbow	1
Shop Keeper	Small Shield	1
Shop Keeper	Soldier's Bane	1
Shop Keeper	Studded Leather Armor	1
Shop Keeper	Studded Leather Boots	1
Shop Keeper	Studded Leather Gloves	1
Shop Keeper	Studded Leather Helm	1
Shop Keeper	Swift Salve	1
Lake Calenhad		
Innkeeper	Apprentice's Amulet	1
Innkeeper	Concentrator Agent	2
Innkeeper	Distillation Agent	4
Innkeeper	Elfroot	7
Innkeeper	Fire Bomb	2
Innkeeper	Fire Crystal	2

Merchant Name	Item Name	Item Quantity
Lake Calenhad (continued)		
Innkeeper	Fire Trap Plans	1
Innkeeper	Flame Coating	1
Innkeeper	Flask	1
Innkeeper	Greater Health Poultice	1
Innkeeper	Greater Warmth Balm	1
Innkeeper	Health Poultice	3
Innkeeper	Incense of Awareness	3
Innkeeper	Injury Kit	1
Innkeeper	Kaddis of the Siege-Breaker	1
Innkeeper	Lesser Health Poultice	2
Innkeeper	Lesser Injury Kit	2
Innkeeper	Lesser Lyrium Potion	5
Innkeeper	Lesser Nature Salve	2
Innkeeper	Lesser Spirit Balm	1
Innkeeper	Lesser Warmth Balm	3
Innkeeper	Lifestone	3
Innkeeper	Lyrium Dust	3
Innkeeper	Lyrium Potion	2
Innkeeper	Metal Shard	2
Innkeeper	Mild Choking Powder Trap Plans	1
Innkeeper	Rock Salve	2
Innkeeper	Shock Bomb	1
Innkeeper	Small Grease Trap Plans	1
Innkeeper	Swift Salve	1
Innkeeper	Toxin Extract	1
Innkeeper	Trap Trigger	8
Innkeeper	Wine	1
Lothering		
Merchant	Acid Flask	2
Merchant	Acidic Coating	1
Merchant	Chainmail	1
Merchant	Chainmail Gloves	1
Merchant	Concentrated Deathroot Extract Recipe	1
Merchant	Concentrated Venom Recipe	1
Merchant	Corrupter Agent	5
Merchant	Crossbow	1
Merchant	Dagger	1
Merchant	Dar'Misu	1
Merchant	Deathroot	7
Merchant	Deep Mushroom	8
Merchant	Dwarven Large Round Shield	1
Merchant	Dwarven Longsword	1
Merchant	Dwarven Mace	1
Merchant	Dwarven Waraxe	1
Merchant	Enchanter's Staff	1
Merchant	Fire Bolt	20
Merchant	Fire Bomb	1
Merchant	Fire Bomb Recipe	1
Merchant	Fire Crystal	3
Merchant	Freeze Bomb Recipe	1
Merchant	Frostrock	2
Merchant	Health Poultice	2
Merchant	Helmet	1
Merchant	Large Wooden Round Shield	1
Merchant	Lesser Ice Salve	1
Merchant	Lesser Injury Kit	2

Vendor Shopping

Basics ~ Character Generation ~ Classes ~ The Party ~ Companions ~ Supporting Cast ~ **Equipment** ~ Bestiary ~ Walkthroughs ~ Side Quests ~ Random Encounters ~ Achievements/Trophies

Merchant Name	Item Name	Item Quantity	Merchant Name	Item Name	Item Quantity
Lothering (continued)			Lothering: Dane's Refuge (continued)		
Merchant	Lesser Warmth Balm	1	Barlin	Thorn of the Dead Gods	1
Merchant	Lifestone	5	Barlin	Trap Trigger	1
Merchant	Lyrium Potion	2	Barlin	Warpaint of the Vanguard	1
Merchant	Maul	1	Orzammar		
Merchant	Scale Armor	1	Alimar	Adder's Kiss Recipe	1
Merchant	Scale Boots	1	Alimar	Antivan Crossbow	1
Merchant	Splintmail Boots	1	Alimar	Arrow of Filth	20
Merchant	Splintmail Gloves	1	Alimar	Ash Warrior Axe	1
Merchant	Swift Salve	1	Alimar	Backhands	1
Merchant	Toxin Extract	4	Alimar	Choking Powder Trap Plans	1
Merchant	Wine	1	Alimar	Concentrated Venom Recipe	1
Lothering: Dane's Refuge			Alimar	Concentrator Agent	3
Barlin	Ale	1	Alimar	Corrupter Agent	1
Barlin	Amulet of Accord	1	Alimar	Crow Dagger	1
Barlin	Distillation Agent	4	Alimar	Crow Poison Recipe	1
Barlin	Elfroot	8	Alimar	Crow Shield	1
Barlin	Fire Arrow	20	Alimar	Dagger	1
Barlin	Flask	1	Alimar	Deathroot	6
Barlin	Glamour Charm	2	Alimar	Deep Mushroom	6
Barlin	Golden Rope Necklace	1	Alimar	Demonic Ichor	3
Barlin	Health Poultice	1	Alimar	Distillation Agent	4
Barlin	Ice Arrow	20	Alimar	Duster Leather Armor	1
Barlin	Incense of Awareness	1	Alimar	Duster Leather Boots	1
Barlin	Incense of Awareness Recipe	1	Alimar	Duster Leather Gloves	1
Barlin	Kaddis of the Courser	1	Alimar	Dwarven Mace	1
Barlin	Large Claw Trap	1	Alimar	Effort's Boots	1
Barlin	Large Claw Trap Plans	1	Alimar	Fire Arrow	40
Barlin	Large Shrapnel Trap Plans	1	Alimar	Fire Crystal	2
Barlin	Leather Boots	1	Alimar	Freeze Bomb Recipe	1
Barlin	Leather Gloves	1	Alimar	Freeze Trap Plans	1
Barlin	Lesser Health Poultice	3	Alimar	Freezing Coating Recipe	1
Barlin	Lesser Injury Kit	2	Alimar	Frostrock	6
Barlin	Lesser Injury Kit Recipe	1	Alimar	Glamour Charm	2
Barlin	Lesser Lyrium Potion	2	Alimar	Ice Bolt	40
Barlin	Lesser Nature Salve	1	Alimar	Imperial Reinforced Gloves	1
Barlin	Lifestone	2	Alimar	Kaddis of the Trickster	1
Barlin	Lightning Rod	1	Alimar	Knockback Bolt	20
Barlin	Longbow	1	Alimar	Lyrium Dust	2
Barlin	Lyrium Dust	3	Alimar	Manual: Bard	1
Barlin	Lyrium Potion Recipe	1	Alimar	Mild Choking Powder Trap Plans	1
Barlin	Mabari Crunch	4	Alimar	Mild Sleeping Gas Trap Plans	1
Barlin	Metal Shard	5	Alimar	Orlesian Bow	1
Barlin	Mild Lure	1	Alimar	Senior Enchanter's Robes	1
Barlin	Mild Lure Plans	1	Alimar	Sleeping Gas Trap Plans	1
Barlin	Rock Salve	1	Alimar	Toxin Extract	4
Barlin	Sailor's Crossbow	1	Alimar	Trap Trigger	1
Barlin	Shiny Gold Ring	1	Figor	Acid Flask	2
Barlin	Shortbow	1	Figor	Concentrator Agent	2
Barlin	Small Claw Trap	3	Figor	Deep Mushroom	8
Barlin	Small Grease Trap	1	Figor	Distillation Agent	3
Barlin	Small Grease Trap Plans	1	Figor	Elfroot	7
Barlin	Small Metal Round Shield	1	Figor	Fire Crystal	3
Barlin	Small Shield	1	Figor	Flask	1
Barlin	Small Shrapnel Trap	2	Figor	Frostrock	3
Barlin	Studded Helmet	1	Figor	Frozen Lightning	2
Barlin	Studded Leather Armor	1	Figor	Greater Health Poultice Recipe	1
Barlin	Studded Leather Boots	1	Figor	Health Poultice	3
Barlin	Studded Leather Gloves	1			

Dragon Age: Origins
PRIMA Official Game Guide

Merchant Name	Item Name	Item Quantity
Orzammar (continued)		
Figor	Health Poultice Recipe	1
Figor	Injury Kit	1
Figor	Lesser Health Poultice	4
Figor	Lesser Ice Salve	1
Figor	Lesser Injury Kit	3
Figor	Lesser Injury Kit Recipe	1
Figor	Lesser Lyrium Potion	3
Figor	Lesser Nature Salve	1
Figor	Lesser Warmth Balm	2
Figor	Lifestone	5
Figor	Lyrium Dust	4
Figor	Magebane	1
Figor	Mild Sleeping Gas Trap	1
Figor	Rock Salve	3
Figor	Small Grease Trap	1
Figor	Spirit Shard	1
Janar	Crossbow	1
Janar	Dwarven Heavy Armor	1
Janar	Dwarven Heavy Boots	1
Janar	Dwarven Heavy Gloves	1
Janar	Dwarven Large Round Shield	1
Janar	Dwarven Longsword	1
Janar	Dwarven Mace	1
Janar	Dwarven Massive Armor	1
Janar	Dwarven Massive Armored Boots	1
Janar	Dwarven Massive Armored Gloves	1
Janar	Dwarven Waraxe	1
Janar	Heavy Dwarven Helmet	1
Janar	Heavy Metal Shield	1
Janar	Large Caltrop Trap Plans	1
Janar	Large Claw Trap Plans	1
Janar	Large Shrapnel Trap Plans	1
Janar	Metal Shard	10
Janar	Rock-Knocker	1
Orzammar: Commons		
Garin	Crossbow	1
Garin	Dagger	1
Garin	Diamond Maul	1
Garin	Dwarven Armor	1
Garin	Dwarven Armored Gloves	1
Garin	Dwarven Heavy Boots	1
Garin	Dwarven Helmet	1
Garin	Dwarven Large Round Shield	1
Garin	Dwarven Longsword	1
Garin	Dwarven Waraxe	1
Garin	Fire Bolt	40
Garin	Gemmed Bracelet	1
Garin	Gold Amulet	1
Garin	Golden Mirror	1
Garin	Heavy Metal Shield	1
Garin	Ice Bolt	40
Garin	Knockback Bolt	20
Garin	Lifegiver	1
Garin	Metal Shard	6
Garin	Precision-Geared Recurve	1
Garin	The Rose's Thorn	1

Merchant Name	Item Name	Item Quantity
Orzammar: Commons (continued)		
Garin	Tome of Physical Technique	1
Legnar	Alley King's Flagon	1
Legnar	Dagger	1
Legnar	Duster Leather Armor	1
Legnar	Duster Leather Boots	1
Legnar	Duster Leather Gloves	1
Legnar	Dwarven Longsword	1
Legnar	Dwarven Mace	1
Legnar	Fire Crystal	3
Legnar	Glamour Charm	4
Legnar	Gold Earrings	1
Legnar	Golden Symbol of Andraste	1
Legnar	Interesting Lure Trap Plans	1
Legnar	Leather Helm	1
Legnar	Mild Lure Plans	1
Legnar	Quicksilver Arming Cap	1
Legnar	Shadow of the Empire	1
Legnar	Silver Demon Head Ring	1
Legnar	Silverhammer's Evaders	1
Legnar	Small Metal Round Shield	1
Legnar	Spirit Shard	2
Legnar	Tome of the Mortal Vessel	1
Ostagar		
Quartermaster	Acid Flask Recipe	1
Quartermaster	Acolyte's Staff	1
Quartermaster	Axe	1
Quartermaster	Backpack	1
Quartermaster	Chainmail	1
Quartermaster	Chainmail Boots	1
Quartermaster	Chainmail Gloves	1
Quartermaster	Concentrated Venom Recipe	1
Quartermaster	Corrupter Agent	3
Quartermaster	Crossbow	1
Quartermaster	Dagger	1
Quartermaster	Deathroot	3
Quartermaster	Deep Mushroom	5
Quartermaster	Distillation Agent	4
Quartermaster	Elfroot	8
Quartermaster	Flask	1
Quartermaster	Greatsword	1
Quartermaster	Health Poultice Recipe	1
Quartermaster	Helmet	1
Quartermaster	Large Claw Trap Plans	1
Quartermaster	Large Wooden Round Shield	1
Quartermaster	Leather Armor	1
Quartermaster	Leather Boots	1
Quartermaster	Leather Gloves	1
Quartermaster	Leather Helm	1
Quartermaster	Lesser Health Poultice	8
Quartermaster	Lesser Injury Kit	3
Quartermaster	Lesser Injury Kit Recipe	1
Quartermaster	Lesser Lyrium Potion	6
Quartermaster	Lifestone	2
Quartermaster	Longsword	1
Quartermaster	Lyrium Dust	3
Quartermaster	Mabari Crunch	2
Quartermaster	Mace	1

106

Vendor Shopping

Basics ~ Character Generation ~ Classes ~ The Party ~ Companions ~ Supporting Cast ~ **Equipment** ~ Bestiary ~ Walkthroughs ~ Side Quests ~ Random Encounters ~ Achievements/Trophies

Merchant Name	Item Name	Item Quantity
Ostagar (continued)		
Quartermaster	Metal Shard	5
Quartermaster	Scale Armor	1
Quartermaster	Scale Boots	1
Quartermaster	Scale Gloves	1
Quartermaster	Shortbow	1
Quartermaster	Small Grease Trap Plans	1
Quartermaster	Small Metal Round Shield	1
Quartermaster	Small Shield	1
Quartermaster	Splintmail	1
Quartermaster	Splintmail Boots	1
Quartermaster	Splintmail Gloves	1
Quartermaster	Studded Helmet	1
Quartermaster	Studded Leather Armor	1
Quartermaster	Studded Leather Boots	1
Quartermaster	Studded Leather Gloves	1
Quartermaster	Toxin Extract	3
Quartermaster	Trap Trigger	8
Quartermaster (second store)	Acid Flask	1
Quartermaster (second store)	Battleaxe	1
Quartermaster (second store)	Concentrated Deathroot Extract Recipe	1
Quartermaster (second store)	Double-Baked Mabari Crunch	1
Quartermaster (second store)	Double-Baked Mabari Crunch Recipe	1
Quartermaster (second store)	Enchanter's Footing	1
Quartermaster (second store)	Enchanter's Staff	1
Quartermaster (second store)	Fire Arrow	20
Quartermaster (second store)	Fire Bolt	20
Quartermaster (second store)	Fire Bomb	1
Quartermaster (second store)	Fire Bomb Recipe	1
Quartermaster (second store)	Glamour Charm	2
Quartermaster (second store)	Health Poultice	3
Quartermaster (second store)	Heavy Chainmail	1
Quartermaster (second store)	Heavy Chainmail Boots	1
Quartermaster (second store)	Heavy Chainmail Gloves	1
Quartermaster (second store)	Ice Arrow	20
Quartermaster (second store)	Ice Bolt	20
Quartermaster (second store)	Injury Kit	2
Quartermaster (second store)	Lesser Nature Salve	1
Quartermaster (second store)	Lesser Warmth Balm	1
Quartermaster (second store)	Longbow	1
Quartermaster (second store)	Lyrium Potion	2
Quartermaster (second store)	Maul	1
Quartermaster (second store)	Metal Kite Shield	1
Quartermaster (second store)	Mild Lure Plans	1
Quartermaster (second store)	Mild Sleeping Gas Trap Plans	1
Quartermaster (second store)	Rock Salve	1
Quartermaster (second store)	Rock Salve Recipe	1
Quartermaster (second store)	Soldier's Helm	1
Quartermaster (second store)	Soulrot Bomb	1
Quartermaster (second store)	Wooden Kite Shield	1
Tranquil Merchant	Incense of Awareness	1
Tranquil Merchant	Lesser Health Poultice	2
Tranquil Merchant	Lesser Lyrium Potion	1
Tranquil Merchant	Lesser Spirit Balm	1
Party Camp		
Bodahn's Wares	Angled Strikers	1
Bodahn's Wares	Backpack	1

Merchant Name	Item Name	Item Quantity
Party Camp (continued)		
Bodahn's Wares	Bard's Dancing Shoes	1
Bodahn's Wares	Blackmetal Torque	1
Bodahn's Wares	Collective Arming Cowl	1
Bodahn's Wares	Concentrator Agent	1
Bodahn's Wares	Conspirator's Foil	1
Bodahn's Wares	Corrupter Agent	1
Bodahn's Wares	Dalish Hunter's Belt	1
Bodahn's Wares	Dalish Pendant	1
Bodahn's Wares	Distillation Agent	1
Bodahn's Wares	Dwarven Merchant's Belt	1
Bodahn's Wares	Earthheart's Portable Bulwark	1
Bodahn's Wares	Ember	1
Bodahn's Wares	Enchanter's Arming Cap	1
Bodahn's Wares	Expert Lightning Rune	1
Bodahn's Wares	Flask	1
Bodahn's Wares	Golden Rope Necklace	1
Bodahn's Wares	Grandmaster Frost Rune	1
Bodahn's Wares	Grandmaster Lightning Rune	1
Bodahn's Wares	Grandmaster Slow Rune	1
Bodahn's Wares	Hailstone	1
Bodahn's Wares	Health Poultice	2
Bodahn's Wares	Imperial Weavers	1
Bodahn's Wares	Journeyman Dweomer Rune	1
Bodahn's Wares	Journeyman Flame Rune	1
Bodahn's Wares	Journeyman Hale Rune	1
Bodahn's Wares	Journeyman Silverite Rune	1
Bodahn's Wares	Lesser Health Poultice	4
Bodahn's Wares	Lesser Injury Kit	4
Bodahn's Wares	Lesser Lyrium Potion	4
Bodahn's Wares	Longbowman's Belt	1
Bodahn's Wares	Lyrium Potion	2
Bodahn's Wares	Mabari Crunch	4
Bodahn's Wares	Manual: Ranger	1
Bodahn's Wares	Manual: Templar	1
Bodahn's Wares	Master Lightning Rune	1
Bodahn's Wares	Novice Cold Iron Rune	1
Bodahn's Wares	Novice Dweomer Rune	1
Bodahn's Wares	Novice Frost Rune	1
Bodahn's Wares	Novice Lighting Rune	1
Bodahn's Wares	Par Vollen Willstone	1
Bodahn's Wares	Proving Helm	1
Bodahn's Wares	Silverhammer's Tackmasters	1
Bodahn's Wares	Spirit Hands	1
Bodahn's Wares	Sylvan's Mercy	1
Bodahn's Wares	The Spellward	1
Bodahn's Wares	The Veshialle	1
Bodahn's Wares	Tome of Arcane Technique	1
Bodahn's Wares	Tome of Physical Technique	1
Bodahn's Wares	Trap Trigger	24
Bodahn's Wares (after Landsmeet)	Arrow of Filth	20
Bodahn's Wares (after Landsmeet)	Axe	1
Bodahn's Wares (after Landsmeet)	Battleaxe	1
Bodahn's Wares (after Landsmeet)	Chainmail	1
Bodahn's Wares (after Landsmeet)	Concentrator Agent	1
Bodahn's Wares (after Landsmeet)	Corrupter Agent	1
Bodahn's Wares (after Landsmeet)	Crossbow	1
Bodahn's Wares (after Landsmeet)	Dagger	1
Bodahn's Wares (after Landsmeet)	Distillation Agent	1

Merchant Name	Item Name	Item Quantity
Party Camp (continued)		
Bodahn's Wares (after Landsmeet)	Double-Baked Mabari Crunch	4
Bodahn's Wares (after Landsmeet)	Dwarven Large Round Shield	1
Bodahn's Wares (after Landsmeet)	Elf-Flight Arrow	40
Bodahn's Wares (after Landsmeet)	Explosive Bolt	20
Bodahn's Wares (after Landsmeet)	Fire Arrow	40
Bodahn's Wares (after Landsmeet)	Fire Bolt	40
Bodahn's Wares (after Landsmeet)	First Enchanter's Cowl	1
Bodahn's Wares (after Landsmeet)	Flask	1
Bodahn's Wares (after Landsmeet)	Grandmaster Frost Rune	1
Bodahn's Wares (after Landsmeet)	Greater Elixir of Grounding	1
Bodahn's Wares (after Landsmeet)	Greater Health Poultice	4
Bodahn's Wares (after Landsmeet)	Greater Ice Salve	1
Bodahn's Wares (after Landsmeet)	Greater Injury Kit	3
Bodahn's Wares (after Landsmeet)	Greater Lyrium Potion	4
Bodahn's Wares (after Landsmeet)	Greater Nature Salve	1
Bodahn's Wares (after Landsmeet)	Greater Spirit Balm	1
Bodahn's Wares (after Landsmeet)	Greater Warmth Balm	1
Bodahn's Wares (after Landsmeet)	Greatsword	1
Bodahn's Wares (after Landsmeet)	Heaven's Wrath	1
Bodahn's Wares (after Landsmeet)	Heavy Chainmail Boots	1
Bodahn's Wares (after Landsmeet)	Heavy Metal Shield	1
Bodahn's Wares (after Landsmeet)	Heavy Plate Gloves	1
Bodahn's Wares (after Landsmeet)	Helmet	1
Bodahn's Wares (after Landsmeet)	Ice Arrow	40
Bodahn's Wares (after Landsmeet)	Ice Bolt	40
Bodahn's Wares (after Landsmeet)	Knockback Bolt	20
Bodahn's Wares (after Landsmeet)	Longbow	1
Bodahn's Wares (after Landsmeet)	Longsword	1
Bodahn's Wares (after Landsmeet)	Mace	1
Bodahn's Wares (after Landsmeet)	Magic Staff	1
Bodahn's Wares (after Landsmeet)	Master Paralyze Rune	1
Bodahn's Wares (after Landsmeet)	Maul	1
Bodahn's Wares (after Landsmeet)	Potent Health Poultice	2
Bodahn's Wares (after Landsmeet)	Potent Lyrium Potion	2
Bodahn's Wares (after Landsmeet)	Scale Armor	1
Bodahn's Wares (after Landsmeet)	Shortbow	1
Bodahn's Wares (after Landsmeet)	Soldier's Helm	1
Bodahn's Wares (after Landsmeet)	Splintmail	1
Bodahn's Wares (after Landsmeet)	Studded Leather Armor	1
Bodahn's Wares (after Landsmeet)	Studded Leather Boots	1
Bodahn's Wares (after Landsmeet)	Studded Leather Gloves	1
Bodahn's Wares (after Landsmeet)	Sureshot Bolt	20
Bodahn's Wares (after Landsmeet)	Tome of Physical Technique	1
Bodahn's Wares (after Landsmeet)	Trap Trigger	1
Sandal's Goods (after Landsmeet)	Arrow of Filth	20
Sandal's Goods (after Landsmeet)	Axe	1
Sandal's Goods (after Landsmeet)	Battleaxe	1
Sandal's Goods (after Landsmeet)	Chainmail Boots	1
Sandal's Goods (after Landsmeet)	Chainmail Gloves	1
Sandal's Goods (after Landsmeet)	Concentrator Agent	1
Sandal's Goods (after Landsmeet)	Corrupter Agent	1
Sandal's Goods (after Landsmeet)	Crossbow	1
Sandal's Goods (after Landsmeet)	Dagger	1
Sandal's Goods (after Landsmeet)	Distillation Agent	1
Sandal's Goods (after Landsmeet)	Double-Baked Mabari Crunch	10

Merchant Name	Item Name	Item Quantity
Party Camp (continued)		
Sandal's Goods (after Landsmeet)	Elf-Flight Arrow	40
Sandal's Goods (after Landsmeet)	Expert Lightning Rune	1
Sandal's Goods (after Landsmeet)	Expert Silverite Rune	1
Sandal's Goods (after Landsmeet)	Explosive Bolt	20
Sandal's Goods (after Landsmeet)	Fire Arrow	40
Sandal's Goods (after Landsmeet)	Fire Bolt	40
Sandal's Goods (after Landsmeet)	Flask	1
Sandal's Goods (after Landsmeet)	Greater Elixir of Grounding	3
Sandal's Goods (after Landsmeet)	Greater Health Poultice	10
Sandal's Goods (after Landsmeet)	Greater Ice Salve	3
Sandal's Goods (after Landsmeet)	Greater Injury Kit	10
Sandal's Goods (after Landsmeet)	Greater Lyrium Potion	10
Sandal's Goods (after Landsmeet)	Greater Nature Salve	3
Sandal's Goods (after Landsmeet)	Greater Spirit Balm	3
Sandal's Goods (after Landsmeet)	Greater Warmth Balm	3
Sandal's Goods (after Landsmeet)	Greatsword	1
Sandal's Goods (after Landsmeet)	Heavy Chainmail	1
Sandal's Goods (after Landsmeet)	Heavy Chainmail Gloves	1
Sandal's Goods (after Landsmeet)	Heavy Plate Armor	1
Sandal's Goods (after Landsmeet)	Heavy Plate Boots	1
Sandal's Goods (after Landsmeet)	Ice Arrow	40
Sandal's Goods (after Landsmeet)	Ice Bolt	40
Sandal's Goods (after Landsmeet)	Knockback Bolt	20
Sandal's Goods (after Landsmeet)	Lesser Spirit Balm	4
Sandal's Goods (after Landsmeet)	Longbow	1
Sandal's Goods (after Landsmeet)	Longsword	1
Sandal's Goods (after Landsmeet)	Mace	1
Sandal's Goods (after Landsmeet)	Magic Staff	1
Sandal's Goods (after Landsmeet)	Master Dweomer Rune	1
Sandal's Goods (after Landsmeet)	Maul	1
Sandal's Goods (after Landsmeet)	Metal Kite Shield	1
Sandal's Goods (after Landsmeet)	Novice Frost Rune	1
Sandal's Goods (after Landsmeet)	Potent Health Poultice	4
Sandal's Goods (after Landsmeet)	Potent Lyrium Potion	4
Sandal's Goods (after Landsmeet)	Scale Boots	1
Sandal's Goods (after Landsmeet)	Scale Gloves	1
Sandal's Goods (after Landsmeet)	Shortbow	1
Sandal's Goods (after Landsmeet)	Small Metal Round Shield	1
Sandal's Goods (after Landsmeet)	Soldier's Heavy Helm	1
Sandal's Goods (after Landsmeet)	Splintmail Boots	1
Sandal's Goods (after Landsmeet)	Splintmail Gloves	1
Sandal's Goods (after Landsmeet)	Studded Leather Helm	1
Sandal's Goods (after Landsmeet)	Sureshot Bolt	20
Sandal's Goods (after Landsmeet)	Trap Trigger	1
Sandal's Goods (after Landsmeet)	Warpaint of the Waking Sea	1
Random Encounter		
Dwarven Merchant	Apprentice's Amulet	1
Dwarven Merchant	Blue Satin Shoes	1
Dwarven Merchant	Ceremonial Armored Boots	1
Dwarven Merchant	Crossbow	1
Dwarven Merchant	Dagger	1
Dwarven Merchant	Diamond Maul	1
Dwarven Merchant	Dwarven Armor	1
Dwarven Merchant	Dwarven Armored Boots	1
Dwarven Merchant	Dwarven Armored Gloves	1

Merchant Name	Item Name	Item Quantity
Random Encounter (continued)		
Dwarven Merchant	Dwarven Heavy Armor	1
Dwarven Merchant	Dwarven Helmet	1
Dwarven Merchant	Dwarven Longsword	1
Dwarven Merchant	Dwarven Mace	1
Dwarven Merchant	Dwarven Waraxe	1
Dwarven Merchant	Explosive Bolt	20
Dwarven Merchant	Fire Bolt	40
Dwarven Merchant	Freeze Trap Plans	1
Dwarven Merchant	Heavy Dwarven Helmet	1
Dwarven Merchant	Ice Bolt	40
Dwarven Merchant	Knockback Bolt	20
Dwarven Merchant	Metal Shard	5
Dwarven Merchant	Ornate Leather Belt	1
Dwarven Merchant	Painting of a Rebel Queen	1
Dwarven Merchant	Shock Trap Plans	1
Dwarven Merchant	Silver Sword of Mercy	1
Dwarven Merchant	Temperament	1
Dwarven Merchant	Tome of Skill and Sundry	1
Redcliffe		
Blacksmith	Axe	1
Blacksmith	Battleaxe	1
Blacksmith	Chainmail Boots	1
Blacksmith	Dwarven Armor	1
Blacksmith	Far Song	1
Blacksmith	Greatsword	1
Blacksmith	Helmet	1
Blacksmith	Large Caltrop Trap Plans	1
Blacksmith	Large Claw Trap Plans	1
Blacksmith	Longsword	1
Blacksmith	Maul	1
Blacksmith	Metal Kite Shield	1
Blacksmith	Metal Shard	5
Blacksmith	Scale Armor	1
Blacksmith	Scale Gloves	1
Blacksmith	Scale Gloves	1
Blacksmith	Small Metal Round Shield	1
Blacksmith	Splintmail Boots	1
Lloyd's Tavern	Ale	1
Lloyd's Tavern	Deep Mushroom	2
Lloyd's Tavern	Double-Baked Mabari Crunch Recipe	1
Lloyd's Tavern	Elfroot	6
Lloyd's Tavern	Flask	1
Lloyd's Tavern	Health Poultice	1
Lloyd's Tavern	Health Poultice Recipe	1
Lloyd's Tavern	Lesser Health Poultice	2
Lloyd's Tavern	Lesser Injury Kit	2
Lloyd's Tavern	Lesser Injury Kit Recipe	1
Lloyd's Tavern	Mabari Crunch	3
Lloyd's Tavern (second store)	Deep Mushroom	2
Lloyd's Tavern (second store)	Double-Baked Mabari Crunch Recipe	1
Lloyd's Tavern (second store)	Elfroot	4
Lloyd's Tavern (second store)	Flask	8
Lloyd's Tavern (second store)	Health Poultice	1
Lloyd's Tavern (second store)	Health Poultice Recipe	1

Merchant Name	Item Name	Item Quantity
Redcliffe (continued)		
Lloyd's Tavern (second store)	Lesser Health Poultice	2
Lloyd's Tavern (second store)	Lesser Injury Kit	2
Lloyd's Tavern (second store)	Lesser Injury Kit Recipe	1
Lloyd's Tavern (second store)	Mabari Crunch	2
Lloyd's Tavern (second store)	Wine	1
Owen	Axe	1
Owen	Dagger	1
Owen	Greatsword	1
Owen	Heavy Chainmail Boots	1
Owen	Heavy Chainmail Gloves	1
Owen	Helmet	1
Owen	Large Caltrop Trap Plans	1
Owen	Large Shrapnel Trap Plans	1
Owen	Longsword	1
Owen	Mace	1
Owen	Metal Kite Shield	1
Owen	Metal Shard	4
Owen	Scale Armor	1
Owen	Scale Boots	1
Owen	Scale Gloves	1
Owen	Small Metal Round Shield	1
Owen	Soldier's Helm	1
Owen	Splintmail	1
Owen	Splintmail Boots	1
Owen	Splintmail Gloves	1
Owen (second store)	Axe	1
Owen (second store)	Battleaxe	1
Owen (second store)	Boots of Diligence	1
Owen (second store)	Chainmail	1
Owen (second store)	Chainmail Boots	1
Owen (second store)	Chainmail Gloves	1
Owen (second store)	Dagger	1
Owen (second store)	Expert Flame Rune	1
Owen (second store)	Expert Frost Rune	1
Owen (second store)	Expert Silverite Rune	1
Owen (second store)	Grandmaster Hale Rune	1
Owen (second store)	Greatsword	1
Owen (second store)	Heavy Chainmail	1
Owen (second store)	Heavy Chainmail Boots	1
Owen (second store)	Heavy Chainmail Gloves	1
Owen (second store)	Heavy Metal Shield	1
Owen (second store)	Heavy Plate Armor	1
Owen (second store)	Helmet	1
Owen (second store)	Large Caltrop Trap Plans	1
Owen (second store)	Large Shrapnel Trap Plans	1
Owen (second store)	Longsword	1
Owen (second store)	Mace	1
Owen (second store)	Maul	1
Owen (second store)	Metal Kite Shield	1
Owen (second store)	Metal Shard	10
Owen (second store)	Poisoned Caltrop Trap Plans	1
Owen (second store)	Pyromancer's Brand	1
Owen (second store)	Soldier's Heavy Helm	1
Owen (second store)	Soldier's Helm	1
Owen (second store)	Warpaint of the West Hills	1

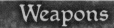

Weapons

If your character loves to hack-and-slash, you'll be happy to scrutinize every weapon. Even if you don't jump into the thick of things often, a weapon can still provide valuable bonuses to attributes and special abilities.

What weapon is the right fit for you? First, identify what sort of weapon you want to carry around: a one-handed melee weapon, a two-hander, or a ranged bow or crossbow for distance damage. Next, check out the weapon's tier level; tiers range from tier 1 to tier 7, and generally the higher tier equals more damage and will prove more useful. Compare the weapon's damage score to other weapons you have in your inventory (or on local vendors) and choose the highest damage score if other bonuses don't matter. See the following tables for more details on the different quality levels.

Weapon Tiers

Axes						
Tier	Material	Damage	Armor Penetration	Critical Chance	Strength Required	N/A
1	Iron	6	2	1	11	—
2	Grey Iron	6.6	2.3	1.1	13	—
3	Steel	7.2	2.6	1.2	15	—
4	Veridium	7.8	2.9	1.3	19	—
5	Red Steel	8.4	3.2	1.4	25	—
6	Silverite	9	3.5	1.5	27	—
7	Dragonbone	9.6	4.2	1.6	31	—

Battleaxes						
Tier	Material	Damage	Armor Penetration	Critical Chance	Strength Required	N/A
1	Iron	10	3	3	18	—
2	Grey Iron	11	3.45	3.3	20	—
3	Steel	12	3.9	3.6	22	—
4	Veridium	13	4.35	3.9	26	—
5	Red Steel	14	4.8	4.2	32	—
6	Silverite	15	5.25	4.5	34	—
7	Dragonbone	16	6.3	4.8	38	—

Crossbows						
Tier	Material	Damage	Armor Penetration	Range	Critical Chance	Strength Required
1	Horn	8	5	40	2	10
2	Ash	8.8	6	42	2.2	12
3	Yew	9.6	7	44	2.4	14
4	Whitewood	10.4	8	46	2.6	18
5	Ironbark	11.2	9	48	2.8	24
6	Sylvanwood	12	10	50	3	26
7	Dragonthorn	12.8	11	52	3.2	30

Daggers						
Tier	Material	Damage	Armor Penetration	Critical Chance	Dexterity Required	N/A
1	Iron	4	4	3	10	—
2	Grey Iron	4.4	4.6	3.3	12	—
3	Steel	4.8	5.2	3.6	14	—
4	Veridium	5.2	5.8	3.9	18	—
5	Red Steel	5.6	6.4	4.2	24	—
6	Silverite	6	7	4.5	26	—
7	Dragonbone	6.4	8.4	4.8	30	—

Greatswords						
Tier	Material	Damage	Armor Penetration	Critical Chance	Strength Required	N/A
1	Iron	11	3	1.5	18	—
2	Grey Iron	12.1	3.45	1.65	20	—
3	Steel	13.2	3.9	1.8	22	—
4	Veridium	14.3	4.35	1.95	26	—
5	Red Steel	15.4	4.8	2.1	32	—

Weapons

Basics ~ Character Generation ~ Classes ~ The Party ~ Companions ~ Supporting Cast ~ **Equipment** ~ Bestiary ~ Walkthroughs ~ Side Quests ~ Random Encounters ~ Achievements/Trophies

Greatswords (continued)

Tier	Material	Damage	Armor Penetration	Critical Chance	Strength Required	N/A
6	Silverite	16.5	5.25	2.25	34	—
7	Dragonbone	17.6	6.3	2.4	38	—

Longbows

Tier	Material	Damage	Armor Penetration	Range	Critical Chance	Dexterity Required
1	Horn	6	4	35	1	14
2	Ash	6.6	4.8	36.75	1.1	16
3	Yew	7.2	5.6	38.5	1.2	18
4	Whitewood	7.8	6.4	40.25	1.3	22
5	Ironbark	8.4	7.2	42	1.4	28
6	Sylvanwood	9	8	43.75	1.5	30
7	Dragonthorn	9.6	8.8	45.5	1.6	34

Longswords

Tier	Material	Damage	Armor Penetration	Critical Chance	Strength Required	N/A
1	Iron	7	2	2	11	—
2	Grey Iron	7.7	2.3	2.2	13	—
3	Steel	8.4	2.6	2.4	15	—
4	Veridium	9.1	2.9	2.6	19	—
5	Red Steel	9.8	3.2	2.8	25	—
6	Silverite	10.5	3.5	3	27	—
7	Dragonbone	11.2	4.2	3.2	31	—

Maces

Tier	Material	Damage	Armor Penetration	Critical Chance	Strength Required	N/A
1	Iron	5	4	0.5	12	—
2	Grey Iron	5.5	4.6	0.55	14	—
3	Steel	6	5.2	0.6	16	—
4	Veridium	6.5	5.8	0.65	20	—
5	Red Steel	7	6.4	0.7	26	—
6	Silverite	7.5	7	0.75	28	—
7	Dragonbone	8	8.4	0.8	32	—

Mauls

Tier	Material	Damage	Armor Penetration	Critical Chance	Strength Required	N/A
1	Iron	9	7	0.5	18	—
2	Grey Iron	9.9	8.05	0.55	20	—
3	Steel	10.8	9.1	0.6	22	—
4	Veridium	11.7	10.15	0.65	26	—
5	Red Steel	12.6	11.2	0.7	32	—
6	Silverite	13.5	12.25	0.75	34	—
7	Dragonbone	14.4	14.7	0.8	38	—

Shortbows

Tier	Material	Damage	Armor Penetration	Range	Critical Chance	Dexterity Required
1	Horn	5	3	20	1	10
2	Ash	5.5	3.6	21	1.1	12
3	Yew	6	4.2	22	1.2	14
4	Whitewood	6.5	4.8	23	1.3	18
5	Ironbark	7	5.4	24	1.4	24
6	Sylvanwood	7.5	6	25	1.5	26
7	Dragonthorn	8	6.6	26	1.6	30

Staves

Tier	Material	Damage	Armor Penetration	Range	Spellpower	Magic Required
1	Iron	4	20	50	1	16
2	Grey Iron	4.4	23	51.25	2	18
3	Steel	4.8	26	52.5	3	20
4	Veridium	5.2	29	53.75	4	24
5	Red Steel	5.6	32	55	5	30
6	Silverite	6	35	56.25	6	32
7	Dragonbone	6.4	40	57.5	7	36

Unique Weapons

Certain weapons have restrictions, such as Spellweaver, a unique sword crafted for a mage who specializes as an arcane warrior. Sell those if you receive one that nobody in your party can use. Below your damage score, critical chance shows you the likelihood of dealing critical strikes, and armor penetration calculates how much more damage you can punch through armor. Higher values in critical chance and armor penetration can lean you toward one weapon over another that may have a similar damage score.

As you level up, more and more weapons (as well as armor and accessories) will come with attribute bonuses and special abilities. Now you must decide: Do you take the weapon with the greater damage score, or do you choose the weapon with the better bonuses? If you're playing pure DPS, damage may be the most important factor; if your play style is more versatile, bonuses tend to be the way to go. Ideally, you will find a weapon that has the maximum damage score for your level range and great bonuses to power your character up.

TIP

Higher-tier weapons may come with one to three rune slots, which you can use to customize your weapon with powers that you choose (damage bonuses, paralysis, spell resistance, etc.). Don't underestimate weapons with rune slots! It may be better to hold a rune-slot weapon with fewer natural bonuses because as you add more powerful runes, the weapon gets more and more powerful.

Axes						
Name	Material	Quality #1	Quality #2	Quality #3	Quality #4	Quality #5	Quality #6
Aodh	Silverite	+3% Melee Critical Chance	+20 Fire Resistance	-5 Cold Resistance	+1 Fire Damage	—	—
Ash Warrior Axe	All Metals	+2 Attack	—	—	—	—	—
Axameter	Silverite	+2 Damage	Lucky	+10% Critical Damage	+2 Damage vs. Dragons		
Axe of the Grey	Silverite	+3% Melee Critical Chance	+4 Armor Penetration	+3 Damage vs. Darkspawn	—	—	—
Biteback Axe	Silverite	+3 Armor Penetration	+15% Critical Damage	Required: Rogue	No Attribute Requirements	—	—
Bloodline	Red Steel	+3 Dexterity	+10 Spirit Resistance	+2 Armor Penetration	+2 Damage vs. Darkspawn	—	—
Dal'Thanu	All Metals	—	—	—	—	—	—
Darkspawn Waraxe	Iron/Grey Iron/Steel	+1 Armor Penetration	-1 Dexterity	—	—	—	—
Deygan's Dal'Thanu	Veridium	+10 Nature Resistance	+4 Attack	—	—	—	—
Everd's Axe	Veridium	—	—	—	—	—	—
The Veshialle	Dragonbone	+2 Strength	+5% Melee Critical Chance	+1.0 Combat Stamina Regeneration	+10% Critical Damage	+2 Nature Damage	—
Battleaxes						
Name	Material	Quality #1	Quality #2	Quality #3	Quality #4	Quality #5	Quality #6
Axe of the Vashoth	Red Steel	+1 Strength	+2 Willpower	+1 Damage	—	—	—
Barbarian Axe	All Metals	—	—	—	—	—	—
Dal'Thanaan	All Metals	—	—	—	—	—	—
Darkspawn Battleaxe	Iron/Grey Iron/Steel	+1 Armor Penetration	-1 Dexterity	—	—	—	—
Faith's Edge	Silverite	+2 Willpower	+5% Critical Damage	—	—	—	—
Griffon's Beak	Silverite	Required: Grey Warden	Item Set 1	—	—	—	—
Maetashear War Axe	Silverite	+1 Damage	+5% Melee Critical Chance	-1 Dexterity	—	—	—
Crossbows						
Name	Material	Quality #1	Quality #2	Quality #3	Quality #4	Quality #5	Quality #6
Antivan Crossbow	All Woods	—	—	—	—	—	—
Darkspawn Crossbow	Ash	+1 Armor Penetration	-1 Dexterity	—	—	—	—
Dwarven Defender	Sylvanwood	+3 Dexterity	+3 Damage vs. Darkspawn	—	—	—	—
Imperium Crossbow	Dragonthorn	—	—	—	—	—	—
Nugbane	Whitewood	+3 Damage	—	—	—	—	—
Precision-Geared Recurve	Sylvanwood	+3 Armor Penetration	+4 Attack	—	—	—	—
Sailor's Crossbow	Sylvanwood	0.2s Faster Aim	—	—	—	—	—

Weapons

Basics ~ Character Generation ~ Classes ~ The Party ~ Companions ~ Supporting Cast ~ Equipment ~ Bestiary ~ Walkthroughs ~ Side Quests ~ Random Encounters ~ Achievements/Trophies

Daggers

Name	Material	Quality #1	Quality #2	Quality #3	Quality #4	Quality #5	Quality #6
Beastman's Dagger	Red Steel	+10% Critical Damage	—	—	—	—	—
Crow Dagger	Iron/Grey Iron/Steel/Silverite/Dragonbone	+15% Critical Damage	—	—	—	—	—
Dar'Misu	All Metals	—	—	—	—	—	—
Darkspawn Dagger	Iron/Grey Iron/Steel	+1 Armor Penetration	-1 Dexterity	—	—	—	—
Enchanted Dagger	Grey Iron	+4 Attack	—	—	—	—	—
Fang	Veridium	+6 Attack	—	—	—	—	—
Gift of the Grey	Silverite	+5% Melee Critical Chance	—	—	—	—	—
Noble's Dagger	Grey Iron	+1 Electricity Damage	—	—	—	—	—
The Rose's Thorn	Dragonbone	+2 Dexterity	+1.0 Combat Health Regeneration	+3 Damage	+5% Melee Critical Chance	+30% Critical Damage	—
Thorn of the Dead Gods	Silverite	+3 Damage	+6 Armor Penetration	—	—	—	—
Thorn of the Dead Gods	Grey Iron	+2 Damage	+4 Armor Penetration	—	—	—	—
Thorn of the Dead Gods	Steel	+1 Damage	+2 Armor Penetration	—	—	—	—
Varathorn's Dar'Misu	Veridium	+4 Armor Penetration	+6 Attack	—	—	—	—

Greatswords

Name	Material	Quality #1	Quality #2	Quality #3	Quality #4	Quality #5	Quality #6
Ageless	Silverite	Weakens Nearby Darkspawn	Messy Kills	+2 Damage vs. Darkspawn	Increases Hostility and Intimidation	+0.25 Combat Stamina Regeneration	
Asala	Steel	+1 Willpower	+3 Armor Penetration	+12 Attack	Required: Sten	—	—
Balanced Greatsword	Iron	—	—	—	—	—	—
Chasind Flatblade	Grey Iron	+1% Melee Critical Chance	+2 Armor Penetration	—	—	—	—
Darkspawn Greatsword	Iron/Grey Iron/Steel	+1 Armor Penetration	-1 Dexterity	—	—	—	—
Everd's Greatsword	Steel	—	—	—	—	—	—
Magic Greatsword	Veridium	+1 Damage	+4% Chance to Ignore Hostile Magic	—	—	—	—
Meteor Sword	Silverite	+2 Strength	+3 Damage	-25 Spirit Resistance	—	—	—
Ornamental Sword	Iron	Lucky	-5 Attack	-1 Damage	—	—	—
Qunari Sword	Red Steel	—	—	—	—	—	—
Shaperate's Blessing	Silverite	+5 Armor Penetration	+6 Attack	—	—	—	—
The Summer Sword	Silverite	+20 Physical Resistance	Chance to Knock Target Back	—	—	—	—
Yusaris	Silverite	+20 Fire Resistance	+5 Damage vs. Dragons	—	—	—	—

Longbows

Name	Material	Quality #1	Quality #2	Quality #3	Quality #4	Quality #5	Quality #6
Antivan Longbow	All Woods	+1% Ranged Critical Chance	—	—	—	—	—
Bow of the Golden Sun	Sylvanwood	+4 Attack	—	—	—	—	—
Dalish Longbow	All Woods	0.1s Faster Aim	—	—	—	—	—
Darkspawn Longbow	Ash	+1 Damage	+1 Dexterity	—	—	—	—
Falon'Din's Reach	Dragonthorn	+2 Damage	0.3s Faster Aim	—	—	—	—
Far Song	Dragonthorn	+2 Damage	0.3s Faster Aim	+3% Ranged Critical Chance	+10 Attack	+10% Critical Damage	—
Longbow	All Woods	—	—	—	—	—	—
Mage's Eye	Dragonthorn	+3% Ranged Critical Chance	+4 Attack	—	—	—	—
Marjolaine's Recurve	Dragonthorn	+3 Cunning	+3 Damage	0.3s Faster Aim	Required: Leliana	—	—
Spear-Thrower	Sylvanwood	0.3s Faster Aim	+5 Armor Penetration	—	—	—	—
Wolf-Killer	Ironbark	—	—	—	—	—	—

Longswords

Name	Material	Quality #1	Quality #2	Quality #3	Quality #4	Quality #5	Quality #6
Dar'Misaan	All Metals						
Darkspawn Longsword	Iron/Grey Iron/Steel	+1 Armor Penetration	-1 Dexterity	—	—	—	—
Dwarven Longsword	Steel/Silverite	—	—	—	—	—	—
Dwyn's Sword	Steel	Messy Kills	+2% Chance to Ignore Hostile Magic				
Family Sword	Grey Iron	+1 Damage	+4 Attack	Required: Warrior or Rogue	No Attribute Requirements	—	—
Fine Dwarven Blade	Grey Iron	+2 Attack	—	—	—	—	—
Gorim's Sword	Red Steel	—	—	—	—	—	—
Imperial Edge	Silverite	+2 Damage	+3% Melee Critical Chance	+6 Attack	—	—	—
Keening Blade	Dragonbone	+4 Armor Penetration	+6 Attack	Required: Warrior	+3 Cold Damage	—	—
King Maric's Blade	Dragonbone	+10 Cold Resistance	+10% to Healing Spells	Required: Warrior	—	—	—
Oathkeeper	Steel	+3 Armor Penetration	+10% to Healing Spells	—	—	—	—
Saw Sword	All Metals	+1 Damage	+1% Melee Critical Chance	—	—	—	—
Ser Garlen's Sword	Grey Iron	+2 Attack	+10 Physical Resistance	—	—	—	—
Spellweaver	Silverite	+5 Magic	+1.0 Combat Mana Regeneration	+10% Chance to Ignore Hostile Magic	Required: Arcane Warrior	No Attribute Requirements	—
The Green Blade	Veridium	+10 Nature Resistance	+3 Damage vs. Beasts	—	—	—	—
Topsider's Honor	Dragonbone	+20 Spirit Resistance	+3 Damage vs. Spirits	—	—	—	—
Warden's Longwsword	All Metals	—	—	—	—	—	—

Maces

Name	Material	Quality #1	Quality #2	Quality #3	Quality #4	Quality #5	Quality #6
Aeducan Mace	Grey Iron	Messy Kills	—				
Barbarian Mace	Iron/Grey Iron/Steel	+1 Strength					
Chevalier's Mace	Steel	+5 Cold Resistance	+5 Spirit Resistance	+2 Cold Damage	—	—	—
Darkspawn Mace	Iron/Grey Iron/Steel	+1 Armor Penetration	-1 Dexterity	—	—	—	—
Dwarven Mace	All Metals	—	—	—	—	—	—
Endrin's Mace	Silverite	+15 Cold Resistance	+10 Mental Resistance	—	—	—	—
Engraved Mace	Veridium	+1 Dexterity	+1 Damage	+5 Mental Resistance	—	—	—
Everd's Mace	Silverite	—	—	—	—	—	—
High Constable's Mace	Silverite	+1.0 Combat Stamina Regeneration	+3 Damage vs. Darkspawn	—	—	—	—
Liberator's Mace	Red Steel	+1 Dexterity	+3% Melee Critical Chance	—	—	—	—
Shaperate's Blessing	Silverite	+4 Attack	—	—	—	—	—
Vanguard	Silverite	+3 Strength	+3 Constitution	+1.0 Combat Stamina Regeneration	—	—	—

Mauls

Name	Material	Quality #1	Quality #2	Quality #3	Quality #4	Quality #5	Quality #6
Chasind Crusher	Iron/Grey Iron/Dragonbone	+3% Melee Critical Chance	-5 Attack	—	—	—	—
Chasind Great Maul	Dragonbone	+5 Damage	+5 Armor Penetration	+0.5 Combat Stamina Regeneration	+75 Stamina	—	—
Darkspawn Maul	Iron/Grey Iron/Steel	+1 Armor Penetration	-1 Dexterity	—	—	—	—

Weapons

Basics ~ Character Generation ~ Classes ~ The Party ~ Companions ~ Supporting Cast ~ **Equipment** ~ Bestiary ~ Walkthroughs ~ Side Quests ~ Random Encounters ~ Achievements/Trophies

Mauls (continued)

Name	Material	Quality #1	Quality #2	Quality #3	Quality #4	Quality #5	Quality #6
Diamond Maul	All Metals	—	—	—	—	—	—
Exalted Maul	Silverite	+2 Willpower	+10 Mental Resistance	+2 Damage vs. Spirits	—	—	—
Forge Master's Hammer	Red Steel	+25 Fire Resistance	+6 Attack	—	—	—	—
Heavy Maul	Steel	+2 Damage	—	—	—	—	—
Spiked Maul	Red Steel	+3 Damage	+2% Melee Critical Chance	-1 Dexterity	—	—	—
Thorval's Luck	Silverite	+10% to Healing Spells	+4 Attack	+10 Physical Resistance	—	—	—
Trian's Maul	Silverite	—	—	—	—	—	—

Shortbows

Name	Material	Quality #1	Quality #2	Quality #3	Quality #4	Quality #5	Quality #6
Darkspawn Shortbow	Ash	+1 Armor Penetration	-1 Dexterity	—	—	—	—
Orlesian Bow	All Woods	—	—	—	—	—	—
Scout's Bow	All Woods	0.1s Faster Aim	—	—	—	—	—
The Dark Moon	Dragonthorn	+2 Willpower	+10 Nature Resistance	+3 Armor Penetration	—	—	—
The Fox's Bow	Sylvanwood	+5 Defense against Missiles	—	—	—	—	—
Whitewood Bow	Whitewood	+3 Damage	+5% Ranged Critical Chance	—	—	—	—
Wilds Bow	Yew	+10 Nature Resistance	—	—	—	—	—

Staves

Name	Material	Quality #1	Quality #2	Quality #3	Quality #4	Quality #5	Quality #6
Acolyte's Staff	Iron	+2 Spellpower	—	—	—	—	Required: Mage
Blackened Heartwood Staff	Iron	+2 Damage	+2 Spellpower	—	—	—	Required: Mage
Darkspawn Staff	Iron	+1 Spellpower	+5% to Spirit Damage	—	—	—	Required: Mage
Enchanter's Staff	All Metals	+1 Magic	+10 Spirit Resistance	+5% to Fire Damage	+5% to Cold Damage	+5% to Electricity Damage	Required: Mage
Harrowmont's Staff	Steel	+1 Magic	+2 Constitution	—	—	—	Required: Mage
Heaven's Wrath	Silverite	+1.0 Combat Mana Regeneration	+5 Spellpower	+10% to Electricity Damage	—	—	Required: Mage
Lightning Rod	Grey Iron	+10 Electricity Resistance	+10% to Electricity Damage	—	—	—	Required: Mage
Magic Staff	Iron/Grey Iron/Steel	+1 Magic	—	—	—	—	Required: Mage
Magister's Staff	Silverite	+1.0 to Combat Mana Regeneration	+5 Spellpower	+10% to Spirit Damage	—	—	Required: Mage
Malign Staff	Veridium	+1.0 to Combat Mana Regeneration	+5 Spellpower	+10% to Spirit Dmaage	+10% to Electricity Damage	-1 Willpower	Required: Mage
Oak Branch	Veridium	+1 Magic	+2 Constitution	+10% to Nature Damage	—	—	Required: Mage
Piece of Wood	Veridium	+1 Constitution	+10 Nature Resistance	—	—	—	Required: Mage
Pyromancer's Brand	Grey Iron	+1 Spellpower	+10% to Fire Damage	—	—	—	Required: Mage
Shaperate's Blessing	Silverite	+2 Willpower	+0.5 Combat Mana Regeneration	+10% to Cold Damage	—	—	Required: Mage
Staff of the Ephemeral Order	Silverite	+3 Willpower	+5% to Spirit Damage	—	—	—	Required: Mage
Staff of the Magister Lord	Dragonbone	+6 Willpower	+2.0 Combat Mana Regeneration	+6 Spellpower	+10% to Fire Damage	+10% to Spirit Damage	Required: Mage
Sylvan's Mercy	Veridium	+5 Nature Resistance	+1 Spellpower	+10% to Nature Damage	—	—	Required: Mage
Torch of Embers	Steel	+10 Fire Resistance	+3 Spellpower	+10% to Fire Damage	—	—	Required: Mage
Valor's Staff	Iron	—	—	—	—	—	Required: Mage
Wintersbreath	Dragonbone	+25 Cold Resistance	+3 Spellpower	+10% to Cold Damage	—	—	Required: Mage

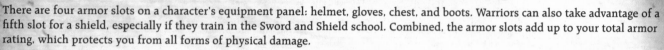

Armor

There are four armor slots on a character's equipment panel: helmet, gloves, chest, and boots. Warriors can also take advantage of a fifth slot for a shield, especially if they train in the Sword and Shield school. Combined, the armor slots add up to your total armor rating, which protects you from all forms of physical damage.

What armor fits you best? First, consider any restrictions your class may have. A mage, for example, cannot wear the more durable armors (with the exception of the arcane warrior mage). Armor may also have a strength or dexterity requirement. Next, check out the armor's tier level; tiers range from tier 1 to tier 7, and generally the higher tiers equal more protection. Compare the armor's damage score to other armor you have in your inventory (or on local vendors) and choose the highest armor score if other bonuses don't matter. See the following tables for more details on the different quality levels.

Armor Tiers

Boots

Tier	Type	Armor	Fatigue	Strength Required
Light Leather				
1	Rough Hide	0.75	0.5	10
2	Cured Hide	1	0.513	11
3	Leather	1.25	0.525	12
4	Hardened Leather	1.5	0.538	14
5	Reinforced Leather	1.75	0.55	17
6	Inscribed Leather	2	0.563	18
7	Drakescale Leather	2.25	0.575	20
Medium Metal				
1	Iron	1	1.5	14
2	Grey Iron	1.2	1.575	16
3	Steel	1.4	1.65	18
4	Veridium	1.6	1.725	22
5	Red Steel	1.8	1.8	28
6	Silverite	2.1	1.875	30
7	Dragonbone	2.6	1.95	34
Heavy Metal				
1	Iron	1.25	2.25	18
2	Grey Iron	1.5	2.363	20
3	Steel	1.75	2.475	22
4	Veridium	2	2.588	26
5	Red Steel	2.25	2.7	32
6	Silverite	2.625	2.813	34
7	Dragonbone	3.25	2.925	38
Massive Metal				
1	Iron	1.5	3	22
2	Grey Iron	1.8	3.15	24
3	Steel	2.1	3.3	26
4	Veridium	2.4	3.45	30
5	Red Steel	2.7	3.6	36
6	Silverite	3.15	3.75	38
7	Dragonbone	3.9	3.9	42

Chest

Tier	Type	Armor	Fatigue	Strength Required
Light Leather				
1	Rough Hide	3	2	10
2	Cured Hide	4	2.05	11
3	Leather	5	2.1	12
4	Hardened Leather	6	2.15	14
5	Reinforced Leather	7	2.2	17
6	Inscribed Leather	8	2.25	18
7	Drakescale Leather	9	2.3	20

Chest (continued)

Tier	Type	Armor	Fatigue	Strength Required
Medium Metal				
1	Iron	4.25	7	14
2	Grey Iron	5.1	7.35	16
3	Steel	5.95	7.7	18
4	Veridium	6.8	8.05	22
5	Red Steel	7.65	8.4	28
6	Silverite	8.925	8.75	30
7	Dragonbone	11.05	9.1	34
Heavy Metal				
1	Iron	6.25	14	18
2	Grey Iron	7.5	14.7	20
3	Steel	8.75	15.4	22
4	Veridium	10	16.1	26
5	Red Steel	11.25	16.8	32
6	Silverite	13.125	17.5	34
7	Dragonbone	16.25	18.2	38
Massive Metal				
1	Iron	8.75	21	22
2	Grey Iron	10.5	22.05	24
3	Steel	12.25	23.1	26
4	Veridium	14	24.15	30
5	Red Steel	15.75	25.2	36
6	Silverite	18.375	26.25	38
7	Dragonbone	22.75	27.3	42

Gloves

Tier	Type	Armor	Fatigue	Strength Required
Light Leather				
1	Rough Hide	0.5	1	10
2	Cured Hide	0.66	1.025	11
3	Leather	0.83	1.05	12
4	Hardened Leather	1	1.075	14
5	Reinforced Leather	1.16	1.1	17
6	Inscribed Leather	1.33	1.125	18
7	Drakescale Leather	1.5	1.15	20
Medium Metal				
1	Iron	0.75	1.25	14
2	Grey Iron	0.9	1.313	16
3	Steel	1.05	1.375	18
4	Veridium	1.2	1.438	22
5	Red Steel	1.35	1.5	28
6	Silverite	1.575	1.563	30
7	Dragonbone	1.95	1.625	34

Armor

Basics ~ Character Generation ~ Classes ~ The Party ~ Companions ~ Supporting Cast ~ **Equipment** ~ Bestiary ~ Walkthroughs ~ Side Quests ~ Random Encounters ~ Achievements/Trophies

Gloves (continued)

Tier	Type	Armor	Fatigue	Strength Required
Heavy Metal				
1	Iron	1	1.75	18
2	Grey Iron	1.2	1.838	20
3	Steel	1.4	1.925	22
4	Veridium	1.6	2.013	26
5	Red Steel	1.8	2.1	32
6	Silverite	2.1	2.188	34
7	Dragonbone	2.6	2.275	38
Massive Metal				
1	Iron	1.25	3	20
2	Grey Iron	1.5	3.15	24
3	Steel	1.75	3.3	26
4	Veridium	2	3.45	30
5	Red Steel	2.25	3.6	36
6	Silverite	2.625	3.75	38
7	Dragonbone	3.25	3.9	42

Helmet

Tier	Type	Armor	Fatigue	Strength Required
Light Leather				
1	Rough Hide	0.75	0	10
2	Cured Hide	1	0	11
3	Leather	1.25	0	12
4	Hardened Leather	1.5	0	14
5	Reinforced Leather	1.75	0	17
6	Inscribed Leather	2	0	18
7	Drakescale Leather	2.25	0	20
Medium Metal				
1	Iron	1	1.5	14
2	Grey Iron	1.2	1.575	16
3	Steel	1.4	1.65	18
4	Veridium	1.6	1.725	22
5	Red Steel	1.8	1.8	28
6	Silverite	2.1	1.875	30
7	Dragonbone	2.6	1.95	34
Heavy Metal				
1	Iron	1.25	2.25	18
2	Grey Iron	1.5	2.363	20
3	Steel	1.75	2.475	22
4	Veridium	2	2.588	26
5	Red Steel	2.25	2.7	32
6	Silverite	2.625	2.813	34
7	Dragonbone	3.25	2.925	38
Massive Metal				
1	Iron	1.5	3	22
2	Grey Iron	1.8	3.15	24
3	Steel	2.1	3.3	26
4	Veridium	2.4	3.45	30
5	Red Steel	2.7	3.6	36
6	Silverite	3.15	3.75	38
7	Dragonbone	3.75	3.9	42

Shield

Tier	Type	Missile Defense	Fatigue	Strength Required
Small Round Metal (1.5 Defense)				
1	Iron	1.5	0	10
2	Grey Iron	1.875	0	12
3	Steel	2.25	0	14
4	Veridium	2.625	0	18
5	Red Steel	3	0	24
6	Silverite	3.375	0	26
7	Dragonbone	4.125	0	30

Shield (continued)

Tier	Type	Missile Defense	Fatigue	Strength Required
Small Round Wooden (1.5 Defense)				
1	Horn	1.5	0	10
2	Ash	1.875	0	12
3	Yew	2.25	0	14
4	Whitewood	2.625	0	18
5	Ironbark	3	0	24
6	Sylvanwood	3.375	0	26
7	Dragonthorn	3.75	0	30
Large Round Metal (3 Defense)				
1	Iron	2.25	2.5	14
2	Grey Iron	2.813	2.625	16
3	Steel	3.375	2.75	18
4	Veridium	3.938	2.875	22
5	Red Steel	4.5	3	28
6	Silverite	5.063	3.125	30
7	Dragonbone	6.1875	3.25	34
Large Round Wooden (3 Defense)				
1	Horn	2.25	2.5	14
2	Ash	2.813	2.563	16
3	Yew	3.375	2.625	18
4	Whitewood	3.938	2.688	22
5	Ironbark	4.5	2.75	28
6	Sylvanwood	5.063	2.813	30
7	Dragonthorn	5.625	2.875	34
Metal Kite (4 Defense)				
1	Iron	3	3.2	18
2	Grey Iron	3.75	3.36	20
3	Steel	4.5	3.52	22
4	Veridium	5.25	3.68	26
5	Red Steel	6	3.84	32
6	Silverite	6.75	4	34
7	Dragonbone	8.25	4.16	38
Wooden Kite (4 Defense)				
1	Horn	3	3.2	18
2	Ash	3.75	3.28	20
3	Yew	4.5	3.36	22
4	Whitewood	5.25	3.44	26
5	Ironbark	6	3.52	32
6	Sylvanwood	6.75	3.6	34
7	Dragonthorn	7.5	3.68	38
Heavy Metal (6 Defense)				
1	Iron	4	4.8	22
2	Grey Iron	5	5.04	24
3	Steel	6	5.28	26
4	Veridium	7	5.52	30
5	Red Steel	8	5.76	36
6	Silverite	9	6	38
7	Dragonbone	11	6.24	42
Heavy Wooden (6 Defense)				
1	Horn	4	4.8	22
2	Ash	5	4.92	24
3	Yew	6	5.04	26
4	Whitewood	7	5.16	30
5	Ironbark	8	5.28	36
6	Sylvanwood	9	5.4	38
7	Dragonthorn	10	5.52	42

Unique Armor

As you level up, most armor will come with attribute bonuses and special abilities. Now you have decisions to make: Do you take the armor with the greater defensive value, or do you choose the armor with the better bonuses? If you're playing the tank role, defense may be the most important factor; if your play style is more versatile, bonuses tend to be the way to go. Ideally, you will find four pieces of armor that have great defense scores for your level range and excellent bonuses.

CAUTION

You can't just look at the highest armor score for your equipment. Armor also comes with a fatigue score; the fatigue percentage equals how much extra a talent will cost in stamina or a spell will cost in mana. A character with a 50 percent fatigue rating from armor will have all of his abilities cost 50 percent more. Balance your need for physical defense with the impact fatigue has on your stamina or mana.

Item Sets

Name	Set Bonus #1	Set Bonus #2
Item Set 1: Griffon	Immunity to Flanking	—
Item Set 2: Effort	-10% Fatigue	—
Item Set 3: Juggernaut Plate	+3 Strength	+3 Constitution
Item Set 4: Imperium Rings	+2 Armor	—
Item Set 5: Legion of the Dead	+3 Damage	+3 Constitution
Item Set 6: Dalish Leather	+5 Defense	—
Item Set 7: Duster Leather	+2 Armor	—
Item Set 8: Wade's Drakeskin	-10% Fatigue	—
Item Set 9: Wade's Dragonskin	-25% Fatigue	—
Item Set 10: Wade's Dragonscale	-20% Fatigue	—
Item Set 11: Wade's Dragonbone Plate	-10% Fatigue	—
Item Set 12: Leather Armor	-5% Fatigue	—
Item Set 13: Studded Leather Armor	+1 Defense	—
Item Set 14: Chainmail	-2.5% Fatigue	—
Item Set 15: Scale Armor	+4.5 Defense vs Missiles	—
Item Set 16: Splint Mail	+1 Armor	—

Name	Set Bonus #1	Set Bonus #2
Item Set 17: Dwarven Medium Armor	+1 Armor	—
Item Set 18: Ancient Elven Armor	+5 Defense	—
Item Set 19: Ceremonial Armor	+6 Defense vs. Missiles	—
Item Set 20: Diligence	+5 Willpower	—
Item Set 21: Dwarven Heavy Armor	+1 Armor	—
Item Set 22: Heavy Chainmail	-3% Fatigue	—
Item Set 23: Chevalier Armor	+3 Willpower	+3 Constitution
Item Set 24: Commander's Plate	+5 Willpower	—
Item Set 25: Dwarven Massive Armor	+2 Armor	—
Item Set 26: Heavy Plate	+7.5 Defense vs Missiles	—
Item Set 27: Wade's Superior Drakeskin	-10% Fatigue	+5 Defense
Item Set 28: Wade's Superior Dragonskin	-25% Fatigue	+5 Defense
Item Set 29: Wade's Superior Dragonscale	-20% Fatigue	+5 Defense
Item Set 30: Wade's Superior Dragonbone Plate	-10% Fatigue	+5 Defense

Something else to keep in mind: if you collect pieces of armor from the same set, you gain item set bonuses. These can range from an immunity to flanking with the Griffon armor items to less fatigue with the regular chainmail set. In general, it's worth collecting an armor set that's in your level range if you can find all the pieces. Some sets, such as the dragon/drake scale armor sets Master Wade crafts you in Denerim's "Drake Scale Armor" side quest, are difficult to obtain but worth the time investment. See the Side Quests chapter for special armor sets that can either be made for you, found on dungeon excursions, or presented as rewards.

Boots							
Name	Material	Quality #1	Quality #2	Quality #3	Quality #4	Quality #5	Quality #6
Light							
Adaia's Boots	Cured Hide	Reduces Hostility	—	—	—	—	—
Antivan Leather Boots	Inscribed Leather	+4% Chance to Ignore Hostile Magic	—	—	—	—	—
Bard's Dancing Shoes	Drakescale	+6 Defense	Reduces Hostility	—	—	—	—
Dalish Boots	All Leathers	+3 Defense	Item Set 6	—	—	—	—
Deygan's Boots	Reinforced Leather	+2 Constitution	—	—	—	—	—
Duster Leather Boots	All Leathers	Item Set 7	—	—	—	—	—
Enchanter's Footing	All Leathers	+3 Defense	Required: Mage	—	—	—	—
Fade Striders	All Leathers	+1 Magic	Required: Mage	—	—	—	—
Imperial Weavers	All Leathers	+10% Chance to Dodge Attacks	Required: Mage	—	—	—	—
Leather Boots	All Leathers	Item Set 12	—	—	—	—	—
Magus War Boots	Drakescale Leather	+12 Defense	Required: Mage	—	—	—	—
Silverhammer's Evaders	All Leathers	+10 Defense against Missile Attacks	Required: Mage	—	—	—	—

Armor

Basics ~ Character Generation ~ Classes ~ The Party ~ Companions ~ Supporting Cast ~ Equipment ~ Bestiary ~ Walkthroughs ~ Side Quests ~ Random Encounters ~ Achievements/Trophies

Boots (continued)

Light (continued)

Name	Material	Quality #1	Quality #2	Quality #3	Quality #4	Quality #5	Quality #6
Silverhammer's Tackmasters	All Leathers	+2 Dexterity	—	—	—	—	—
Studded Leather Boots	All Leathers	Item Set 13	—	—	—	—	—
Wade's Drakeskin Boots	Drakescale	+5 Fire Resistance	Item Set 8	—	—	—	—
Wade's Superior Drakeskin Boots	Drakescale	+1 Dexterity	+10 Fire Resistance	Item Set 27	—	—	—

Medium

Name	Material	Quality #1	Quality #2	Quality #3	Quality #4	Quality #5	Quality #6
Ancient Elven Boots	Veridium	+1 Constitution	Item Set 18	—	—	—	—
Chainmail Boots	All Metals	Item Set 14	—	—	—	—	—
Dwarven Armored Boots	All Metals	Item Set 17	—	—	—	—	—
Dwarven Noble Armored Boots	All Metals	—	—	—	—	—	—
Everd's Boots	Grey Iron	—	—	—	—	—	—
Scale Boots	All Metals	Item Set 15	—	—	—	—	—
Splintmail Boots	All Metals	Item Set 16	—	—	—	—	—
Wade's Dragonskin Boots	Dragonbone	+5 Fire Resistance	Item Set 9	—	—	—	—
Wade's Superior Dragonskin Boots	Dragonbone	+10 Fire Resistance	+0.5 Combat Stamina Regeneration	Item Set 28	—	—	—

Heavy

Name	Material	Quality #1	Quality #2	Quality #3	Quality #4	Quality #5	Quality #6
Boots of Diligence	Silverite	+6 Defense	+2 Armor	Item Set 20	—	—	—
Ceremonial Armored Boots	Red Steel	Item Set 19	—	—	—	—	—
Dwarven Heavy Boots	All Metals	Item Set 21	—	—	—	—	—
Heavy Chainmail Boots	All Metals	Item Set 22	—	—	—	—	—
Wade's Heavy Dragonscale Boots	Dragonbone	+5 Fire Resistance	Item Set 10	—	—	—	—
Wade's Superior Heavy Dragonscale Boots	Dragonbone	+10 Fire Resistance	+0.5 Combat Stamina Regeneration	Item Set 29	—	—	—

Massive

Name	Material	Quality #1	Quality #2	Quality #3	Quality #4	Quality #5	Quality #6
Armor of the River Dane Boots	Silverite	+1 Strength	+1 Willpower	Required: Champion	Required: Loghain	Item Set 24	—
Boots of the Legion	Dragonbone	Item Set 5	—	—	—	—	—
Chevalier's Boots	All Metals	Item Set 23	—	—	—	—	—
Commander's Plate Boots	All Metals	Item Set 24	—	—	—	—	—
Dwarven Massive Armored Boots	All Metals	Item Set 25	—	—	—	—	—
Effort's Boots	Silverite	+1 Armor	Item Set 2	—	—	—	—
Heavy Plate Boots	All Metals	Item Set 26	—	—	—	—	—
Juggernaut Plate Boots	Silverite	+5 Fire Resistance	+5 Cold Resistance	+5 Electricity Resistance	+5 Nature Resistance	+5 Spirit Resistance	Item Set 3
Templar Boots	All Metals	—	—	—	—	—	—
Wade's Dragonbone Plate Boots	Dragonbone	+5 Fire Resistance	Item Set 11	—	—	—	—
Wade's Superior Dragonbone Plate Boots	Dragonbone	+10 Fire Resistance	+0.5 Combat Stamina Regeneration	Item Set 30	—	—	—

Chest

Light

Name	Material	Quality #1	Quality #2	Quality #3	Quality #4	Quality #5	Quality #6
Dalish Armor	All Leathers	+1 Dexterity	Item Set 6	—	—	—	—
Duster Leather Armor	All Leathers	Item Set 7	—	—	—	—	—
Leather Armor	All Leathers	Item Set 12	—	—	—	—	—
Shadow of the Empire	Drakescale	+2 Strength	+2 Dexterity	+1.0 Combat Stamina Regeneration	—	—	—
Studded Leather Armor	All Leathers	Item Set 13	—	—	—	—	—

Name	Material	Quality #1	Quality #2	Quality #3	Quality #4	Quality #5	Quality #6
Chest (continued)							
Light (continued)							
The Felon's Coat	Drakescale	+6 Dexterity	+9 Defense	+4 Armor	+1.0 Combat Stamina Regeneration	+15 Physical Resistance	—
Wade's Drakeskin Leather Armor	Drakescale	+25 Fire Resistance	Item Set 8	—	—	—	—
Wade's Superior Drakeskin Leather Armor	Drakescale	+2 Dexterity	+50 Fire Resistance	Item Set 27	—	—	—
Name	**Material**	**Quality #1**	**Quality #2**	**Quality #3**	**Quality #4**	**Quality #5**	**Quality #6**
Medium							
Ancient Elven Armor	Veridium	+2 Dexterity	+2 Armor	+10 Spirit Resistance	Item Set 18	—	—
Chainmail	All Metals	Item Set 14	—	—	—	—	—
Dwarven Armor	All Metals	Item Set 17	—	—	—	—	—
Dwarven Noble Armor	All Metals	—	—	—	—	—	—
Everd's Armor	Grey Iron	+2.5 Combat Stamina Regeneration	—	—	—	—	—
Scale Armor	All Metals	Item Set 15	—	—	—	—	—
Shielded Dwarven Armor	Steel	+1 Constitution	+4% Chance to Ignore Hostile Magic	—	—	—	—
Splintmail	All Metals	Item Set 16	—	—	—	—	—
Varathorn's Armor	Silverite	+3 Armor	+20 Nature Resistance	+25 Stamina	—	—	—
Wade's Dragonskin Armor	Dragonbone	+25 Fire Resistance	Item Set 9	—	—	—	—
Wade's Superior Dragonskin Armor	Dragonbone	+50 Fire Resistance	+1.0 Combat Stamina Regeneration	+25 Stamina	Item Set 28	—	—
Name	**Material**	**Quality #1**	**Quality #2**	**Quality #3**	**Quality #4**	**Quality #5**	**Quality #6**
Heavy							
Armor of Diligence	Silverite	+0.5 Combat Health Regeneration	+2 Armor	Item Set 20	—	—	—
Ceremonial Armor	Red Steel	-3 Armor	+10 Mental Resistance	Item Set 19	—	—	—
Dwarven Guard Armor	Iron	+1 Armor	—	—	—	—	—
Dwarven Heavy Armor	All Metals	Item Set 21	—	—	—	—	—
Evon the Great's Mail	Dragonbone	+1.0 Combat Health Regeneration	+6 Armor	+10% Chance to Dodge Attacks	+1.0 Combat Stamina Regeneration	+10 Missile Defense	—
Heavy Chainmail	All Metals	Item Set 22	—	—	—	—	—
Heavy Chainmail	Red Steel	—	—	—	—	—	—
Superior Dwarven Guard Armor	Grey Iron	+1 Armor	+10 Physical Resistance	—	—	—	—
Wade's Heavy Dragonscale Armor	Dragonbone	+25 Fire Resistance	Item Set 10	—	—	—	—
Wade's Superior Heavy Dragonscale Armor	Dragonbone	+50 Fire Resistance	+1.0 Combat Stamina Regeneration	+25 Stamina	Item Set 29	—	—
Name	**Material**	**Quality #1**	**Quality #2**	**Quality #3**	**Quality #4**	**Quality #5**	**Quality #6**
Massive							
Armor of the Divine Will	Silverite	+20% Chance to Ignore Hostile Magic	-5 Magic	Required: Templar	—	—	—
Armor of the Legion	Dragonbone	+3 Willpower	Item Set 5	—	—	—	—
Armor of the River Dane	Silverite	+3 Strength	+3 Willpower	+1.25 Combat Stamina Regeneration	Required: Loghain	—	—
Chevalier's Armor	All Metals	Item Set 23	—	—	—	—	—
Commander's Plate Armor	All Metals	Item Set 24	—	—	—	—	—
Dwarven Massive Armor	All Metals	+1 Armor	Item Set 25	—	—	—	—

Armor

Basics ~ Character Generation ~ Classes ~ The Party ~ Companions ~ Supporting Cast ~ Equipment ~ Bestiary ~ Walkthroughs ~ Side Quests ~ Random Encounters ~ Achievements/Trophies

Chest (continued)

Name	Material	Quality #1	Quality #2	Quality #3	Quality #4	Quality #5	Quality #6
			Massive (continued)				
Effort	Silverite	+15% to Healing Spells	Item Set 2	—	—	—	—
Heavy Plate Armor	All Metals	Item Set 26	—	—	—	—	—
Juggernaut Plate Armor	Silverite	+10 Fire Resistance	+10 Cold Resistance	+10 Electricity Resistance	+10 Nature Resistance	+10 Spirit Resistance	Item Set 3
Knight Commander's Plate	Silverite	+5 Willpower	+40% Chance to Ignore Hostile Magic	+10 Mental Resistance	Required: Templar	—	—
Templar Armor	Steel	+3 Willpower	+20% Chance to Ignore Hostile Magic	+5 Mental Resistance	Required: Templar	—	—
Wade's Dragonbone Plate Armor	Dragonbone	+25 Fire Resistance	Item Set 11	—	—	—	—
Wade's Superior Dragonbone Plate Armor	Dragonbone	+50 Fire Resistance	+1.0 Combat Stamina Regeneration	+25 Stamina	Item Set 30	—	—
Name	Material	Quality #1	Quality #2	Quality #3	Quality #4	Quality #5	Quality #6
			Mage				
Apprentice Robes	Robes	+1 Willpower	—	—	—	—	—
Archon Robes	Robes	+0.75 Combat Health Regeneration	+3 Armor	+2 Spellpower	—	—	—
Chasind Robes	Robes	+6 Defense	—	—	—	—	—
First Enchanter Robes	Robes	+3 Willpower	+3 Magic	+9 Defense	—	—	—
Lesser Tevinter Robe	Robes	+0.25 Combat Mana Regeneration	+1 Spellpower	—	—	—	—
Mage Robes	Robes	+1 Willpower	+1 Magic	—	—	—	—
Morrigan's Robes	Robes	+2 Magic	+10% Cold Damage	Required: Morrigan	—	—	—
Reaper's Vestments	Robes	+6 Constitution	+20 Fire Resistance	+16% Chance to Ignore Hostile Magic	+10% Chance to Dodge Attacks	+12 Armor	—
Robe of the Witch	Robes	+10 Cold Resistance	+5% Chance to Dodge Attacks	+3 Armor	—	—	—
Robes of Possession	Robes	+5 Magic	+12 Defense	+8% Chance to Ignore Hostile Magic	+20% Cold Damage	-1 Willpower	Required: Morrigan
Robes of the Gifted	Robes	+6% Chance to Ignore Hostile Magic	Reduces Hostility	—	—	—	—
Robes of the Magister Lords	Robes	+5 Willpower	+10 Fire Resistance	+10 Cold Resistance	—	—	—
Senior Enchanter's Robes	Robes	+2 Willpower	+2 Magic	+6 Defense	—	—	—
Tevinter Enchanter's Robes	Robes	+0.5 Combat Mana Regeneration	+3 Spellpower	+10% Chance to Dodge Attacks	—	—	—
Tevinter Mage Robes	Robes	+1.0 Combat Mana Regeneration	+4% Chance to Ignore Hostile Magic	+5 Spellpower	—	—	—
Tevinter Robe	Robes	+0.5 Combat Mana Regeneration	+3 Spellpower	—	—	—	—

Gloves

Name	Material	Quality #1	Quality #2	Quality #3	Quality #4	Quality #5	Quality #6
			Light				
Angled Strikers	Rough Hide	+5% Critical Damage	Required: Rogue	—	—	—	—
Ashen Gloves	Inscribed Leather	+20% to Cold Damage	Required: Mage	—	—	—	—
Backhands	Hardened Leather	+10% Critical Damage	Required: Rogue	—	—	—	—
Black Hand Gauntlets	Inscribed Leather	+20% to Spirit Damage	Required: Mage	—	—	—	—
Charged Mitts	Hardened Leather	+10% to Electricity Damage	Required: Mage	—	—	—	—

Gloves (continued)

Name	Material	Quality #1	Quality #2	Quality #3	Quality #4	Quality #5	Quality #6
Light (continued)							
Cinderfel Gauntlets	Inscribed Leather	+20% to Fire Damage	Required: Mage	—	—	—	—
Coarse Cut Gauntlets	Rough Hide	+2% Melee Critical Chance	Required: Rogue	—	—	—	—
Dalish Gloves	All Leathers	+1 Dexterity	Item Set 6	—	—	—	—
Duster Leather Gloves	All Leathers	Item Set 7	—	—	—	—	—
Elementalist's Grasp	Inscribed Leather	+5% to Fire Damage	+5% to Cold Damage	+5% to Electricity Damage	+5% to Nature Damage	+5% to Spirit Damage	Required: Mage
Gloves of Guile	Drakescale	+5 Armor Penetration	—	—	—	—	—
Imperial Reinforced Gloves	Rough Hide	+1 Armor Penetration	—	—	—	—	—
Katriel's Grasp	Drakescale	+3% Melee Critical Chance	—	—	—	—	—
Leather Gloves	All Leathers	Item Set 12	—	—	—	—	—
Lend of the Lion	Hardened Leather	+10% to Nature Damage	Required: Mage	—	—	—	—
Pocketed Searing Gloves	Hardened Leather	+10% to Fire Damage	Required: Mage	—	—	—	—
Polar Gauntlets	Hardened Leather	+10% to Cold Damage	Required: Mage	—	—	—	—
Pushback Strikers	Drakescale	+5% Melee Critical Chance	Required: Rogue	—	—	—	—
Qunari Siege Gauntlets	Hardened Leather	+3 Armor Penetration	—	—	—	—	—
Red Jenny Seekers	Drakescale	+15% Critical Damage	Required: Rogue	—	—	—	—
Silk Weave Gloves	Inscribed Leather	+20% to Nature Damage	Required: Mage	—	—	—	—
Spirit Hands	Hardened Leather	+10% to Spirit Damage	Required: Mage	—	—	—	—
Storm Talons	Inscribed Leather	+20% to Electricity Damage	Required: Mage	—	—	—	—
Studded Leather Gloves	All Leathers	Item Set 13	—	—	—	—	—
Wade's Drakeskin Gloves	Drakescale	+5 Fire Resistance	Item Set 8	—	—	—	—
Wade's Superior Drakeskin Gloves	Drakescale	+1 Dexterity	+10 Fire Resistance	Item Set 27	—	—	—
Name	**Material**	**Quality #1**	**Quality #2**	**Quality #3**	**Quality #4**	**Quality #5**	**Quality #6**
Medium							
Ancient Elven Gloves	Veridium	+2 Armor	+8% Chance to Ignore Hostile Magic	Item Set 18	—	—	—
Chainmail Gloves	All Metals	Item Set 14	—	—	—	—	—
Dwarven Armored Gloves	All Metals	Item Set 17	—	—	—	—	—
Dwarven Noble Armored Gloves	All Metals	—	—	—	—	—	—
Everd's Gloves	Grey Iron	—	—	—	—	—	—
Scale Gloves	All Metals	Item Set 15	—	—	—	—	—
Splintmail Gloves	All Metals	Item Set 16	—	—	—	—	—
Wade's Dragonskin Gloves	Dragonbone	+5 Fire Resistance	Item Set 9	—	—	—	—
Wade's Superior Dragonskin Gloves	Dragonbone	+10 Fire Resistance	+0.5 Combat Stamina Regeneration	Item Set 28	—	—	—
Name	**Material**	**Quality #1**	**Quality #2**	**Quality #3**	**Quality #4**	**Quality #5**	**Quality #6**
Heavy							
Ceremonial Armored Gloves	Red Steel	Item Set 19	—	—	—	—	—
Dwarven Heavy Gloves	All Metals	Item Set 21	—	—	—	—	—
Gloves of Diligence	Silverite	+4 Armor	Item Set 20	—	—	—	—
Heavy Chainmail Gloves	All Metals	Item Set 22	—	—	—	—	—

Armor

Basics ~ Character Generation ~ Classes ~ The Party ~ Companions ~ Supporting Cast ~ **Equipment** ~ Bestiary ~ Walkthroughs ~ Side Quests ~ Random Encounters ~ Achievements/Trophies

Gloves (continued)

Name	Material	Quality #1	Quality #2	Quality #3	Quality #4	Quality #5	Quality #6
Heavy (continued)							
Wade's Heavy Dragonscale Gloves	Dragonbone	+5 Fire Resistance	Item Set 10	—	—	—	—
Wade's Superior Heavy Dragonscale Gloves	Dragonbone	+10 Fire Resistance	+0.5 Combat Stamina Regeneration	Item Set 29	—	—	—

Name	Material	Quality #1	Quality #2	Quality #3	Quality #4	Quality #5	Quality #6
Massive							
Armor of the River Dane Gloves	Silverite	+1 Strength	+1 Willpower	Required: Loghain	—	—	—
Chevalier's Gloves	All Metals	Item Set 23	—	—	—	—	—
Commander's Plate Gloves	All Metals	Item Set 24	—	—	—	—	—
Dwarven Massive Armored Gloves	All Metals	Item Set 25	—	—	—	—	—
Effort's Gloves	Silverite	+1 Strength	Item Set 2	—	—	—	—
Gloves of the Legion	Dragonbone	+4 Attack	Item Set 5	—	—	—	—
Heavy Plate Gloves	All Metals	Item Set 26	—	—	—	—	—
Juggernaut Plate Gloves	Silverite	+5 Fire Resistance	+5 Cold Resistance	+5 Electricity Resistance	+5 Nature Resistance	+5 Spirit Resistance	Item Set 3
Wade's Dragonbone Plate Gloves	Dragonbone	+5 Fire Resistance	Item Set 11	—	—	—	—
Wade's Superior Dragonbone Plate Gloves	Dragonbone	+10 Fire Resistance	+0.5 Combat Stamina Regeneration	Item Set 30	—	—	—

Helmet

Name	Material	Quality #1	Quality #2	Quality #3	Quality #4	Quality #5	Quality #6
Light							
Armsman's Tensioner	Inscribed Leather	0.3s Faster Aim	+6 Attack	—	—	—	—
Conspirator's Foil	Inscribed Leather	+20 Mental Resistance	—	—	—	—	—
Free Scout Arming Cap	Hardened Leather	+2 Dexterity	—	—	—	—	—
Leather Helm	All Leathers	—	—	—	—	—	—
Longrunner's Cap	Reinforced Leather	+0.5 Combat Stamina Regeneration	—	—	—	—	—
Orzammar Guard Helmet	Iron	—	—	—	—	—	—
Owen's Remasterwork	Grey Iron	+1 Armor	—	—	—	—	—
Quicksilver Arming Cap	Hardened Leather	+2 Cunning	—	—	—	—	—
Qunari Thickened Cap	Reinforced Leather	+10 Mental Resistance	—	—	—	—	—
Studded Helmet	All Leathers	+3 Physical Resistance	—	—	—	—	—
Studded Leather Helm	All Leathers	+2 Physical Resistance	—	—	—	—	—
The Long Sight	Drakescale	+5% Ranged Critical Chance	—	—	—	—	—

Name	Material	Quality #1	Quality #2	Quality #3	Quality #4	Quality #5	Quality #6
Medium							
Ancient Elven Helm	Veridium	+25 Spirit Resistance	Item Set 18	—	—	—	—
Barbarian Helmet	All Metals	+2 Attack	—	—	—	—	—
Camenae's Barbute	Silverite	0.3s Faster Aim	+1 Defense against Missiles	—	—	—	—
Dead Metal Bucket	Silverite	+25 Mental Resistance	—	—	—	—	—
Dwarven Helmet	All Metals	+2 Physical Resistance	—	—	—	—	—
Helmet	All Metals		—	—	—	—	—
Qunari Infantry Helm	All Metals	+2 Mental Resistance	—	—	—	—	—

Name	Material	Quality #1	Quality #2	Quality #3	Quality #4	Quality #5	Quality #6
Heavy							
Commander's Helm	All Metals	—	—	—	—	—	—
Executioner's Helm	All Metals	+25 Stamina	—	—	—	—	—
Grey Warden Helmet	All Metals	—	—	—	—	—	—

Dragon Age ORIGINS
PRIMA Official Game Guide

Helmet (continued)

Name	Material	Quality #1	Quality #2	Quality #3	Quality #4	Quality #5	Quality #6
			Heavy (continued)				
Griffon's Helm	Silverite	+15 Electricity Resistance	Item Set 1	—	—	—	—
Heavy Dwarven Helmet	All Metals	—	—	—	—	—	—
Helm of the Legion	Dragonbone	—	—	—	—	—	—
Helm of the Red	Steel	+1 Dexterity	+10 Fire Resistance	—	—	—	—
Proving Helm	Iron	+1 Willpower	+1 Constitution	—	—	—	—
Qunari Commander Helm	All Metals	—	—	—	—	—	—
Soldier's Helm	All Metals	—	—	—	—	—	—
Thane Helmet	All Metals	+3 Defense	—	—	—	—	—
Name	Material	Quality #1	Quality #2	Quality #3	Quality #4	Quality #5	Quality #6
			Massive				
Corruption	Dragonbone	+5 Dexterity	+1 Armor	+75 Spirit Resistance	-1 Willpower	—	—
Duty	Silverite	+2 Constitution	Item Set 2	—	—	—	—
Heavy Infantry Helmet	All Metals	—	—	—	—	—	—
Juggernaut Helm	Silverite	+1 Armor	+10 Mental Resistance	Item Set 3	—	—	—
Knight-Commander's Helm	All Metals	+5 Physical Resistance	—	—	—	—	—
Rock-Knocker	Red Steel	+25 Physical Resistance	—	—	—	—	—
Soldier's Heavy Helm	All Metals	—	—	—	—	—	—
Standard Bearer's Helm	All Metals	+2 Mental Resistance	—	—	—	—	—
Name	Material	Quality #1	Quality #2	Quality #3	Quality #4	Quality #5	Quality #6
			Mage				
Apprentice Cowl	Cowl	+5 Mental Resistance	—	—	—	—	—
Cameo Cowl	Cowl	+2 Cunning	+0.5 Combat Health Regeneration	—	—	—	—
Collective Arming Cowl	Cowl	+2 Constitution	—	—	—	—	—
Enchanter Cowl	Cowl	+5 Cold Resistance	+5 Nature Resistance	+5 Spirit Resistance	+5 Mental Resistance	—	—
Enchanter's Arming Cap	Cowl	+1 Willpower	+10 Mental Resistance	—	—	—	—
First Enchanter's Cowl	Cowl	+4% Chance to Ignore Hostile Magic	+10% Chance to Dodge Attacks	—	—	—	—
Reinforced Magus Cowl	Cowl	+2 Willpower	+20 Mental Resistance	-1 Dexterity	—	—	—
The Libertarian's Cowl	Cowl	+12 Defense	+0.25 Combat Mana Regeneration	—	—	—	—

Shield

Name	Material	Quality #1	Quality #2	Quality #3	Quality #4	Quality #5	Quality #6
			Round, Small				
Aeducan Shield	Iron	+1 Strength	—	—	—	—	—
Bloodstained Shield	All Woods	—	—	—	—	—	—
Caridin's Shield	Silverite	+10 Cold Resistance	+10 Electricity Resistance	+10 Spirit Resistance	—	—	—
Carta Shield	All Woods	—	—	—	—	—	—
Clan Shield	Horn	—	—	—	—	—	—
Crow Shield	All Woods	—	—	—	—	—	—
Dalish Shield	Ironbark	—	—	—	—	—	—
Gorim's Shield	Iron	+0.25 Combat Health Regeneration	—	—	—	—	—
Harrowmont Guard Shield	All Metals	—	—	—	—	—	—
Howe Guard Shield	All Metals	—	—	—	—	—	—
Mythal's Blessing	Whitewood	+1% Melee Critical Chance	+10% to Healing Spells	—	—	—	—
Orzammar Guard Shield	Iron	—	—	—	—	—	—
Ruck's Shield	Steel	+4 Attack	+10 Spirit Resistance	—	—	—	—

Armor

Basics ~ Character Generation ~ Classes ~ The Party ~ Companions ~ Supporting Cast ~ **Equipment** ~ Bestiary ~ Walkthroughs ~ Side Quests ~ Random Encounters ~ Achievements/Trophies

Shield (continued)

Name	Material	Quality #1	Quality #2	Quality #3	Quality #4	Quality #5	Quality #6
Round, Small (continued)							
Small Darkspawn Shield	All Metals	—	—	—	—	—	—
Small Metal Round Shield	All Metals	—	—	—	—	—	—
Small Shield	All Woods	—	—	—	—	—	—
Warden Recruit Shield	All Woods	—	—	—	—	—	—
Name	Material	Quality #1	Quality #2	Quality #3	Quality #4	Quality #5	Quality #6
Round, Large							
Aeducan Family Shield	Silverite	+1 Cunning	+1 Constitution	+9 Defense	—	—	—
Aeducan Shield	Steel	+3 Defense	—	—	—	—	—
Branka's Shield	Silverite	—	—	—	—	—	—
Champion's Shield	Silverite	+12 Defense	—	—	—	—	—
Dead Coat of Arms	Silverite	+1 Constitution	+1.0 Combat Stamina Regeneration	—	—	—	—
Dwarven Large Round Shield	All Metals	—	—	—	—	—	—
Everd's Shield	Steel	—	—	—	—	—	—
Large Darkspawn Shield	All Metals	—	—	—	—	—	—
Large Wooden Round Shield	All Woods	—	—	—	—	—	—
Shield of the Legion	Dragonbone	+10 Mental Resistance	—	—	—	—	—
Tevinter Shield	All Woods	—	—	—	—	—	—
Name	Material	Quality #1	Quality #2	Quality #3	Quality #4	Quality #5	Quality #6
Kite							
Cousland Guard Shield	All Woods	—	—	—	—	—	—
Eamon's Shield	Steel	+6 Defense	+25 Stamina	—	—	—	—
Havard's Aegis	Yew Wood	+4% Chance to Ignore Hostile Magic	+5 Defense against Missiles	—	—	—	—
Knight-Commander's Shield	All Metals	—	—	—	—	—	—
Loghain's Guardsmen	Yew Wood	—	—	—	—	—	—
Loghain's Shield	Silverite	+20 Physical Resistance	Required: Loghain	—	—	—	—
Metal Kite Shield	All Metals	—	—	—	—	—	—
Redcliffe Elite Shield	Red Steel	+1 Willpower	+3 Defense	+15 Electricity Resistance	+2 Attack	—	—
Redcliffe Shield	All Woods	—	—	—	—	—	—
Shield of Highever	Grey Iron	+4 Attack	—	—	—	—	—
Swiftrunner's Shield	Whitewood	+10 Nature Resistance	+10 Spirit Resistance	—	—	—	—
Templar Shield	All Woods	—	—	—	—	—	—
Wooden Kite Shield	All Woods	—	—	—	—	—	—
Name	Material	Quality #1	Quality #2	Quality #3	Quality #4	Quality #5	Quality #6
Heavy							
Denerim Guard Shield	All Metals	—	—	—	—	—	—
Duncan's Shield	Silverite	+3 Willpower	+6 Defense	+1.0 Combat Stamina Regeneration	—	—	—
Earthheart's Portable Bulwark	Red Steel	+1 Strength	+1 Dexterity	+1 Constitution	—	—	—
Fade Wall	Silverite	+3 Defense	+20% to Healing Spells	+1.0 Combat Stamina Regeneration	+25 Stamina	—	—
Greagoir's Shield	Whitewood	+6 Defense	+10 Fire Resistance	+4% Chance to Ignore Hostile Magic	—	—	—
Heavy Metal Shield	All Metals	—	—	—	—	—	—
Heavy Wooden Shield	All Woods	—	—	—	—	—	—
Howe's Shield	Silverite	+12 Defense	+10 Fire Resistance	+10 Cold Resistance	-2 Willpower	—	—
King's Shield	Silverite	—	—	—	—	—	—

Accessories

Belts, amulets, and rings fall into the accessories category, and each provides more magical bonuses to augment your characters' attributes and skills. The Magister's Cinch in the belt slot, for example, reduces hostility and grants a 10 percent bonus to healing effects. Depending on how you want to build up your character, you may opt for the Warden's Oath amulet to provide 2 more constitution points, or a Ring of Faith with its +10 percent fire damage for a Fireball-happy mage. When you receive a new accessory, you may not want to drop it on your main PC each time; think about which party member it benefits the most and give it to them. Giving an item granting extra defense to the tank benefits the party more than giving it to your PC rogue who barely needs it.

Amulets					
Name	Quality #1	Quality #2	Quality #3	Quality #4	Quality #5
Amulet of Accord	Reduces Hostility	+10 Physical Resistance	—	—	—
Aneirin's Token	+10 Electricity Resistance	+10 Nature Resistance	+10 Spirit Resistance	—	—
Apprentice's Amulet	+5 Fire Resistance	+5 Cold Resistance	+1 Armor	—	—
Athras's Pendant	+4% Chance to Ignore Hostile Magic	—	—	—	—
Caridin's Cage	+20 Electricity Resistance	-1 Cunning	—	—	—
Charm of Flame	+5% to Fire Damage	—	—	—	—
Charm of Still Waters	+1 Willpower	—	—	—	—
Dalish Pendant	+10 Nature Resistance	—	—	—	—
Deadhead Charge	+20 Physical Resistance	-1 Willpower	—	—	—
Faulty Amulet	+20 Mental Resistance	+20 Physical Resistance	-3 Armor	—	—
Gateway Amulet	+20 Spirit Resistance	-1 Willpower	—	—	—
Halla Horn	+10 Mental Resistance	—	—	—	—
Heart of Witherfang	+1 Strength	+1 Magic	+50 Nature Resistance	—	—
Hearthstone Pendant	+10 Cold Resistance	—	—	—	—
Heirloom Necklace	+10 Spirit Resistance	—	—	—	—
Lifedrinker	+4 Spellpower	Required: Blood Mage	—	—	—
Magister's Shield	+6 Defense	+4% Chance to Ignore Hostile Magic	+6 Defense vs. Missiles	-10 Nature Resistance	—
Mud Idol	+10 Cold Resistance	—	—	—	—
North Ward	+20 Mental Resistance	-1 Strength	—	—	—
Par Vollen Willstone	+2 Willpower	—	—	—	—
Reflection	+1 Constitution	+15% to Healing Spells	—	—	—
Sailor's Charm	+10 Electricity Resistance	—	—	—	—
Seeker's Circle	+1 Cunning	+10 Mental Resistance	Required: Leliana	—	—
Shaper's Amulet	+2 Willpower	—	—	—	—
Shiver	+20 Cold Resistance	-1 Dexterity	—	—	—
Silver Cord	+5 Spirit Resistance	+2% Chance to Ignore Hostile Magic	—	—	—
Smith's Heart	+20 Fire Resistance	-1 Dexterity	—	—	—
Spirit Charm	+10 Fire Resistance	—	—	—	—
Spirit Ward	+10 Spirit Resistance	—	—	—	—
Temperament	+10 Mental Resistance	—	—	—	—
The Spellward	+5 Willpower	+2.0 Exploration Health Regeneration	+30% Chance to Ignore Hostile Magic	+10% Chance to Dodge Attacks	+6 Defense vs. Missiles
Varathorn's Amulet	+20 Nature Resistance	-1 Constitution	—	—	—
Warden's Oath	+2 Constitution	Required: Player Only	—	—	—
Wildstone Clasp	+1 Willpower	+10 Mental Resistance	Required: Morrigan	—	—

Belts					
Name	Quality #1	Quality #2	Quality #3	Quality #4	Quality #5
Andruil's Blessing	+2 to All Attributes	+20 Nature Resistance	+1.0 Combat Mana Regeneration	+1.0 Combat Stamina Regeneration	+10 Physical Resistance
Archivist's Sash	Increased XP from Codex	Required: Player Only	—	—	—
Belt of the Magister Lords	+3 Spellpower	—	—	—	—
Borders Yet to Be	+2 Willpower	Required: Loghain	—	—	—
Buckle of the Winds	+3 Defense	—	—	—	—
Creationist's Cord	+10 Fire Resistance	+10% to Healing Spells	—	—	—
Dalish Hunter's Belt	+0.75 Combat Stamina Regeneration	Required: Warrior or Rogue	—	—	—
Dalish Leather Belt	+0.75 Combat Stamina Regeneration	Required: Warrior or Rogue	—	—	—
Destructionist's Belt	+0.5 Combat Mana Regeneration	+3 Spellpower	Required: Mage	—	—

Accessories

Basics ~ Character Generation ~ Classes ~ The Party ~ Companions ~ Supporting Cast ~ **Equipment** ~ Bestiary ~ Walkthroughs ~ Side Quests ~ Random Encounters ~ Achievements/Trophies

Belts (continued)

Name	Quality #1	Quality #2	Quality #3	Quality #4	Quality #5
Dwarven Merchant's Belt	Increased Monetary Gain	—	—	—	—
Dwarven Smith's Belt	+1 Armor	—	—	—	—
Dwarven Warrior's Belt	+1 Strength	+1 Armor	—	—	—
Earthen Cinch	+1 Armor	+5% to Nature Damage	—	—	—
Elfrope	+20 Nature Resistance	Required: Warrior or Rogue	—	—	—
Ephemeralist's Belt	+1 Spirit Resistance	—	—	—	—
Fencer's Cinch	+4 Attack	—	—	—	—
Hardy's Belt	+1 Constitution	—	—	—	—
Longbowman's Belt	+2% Ranged Critical Chance	—	—	—	—
Magister's Cinch	Reduces Hostility	+10% to Healing Spells	—	—	—
Mixed Metal Rounds	+2 Dexterity	Required: Zevran	—	—	—
One for the Ditch	+1 Constitution	+10 Physical Resistance	Required: Oghren	—	—
Ornate Leather Belt	+1 Strength	—	—	—	—
Silver Aron	+2 Magic	Required: Wynne	—	—	—
Sword Belt	+2 Armor Penetration	—	—	—	—
Swordsman's Girdle	+2% Melee Critical Chance	—	—	—	—

Rings

Name	Quality #1	Quality #2	Quality #3	Quality #4	Quality #5
Blood Ring	Improves Blood Magic	+5% to Spirit Damage	Required: Blood Mage	—	—
Dalish Battery	+10% to Electricity Damage	—	—	—	—
Dawn Ring	+4 Strength	-1 Cunning	Item Set 4	—	—
Dreamsever	+10% to Spirit Damage	—	—	—	—
Dusk Ring	+3 Cunning	-1 Strength	Item Set 4	—	—
Ember	+5% to Fire Damage	—	—	—	—
Focus Ring	+5% to Spirit Damage	—	—	—	—
Frostshear	+10% to Cold Damage	—	—	—	—
Golden Ring	+1 Constitution	—	—	—	—
Hailstone	+5% to Cold Damage	—	—	—	—
Iced Band	+10 Cold Resistance	—	—	—	—
Keeper's Ring	+1 Dexterity	—	—	—	—
Key to the City	+2 to All Attributes	+4% to Ignore Hostile Magic	+10% to Healing Spells	—	—
Lifegiver	+10 Constitution	+3.0 Combat Health Regeneration	+2.5 Exploration Health Regeneration	+3 Armor	+20% to Healing Spells
Lloyd's Magic Ring	+2 Strength	-1 Cunning	—	—	—
Memory Band	+1% to Experience	—	—	—	—
Morrigan's Ring	+2 Willpower	—	—	—	—
Ring of Ages	+20 Fire Resistance	+20 Cold Resistance	+20 Electricity Resistance	+20 Nature Resistance	+20 Spirit Resistance
Ring of Faith	+10% to Fire Damage	Required: Mage	—	—	—
Ring of Resistance	+1 Willpower	+1 Constitution	—	—	—
Ring of Selection	+10% to Nature Damage	—	—	—	—
Ring of Study	+1 Magic	—	—	—	—
Ring of the Warrior	+2 Strength	+2 Dexterity	—	—	—
Runic Worry Token	+1 Willpower	+10 Mental Resistance	Required: Alistair	—	—
Seal of Rat Red	+10 Mental Resistance	+10 Physical Resistance	—	—	—
Silverleaf	+1 Cunning	—	—	—	—
Spiral Band	+5% to Spirit Damage	—	—	—	—
Surveyor	+1 Willpower	—	—	—	—
Thorn	+5% to Nature Damage	—	—	—	—
Twitch	+5% to Electricity Damage	—	—	—	—

Dog Collars

Name	Quality #1	Quality #2	Quality #3	Quality #4	Quality #5
Black Leather Collar	+1 Armor Penetration	+2 Armor	—	—	—
Blackmetal Torque	+6 Attack	+6 Armor	—	—	—
Lord's Hunting Jabot	+4 Attack	+4 Armor	—	—	—
Mabari Dog Chain	+2 Armor Penetration	+4 Armor	—	—	—
Mabari War Harness	+4 Armor Penetration	+8 Armor	—	—	—
Pure Bitch Braid	+8 Attack	+8 Armor	—	—	—
Steel Spiked Collar	+3 Armor Penetration	+6 Armor	—	—	—
Throwback Harness	+2 Attack	+2 Armor	—	—	—
Worn Studded Braid	+2 Constitution	—	—	—	—

Dog Warpaint					
Name	Quality #1	Quality #2	Quality #3	Quality #4	Quality #5
Kaddis of Hakkon Wintersbreath	+30 Cold Resistance	—	—	—	—
Kaddis of the Courser	+2 Dexterity	—	—	—	—
Kaddis of the King's Hounds	+30 Nature Resistance	—	—	—	—
Kaddis of the Lady of the Skies	+30 Physical Resistance	—	—	—	—
Kaddis of the Mountain-Father	+20 Nature Resistance	+20 Spirit Resistance	—	—	—
Kaddis of the Siege-Breaker	+30 Fire Resistance	—	—	—	—
Kaddis of the Trickster	+3 Damage	—	—	—	—
Warpaint of the Tempest	+30 Electricity Resistance	—	—	—	—
Warpaint of the Vanguard	+1.0 Combat Stamina Regeneration	—	—	—	—
Warpaint of the Waking Sea	+0.25 Combat Health Regeneration	—	—	—	—
Warpaint of the West Hills	+9 Defense	—	—	—	—
Warpaint of the Wolfhound	None	—	—	—	—

Ammo					
Name	Quality #1	Quality #2	Quality #3	Quality #4	Quality #5
Andraste's Arrows	Mage Slayer—Interrupts Spellcasting	—	—	—	—
Arrow of Filth	+3 Nature Damage	—	—	—	—
Elf-Flight Arrow	+6 Attack	Chance to Stun	—	—	—
Explosive Bolt	+4 Fire Damage	—	—	—	—
Fire Arrow	+2 Fire Damage	—	—	—	—
Fire Bolt	+3 Fire Damage	—	—	—	—
Ice Arrow	+2 Cold Damage	—	—	—	—
Ice Bolt	+3 Cold Damage	—	—	—	—
Knockback Bolt	Chance to Knock Target Back	—	—	—	—
Sureshot Bolt	Massive Damage to Darkspawn				

Rune Enchanting

Bodahn's son, Sandal, enchants weapons for you at party camp. Any time you find or buy a rune, check back with Sandal to see about slotting the rune in your present equipment. You can use a rune if your weapon has an open slot (most lower-tier weapons do not have rune slots; many higher-tier weapons do). When you speak to Sandal, the rune interface will show you which weapons have rune slots in your inventory, who wields the weapon, and the available runes with which to enchant. Simply drag the rune into the open weapon slot to add its ability to the weapon. If you want to make a change, drag the active rune back to the rune inventory section and add a new rune to the weapon.

Runes

There are five rune categories, which increase in potency with each level: novice, journeyman, expert, master, and grandmaster. A novice flame rune, for example, grants +1 fire damage, while a grandmaster flame rune gives +5. There are nine different rune abilities as well: cold iron (damage vs. undead), dweomer (spell resistance), flame (added fire damage), frost (added cold damage), hale (added physical resistance), lightning (added electrical damage), paralyze (chance to root target), silverite (damage vs. darkspawn), and slow (reduce movement speed).

As you collect runes and add them to your weapons, parcel them out based on party needs and class specialties. The damage-based runes generally go to DPS characters or the tank. Hale, of course, goes to a tank, while dweomer tends to go on mage weapons or ranged DPSers (they tend to draw the return fire from enemy spellcasters in the rear). Paralyze and slow runes are excellent on a tank or DPSer weapon to keep the enemy in place while they wallop on them. As with everything, play to your party's strengths and mind their weaknesses. If your tank keeps getting hurt by enemy spellcasters, naturally give him the dweomer rune.

Accessories - Crafting

Basics ~ Character Generation ~ Classes ~ The Party ~ Companions ~ Supporting Cast ~ **Equipment** ~ Bestiary ~ Walkthroughs ~ Side Quests ~ Random Encounters ~ Achievements/Trophies

Name	Bonuses	Name	Bonuses
Novice Cold Iron Rune	Damage +2 vs. Undead	Expert Lightning Rune	+3 Electricity Damage
Novice Dweomer Rune	+2% Chance to Ignore Hostile Magic	Expert Paralyze Rune	Chance of Paralysis
Novice Flame Rune	+1 Fire Damage	Expert Silverite Rune	Damage +6 vs. Darkspawn
Novice Frost Rune	+1 Cold Damage	Expert Slow Rune	Chance to Reduce Movement Speed
Novice Hale Rune	+5 Physical Resistance	Master Cold Iron Rune	Damage +8 vs. Undead
Novice Lightning Rune	+1 Electricity Damage	Master Dweomer Rune	+8% Chance to Ignore Hostile Magic
Novice Paralyze Rune	Chance of Paralysis	Master Flame Rune	+4 Fire Damage
Novice Silverite Rune	Damage +2 vs. Darkspawn	Master Frost Rune	+4 Cold Damage
Novice Slow Rune	Chance to Reduce Movement Speed	Master Hale Rune	+20 Physical Resistance
Journeyman Cold Iron Rune	Damage +4 vs. Undead	Master Lightning Rune	+4 Electricity Damage
Journeyman Dweomer Rune	+4% Chance to Ignore Hostile Magic	Master Paralyze Rune	Chance of Paralysis
Journeyman Flame Rune	+2 Fire Damage	Master Silverite Rune	Damage +8 vs. Darkspawn
Journeyman Frost Rune	+2 Cold Damage	Master Slow Rune	Chance to Reduce Movement Speed
Journeyman Hale Rune	+10 Physical Resistance	Grandmaster Cold Iron Rune	Damage +10 vs. Undead
Journeyman Lightning Rune	+2 Electricity Damage	Grandmaster Dweomer Rune	+10% Chance to Ignore Hostile Magic
Journeyman Paralyze Rune	Chance of Paralysis	Grandmaster Flame Rune	+5 Fire Damage
Journeyman Silverite Rune	Damage +4 vs. Darkspawn	Grandmaster Frost Rune	+5 Cold Damage
Journeyman Slow Rune	Chance to Reduce Movement Speed	Grandmaster Hale Rune	+25 Physical Resistance
Expert Cold Iron Rune	Damage +6 vs. Undead	Grandmaster Lightning Rune	+5 Electricity Damage
Expert Dweomer Rune	+6% Chance to Ignore Hostile Magic	Grandmaster Paralyze Rune	Chance of Paralysis
Expert Flame Rune	+3 Fire Damage	Grandmaster Silverite Rune	Damage +10 vs. Darkspawn
Expert Frost Rune	+3 Cold Damage	Grandmaster Slow Rune	Chance to Reduce Movement Speed
Expert Hale Rune	+15 Physical Resistance		

Crafting

Herbalism, Trap-Making, and Poison-Making contribute to craft items. When you gain the Herbalism skill, you can craft medicinal items, such as health poultices, lyrium potions, and injury kits. Trap-Making creates simple but effective mechanisms for snaring and injuring enemies, such as claw traps and caltrop traps. Poison-Making extracts potent poisons from deadly plants and venom from reptiles to coat weapons with various effects detrimental to your enemies. Herbalism is absolutely essential in any group, and usually a mage will take up the craft due to their high magic score. Trap-Making is a nice luxury if you have the extra skill points to spend on it. Any warrior or rogue who wants a little extra AoE and root/snaring effects can dabble here. Poison-Making will improve DPS, which fits with a rogue or damage-dealing warrior. You main PC should probably spend skill points on the critical talents, such as Coercion and Combat Training (for warriors and rogues), while each companion can take one of the crafting skills to maximize your item output in the various crafting areas.

Crafting Recipes

So you've decided you want to study up on Herbalism, Poison-Making, or Trap-Making. What reagents to you need, and at what rank can you make each crafting item? Read through the following table for the essentials you need to craft every item in the game.

primagames.com

Herbalism

Item Name	Craft	Ingredient 1	Count 1	Ingredient 2	Count 2	Ingredient 3	Count 3	Ingredient 4	Count 4
Lesser Health Poultice	Herbalism	Elfroot	1	Flask	1	—	0	—	0
Lesser Lyrium Potion	Herbalism	Lyrium Dust	1	Flask	1	—	0	—	0
Mabari Crunch	Herbalism	Elfroot	1	Deep Mushroom	1	—	0	—	0
Double-Baked Mabari Crunch	Herbalism (Improved)	Elfroot	2	Deep Mushroom	2	—	0	—	0
Health Poultice	Herbalism (Improved)	Elfroot	3	Flask	1	Distillation Agent	1	—	0
Incense of Awareness	Herbalism (Improved)	Lyrium Dust	1	Deep Mushroom	1	Flask	1	Distillation Agent	1
Lyrium Potion	Herbalism (Improved)	Lyrium Dust	2	Flask	1	Distillation Agent	1	—	0
Minor Injury Repair Kit	Herbalism (Improved)	Elfroot	2	Deep Mushroom	2	Distillation Agent	1	—	0
Rock Salve	Herbalism (Improved)	Deep Mushroom	2	Flask	1	Distillation Agent	1	—	0
Greater Health Poultice	Herbalism (Expert)	Elfroot	4	Flask	1	Distillation Agent	2	Concentrator Agent	1
Greater Lyrium Potion	Herbalism (Expert)	Lyrium Dust	3	Flask	1	Distillation Agent	2	Concentrator Agent	1
Injury Repair Kit	Herbalism (Expert)	Elfroot	3	Deep Mushroom	3	Distillation Agent	2	Concentrator Agent	1
Lesser Elixir of Grounding	Herbalism (Expert)	Frozen Lightning	1	Flask	1	Concentrator Agent	1	—	0
Lesser Ice Salve	Herbalism (Expert)	Frostrock	1	Flask	1	Concentrator Agent	1	—	0
Lesser Nature Salve	Herbalism (Expert)	Lifestone	1	Flask	1	Concentrator Agent	1	—	0
Lesser Spirit Balm	Herbalism (Expert)	Spirit Shard	1	Flask	1	Concentrator Agent	1	—	0
Lesser Warmth Balm	Herbalism (Expert)	Fire Crystal	1	Flask	1	Concentrator Agent	1	—	0
Swift Salve	Herbalism (Expert)	Lyrium Dust	2	Deep Mushroom	2	Flask	1	Concentrator Agent	1
Dwarven Regicide Antidote	Herbalism (Master)	Elfroot	4	Lifestone	2	Flask	1	Concentrator Agent	2
Greater Elixir of Grounding	Herbalism (Master)	Frozen Lightning	2	Flask	1	Distillation Agent	1	Concentrator Agent	2
Greater Ice Salve	Herbalism (Master)	Frostrock	2	Flask	1	Distillation Agent	1	Concentrator Agent	2
Greater Nature Salve	Herbalism (Master)	Lifestone	2	Flask	1	Distillation Agent	1	Concentrator Agent	2
Greater Spirit Balm	Herbalism (Master)	Spirit Shard	2	Flask	1	Distillation Agent	1	Concentrator Agent	2
Greater Warmth Balm	Herbalism (Master)	Fire Crystal	2	Flask	1	Distillation Agent	1	Concentrator Agent	2
Major Injury Repair Kit	Herbalism (Master)	Elfroot	4	Deep Mushroom	4	Distillation Agent	2	Concentrator Agent	2
Potent Health Poultice	Herbalism (Master)	Elfroot	5	Flask	1	Distillation Agent	2	Concentrator Agent	2
Potent Lyrium Potion	Herbalism (Master)	Lyrium Dust	4	Flask	1	Distillation Agent	2	Concentrator Agent	2

Poison-Making

Item Name	Craft	Ingredient 1	Count 1	Ingredient 2	Count 2	Ingredient 3	Count 3	Ingredient 4	Count 4
Deathroot Extract	Poison-Making	Deathroot	1	Flask	1	—	0	—	0
Venom	Poison-Making	Toxin Extract	1	Flask	1	—	0	—	0
Acid Flask	Poison-Making (Improved)	Lifestone	1	Flask	1	Corrupter Agent	1	—	0
Concentrated Death-root Extract	Poison-Making (Improved)	Deathroot	2	Flask	1	Distillation Agent	1	—	0
Concentrated Venom	Poison-Making (Improved)	Toxin Extract	2	Flask	1	Distillation Agent	1	—	0
Crow Poison	Poison-Making (Improved)	Toxin Extract	2	Deathroot	2	Flask	1	Distillation Agent	1

Crafting

Basics ~ Character Generation ~ Classes ~ The Party ~ Companions ~ Supporting Cast ~ **Equipment** ~ Bestiary ~ Walkthroughs ~ Side Quests ~ Random Encounters ~ Achievements/Trophies

Poison-Making (continued)

Item Name	Craft	Ingredient 1	Count 1	Ingredient 2	Count 2	Ingredient 3	Count 3	Ingredient 4	Count 4
Fire Bomb	Poison-Making (Improved)	Fire Crystal	1	Flask	1	Corrupter Agent	1	—	0
Freeze Bomb	Poison-Making (Improved)	Frostrock	1	Flask	1	Corrupter Agent	1	—	0
Shock Bomb	Poison-Making (Improved)	Frozen Lightning	1	Flask	1	Corrupter Agent	1	—	0
Soulrot Bomb	Poison-Making (Improved)	Spirit Shard	1	Flask	1	Corrupter Agent	1	—	0
Acidic Coating	Poison-Making (Expert)	Lifestone	2	Flask	1	Corrupter Agent	2	Concentrator Agent	1
Adder's Kiss	Poison-Making (Expert)	Toxin Extract	3	Flask	1	Distillation Agent	2	Concentrator Agent	1
Concentrated Crow Poison	Poison-Making (Expert)	Toxin Extract	3	Deathroot	3	Flask	1	Concentrator Agent	1
Demonic Poison	Poison-Making (Expert)	Demonic Ichor	1	Flask	1	Concentrator Agent	1	—	0
Flaming Coating	Poison-Making (Expert)	Fire Crystal	2	Flask	1	Corrupter Agent	2	Concentrator Agent	1
Fleshrot	Poison-Making (Expert)	Deathroot	3	Flask	1	Distillation Agent	2	Concentrator Agent	1
Freezing Coating	Poison-Making (Expert)	Frostrock	2	Flask	1	Corrupter Agent	2	Concentrator Agent	1
Magebane	Poison-Making (Expert)	Lyrium Dust	3	Flask	1	Corrupter Agent	2	Concentrator Agent	1
Shock Coating	Poison-Making (Expert)	Frozen Lightning	2	Flask	1	Corrupter Agent	2	Concentrator Agent	1
Soldier's Bane	Poison-Making (Expert)	Deep Mushroom	3	Flask	1	Corrupter Agent	2	Concentrator Agent	1
Soulrot Coating	Poison-Making (Expert)	Spirit Shard	2	Flask	1	Corrupter Agent	2	Concentrator Agent	1
Concentrated Demonic Poison	Poison-Making (Master)	Demonic Ichor	2	Flask	1	Concentrator Agent	2	—	0
Concentrated Magebane	Poison-Making (Master)	Lyrium Dust	4	Flask	1	Corrupter Agent	2	Concentrator Agent	2
Concentrated Soldier's Bane	Poison-Making (Master)	Deep Mushroom	4	Flask	1	Corrupter Agent	2	Concentrator Agent	2
Quiet Death	Poison-Making (Master)	Toxin Extract	4	Deathroot	4	Flask	1	Concentrator Agent	2

Trap-Making

Item Name	Craft	Ingredient 1	Count 1	Ingredient 2	Count 2	Ingredient 3	Count 3	Ingredient 4	Count 4
Rope Trap	Trap-Making	Trap Trigger	1	—	0	—	0	—	0
Small Caltrop Trap	Trap-Making	Metal Shard	1	—	0	—	0	—	0
Small Claw Trap	Trap-Making	Metal Shard	1	Trap Trigger	1	—	0	—	0
Small Shrapnel Trap	Trap-Making	Metal Shard	1	Trap Trigger	1	—	0	—	0
Large Caltrop Trap	Trap-Making (Improved)	Metal Shard	2	—	0	—	0	—	0
Large Claw Trap	Trap-Making (Improved)	Metal Shard	2	Trap Trigger	1	—	0	—	0
Large Shrapnel Trap	Trap-Making (Improved)	Metal Shard	2	Trap Trigger	1	—	0	—	0
Mild Choking Powder Trap	Trap-Making (Improved)	Toxin Extract	1	Corrupter Agent	1	Trap Trigger	1	—	0
Mild Sleeping Gas Trap	Trap-Making (Improved)	Deathroot	1	Corrupter Agent	1	Trap Trigger	1	—	0
Small Grease Trap	Trap-Making (Improved)	Lifestone	1	Distillation Agent	1	Trap Trigger	1	—	0
Small Lure	Trap-Making (Improved)	Glamour Charm	1	—	0	—	0	—	0
Acidic Trap	Trap-Making (Expert)	Lifestone	1	Corrupter Agent	1	Trap Trigger	1	—	0
Choking Powder Trap	Trap-Making (Expert)	Toxin Extract	2	Corrupter Agent	2	Concentrator Agent	1	Trap Trigger	1
Fire Trap	Trap-Making (Expert)	Fire Crystal	1	Corrupter Agent	1	Trap Trigger	1	—	0

primagames.com

Trap-Making (continued)

Item Name	Craft	Ingredient 1	Count 1	Ingredient 2	Count 2	Ingredient 3	Count 3	Ingredient 4	Count 4
Freeze Trap	Trap-Making (Expert)	Frostrock	1	Corrupter Agent	1	Trap Trigger	1	—	0
Large Grease Trap	Trap-Making (Expert)	Lifestone	2	Distillation Agent	2	Concentrator Agent	1	Trap Trigger	1
Large Lure	Trap-Making (Expert)	Glamour Charm	2	—	0	—	0	—	0
Poisoned Caltrop Trap	Trap-Making (Expert)	Metal Shard	2	Lifestone	1	Corrupter Agent	1	—	0
Shock Trap	Trap-Making (Expert)	Frozen Lightning	1	Corrupter Agent	1	Trap Trigger	1	—	0
Sleeping Gas Trap	Trap-Making (Expert)	Deathroot	2	Corrupter Agent	2	Concentrator Agent	1	Trap Trigger	1
Soulrot Trap	Trap-Making (Expert)	Spirit Shard	1	Corrupter Agent	1	Trap Trigger	1	—	0
Acidic Grease Trap	Trap-Making (Master)	Lifestone	3	Corrupter Agent	2	Concentrator Agent	2	Trap Trigger	1
Choking Powder Cloud Trap	Trap-Making (Master)	Toxin Extract	3	Corrupter Agent	2	Concentrator Agent	2	Trap Trigger	1
Irresistable Lure	Trap-Making (Master)	Glamour Charm	3	—	0	—	0	—	0
Sleeping Gas Cloud Trap	Trap-Making (Master)	Deathroot	3	Corrupter Agent	2	Concentrator Agent	2	Trap Trigger	1

Recipes and Plans

Item Name	Location	Merchant Name
Acid Flask Recipe	Dalish Camp	Varathorn's Goods
Acid Flask Recipe	Dalish Camp	Varathorn's Goods (second store)
Acid Flask Recipe	Haven	New Shop Keeper
Acid Flask Recipe	Haven	Shop Keeper
Acid Flask Recipe	Ostagar	Quartermaster
Acidic Coating Recipe	Dalish Camp	Varathorn's Goods
Acidic Coating Recipe	Dalish Camp	Varathorn's Goods (second store)
Acidic Coating Recipe	Haven	New Shop Keeper
Acidic Coating Recipe	Haven	Shop Keeper
Acidic Grease Trap Plans	Dalish Camp	Varathorn's Goods (second store)
Acidic Trap Plans	Dalish Camp	Varathorn's Goods
Acidic Trap Plans	Dalish Camp	Varathorn's Goods (second store)
Adder's Kiss Recipe	Orzammar	Alimar
Choking Powder Cloud Trap Plans	Orzammar	Alarith's Store (after Landsmeet)
Choking Powder Trap Plans	Haven	New Shop Keeper
Choking Powder Trap Plans	Orzammar	Alimar
Concentrated Crow Poison Recipe	Denerim Market District	Cesar
Concentrated Crow Poison Recipe	Denerim Market District	Cesar (second store)
Concentrated Deathroot Extract Recipe	Frostback Mountains	Faryn
Concentrated Deathroot Extract Recipe	Lothering	Merchant
Concentrated Deathroot Extract Recipe	Ostagar	Quartermaster (second store)
Concentrated Demonic Poison Recipe	Denerim Market District	Cesar (second store)
Concentrated Magebane Recipe	Denerim Market District	Cesar (second store)
Concentrated Soldier's Bane Recipe	Denerim Market District	Cesar (second store)

Recipes and Plans

Item Name	Location	Merchant Name
Concentrated Venom Recipe	Lothering	Merchant
Concentrated Venom Recipe	Orzammar	Alimar
Concentrated Venom Recipe	Ostagar	Quartermaster
Crow Poison Recipe	Orzammar	Alimar
Demonic Poison Recipe	Denerim Market District	Cesar
Demonic Poison Recipe	Denerim Market District	Cesar (second store)
Double-Baked Mabari Crunch Recipe	Ostagar	Quartermaster (second store)
Double-Baked Mabari Crunch Recipe	Redcliffe	Lloyd's Tavern
Double-Baked Mabari Crunch Recipe	Redcliffe	Lloyd's Tavern (second store)
Fire Bomb Recipe	Circle Tower	Quartermaster
Fire Bomb Recipe	Lothering	Merchant
Fire Bomb Recipe	Ostagar	Quartermaster (second store)
Fire Trap Plans	Lake Calenhad	Innkeeper
Flame Coating Recipe	Circle Tower	Quartermaster
Flame Coating Recipe	Orzammar	Alarith's Store (after Landsmeet)
Fleshrot Recipe	Frostback Mountains	Faryn
Freeze Bomb Recipe	Lothering	Merchant
Freeze Bomb Recipe	Orzammar	Alimar
Freeze Trap Plans	Orzammar	Alimar
Freeze Trap Plans	Random Encounter	Dwarven Merchant
Freezing Coating Recipe	Orzammar	Alarith's Store (after Landsmeet)
Freezing Coating Recipe	Orzammar	Alimar
Greater Elixir of Grounding Recipe	Haven	New Shop Keeper
Greater Health Poultice Recipe	Dalish Camp	Varathorn's Goods
Greater Health Poultice Recipe	Dalish Camp	Varathorn's Goods (second store)
Greater Health Poultice Recipe	Denerim Market District	Gnawed Noble Tavern (after Landsmeet)

Crafting

Basics ~ Character Generation ~ Classes ~ The Party ~ Companions ~ Supporting Cast ~ Equipment ~ Bestiary ~ Walkthroughs ~ Side Quests ~ Random Encounters ~ Achievements/Trophies

Recipes and Plans

Item Name	Location	Merchant Name
Greater Health Poultice Recipe	Orzammar	Figor
Greater Ice Salve Recipe	Denerim Market District	Wonders of Thedas (after Landsmeet)
Greater Injury Kit Recipe	Orzammar	Alarith's Store (after Landsmeet)
Greater Lyrium Potion Recipe	Denerim Market District	Wonders of Thedas (after Landsmeet)
Greater Lyrium Potion Recipe	Frostback Mountains	Faryn
Greater Nature Salve Recipe	Dalish Camp	Varathorn's Goods (second store)
Greater Spirit Balm Recipe	Dalish Camp	Varathorn's Goods (second store)
Greater Warmth Balm Recipe	Denerim Market District	Wonders of Thedas (after Landsmeet)
Health Poultice Recipe	Dalish Camp	Varathorn's Goods
Health Poultice Recipe	Dalish Camp	Varathorn's Goods (second store)
Health Poultice Recipe	Denerim Market District	Gnawed Noble Tavern (after Landsmeet)
Health Poultice Recipe	Orzammar	Figor
Health Poultice Recipe	Ostagar	Quartermaster
Health Poultice Recipe	Redcliffe	Lloyd's Tavern
Health Poultice Recipe	Redcliffe	Lloyd's Tavern (second store)
Incense of Awareness Recipe	Circle Tower	Quartermaster
Incense of Awareness Recipe	Lothering: Dane's Refuge	Barlin
Injury Kit Recipe	Circle Tower	Quartermaster
Injury Kit Recipe	Denerim Market District	Gnawed Noble Tavern (after Landsmeet)
Interesting Lure Trap Plans	Haven	New Shop Keeper
Interesting Lure Trap Plans	Orzammar: Commons	Legnar
Large Caltrop Trap Plans	Orzammar	Janar
Large Caltrop Trap Plans	Redcliffe	Blacksmith
Large Caltrop Trap Plans	Redcliffe	Owen
Large Caltrop Trap Plans	Redcliffe	Owen (second store)
Large Claw Trap Plans	Lothering: Dane's Refuge	Barlin
Large Claw Trap Plans	Orzammar	Janar
Large Claw Trap Plans	Ostagar	Quartermaster
Large Claw Trap Plans	Redcliffe	Blacksmith
Large Grease Trap Plans	Dalish Camp	Varathorn's Goods
Large Grease Trap Plans	Dalish Camp	Varathorn's Goods (second store)
Large Grease Trap Plans	Frostback Mountains	Faryn
Large Shrapnel Trap Plans	Lothering: Dane's Refuge	Barlin
Large Shrapnel Trap Plans	Orzammar	Janar
Large Shrapnel Trap Plans	Redcliffe	Owen
Large Shrapnel Trap Plans	Redcliffe	Owen (second store)
Lesser Elixir of Grounding Recipe	Haven	New Shop Keeper
Lesser Elixir of Grounding Recipe	Haven	Shop Keeper
Lesser Ice Salve Recipe	Frostback Mountains	Faryn
Lesser Ice Salve Recipe	Haven	New Shop Keeper
Lesser Injury Kit Recipe	Denerim Market District	Gnawed Noble Tavern (after Landsmeet)
Lesser Injury Kit Recipe	Lothering: Dane's Refuge	Barlin
Lesser Injury Kit Recipe	Orzammar	Figor
Lesser Injury Kit Recipe	Ostagar	Quartermaster
Lesser Injury Kit Recipe	Redcliffe	Lloyd's Tavern

Recipes and Plans

Item Name	Location	Merchant Name
Lesser Injury Kit Recipe	Redcliffe	Lloyd's Tavern (second store)
Lesser Nature Salve Recipe	Dalish Camp	Varathorn's Goods
Lesser Nature Salve Recipe	Dalish Camp	Varathorn's Goods (second store)
Lesser Nature Salve Recipe	Orzammar	Alarith's Store (after Landsmeet)
Lesser Spirit Balm Recipe	Circle Tower	Quartermaster
Lesser Spirit Balm Recipe	Dalish Camp	Varathorn's Goods
Lesser Spirit Balm Recipe	Dalish Camp	Varathorn's Goods (second store)
Lesser Warmth Balm Recipe	Circle Tower	Quartermaster
Lesser Warmth Balm Recipe	Orzammar	Alarith's Store (after Landsmeet)
Lyrium Potion Recipe	Circle Tower	Quartermaster
Lyrium Potion Recipe	Haven	New Shop Keeper
Lyrium Potion Recipe	Haven	Shop Keeper
Lyrium Potion Recipe	Lothering: Dane's Refuge	Barlin
Magebane Poison Recipe	Denerim Market District	Cesar
Magebane Poison Recipe	Denerim Market District	Cesar (second store)
Magebane Poison Recipe	Haven	New Shop Keeper
Mild Choking Powder Trap Plans	Haven	New Shop Keeper
Mild Choking Powder Trap Plans	Haven	Shop Keeper
Mild Choking Powder Trap Plans	Lake Calenhad	Innkeeper
Mild Choking Powder Trap Plans	Orzammar	Alimar
Mild Lure Plans	Haven	New Shop Keeper
Mild Lure Plans	Haven	Shop Keeper
Mild Lure Plans	Lothering: Dane's Refuge	Barlin
Mild Lure Plans	Orzammar: Commons	Legnar
Mild Lure Plans	Ostagar	Quartermaster (second store)
Mild Sleeping Gas Trap Plans	Orzammar	Alimar
Mild Sleeping Gas Trap Plans	Ostagar	Quartermaster (second store)
Overpowering Lure Trap Plans	Denerim Market District	Wonders of Thedas (after Landsmeet)
Poisoned Caltrop Trap Plans	Redcliffe	Owen (second store)
Potent Health Poultice Recipe	Dalish Camp	Varathorn's Goods (second store)
Potent Lyrium Potion Recipe	Denerim Market District	Wonders of Thedas (after Landsmeet)
Quiet Death Recipe	Denerim Market District	Cesar (second store)
Rock Salve Recipe	Orzammar	Alarith's Store (after Landsmeet)
Rock Salve Recipe	Ostagar	Quartermaster (second store)
Shock Bomb Recipe	Denerim Market District	Wonders of Thedas (after Landsmeet)
Shock Coating Recipe	Denerim Market District	Wonders of Thedas (after Landsmeet)
Shock Trap Plans	Random Encounter	Dwarven Merchant
Sleeping Gas Cloud Trap Plans	Orzammar	Alarith's Store (after Landsmeet)
Sleeping Gas Trap Plans	Orzammar	Alimar
Small Grease Trap Plans	Dalish Camp	Varathorn's Goods
Small Grease Trap Plans	Dalish Camp	Varathorn's Goods (second store)

Recipes and Plans

Item Name	Location	Merchant Name
Small Grease Trap Plans	Frostback Mountains	Faryn
Small Grease Trap Plans	Lake Calenhad	Innkeeper
Small Grease Trap Plans	Lothering: Dane's Refuge	Barlin
Small Grease Trap Plans	Ostagar	Quartermaster
Soldier's Bane Recipe	Denerim Market District	Cesar
Soldier's Bane Recipe	Denerim Market District	Cesar (second store)
Soldier's Bane Recipe	Haven	New Shop Keeper
Soulrot Bomb Recipe	Dalish Camp	Varathorn's Goods (second store)

Recipes and Plans

Item Name	Location	Merchant Name
Soulrot Coating Recipe	Dalish Camp	Varathorn's Goods (second store)
Soulrot Trap Plans	Dalish Camp	Varathorn's Goods (second store)
Soulrot Trap Plans	Frostback Mountains	Faryn
Swift Salve Recipe	Denerim Market District	Wonders of Thedas (after Landsmeet)
Swift Salve Recipe	Frostback Mountains	Faryn

Usable Items

Anything you can craft, and many of the crafting components, can be considered usable items. The most common ones are health poultices and lyrium potions (Herbalism), poisons from Poison-Making, and trap kits from Trap-Making. Click on the item and you gain the effect, using up one of the item in the process. If you use an item often, add it to your quickbar/shortcut for easy access. Something that early adventurers may not be aware of is that crafting reagents also have effects if used directly. For example, Deep Mushroom restores 10 stamina, while Lifestone gives +10 nature resistance for one minute. In general, though, if you plan on crafting, hold off on the small one-time reagent effects to gain the larger effects from crafted items.

Dog Food

Name	Quality #1	Quality #2	Quality #3
Double-Baked Mabari Crunch	+16.0 Health Regeneration for 10 seconds	+16.0 Stamina Regeneration for 10 seconds	Removes 3 Injuries
Mabari Crunch	+8.0 Health Regeneration for 10 seconds	+8.0 Stamina Regeneration for 10 seconds	Removes 1 Injury

Grenades

Name	Quality #1	Quality #2	Quality #3
Acid Flask	Deals 80 Nature Damage to creatures in the area of effect	—	—
Fire Bomb	Deals 80 Fire Damage to creatures in the area of effect	—	—
Freeze Bomb	Deals 80 Cold Damage to creatures in the area of effect	—	—
Shock Bomb	Deals 80 Electricity Damage to creatures in the area of effect	—	—
Soulrot Bomb	Deals 80 Spirit Damage to creatures in the area of effect	—	—

Health Potions

Name	Quality #1	Quality #2	Quality #3
Lesser Health Poultice	Restores 50+ Health	—	—
Health Poultice	Restores 100+ Health	—	—
Greater Health Poultice	Restores 150+ Health	—	—
Potent Health Poultice	Restores 200+ Health	—	—
Shimmering Orb	Restores 50+ Health	—	—

Injury Repair Kits

Name	Quality #1	Quality #2	Quality #3
Lesser Injury Kit	Restores 10 Health	Removes 1 Injury	—
Injury Kit	Restores 20 Health	Removes 3 Injuries	—
Greater Injury Kit	Restores 40 Health	Removes All Injuries	—

Mana Potions

Name	Quality #1	Quality #2	Quality #3
Lesser Lyrium Potion	Restores 50+ Mana	—	—
Lyrium Potion	Restores 100+ Mana	—	—
Greater Lyrium Potion	Restores 150+ Mana	—	—
Potent Lyrium Potion	Restores 200+ Mana	—	—

Poisons

Name	Quality #1	Quality #2	Quality #3
Deathroot Extract	+1 Nature Damage for 60 seconds	Chance to stun target for 60 seconds	—
Venom	+1 Nature Damage for 60 seconds	Chance to slow target for 60 seconds	—
Concentrated Deathroot Extract	+2 Nature Damage for 60 seconds	Chance to stun target for 60 seconds	—
Concentrated Venom	+2 Nature Damage for 60 seconds	Chance to slow target for 60 seconds	—
Adder's Kiss	+3 Nature Damage for 60 seconds	Chance to slow target for 60 seconds	—
Crow Poison	+3 Nature Damage for 60 seconds	Chance to stun target for 60 seconds	—

Crafting - Usable Items

Basics ~ Character Generation ~ Classes ~ The Party ~ Companions ~ Supporting Cast ~ **Equipment** ~ Bestiary ~ Walkthroughs ~ Side Quests ~ Random Encounters ~ Achievements/Trophies

Poisons (continued)

Name	Quality #1	Quality #2	Quality #3
Fleshrot	+3 Nature Damage for 60 seconds	Chance to stun target for 60 seconds	—
Demonic Poison	+5 Spirit Damage for 60 seconds	—	—
Magebane	+5 Mana Damage for 60 seconds	—	—
Soldier's Bane	+5 Stamina Damage for 60 seconds	—	—
Concentrated Crow Poison	+6 Nature Damage for 60 seconds	Chance to stun target for 60 seconds	—
Concentrated Demonic Poison	+10 Spirit Damage for 60 seconds	—	—
Concentrated Magebane	+10 Mana Damage for 60 seconds	—	—
Concentrated Soldier's Bane	+10 Stamina Damage for 60 seconds	—	—
Quiet Death	+10 Nature Damage for 60 seconds	Chance to stun target for 60 seconds	Chance to instantly kill weak, injured creatures

Reagents

Name	Quality #1	Quality #2	Quality #3
Deep Mushroom	Restores 10 Stamina	—	—
Elfroot	Restores 10 Health	—	—
Fire Crystal	+10 Fire Resistance for 60 seconds	—	—
Frostrock	+10 Cold Resistance for 60 seconds	—	—
Frozen Lightning	+10 Electricity Resistance for 60 seconds	—	—
Lifestone	+10 Nature Resistance for 60 seconds	—	—
Lyrium Dust	Restores 10 Mana	—	—
Spirit Shard	+10 Spirit Resistance for 60 seconds	—	—

Resistance Potions

Name	Quality #1	Quality #2	Quality #3
Lesser Elixir of Grounding	+30 Electricity Resistance for 180 seconds	—	—
Lesser Ice Salve	+30 Cold Resistance for 180 seconds	—	—
Lesser Nature Salve	+30 Nature Resistance for 180 seconds	—	—
Lesser Spirit Balm	+30 Spirit Resistance for 180 seconds	—	—
Lesser Warmth Balm	+30 Fire Resistance for 180 seconds	—	—
Greater Elixir of Grounding	+60 Electricity Resistance for 180 seconds	—	—
Greater Ice Salve	+60 Cold Resistance for 180 seconds	—	—
Greater Nature Salve	+60 Nature Resistance for 180 seconds	—	—
Greater Spirit Balm	+60 Spirit Resistance for 180 seconds	—	—
Greater Warmth Balm	+60 Fire Resistance for 180 seconds	—	—

Trap Kits

Name	Quality #1	Quality #2	Quality #3
Acidic Grease Trap	Movement speed reduced	Chance to slip	Constant Nature Damage
Acidic Trap	100 Nature Damage	—	—
Choking Powder Cloud Trap	Cloud remains for 20 seconds	Dazed	Movement speed reduced
Choking Powder Trap	Dazed	Movement speed reduced	—
Fire Trap	100 Fire Damage	—	—
Freeze Trap	100 Cold Damage	—	—
Interesting Lure	Middle rank creatures are drawn to the lure	Lure disappears after being touched	—
Large Caltrop Trap	Movement speed reduced	Enemies take constant Physical Damage	—
Large Claw Trap	Immobilized	150 Physical Damage	—
Large Grease Trap	Movement speed reduced	Chance to slip	—
Large Shrapnel Trap	80 Physical Damage	—	—
Mild Choking Powder Trap	Dazed	Movement speed reduced	—
Mild Lure	Lower rank creatures are drawn to the lure	Lure disappears after being touched	—
Mild Sleeping Gas Trap	Put to sleep	—	—
Overpowering Lure	Most creatures are drawn to the lure	Lure disappears 30 seconds after being touched	—
Poisoned Caltrop Trap	Movement speed reduced	Enemies take constant Physical and Nature Damage	—
Shock Trap	100 Electricity Damage	—	—
Sleeping Gas Cloud Trap	Cloud remains for 20 seconds	Put to sleep	—
Sleeping Gas Trap	Put to sleep	—	—
Small Caltrop Trap	Movement speed reduced	Enemies take constant Physical Damage	—
Small Claw Trap	Immobilized	100 Physical Damage	—
Small Grease Trap	Movement speed reduced	Chance to slip	—
Small Shrapnel Trap	60 Physical Damage	—	—
Soulrot Trap	100 Spirit Damage	—	—
Spring Trap	Chance to slip	—	—

Weapon Coatings			
Name	Quality #1	Quality #2	Quality #3
Acidic Coating	+2 Nature Damage for 60 seconds	—	—
Flame Coating	+2 Fire Damage for 60 seconds	—	—
Freezing Coating	+2 Cold Damage for 60 seconds	—	—
Shock Coating	+3 Electricity Damage for 60 seconds	—	—
Soulrot Coating	+2 Spirit Damage for 60 seconds	—	—

Misc			
Name	Quality #1	Quality #2	Quality #3
Dwarven Regicide Antidote	Dispels magical effects	—	—
Formari Tome	Character gains +1 Skill point	—	—
Greater Tome of the Mortal Vessel	Character gains +2 Attribute points	—	—
Incense of Awareness	+10 Defense for 120 seconds	-10 Mental Resistance for 120 seconds	—
Kolgrim's Horn	Summons High Dragon	—	—
Litany of Andralla	Stops Mind-Controlling Blood Magic	—	—
Rock Salve	+5 Armor for 120 seconds	+10 Physical Resistance for 120 seconds	Movement speed slowed for 120 seconds
Swift Salve	Movement speed increase for 60 seconds	Attack speed increase for 60 seconds	Aim speed increase for 60 seconds
Tome of Arcane Technique	Character gains +1 Talent point	Required: Mage	—
Tome of Ethereal Suggestion	Character gains +1 Talent point	—	—
Tome of Physical Technique	Character gains +1 Talent point	Required: Warrior or Rogue	—
Tome of Skill and Sundry	Character gains +1 Skill point	—	—
Tome of the Mortal Vessel	Character gains +1 Attribute point	—	—

Gifts

Everyone loves to receive gifts, even rugged, never-smiling companions such as Sten. Presenting a gift to a companion raises their approval rating, and you always want your approval rating with a companion as high as possible. Approval rating affects how the companion responds to you, including sharing specializations, inviting you on personal quests, starting up romantic intentions, following your lead, or even leaving the group permanently.

NOTE

See the "Gifts" sections of the Companions chapter for the complete rundown on gifts, approval ratings, distribution recommendations, and more.

As you journey around the land, you will find or buy gifts. Consult the gift charts beginning on this page for the companion who would best benefit from the new gift you have. If you deliver the gift to the correct companion, you will gain a big approval boost for that companion; if you give the special gift to another companion, expect only a minor approval boost (after a while it will only be +1). If you don't care too much about a companion—for example, you only use Alistair instead of Oghren—feel free to give that companion's gifts away to whoever you want to improve relationships with more. There are also many gifts, such as ale in a tavern, that provide a small approval boost but can be given to any companion. You'll need all the gifts you can get to raise a companion's level up to 100 if you ever want to max out a companion's affection for you. Romance ensues.

Alistair			
Name	Plot Gift or Normal	Found In	Location
Alistair's Mother's Amulet	Plot	Desk	Castle Redcliffe: Main Floor
Black Runestone	Normal	Chest	Aeducan Thaig
Duncan's Shield	Plot	Armor Stand	Market Warehouse
Onyx Demon Statuette	Normal	Pile of Bones	East Brecilian Forest
Small Carved Statuette	Normal	Crate	Lothering
Stone Dragon Statuette	Normal	Chest	Castle Redcliffe: Upper Floor
Stone Warrior Statuette	Normal	Pile of Dragon Filth	Caverns (Haven)
White Runestone	Normal	Abomination	Third Floor of Circle Tower

Dog			
Name	Plot Gift or Normal	Found In	Location
Beef Bone	Normal	Sacks / Chest	Ostagar / Templar's Quarters in Circle Tower
Lamb Bone	Normal	Chest	Castle Redcliffe: Main Floor
Large Bone	Normal	Corpse	Village Store (Haven)
Ox Bone	Normal	Rubble	West Brecilian Forest
Veal Bone	Normal	Chest	Run-down Apartments (Denerim Alienage)

Leliana			
Name	Plot Gift or Normal	Found In	Location
Andraste's Grace	Plot	Flower	Redcliffe Village (near mill), West Brecilian Forest, or Elven Alienage (near giant tree)
Bronze Symbol of Andraste	Normal	Chest	Lothering Chantry

Leliana (continued)

Name	Plot Gift or Normal	Found In	Location
Chantry Amulet	Normal	Templar Corpse	Senior Mage Quarters in Circle Tower
Etched Silver Symbol	Normal	Ruck	Ortan Thaig
Golden Symbol of Andraste	Normal	Legnar's Store	Orzammar Commons
Nug	Plot	Nug Wrangler	Orzammar Commons
Silver Sword of Mercy	Normal	Dwarven Vendor	Random Encounter
Steel Symbol of Andraste	Normal	Chest	Brother Genitivi's Home in Denerim Market

Loghain

Name	Plot Gift or Normal	Found In	Location
Ancient Map of the Imperium	Normal	Wonders of Thedas Store	Denerim Market District
Botanist's Map of Thedas	Normal	Chest on Main Floor (after the Landsmeet)	Castle Redcliffe
Current Map of Ferelden	Normal	Alarith's Store	Elven Alienage in Denerim
Map of the Anderfels	Normal	Gorim	Denerim Market District
Map of Occupied Ferelden	Normal	Chest in the Upper Floor Guest Room	Redcliffe Castle

Morrigan

Name	Plot Gift or Normal	Found In	Location
Black Grimoire	Plot	Irving's Quarters	Circle Tower
Flemeth's Grimoire	Plot	Chest	Flemeth's Hut
Gold Amulet	Normal	Garin	Orzammar Commons
Golden Demon Pendant	Normal	Corpse	Urn of Sacred Ashes Room
Golden Mirror	Plot	Garin	Orzammar Commons
Golden Rope Necklace	Normal	Barlin	Dane's Refuge in Lothering
Locket	Normal	Locked Chest	Village Store in Haven
Silver Brooch	Normal	Varathorn	Dalish Camp
Silver Chain	Normal	Vanity	Senior Mage Quarters in Circle Tower
Silver Medallion	Normal	Dragon Hoard	Upper Level of Elven Ruins
Tribal Necklace	Normal	Barrel	Top Floor of Tower of Ishal

Oghren

Name	Plot Gift or Normal	Found In	Location
Alley King's Flagon	Normal	Legnar's Store	Orzammar Commons
Chasind Sack Mead	Normal	Dusty Scrolls	Ruined Temple
Garblog's Backcountry Reserve	Normal	Dog	Random chance he'll fetch it
Golden Scythe 4-90 Black	Normal	Crate	Lothering
Legacy White Shear	Normal	Sarcophagus	Lower Ruins
Sun Blonde Vint-1	Normal	Vanity	Templar Quarters

Sten

Name	Plot Gift or Normal	Found In	Location
Painting of a Rebel Queen	Normal	Dwarven Merchant	Random Encounter
Portrait of a Goosegirl	Normal	Faryn	Frostback Mountains
Silver Framed Still-Life	Normal	Chest	Upper Level of Castle Redcliffe
Sten's Sword	Plot	Scavenger near Lake Calenhad Docks, then Faryn in Frostback Mountains	Dwyn in Redcliffe Village (kill him, pay him, or convince him to give it to you)
Totem	Normal	Chest	Caridin's Cross
Water-stained Portrait	Normal	Charred Corpse	Senior Mage Quarters in Circle Tower

Wynne

Name	Plot Gift or Normal	Found In	Location
Discovering Dragon's Blood: Potions, Tinctures, and Spicy Sauces*	Normal	Bookshelf	Ruined Temple
Fancy Scroll	Normal	Sarcophagus	Lower Ruins
Tattered Notebook	Normal	Dog	Random chance he'll fetch it
The Guerrins of Ferelden: A Genealogical History*	Normal	Bookshelf	Upper Level of Castle Redcliffe
The Rose of Orlais	Normal	Pile of Books	Senior Mage Quarters of Circle Tower
The Search for the True Prophet	Normal	Locked Chest	Shaperate in Orzammar

Zevran

Name	Plot Gift or Normal	Found In	Location
Antivan Leather Boots	Plot	Iron Chest	Village Store (Haven)
Dalish Gloves	Plot	Chest	West Brecilian Forest
Medium Gold Bar	Normal	Treasure Pile	Arl of Denerim's Estate—Interior
Medium Silver Bar	Normal	Chest	Anvil of the Void
Small Gold Bar	Normal	Charmed Templar	Templar's Quarters in Circle Tower
Small Silver Bar	Normal	Inscribed Chest	Haven Chantry

*Name shortened on console version.

prima games.com

PRIMA Official Game Guide

Downloadable Content Items

Two new quest lines, "Warden's Keep" and "The Stone Prisoner," add more items to the world of Ferelden if you download the special content. Scan through the lists below for new weapons, armor, accessories, gifts, and more. Note that additional runes, recipes, plans, and a Spirit Healer manual are available from Levi at the Warden's Keep in Soldier's Peak.

Warden's Keep Merchant Vendor Lists (DLC only)

Location	Merchant	Item Name	Item Quantity	Location	Merchant	Item Name	Item Quantity
Soldier's Peak	Levi's Shop	Acid Flask	1	Soldier's Peak	Levi's Shop	Soulrot Coating	2
Soldier's Peak	Levi's Shop	Charm of Still Waters	1	Soldier's Peak	Levi's Shop	Soulrot Coating Recipe	1
Soldier's Peak	Levi's Shop	Concentrator Agent	1	Soldier's Peak	Levi's Shop	Soulrot Trap Plans	1
Soldier's Peak	Levi's Shop	Corrupter Agent	6	Soldier's Peak	Levi's Shop	Spirit Shard	8
Soldier's Peak	Levi's Shop	Demonic Ichor	2	Soldier's Peak	Levi's Shop	Toxin Extract	1
Soldier's Peak	Levi's Shop	Distillation Agent	4	Soldier's Peak	Mikhael's Smithy	Axe	1
Soldier's Peak	Levi's Shop	Expert Frost Rune	1	Soldier's Peak	Mikhael's Smithy	Battleaxe	1
Soldier's Peak	Levi's Shop	Fire Crystal	1	Soldier's Peak	Mikhael's Smithy	Crossbow	1
Soldier's Peak	Levi's Shop	Flask	5	Soldier's Peak	Mikhael's Smithy	Dagger	1
Soldier's Peak	Levi's Shop	Freeze Bomb	3	Soldier's Peak	Mikhael's Smithy	Greatsword	1
Soldier's Peak	Levi's Shop	Freeze Bomb Recipe	1	Soldier's Peak	Mikhael's Smithy	Grey Warden Helmet	4
Soldier's Peak	Levi's Shop	Freeze Trap	5	Soldier's Peak	Mikhael's Smithy	Grey Warden Shield	4
Soldier's Peak	Levi's Shop	Freeze Trap Plans	1	Soldier's Peak	Mikhael's Smithy	Heavy Chainmail	4
Soldier's Peak	Levi's Shop	Freezing Coating	3	Soldier's Peak	Mikhael's Smithy	Heavy Chainmail Boots	4
Soldier's Peak	Levi's Shop	Freezing Coating Recipe	1	Soldier's Peak	Mikhael's Smithy	Heavy Chainmail Gloves	4
Soldier's Peak	Levi's Shop	Frostrock	7	Soldier's Peak	Mikhael's Smithy	Heavy Metal Shield	2
Soldier's Peak	Levi's Shop	Frozen Lightning	6	Soldier's Peak	Mikhael's Smithy	Heavy Plate Armor	4
Soldier's Peak	Levi's Shop	Glamour Charm	1	Soldier's Peak	Mikhael's Smithy	Heavy Plate Boots	4
Soldier's Peak	Levi's Shop	Grandmaster Cold Iron Rune	1	Soldier's Peak	Mikhael's Smithy	Heavy Plate Gloves	4
Soldier's Peak	Levi's Shop	Grandmaster Frost Rune	1	Soldier's Peak	Mikhael's Smithy	Helmet	4
Soldier's Peak	Levi's Shop	Greater Ice Salve Recipe	1	Soldier's Peak	Mikhael's Smithy	Ice Arrow	50
Soldier's Peak	Levi's Shop	Greater Warmth Balm Recipe	1	Soldier's Peak	Mikhael's Smithy	Ice Bolt	50
Soldier's Peak	Levi's Shop	Health Poultice	3	Soldier's Peak	Mikhael's Smithy	Longbow	1
Soldier's Peak	Levi's Shop	Iced Band	1	Soldier's Peak	Mikhael's Smithy	Longsword	1
Soldier's Peak	Levi's Shop	Injury Kit	1	Soldier's Peak	Mikhael's Smithy	Mace	1
Soldier's Peak	Levi's Shop	Journeyman Cold Iron Rune	1	Soldier's Peak	Mikhael's Smithy	Maul	1
Soldier's Peak	Levi's Shop	Journeyman Frost Rune	1	Soldier's Peak	Mikhael's Smithy	Metal Kite Shield	4
Soldier's Peak	Levi's Shop	Journeyman Slow Rune	1	Soldier's Peak	Mikhael's Smithy	Shortbow	1
Soldier's Peak	Levi's Shop	Lesser Health Poultice	4	Soldier's Peak	Mikhael's Smithy	Soldier's Heavy Helm	4
Soldier's Peak	Levi's Shop	Lesser Injury Kit	10	Soldier's Peak	Mikhael's Smithy	Splintmail	4
Soldier's Peak	Levi's Shop	Manual: Spirit Healer	1	Soldier's Peak	Mikhael's Smithy	Splintmail Boots	4
Soldier's Peak	Levi's Shop	Metal Shard	5	Soldier's Peak	Mikhael's Smithy	Splintmail Gloves	4
Soldier's Peak	Levi's Shop	Novice Frost Rune	1	Soldier's Peak	Mikhael's Smithy	Studded Helmet	4
Soldier's Peak	Levi's Shop	Potent Health Poultice	2	Soldier's Peak	Mikhael's Smithy	Studded Leather Armor	4
Soldier's Peak	Levi's Shop	Shaper's Amulet	1	Soldier's Peak	Mikhael's Smithy	Studded Leather Boots	4
Soldier's Peak	Levi's Shop	Soulrot Bomb	2	Soldier's Peak	Mikhael's Smithy	Studded Leather Gloves	4
Soldier's Peak	Levi's Shop	Soulrot Bomb Recipe	1	Soldier's Peak	Mikhael's Smithy	Warden Recruit Shield	4

Stone Prisoner Items (DLC only)

Items from a massive constitution amulet to a helm that buffs all your attributes, even a unique cheese knife, can be found in the golem-themed "Stone Prisoner" downloadable content. Check out all the items here.

Name	Material	Quality #1	Quality #2	Quality #3	Quality #4	Quality #5
Blood Gorged Amulet	Inscribed Leather	Constitution +12	Strength -3	Willpower -3	—	—
Cadash Stompers (boots)	Inscribed Leather	Dexterity +2	Armor +2	Critical Hit Chance +2	—	—
Cord of Shattered Dreams	Hardened Leather	Willpower +3	Mental Resistance +10	Required: Mage	—	—
Dead Thaig Shanker (dagger)	Silverite	Cunning +5	Armor Penetration +1	Attack Power +6	—	—
Harvest Festival Ring	Silverite	Strength +2	Dexterity +2	Attack Power +4	Required: Warrior or Rogue	—
Helm of Honnleath	Red Steel	All Attributes +2	Armor +3	—	—	—
Oalf's Prized Cheese Knife	Red Steel	Armor Penetration +2	—	—	—	—
Wilhelm's Magus Staff	Red Steel	Willpower +3	Fire Resistance +25	Fire Damage +10%	Lightning Damage +10%	Required: Mage

Warden's Keep Items (DLC only)

Some major items, including the threat-reducing Shadow Belt and new tier 8 star metal weapons, come from the "Warden's Keep" downloadable content. See the Random Encounters chapter for details on the star metal quest, while stats for all the rest of the "Warden's Keep" items can be found here.

Name	Material	Quality #1	Quality #2	Quality #3	Quality #4
Antique Warden Crossbow	Ironbark	Damage +1	Faster Aim by 0.5 seconds	—	—
Asturian's Might	Silverite	Damage +2	Armor Penetration +2	Weakens Nearby Darkspawn	—
Robes of Avernus	Cloth	Willpower +3	Armor +3	Blood Magic +1	—
Shadow Belt	Iron	Melee Crit Chance +3	Reduces Hostility	—	—
Starfang (greatsword)	Star Metal	Strength +3	Armor Penetration +5	Attack +8	—
Starfang (longsword)	Star Metal	Dexterity +3	Damage +3	Armor Penetration +5	—
Warden Commander Armor*	Silverite	Armor +1	Combat Stamina Regen +0.50	Crit Damage +15%	Physical Resistance +10
Warden Commander Boots*	Steel	Stamina +50	—	—	—
Warden Commander Gloves*	Steel	Fire Resistance +10	—	—	—
Winter's Breath	Dragonbone	Cold Resistance +25	Cold Damage +15%	Required: Mage	—

*When the Warden boots, gloves, and chest armor are combined in a set on the character, he or she receives a bonus to health. In addition, spells or talents cost less to use.

Shale's Gifts (DLC only)

Remarkable gemstones attract Shale's eye, so if you want to bump up Shale's approval rating, you'll want to collect as many of these gifts for the downloadable golem companion.

Gift	Plot Gift or Normal	Found In	Location
Remarkable Amethyst	Normal	Alimar's Emporium	Orzammar's Dust Town
Remarkable Diamond*	Normal	Garin's Gem Store	Orzammar Commons
Remarkable Emerald	Normal	Figor's Store	Orzammar Commons
Remarkable Garnet	Normal	Wonders of Thedas Store	Denerim Market District
Remarkable Greenstone	Normal	Cellars	Village of Honnleath
Remarkable Malachite	Normal	Shaperate Store	Circle Tower
Remarkable Ruby	Normal	Alarith's Store	Denerim's Elven Alienage
Remarkable Sapphire	Normal	Legnar's Store	Orzammar Commons
Remarkable Topaz	Normal	Faryn's Store	Frostback Mountains

*Console Version Only.

Shale's Crystals (DLC only)

Unlike other companions, Shale uses crystals as weapons and armor. When wearing a matching set of a particular element, Shale gets an additional bonus to damage and resistance for that element.

Size	Quality	Type	Bonus 1	Bonus Value	Bonus 2	Bonus Value	Bonus 3	Bonus Value	Bonus 4	Bonus Value
Large	Chipped	Fire	Fire Resistance	10%	—	—	—	—	—	—
Large	Flawed	Fire	Fire Resistance	20%	—	—	—	—	—	—
Large	Clear	Fire	Fire Resistance	30%	Defense	3	Strength	1	Combat Stamina Regen	4
Large	Flawless	Fire	Fire Resistance	40%	Defense	6	Strength	2	Combat Stamina Regen	8
Large	Brilliant	Fire	Fire Resistance	50%	Defense	9	Strength	4	Combat Stamina Regen	12
Large	Chipped	Ice	Cold Resistance	10%	—	—	—	—	—	—
Large	Flawed	Ice	Cold Resistance	20%	—	—	—	—	—	—
Large	Clear	Ice	Cold Resistance	30%	Defense	6	Combat Health Regen	1	Increase Healing Spells	5%
Large	Flawless	Ice	Cold Resistance	40%	Defense	9	Combat Health Regen	3	Increase Healing Spells	10%
Large	Brilliant	Ice	Cold Resistance	50%	Defense	15	Combat Health Regen	5	Increase Healing Spells	15%
Large	Chipped	Lightning	Electricity Resistance	10%	—	—	—	—	—	—
Large	Flawed	Lightning	Electricity Resistance	20%	—	—	—	—	—	—
Large	Clear	Lightning	Electricity Resistance	30%	Dexterity	2	Chance to Dodge Attacks	5%	Defense Against Missiles	4
Large	Flawless	Lightning	Electricity Resistance	40%	Dexterity	3	Chance to Dodge Attacks	10%	Defense Against Missiles	8
Large	Brilliant	Lightning	Electricity Resistance	50%	Dexterity	4	Chance to Dodge Attacks	15%	Defense Against Missiles	12
Large	Chipped	Natural	Nature Resistance	10%	—	—	—	—	—	—
Large	Flawed	Natural	Nature Resistance	20%	—	—	—	—	—	—
Large	Clear	Natural	Nature Resistance	30%	Armor	2	Physical Resistance	10%	—	—
Large	Flawless	Natural	Nature Resistance	40%	Armor	3	Physical Resistance	15%	Constitution	1
Large	Brilliant	Natural	Nature Resistance	50%	Armor	4	Physical Resistance	25%	Constitution	2
Large	Chipped	Spirit	Spirit Resistance	10%	—	—	—	—	—	—
Large	Flawed	Spirit	Spirit Resistance	20%	—	—	—	—	—	—
Large	Clear	Spirit	Spirit Resistance	30%	Chance to Ignore Hostile Magic	8%	Mental Resistance	5%	—	—
Large	Flawless	Spirit	Spirit Resistance	40%	Chance to Ignore Hostile Magic	12%	Mental Resistance	15%	All Attributes	1
Large	Brilliant	Spirit	Spirit Resistance	50%	Chance to Ignore Hostile Magic	16%	Mental Resistance	25%	All Attributes	1
Small	Chipped	Fire	Fire Damage	5%	—	—	—	—	—	—
Small	Flawed	Fire	Fire Damage	10%	—	—	—	—	—	—
Small	Clear	Fire	Fire Damage	15%	Melee Crit Chance	2	Damage	3	—	—

Downloadable Content Items

Basics ~ Character Generation ~ Classes ~ The Party ~ Companions ~ Supporting Cast ~ Equipment ~ Bestiary ~ Walkthroughs ~ Side Quests ~ Random Encounters ~ Achievements/Trophies

Size	Quality	Type	Bonus 1	Bonus Value	Bonus 2	Bonus Value	Bonus 3	Bonus Value	Bonus 4	Bonus Value
Small	Flawless	Fire	Fire Damage	22.50%	Melee Crit Chance	3	Damage	4	—	—
Small	Brilliant	Fire	Fire Damage	30%	Melee Crit Chance	5	Damage	5	—	—
Small	Chipped	Ice	Ice Damage	5%	—	—	—	—	—	—
Small	Flawed	Ice	Ice Damage	10%	—	—	—	—	—	—
Small	Clear	Ice	Ice Damage	15%	Armor Penetration	2	Critical Damage	5%	—	—
Small	Flawless	Ice	Ice Damage	22.50%	Armor Penetration	4	Critical Damage	10%	—	—
Small	Brilliant	Ice	Ice Damage	30%	Armor Penetration	6	Critical Damage	15%	—	—
Small	Chipped	Lightning	Lightning Damage	5%	—	—	—	—	—	—
Small	Flawed	Lightning	Lightning Damage	10%	—	—	—	—	—	—
Small	Clear	Lightning	Lightning Damage	15%	Dexterity	2	Attack Power	4	—	—
Small	Flawless	Lightning	Lightning Damage	22.50%	Dexterity	4	Attack Power	6	—	—
Small	Brilliant	Lightning	Lightning Damage	30%	Dexterity	6	Attack Power	10	—	—
Small	Chipped	Natural	Nature Damage	5%	—	—	—	—	—	—
Small	Flawed	Natural	Nature Damage	10%	—	—	—	—	—	—
Small	Clear	Natural	Nature Resistance	15%	Constitution	2	Combat Health Regen	8	—	—
Small	Flawless	Natural	Nature Resistance	22.50%	Constitution	4	Combat Health Regen	16	—	—
Small	Brilliant	Natural	Nature Resistance	30%	Constitution	6	Combat Health Regen	24	—	—
Small	Chipped	Spirit	Spirit Damage	5%	—	—	—	—	—	—
Small	Flawed	Spirit	Spirit Damage	10%	—	—	—	—	—	—
Small	Clear	Spirit	Spirit Damage	15%	All Attributes	1	Armor Penetration	2	—	—
Small	Flawless	Spirit	Spirit Damage	22.50%	All Attributes	2	Armor Penetration	3	—	—
Small	Brilliant	Spirit	Spirit Damage	30%	All Attributes	3	Armor Penetration	4	—	—

The Bestiary

Monsters most foul and fiendish inhabit the dark corners of Ferelden and swell the ranks of the Blight. In *Dragon Age: Origins*, statistics for monsters are dynamic; they scale to the player's level. This makes for a challenging experience, because you won't run into an area way too easy or way too difficult; you can enjoy the game play right along with the story.

TIP

Monster levels scale to a party the first time they enter an area. Visit a particularly difficult area early, leave and come back a few levels later and your party will have a much easier time conquering the place.

The following Bestiary showcases the game's monsters, including its rank, class, primary stats, description, and play tips on how to avoid the monsters' attacks and how to defeat

the diabolical denizens. Each creature falls in one of seven ranks. Normal is on par with the PC. Weak Normal, Critter, and One-Hit descend in power from a creature barely a challenge to the PC to a creature you can eliminate in a single stroke. On the other side, Lieutenant is a creature slightly above the PC's level, Boss is a creature meant to take on an entire party, and Elite Boss is the toughest of the tough and taking it down will require an expert party and all their skills.

NOTE

There are many monster variants among the creatures of Ferelden. For example, you could have a skeleton warrior or an Arland skeleton, but both are still skeletons. The basic monster type remains the same and the different monster looks do not affect your play strategy against them.

Rank Type	Monster Ranks								
Label	Health Scaling	Bonus Stat Points	Level Scaling	Damage Capability	Resistance to Various Attacks	Resistance Maximum	Loot Drops	Chance to Steal From	Stealth Detection
One-Hit Kill	Very Low	N/A	2 behind player	Very Low	Average	0	Very Low	Very High	Average
Critter	Low	N/A	3 behind player	Very Low	Average	0	Very Low	Very High	Average
Weak Normal	Fair	N/A	2 behind player	Low	Fair	25%	Low	Very High	Average
Normal	Moderate	N/A	1 behind player	Moderate	Average	50%	Fair	Moderate	Average
Player	Average	N/A	Average	Average	Average	75%	N/A	Very High	Moderate
Lieutenant	Above Average	Fair	Average	Average	Above Average	75%	Above Average	Fair	Above Average
Boss	High	Above Average	1 ahead of player	Average	High	100%	High	Low	High
Elite Boss	Very High	Very High	2 ahead of player	Very High	Very High	100%	Very High	Very Low	Very High

The higher the rating, the higher the health.

The higher the rating, the more stat points each target gets.

Level target is compared to the PC.

The higher the rating, the more damage the target does.

The higher the rating, the greater the resistance to an array of things.

The maximum amount of damage this rank could possibly resist from a certain type of attack (in percentage).

The higher the ratings here, the better chance of loot drops.

The higher the rating, the harder it is to steal from the target.

The higher the rating, the easier it is for the enemy to detect a stealthed character.

The creature's class fits in a general category and defines its key combat component, such as warrior, rogue, high damage, spellcaster, tank, agile, etc. The class, in turn, defines the general range of the creature's attributes, going from Very low up to superior rankings. By glancing at the creature's attributes you can see where their strengths and weaknesses lie. A creature with a high strength score, for example, will deal significant melee damage and take less in return. A creature with a high magic score will lean toward spells in combat. A creature with low willpower won't have much stamina or mana and will not be able to continuously hit you with abilities.

After each monster description, look for play tips on how to overcome the creature's abilities and how to defeat the beast. After you encounter a monster several times you'll probably know what to expect, but it's useful to study up on creatures for your first few encounters. When you want to know more about the creatures that inhabit Ferelden, check out your codex. Each time you encounter a monster for the first time, you gain a codex entry, and you can learn about the psychic abilities of revenants or how hurlock emissaries are the only darkspawn capable of human speech.

Abomination - Bear

Basics ~ Character Generation ~ Classes ~ The Party ~ Companions ~ Supporting Cast ~ Equipment ~ **Bestiary** ~ Walkthroughs ~ Side Quests ~ Random Encounters ~ Achievements/Trophies

Abomination

Rank: Normal

Class: Spellcaster

Prime Location: Circle Tower

Special Abilities: Rage, Triple Strike

Description: An abomination is a mage possessed by a rage, hunger, sloth, or desire demon.

Play Tips: In the "Broken Circle" quest, the Litany of Andralla artifact destroys the demonic link between host and victim and prevents the creation of new abominations.

Attributes

Strength	Dexterity	Willpower	Magic	Cunning	Constitution
Meager	Moderate	Very High	Very High	High	Moderate

Arcane Horror

Rank: Boss

Class: Spellcaster

Prime Location: The Fade

Special Abilities: Ranged spells

Description: An arcane horror is a skeleton possessed by a pride demon.

Play Tips: Interrupt an arcane horror's casting as much as possible. Up close, abilities such as Dirty Fighting and Mind Blast work great. At range, Paralyze, Pinning Shot, or Scattershot can break the thing's concentration.

Attributes

Strength	Dexterity	Willpower	Magic	Cunning	Constitution
Meager	Moderate	Superior	Superior	High	Meager

Archdemon

Rank: Elite Boss

Class: Tank

Prime Location: Denerim

Special Abilities: Enough to kill you quick (see "The Final Onslaught" walkthrough section)

Description: This is a corrupted version of the standard dragon, bred by the darkspawn. This tainted dragon is the big elite boss at the end of the game. His name is Urthemiel and was once known as the "Dragon of Beauty."

Play Tips: Arm yourself with the best gear possible. Select your most veteran party. Cross your fingers. (See "The Final Onslaught" walkthrough section for complete details on how to beat the archdemon.)

Attributes

Strength	Dexterity	Willpower	Magic	Cunning	Constitution
Very High	High	Above Avg.	Above Avg.	Above Avg.	Very High

Ash Wraith

Rank: Lieutenant

Class: Spirit

Prime Location: Circle Tower

Special Abilities: Life Drain

Description: A wraith is a powerful version of a shade, a spirit that has entered the physical world but does not possess a physical body. In the case of the ash wraith, the spirit has formed a quasi-material body for itself out of ashes (usually the ashes of burnt corpses, but not necessarily). This allows it to interact with and affect the physical world, but the wraith is not dependent on the ashes to survive. If wounded, it can disperse at will and reform later. Such wraiths occasionally use other materials to form their physical bodies such as bones, mold, and even blood.

Play Tips: Watch out for rear or flank attacks, as these creatures can materialize behind or on your side. High spirit resistance will reduce the damage taken from the wraith's main attacks.

Attributes

Strength	Dexterity	Willpower	Magic	Cunning	Constitution
Very High	Very High	Above Avg.	Very Low	Meager	Very High

Bear

Rank: Critter

Class: Tank

Prime Location: Any outdoor location

Special Abilities: Overwhelm

Description: Bears live in forests, often near settlements. They are known for breaking into cabins and stealing food. They have a special fondness for honey. There is also a trained bear with a trainer at the Pearl brothel in Denerim.

Play Tips: Any bear form is vulnerable to magic, so mages deliver serious damage. The mage's shapeshifter specialization transforms the caster into a bear, so you can experience its abilities firsthand.

Attributes

Strength	Dexterity	Willpower	Magic	Cunning	Constitution
Very High	High	Above Avg.	Very Low	Meager	Very High

Bereskarn

The bereskarn variant, including the boss in the Dalish Elf origin, is a lieutenant with twice as much health as the average PC.

Black Bear

Most bears you meet will be of the more common black bear variety.

Giant Bear

The great bear variant is a more formidable adversary, with lots more health, deadlier claws, and an Overwhelm ability.

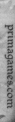

Bronto

Rank: Lieutenant

Class: Tank

Prime Location: Wyrmling Lair

Special Abilities: Charge

Description: A bronto is a huge rhino-like beast based on the real world brontothere (an animal that lived more than 10,000 years ago).

Play Tips: You don't want to be in its way when this creature charges. Attack from its flank or rear and with magic whenever possible.

Attributes

Strength	Dexterity	Willpower	Magic	Cunning	Constitution
Very High	High	Above Avg.	Very Low	Meager	Very High

Broodmother

Rank: Boss

Class: Tank

Prime Location: Dead Trenches

Special Abilities: Burrowing Tentacles

Description: Tainted females of the surface species are affected differently from males, undergoing great pain and gross mutations, which cause most of them to perish. Those who survive, however, become the egg-laying broodmothers. These broodmothers spawn many infertile offspring at a time, over and over throughout their lifetime. One broodmother, in fact, can create thousands of darkspawn…and it is from these broodmothers that all darkspawn originate. Like bees, the broodmothers are the "queens" and nominal rulers of the darkspawn races during the periods when a Blight is not in progress. There is no evidence to suggest much in the way of actual organization, however. Elven broodmothers birth shrieks, qunari broodmothers birth ogres, dwarven broodmothers birth genlocks, and human broodmothers birth hurlocks.

Play Tips: Go for the tentacles first. Chop away one at a time, and when the tentacles dip beneath the ground, aim as much damage as you can directly on the broodmother.

Attributes

Strength	Dexterity	Willpower	Magic	Cunning	Constitution
Very High	High	Above Avg.	Very Low	Meager	Very High

Corpse

Rank: Normal

Class: Tank

Prime Location: Redcliffe

Special Abilities: Rise from the dead

Description: Weaker demons crossing over from the Fade may be able to possess a living target. Unable to distinguish that which was once living from that which still is, they sometimes end up in a corpse instead.

Play Tips: Beware of dead bodies strewn upon the ground. Frequently, what appears as the grisly remnants of a massacre is actually an ambush by the various corpse forms.

Attributes

Strength	Dexterity	Willpower	Magic	Cunning	Constitution
Very High	High	Above Avg.	Very Low	Meager	Very High

Devouring Corpse

Devouring corpses are corpses possessed by a hunger demon. These attempt to feed on living victims as quickly as possible.

Enraged Corpse

Enraged corpses are corpses possessed by a rage demon. These go berserk and simply wade into opponents mindlessly.

Shambling Corpse

Shambling corpses are corpses possessed by a sloth demon. These cause enemies to become weak and fatigued.

Deepstalker

Rank: Critter

Class: Agile

Prime Location: Deep Roads

Special Abilities: Camouflage

Description: This bizarre creature evolved in the deep caverns beneath the dwarven cities. When rolled up, the creature resembles a large rock; stalkers often look like boulders strewn through the dwarven tunnels. Once prey approaches, they unroll and leap at their victims.

Play Tips: Deepstalkers hunt in packs. If you see one, others are nearby ready to pounce. Try to spot the large group and raze them with AoE damage.

Attributes

Strength	Dexterity	Willpower	Magic	Cunning	Constitution
Very High	Very High	Above Avg.	Very Low	Meager	High

Deepstalker Leader

The leader ranks as normal with slightly higher attack and defense values.

Deepstalker Spitter

The spitter has a ranged poison attack. Where other deepstalkers charge into melee, this one will hang back and spit, then engage.

Desire Demon

Rank: Lieutenant

Class: Balanced Mental

Prime Location: Circle Tower

Special Abilities: Enthrallment

Description: Of all the threats from beyond the Veil, few are more insidious and deceptively deadly than the desire demon. In popular folklore, such demons are characterized most commonly as peddlers of lust, luring their prey into a sexual encounter where they are slain at the culmination. While a desire demon can indeed deal in pleasure, in truth they deal with any manner of desire that humans can possess: wealth, power, and beauty to name a few. Far more intelligent than the bestial hunger and rage demons, and more ambitious than the demons of sloth, these dark spirits are among the greatest at tempting mages into possession. Many who serve the whims of a desire demon never realize it. They are manipulated by illusions and deceit if not outright mind control, though these demons are reluctant to resort to such crude measures. Instead, they seem to take great pleasure in corruption. The greater the deceit, the greater their victory.

Play Tips: Once a desire demon has someone in her thrall, you must treat them as an enemy and destroy them along with the desire demon.

Attributes

Strength	Dexterity	Willpower	Magic	Cunning	Constitution
Meager	Moderate	Very High	Very High	Very High	Meager

Dragon

Rank: Elite Boss

Class: Balanced Physical

Prime Location: Mountaintop outside the Gauntlet

Special Abilities: Fire Breathing

Description: At about 100 years of age, female dragonlings undergo a metamorphosis, darkening in color and growing wings. After their wings grow, these dragon females become very adventurous, traveling long distances from their original hatching grounds and feeding widely on wild beasts and livestock as they range out to find their own burrows. Human encounters happen most often with these nomadic adult females. Adult dragons are the most aggressive and commonly seen; however, while deadly, they are not regarded with the awe usually reserved for high dragons.

Play Tips: Everyone stand back except the tank. Send your tank in to pull as much threat as possible. When the dragon gets angry enough to unload its fire breath on the tank, have a mage cast Force Field to shield the tank for the duration of the attack. Everyone else unloads high-powered damage on the dragon while it concentrates on the invulnerable tank.

Attributes

Strength	Dexterity	Willpower	Magic	Cunning	Constitution
Very High	Very High	Above Avg.	Very Low	Meager	Very High

Dragonling

Baby dragons of both genders hatch from eggs into dragonlings, which are roughly the size of a deer. These dragonlings are wingless and slender and are born in vast numbers because they are still very vulnerable to predation. At this age, males and females are identical. The dragonlings stay for a short time in their mothers' lairs, then venture out into the world where they spend several decades in their small, vulnerable state.

High Dragon

Any dragon is a formidable adversary, but a high dragon is even more: an elite boss. High dragons are adult female dragons, the mountainous classic dragons into which the dragons mature. Relatively few dragons survive to this stage of adulthood. When they do, they take possession of a burrow (either an abandoned tunnel complex that they further hollow out, or the lair of another high dragon who they challenge and displace). The high dragons then spend most of their time sleeping and mating, living off the prey that their drakes hunt and bring back.

primagames.com

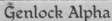
Drake

Rank: Lieutenant

Class: Balanced Physical

Prime Location: Wyrmling Lair

Special Abilities: Fire Breathing

Description: At about 50 years of age, male dragonlings undergo a metamorphosis, as the skin of their forelimbs stretches and grows into wings, leaving them with no separate forelegs. These drakes immediately begin searching for mates, seeking out the lairs of adult female high dragons (which are many times larger). When they find high dragon mates, drakes move into the female's lair and spend the rest of their lives there, emerging only to hunt and bring food back for the female and dragonlings. For any given high dragon, usually a dozen or so drakes live in her lair and fight among themselves for the right to mate. If the high dragon or dragonlings are attacked, the drakes defend the lair. Drakes live only about 100 years, and often much less when the casualties of combat are considered.

Play Tips: Collect three drake scales and return to Wade's Emporium in the Denerim Market District. Master Wade will craft a special piece of armor for you, and you'll complete the "Drake Scale Armor" side quest.

Attributes

Strength	Dexterity	Willpower	Magic	Cunning	Constitution
Very High	Very High	Above Avg.	Very Low	Meager	Very High

Genlock

Rank: Normal

Class: Default Warrior, Ranged Warrior (for archers), Spellcaster (for emissaries)

Prime Location: Anywhere

Special Abilities: Alpha (Dual Wield), Emissary (Spells)

Description: Genlocks originate from dwarven broodmothers and are the most numerous of all the darkspawn. They have stocky dwarven bodies and a robust appearance. Their skin is pale white or yellow, and their heads are large and bald, with sunken eyes and cheeks. Genlocks have both the strength and hardiness of their dwarven origins and are difficult to kill. They also commonly possess the dwarven resistance to magic, though this trait is strongest in alpha and emissary genlocks.

Play Tips: Load up on silverite runes if you know you're about to battle darkspawn. Even a novice silverite rune grants +2 damage against the fiends, and a grandmaster silverite rune gives +10!

Attributes

Strength	Dexterity	Willpower	Magic	Cunning	Constitution
Very High	High	Above Avg.	Very Low	Meager	Very High

Genlock Alpha

Alphas are more cunning versions of the base genlock and have higher magic resistance. They are ranked as lieutenants and can dual wield.

Genlock Emissary

Genlock emissaries are the most intelligent genlock and have the highest magic resistance. They are ranked as lieutenants.

Ghoul

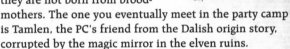

Rank: Lieutenant

Class: High Damage

Prime Location: Brecilian Ruins

Special Abilities: Life Drain

Description: A ghoul is a man or woman twisted and corrupted by the darkspawn taint. This differs from regular darkspawn in that they are not born from brood-mothers. The one you eventually meet in the party camp is Tamlen, the PC's friend from the Dalish origin story, corrupted by the magic mirror in the elven ruins.

Play Tips: Invest in cold iron runes to fight undead. A novice cold iron rune grants +2 damage against ghouls and other undead, and a grandmaster cold iron rune adds 10 more damage per hit!

Attributes

Strength	Dexterity	Willpower	Magic	Cunning	Constitution
Very High	High	Above Avg.	Very Low	Meager	Very High

Golem

Rank: Lieutenant

Class: Tank

Prime Location: Anvil of the Void

Special Abilities: Quake

Description: Dwarves built golems, creatures of hewn stone or sheets of metal animated with a spark of lyrium. They were once a crucial part of Orzammar's defenses, but the secret to their manufacture was lost over 1,000 ago. What few golems remain are guarded closely by the Shaperate of Golems, and only brought out when the battle with the darkspawn grows desperate enough to risk their loss. No one now would sell a golem for any price, but in ancient times, dwarves sold many golems to the magister lords of the Tevinter Imperium. A magical, not mechanical, process animates the golem, making it more of a living "iron/stone creature."

Play Tips: The warrior's Shattering Blows talent increases damage against golems and other constructs. A warrior heading into the Deep Roads might be wise to spend a few points in the Two-Handed school.

Attributes

Strength	Dexterity	Willpower	Magic	Cunning	Constitution
Very High	High	Above Avg.	Very Low	Meager	Very High

Drake - Mabari War Hound

Basics ~ Character Generation ~ Classes ~ The Party ~ Companions ~ Supporting Cast ~ Equipment ~ **Bestiary** ~ Walkthroughs ~ Side Quests ~ Random Encounters ~ Achievements/Trophies

Halla

Rank: Critter

Class: Warrior

Prime Location: Brecilian Forest

Special Abilities: Moving Dalish landships

Description: These Dalish white stags are much larger and swifter than the normal wild stags (having been bred for this purpose by the elves for several millennia). It is standard for a halla's keeper to carve its antlers as they grow, making them curve into unique and aesthetic shapes (the antlers fetch a high price in the Imperium). Since the fall of the Dales, the halla have been used less as mounts and more to pull the aravels (called "landships" by humans) of the Dalish.

Play Tips: They make good eating, but you don't have much reason to battle these creatures. In the Dalish camp, you can save one and complete the "Elora's Halla" side quest.

Attributes

Strength	Dexterity	Willpower	Magic	Cunning	Constitution
High	High	High	Low	Low	High

Hurlock

Rank: Normal

Class: Warrior

Prime Location: Anywhere

Special Abilities: Alpha (Weapon and Shield, Two-Handed), Emissary (Spells)

Description: Hurlocks originate from human broodmothers. Muscular and tough, they are the most common foot soldiers of the darkspawn during a Blight. They are tanks, easily equaling a qunari's raw physical power. They are the shock troops of the darkspawn and often form the strongest part of their armies, wielding primitive swords and axes and wearing patchwork armor. Hurlock skin ranges from pale white to dark brown; there is generally a lot of variance, and most do not possess hair (it is always black in those who do). Hurlocks consider themselves superior to other darkspawn races, treating them roughly and adorning themselves in crudely carved tattoos to keep track of kills and deeds.

Play Tips: Identify hurlocks as soon as a fight ensues. Emissaries are your immediate priority. Alphas can be trouble, but you'll probably want to eliminate the regular hurlocks first and reduce the numbers against you.

Attributes

Strength	Dexterity	Willpower	Magic	Cunning	Constitution
High	High	High	Low	Low	High

Hurlock Alpha

Darkspawn childer hatched by a broodmother have to fight among themselves for food during the first month of life; usually, a tenth to a quarter of the litter will survive. Occasionally one childer will prove stronger than the rest of its siblings and be the only one remaining at the end of the month. This is indicative of a superior version of the race and it will be known as an "alpha." Alphas are generally taller, stronger, and much more intelligent than others of their kind. They will be the commanders and generals who direct the others in combat and are intelligent enough to direct the slavery of humanoid races in lands they conquer. As lieutenants, they act as warriors with the Weapon and Shield and Two-Handed talents.

Hurlock Emissary

A very few alphas have proven themselves to be not only incredibly intelligent, but also naturally gifted with magical abilities that seem similar to blood magic in their effects. These few are known as "emissaries." Emissary lieutenants tend to appear only during the Blights and are the most feared of the darkspawn, the ones who watch the commanders and generals to make sure that those cunning alphas serve the archdemon's interests and not their own. Darkspawn armies are fairly disorganized, but the different races usually group together (genlocks with genlocks, hurlocks with hurlocks, etc.).

Mabari War Hound

Rank: Normal

Class: Default Dog

Prime Location: Ostagar

Special Abilities: Bite

Description: Dogs are an essential part of Fereldan culture, and no dog is more prized than the Mabari. The breed is as old as myth, said to have been bred from the wolves who served the legendary hero, Dane. Prized for their intelligence and loyalty, these dogs are more than mere weapons or status symbols: The hounds choose their masters, and pair with them for life. To be the master of a Mabari anywhere in Ferelden is to be recognized instantly as a person of worth. The Mabari are also an essential part of Ferelden military strategy. Trained hounds can easily pull knights from horseback or break lines of pike men, and the sight and sound of a wave of war dogs, howling and snarling, has been known to cause panic among even the most hardened infantry soldiers.

Play Tips: You will battle Mabari war dogs in your travels; however, one of them becomes your friendliest ally either in the Human Noble origin or as a side quest beginning in Ostagar.

Attributes

Strength	Dexterity	Willpower	Magic	Cunning	Constitution
Superior	Above Avg.	Moderate	Very Low	Fair	Superior

primagames.com

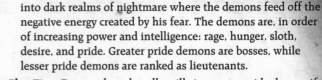

Dragon Age

ORIGINS

PRIMA Official Game Guide

Nug

Rank: Critter

Class: Warrior

Prime Location: Orzammar

Special Abilities: Nibble

Description: Sometimes called "mudsplashers" by the dwarves, these small, hairless creatures resemble small pigs, with pointed snouts for digging. Nearly blind, they populate the underground tunnels of the dwarves.

Play Tips: Collect these for Nug Wrangler Boermor in the Orzammar Commons area. Corral 11 of them for a prize.

Attributes

Strength	Dexterity	Willpower	Magic	Cunning	Constitution
High	High	High	Low	Low	High

Ogre

Rank: Lieutenant or Normal

Class: High Damage

Prime Location: Brecilian Forest

Special Abilities: Grab and Throttle

Description: Ogres originate from qunari broodmothers; they are rare, but growing in number. They are massive: taller and broader than even hurlock alphas, with dark, rough-colored skin covered in patches of thick fur. They possess huge, curved horns and are said to charge their enemies like bulls, slamming into them with devastating effect: they can even barrel through thick stone walls. Tougher ogres are ranked as lieutenants, while the smaller grunts are normal difficulty.

Play Tips: Avoid the ogre's long reach: an ogre can grab and choke the life out of you. If the ogre grabs a companion, stun it immediately to cease the continuous damage.

Attributes

Strength	Dexterity	Willpower	Magic	Cunning	Constitution
Very High	High	Above Avg.	Very Low	Meager	Very High

Pride Demon

Rank: Boss (lesser is ranked Lieutenant)

Class: High Damage

Prime Location: The Fade

Special Abilities: Possession

Description: Demons can exist in both the real world (through possession) and in the Fade. Demons spend their time searching out new territory and pushing their boundaries. For this reason, they are the Fade dwellers most commonly seen in the mortal realm. While in the Fade, demons rail at a sleeper, forcing him into dark realms of nightmare where the demons feed off the negative energy created by his fear. The demons are, in order of increasing power and intelligence: rage, hunger, sloth, desire, and pride. Greater pride demons are bosses, while lesser pride demons are ranked as lieutenants.

Play Tips: Damage-based spells will rip apart a pride demon if you can keep the pressure on. Cycle through a spell rotation so you aren't waiting on any cooldown effects.

Attributes

Strength	Dexterity	Willpower	Magic	Cunning	Constitution
Very High	High	Above Avg.	Very Low	Meager	Very High

Rage Demon

Rank: Lieutenant (lesser is ranked Critter)

Class: Spirit

Prime Location: The Fade

Special Abilities: Flame Blast

Description: Demons can exist in both the real world (through possession) and in the Fade. Demons spend their time searching out new territory and pushing their boundaries. For this reason, they are the Fade dwellers most commonly seen in the mortal realm. While in the Fade, demons rail at a sleeper, forcing him into dark realms of nightmare where the demons feed off the negative energy created by his fear. The demons are, in order of increasing power and intelligence: rage, hunger, sloth, desire, and pride. Greater rage demons are lieutenants, while lesser rage demons are ranked as critters.

Play Tips: Stick to the cold-based spells to deal extra damage. Cone of Cold or Blizzard can freeze them solid and deal significant damage; even Winter's Grasp can be effective.

Attributes

Strength	Dexterity	Willpower	Magic	Cunning	Constitution
Very High	Very High	Above Avg.	Very Low	Meager	Very High

Rat

Rank: Critter

Class: Warrior

Prime Location: Underground

Special Abilities: Gnaw

Description: Any of several long-tailed rodents of the family Muridae, of the genus Rattus; distinguished from the mouse by being larger. Only the giant ones fight.

Play Tips: It doesn't take much to squash them. Watch out for rats' swarm tactics; keep your flanks defended by companions or obstacles.

Attributes

Strength	Dexterity	Willpower	Magic	Cunning	Constitution
High	High	High	Low	Low	High

Nug - Skeleton

Basics ~ Character Generation ~ Classes ~ The Party ~ Companions ~ Supporting Cast ~ Equipment ~ **Bestiary** ~ Walkthroughs ~ Side Quests ~ Random Encounters ~ Achievements/Trophies

Revenant

Rank: Lieutenant

Class: High Damage

Prime Location: Brecilian Forest

Special Abilities: Telekinetic Pull

Description: A revenant is a corpse possessed by a pride demon. Many possess spells, but most are armed and armored and prefer to use their martial talents.

Play Tips: A challenging foe, the revenant can pull you toward it with telekinesis; ranged DPS and healing won't be safe at the edge of the battlefield. Don't waste time on ranged positioning. If the revenant does pull, it sets aside its massive blade, which is prime time for melee combatants to get in some licks.

Attributes

Strength	Dexterity	Willpower	Magic	Cunning	Constitution
Very High	High	Above Avg.	Very Low	Meager	Very High

Shade

Rank: Lieutenant (lesser version is ranked Normal)

Class: Spirit

Prime Location: The Fade

Special Abilities: Life Drain

Description: Shades are spirits of the dead that have come into the mortal world but have not possessed living beings. Over time, they become so jealous of the living that they begin to draw the energy of life itself into themselves through their touch. They become humanoid shadows, lingering in dead places and being devoid of any thought but draining life whenever it draws near. More powerful versions of these shades, those who have fed on a great deal of life energy, are known as "wraiths." Wraiths regain a bit of their intelligence and can use their power to affect the mortal world, usually through control over the elements and by affecting the minds of the living.

Play Tips: Mundane weapons may have a lesser effect, but spells can put a hurt on a shade. Keep your spellcasters protected and let them fire away while the tank and melee DPS hold them at bay.

Attributes

Strength	Dexterity	Willpower	Magic	Cunning	Constitution
Very High	Very High	Above Avg.	Very Low	Meager	Very High

Shriek

Rank: Lieutenant (Normal shriek is ranked Normal)

Class: High Damage

Prime Location: Dead Trenches

Special Abilities: Stealth

Description: Thought of as horrors of the night more than as darkspawn, shrieks are tall, lean creatures renowned for their speed, incredible agility, and stealth. Indeed, shrieks have been known to run (with their strange, loping gait: their arms are as long as their legs) as fast as a horse and disappear just as quickly into the shadows. Shrieks' talons and teeth are incredibly sharp, as their favorite tactic is to leap on their prey and tear it to ribbons within seconds; in fact, they fight with long sharpened blades attached to their forearms. Shrieks originate from elven broodmothers, and retain both a natural elven agility and relative fragility. Only couple solid strikes are needed to kill the creature—getting that strike, however, tends to be the problem. Physically, shrieks stand between six and seven feet tall but weigh only perhaps 100 to 120 pounds. They are thin, with bark-like skin that ranges from light green to dark brown in color. Their faces are twisted, with long wild-looking hair and eyes that are sunken into their skull, appearing to be black holes with pricks of dim light shining from within.

Play Tips: Set up a defensive perimeter where each companion can watch the other's backs. Shrieks can materialize out of thin air, and you don't want them ripping and tearing at your exposed side.

Attributes

Strength	Dexterity	Willpower	Magic	Cunning	Constitution
Very High	High	Above Avg.	Very Low	Meager	Very High

Skeleton

Rank: Normal

Class: Warrior

Prime Location: Redcliffe

Special Abilities: Archer (ranged), Fanged (Dual Weapon), Normal (Weapon and Shield), Shambling (Two-Handed)

Description: Demons that possess flesh form walking corpses; demons that possess bones form skeletons.

Play Tips: Employ standard party tactics as you would for any melee combatant or enemy archer. The shambling skeletons generally deal more damage and should be a priority.

Attributes

Strength	Dexterity	Willpower	Magic	Cunning	Constitution
Very High	High	Above Avg.	Very Low	Meager	Very High

Archer

Archer skeletons are bones possessed by a rage demon. They use ranged bows.

Fanged

Fanged skeletons are bones possessed by a hunger demon. They act as warriors with the Dual Weapon talents.

Normal

Normal skeletons are bones possessed by a rage demon. They act as warriors with the Weapon and Shield talents.

Shambling

Shambling skeletons are bones possessed by a sloth demon. They act as warriors with the Two-Handed talents.

Sloth Demon

Rank: Boss or Normal

Class: Tank

Prime Location: The Fade

Special Abilities: Spells

Description: The sloth demon is a shapechanger with no true form (that is known, anyway). It takes existing forms, usually from dreams of the dreamer. In the Magi origin story, the sloth demon appears as a bereskarn.

Play Tips: Normal sloth demons adopt similar tactics as the arcane horror. Avoid its big spells with well-timed stuns or debilitating spells such as Crushing Prison.

Attributes

Strength	Dexterity	Willpower	Magic	Cunning	Constitution
Very High	High	Above Avg.	Very Low	Meager	Very High

Spider

Rank: Normal

Class: Agile

Prime Location: Underground

Special Abilities: Poison, Web, Overwhelm

Description: These creatures (also called "deep crawlers" by the dwarves) grew in the depths of the dwarven Deep Roads, once having been encouraged to multiply to feed on the numerous species of large bats that the dwarves considered pests. Once the Deep Roads were lost to the darkspawn, these spiders began to feed on genlocks as well as bats, and their numbers were no longer controlled. Some moved up to make their lairs in the surface forests, but most have remained below ground.

Play Tips: Support each other whenever spiders arrive. If you end up apart, a spider's web or Overwhelm attack can incapacitate a lone companion. When webbed, the companions who aren't trapped should defend their comrade. Against an Overwhelm attack, everyone else should immediately focus on the charging spider to kill it before it kills your companion.

Attributes

Strength	Dexterity	Willpower	Magic	Cunning	Constitution
Very High	Very High	Above Avg.	Very Low	Meager	High

Corrupted Spider

Corrupted Spiders are giant spiders that have fed on the flesh of darkspawn. Unlike other animals so tainted, giant spiders don't become darkspawn ghouls. But they are forever changed after having feasted on darkspawn gore: they are more aggressive and stronger than standard spider kin.

Giant Spider

These are the most common variety of dungeon spider and will threaten you with an Overwhelm ability.

Poisonous Spider

These spiders can shoot poison at medium range and deal damage over time.

Werewolf

Rank: Normal

Class: High Damage

Prime Location: Brecilian Forest

Special Abilities: Claws, Stealth

Description: Ferelden lore is full of instances where these creatures have plagued the countryside: wolves possessed by rage demons and transformed into humanoid monsters with incredible speed and strength, able to spread a curse to those they bit that would drive them mad with rage. Indeed, the ability of normal dogs to detect a werewolf even when it is in a human guise is what first led Fereldans to adopt dogs as an indispensable companion in every farmhold. The hero Dane led a crusade to eliminate this threat once and for all, and while werewolves have never assumed the same prominence since, there have still been reports of individual packs lurking in remote forests. In recent years, some have even been reported to have developed an uncanny willpower and intelligence.

Play Tips: Werewolves are very fast, and some use stealth. At least one point in Survival will help drastically in detecting werewolves on your mini-map before they are on you.

Attributes

Strength	Dexterity	Willpower	Magic	Cunning	Constitution
Very High	High	Above Avg.	Very Low	Meager	Very High

Sloth Demon - Wolf

Basics ~ Character Generation ~ Classes ~ The Party ~ Companions ~ Supporting Cast ~ Equipment ~ Bestiary ~ Walkthroughs ~ Side Quests ~ Random Encounters ~ Achievements/Trophies

Werewolf Leader

Werewolf leaders are lieutenants and stronger, more resilient versions of the core werewolves. Swiftrunner, leader of the werewolves in the "Nature of the Beast" quest, is more intelligent than the others. He is still little more than a vicious beast, however, and very easily gives in to his bestial temper. If the player frees the werewolves, he is restored to his former human self.

Rabid Werewolf

An extremely nasty, savage variant of the regular werewolf

Shadow Werewolf

These werewolves use stealth to go invisible and sneak up on the unsuspecting.

Wild Sylvan

Rank: Lieutenant

Class: Tank

Prime Location: Brecilian Forest

Special Abilities: Camouflage

Description: In forests where the Veil between this plane and the Fade has become thin, the forest is "alive" with vengeful spirits who have possessed trees. These creatures are called "wild sylvans." Sylvans can retain some of the intelligence and even memories of the possessing spirit, which sometimes grow over time. More often, sylvans retain only a smattering of intelligence and are filled with an extreme jealousy of other living things. They kill any who enter their domain, animating branches to swing as fists, enveloping the living in their roots, or uprooting themselves briefly to walk (slowly). Sylvans are heavily resistant to physical damage.

Play Tips: Tread slowly when in a forest around sylvans. The tree creatures blend in with the non-hostile forest and suddenly spring to life as you near. Fire-based attacks do extra damage.

Attributes

Strength	Dexterity	Willpower	Magic	Cunning	Constitution
Very High	High	Above Avg.	Very Low	Meager	Very High

Grand Oak

The rhyming spirit of a great oak tree, this sylvan boss helps the player after the player recovers his stolen acorn.

Wisp

Rank: Critter

Class: Spirit

Prime Location: The Fade

Special Abilities: Lightning

Description: Wisps are small glowing balls of electrical energy. It is not certain whether they are demon, spirit, or just a Fade disturbance of some kind.

Play Tips: When a wisp detects you, it will begin firing lightning at you. Close quickly if you rely on melee; otherwise, it will sizzle you from long range. If you attack at range, out-damage wisps with a barrage of spells or arrows.

Attributes

Strength	Dexterity	Willpower	Magic	Cunning	Constitution
Very High	Very High	Above Avg.	Very Low	Meager	Very High

Wolf

Rank: Critter

Class: Agile

Prime Location: Outdoors

Special Abilities: Bite, Overwhelm

Description: These wolves are large and imposing. They hunt in packs and take advantage of large numbers to take down tougher targets.

Play Tips: Wolves hunt in packs and will attempt to swarm you. Try not to get flanked and have the party concentrate firepower on one at a time as you trim down the numbers against you. Also watch out for their Overwhelm ability, which can take a party member down quickly if you're not prepared.

Attributes

Strength	Dexterity	Willpower	Magic	Cunning	Constitution
Very High	Very High	Above Avg.	Very Low	Meager	High

Alpha Wolf

A stronger variant of the wolf, this lieutenant will lead the wolf charge as a dangerous pack closes in.

Witherfang

The fighting form of the Lady of the Forest (the spirit of a dryad that Zathrian captured and trapped in the body of a wolf). She is the originator of the werewolf curse in the Brecilian Forest. She is a massive, white dire wolf boss.

Tour of Ferelden

The vast wilderness and cultural centers of Ferelden live and breathe each day that passes on your mission to stop the Blight. You can immerse yourself in the world and enjoy much that it has to offer, but Ferelden is so huge that it will take several plays to fully explore its majesty. For those who want a sneak peek of what's in store or want a guide to the essential quests, NPCs, items, and skills that you'll encounter on your travels, look no further.

Essential Locations

Ostagar

After your origin story, Duncan guides you to King Cailan and the rest of the Grey Wardens at this ancient fortress. You meet companions Alistair and Morrigan, as well as a couple of Grey Warden trainees who travel with you temporarily as you quest for the elements of the Joining. As part of the prelude quests, you must complete all of Ostagar before you go anywhere else. Your adventures will take you into neighboring Korcari Wilds and Flemeth's Hut before setting off into the wide open world.

Lothering

A small town on your way up the Imperial Highway, Lothering supplies you with lots of side quests to build up your novice characters. You meet companions Leliana and Sten inside the village limits, and you gain a dwarven merchant and his enchanter son for your party camp after you leave. Be sure to do all Lothering quests before leaving the town; once you complete one of the major quest lines, darkspawn destroy Lothering and you can never return.

Circle Tower

Home to the Circle of Magi, the tower falls prey to abominations and the dark lure of the dreamworld, the Fade. You gain the services of spirit healer Wynne inside the tower, and she should be a permanently part of any group that doesn't already have a healer. To reach the tower, you must first convince the guard on the Lake Calenhad Docks to let you pass. When you finish the "Broken Circle" quests here, you choose either mages or templars to serve in your army against the archdemon.

Redcliffe

The "Arl of Redcliffe" quest line takes place in Redcliffe Village and Redcliffe Castle. Undead plague the area, and another demon has imprisoned the royal family. Your travels take you through the village, basement, courtyard and both floors of the castle. You need Arl Eamon to call the Landsmeet for the finale, but you cannot save the arl until you also complete the "Urn of Sacred Ashes" quest line.

Denerim

Visit the game's largest city early to partake in the market district's many vendors and to accept a wealth of side quests. The experience and rewards from these side quests will help your characters develop their talents and gear. Later in the story, after Arl Eamon calls the Landsmeet, Denerim serves as the final battleground for the events leading up to the confrontation with the archdemon.

Sequence of Events

The following three quest lines serve as the introduction to the game and must be completed in order:

- Your Origin
- Ostagar
- Lothering

The following four "Ancient Treaties" quest lines can be completed in any order, though they are listed in most practical order:

- Broken Circle (Circle Tower)
- Arl of Redcliffe/Urn of Sacred Ashes (Redcliffe)
- Paragon of Her Kind (Orzammar)
- Nature of the Beast (Brecilian Forest)

The capital city, Denerim, serves as a home base with lots of vendors and side quests. You generally want to visit this early in your pursuit for the "Ancient Treaties" quests, and return often.

- Denerim

Once you have completed all the "Ancient Treaties" quests, you can speak with Arl Eamon to trigger the final two quest lines to end the game:

- Landsmeet (Denerim)
- The Final Onslaught

Urn of Sacred Ashes

Part two of the effort to save Arl Eamon eventually brings you to the remote location of Haven. The cultists in the town and connecting dungeons want to keep strangers in the dark at all costs. Ultimately, though, the Urn of Sacred Ashes resides at

Essential Locations - How to Use the Walkthrough

Basics ~ Character Generation ~ Classes ~ The Party ~ Companions ~ Supporting Cast ~ Equipment ~ Bestiary ~ **Walkthroughs** ~ Side Quests ~ Random Encounters ~ Achievements/Trophies

the end of a trio of dungeons: Ruined Temple, Wyrmling Lair, and the Gauntlet. When you finish the "Arl of Redcliffe/Urn of Sacred Ashes" quests, the arl promises you his men to serve in your final army against the archdemon.

Orzammar

The mountain home of the dwarves is also home to the "Paragon of Her Kind" quest line. Delve into dwarven politics and the lost secrets of the Deep Roads to earn the graces of the next dwarven king. During your travels, you pick up the warrior Oghren for your party. If you can survive darkspawn and golems within the underground catacombs, the dwarves will come to your aid in the final battle against the archdemon.

Brecilian Forest

Hidden in the lust forests, a lone Dalish camp holds out against werewolf attacks. But is all what it seems? Discover the secrets of the forest and its denizens as you adventure through the "Nature of the Beast" quest line. When you uncover the final answers, you choose either elves or werewolves to join your army against the archdemon.

Landsmeet and Final Battle

After you complete all of the main quests in Circle Tower, Redcliffe, Orzammar, and the Brecilian Forest, Arl Eamon will call the Landsmeet to select a new ruler of Ferelden. Aid Arl Eamon in the task of discrediting the traitor Loghain and drumming up support for your chosen candidate to take the throne. Once the Landsmeet is resolved, you have one last hurdle: Slay the archdemon before the Blight consumes all of Ferelden.

NOTE

Side quests and random encounters have dedicated chapters after this walkthrough section covering all the main quests. See the Side Quests chapter and the Random Encounters chapter for all the details.

How to Use the Walkthrough

Main quests as you travel around Ferelden can sometimes seem complex and daunting. The following walkthroughs provide in-depth, precise explanations for every main quest line in the game. If it doesn't appear in this chapter, it's not a main quest and will appear in the Side Quests or Random Encounters chapters. The walkthroughs that follow this introduction are presented in the most efficient sequence, from your origin and the prelude to the various "Ancient Treaties" quests to secure the aid of the Ferelden races to "Landsmeet" endgame quests. Here's a quick breakdown of what's in each walkthrough:

Map

Each walkthrough contains all the necessary maps to navigate from the quest's starting point to ending point. Labels on the maps indicate NPCs, enemies, quest spots, treasure locations, general points of interest, and runthrough markings to show the best route through the area. A walkthrough will generally contain multiple maps to all the important locations.

Legend

◆ Runthrough markings that correspond to the runthrough boxes and walkthrough text	X Side quest locations or points of interest
◆ NPCs	⚠ Loot or side quest related items
▦ Enemies	◯ Additional info (traps, etc.)

Runthrough

This small sidebar boils the walkthrough down to essential steps. The steps are marked on the map in orange letters. To progress through an area effectively, start with "A" and continue in alphabetical order to the last letter. If you're familiar with an area, you can use the runthrough as a guide to moving through a map very quickly.

Cheatsheet

Each main map has a cheatsheet that tracks the main quest, important NPCs, key items, monsters, and side quests. Use this cheatsheet to make sure you didn't miss anything critical on your journey, or to scout out what you need to accomplish in the area.

Walkthrough Text

We pack as much comprehensive strategy and expert guidance as we can into each section. The runthrough can give you a nice overview, but if you really want to know how to avoid the traps, tackle the monsters, and collect the important items, read the walkthrough. Whenever you encounter a really difficult enemy—whether it be a boss or other ranked, troublesome adversary—we'll give you tips on its battle tendencies and how to defeat it.

Reference the world map for your global questions, then flip to the appropriate walkthrough section for the nitty gritty of that quest line. You might scratch your head at the Gauntlet's riddles or wonder how to escape the Fade that has enveloped the Circle Tower; with these walkthrough, though, you won't waste time for long.

primagames.com

Dragon Age ORIGINS

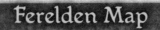

PRIMA Official Game Guide

Ferelden Map

Ferelden Map

Basics ~ Character Generation ~ Classes ~ The Party ~ Companions ~ Supporting Cast ~ Equipment ~ Bestiary ~ **Walkthroughs** ~ Side Quests ~ Random Encounters ~ Achievements/Trophies

Ferelden Highlights

1 Ostagar
- Prelude quests ("Joining the Grey Wardens")
- Alistair (companion)
- Mabari hound (companion)

2 Korcari Wilds
- Prelude quests ("Joining the Grey Wardens")
- Ancient Treaties

3 Flemeth's Hut
- Prelude quests ("Joining the Grey Wardens")
- Morrigan (companion)

4 Lothering
- Many side quests
- Leliana (companion)
- Sten (companion)
- Bodahn Feddic (merchant)
- Sandal Feddic (enchanter)

5 Lake Calenhad Docks
- "Broken Circle" quest line

6 Circle Tower
- "Broken Circle" quest line
- Wynne (companion)
- Black Grimoire
- Blood mage specialization
- Fade attribute bonuses
- Mage or templar army

7 Redcliffe Village
- "Arl of Redcliffe" quest line
- Sten's Sword
- The Green Blade

8 Redcliffe Basement
- "Arl of Redcliffe" quest line

9 Redcliffe Castle
- "Arl of Redcliffe" quest line
- Alistair's Mother's Necklace
- Champion specialization
- Redcliffe army

10 Denerim
- Many side quests
- Goldanna (Alistair's sister)
- Drake/Dragon scale armor
- Assassin specialization (Alarith's Store)
- Berserker specialization (Gorim)
- Duelist specialization (Isabela)
- Spirit healer specialization (Wonders of Thedas)

11 Village of Haven
- "Urn of the Sacred Ashes" quest line
- Brother Genitivi

12 Ruined Temple
- "Urn of the Sacred Ashes" quest line

13 Wyrmling Lair
- "Urn of the Sacred Ashes" quest line
- Urn of Sacred Ashes
- Reaver specialization

14 Frostback Mountains
- "Paragon of Her Kind" quest line

15 Orzammar
- "Paragon of Her Kind" quest line
- Oghren (companion)
- Bard specialization (Alimar)
- Dwarven or golem army
- Legion of the Dead army

16 Aeducan Thaig
- "Paragon of Her Kind" quest line

17 Caridin's Cross
- "Paragon of Her Kind" quest line

18 Ortan Thaig
- "Paragon of Her Kind" quest line

19 The Dead Trenches
- "Paragon of Her Kind" quest line

20 Brecilian Outskirts
- "Nature of the Beast" quest line

21 Dalish Camp
- "Nature of the Beast" quest line
- Shapeshifter specialization (Varathorn)
- Elven army

22 Brecilian Forest
- "Nature of the Beast" quest line
- Anerin (Wynne's apprentice)

23 Brecilian Ruins
- "Nature of the Beast" quest line

24 Elven Tomb
- "Nature of the Beast" quest line
- Arcane warrior specialization

25 Werewolf Lair
- "Nature of the Beast" quest line
- Werewolf army

26 Landsmeet & Final Battle
- "Landsmeet" quest line (in Denerim)
- Final Battle (against the archdemon in Denerim)

~~~~~~~~~~~~~~~~~~~~~~~~~~~~~~~~~~~~~

A Party Camp

B Refugees

C Battlefield

D Civil War

E Caravan

F Kadan-Fe Hideout

~~~~~~~~~~~~~~~~~~~~~~~~~~~~~~~~~~~~~

DLC Only

1 Soldier's Peak
- "Soldier's Peak" quest line
- New class talents/spells
- Party storage chest

2 Sulcher's Pass
- "The Golem in Honnleath" quest line

3 Honnleath
- "The Golem in Honnleath" quest line
- Shale (companion)

maranthine Ocean

primagames.com

Dragon Age Origins

PRIMA Official Game Guide

Dwarf Commoner Origin

Home

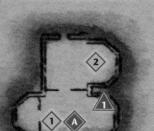

Home Cheatsheet

Main Plot Quests
- On the Streets of Dust Town

Important NPCs
- Beraht
- Kalah
- Rica

Key Items
- None

Monsters
- None

Side Quests
- None

Runthrough (Home)

Summary: Talk to your sister and mother and learn about how rough life can be in Dust Town.

A. Beraht pays you a visit. Listen to what he has to say and then talk with your family before exiting to Dust Town.

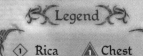

Legend
- ① Rica
- ② Kalah
- ▲ Chest

A As your story begins, Beraht, an infamous crime lord in Dust Town, drops in to say hello to you and your sister Rica. He has you on the payroll to run small "errands," and he wants your sister to find a nobleman and get pregnant so he can share in the rewards when your family becomes of noble blood. After Beraht leaves, speak with your sister and mother and then meet your friend Leske outside your door.

Dust Town

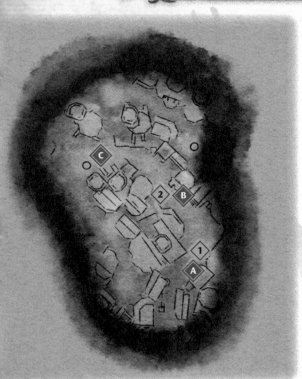

Runthrough (Dust Town)

Summary: Talk Goilinar before exiting Dust Town for the Commons.

A. Leske teams up with you to begin your first task for Beraht.

B. Speak with Goilinar about Oskias.

C. Exit Dust Town and head into the Commons in search of the Tapster's Tavern.

Dust Town Cheatsheet

Main Plot Quests
- On the Streets of Dust Town

Important NPCs
- Goilinar
- Leske

Key Items
- None

Monsters
- None

Side Quests
- None

Legend
- ① Leske
- ② Goilinar

A Your friend and partner-in-crime Leske hooks up with you outside your home. He explains that Beraht wants you to teach someone a lesson: a surfacer by the name of Oskias who has been selling shipments topside that never make it to Beraht's ears down in Dust Town.

B Look for the beggar Goilinar in the streets. Ask him about Oskias. He can either be intimidated or given money to talk. A little extra information on your target is always a good thing.

C Leave Dust Town and head to the Commons area and find Tapster's Tavern.

Commons

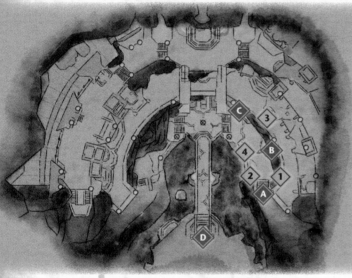

Legend

1. Kasch
2. Olinda (vendor)
3. Unna
4. Ademaro (vendor)

Runthrough (Commons)

Summary: In the Commons, you hit all your major quest locations: Tapster's Tavern, Beraht's Shop, and the Proving Grounds.

A. Enter the Commons.

B. Proceed to Tapster's Tavern.

C. Stop by Beraht's Shop after visiting the tavern.

D. Visit the Proving Grounds after Beraht's Shop.

Commons Cheatsheet

Main Plot Quests
- On the Streets of Dust Town

Important NPCs
- Beraht
- Kasch
- Olinda
- Oskias
- Unna

Key Items
- Lyrium Nuggets

Monsters
- None

Side Quests
- None

A Enter the Commons and scout around if you like. You can talk to a tooth-pulling merchant, visit Olinda's shop for some goods (though you probably don't have much money to spend at this point), and get chastised by a clothes washer.

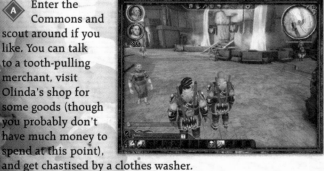

B When you're ready to continue with your mission, proceed to Tapster's Tavern.

primagames.com

Legend

1. Bartender
2. Oskias

You can speak with the bartender first if you like, and he'll back down to your threats and let you handle Oskias any way that you want. Oskias sits at the table nearby, nursing an ale. Question him and you'll hear that he's been hoarding lyrium on the side. At first, Oskias will offer you a lyrium nugget to let this whole thing slide. You can intimidate him for two nuggets. You can also kill Oskias and take the lyrium from his dead body, or let him go and scare him into giving you both nuggets.

Beraht will ask you for Oskias's profits. You can hand them over, or try to persuade him with a lie that allows you to keep one or both of the lyrium nuggets. If you persuade him and keep one or both of the nuggets, Leske will propose selling them to Olinda when you leave. You can split the profits 50–50 with Leske, or talk him down to 75–25. Beraht also sends you on your next assignment: enter the Proving Grounds to drug a fighter so that his fighter wins the day.

Legend

1. Beraht
2. Jarvia
3. Shopkeeper

C. Look for Beraht's Shop in this section of the Commons. After you obtain the lyrium from Oskias, seek out the boss at his shop.

D. The doors to the Proving Grounds lie closed here. The casteless are not allowed inside the arena, so you'll have to come back once Beraht hands you a pass when you complete the Oskias task.

Proving Grounds

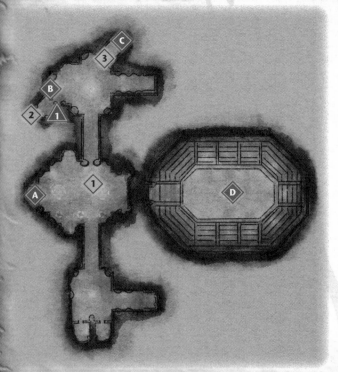

Runthrough (Proving Grounds)

Summary: Ensure that Beraht wins the contest by fighting in Everd's place.

A. Enter the Proving Grounds.

B. Find Everd. He's drunk, so you'll have to put on his armor and fight instead.

C. Drug Mainar.

D. Fight in the Proving Grounds arena.

Proving Grounds Cheatsheet

Main Plot Quests
- On the Streets of Dust Town

Important NPCs
- Duncan
- Everd
- Mainar

Key Items
- Everd's Arena Gear

Monsters
- Proving Grounds Opponents

Side Quests
- None

Legend

① Duncan ③ Mainar
② Everd ⚠ Everd's Armor Chest

A Enter the Proving Grounds on Beraht's mission to ensure that he gets his money by betting on the winning combatant. In the main foyer, speak to Duncan and he'll give you a preview of what it's like to be a Grey Warden. You'll also unlock the Duncan codex entry.

B Find Everd. Unfortunately for you, he's stone-cold drunk, passed out on the floor. You concoct a plan to put on his armor and fight in his stead. Don't put on the armor in his chest until you are ready to enter the arena.

C While speaking with Leske over Everd's drunk body, you must decide to drug Mainar or not. You can leave Mainar alone and battle him without aid, ask Leske to drug Mainar, talk to Mainar to distract him while Leske sneaks into his room, distribute the drug yourself by pouring it into the water basin in Mainar's room, use stealth to sneak into Mainar's room to pour the drug, or persuade Mainar into letting you in through dialogue choices.

D Put on Everd's armor and talk to the Proving Grounds guard to the east. The Proving will begin. After you win the third fight, Everd will stagger out into the arena looking for his armor. You've been discovered! You put up a grand fight, but eventually you succumb to the guards and wake up in a cell.

Beraht's Hideout

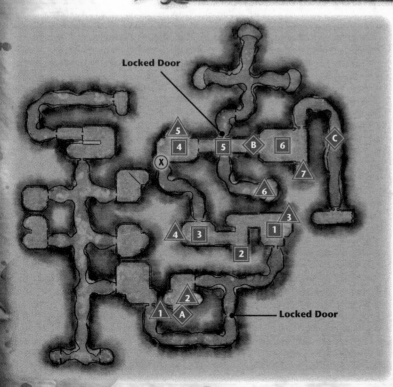

Locked Door

Locked Door

Runthrough (Beraht's Hideout)

Summary: You are locked in a cell in Beraht's Hideout and must escape.

A. Escape from your cell.

B. Reach the crime lord's chamber.

C. Take the secret passage into Beraht's Shop.

Legend

1 Thugs		**⚠1** Rubble	
2 Thugs		**⚠2** Confiscated Belongings	
3 Thugs		**⚠3** Chest & Barrels	
4 Thugs		**⚠4** Barrels	
5 Thugs		**⚠5** Crate & Barrels	
6 Beraht & Thugs		**⚠6** Chest (locked)	
ⓧ Trap		**⚠7** Chest (locked)	

primagames.com

Beraht's Hideout Cheatsheet

Main Plot Quests
- On the Streets of Dust Town

Important NPCs
- Leske

Key Items
- None

Monsters
- None

Side Quests
- None

You awake in a cell in Beraht's Hideout. In a few hours Beraht is coming to kill you, so you must escape your cell before it's too late. There are several ways to get out of the cell: steal the key from the guard, pick the lock on the door (if you're a rogue), trick the guard into coming close to the cell and then knock him out, fake an illness to trick the guard into opening the door. A nearby rubble pile contains splinters that you can give to Leske to pick his door.

Battle through Beraht's thugs to reach the crime lord's chamber. Watch out for a trap in the fourth encounter, and because Beraht's men usually have superior numbers, avoid getting flanked or attacked from behind.

When you reach Beraht, concentrate on the bodyguard thugs first. They are easier to kill and fewer blows will be swinging at your heads. Use Leske's Dirty Fighting on Beraht to slow him down and any stunning talents that your PC may have. Beraht is your first ranked foe, so he will be very difficult to bring down. Rely on health poultices to keep you in the fight long enough to finally kill the slimeball.

After the battle, exit through the northern door and keep going until you find the secret passage into Beraht's Shop. Take the door back out into the Commons. You will be captured by the city guard, but Duncan steps in to save you and offer you a place in the Grey Wardens. Accept to fulfill your greater destiny.

Dwarf Commoner Origin - Dwarf Noble Origin

Basics ~ Character Generation ~ Classes ~ The Party ~ Companions ~ Supporting Cast ~ Equipment ~ Bestiary ~ **Walkthroughs** ~ Side Quests ~ Random Encounters ~ Achievements/Trophies

Dwarf Noble Origin

Orzammar Royal Palace

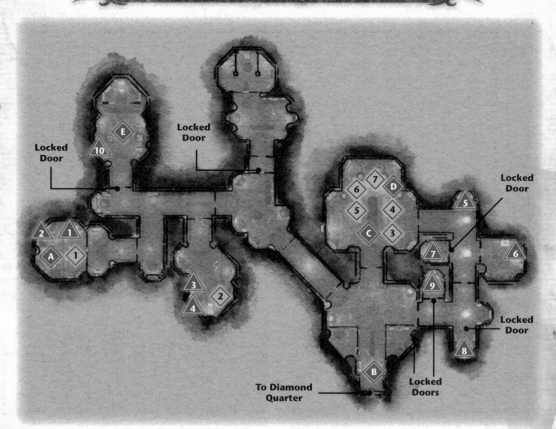

Runthrough (Royal Palace)

Summary: Attend a feast in your honor in the throne room once you've tired of other distractions.

A. You begin your chambers. Speak with your friend Gorim.

B. Then exit to the Diamond Quarters. You may use this to reach the market area and then the Proving Grounds.

C. Engage in a game of politics with Lord Dace.

D. Let the king know that you are ready for your honors.

E. Seek out Trian (in his quarters or at the Proving Grounds).

Royal Palace Cheatsheet

Main Plot Quests
- The Pride of Aeducan

Important NPCs
- Duncan
- Gorim
- King Endrin Aeducan
- Lady Helmi
- Lord Bemot
- Lord Harrowmont

- Lord Meino
- Lord Ronus Dace

Key Items
- None

Monsters
- None

Side Quests
- None

Legend

① Gorim	⑦ King Endrin Aeducan	⑥ Barrel
② Mistress	① Vanity	⑦ Barrel
③ Lord Ronus Dace	② Chest	⑧ Vase & Chest (locked)
④ Duncan	③ Pile of Books	⑨ Barrel
⑤ Lady Helmi	④ Chest (locked) & Armoire	⑩ Chest (locked)
⑥ Lord Harrowmont, Lord Bemot, & Lord Meino	⑤ Book	

primagames.com

A Speak with your friend Gorim at the start. He'll tell you that a feast is being held in your honor in the throne room, but he'll also mention the Proving Grounds if you want a little fighting action (and some extra experience). If you want to go to the Proving Grounds, head to the main doors (marked diamond B on the map) and then find the Proving Grounds stairs in the Diamond Quarter. If you want to skip the Proving Grounds for now (you'll go there later), head to the throne room (diamond C).

B This is the exit from the palace. Leave through here if you would like to explore among the merchants in the Diamond Quarter, or if you want to visit the Proving Grounds.

C Once you decide to enter the throne room, seek out Lord Ronus Dace to your right. He asks for your support in an upcoming vote involving the surface caste. You can speak out for the surface caste by agreeing to help Lord Dace. When being presented at the feast, when Lord Dace asks about the rights for the surfacers, agree that they should have the same rights as everyone else. If you speak to Lord Dace again and you arranged it when you first spoke with Lord Dace, you receive either information or a reward (note of credit) for aiding Lord Dace. If you want to humiliate Lord Dace instead, agree to help him and then do not support the surface caste's rights at the feast.

If you suspect all is not what it seems, you are correct. After speaking with Lord Dace the first time, talk to Lady Helmi. She tells you that Lord Dace has lost a considerable amount of money to the surfacers and if this deal went through, the surface caste would be obligated to repay him, including some of your relatives. After learning this, return to Lord Dace and tell him what you have heard from Lady Helmi. When he goes to excuse himself, choose "Not so fast" and then "Your schemes are an insult to House Aeducan." This triggers an Honor Proving, and you automatically move to the Proving Grounds and fight Lord Dace's son, Mandar Dace. Defeat Mandar Dace and you will leave Lord Dace a broken man.

D When you finally talk to your father, he will begin the ceremony honoring you. After you have been made commander, your father tasks you with finding your brother. If you have already been to the Proving Grounds, your brother Trian will be in his room (the chamber nearest yours behind the locked door). If you haven't been to the Proving Grounds, Trian and your brother Bhelen will be found watching the festivities there.

E If you have completed the Proving Grounds, after the feast you will find Trian in his quarters (otherwise, he is at the Proving Grounds). Speak with him, and after Trian denigrates you a bit, he leaves you to talk with your other brother, Bhelen. Bhelen warns you that Trian plots to kill you so you won't be a threat to his taking the throne. You can choose to give the order to kill Trian, wait and see what he does, or refuse to fight your brother. All choices lead to a similar outcome, so choose what appeals to you most.

Dwarf Noble Origin

Basics ~ Character Generation ~ Classes ~ The Party ~ Companions ~ Supporting Cast ~ Equipment ~ Bestiary ~ **Walkthroughs** ~ Side Quests ~ Random Encounters ~ Achievements/Trophies

Diamond Quarter

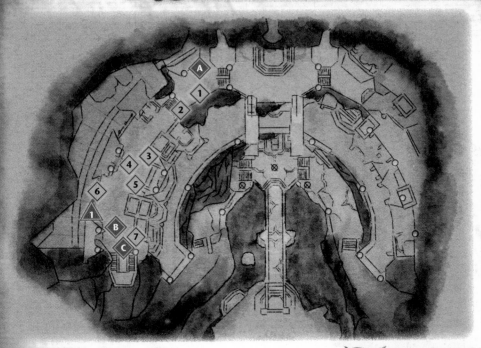

Diamond Quarter Cheatsheet

Main Plot Quests
- The Pride of Aeducan

Important NPCs
- Bruntin Vollney
- Scholar Gertek
- Weapons Merchant

Key Items
- Noble's Dagger

Monsters
- None

Side Quests
- Scholar Argument
- Weapons Merchant

Legend

1. Scholar Gertek
2. Bruntin Vollney
3. Silk Merchant
4. Trian & Bhelen
5. Armor Merchant
6. Mardy & Teli
7. Magic Merchant
1. Barrels

Runthrough (Diamond Quarter)

Summary: Wander about the merchant area on your way to the Proving Grounds.

A. Break up an argument between Scholar Gertek and Bruntin Vollney.

B. Visit the weapon merchant for a special gift or to restore family honor.

C. Ask the guards to take you to the Proving Grounds.

A Outside the royal palace, two dwarves, Scholar Gertek and Bruntin Vollney, argue about the merits of historic truth. If you side with Vollney and defend his family's honor, you can allow Vollney to kill the scholar or force Vollney to let him live. If you side with Gertek and his research into the past, you drive Vollney off and can choose to have Gorim kill Vollney or not. You can then either demand a monetary reward from Scholar Gertek or gain the book "A History of Aeducan: Paragon, King, and Peacemaker" as a token of good faith.

Feel free to wander around the rest of the marketplace. You can shop at various vendors, pick up some loot in a collection of barrels, interact with some "noble hunter" women for a possible good time, and halfway through the area you'll encounter your brothers Trian and Bhelen (if you haven't gone to the feast yet).

B Stop by the weapons merchant here. Speak with him and he tells you of a special dagger he has crafted for you on your big day. You can either accept the gift or kill him for his insolence in speaking out of turn. The Noble's Dagger is a fine dagger, with decent DPS and magical electricity damage.

C Once you are finished with the market area, speak with the guards in the southwestern corner. They will escort you to the Proving Ground.

primagames.com

Proving Grounds

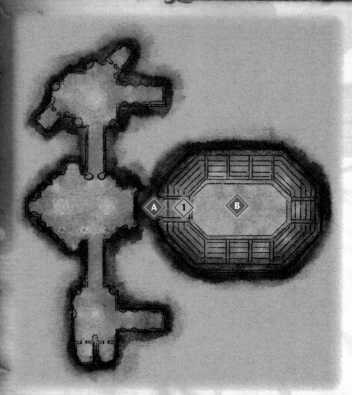

Runthrough (Proving Grounds)

Summary: Defeat four opponents in the arena to earn the Proving Helm.

A. Speak with the Proving Master.

B. Battle three opponents in the arena.

Proving Grounds Cheatsheet

Main Plot Quests
- The Pride of Aeducan

Important NPCs
- Bhelen (only if you attended the feast)
- Proving Master
- Trian (only if you attended the feast)

Key Items
- Proving Helm

Monsters
- Proving Grounds Opponents

Side Quests
- None

Legend

① Proving Master

A When you arrive at the Proving Grounds, talk to the Proving Master. You may either watch the action or partake in it yourself. If you watch, talk to the royal escort guards when you are ready to leave. If you enter the arena, you must slay four opponents in a row. Do so to survive and earn a reward: the Proving Helm.

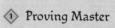

B You should be able to beat the first opponent just by trading blows. The rest of your opponents get tougher. You may need to keep your distance and do some ranged attacks to help supplement damage, or rely on some healing poultices. Talents such as Dirty Fighting that stun your opponent prove invaluable.

Ruined Thaig

~ See map on next page ~

Runthrough (Ruined Thaig)

Summary: Find the Aeducan Shield while battling darkspawn and dwarven treachery.

A. Begin your journey into the Deep Roads and head into the nearby tunnel.

B. Meet Frandlin Ivo and have him join your party.

C. Meet the scout and have him join your party.

D. Fight through the genlocks and their traps.

E. Overcome the mercenary ambush.

F. Find the Thaig Chamber and solve the floor puzzle to gain the Aeducan Shield. Return to the crossroads and become unjustly imprisoned for the death of Trian.

Dwarf Noble Origin

Basics ~ Character Generation ~ Classes ~ The Party ~ Companions ~ Supporting Cast ~ Equipment ~ Bestiary ~ **Walkthroughs** ~ Side Quests ~ Random Encounters ~ Achievements/Trophies

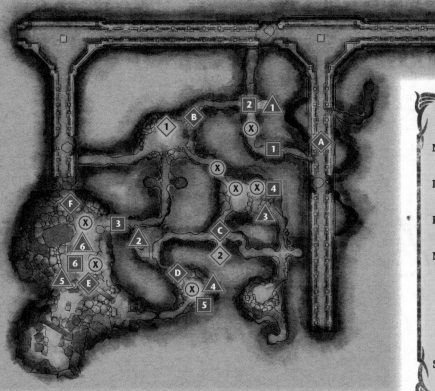

Ruined Thaig Cheatsheet

Main Plot Quests
• The Pride of Aeducan

Important NPCs
• Frandlin Ivo

Key Items
• Aeducan Shield

Monsters
• Deepstalkers
• Genlock Alpha
• Genlocks
• Giant Spider
• Mercenaries

Side Quests
• None

Legend

◇ Frandlin Ivo	5 Genlock Alpha & Genlocks	▲ Chest (locked)
◇ Scout	6 Mercenaries	▲ Chest (locked)
1 Giant Spider	▲ Dwarf Corpse	▲ Dwarf Corpse
2 Genlocks	▲ Dwarf Corpse	⊗ Trap
3 Deepstalkers	▲ Wooden Crate & Chest (locked)	
4 Genlocks		

A Your first quest against the darkspawn is to find the Shield of the Paragon Aeducan. The king and his council tell you that it's rumored to be in a ruined thaig, and it's your mission to return the shield for the greater glory of your family. Two scouts are already inside to aid you. Head toward the first crossroads (marked diamond B on the map) to rendezvous with the first scout, Frandlin Ivo. Beware of traps and enemies along the way.

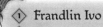

B Meet the first scout, Frandlin Ivo. Invite him to join your party so you are now three strong against the darkspawn forces.

C Rendezvous with the second scout. Add him to your party and proceed to the west.

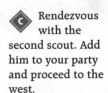

primagames.com

D Your party has a tough battle ahead against a gang of genlocks and their genlock alpha leader. Beware of the traps they have set around the cavern. Avoid those while flanking whatever genlock charges at you, usually the genlock alpha. Coordinate your efforts on the charging genlocks, then go after one archer at a time until they're all down and out.

E Over the stone bridge, you discover a band of mercenaries lying in wait for you. Don't get too confident and plow into the chamber. There are more mercenaries than members of your party. Plus, the

mercenaries have set bear traps around the chamber to pin you in one spot, and they have a ballista aimed at the center to deal big damage (and knockdown) to anyone who enters its area of fire. Pull them toward the entrance and fight from cover there. Coordinate attacks on the nearest mercenary and work your way through them. If things look dire, save your health poultices for your PC and let your scouts fall. If you win, they will recover, albeit with some minor injuries. Because you're nearing the end, it won't matter too much. On one of the dead mercenaries you find a House Aeducan signet ring and figure it must have been given to the mercenaries by Trian to enter this place and lie in ambush.

You can use the ancient ballista to get access to another passage back to the meeting point. The bolt you need to fire it with is in the barrel behind the ballista the mercenaries are firing at you when you get ambushed. The passageway opened by the ancient ballista opens into the path filled with the deepstalkers.

F Enter the Thaig Chamber and solve the floor puzzle. Three of the stone tiles are different from the rest. Have each of your followers stand on a tile. This unlocks the sarcophagus in the middle and

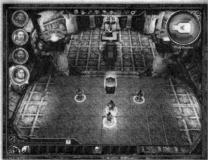

you are free to retrieve the Aeducan Shield inside. Only the PC can get the shield because you have the Aeducan signet ring. Prepare for a genlock ambush when you leave the shield chamber. Return to the crossroads (diamond B on the map, where you first met Frandlin Ivo) after you defeat genlocks. If you had decided to kill Trian earlier, Trian will be at the crossroads with his guards and you will have to fight and kill Trian. If you decided to wait to see how Trian would act, you come across Trian's dead body at the crossroads. The king and his entourage find you, and the two scouts betray you with lies about how you slew Trian dishonestly. You are dragged back to Orzammar Prison to await judgment.

Orzammar Prison

In prison, you get to say goodbye to Gorim one last time. Lord Harrowmont pronounces sentence on you and condemns you to exile in the Deep Roads until the darkspawn overrun you. You can either be defiant or proclaim your innocence. If you leave on good terms with Harrowmont, you will receive a slightly better dwarven longsword than the regular one the guard will hand to you.

Dwarf Noble Origin

Basics ~ Character Generation ~ Classes ~ The Party ~ Companions ~ Supporting Cast ~ Equipment ~ Bestiary ~ **Walkthroughs** ~ Side Quests ~ Random Encounters ~ Achievements/Trophies

Outskirts

Runthrough (Outskirts)

Summary: Survive darkspawn attacks and find the Grey Wardens.

A. Begin your journey into the outskirts of the Deep Roads.

B. Discover Duncan and the other Grey Wardens. Join their cause.

Outskirts Cheatsheet

Main Plot Quests
- The Pride of Aeducan

Important NPCs
- Duncan

Key Items
- None

Monsters
- Deepstalkers
- Genlocks
- Giant Spiders

Side Quests
- None

Legend

① Duncan & Grey Wardens	④ Giant Spider	⚠1 Corpse	⚠5 Dead Dwarf
1 Wardens	5 Deepstalkers	⚠2 Dead Dwarf	⚠6 Dwarf Corpses
2 Giant Spider	6 Genlocks	⚠3 Wooden Crate & Chest (locked)	Ⓧ Trap
3 Genlocks	7 Deepstalkers	⚠4 Darkspawn Corpse	

TIP

It's important to scavenge early in the outskirts. Because you have no quality armor or weapons, search for treasure often to upgrade to decent fighting gear.

A At the entrance to the outskirts, take the tunnel to your left. Giant spiders, genlocks, and deepstalkers will harass your every step in these tunnels, but it's the only route to Duncan and freedom. Go slowly and try to take on one foe at a time, at least until you've scavenged enough equipment to gear up. There are a few traps set by genlocks; if you aren't a rogue and can't deactivate them, go even slower so you aren't caught unawares.

B Continue south through the tunnels until you exit them at the main corridor again. Duncan and the other Grey Wardens are here. Speak with Duncan and he will invite you into the Grey Wardens to continue your noble pursuits elsewhere in the human lands.

primagames.com

City Elf Origin

Home

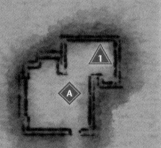

Runthrough (Home)

Summary: The player is a city elf living in the Alienage, a segregated community of elves within Denerim. Life in the Alienage allows some freedom, but not like that of the humans, because most city elves are servants. You begin on your wedding day, which is interrupted by an arl's son, and you set out to rescue the captured women (and yourself, if you're a female elf).

A. Your father Cyrion is waiting here for any last minute questions you have before the wedding.

Home Cheatsheet

Main Plot Quests
- Life in the Alienage—A Day for Celebration

Important NPCs
- Cyrion
- Shianni

Key Items
- Adaia's Boots
- Wedding Clothes in Footlocker

Monsters
- None

Side Quests
- None

Legend

1 Footlocker (wedding clothes)

A Speak to your father Cyrion who will answer any questions you have, and explain to you that your arranged marriage is tradition. He also tells you to keep your combat training (which you received from your deceased mother) a secret. Lastly he gives you a gift left from your mother, Adaia's Boots. You can grab some wedding clothes from the nearby footlocker.

Elven Alienage

~ See map on next page ~

Runthrough (Elven Alienage)

Summary: Your betrothed Nesiara is taken by an arl's son and you set out to rescue her (or rescue yourself, if a female elf).

A. Nessa's family has been evicted and is moving. You can help them by giving them some silver.

B. Meet with Soris and he joins up to go meet your bride-to-be (male elf) or groom-to-be (female elf).

C. The arl's son Vaughan starts roughing up some elven women. Shianni knocks him out with a bottle and they leave. You meet your betrothed.

D. You meet with Duncan to find out why he is here.

E. The wedding ceremony is interrupted by the return of Vaughan with some guards. He knocks you out and takes the women (and you, if you're a female elf).

Male Elves only:

F. Meeting of the elders to decide what to do.

G. An elf servant sneaks you into the castle.

Elven Alienage Cheatsheet

Main Plot Quests
- Life in the Alienage—A Day for Celebration

Important NPCs
- Duncan
- Nesiara (or Nelaros)
- Nessa's Father
- Shianni
- Soris
- Valendrian

Key Items
- None

Monsters
- None

Side Quests
- None

City Elf Origin

Basics ~ Character Generation ~ Classes ~ The Party ~ Companions ~ Supporting Cast ~ Equipment ~ Bestiary ~ **Walkthroughs** ~ Side Quests ~ Random Encounters ~ Achievements/Trophies

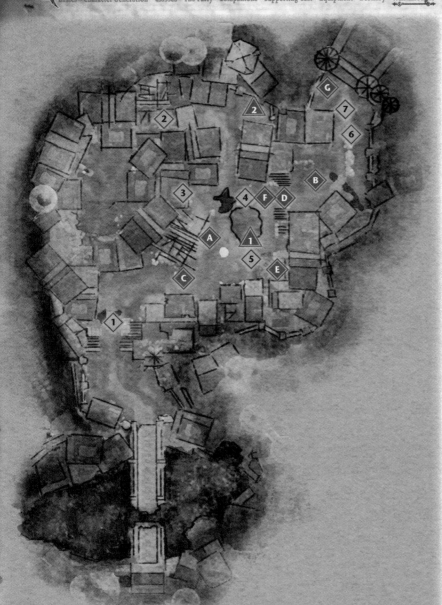

Legend

① Drunken Elves
② Elf Kids
③ Alarith's Store
④ Taeodor
⑤ Dilwyn
⑥ Elva
⑦ Beggar
△1 Alienage Tree Codex
△2 Elfroot

A Speak with Nessa's father and he tells you they have been evicted and have to leave. If you offer to help, you are turned down and wish them well. While leaving, the daughter asks you for help. You can give her 10 silver so that they can stay. The nearby couple (Dilwyn) will give you 15 silver for your wedding, so if you speak to them first, you can help Nessa.

B You meet with Soris who doesn't sound pleased about his future "mouse" wife. He joins your party and you are tasked with meeting your future bride (or groom).

C There is a disturbance here as the arl's son Vaughan starts pushing around some of the elven women. Shianni defends herself by knocking out Vaughan with a bottle, driving the humans away. Afterward Soris introduces you to the person you are marrying.

primagames.com

D Speak with Duncan to find out why he is in the Alienage. He doesn't tell you much, but an elder shows up and tells you Duncan is a Grey Warden and a friend. Duncan is vague about what his business is here, but it can wait until after the wedding.

E The wedding ceremony commences. Just after it begins, Vaughan returns with an armed escort. He knocks you out and takes the women (including you, if you're a female elf) back to the castle.

NOTE
This part of the origin story occurs only if you are playing a male elf. A female elf starts her rampage inside the mansion, as she is taken by the guards.

F A crowd of elves has formed to decide what should be done. You can offer to go after the women, and an elf who serves inside the arl's estate will sneak you in.

G You meet the elf servant who will sneak you through the gate to the arl's estate.

Arl of Denerim's Estate (Exterior)

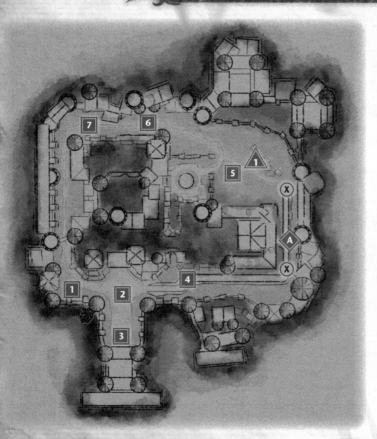

Runthrough
(Arl of Denerim's Estate: Exterior)

Summary: After being snuck through the main gates, head through the courtyard of the arl's estate.

A. When you reach the door to the arl's palace, the elf servant sees you off.

Arl of Denerim's Estate: Exterior Cheatsheet

Main Plot Quests
- Life in the Alienage—A Day for Celebration

Important NPCs
- None

Key Items
- None

Monsters
- Guards
- Mabari

Side Quests
- None

City Elf Origin

Basics ~ Character Generation ~ Classes ~ The Party ~ Companions ~ Supporting Cast ~ Equipment ~ Bestiary ~ **Walkthroughs** ~ Side Quests ~ Random Encounters ~ Achievements/Trophies

Legend

1	Guard	**6**	Mabari
2	Guard & Mabari	**7**	Mabari
3	Guard	**△1**	Deathroot
4	Mabari	**✕**	Trap
5	Mabari		

A Once you reach the door to the arl's palace, the elf servant answers a few last questions and then leaves you. Try not to get into too much trouble on the grounds; it will only alert guards to your presence. Enter the door when you're ready to tackle the estate interior.

Arl of Denerim's Estate (Interior)

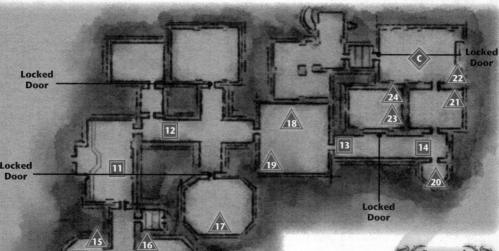

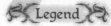

Legend

1	Sleeping Guard	**△5**	Storage Cabinet
2	Off-Duty Guard	**△6**	Wine Rack
3	Guard	**△7**	Barrel
4	Guard	**△8**	Armor Stand
5	Guard Captain & Guards	**△9**	Weapon Rack
6	Guard	**△10**	Weapon Rack
7	Dog Trainers & Mabari	**△11**	Cabinet
8	Locked Kennel with Hostile Mabari	**△12**	Wooden Crate
9	Off-Duty Guards	**△13**	Books
10	Off-Duty Guards	**△14**	Iron Footlocker (locked)
11	Guards	**△15**	Footlocker (locked)
12	Guard	**△16**	Footlocker (locked)
13	Fireball Trap	**△17**	Ornate Chest
14	Bodyguard	**△18**	Jars
△1	Barrel	**△18**	Armoire
△2	Shelves	**△20**	Wooden Crate
△3	Liquor Cabinet (locked)	**△21**	Vase
△4	Pile of Sacks	**△22**	Armor Stand
		△23	Shelves
		△24	Book

primagames.com

Runthrough (Arl of Denerim's Estate: Interior)

Summary: Search the arl's estate for Vaughan and the captured elven maidens.

A. The cook sees you and threatens to call for the guards, but his elven assistant knocks him out and lets you pass.

B. A guard captain and two guards have just slain an elf maiden.

C. Vaughan, his friends, and Shianni are here.

Arl of Denerim's Estate (Interior) Cheatsheet

Main Plot Quests
- Life in the Alienage—A Day for Celebration

Important NPCs
- Shianni

Key Items
- None

Monsters
- Bodyguard
- Dog Trainers

- Guard Captain
- Guards
- Lord Braden
- Lord Jonaley
- Mabari
- Off-Duty Guards
- Vaughan

Side Quests
- None

 A cook sees you and threatens to call for the guards, but his elven assistant knocks him out and lets you pass.

C You finally meet Vaughan and two of his friends, Lord Jonaley and Lord Braden. Shianni is here as well. Vaughan, aware of what you have done to his guards to get here, tries to talk you out of killing him. If you take the deal and leave without the women, he will set the guards on you (and they'll take the money back if you don't hide it outside the arl's estate, where you can find it during the "Landsmeet" quest line later on). Soris will always be imprisoned if you take this route. Also, all your friends and family will hate you later on. If you don't take the deal, kill Vaughan and his men. Soris will leave to find the other women.

B A guard captain and two guards make jokes over the body of one of the elf maidens. Be sure to remove the two guards first, because they will drop faster. Don't let them flank you early in the fight.

After the battle, you can speak to Shianni. She is beaten but will live, and she's happy that you took care of the humans. Soris returns with the other women and you leave the castle.

Ending

After returning to the Alienage, you inform the elder and Duncan of what happened. Shortly after, guards arrive demanding to know who is responsible for Vaughan's death. You can step forward to take the blame, and Duncan invokes the Grey Warden's right of conscription to take you out of their custody and to become a member of the Grey Wardens. Duncan allows you to say your goodbyes to anyone you want to in the Alienage and when you are ready to leave, speak with Duncan again.

City Elf Origin - Dalish Elf Origin

Basics ~ Character Generation ~ Classes ~ The Party ~ Companions ~ Supporting Cast ~ Equipment ~ Bestiary ~ **Walkthroughs** ~ Side Quests ~ Random Encounters ~ Achievements/Trophies

Dalish Elf Origin

Forest Clearing

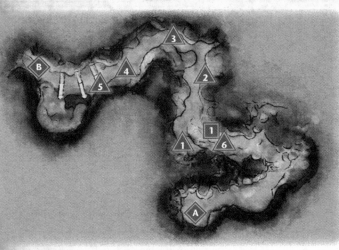

Runthrough (Forest Clearing)

Summary: The player is a member of a traveling Dalish elf camp. While hunting with your friend Tamlen, you stumble upon three humans wandering about the woods.

A. Interrogate the three wandering humans to learn about nearby elvish ruins.

B. Stop at cave entrance. Tamlen wants to explore before going back for help.

Forest Clearing Cheatsheet

Main Plot Quests
- A Child of the Dalish—The Lost Mysteries of the Ancients

Important NPCs
- Tamlen (follower)

Key Items
- None

Monsters
- Wolf

Side Quests
- None

Legend

1	Wolves	3	Elfroot
🔒	Chest (locked)	4	Elfroot
2	Tree Stump	5	Rubble
		6	Dead Halla

A The Dalish Elf origin story starts with you hunting alongside your friend Tamlen. You run into three humans in the woods who claim they have been to nearby elven ruins. One of the humans gives Tamlen a carving with elven writing on it and claims a demon chased them away from the ruins. You can then release or kill the humans before going to explore the ruins.

B You arrive at the cave entrance, which is unfamiliar territory for both of you. Tamlen wants to go inside and take a look before you go back to camp and tell anyone.

Elven Ruins

~ See map on next page ~

Runthrough (Elven Ruins)

Summary: Alongside Tamlen, you explore the elven ruins.

A. Tamlen discovers a statue that reminds him of ancient elven tales.

B. Kill the bereskarn and then Tamlen inspects the mirror.

Elven Ruins Cheatsheet

Main Plot Quests
- A Child of the Dalish—The Lost Mysteries of the Ancients

Important NPCs
- Tamlen (follower)

Key Items
- None

Monsters
- Bereskarn
- Giant Spiders
- Skeletons

Side Quests
- None

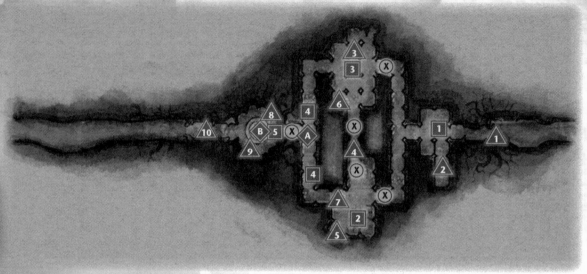

Legend

1 Giant Spiders	**5** Bereskarn	**4** Pile of Bones	**8** Rubble
2 Giant Spiders	**1** Cocoon	**5** Cocoon	**9** Sarcophagus
3 Giant Spiders	**2** Chest (locked)	**6** Cocoon	**10** Chest (locked)
4 Skeletons	**3** Pile of Bones	**7** Locked Door	**X** Trap

A While exploring the elven ruins, Tamlen notices a statue that reminds him of ancient elven teachings. There is a large poison trap nearby and two skeletons rise and attack when you trigger it. Work as a team to dispatch the relatively easy skeletons.

B When you open the door to the large circular chamber, a bereskarn attacks you. After killing it, you see a large mirror in the center of the room. There is a path leading out from the room, but if you try to leave, Tamlen will inspect the mirror. Tamlen seems entranced with the reflecting surface and walks up to touch it. He places his hand on it and begins to see things through it. Shortly after, Tamlen becomes frightened and an explosion knocks you out.

Dalish Elf Camp

~ See map on next page ~

Runthrough (Dalish Elf Camp)

Summary: You wake up back at the Dalish Elf camp, with no memory of what happened since encountering the mirror with Tamlen.

A. You wake up and are greeted by Fenarel.

B. Talk to Fenarel and have him join you.

C. Talk to Merrill when you are ready to leave camp and search for Tamlen.

Dalish Elf Camp Cheatsheet

Main Plot Quests
- A Child of the Dalish— The Lost Mysteries of the Ancients

Important NPCs
- Fenarel (follower)
- Keeper Marethari
- Merrill (follower)
- Ilen (shop)

Key Items
- None

Monsters
- None

Side Quests
- None

Dalish Elf Origin

Basics ~ Character Generation ~ Classes ~ The Party ~ Companions ~ Supporting Cast ~ Equipment ~ Bestiary ~ **Walkthroughs** ~ Side Quests ~ Random Encounters ~ Achievements/Trophies

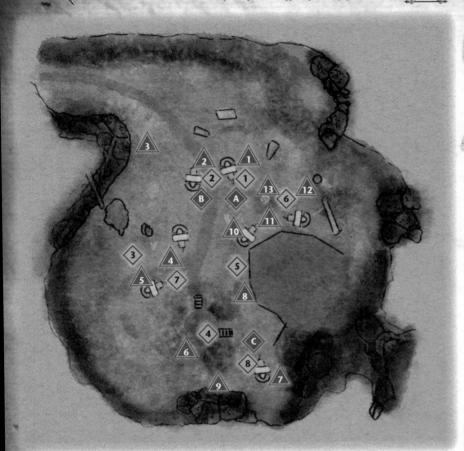

Legend

1. Keeper Marethari
2. Fenarel
3. Junar & Pol
4. Ashalle
5. Maren
6. Paivel
7. Ilen
8. Merrill

1. Pile of Sacks
2. Sack
3. Fen'Harel Codex
4. Small Wooden Crate & Dusty Scroll
5. God of the Craft Codex
6. Chest (locked)
7. Note
8. Ghilan'nain Codex
9. Scroll
10. Eldest of the Sun Codex
11. Chests (locked), Crate, & Scroll
12. Book
13. Small Scroll

A You wake up back at the Dalish Elf camp, with no memory of what happened since encountering the mirror with Tamlen. Fenarel asks you how you feel and tells you that you were brought to camp two days ago by a human Grey Warden named Duncan. You speak with Keeper Marethari who has used her powers to help you recover from the dark curse you received from the mirror. You are told to meet with Merrill and go find Tamlen.

B After speaking with the Keeper, you can talk to Fenarel and find out that he wants to help find Tamlen too. Speak with the Keeper and she will allow him to go with you.

C Talk to Merrill when you are ready to leave camp and go look for Tamlen.

Return to the Forest Clearing

Runthrough
(Return to the Forest Clearing)

Summary: You join Merrill (and possibly Fenarel) to search for Tamlen.

A. Genlock ambush.

B. Find a campsite and another genlock ambush.

Return to the Forest Clearing Cheatsheet

Main Plot Quests
- A Child of the Dalish—The Lost Mysteries of the Ancients

Important NPCs
- Fenarel (follower)
- Merrill (follower)

Key Items
- None

Monsters
- Genlocks

Side Quests
- None

Legend

1 Genlocks **2** Genlocks

A You are ambushed by two genlocks. Concentrate fire on one of the genlocks to bring it down first. You shouldn't need any healing if you coordinate your efforts.

B You find a fresh campfire and are ambushed by more genlocks. Repeat the same battle tactics as the first genlock skirmish.

Return to the Elven Ruins

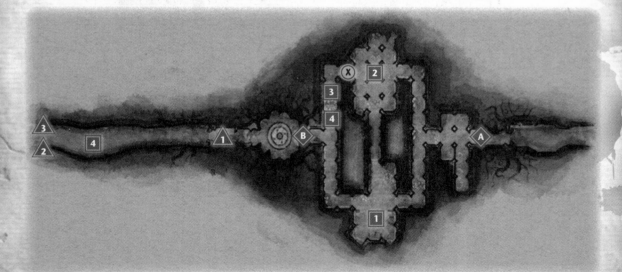

Dalish Elf Origin

Basics ~ Character Generation ~ Classes ~ The Party ~ Companions ~ Supporting Cast ~ Equipment ~ Bestiary ~ **Walkthroughs** ~ Side Quests ~ Random Encounters ~ Achievements/Trophies

Runthrough (Return to the Elven Ruins)

Summary: You return to the elven ruins to find Tamlen

A. Merrill observes the ruins.

B. Meet with Duncan to find out what happened.

Legend

1 Genlocks	**1** Chest (locked)
2 Genlocks	**2** Chest (locked)
3 Genlock Emissary & Genlocks	**3** Strange Statue
4 Skeletons & Skeleton Archers	**X** Trap

Return to the Elven Ruins Cheatsheet

Main Plot Quests
- A Child of the Dalish— The Lost Mysteries of the Ancients

Important NPCs
- Fenarel (follower)
- Merrill (follower)
- Duncan

Key Items
- None

Monsters
- Genlock Emissary
- Genlocks
- Skeletons
- Skeleton Archers

Side Quests
- None

A You return to the ruins. Merrill doesn't think the chances are good that Tamlen is still alive.

B Duncan is waiting for you in the Mirror Chamber. You find out that the mirror is responsible for the darkspawn and that Tamlen will not be saved. Duncan also tells you that you have the darkspawn plague and that the Keeper has helped you recover from it, but you are not cured. He smashes the mirror to prevent any more damage from the foul thing and bids you to return to camp. You can look around more if you wish before returning.

Return to Dalish Elf Camp

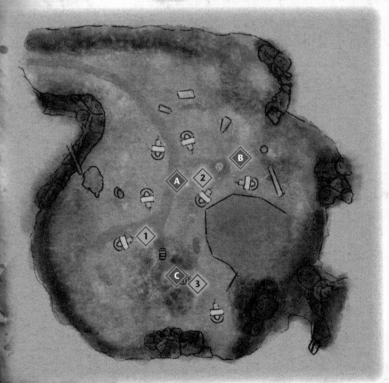

Legend

- **1** Ilen
- **2** Fenarel
- **3** Ashalle

Runthrough (Return to the Dalish Elf Camp)

Summary: After you return from the ruins with Duncan, the Keeper speaks with him to find out what happened.

A. Talk to the Keeper. She leaves with Duncan and tells you to speak with Hahren Paivel about funeral services.

B. Talk to Paivel and arrange a funeral for Tamlen.

C. Talk to Duncan and leave with him to join the Grey Wardens.

primagames.com

Return to the Dalish Elf Camp Cheatsheet

Main Plot Quests
- A Child of the Dalish—The Lost Mysteries of the Ancients

Important NPCs
- Fenarel (follower)
- Keeper Marethari
- Merrill (follower)
- Ilen (shop)
- Duncan
- Paivel

Key Items
- None

Monsters
- None

Side Quests
- None

B Talk to Paivel and tell him Tamlen's fate. Deliver the Keeper's request for a funeral for Tamlen.

C Duncan invites you to join the order of the Grey Wardens. This is the only way you can be cured of the darkspawn plague. You have to leave your friends at the camp and journey to a strange place: Ostagar.

A You return from the ruins with Duncan. You tell the Keeper that Tamlen is gone and Duncan has smashed the mirror so that no more darkspawn can come through. The Keeper wants to speak to Duncan about what happened and tells you to find Paivel and arrange funeral services for Tamlen.

Mage Origin

The Harrowing

~ See map on next page ~

Runthrough (The Harrowing)

Summary: All mages must enter the demon dream realm, the Fade, and test themselves in a dangerous ritual called the Harrowing. You must defeat a demon in the hellish dreamscape to survive.

A. You enter the Fade. The Harrowing has begun.

B. Meet Mouse and listen to his experiences in the Fade.

C. Retrieve Valor's Staff from the Spirit of Valor (through dialogue or battle).

D. Defeat the sloth demon and gain bear form for Mouse.

E. Defeat the Spirit of Rage and escape the Fade.

Harrowing Cheatsheet

Main Plot Quests
- In the High Tower of the Mages

Important NPCs
- Irving
- Greagoir
- Mouse
- Spirit of Valor
- Sloth Demon

Key Items
- Valor's Staff

Monsters
- Wisp Wraiths
- Spirit Wolves
- Spirit of Rage

Side Quests
- None

Dalish Elf Origin ~ Mage Origin

Basics ~ Character Generation ~ Classes ~ The Party ~ Companions ~ Supporting Cast ~ Equipment ~ Bestiary ~ **Walkthroughs** ~ Side Quests ~ Random Encounters ~ Achievements/Trophies

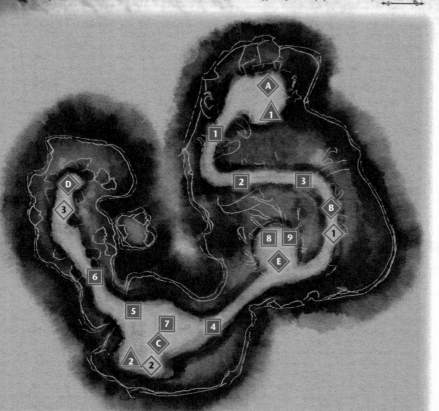

A — As an apprentice in the mages' Circle Tower, you must undergo the ritual of the Harrowing. Every mage channels great power, but also risks possession by the demons of the dream realm called the Fade. First Enchanter Irving and Knight-Commander Greagoir, leader of the Chantry templars, send you into the Fade to conquer your fears and master the powers within yourself. You unlock the Harrowing codex entry as soon as you arrive. Before you leave the area, make sure you access the Vase of Healing to your left and add three shimmering orbs of light to your inventory. The orbs act like health poultices in the Fade (These are health poultices in the console version of the game). Also, if you click on the disturbing statue on the stone landing, you unlock the Beyond the Veil: Spirits and Demons codex entry.

As you descend the path from the starting area, you'll encounter your first monster: a wisp wraith. These wraiths can fire an electrical barrage at you, so return fire with Arcane Bolts quickly. The wisps move about, sometimes retreating, so you can supplement Arcane Bolt with other spells such as Lightning or Winter's Grasp while you wait for Arcane Bolt to recharge. If you've chosen Heal, mix a healing spell into your rotation should your health drop below 50 percent. You'll fight several more wisps in the Fade so pick a spell rotation that works for you and stick with it.

B — You meet Mouse here. Speak with him about the Fade and he tells you about your test against a demon that hunts you and the other spirits lurking about. Mouse offers to tag along on your journey (but he doesn't join your party), and he'll give you hints as you wander through the Fade. If you would like to unlock the Lyrium codex entry, examine the lyrium vein in the fiery grotto to the right after meeting Mouse.

C — In the southern alcove, the Spirit of Valor stands proud. Through sheer force of will, the Spirit of Valor creates ethereal weapons in the Fade to show his prowess. You need one of these weapons, Valor's Staff, to defeat the threat ahead. You can gain the staff in one of two ways: 1) Talk the Spirit of Valor into giving it to you; or 2) Duel the Spirit of Valor for it. If you want to skip the combat (the spirit is no slouch!), speak with the spirit until the Willpower dialogue choice appears. After that, ask the spirit to help you against the demon threat in the

primagames.com

Fade and he will give you Valor's Staff. If not, accept the spirit's duel request and you'll fight. Rely on whatever spell rotation has worked for you against the wisps; however, this battle will be closer than your ranged battles against the wisps, so you can cast spells such as Flame Blast that have a shorter range. Once you defeat the spirit, he hands you Valor's Staff. As a bloodthirsty option, if you chose to duel the Spirit of Valor and beat him, you can attack him again to kill him permanently.

TIP

At any point during a fight, don't hesitate to use a shimmering orb of light to gain health. The orbs only work in the Fade, so you cannot use them back in the real world.

At the far edge of the Fade, you meet a sloth demon. The demon wants nothing to do with you really, he's content to lie around and do nothing. You need to convince him to help you out by teaching Mouse the demon's bear form. Mouse will then join your party and fight as a bear. You can do this in one of two ways: 1) Solve the sloth demon's three riddles. The answers are: a map, my tongue, and a dream; or 2) Fight the sloth demon and defeat it. Note that if you fail to answer one of the riddles correctly, you must fight the sloth demon to earn Mouse the bear form.

CAUTION

When you double-back to your final challenge, beware of a spirit wolf ambush in the Spirit of Valor area (marked square 7 on the map). Four spirit wolves will appear out of nowhere and test your partnership with Mouse in combat. Target the same wolf together and you will bring them down faster.

Though it wasn't there when you first passed the fiery grotto, the Spirit of Rage has now decided to take form and challenge you directly. No matter your dialogue with the demon, the outcome is a fight to the death. Fortunately, you have Mouse and his bear form on your side. When the demon attacks, let Mouse grab the initial threat and tank the Spirit of Rage. You'll survive longer if the spirit's attacks are concentrated on the tougher bear. If you have Heal, pop a few off on Mouse to keep him healthy, then throw offensive spells at the demon as often as possible. If the spirit attacks you, use your remaining shimmering orbs to stay in the fight.

TIP

The Spirit of Rage brings four wisp wraiths with it to the fight. Though the wisps will hit you with damage from time to time, ignore them and concentrate all firepower on the demon. When the demon falls, the encounter ends and wisps disappear.

After the fight, Mouse congratulates you on finally destroying the demon that has tormented him for so long. But you sense something is not right. Eventually your dialogue will uncover that Mouse is not what he seems to be. He is not a helpless soul lost in the Fade, but rather a power-hungry demon looking for a way out with your unwitting help. It turns out that Mouse is your true test in the Harrowing. That you are able to resist the temptation and careless trust that Mouse symbolizes means you are finally ready to become a mage.

The Circle Tower

~ See maps on next page ~

Runthrough (Circle Tower)

Summary: After surviving the Harrowing in the Fade, you return to the Circle Tower. You become involved in a plot to free your friend Jowan from his mage responsibilities so he can marry his love, Lily.

A. You wake up back in the Circle Tower. Your Harrowing is finished, and Jowan lets you know Irving is looking for you.

B. Answer First Enchanter Irving's summons in his room.

C. Escort Duncan back to the guest quarters.

D. Speak with Jowan and Lily in the chapel.

E. Obtain the rod of fire.

Circle Tower Cheatsheet

Main Plot Quests
- In the High Tower of the Mages

Important NPCs
- Jowan
- Owain
- Irving
- Greagoir
- Duncan
- Lily
- Leorah

Key Items
- Magic Staff
- Mage Robes
- Ring of Study
- Rod of Fire

Monsters
- Giant Spiders
- Poisonous Spiders

Side Quests
- Spider Caves

Mage Origin

Basics ~ Character Generation ~ Classes ~ The Party ~ Companions ~ Supporting Cast ~ Equipment ~ Bestiary ~ **Walkthroughs** ~ Side Quests ~ Random Encounters ~ Achievements/Trophies

~ First Floor ~

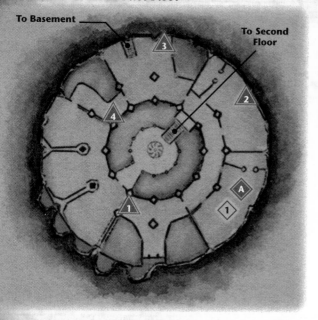

~ Second Floor ~

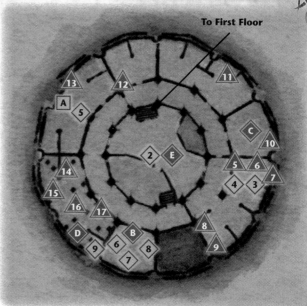

Legend

① Jowan	③ Cabinet
Ⓐ Vase	Ⓐ Shelves
② Chest	

Legend

- ② Owain
- ③ Niall
- ④ Torrin
- ⑤ Leorah
- ⑥ Irving
- ⑦ Duncan
- ⑧ Greagoir
- ⑨ Lily
- Ⓐ The Four Schools of Magic: Spirit Codex
- Ⓐ History of the Circle Codex
- Ⓐ The Four Schools of Magic: Entropy Codex
- Ⓐ The Four Schools of Magic: Primal Codex
- Ⓐ The Four Schools of Magic: Creation Codex & Hierarchy of the Circle Codex
- ⑩ Armoire
- ⑪ Chest
- ⑫ Shelves
- ⑬ Storage Cabinet
- ⑭ Rite of Annulment Codex
- ⑮ Founding of the Chantry Codex
- ⑯ Andraste: Bride of the Maker Codex
- ⑰ Chant of Light & The Maker Codex
- Ⓐ "Spider Caves"

Ⓐ You wake up in your own bed after the Harrowing. Your friend Jowan lets you know that First Enchanter Irving would like to see you. He's on the second floor (marked diamond B on the map). You can tell something is bothering Jowan, but he says he'll speak with you later about it. Be sure to check out a few of the loot spots on the first floor for some more goods for your inventory.

Ⓑ Head upstairs to the second floor and seek out Irving here. Along the way, examine the treasure spots on the second floor, mostly to unlock codex entries. Irving is in a meeting with Greagoir and Duncan, a member of the famed Grey Wardens who safeguard the land against the darkspawn. Question Irving and Duncan for some good information about the Circle and the coming war. At the end of the conversation, Irving asks you to escort Duncan back to the guest quarters, but not before he gives you a Magic Staff, Mage Robes, and Ring of Study. You now have some magic items to beef up your wardrobe.

primagames.com

C Run Duncan back to the guest quarters. When you spoke with Duncan earlier, you automatically unlocked the Duncan codex entry, and now you unlock the Grey Wardens entry when you reach his chambers. You can question Duncan more about what's going on outside the tower, the king's army, blood magic, the Tranquil and more. You unlock the Darkspawn codex entry if you listen to Duncan's tale about the foul creatures.

D Jowan will be waiting for you outside Duncan's room. Speak with him and he'll take you to the back corner of the chapel for a private talk. He introduces you to his lady love, Lily, a Chantry initiate. Their love is forbidden by tower rule. They ask you to join them in a scheme to free both of them from the tower. Jowan and Lily plan to slip into the basement, destroy Jowan's phylactery so he can't be tracked by the templars, and escape from the tower. Jowan claims that the mages want to turn him into a Tranquil against his will. In order to break into the phylactery vault, they ask you to obtain a rod of fire from the stockroom.

E Visit Owain at the stockroom and ask for the rod of fire. You learn that the rod can only be released with signed papers from a senior enchanter. There are two main methods of obtaining the release form signature. You can return to Irving and spill the beans on the plan. Irving will ask you to betray the pair, but only after he signs the form and instructs you to carry out their scheme so he can catch them at the end red-handed. You can also engage him in conversation in the library and humor him to get the release form.

If you want to bypass Irving altogether, seek out Senior Enchanter Leorah and interrogate her about why the storage caves are locked (marked square A on the map). She will tell you about the spider infestation. Enter the spider cave and kill all the spiders. Upon doing so, Leorah will sign the release form. If you already have the form signed, she will give you some potions instead.

◄═══ CAUTION ═══►

If you want to do the "Spider Caves" side quest, do not return to Jowan and Lily until after you've completed the quest. Once Jowan and Lily join your party, it is too late to vanquish the spiders.

Once you have a signed release form, return to Owain and he will give you the rod of fire. With the rod in hand, seek out Jowan and Lily in the chapel and trigger the final stage of the quest in the basement.

The Repository

~ Spider Caves ~

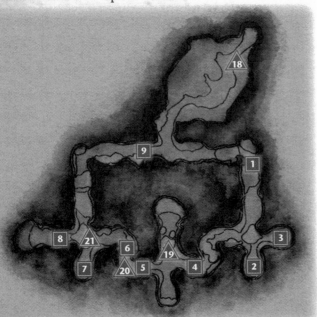

◄═══ Legend ═══►

1	Giant Spider	**8**	Giant Spider
2	Poisonous Spider	**9**	Giant Spider
3	Giant Spider	**18**	Chests
4	Giant Spider	**19**	Chest
5	Giant Spider	**20**	Cocoon
6	Giant Spider	**21**	Cocoon
7	Giant Spider		

Mage Origin
Basics ~ Character Generation ~ Classes ~ The Party ~ Companions ~ Supporting Cast ~ Equipment ~ Bestiary ~ **Walkthroughs** ~ Side Quests ~ Random Encounters ~ Achievements/Trophies

~ Basement ~

Legend

1. Sentinel
2. Sentinels
3. Sentinels
4. Robed Sentinels
5. Deepstalkers
6. Sentinels
7. Sentinels
8. Robed Sentinels
9. Sentinel Guardian & Sentinels

1. Wooden Crate
2. Chest
3. Wooden Crate & Chest
4. Storage Cabinet
5. Wooden Crate & Chest
6. Wooden Crate
7. Chest
8. Blackened Heartwood Staff
9. Tevinter Imperium Codex
10. Chest

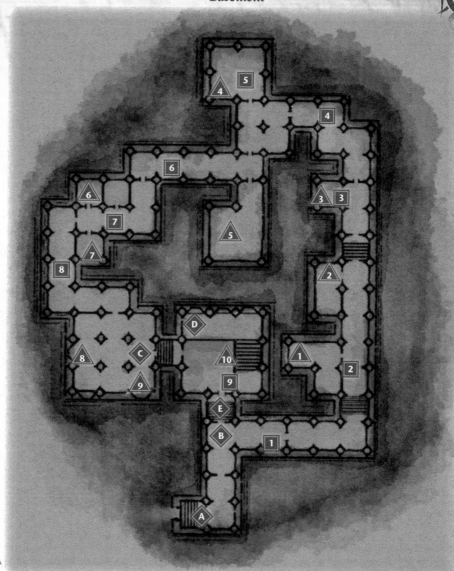

Runthrough (Repository)

Summary: You must stage a break in to the repository so that Jowan can destroy his phylactery. The couple plans to escape, but there are many surprises in store.

A. Enter the basement with the rod of fire and Jowan and Lily in your party.

B. Attempt to break through the magical door.

C. Reach the repository.

D. Slay the sentinel guardian.

E. Try to escape.

Repository Cheatsheet

Main Plot Quests
- In the High Tower of the Mages

Important NPCs
- Jowan
- Irving
- Greagoir
- Duncan
- Lily

Key Items
- Rod of Fire
- Blackened Heartwood Staff

Monsters
- Sentinels
- Robed Sentinels
- Deepstalkers
- Sentinel Guardian

Side Quests
- None

A You, Jowan, and Lily should enter the basement with the rod of fire. Open the Victim's Door a few paces into the basement with your magic touch and Lily's sweet tongue. It's a long trek to the repository proper, so pace yourself. Heal after each fight and save your health poultices and lyrium potions for key moments.

B Use the rod of fire on the magic door here. Alas, it won't work due to the anti-magic field in the immediate area. You have to find a way around to the other side of the basement. Continue to follow the corridor to your right and keep an eye on the statue in the hallway. It's actually a magical sentinel and will animate after you melt the door lock with the rod of fire. Defeat the sentinel and watch for more defenders as you continue through the passages.

C After battling through most of the basement, you finally reach the repository. Search the chest and statue in the room to gain a magic staff and a new codex entry. Once you are ready to break into the phylactery vault, examine the bookcase on the eastern wall. You notice a weak spot in the wall behind it. Together you and Jowan slide the bookcase out of the way. Next, examine the dog statue directly in front of the bookcase. By using the rod of fire on the statue, you can blast a hole through the repository wall and into the phylactery vault.

D Enter the repository and prepare for a difficult fight. Two sentinels swarm you, followed by the sentinel guardian. Dispatch the two sentinels first, then gang up on the guardian. It will take several Heal spells, and probably a few health poultices and lyrium potions to deal enough damage to kill the guardian. Lily's Dirty Fighting will stun the guardian, and it's very useful to back away momentarily, heal up, and coordinate a new round of attacks on your foe.

E When you finally defeat the sentinel guardian, climb the stairs and find Jowan's phylactery on the end. Jowan will destroy it

Leave via the magic door (now unlocked) that you originally couldn't get through because of the anti-magic field. Return to the basement entrance and head back up to the first level. Irving and Greagoir intercept you as soon as you arrive topside. They expose the whole plot. Greagoir orders the templars to imprison Lily, and Jowan, in his anger, reveals the full extent of his blood mage power. He kills several templars and rushes out of the tower after a shocked Lily scorns his evil-doing. Greagoir and Irving question you. It's possible to keep the Blackened Heartwood Staff if you use Persuade skill and say that you didn't steal anything from the repository. As Greagoir and Irving argue over what to do with you, Duncan arrives and insists on recruiting you to the Grey Wardens. Irving sides with Duncan—you did not, after all, know that Jowan was a blood mage—and you are sent with the Grey Warden to Ostagar. Your power will be better served outside the tower.

Mage Origin - Human Noble Origin

Basics ~ Character Generation ~ Classes ~ The Party ~ Companions ~ Supporting Cast ~ Equipment ~ Bestiary ~ **Walkthroughs** ~ Side Quests ~ Random Encounters ~ Achievements/Trophies

Human Noble Origin

Castle Cousland by Day

Castle Day Cheatsheet

Main Plot Quests
- The Couslands of Highever

Important NPCs
- Teryn Cousland (father)
- Arl Howe
- Duncan
- Ser Gilmore (follower)
- Dog (follower)
- Teryna Eleanor (mother)
- Fergus (brother)

Key Items
- None

Monsters
- Giant Rats

Side Quests
- Sweet Iona (or Sweet Dairren)

Legend

1. Teryn Cousland
2. Arl Howe
3. Duncan
4. Ser Gilmore
5. Nan
6. Dog
7. Teryna Eleanor
8. Lady Landra, Iona, & Dairren
9. Mother Mallol
10. Treasury Guards
11. Aldous
12. Fergus
- **1** Giant Rats
- **1** Crate & Sack
- **2** Sacks (locked room)
- **3** Chest (locked room)
- **4** Chest (locked room)
- **5** Chests & Weapon Stand (locked room)
- **A** Seduction side quests

Runthrough (Castle Cousland by Day)

Summary: The player is the son or daughter of Byron Cousland, the Teyrn of Highever. His/her father and older brother are going off to join King Cailan at Ostagar on the morrow—or so they think. During the day, things are peaceful; giant rats in the kitchen pantry are the only enemies to fight.

A. Talk to your father, Arl Howe, and the Grey Warden Duncan. Your father asks you to speak with your brother Fergus.

B. You meet Ser Roderick Gilmore. He asks you to head to the kitchen to deal with your Mabari war hound that is supposedly terrorizing the staff. Ser Gilmore joins your party temporarily.

C. After speaking with Nan, enter the pantry and join up with your dog. He has actually been guarding the kitchen against a giant rat invasion. Slay the giant rats and earn some small rewards.

D. Speak with your mother and her guests Lady Landra, Iona, and Dairren. If you have any other business in the castle, conduct it before finding your brother.

E. Give Fergus your father's message about leaving early for the war. Your father and mother join you at the end of this conversation, and when you leave the room, the night portion of the adventure begins.

primagames.com

The Human Noble origin story takes place in Castle Cousland in two parts: day and night. In this section (day), you can talk with friends and family around the castle, learn about your family's place in the world events, and collect some experience points and treasure before the action gets intense. Explore the entire castle before speaking with Fergus (diamond E) or you will lose your chance and trigger the night's events.

 You begin the game in conversation with your father, Teryn Cousland of Highever, and his ally Arl Howe. Your father explains that he would like you to stay home and guard the castle while he and your brother, Fergus, head off to join King Cailan's army at Ostagar. He asks you to take a message to your brother: Fergus is to leave ahead of your father and press for Ostagar sooner than expected.

Midway through the conversation, Duncan, a member of the famed Grey Wardens who pledge their service against the darkspawn, enters the main hall. All your dialogue choices here will result in the same: You gain a short quest to speak with Fergus and unlock the codex entries for Highever and Duncan.

 At this point you are free to explore the castle. If you are a rogue, make sure you visit the locked rooms in the castle's eastern half to gain a tiny bit more experience and extra loot (marked triangles 2–5 on the map). Leave from the door in the north if you'd like to pursue some more of the main origin story. At the intersection just to the west, Ser Roderick Gilmore intercepts you. Apparently, your Mabari war hound is up to no good in the kitchen. Ser Gilmore joins your party for the "Mischief in the Larder" quest and the two of you head off.

 Head north and take the first door on the left. Talk with Nan and she'll holler a bit about your dog locked in the pantry behind her. Once you calm her down, you can enter the pantry and Dog joins your party (you can name the Mabari hound whatever you like; we'll call him Dog for the purposes of the walkthrough). It turns out the pantry has an infestation of giant rats, which attack shortly after you enter. Together, you, Ser Gilmore, and Dog battle the giant rats in your first combat encounter. You should have no

problem squashing them all, but if you run into any trouble, remember to pause the battle and issue precise orders to each of your party members. You start with three lesser health poultices, so use one if your health gets low.

Ser Gilmore leaves the party after you slay the giant rats. By finding Dog, you unlock the Dogs in Ferelden codex entry, and don't forget to raid a special crate and sack in the pantry for some minor rewards.

Your mother, Teryna Eleanor, chats here with guests Lady Landra, her lady-in-waiting Iona, and her son Dairren in the hallway. Engage in a few pleasantries, and shortly Lady Landra will excuse herself, and Iona and Dairren will retire to the study (the small room south of Aldous's library).

CAUTION

After you talk to your mother and her guests, you are free to speak with your brother in the southwest wing. However, once you do that, day ends and night begins. You will be unable to complete most of the encounters around the castle. Talk to all NPCs and explore all rooms before speaking with Fergus.

Once you say goodbye to your mother, go back into the castle and explore anywhere you haven't yet. Highlights include praying (or not) with Mother Mallol in the chapel (marked diamond 9 on the map), which unlocks the Maker and Commandments of the Maker codex entries; catching two guards gambling at the guard post outside the treasury (diamond 10); and learning about history from Scribe Aldous (diamond 11), which unlocks the Geography of Ferelden and Noble Families of Ferelden codex entries. If you're the flirtatious type, you can also seduce either Iona or Dairren (gender preference doesn't matter). Both are in the study (marked square 1). Talk with either and always choose compliments throughout the dialogue. When the dialogue option pops up to invite them back to your room, choose that and you'll have a bedroom encounter at night. If you try to meet up with both of them, however, they will take offense and leave you with the cold shoulder.

When you are finally ready to talk to Fergus, head to the room in the far southwest corner (marked diamond 12). Give Fergus your father's message and talk with his family for a bit. Your father and mother join you at the end of the conversation, and you have a warm family moment—unfortunately, it will be your last! Treasure it, for when you leave the room, day ends and night begins in the castle.

Castle Cousland by Night

Castle Night Cheatsheet

Main Plot Quests
- The Couslands of Highever

Important NPCs
- Dog (follower)
- Teryna Eleanor (follower)
- Ser Gilmore
- Teryn Cousland (father)
- Duncan

Key Items
- Family Sword
- Shield of Highever

Monsters
- Howe Soldiers
- Howe Archers

Side Quests
- The Cousland Treasury

Legend

◇1	Teryna Eleanor	△1	Chest (your room)
◇2	Ser Gilmore	△2	Chest & Trunk
◇3	Teryn Cousland	△3	Chest (locked)
◇4	Duncan	△4	Chest (locked)
☐1	Howe's Men	△5	Knight's Corpse
☐2	Howe's Men	△6	Rubble
☐3	Howe's Men	△7	Chest (locked)
☐4	Howe's Men	△8	Rubble
☐5	Howe's Men	△9	Knight Corpse
☐6	Howe's Men	A	"The Cousland Treasury"
☐7	Howe Knight		

The Human Noble origin story takes place in Castle Cousland in two parts: day and night. In this section (night), you battle for survival against Arl Howe's brutal treachery. You must escape the castle and join Duncan on the road to becoming a Grey Warden.

Runthrough (Castle Cousland by Night)

Summary: Unbeknownst to the Couslands, their long-time rival and ally, Arl Howe, has conspired to lay siege to the castle. Before the night is over, your mother and father will be dead, your brother's family will be murdered, and you will be conscripted into the Grey Wardens to save your life.

A. You are under attack! Defend yourself with Dog at your side.

B. Defeat Howe's men in the hallway and join your mother. Teryna Eleanor becomes a member of your party.

C. When your mother pauses to speak with you, ask her what else you can do. She will give you the treasury key. Recover the family sword and shield from inside the treasury.

D. Fight to the main hall. Ser Gilmore holds the doors and tells you that your father escaped to the pantry.

E. Battle to the pantry. Your father lies mortally wounded, and your mother chooses to stay by his side in the final moments before Howe's men overrun the castle. Duncan enlists you in the Grey Wardens and convinces you to flee to safety.

A Night falls, and you awake to Dog barking at your bedroom door. When the door opens a Howe archer kills Iona or Dairren (if you seduced them) or a servant warning you. Another Howe soldier charges at you. Dog and you must fight off the first two of Howe's men while gathering your wits and clothes.

TIP

You don't have to slug it out with Howe's men naked. Hit your Inventory button and put on armor and weapons in the middle of the fight!

B Two more of Howe's men stand at the southern portion of the hallway in front of your mother's room. If you don't want to engage them right away, lure the first two enemies into your room to fight. After you slay the second two, your mother rushes out of her room and the two of you figure out that Howe's men have besieged the castle. Unfortunately, they have already killed Fergus's wife and child. Your father and brother are missing.

TIP

Besides gathering loot from the downed soldiers, don't forget to raid the chests in both your room and your mother's room. With so little in your possession during this attack, every little bit counts and some better weapons are stashed in the chest in your mother's bedroom, including a longbow that she's rather good at using.

C After wading through the first wave of Howe's men, your mother stops you in the corridor outside the southwest wing. When the dialogue choice, "Is there nothing else we can do?" comes up, choose that. It opens "The Cousland Treasury" side quest. Even though it's a side quest, treat it like the main story. You want the sword and shield in the treasury, and you certainly don't want it to fall into Howe's grimy hands. Before you leave, search the knight's corpse in the circular room to your left for some loot.

Battle through to the treasury (marked square A on the map) and recover the family heirlooms. Be careful, though, at the following intersection (square 4). A large group of Howe's soldiers patrol to the north and south of here. An unarmed castle worker will run in your direction, and if you try to persuade him, you can get him to join with some other Cousland loyalists to fight Howe's men to the north. You can either slay the south enemies (including those at square 5) and make a run for the treasury, or take on the enemies up north too.

D After gaining the family sword and shield, walk back up the corridor to the main hall to the northeast. Watch out for more of Howe's men along the way. Inside the main hall, Ser Gilmore and a handful of men hold the room against Howe's forces. Swarm into the room to aid Ser Gilmore. Keep him alive as best as you can. Generally, your party should attack as a group on any soldier slashing at Ser Gilmore. Howe's men have a single Howe mage in the midst, and the mage's Lightning attacks can devastate the Cousland side. As soon as you spot the mage, charge the spellcaster and strike him down quickly. Even if you use up a few lesser health poultices to bring down the mage, it's worth it. Once the battle ends, Ser Gilmore tells you that your father has been badly wounded and went to the pantry near the secret escape out of the castle.

E Fight toward the kitchen pantry, where you and Dog fought the giant rats earlier. You meet your first ranked foe in the enemy group outside the kitchen door: the Howe knight. Concentrate your party's attacks on the lesser Howe men first to reduce the strikes against you. When the Howe knight remains, gang up all three of your attacks on him and let Dog take most of the beating at first. Step in when Dog's health gets low and take the remaining knight damage on yourself. When your health gets low, pop a health poultice.

Slay the Howe knight and his gang and you can reach the pantry. The teryn lies mortally wounded on the floor. There will be no escape for him. Your mother chooses to fight by his side to the death, no matter how much you plead. Duncan arrives and offers you a chance to escape: Join the Grey Wardens with him and he will guide you to safety outside the castle. Your father and mother agree as it is the only hope for their child. You are on the road to Ostagar, where the Grey Wardens gather for King Cailan, and it will become even more dangerous than Castle Cousland soon enough.

Human Noble Origin - Ostagar

Basics ~ Character Generation ~ Classes ~ The Party ~ Companions ~ Supporting Cast ~ Equipment ~ Bestiary ~ Walkthroughs ~ Side Quests ~ Random Encounters ~ Achievements/Trophies

Ostagar

NOTE

After your origin story, all characters arrive in Ostagar with Duncan. You must complete the quests leading up to becoming a Grey Warden to advance out into the full world map.

King's Camp

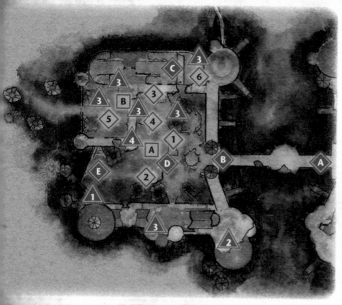

Legend

1. Wynne
2. Duncan
3. Quartermaster
4. Daveth
5. Jory
6. Alistair

1. Elfroot
2. Sack
3. Chest (locked)
4. Note

A. Kennel Master for "The Mabari Hound"
B. "Hungry Deserter"

Runthrough (King's Camp)

Summary: Duncan recruits you to join the Grey Wardens. He takes you to Ostagar to meet King Cailan and prepare for your initiation into the Grey Wardens.

A. You meet King Cailan and learn that the fight against the darkspawn is going well, though Duncan fears it isn't as easy as it seems. Duncan tells you to look around the camp and find Alistair.

B. A soldier here will greet you and give you basic directions and info about the camp.

C Meet Alistair.

D. Speak with Duncan and get your mission out into the Korcari Wilds.

E. The guard at the gate lets you out of camp.

King's Camp Cheatsheet

Main Plot Quests
- Joining the Grey Wardens

Important NPCs
- Alistair
- Duncan
- Daveth
- Jory
- King Cailan

- Wynne

Key Items
- None

Monsters
- None

Side Quests
- Hungry Deserter
- Mabari Hound

A You arrive in Ostagar with Duncan and meet King Cailan. The king seems a bit disappointed that there aren't more darkspawn, though Duncan thinks things may not be going as well as they seem. After you finish your introductions, Duncan asks you to look around camp and find Alistair.

B A soldier here will greet you and give you basic directions and info about the camp. If it's your first time visiting Ostagar, the directions are helpful.

TIP

Seek out the quartermaster if you want to purchase your first backpack.

primagames.com

C You arrive to see Alistair and a mage arguing. Alistair greets you after and figures that you're Duncan's new recruit. He also mentions that he used to be a templar, or mage hunter. After joining you as a companion, he suggests going back to Duncan. Depending on the eventual makeup of your party, Alistair may become your main tank, so if he happens to level during your adventures in Ostagar and the Korcari Wilds, spend your points accordingly.

D When you return to Duncan, he tasks you with going out into the Korcari Wilds to find three vials of darkspawn blood, one for each recruit ("Tainted Blood" quest). He also wants you to find an abandoned Grey Warden archive and retrieve any magical scrolls found there ("The Grey Wardens' Cache" quest).

E After Duncan gives you the Korcari Wilds tasks, seek out the guard at the side gate. He will let you into the Wilds.

Korcari Wilds

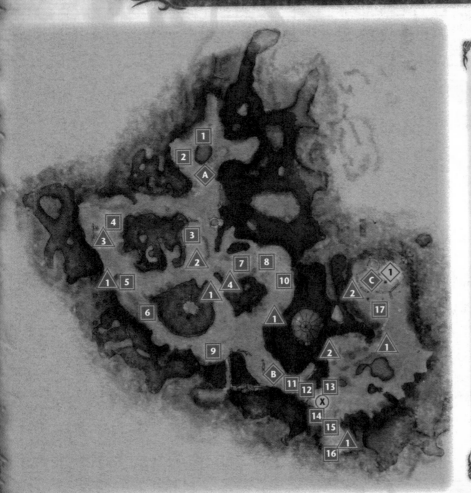

Legend

- ① Morrigan
- **1** Wolf
- **2** Wolves
- **3** Genlocks & Hurlocks
- **4** Genlocks & Hurlocks
- **5** Genlocks & Hurlocks
- **6** Genlock Rogues
- **7** Genlocks & Hurlocks
- **8** Genlock Rogues
- **9** Genlock, Hurlock, & Wolves
- **10** Genlock Rogues
- **11** Genlock Rogues
- **12** Hurlock Emissary
- **13** Hurlock Archer
- **14** Genlock
- **15** Hurlocks
- **16** Alpha Wolf & Wolves
- **17** Alpha Hurlock & Hurlocks
- △1 Elfroot
- △2 Deathroot
- △3 Chest
- △4 Wooden Crates & Chest (locked)
- Ⓧ Trap

Ostagar

Basics ~ Character Generation ~ Classes ~ The Party ~ Companions ~ Supporting Cast ~ Equipment ~ Bestiary ~ **Walkthroughs** ~ Side Quests ~ Random Encounters ~ Achievements/Trophies

Runthrough (Korcari Wilds)

Summary: Enter the Korcari Wilds to retrieve three vials of darkspawn blood and ancient Grey Wardens treaties.

A. You find a dying soldier who warns you of danger ahead.

B. A hurlock emissary leads a large ambush when you arrive at the bridge here.

C. You reach the abandoned Grey Warden ruins and the Warden's Cache still exists. You meet Morrigan.

Korcari Wilds Cheatsheet

Main Plot Quests
- Tainted Blood
- The Grey Wardens' Cache

Important NPCs
- Morrigan

Key Items
- Ancient Treaties

Monsters
- Alpha Wolf
- Genlocks
- Genlock Archers

- Genlock Rogues
- Hurlocks
- Hurlock Alpha
- Hurlock Archers
- Hurlock Emissary
- Wolves

Side Quests
- Last Will and Testament
- The Mabari Hound
- The Missionary
- A Pinch of Ashes

A You find a dying soldier, who was part of a patrol that was ambushed by darkspawn. You can bandage him up and he will go back to the camp after warning you that danger is ahead.

B A hurlock emissary leads a large ambush when you arrive at the bridge here. The emissary is a mage, so take him out fast or he'll hang back and rip you apart. There are a lot of traps at the other side of the bridge; be careful not to be drawn into the traps and caught in a crossfire. During this fight (or with nearby darkspawn afterward), you should easily get enough blood vials to fulfill the "Tainted Blood" quest.

C You reach the abandoned Grey Warden ruins and meet Morrigan, daughter to a mysterious witch of the Wilds, Flemeth. Morrigan tells you that the Warden's Cache still exists and takes you to her mother Flemeth. After a bit of convincing, Flemeth returns the scrolls and Morrigan brings you back to King's Camp.

Return to King's Camp

~ See map on next page ~

Runthrough (Return to King's Camp)

Summary: You return to the camp and are tasked with heading to the Tower of Ishal once the battle starts.

A. Return to Duncan with the blood vials and scrolls.

B. You must go to the Tower of Ishal and light a signal fire.

C. Outside the tower courtyard, a guard and soldier tell you the tower has been taken over.

D. Defeat a few packs of darkspawn, then enter the tower.

Return to King's Camp Cheatsheet

Main Plot Quests
- Joining the Grey Wardens

Important NPCs
- Duncan
- King Cailan
- Wynne

Key Items
- None

Monsters
- Genlocks
- Hurlock Alpha
- Hurlocks

Side Quests
- Hungry Deserter
- Mabari Hound

Legend

- ① Wynne
- ② Duncan
- ③ Quartermaster
- 1 Genlocks & Hurlocks
- 2 Genlocks
- 3 Genlocks & Hurlocks
- 4 Genlocks
- 5 Hurlock Alpha
- △1 Elfroot
- △2 Sack
- △3 Chest (locked)
- △4 Note
- △5 Deathroot
- △6 Wooden Crates
- △7 Barrels & Wooden Crate
- △8 Wooden Crate
- A Kennel Master for "The Mabari Hound"
- B "Hungry Deserter"

A You return to Duncan with the Ancient Treaties and vials of blood. Then you have the Ritual of Joining. It's a grueling affair, and only you survive.

Congratulations, you are now a Grey Warden and receive an extra spell/talent for surviving your ordeal! Duncan wants you to meet with him and the king to discuss the imminent battle against the invading darkspawn.

B After you survive the Joining, Duncan tells you to meet him at the War Council. There is going to be a large battle with the darkspawn, and your task is to go

with Alistair to the Tower of Ishal to light a signal fire so that Loghain's troops know when to attack.

C When you arrive at the tower, a tower guard and soldier inform you that the tower has been taken by darkspawn. The guard and soldier join your party, and you must take the tower back.

D Approach the tower slowly. Several darkspawn mobs guard the steps and surrounding area. If you charge in, you will alert multiple groups and have a much tougher fight on your hands. The guard and soldier that join your party are temporary allies; you don't want to die for the king, but if they have to, so be it. After fighting past the packs of darkspawn and a slightly tougher hurlock alpha at the tower door, enter the tower.

Ostagar

Basics ~ Character Generation ~ Classes ~ The Party ~ Companions ~ Supporting Cast ~ Equipment ~ Bestiary ~ **Walkthroughs** ~ Side Quests ~ Random Encounters ~ Achievements/Trophies

Tower of Ishal

~ First Floor ~

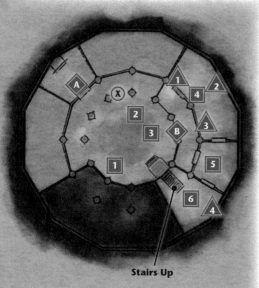

Stairs Up

Runthrough (Tower of Ishal)

Summary: You enter the Tower of Ishal, which has been taken over by darkspawn. You must get to the top and light the signal fire.

A. Avoid the tripwire Grease trap followed by emissary fireball.

B. Be on guard for two-room pull with ambush by hurlocks and genlocks.

C. Another large ambush is triggered.

D. Fight in the dog pen.

E. Reach the top of the tower and battle the ogre.

Tower of Ishal Cheatsheet

Main Plot Quests	Key Items	• Genlocks
• The Tower of Ishal	• Havard's Aegis	• Hurlocks
	Monsters	• Ogre
Important NPCs	• Genlock Alpha	**Side Quests**
• Soldier	• Genlock Emissary	• None
• Tower Guard		

Legend (1F)

1	Hurlocks	6	Genlocks
2	Hurlocks	△1	Chest (locked)
3	Genlock Emissary	△2	Wooden Crates
4	Hurlocks	△3	Chest
5	Genlocks	△4	Chest (locked)
		Ⓧ	Trap

~ Second Floor ~

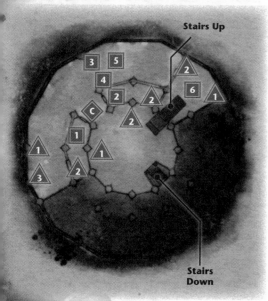

Stairs Up

Stairs Down

A When you enter the large circular room, several barricades are on fire. You can only pass through the area marked with a gray X on the map, and, unfortunately, there is a tripwire trap here that sets off a Grease spell if triggered. Unless you are a skilled rogue and avoid the tripwire, this will probably knock you down, and it will slow you. Right after you pass here, the nearby genlock emissary shoots a Fireball at your feet. If the Grease trap was triggered, the Fireball will ignite the oily surface, damaging anyone standing in it until the Grease burns off. Send in one person to disarm or trigger this trap first, draw threat from the hurlocks (who prefer to use archery in here), and return to the entrance room. You can probably get a couple of the hurlocks to follow you back to the entrance, and take them out easily. You can then send someone in again to try to draw more of them back to the entrance, or just charge in as a group and finish them. The genlock emissary is a fairly strong mage, so make him the priority target.

Legend (2F)

1	Hurlocks	5	Genlocks
2	Hurlocks	6	Genlocks
3	Genlock Emissary	△1	Chest (locked)
4	Hurlocks	△2	Wooden Crates
		△3	Discarded Book

primagames.com

B This hallway has two doors. The larger room to the left contains a group of hurlocks and the smaller room to the right has a group of genlocks. No matter which door you go in, the mobs from the other room come out and join the fight. You can either rush one of the rooms and try to take a few out before the other group joins, or, if you have good AoE damage, send one person in to open one of the doors and pull the mobs. Then return to the large central room and use the choke point archway at "B" on the map to get them all together and AoE them down. Proceed through the genlock room to final room with another genlock group and defeat them to get to the stairs.

C This area is the trigger point for a massive ambush. The doors to your right and left can be opened ahead of time to kill the darkspawn waiting inside (marked squares 1 and 2 on the map). If you don't clear them out first, they will open their doors and join the fight once

you cross into sight of the small army around the corner. There are nearly a dozen darkspawn around the corner (squares 3–5), which are much easier to take out with AoE damage, because they are so close together. Also, you have access to two ballistas to your immediate left, which you can interact with to fire arrows at the large darkspawn horde. If you have little AoE, you can sneak around to the left and start the fight from behind the ballistas, using them to get some extra hits on the darkspawn before they get to you.

D Even though there is a ranked genlock alpha in this battle, it only gets difficult if you fail to take advantage of your surroundings. The floor switch in the room's north side will open the dog cages scattered around the room. Several of the dogs come out and assist you in the fight. The dogs can stun and draw the attention of the genlocks while you can pick them off one at a time, or AoE them all down if they bunch up. If any dogs survive, they help with the fight in the next hallway, which holds three doors. These doors all open once you open any one of them. Each room has three darkspawn, so you have nine total once the fight begins. You can opt to have one party member open the door and pull the darkspawn back to the group defending near the dog cages.

~ Third Floor ~

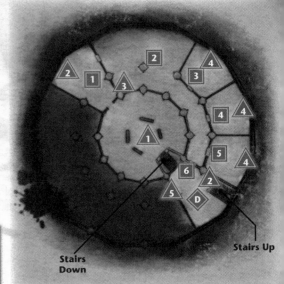

Stairs Down

Stairs Up

Legend (3F)

1 Genlocks	**6** Genlocks & Hurlock
2 Genlock Alpha & Genlocks	**△1** Pile of Bones
3 Genlock & Hurlocks	**△2** Weapon Stand
4 Genlocks	**△3** Weapon Crate (locked)
5 Genlock & Hurlocks	**△4** Crates
	△5 Chest (locked)

~ Fourth Floor ~

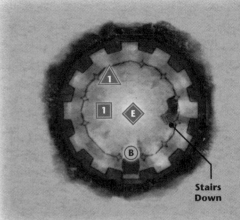

Stairs Down

Legend (4F)

1 Ogre
△ Barrels
ⓑ Beacon

Ostagar

Basics ~ Character Generation ~ Classes ~ The Party ~ Companions ~ Supporting Cast ~ Equipment ~ Bestiary ~ **Walkthroughs** ~ Side Quests ~ Random Encounters ~ Achievements/Trophies

E You've finally reached the top of the tower, but before you can ignite the signal fire, you have a big, bad ogre standing in your path. Ranged damage helps a lot in this fight, as the ogre's smash move can hit everyone around him. If you're a ranged DPSer, have Alistair pull him around the circular chamber, while you take him down with steady damage. If the ogre threatens you, have one of the warriors try to pull him back and continue shooting at him from range. Use health poultices to keep your health high.

After you kill the ogre, loot him for Havard's Aegis (magic shield). Loot a couple barrels as well, then you can light the beacon to the south and watch the ensuing chaos.

Flemeth's Hut

After you light the beacon, the traitor Loghain leaves the battle and the king's army is wiped out. Friends and allies are murdered, including your mentor, Duncan.

In the tower, darkspawn overrun you. Due to timely intervention by Flemeth, you awake back in the Wilds where Morrigan tells you what happened. Flemeth is outside with Alistair and wants to speak with you.

Flemeth says she saved you so that the Grey Wardens will continue to fight the Blight, which is a threat to everyone, including her. She suggests raising an army to fight the Blight, and Alistair realizes that you can use the treaties to go and ask for help from various cities. You now can call on the dwarves, humans, elves, and mages to come to your aid in the final battle. Flemeth offers Morrigan to join your party, and after you set off, Morrigan suggests starting your long journey at the nearby town of Lothering.

Lothering

NOTE

After Ostagar, Morrigan leads you north to the small town of Lothering. Complete as many side quests as you can here to gear up for the main quests soon on the world map. Be sure to pick up the two companions in Lothering: the rogue Leliana and the warrior Sten.

CAUTION

Once you leave Lothering and complete one of the main quest lines—"Broken Circle," "Arl of Redcliffe," "Paragon of Her Kind," or "Nature of the Beast"—the darkspawn invade Lothering and destroy the whole town. You can't go back once this occurs, so complete everything you can before the catastrophe.

Lothering

~ See map on next page ~

Runthrough (Lothering)

Summary: You head to the small village of Lothering to re-supply and get news on what has happened since the battle.

A. Bandits greet your arrival at Lothering and demand that you pay a toll.

B. After you deal with the bandits, you find the body of a templar nearby.

C. Before entering the town, Alistair tells you about the three treaties and where you can go to ask for help.

D. A farmer here warns you about staying in town, because there is now a bounty on Grey Wardens.

E. Dane's Refuge. You are attacked by Loghain's men and can recruit Leliana after.

F. You get the side quest "Scraping the Barrel."

G. You get the side quest "Dereliction of Duty."

H. "A Poisonous Proposition" side quest.

I. Settle an argument between a merchant and refugees.

J. Orphan boy.

K. A family that was attacked by bandits.

L. Doomsayer.

M. Allison for "Traps Are a Girl's Best Friend" side quest.

N. "More Than Just Plants" side quest.

O. "Bandits, Bandits, Everywhere" side quest.

P. Refugee ambush.

Q. Save merchants from darkspawn.

R. Blood mage corpse with letter.

S. Release Sten from cage and he joins party.

T. "When Bears Attack" side quest.

U. "A Last Keepsake" side quest.

V. Leave Lothering.

Lothering Cheatsheet

Main Plot Quests
- Lothering and the Imperial Highway

Important NPCs
- Allison
- Barlin ("A Poisonous Proposition")
- Bodahn Feddic
- Chanter Devons
- Elder Miriam
- Leliana
- Patter Gritch ("Scraping the Barrel")
- Sandal
- Ser Bryant
- Ser Donall
- Sten

Key Items
- Knight's Locket ("A Fallen Templar")
- Sealed Letter

Monsters
- Bandit
- Bandit Leader
- Black Bear
- Commander

- Genlock
- Hurlock
- Hurlock Alpha
- Mabari
- Mercenary
- Mercenary Archer
- Rogue
- Soldier
- Wolves

Side Quests
- A Fallen Templar
- A Last Keepsake (Chanter's Board)
- A Poisonous Proposition
- Bandits on the Road
- Bandits, Bandits, Everywhere (Chanter's Board)
- Dereliction of Duty
- More Than Just Plants
- Scraping the Barrel
- The Qunari Prisoner
- Traps Are a Girl's Best Friend
- When Bears Attack (Chanter's Board)

Lothering

Basics ~ Character Generation ~ Classes ~ The Party ~ Companions ~ Supporting Cast ~ Equipment ~ Bestiary ~ **Walkthroughs** ~ Side Quests ~ Random Encounters ~ Achievements/Trophies

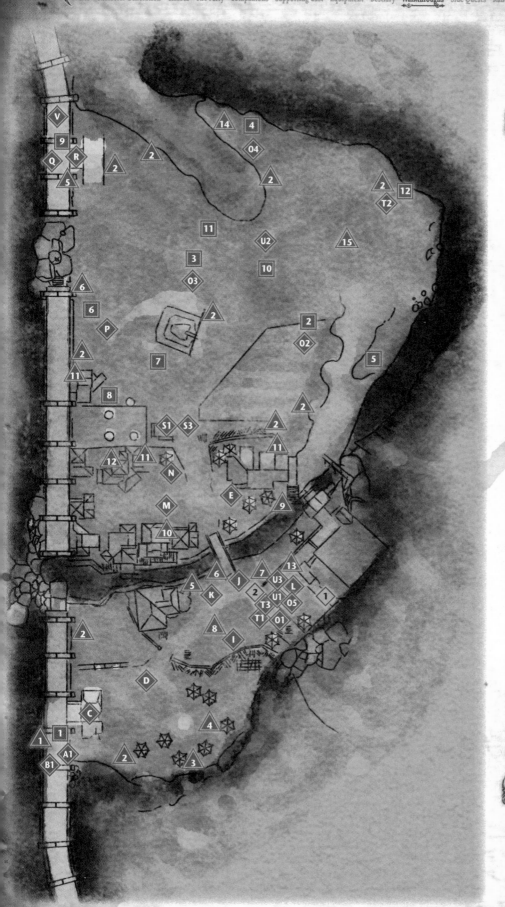

Legend

1. Ser Maron
2. Chanter Devons
1. Bandit Leader & Bandits
2. Bandits & Mercenary Archer
3. Bandits, Mabari, Rogue, Mercenary Archer
4. Bandits, Mabari, Mercenary, Bandit Leader
5. Giant Spiders
6. Refugees
7. Refugees
8. Refugee
9. Genlocks, Hurlocks, Hurlock Alpha
10. Wolves
11. Wolves
12. Black Bears
1. Crates
2. Elfroot
3. Broken Crates
4. Broken Crate
5. Crate
6. Rubble
7. Wooden Crates
8. Barrel & Chest (locked)
9. Wooden Crate
10. Barrel
11. Chest (locked)
12. Pile of Filth & Sack
13. Pile of Sacks
14. Sack & Chest (locked)
15. Deathroot

primagames.com

("Bandits on the Road")

(inside the Chantry)

("A Fallen Templar")

A1 When you arrive at Lothering, bandits confront you and ask for a toll to cross the bridge. You can either pay 10 silver, intimidate them, or fight them. When the bandit leader gets low on health, he surrenders. You can collect some money from him (1 gold, 50 silver) and then either finish them off or let them go (the other options lead to fighting).

A2 Ser Bryant will reward you 20 silver and the key to a locked cabinet.

B1 Here you find the body of a dead templar. On his body you find a knight's locket and knight's note. The note says that he was searching for the Urn of Sacred Ashes. Ser Donall in Lothering awaits his report.

~ Lothering Chantry ~

(inside the Chantry)

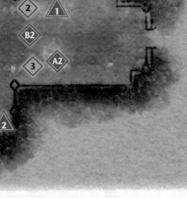

B2 You can talk to Ser Donall here and return the knight's locket. If you ask for a reward, he will give you 1 gold. He will also tell you about Arl Eamon's illness and the search for the Urn of Sacred Ashes.

C Before entering the town, Alistair tells you about the three treaties and where you can go to ask for help.

D A farmer here warns you about staying in town, because there is now a bounty on Grey Wardens.

Legend

①	Revered Mother	△1	Book
②	Ser Donall	△2	Chest (locked)
③	Ser Bryant	△3	Locked Cabinet
		△4	Bookshelf (codex)

(Dane's Refuge)

E When you enter Dane's Refuge, some of Loghain's men recognize you as a Grey Warden and attack. When the commander gets low on health, he will surrender and you can choose to finish him or let him go. Releasing him will gain favor with the rogue Leliana and she will join your party as a new companion.

("Scraping the Barrel," from Blackstone Irregulars' box in Dane's Refuge)

F1 You need to deliver three letters to people spread across the land: Dernal Garrison in Redcliffe, Patter Gritch in Lothering, and Varel Baern in Denerim's Alienage.

(inside the Chantry)

F2 Deliver the letter to Patter Gritch in the Lothering Chantry. The remainder of the quest is completed much later in the game.

("Dereliction of Duty," from Blackstone Irregulars' box in Dane's Refuge)

G You have to track down three deserters and "deal with them." The deserters are Sammael in Lake Calenhad, Layson in Denerim, and Tornas in the Frostback Mountains. This quest is completed later, outside Lothering.

("A Poisonous Proposition" in Dane's Refuge)

H Barlin in Dane's Refuge wants you to make him three vials of venom. You receive 75 silver reward for completing this. Giant spiders northeast of town drop toxin extracts.

~ Dane's Refuge ~

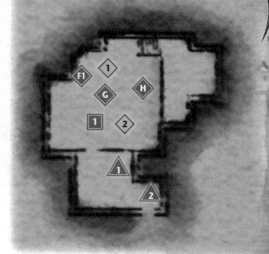

Legend

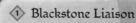

1 Blackstone Liaison
2 Leliana (companion)
1 Commander & Soldiers
1 Pile of Sacks
2 Barrel & Chest (locked)

I Here you see a merchant arguing with some refugees over his high prices. You can settle the dispute by siding with the merchant for 100 silver and a discount on his goods. You can also persuade or intimidate him into lowering his prices, or just have him leave.

J A boy here has lost his mother, who was probably killed by bandits. There isn't any award or penalty regardless of what you tell him to do.

K A family here was attacked by the highway bandits. If you took care of the bandits, you can tell them and they'll go try to get back their stuff.

L A doomsayer is making a scene here and scaring everyone. You can convince him he's wrong (he's not!), or let him be.

("Traps Are a Girl's Best Friend")

M Allison needs some help and has a quest for you to hand in traps (similar to H).

("More Than Just Plants")

N Elder Miriam needs your help if you know Herbalism. She wants you to bring her three lesser health poultices. You get 50 silver for turning them in.

("Bandits, Bandits, Everywhere" from the Chanter's Board)

01 You get a quest on the Chanter's Board to kill three groups of bandits in Lothering.

02 One group of bandits is here (five bandits and one mercenary archer). One or two of the bandits hang back and use archery. Pull the melee bandits back away from the rest of the group if you are having trouble. Use the nearby hill as cover.

03 Another group of bandits here consists of three bandits, two Mabari hounds, one rogue, and one mercenary archer. Same deal here: pull a few out if needed.

04 The last group of bandits consists of three bandits, one Mabari, one mercenary, and the ranked bandit leader. This is a tough fight. If you have stunning capabilities, stun the leader and concentrate your party's damage one of the lesser foes, picking them off one by one. A mage with Fireball or Cone of Cold can help tremendously with AoE damage.

05 Turn in the quest here to Chanter Devons. You are rewarded with 3 gold.

Lothering

Basics ~ Character Generation ~ Classes ~ The Party ~ Companions ~ Supporting Cast ~ Equipment ~ Bestiary ~ **Walkthroughs** ~ Side Quests ~ Random Encounters ~ Achievements/Trophies

P A group of desperate refugees here has heard about your bounty and decided to try to kill you for it. You are ambushed by the five refugees ahead, as well as a group of three to the southeast and another single one south (marked squares 6, 7, and 8 on map).

Q A group of darkspawn attacks a pair of dwarves here. After you kill the darkspawn, the dwarf introduces himself as Bodahn Feddic and his son Sandal. They are traveling merchants who will join you later as vendors in your party camp.

R You find the corpse of a blood mage. A sealed letter on her corpse says some items are hidden in a cache in the Circle Tower study area, middle alcove.

("The Qunari Prisoner")

S1 Imprisoned here stands a qunari warrior named Sten. He has been left to die after killing a family, but you can convince him that he can seek atonement for what he has done by joining you and helping to defeat the Blight. You need to ask the Revered Mother in the Chantry to release him.

(in the Chantry)

S2 To free Sten, you need the key to his cage. You can acquire it in various ways:

- In dialogue with the Revered Mother, you can persuade her to free Sten. This is easier depending on the amount of money you donate (5, 10, or 30 silver) to the Chantry when talking to the Revered Mother for the first time. With Leliana in the party, the Revered Mother will automatically free Sten when asked.
- A character with the Stealing skill can pickpocket the Revered Mother.
- A character with a high enough lockpicking ability can pick the lock on Sten's cage.

S3 Return to Sten's cage with the key and release him. He then joins your party if you ask him.

("When Bears Attack" from the Chanter's Board)

T1 After completing the bandit quest, two more quests open on the Chanter's Board. The first quest is to kill some Blight-infected bears.

T2 Three black bears live in this area. They are a bit stronger than normal mobs, so take it easy and pull them toward you and you can pelt them with extra ranged damage.

primagames.com

T3 Return to Chanter Devons and receive a reward of 1 gold and the Oathkeeper sword, which has a socket and increases healing received.

("A Last Keepsake" from the Chanter's Board)

U1 The other Chanter's Board quest is to find the body of the orphaned boy's mother, Sarha.

U2 Seven wolves guard the body of Sarha, with another pack of six wolves nearby to the northwest. You should be able to pull each group separately,

though they are weak. After you defeat the animals, search the body for a keepsake to bring back to Chanter Devons.

U3 Return to Chanter Devons and receive a 50 silver reward.

V When you are finished in town, exit using the highway in the northwest corner. Going here ends the "Lothering and the Imperial Highway" quest.

The wide open world map now becomes available to you and you end up in your party camp where you can decide what main quest you want to choose next.

NOTE

The main quest lines—"Broken Circle" (mage), "Arl of Redcliffe/Urn of Sacred Ashes" (human), "Paragon of Her Kind" (dwarf), and "Nature of the Beast" (elf)—can be completed in any order. We've listed them in a logical order, but review the following to see what order best suits your party's needs.

Broken Circle: This quest gives you access to the spirit healer Wynne and allows you to enhance your attributes with all the essences you find in the Fade.

Arl of Redcliffe/Urn of Sacred Ashes: These quests take you into Denerim for access to lots of vendors and rewarding side quests, as well as possibly encompassing the "Broken Circle" quest line.

Paragon of Her Kind: Oghren joins your party in Orzammar, providing a tank or extra melee DPS companion.

Nature of the Beast: If you are a mage and would like the arcane warrior specialization, complete the Dalish elf quest line early, possibly after "Broken Circle."

NOTE

The "Warden's Keep" and "Stone Prisoner" quest lines, available as downloadable content, can be picked up any time after leaving Lothering when the wide open world map becomes available. See their respective walkthroughs for more info.

Lothering - Broken Circle

Basics ~ Character Generation ~ Classes ~ The Party ~ Companions ~ Supporting Cast ~ Equipment ~ Bestiary ~ **Walkthroughs** ~ Side Quests ~ Random Encounters ~ Achievements/Trophies

Broken Circle

❧ NOTE ❧

The main quest lines—"Broken Circle" (mage), "Arl of Redcliffe/Urn of Sacred Ashes" (human), "Paragon of Her Kind" (dwarf), and "Nature of the Beast" (elf)—can be completed in any order. However, it's probably best to finish Broken Circle first to gain the spirit healer Wynne and enhance your attributes with all the essences you find in the Fade.

Lake Calenhad Docks

Legend

① Kester
② Carroll
△ Barrels

Ⓐ The Spoiled Princess (Brother Genitivi)
Ⓑ Mages' Collective

Runthrough (Lake Calenhad Docks)

Summary: Inspect the docks and discover a way across the lake to the mages' Circle Tower.

A. You begin on the hill overlooking the lake.

B. Speak with Carroll. Convince him to let you cross to the Circle Tower.

Lake Calenhad Cheatsheet

Main Plot Quests
• Broken Circle

Important NPCs
• Carroll

Key Items
• None

Monsters
• None

Side Quests
• Blackstone Irregulars
• Brother Genitivi
• Mages' Collective

Ⓐ You begin your quest for the mages' help here at the Lake Calenhad Docks. It's a small area serving as a bridge between the mainland and the mages' Circle Tower. Check out the Mages' Collective if you're working on those side quests, and visit the Spoiled Princess inn to replenish supplies (the innkeeper also has information on Brother Genitivi for the "Urn of Sacred Ashes" quest line).

❧ CAUTION ❧

Once you enter the Circle Tower and begin the main section of the quest, you cannot leave until you finish the mage quest line. Before you depart Lake Calenhad Docks, be sure your party is fully geared and stocked for a long adventure.

Ⓑ Speak with Carroll. He takes a bit of convincing to let you ferry across to the Circle Tower. If you have a high Persuade skill, you can ask about his superiors and he will let you in, or you can try to intimidate him by saying your patience is wearing thin. If you fail at one option, you will always succeed on the other. Also, if you try to work something out with Carroll, he will let you in if you have Sten, Morrigan, or Leliana in your party. Once you get him to agree to let you pass, you begin the main quest line in the tower.

primagames.com

The Circle Tower (First Floor)

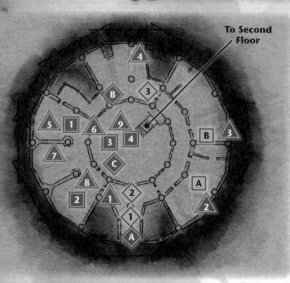

To Second Floor

Legend

① Greagoir
② Quartermaster
③ Wynne (companion)
1 Abominations
2 Abominations
3 Abominations
4 Greater Rage Demon
△**1** Vase
△**2** Chest (locked)
△**3** Chest (locked)

④ Chest (locked)
⑤ Pile of Books
⑥ Soldier Corpse
⑦ Soldier Corpse
⑧ Promises of Pride Codex
⑨ Corpses
Ⓐ Watchguard of the Reaching
Ⓑ Watchguard of the Reaching

Runthrough (Circle Tower: First Floor)

Summary: Enter the tower, which has been overrun by abominations, and slay Uldred, the source of the demon power. You are on the first floor; find the door to the second floor.

A. Speak with Greagoir. He explains that demons have invaded the tower and lets you in to stop them.

B. Pass through the magical barrier. Get Wynne to join your party.

C. Defeat the greater rage demon and ascend to the second floor.

Circle Tower (First Floor) Cheatsheet

Main Plot Quests
• Broken Circle

Important NPCs
• Greagoir
• Quartermaster
• Wynne (follower)

Key Items
• None

Monsters
• Desire Abominations
• Greater Rage Demon
• Hunger Abominations
• Lesser Rage Abominations
• Rage Abominations

Side Quests
• Watchguard of the Reaching

Ⓐ When you arrive at the Circle Tower, Greagoir greets you and explains that the templars have lost control of the tower and it's now overrun by demons. He will grant you permission to enter the tower, but warns that once you do, there is no turning back. Check in the vase to your left for loot, and visit the quartermaster for your last chance to stock up your inventory before your tower adventure.

Ⓑ Leave the entry chamber through the east door and head up the hallway to the next door. If you want to do the "Watchguard of the Reaching" side quest, pick up the first two parts in the apprentice's chests in the rooms to your right (and open two locked chests if you have a competent rogue). You meet Wynne when you enter the room with the stairs heading down into the basement, which you don't have to bother with for the main quest line. Offer to help her rectify the tower situation and Wynne will join your party. It's worth dropping one of your current members for Wynne to give you much more healing power.

TIP

You want Wynne in your party! She is a spirit healer, who comes with the incredible Group Heal talent ready to go. She will prove invaluable in the countless battles ahead. Remember, you can have only four party members at once. Dropped party members return to party camp and are always available at a later time.

Broken Circle

Basics ~ Character Generation ~ Classes ~ The Party ~ Companions ~ Supporting Cast ~ Equipment ~ Bestiary ~ **Walkthroughs** ~ Side Quests ~ Random Encounters ~ Achievements/Trophies

C Fight through to the center of the level. Here you'll spot a handful of abominations and the much tougher greater rage demon. Pick off the abominations as quickly as you can, then have the party focus on the greater rage demon. Alistair, or another tank, should engage the greater rage demon and hold its attention so it doesn't rip into a mage or rogue and slay them before you can blink. You may consider playing Wynne for most of the fight, with one finger on the Group Heal to give a crucial health boost when multiple members get roughed up. At battle's end, collect your loot and head up the stairs to the second level.

The Circle Tower (Second Floor)

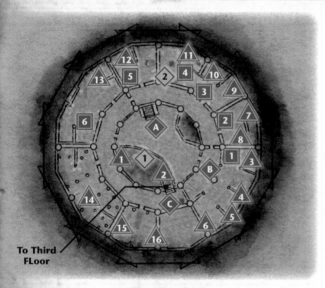

To Third FLoor

Legend

① Owain
② Godwin (in closet)
▫1 Blood Mages
▫2 Hunger Abominations
▫3 Shambling Corpses
▫4 Rage Abominations
▫5 Blood Mages & Abominations
▫6 Abominations
△1 Pile of Filth
△2 Charred Corpses
△3 Pile of Books
△4 Bel's Cache
△5 Chest (locked)

△6 Scroll of Banastor
△7 Charred Corpse
△8 Pile of Books
△9 Chest (locked)
△10 Armoire
△11 Vanity
△12 Pile of Books & Chest (locked)
△13 Scrolls & Armoire
△14 Corpses
△15 Irving's Chest & Desk
△16 Cabinet & Chest (locked)

Runthrough (Circle Tower: Second Floor)

Summary: More demonic abominations siege the tower. Battle through them and find the third floor stairs.

A. Enter the second level and speak with Owain.

B. You are blocked from proceeding by a magical barrier. Slay the blood mages in the room to continue.

C. Find the third floor stairs at the end of the hall.

Circle Tower (Second Floor) Cheatsheet

Main Plot Quests
- Broken Circle

Important NPCs
- Owain

Key Items
- Black Grimoire
- Chantry Amulet
- Scroll of Banastor
- Silver Chain

- Small Painted Box
- The Rose of Orlais
- Water-stained Portrait

Monsters
- Blood Mages
- Hunger Abominations
- Shambling Corpses

Side Quests
- None

A As soon as you enter the second floor you'll meet up with Owain. He's hiding out in the stockroom and mentions that Niall is out there somewhere trying to put a stop to the demon mess. Grab the loot in the area and exit through the southeast doorway. Prepare for more fighting ahead.

B In the hallway beyond Owain's room, the way is blocked by a magical barrier. Three blood mages have erected the barrier, and you will have to battle them to dissipate it. At the end of the fight, the last blood mage will beg for mercy. It's your choice whether you want to put her to the sword (combat continues) or show mercy and let her escape.

C Circle counter-clockwise around the hallway to reach the third floor stairs on the far end. The outer rooms are filled with mobs and treasure, if you are so inclined to partake in some hack-and-slash for reward. You can run down the hall for a quick escape; however, watch out for opening doors, especially at the shambling corpses location (marked square 3 on the map).

The Circle Tower (Third Floor)

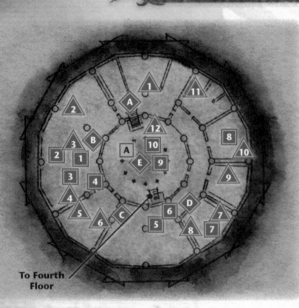

To Fourth Floor

Legend

1 Enraged Corpses
2 Devouring Corpses
3 Shambling Corpses
4 Arcane Horror
5 Abominations
6 Lesser Rage Demons
7 Possessed Templars
8 Desire Demon & Charmed Templars
9 Abomination & Skeletons
10 Lesser Shades

1 Chest (locked)
2 Ancient Texts
3 Charred Corpses
4 Pile of Books
5 Chest (locked)
6 Charred Corpse
7 Pile of Books
8 Closet
9 Cabinet
10 Armoire
11 Chest (locked)
12 Charred Corpse
A Watchguard of the Reaching

Runthrough (Circle Tower: Third Floor)

Summary: Continue up the tower to the fourth floor.

A. You begin here on the third floor.

B. A massive battle against corpses triggers here when you venture halfway across the room.

C. Avoid the bear trap and battle the demons within the room.

D. Beware of another bear trap in the possessed templars' room.

E. Battle the abomination and skeletons to reach the fourth floor stairs.

Circle Tower (Third Floor) Cheatsheet

Main Plot Quests
• Broken Circle

Important NPCs
• None

Key Items
• Small Gold Bar
• White Runestone

Monsters
• Abominations
• Arcane Horror
• Charmed Templars

• Desire Demon
• Devouring Corpses
• Enraged Corpses
• Lesser Rage Demons
• Possessed Templars
• Shambling Corpses
• Skeleton Archers
• Shambling Skeleton

Side Quests
• Watchguard of the Reaching

Broken Circle

Basics ~ Character Generation ~ Classes ~ The Party ~ Companions ~ Supporting Cast ~ Equipment ~ Bestiary ~ **Walkthroughs** ~ Side Quests ~ Random Encounters ~ Achievements/Trophies

A You have reached the third floor. Take a moment to collect your thoughts, and if you have a rogue in the party, open the chest out of sight behind the center pillar.

B All looks peaceful in the second room. Dead bodies on the floor, overturned furniture, a few loot items— you've seen this before in lots of other tower rooms. Except, this one is a trap. When you cross the halfway point (marked diamond B on the map), hordes of corpses animate and you have a large-scale battle all around you. Your tank should grab as much threat as possible, and healers should retreat to the entry doorway. Battle back to the entry if the corpses start to flank you. When the first wave ends, a second will begin almost immediately. Continue taking down corpses and watch for the appearance of an arcane horror near the exit doorway on the far side of the room. Once the arcane horror shows up, concentrate long-range damage on it; you can't let the thing casts spells on you or the group can die in seconds. When the tank cleans up all the corpses, send him at the arcane horror for the finishing blows.

C On the other side of this closed door lies a hidden bear trap. If you have a rogue, see if you can avoid the trap; otherwise, it will pin anyone who steps on it, which is usually your warrior charging

into battle. If someone gets trapped, lure the mobs back toward the doorway and fight them there. Once in the chamber, you have plenty of room to out-flank the abominations. Eventually, lesser rage demons will show up as reinforcements from the exit doorway on the opposite side of the room.

D Beware of another bear trap in front of the possessed templars' door. Sidestep it or disarm it if you can. Defeat the templars and collect extra loot from pile of books and closet inside.

E In the center chamber where some ungodly acts have taken place, battle the abomi- nation, skeletons, and lesser shades to finally win the fourth floor stairs. A few ranged spells and arrows can take out the skeletons. The lesser shades battle alongside the abomi- nation. Concentrate party fire on one lesser shade at a time until they both fall, then switch attention to the abomination. Keep a constant flow of healing going; it's a long fight. At the end, look for some loot in the shadowy corner of the room. There's also a statue near the center. Be careful: it burns you for damage whenever you interact with it unless you have activated the other items in the "Watchguard of the Reaching" side quest (see the Side Quests chapter for more info).

The Circle Tower (Fourth Floor)

~ See map on next page ~

Runthrough (Circle Tower: Fourth Floor)

Summary: Continue toward the Harrowing Chamber; however, in the central chamber, you will meet Sloth and be cast into the Fade.

A. You arrive on the fourth floor at the southern stairs.

B. Optional enemies down this side path, but good loot.

C. Succumb to Sloth's power and slip into the Fade.

Circle Tower (Fourth Floor) Cheatsheet

Main Plot Quests
• Broken Circle

Important NPCs
• None

Key Items
• Sun Blonde Vint-I

Monsters
• Bewitched Templar

• Blood Mage
• Desire Demon
• Possessed Templars
• Shambling Corpses
• Sloth

Side Quests
• None

primagames.com

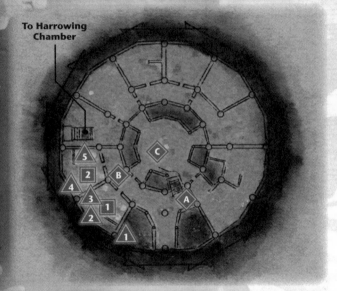

To Harrowing Chamber

Legend

1 Desire Demon & Bewitched Templars

2 Blood Mage & Possessed Templars

⚠ Chest (locked)

2 Vanity

3 Closet

4 Chest (locked)

5 Closet

A You've made it to the fourth level. The staircase lies in the south and you must weave through the chamber to reach the northern portion. Rest up here if you're not at full strength.

B The two mobs on the side passage are optional, but they do provide some good experience and loot. In the first room, a desire demon has enslaved a templar and perverts his dreams. The fight can be a tough one if you don't coordinate your troops well. To trigger the encounter, you have to fully enter the room, so no long-range bombing with a Fireball or anything like that. The templar hits hard, so make sure the tank locks on to him. The rest of the party should concentrate on the desire demon. A couple of shambling corpses animate as well. Pick them off as you see opportunities.

A blood mage and his enthralled templars camp out in the next room. Watch out for the bear trap at the entrance, and take out the blood mage first if you can bash through the templars. If you leave the blood mage alone, he will pepper the party with Fireballs and Arcane Bolts, and someone is bound to go down.

C When you enter the central chamber, you confront the nasty looking demon Sloth. He puts you to sleep and casts you into the demon dream world, the Fade. There's nothing you can do about it, except to escape the Fade through a series of difficult trials.

NOTE

When you meet Sloth, you get cast into the Fade. You must play through all the Fade maps before returning to battle Sloth on the tower's fourth floor.

Surviving the Fade

To escape the Fade you have to dance back and forth between several "island realms," such as the Darkspawn Invasion and the Burning Tower. Below is handy list for the sequence of events. Follow these steps and you'll maximize your chances of survival in this deadly dream realm.

1. Weisshaupt
2. The Raw Fade (A-E). Gain mouse form.
3. Darkspawn Invasion (A-E). Gain spirit form.
4. Return to the Raw Fade (F). Slay Yevena.
5. Burning Tower (A-D). Gain burning man form.
6. Mages Asunder. Gain golem form and defeat Slavren.
7. Return to Darkspawn Invasion (F). Slay Uthkiel the Crusher.
8. Return to Burning Tower (E). Beat Rhagos.
9. Templar Nightmare. Slay Vereveel.
10. Free any followers along the way.
11. Inner Sanctum. Defeat Sloth.

Broken Circle

Basics ~ Character Generation ~ Classes ~ The Party ~ Companions ~ Supporting Cast ~ Equipment ~ Bestiary ~ Walkthroughs ~ Side Quests ~ Random Encounters ~ Achievements/Trophies

The Fade (Weisshaupt)

~ Weisshaupt ~

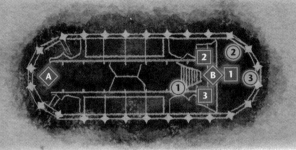

Legend

1	Duncan	①	Essence of Willpower
2	Warden	②	Lyrium Vein
3	Warden	③	Fade Pedestal

A Sloth puts you into a dream sleep and you fall into the Fade. To overcome Sloth's magic, you must wander through the Fade in search of your missing companions. You begin in Weisshaupt, the ancient Grey Warden fortress. Walk down the aisle to the end of the chamber where an illusionary Duncan awaits.

B The fake Duncan tries to convince you to retire and stay with him, but your dialogue choices will see through the illusion. As the battle begins, the two wardens you passed join in to defeat you. Duncan hits harder, so stay on him with your melee attacks or spells until he drops. Pop a health poultice or cast a Heal after defeating Duncan, then turn your attention on the two wardens. Talents such as Dirty Fighting or spells such as Mind Blast can buy you the time you need by stunning one (or both!) while you finish off the second.

TIP

A lyrium vein lies in the back corner behind Duncan. Use it to regain vital health and mana during the fight.

Runthrough (The Fade: Weisshaupt)

Summary: Trapped in the Fade, you must find a way out. You begin in the ancient fortress of the Grey Wardens, Weisshaupt, and must battle your old friend, Duncan.

A. Your journey into the Fade begins here.

B. Destroy Duncan and his wardens. Use the Fade Pedestal to enter the next part of the Fade.

The Fade (Weisshaupt) Cheatsheet

Main Plot Quests
- Lost in Dreams

Important NPCs
- None

Key Items
- Essence of Willpower

Monsters
- Duncan
- Wardens

Side Quests
- None

When you click on the Fade Pedestal that appears once you defeat Duncan, the Fade map will appear. You are at the top in Weisshaupt Fortress. You eventually want to get to the middle: the Inner Sanctum. Your followers are trapped along the outer edges in "A Nightmare" locations. There are five Fade islands that separate you from your followers and, if you complete all of them, the Inner Sanctum. The main Fade locations are the Raw Fade, Darkspawn Invasion, Templar's Nightmare, Mage Asunder, Burning Tower. You can navigate from one to the next, and if you reach A Nightmare, you can set one of your companions free. Note that they won't join you until after you exit the Fade to fight Sloth; you can skip freeing a follower, but they will not be available then for the fight against Sloth. See the following Fade sections for the most advantageous paths to your followers and the Inner Sanctum.

primagames.com

The Raw Fade

~ The Raw Fade ~

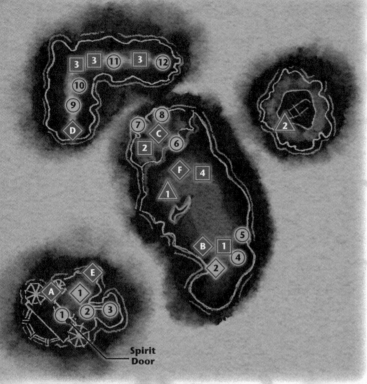

Runthrough
(The Raw Fade)

Summary: After speaking with Niall, kill all demons in the Raw Fade. Return to the Raw Fade after you have spirit form to slay Yevena.

A. Speak with Niall, who will explain how you navigate the Fade. Exit the first part of the Raw Fade via the Fade Portal.

B. Defeat the rage demon and gain mouse form from the dying Mouse.

C. Slay the lesser rage demon (or slip by it using stealth) and use the Fade Portal.

D. Slay three demons to reach the next Fade Portal.

E. Speak with Niall and unlock the Fade Pedestal again.

F. Defeat the demoness Yevena.

The Raw Fade Cheatsheet

Main Plot Quests	Monsters
• Lost in Dreams	• Rage Demon
Important NPCs	• Shades
• Niall	• Yevena
• Mouse	**Side Quests**
Key Items	• None
• Essence of Willpower	

Legend

- ◇1 Niall
- ◇2 Mouse
- ▣1 Rage Demon
- ▣2 Lesser Rage Demon
- ▣3 Lesser Demons
- ▣4 Yevena & Shades
- ▲1 Essence of Willpower
- ▲2 Essence of Dexterity
- ① Spirit Door
- ② Fade Pedestal
- ③ Fade Pedestal
- ④ Lyrium Vein
- ⑤ Mouse Hole (to Gray 6)
- ⑥ Mouse Hole (to Gray 5)
- ⑦ Fade Portal
- ⑧ Lyrium Vein
- ⑨ Fade Portal
- ⑩ Spirit Door
- ⑪ Lyrium Vein
- ⑫ Fade Portal

Spirit Door

A When you first arrive in the Raw Fade, speak with Niall. He explains that he's been trapped in the Fade and that you must defeat the obstacles on the various islands in the Fade to eventually escape. Leave this first area through the Fade Portal to the east.

B You teleport into the middle of a battle against a rage demon and a mouse. Defeat the rage demon. It shouldn't be too difficult one on one. When you speak with the mouse, you realize he's dying, but not before he imparts mouse form, the first of four shape-shifting forms you'll gain in the Fade. You can use mouse form for stealth and slipping in and out of mouse hole shortcuts. Take the nearby mouse hole to the next Fade section.

Broken Circle

Basics ~ Character Generation ~ Classes ~ The Party ~ Companions ~ Supporting Cast ~ Equipment ~ Bestiary ~ **Walkthroughs** ~ Side Quests ~ Random Encounters ~ Achievements/Trophies

Fade Shapeshifting: Mouse Form

Abilities: Mouse Form, Stealth

Inside the Fade, you can gain the power to shapechange into four different creature forms, each with its own strengths and weaknesses. Though not ideal for combat, mouse form allows you to pass through openings that are normally too small for anything else. It also allows you to remain hidden and pass through certain areas unnoticed. Look for mouse holes to use as shortcuts between areas.

C Stay in mouse form if you want to sneak around the lesser rage demon for better position. If you proceed cautiously, you can reach your maximum range and pick off the rage demon with ranged attacks in your true form. After slaying the demon, combat ends and you can use the Fade Portal nearby.

D You battle a series of three demons as you progress down this L-shaped area. Rest after each one to fully heal back up, and replenish with a lyrium vein halfway to the next Fade Portal.

E Return to the original area with Niall. Speak with him and tell him about your adventures in mouse form. He suggests gaining other forms, and the Fade Pedestal next to him opens again and you can reach any of the other four main islands. After you gain spirit form from the Darkspawn Invasion island, you can return to the Raw Fade to battle Yevena in the final area (marked diamond F on the map).

NOTE

You can only reach Yevena after you have obtained spirit form from the Darkspawn Invasion island.

F Return from the Darkspawn Invasion and enter the spirit door adjacent to you when you arrive. The spirit door puts you smack dab in the middle of combat with Yevena and her two shades. In spirit form, throw Crushing Prison on Yevena and hurl Winter's Grasp at each shade until it perishes. Before Yevena reaches you, cast Regeneration on yourself and then attack her with Winter's Grasps when they're available or slip back into your class form and pound her with your normal talents or spells. One major demon is down, although there are a lot more to go. Don't forget the essence of willpower in the corner before you leave.

Darkspawn Invasion

~ See map on next page ~

Runthrough (Darkspawn Invasion)

Summary: Use mouse form to navigate most of the Darkspawn Invasion island. Save the Templar Spirit to gain spirit form. Return to finish it once you have golem form.

A. Enter the Darkspawn Invasion island and use mouse form for shortcuts.

B. Take the long way and battle some genlocks and hurlocks.

C. Take the shortcut and skip halfway through the dungeon.

D. Another shortcut gets you past a fire barrier.

E. Save the Templar Spirit and gain spirit form. Exit this island via the Fade Pedestal.

~ Darkspawn Invasion ~

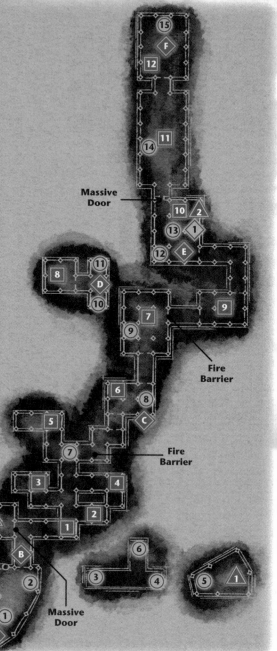

Massive Door

Fire Barrier

Fire Barrier

Massive Door

A You start on this island in a nearly empty room to the south. Take the mouse hole in the northeast corner and follow the next passage straight to the end. Enter a second mouse hole and you'll pop up in an isolated room with the essence of cunning. Click on the essence of cunning to gain +1 cunning permanently. Return to the corridor you just came from. You can either turn right for a shortcut mouse hole to advance farther into the dungeon, or you can return to the original room and exit via the main door.

NOTE

Throughout the Fade there are glowing containers (a cauldron, combat dummy, broken chest, pile of books, weapon rack, or golden apparatus) that contain essences which increase your attributes. Each essence increases the appropriate attribute permanently by one point. Some may require a certain shapeshifting form to reach or interact with, but the stat boosts are well worth it. Try to collect as many of these as you can to power up your main character.

Legend

① Templar Spirit	⑧ Genlocks	① Fade Pedestal	⑨ Mouse Hole (to Gray 10)
① Hurlocks	⑨ Flaming Darkspawn	② Mouse Hole (to Gray 3)	⑩ Mouse Hole (to Gray 9)
② Genlock Alpha	⑩ Darkspawn Spirits	③ Mouse Hole (to Gray 2)	⑪ Lyrium Vein
③ Genlocks	⑪ Genlocks, Hurlocks, & Darkspawn Emissary	④ Mouse Hole (to Gray 5)	⑫ Fade Portal
④ Hurlocks	⑫ Uthkiel the Crusher	⑤ Mouse Hole (to Gray 4)	⑬ Fade Portal
⑤ Hurlocks	△ Essence of Cunning	⑥ Mouse Hole (to Gray 8)	⑭ Lyrium Vein
⑥ Flaming Darkspawn	△ Essence of Willpower	⑦ Lyrium Vein	⑮ Fade Pedestal
⑦ Hurlock Emissary & Hurlocks	△ Font of Strength	⑧ Mouse Hole (to Gray 6)	

Broken Circle

Basics ~ Character Generation ~ Classes ~ The Party ~ Companions ~ Supporting Cast ~ Equipment ~ Bestiary ~ **Walkthroughs** ~ Side Quests ~ Random Encounters ~ Achievements/Trophies

B If you skip the mouse hole shortcut, you've set your heart on some fighting. However, you will be forced to return to the mouse holes eventually (unless you already have the burning man form). Around the first turn, prepare for a group of hurlocks to your right and a genlock alpha behind them. A long-range Fireball or large AoE spell will whittle them down in no time. If you're hacking through them, lure them back to the first corner and battle there. You may avoid pulling the genlock alpha; it's better to fight them separately than together. Around the second turn, prepare for more hurlocks and genlocks. To the right of the lyrium vein, you encounter a fire barrier. This forces you to take the mouse holes leading from the entry room.

NOTE

You cannot open massive doors until you have golem form, and you cannot pass through fire barriers until you have burning man form. Skip those doors and barriers for now and return once you have those abilities.

C If you take the mouse hole shortcut, you appear next to two flaming darkspawn. Return to your true form to dispatch them. You can hide behind the room's pillar as you do so to avoid alerting them to your immediate presence. In the next room, you face a hurlock emissary and some lackeys. Don't let the emissary heave spells at you. If you're a warrior or rogue, charge at the emissary and take it down first. If you're a mage, hurl a Fireball through the doorway or crush the emissary with an AoE spell that will also hit his hurlock buddies. You must choose the mouse hole on the west wall if you don't have burning man form yet.

D Take the mouse hole shortcut through this small area. A trio of genlocks will challenge you from the left as you pass into the open, heading for the next mouse hole. Cut them down and continue.

E In this large chamber you see the Templar Spirit. As you approach, darkspawn spirits besiege him, and it's up to you to bail him out. Help the Templar Spirit slay the evil spirits and he will grant you spirit form. Use the Fade Pedestal to go to the next Fade island on your circuit: the Burning Tower.

Fade Shapeshifting: Spirit Form

Abilities: Spirit Form, Winter's Grasp, Crushing Prison, Regeneration

Inside the Fade, you can gain the power to shapechange into four different creature forms, each with its own strengths and weaknesses. Spirit form allows you to interact with ethereal objects that would normally be hidden from you. Look for spirit doors to use as shortcuts between areas. In combat, spirit form can be brutal against single opponents. Throw your Crushing Prison on your foe and most will die just from that. Follow it up with Winter's Grasp, which deals solid damage and freezes your adversary, to buy more time. When running low on health, cast Regeneration on yourself and return to your offensive spells.

NOTE

Once you gain spirit form, leave Darkspawn Invasion temporarily to gain the other two shapeshifting forms. Once you have golem form, you can return to finish off the level.

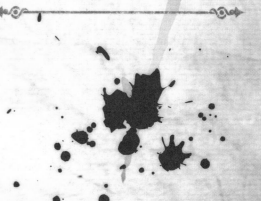

F Once you return to this chamber after gaining golem form in Mage Asunder, smash open the massive door in your new uber form. Stay in golem form for the rest of the level, unless you need to drop out for some healing. The next room is a huge area, with lots of genlocks, hurlocks, and a mean darkspawn emissary. Fortunately, in golem form, you have great crowd control with Quake and Hurl. When the enemies swarm you, knock them off their feet with Quake. The first to stand up gets a Slam, then the next gets a Hurl. Slam the darkspawn emissary when it gets close and keep pummeling until the thing dies.

In the final room, you go up against the ogre Uthkiel the Crusher. It's a great slugfest with your golem form. Alternate Quake and Hurl to stun Uthkiel, then smack it with a Slam as soon as it's ready to go. It might take longer than the average battle, but it's lots of fun to trade punches with another big monster. When you finish off Uthkiel, head to the Burning Tower to complete that island next.

Burning Tower

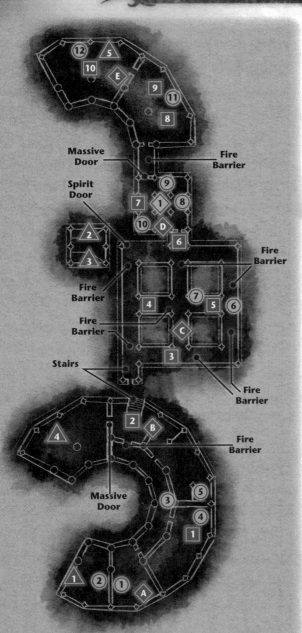

Massive Door
Fire Barrier
Spirit Door
Fire Barrier
Fire Barrier
Stairs
Fire Barrier
Fire Barrier
Massive Door

Runthrough (Burning Tower)

Summary: Use mouse form to navigate most of the Burning Tower. Beat the Dreaming Templar to gain burning man form. Return to finish it once you have golem form.

A. Enter the Burning Tower here.

B. Beat the burning templars to reach the stairs.

C. Weave through the maze to reach the mouse hole.

D. Defeat the Dreaming Templar to gain burning man form.

E. Slay Rhagos.

Legend

◇ Dreaming Templar	△3 Essence of Cunning
■1 Burning Templars	△4 Essence of Magic
■2 Burning Templars	△5 Font of Strength
■3 Burning Hounds	①① Mouse Hole (to Gray 2)
■4 Burning Templar & Hound	②② Mouse Hole (to Gray 1)
■5 Burning Hounds	③③ Lyrium Vein
■6 Burning Hound	④④ Mouse Hole (to Gray 5)
■7 Burning Demon	⑤⑤ Mouse Hole (to Gray 4)
■8 Shambling Corpses	⑥⑥ Mouse Hole (to Gray 8)
■9 Burning Templars	⑦⑦ Lyrium Vein
■10 Rhagos	⑧⑧ Mouse Hole (to Gray 6)
△1 Essence of Cunning	⑨⑨ Lyrium Vein
△2 Essence of Constitution	⑩⑩ Fade Pedestal
	⑪⑪ Lyrium Vein
	⑫⑫ Fade Pedestal

Broken Circle

Basics ~ Character Generation ~ Classes ~ The Party ~ Companions ~ Supporting Cast ~ Equipment ~ Bestiary ~ **Walkthroughs** ~ Side Quests ~ Random Encounters ~ Achievements/Trophies

Burning Tower Cheatsheet

Main Plot Quests
- Lost in Dreams

Important NPCs
- Dreaming Templar

Key Items
- Burning Man Form
- Essence of Cunning (x2)
- Essence of Constitution

- Essence of Magic
- Font of Strength

Monsters
- Burning Demon
- Burning Hounds
- Burning Templars
- Rhagos
- Shambling Corpses

Side Quests
- None

A You begin at the south end of the Burning Tower. Change into mouse form and go through the hole to the west. You crawl into a small, self-contained room with an essence of cunning within. Gain your +1 cunning and return to the original room. Change back into your true form and open the door out into the corridor.

B Continue down the corridor to the second door on the right. You can open the first door on the right if you want to fight an extra pair of burning templars, but it's not necessary. Enter the room and open the door on your immediate left. Two more burning templars guard the stairs to the next level. If you're in spirit form, use Crushing Prison on one of the templars and Winter's Grasp on the other. Climb the stairs to the next level.

C Turn right at the first inter-section (you can't go straight because of the fire barrier). You'll enter a maze of twisting corridors and fire barriers. Go left then right to find the mouse hole out of the maze. You are also surrounded by burning hounds and one burning templar. Be on your guard: these creatures are not affected by the fire barriers and will rush at you from any side. The spirit form's Winter's Grasp works especially well against these fire beings.

D When you crawl out of the mouse hole, you'll be face to face with the Dreaming Templar. Enthralled by anger, he attacks you a few seconds later, along with the burning demon by his side. In spirit form, lock down either one with Crushing Prison and immediately attack the other with Winter's Grasp. You may require an early Regeneration to keep your health high, or drop out into your true form and pop a health poultice. When you defeat the Dreaming Templar, he grants you the burning man form and disappears. Before you leave the island via the Fade Pedestal that has appeared in the room, take a short trip out the south door and through the flames in burning man form. Switch to spirit form to enter the spirit door down the corridor to your right. It's worth the trip as you gain an essence of cunning and essence of constitution from the small side room.

NOTE

You cannot open massive doors until you have golem form. Skip those doors on the level and return after you have golem form from the Mage Asunder island.

Fade Shapeshifting: Burning Man Form

Abilities: Burning Man Form, Fireball, Flame Blast

Inside the Fade, you can gain the power to shapechange into four different creature forms, each with its own strengths and weaknesses. Burning Man form makes you immune to fire and you can pass through fire unharmed. However, this form is physically weak and vulnerable to cold damage, but it is the fastest of the Fade forms. Look for any fire barriers to pass through.

primagames.com

E After you return from Mage Asunder with the golem form, you can bash into the last two rooms (you can also double-back to the massive door down in the south and pick up an essence of magic). Some shambling corpses and burning templars block your way in the first room. In golem form, use Quake to stun as many as you can, followed by a Hurl to knock anyone else to the ground. Whoever stands gets a Slam or a rocky punch. The second room holds Rhagos, the final boss on this level. You can stay in golem form to dish out good damage against Rhagos, or switch to burning man if Rhagos's fire damage gets too much. You also have the option of spirit form's Crushing Prison to put him in his place.

Mage Asunder

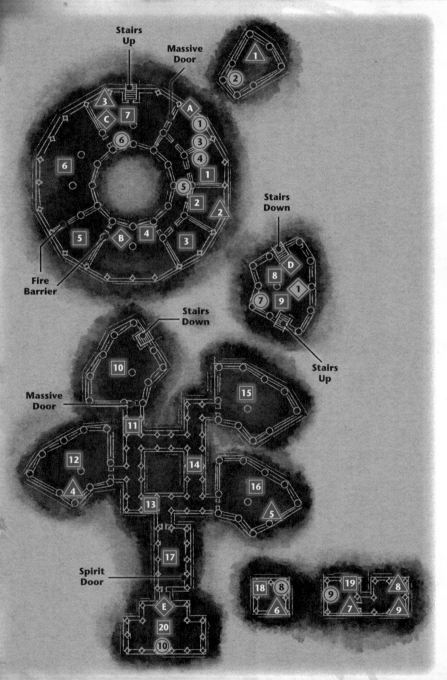

Legend

- ◇ Cursed Dreamer
- **1** Mages
- **2** Mages
- **3** Crazy Mages
- **4** Servants
- **5** Lesser Rage Demons
- **6** Mages
- **7** Mage Instructors & Pupils
- **8** Chantry Priests
- **9** Stone Golems
- **10** Mages & Stone Golem
- **11** Mage & Priest
- **12** Priest & Stone Golem
- **13** Stone Golem
- **14** Stone Golem
- **15** Priests
- **16** Stone Golems
- **17** Arcane Horrors
- **18** Stone Golem
- **19** Stone Golems
- **20** Slavren
- △1 Font of Strength
- △2 Essence of Magic
- △3 Bookcase
- △4 Essence of Willpower
- △5 Font of Strength
- △6 Essence of Dexterity
- △7 Essence of Cunning
- △8 Essence of Constitution
- △9 Essence of Dexterity
- ① Mouse Hole (to Gray 2)
- ② Mouse Hole (to Gray 1)
- ③ Mouse Hole (to Gray 4)
- ④ Mouse Hole (to Gray 3)
- ⑤ Lyrium Vein
- ⑥ Lyrium Vein
- ⑦ Fade Pedestal
- ⑧ Mouse Hole (to Gray 9)
- ⑨ Mouse Hole (to Gray 8)
- ⑩ Fade Pedestal

Broken Circle

Basics ~ Character Generation ~ Classes ~ The Party ~ Companions ~ Supporting Cast ~ Equipment ~ Bestiary ~ **Walkthroughs** ~ Side Quests ~ Random Encounters ~ Achievements/Trophies

Runthrough (Mage Asunder)

Summary: Use mouse form and burning man form to navigate Mage Asunder. Free the Cursed Dreamer to gain golem form. Defeat Slavren.

A. Enter Mage Asunder here.

B. Use burning man form to bypass the fire barriers.

C. Defeat the mages and climb the stairs.

D. Free the Cursed Dreamer and gain golem form.

E. Slay Slavren.

Mage Asunder Cheatsheet

Main Plot Quests
- Lost in Dreams

Important NPCs
- Cursed Dreamer

Key Items
- Essence of Constitution
- Essence of Cunning
- Essence of Dexterity (x2)
- Essence of Magic
- Essence of Willpower

- Font of Strength (x2)
- Golem Form

Monsters
- Arcane Horrors
- Chantry Priests
- Crazy Mages
- Lesser Rage Demons
- Mages
- Stone Golems

Side Quests
- None

A You begin at the northeast corner of the map. Take the mouse shortcut to your immediate left and pick up the +1 strength in the side room. Return to the original room and take the second mouse hole. This will sneak you into the next room where a pair of mages plot. Because you've come in stealthed, you can change form in their midst and get the jump on them. In the third room, you aren't so lucky; you'll have to beat the two mages the old-fashioned way through hard work and skill. Pick up the +1 magic bonus in this room.

The third room has a circle of crazy mages that immediately attack. Use your burning man form to hurl a Fireball in the center of the circle. With any luck, you should incinerate two to three of them on the spot, and severely burn the rest. Follow up with a Flame Blast or two, or switch to spirit form for some icy fun.

The fourth room has "lowly" servants, but watch out! One servant will charge you when you open the door, and two others are invisible, waiting to backstab you as soon as they get a chance. A burning man's Fireball at the first servant may get two in the process. Use spirit form or your true form to handle the rogue servants.

B Switch to burning man form to pass the fire barrier on the opposite side of the servants' quarters. Three lesser rage demons will appear and attack in the next room. Switch out of burning man form and into spirit form. Root one with Crushing Prison and battle the second with Winter's Grasp. The third will arrive after a delay, possibly long enough for you to finish off the first two. Switch back to burning man form to open the next door. Hurl a Fireball into the room in the midst of the enemy mages near the center of the next room. If anyone gets up, burn them back down with Flame Blast.

C Mage instructors and mage pupils inhabit this room. Stay in burning man form for this encounter! The mages are Fireball happy, and you can protect yourself from a lot of damage with the burning man's fire immunity. A Fireball or two at strategic locations should do the trick. After searching the bookcase, take the stairs up to the next level.

D When you enter the next floor, you stumble upon Chantry priests and two stone golems attacking the Cursed Dreamer. You'll have to be on the move for this fight; if you stand still and get whacked by a golem or Chantry spell, it could be all over. In burning man form, chuck a Fireball at whichever group you can strike without causing friendly fire to the Dreamer or yourself. Switch to spirit form and imprison one of the golems with Crushing Prison and then use a Winter's Grasp on one of the Chantry priests (or the second golem if its health is low). Hit Regeneration on yourself and circle around the room. Wait for Winter's Grasp to become active and fire another off. When Crushing Prison becomes available again, throw it on the strongest foe. Eventually, you will wear them down and save the Cursed Dreamer. As a reward, he gives you the golem form. Ignore the new Fade Pedestal that has appeared and take the stairs up to the next level instead. Kill the mages and stone golem in the next room, then switch to golem form to smash through the massive door blocking your path. You now have access to the southern section of the map.

primagames.com

Fade Shapeshifting: Golem Form

Abilities: Golem Form, Slam, Quake, Hurl

Inside the Fade, you can gain the power to shapechange into four different creature forms, each with its own strengths and weaknesses. Golem form has enormous strength and can smash doors you would not normally be able to budge. It is highly resistant to physical attacks, but vulnerable to magic. Your Slam attack will cause critical damage on each hit and knock the target down. Quake is an AoE attack that damages all nearby foes (and friends) and stuns them unless they pass a physical resistance check. Hurl throws a chunk of rock at a target and damages all nearby targets. It also knocks down enemies hit. You can now smash open massive doors.

(E) In the southern section of the map, there are six essences to earn. It's well worth the effort of cleaning up some stone golems, mages, and priests. When you're ready to tackle Slavren, head down to the southern tip and fight the arcane horrors (square 17). After you defeat the horrors, change to spirit form and take the side passages to earn more essences. You only have to vanquish three stone golems for four essences—a nice trade.

As soon as you enter the last room, Slavren will charge. You can go for the Crushing Prison, but if Slavren resists it your spirit form will get torn to shreds. It's better to pound at him in golem form, then switch to your true form for some healing (either if you're a mage or with a health poultice). You can also hit Slavren with a point-blank Fireball if you're in burning man form. Take him down and another island falls. Now return to Darkspawn Invasion and Burning Tower to complete those islands.

Templar's Nightmare

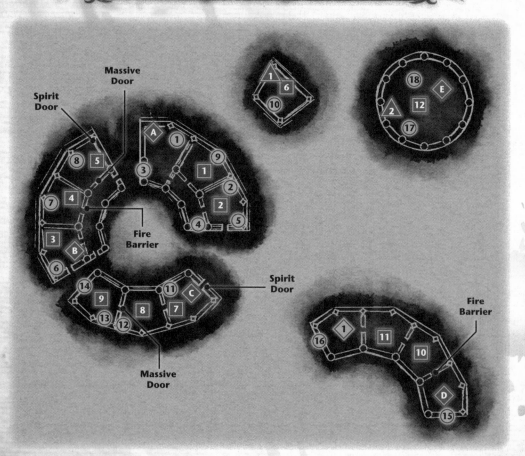

Broken Circle

Basics ~ Character Generation ~ Classes ~ The Party ~ Companions ~ Supporting Cast ~ Equipment ~ Bestiary ~ **Walkthroughs** ~ Side Quests ~ Random Encounters ~ Achievements/Trophies

Runthrough (Templar's Nightmare)

Summary: Use all of your forms to traverse the dungeon and slay Vereveel.

A. Enter Templar's Nightmare here.

B. Use the mouse holes to sneak up on the ogre.

C. Hop through the spirit door to reach the third hub.

D. Stay in burning man form to avoid a fire trap and then clean out the fourth hub.

E. Slay Vereveel.

Templar's Nightmare Cheatsheet

Main Plot Quests
- Lost in Dreams

Important NPCs
- Templar's Body

Key Items
- Essence of Cunning
- Essence of Dexterity

Monsters
- Arcane Horror
- Blight Wolf
- Desire Abominations
- Hunger Abominations
- Ogre
- Rage Abominations
- Shambling Corpses
- Sloth Demons
- Vereveel

Side Quests
- None

Legend

- ① Templar's Body
- ◼ Sloth Demons
- ◼2 Arcane Horror
- ◼3 Ogre
- ◼4 Hunger Abominations
- ◼5 Rage Abominations
- ◼6 Blight Wolf
- ◼7 Rage Abominations
- ◼8 Hunger Abominations
- ◼9 Arcane Horror & Shambling Corpses
- ◼10 Desire Abominations
- ◼11 Arcane Horror & Shambling Corpses
- ◼12 Vereveel
- △1 Essence of Dexterity
- △2 Essence of Cunning

- ① Mouse Hole (to Gray 2)
- ② Mouse Hole (to Gray 1)
- ③ Fade Portal (to Gray 4)
- ④ Fade Portal (to Gray 3)
- ⑤ Mouse Hole (to Gray 6)
- ⑥ Mouse Hole (to Gray 5)
- ⑦ Mouse Hole (to Gray 8)
- ⑧ Mouse Hole (to Gray 7)
- ⑨ Mouse Hole (to Gray 10)
- ⑩ Mouse Hole (to Gray 9)
- ⑪ Lyrium Vein
- ⑫ Mouse Hole (to Gray 13)
- ⑬ Mouse Hole (to Gray 12)
- ⑭ Fade Portal (to Gray 15)
- ⑮ Fade Portal (to Gray 14)
- ⑯ Mouse Hole (to Gray 17)
- ⑰ Mouse Hole (to Gray 16)
- ⑱ Fade Pedestal

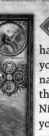

A You must have all your forms to navigate through the Templar's Nightmare; if not, you'll get frustrated or stuck in many areas. In the initial chamber, change to mouse form and take hole #1 to hole #2. When you reach the room with the arcane horror, you'll trigger a poison trap. Forget it for now and change quickly into spirit form. Use Crushing Prison on the horror and it's over for the creature. Cast Regeneration to offset the poison.

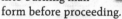

B In the arcane horror room, change to mouse form again and take hole #5 to hole #6. You'll appear behind monstrous ogre. Due to the element of surprise, you have your pick on how to handle the ogre. You can use Crushing Prison on him in spirit form, or bash fists in golem form. You could even Fireball him with burning man form. One or two hunger abominations from the next room may hear the commotion and attack as backup for the ogre. Deal with them using Winter's Grasp, Quake, or Flame Blast, according to your form.

Change to burning man form and bypass the fire barrier in the next room. Next, change to mouse form and take hole #7 to hole #8 in the next room (or you could just bash in the door in golem form). Dispatch the rage abominations in the room and switch to spirit form so you can use the spirit door within.

C Fight through a series of creatures in the next three rooms. Stick with the forms that have been working best for you, and restock at the lyrium vein if you get low on health or mana. Turn into burning man form before proceeding.

D When you reach this room via the Fade Portal, make sure you are in burning man form. A fire trap triggers and engulfs the whole room in flames. Pull the desire abominations toward you by lobbing a Fireball at the nearest one. The flames in the room will take care of the rest. In the third room, shambling corpses run interference for an arcane horror. Don't let the horror cast deadly spells on you. Burning man form gives you Fireball as a great counterattack, or spirit form's Crushing Prison can silence the arcane horror forever. Take the mouse hole at the end to the final area.

E Vereveel leads you into a circular chamber with no exits. It's do or die time here. Try to catch her with a Crushing Prison if you can, or lob a Fireball in her direction. Avoid golem form; it takes too much damage from her spell attacks. Use your true form to cast healing or use poultices throughout the fight to stay alive. Once you defeat Vereveel, you will have unlocked the Inner Sanctum, where you can go after Sloth. However, first you need to free your followers for the coming finale.

A Nightmare (Freeing Your Followers)

Before you go battle Sloth in the Inner Sanctum, visit each of the three Nightmare realms on the Fade outskirts. Your followers are trapped in them, and you need to free them for the battle against Sloth. Talk to each companion and help them snap out of their nightmares. You should know your followers well by now, so it's a snap to answer the correct dialogue choices and get each one to fight free. A short battle will occur, and once the two of you defeat the enemies, your follower will be available for the final battle.

The Inner Sanctum

Prepare your party for one of the toughest battles in the entire game. Sloth changes form, so you must defeat him four different times to win. After playing solo for a while, get back into party mode and work your standard tactics—tank on Sloth, healer primarily on the tank, and DPS chipping in whenever possible. Your PC should use his golem form for most of the fight. It does solid damage and reduces the physical damage from Sloth's attacks. Spirit form can also add another healer to your party when you start throwing Regeneration around.

It's a long fight. Ration your spell-casting to only essential spells: ones that damage Sloth heavily, and ones that heal your party. Keep several lyrium potions handy to fill up your mana reserve on healers. If a party member drops to near dying, retreat and use a health poultice, especially if the healer's mana is running low.

Broken Circle

Basics ~ Character Generation ~ Classes ~ The Party ~ Companions ~ Supporting Cast ~ Equipment ~ Bestiary ~ **Walkthroughs** ~ Side Quests ~ Random Encounters ~ Achievements/Trophies

In his final form, Sloth will freeze the entire party, which paralyzes you in place and deals cold damage over time. It's brutal if you don't have healing at this point. If you have Wynne, she should kick off a Group Heal immediately after the effect to try to pump up everyone's health before Sloth kills them one by one. With some good party tactics and some timely healing, Sloth will eventually succumb to your weapons and you'll finally be free of the Fade. You now return to Templar Quarters on the fourth level of the Circle Tower. You have one more major enemy to kill.

The Circle Tower (Fourth Floor: After Fade)

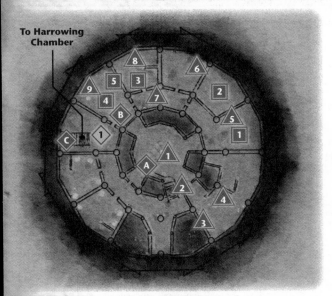

To Harrowing Chamber

Legend

① Cullen
▣ Dragonlings
② Rage Abominations
③ Sloth Abominations
④ Greater Rage Demon
⑤ Lesser Shades
△ Litany of Andralla
△ Soldier's Corpse

△ Cabinet
△ Charred Corpse
△ Chest
△ Chest (locked)
△ Soldier's Corpse
△ Vase & Chest (locked)
△ Soldier's Corpse & Chest (locked)

Runthrough (Circle Tower: Fourth Floor—After the Fade)

Summary: After returning from the Fade, you must seek out Uldred and end the Circle Tower nightmare.

A. Back on the fourth floor of the Circle Tower, pick up the Litany of Andralla from Niall's dead body.

B. A trap triggers by this treasure and surrounds you with demons.

C Speak with Cullen and then head into the Harrowing Chamber.

Circle Tower (Fourth Floor: After the Fade) Cheatsheet

Main Plot Quests
• Broken Circle

Important NPCs
• Cullen

Key Items
• Litany of Andralla

Monsters
• Dragonlings
• Greater Rage Demon
• Lesser Shades
• Rage Abominations
• Sloth Abominations

Side Quests
• None

A After exiting the Fade, you arrive back on the fourth level. Before you leave the central room in search of the Harrowing Chamber, loot Niall's dead body for the Litany of Andralla. It will protect you against mind control before the adventure ends.

B In the room with the giant globe, you'll see a soldier's corpse and a locked chest at the end opposite the entrance. It appears as any other empty room, until you touch the treasure. A greater shade, a few

lesser shades, and a greater rage demon materialize around you and attack. Retreat to one corner and fight there so you don't get flanked by demons. The lesser shades go down easier; concentrate on them to reduce the number, then apply your full party strength against whichever of the two bigger threats is weaker. When you finish off the second ranked foe, grab your treasure and be on your way.

primagames.com

C The last room before Harrowing Chamber holds Cullen. Inside a magical circle of protection, the templar pleads with you to destroy everyone in the Harrowing Chamber, unsure of what they've become. You can choose to see for yourself what's up there before making a decision, or you can choose on the spot to side with the mages (don't kill them) or side with the templars (kill all mages). After speaking with Cullen, proceed up the stairs to the Harrowing Chamber.

The Harrowing Chamber

Runthrough (Harrowing Chamber)

Summary: Slay Uldred and bring the Circle Tower's madness to an end.

A. Slay Uldred.

Legend

1 Uldred
2 Abominations

Harrowing Chamber Cheatsheet

Main Plot Quests
• Broken Circle

Important NPCs
• First Enchanter Irving

Key Items
• None

Monsters
• Abominations
• Uldred

Side Quests
• None

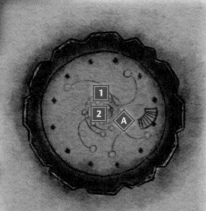

A Uldred has made mass murder even more repulsive, if that's possible. He has converted many of the mages into abominations, and plans on doing the same to you and everyone left in the tower. The only way to cleanse the tower is to kill Uldred. During the fight, as Uldred begins to convert a mage into an abomination (which will add that abomination to the fight against you), you can use the Litany of Andralla to deny the conversion. If Wynne is still alive in the party, she will give you a voice cue when to use it, or you can watch for a white glow around the wounded mages around the outer edge of the chamber. Using the Litany saves the mage, and if you do it at least once, then you have chosen to save all the mages in the Tower as the ultimate outcome. If you don't have the Litany or choose not to use it, then all the mages die at the end of the battle and you have ultimately sided with the templars.

◆ NOTE ◆

Choosing to side with the mages means you will gain a mage army in the final battle against the archdemon at game's end. Choosing to side with the templars gives you a templar army in the final battle against the archdemon. Both will aid you in the final battle, though siding with the mages now prevents Uldred from gaining allies in the current fight and makes for an easier encounter.

Broken Circle

Basics ~ Character Generation ~ Classes ~ The Party ~ Companions ~ Supporting Cast ~ Equipment ~ Bestiary ~ **Walkthroughs** ~ Side Quests ~ Random Encounters ~ Achievements/Trophies

Match your tank up against Uldred from the start. Send an off-tank against one of the abominations and have your party concentrate on destroying that abomination quickly. While preventing Uldred from creating abominations (the Litany stops this), slay the remaining abominations so you only have to face Uldred. In his demon form, Uldred can smack characters around for heavy damage. Your party healer should rotate through healing spells, such as Heal, Regeneration, and Group Heal (if they are a spirit healer and others in the party have taken damage too). If anyone in the party drops below 50 percent health and the healer can't keep up with the damage, they should immediately use a health poultice to stay out of the danger zone. Watch out for Uldred's ice attack which freezes everyone solid. It effectively acts like a stun, which means you can't deal damage or heal for several seconds. None of your party members can be low on health at this time or he may slay them.

Pour the damage on Uldred. Ranged attackers should stay clear of his long, sweeping demon claws. If you can outrace the damage Uldred deals, and minimizes how many extra abominations enter the fight, you should come out on top.

❖ TIP ❖
If you have a healer with Revive, don't forget to resurrect a fallen companion in the middle of battle to keep your party whole.

After the battle, speak with First Enchanter Irving. He will take you down to talk with Greagoir and thank you for saving the Circle Tower. You will gain your army for the final battle at this point. Wynne will also join your party permanently if you choose to invite her, and provided you are not a blood mage specialist. If you've chosen to specialize as a blood mage, Wynne will confront you at the base of the tower. If you admit you are a blood mage and choose to fight, then you will battle all the remaining templars and any mages alive (including Wynne). If you survive, you will gain neither the mages nor the templars for the final battle against the archdemon.

❖ CAUTION ❖

If Morrigan is in the party, at the end dialogue (in any outcome), it is possible to mention that she is an apostate mage. At this stage you can get her to leave the party in the same way as if you told her to directly leave the party.

Mage Army

If you have saved all the mages in the tower or have chosen not to lock the mages away, then the mages join the Grey Warden army for the final battle against the archdemon. The mages of the Circle are capable of unleashing deadly spells at any range, but are very weak in melee combat.

Templar Army

If you have killed all the mages in the tower or have chosen to lock the mages away, then the templars join the Grey Warden army for the final battle against the archdemon. The templars are an elite force of well-rounded fighters. Because they are capable of disrupting magic, they excel against spellcasters.

Arl of Redcliffe

NOTE

The main quest lines—"Broken Circle" (mage), "Arl of Redcliffe/Urn of Sacred Ashes" (human), "Paragon of Her Kind" (dwarf), and "Nature of the Beast" (elf)—can be completed in any order. However, it's probably best to finish the "Arl of Redcliffe/Urn of Sacred Ashes" quests second because, unlike the elf quests or the dwarf quests, these take you into Denerim, and you want to explore Denerim early in the game for access to lots of vendors and rewarding side quests.

Redcliffe Village (Day)

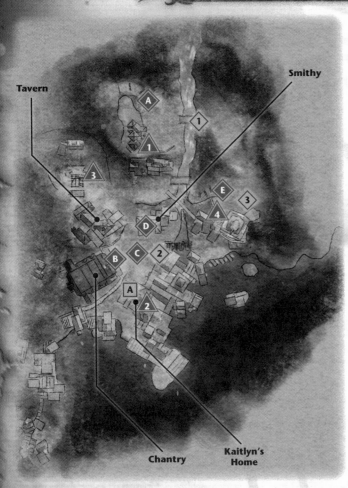

Tavern

Smithy

Chantry

Kaitlyn's Home

Runthrough (Redcliffe Village: Day)

Summary: Help the villagers prepare for the night's fight against the undead.

A. Enter the village and speak with Tomas.

B. Visit the village Chantry and speak with all inside.

C. Speak with Murdock.

D. Convince Owen to join the cause.

E. Speak with Ser Perth.

Redcliffe Village (Day) Cheatsheet

Main Plot Quests
- A Village Under Siege

Important NPCs
- Bann Teagan
- Kaitlyn
- Mother Hannah
- Murdock
- Owen
- Ser Perth
- Tomas

Key Items
- The Green Blade

Monsters
- None

Side Quests
- A Missing Child
- A Stiff Drink to Dull the Pain
- Every Little Bit Helps
- Lost in the Castle
- The Dwarven Veteran
- The Maker's Shield
- Spy!

Legend

① Tomas

② Murdock

③ Ser Perth

△1 Deathroot

△2 The Green Blade

△3 Deathroot

△4 A Landmark Tree

Ⓐ Bevin for "A Missing Child"

Ⓐ You arrive at Redcliffe from the northwest staircase. Travel across the open field and over the bridge to talk to Tomas. He explains that there is trouble at the castle and guides you down into the village.

Arl of Redcliffe

Basics ~ Character Generation ~ Classes ~ The Party ~ Companions ~ Supporting Cast ~ Equipment ~ Bestiary ~ **Walkthroughs** ~ Side Quests ~ Random Encounters ~ Achievements/Trophies

B Tomas takes you to talk to Bann Teagan in the Chantry. You discover that the village is under siege at night by undead monsters. After speaking with Teagan, you can also chat with Mother Hannah and Kaitlyn. If you choose, Kaitlyn gives you the "A Missing Child" side quest to find her brother Bevin. Find the boy hiding in the dresser at Kaitlyn's home. You can persuade/intimidate Bevin into giving you the key to a locked chest on the second floor that contains the magic family sword: The Green Blade. There is also a book in the house for another codex entry: The Legend of Calenhad: Chapter 1.

~ Village Chantry ~

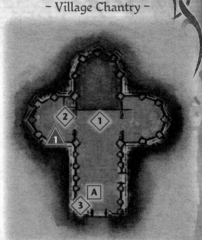

Legend

1. Bann Teagan
2. Mother Hannah
3. Kaitlyn
1. Book
A. "A Missing Child"

CAUTION

If you leave Redcliffe after speaking with Bann Teagan, you abandon the village to a grisly fate. When you return, the village will be empty and only the castle will remain.

C In the town square, Murdock orders men back and forth. He tells you that the village defenders are poorly outfitted and need repairs badly. He directs you to speak with the local blacksmith, Owen, who is reluctant to help. Talk to Owen in the smithy, then report back to Murdock.

D The smithy door is locked. To gain entrance, you need to persuade or intimidate Owen to let you in. Failing that, you can have a rogue try to pick the lock or simply smash it in by brute force. Convince Owen to carry out the equipment repairs by promising to look for his daughter Valena in the castle and accepting the side quest, "Lost in the Castle" (see the Side Quests chapter for details). After Owen has agreed to help, search the corner for a stash of equipment. It's under the crate, and you'll need Owen's key to open the hidden trapdoor.

If you don't want Owen's help, it's possible to refuse the "Lost in the Castle" quest. You can still gain the equipment stash, but only if you kill Owen and take his trapdoor key. With Owen dead, you can choose to give the hidden equipment to Murdock and his men; however, the hidden equipment is inferior to the repaired equipment Owen would have given the men. You can also tell Murdock that there is no way to acquire better equipment and the militia will fight using only the equipment they have.

~ Smithy ~

Legend

1. Owen
1. Hidden Trapdoor (under crate)
A. "Lost in the Castle"

TIP

If you've killed the blacksmith Owen, he will be replaced with a new smith after the battle. You can lie to the new smith and trick him into giving you one of Owen's items.

E Speak with Ser Perth on the hill and confirm that his knights are ready for battle. The night's battle against the undead will begin as soon as you also confirm with Murdock that his men are ready.

NOTE

There are several side quests you can complete in Redcliffe Village to strengthen the defenses before nighttime. These include "The Dwarven Veteran" (add more men to the fray), "The Maker's Shield" (boost the militia's morale), "Every Little Bit Helps" (add fire to village defenses), and "A Stiff Drink to Dull the Pain" (boost morale). You can also investigate "Spy!" to mess up Loghain's schemes. See the Side Quests chapter for complete details.

Redcliffe Village (Night)

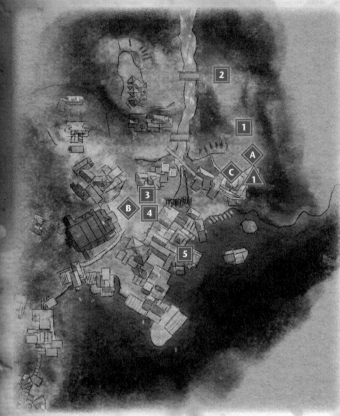

Runthrough (Redcliffe Village: Night)

Summary: Help the villagers defend against the undead.
A. Battle walking corpses by the mill.
B. Battle walking corpses in the town square.
C. Speak with Bann Teagon to discover a secret passage into the castle.

Redcliffe Village (Night) Cheatsheet

Main Plot Quests
• The Attack at Nightfall

Important NPCs
• None

Key Items
• None

Monsters
• Walking Corpses

Side Quests
• None

Legend

1 Walking Corpses 4 Walking Corpses
2 Walking Corpses 5 Walking Corpses
3 Walking Corpses ⚠ Wooden Crate

A As night falls, the walking corpses shamble out of the castle and down into the village. You first encounter them up at the mill. Use the barricades at the bottom of the mountain pass as cover. Position your warrior and other DPSers alongside the top one, or in between the two back barricades, to prevent the hordes of walking corpses from flanking you. Position your spellcasters in the rear. If the walking corpses begin to swarm you, retreat toward the mill and the knights will rally out to protect you. Use your standard combat procedures and repeat as each undead wave hits. When only a few remain, climb the hill and finish them off.

B Once the mill is safe, a villager alerts you to the undead forces attacking the town square. Rush down the hill toward the Chantry and aid the men who're battling walking corpses on

all sides. Slay all the walking corpses in town as they charge from the outskirts. Eventually, you have to hunt down a few straggler undead. It helps to have the Survival skill here to spot the undead from afar.

TIP
If no defenders are killed during the fight, Teagan will give you an extra reward. If you have Dwyn's thugs in the group, they do not count and can die without cutting off the reward.

C Return to Bann Teagan up on the hill by the mill. He and Lady Isolde plan to enter the castle through the main gates, while he asks you to slip into the castle via a secret passage in the windmill. Teagan

offers you his signet ring to open the secret door. Accept to go save Arl Eamon.

Arl of Redcliffe

Basics ~ Character Generation ~ Classes ~ The Party ~ Companions ~ Supporting Cast ~ Equipment ~ Bestiary ~ **Walkthroughs** ~ Side Quests ~ Random Encounters ~ Achievements/Trophies

Redcliffe Village (Basement)

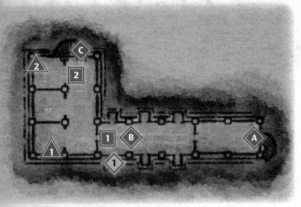

Legend

① Jowan
▲ Pile of Filth
🟦1 Enraged Corpses
▲2 Pile of Bones
🟦2 Shambling Corpses

Runthrough (Redcliffe Village: Basement)

Summary: Enter the castle and find the stairs to the first floor.

A. Slay the enraged corpses near the prison cells.

B. Speak to the blood mage Jowan. Release or kill him.

C. Battle the shambling corpses and go up the stairs to the first floor.

Redcliffe Castle (Basement) Cheatsheet

Main Plot Quests
- The Trouble with Castle Redcliffe

Important NPCs
- Jowan

Key Items
- None

Monsters
- Enraged Corpses
- Shambling Corpses

Side Quests
- None

A You enter the castle through the secret passage in the mill. It brings you into the basement level, and before you can take a few steps, a group of enraged corpses attack from down the corridor. Switch to your ranged weapons and plug them with arrows, or a fireball, or any AoE damage that won't catch your party too. By the time they reach you, the corpses should be halfway down, and a few sword swings and staff missiles should do the rest.

B Look for the blood mage Jowan in his cell. You can release Jowan and let him run ahead on his own, leave him in his cell, kill him, or force him to leave the castle permanently. If you choose to kill him or force him to leave the castle, Jowan will not be able to perform the blood magic ritual at the end of the quest. If you don't plan to enact blood magic, then do with him as you will.

C Watch out for the shambling corpses that rise up around you before the stairs. You won't have the same chance to do ranged damage as you did with the enraged corpses. Instead, back into a corner so the corpses can't flank you and have your tank hold as much threat as possible. The party deals damage on the corpses held by the tank, unless you order an off-tank to pick up any strays. Healers should be active keeping everyone healthy, and a spirit healer with Group Heal makes all the difference in this fight.

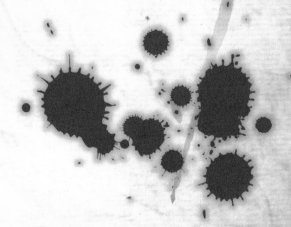

Redcliffe Castle (First Floor)

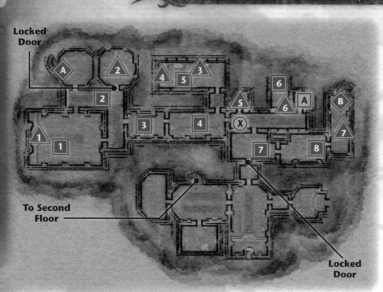

Runthrough (Redcliffe Castle: First Floor)

Summary: Progress through the first floor, down into the cellar, and out into the courtyard.

A. Enter the first floor.

B. Battle through corpses until you reach the stairs to the cellar.

Redcliffe Castle (First Floor) Cheatsheet

Main Plot Quests
- The Trouble with Castle Redcliffe

Important NPCs
- Valena

Key Items
- None

Monsters
- Devouring Corpses
- Enraged Corpses
- Greater Shade
- Lesser Shades
- Mabari
- Shambling Corpse

Side Quests
- Lost in the Castle

Legend

1. Greater Shade & Lesser Shades
2. Shambling Corpse
3. Shambling Corpses
4. Corpses
5. Mabari
6. Shambling Corpses
7. Enraged Corpse
8. Shambling Corpses
1. Book
2. Weapon Stands, Armor Stands, Chest
3. Chest
4. Charred Corpse
5. Cabinets
6. Armoire
7. Wooden Crates
A. Valena for "Lost in the Castle"
X. Trap

~ Cellar ~

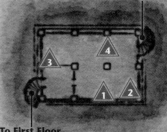

To Courtyard

To First Floor

Legend

1. Chest (locked)
2. Vase
3. Chest
4. Pile of Junk

A You come up on the first floor in the northwest corner. It's an empty room, but outside the door is a shambling corpse that wanders the hallway. If you have Survival and can track the corpse on your mini-map, open the door exactly when the creature is in front of it. You'll surprise it and lure the thing in to fight your party out of harm's way. Fight it in the hallway and it may draw other corpses from down the hall.

If you have a rogue with nimble fingers, it's worth picking the locked door on your left down the hallway. The secure room holds a treasure trove of items. After you dispatch more shambling corpses in the next room, begin to travel east as best you can.

B Continue battling through corpse after corpse. If you want to finish the "Lost in the Castle" side quest, rescue Valena from the small room near the end of the hall (marked square A on the map). In the northeast corner of the floor you'll find the stairs going down to the cellar.

Down in the cellar, sweep the floor clean of all the treasure in chests, a vase, and a pile of junk. Take the stairs in the northeast corner up to the courtyard.

Arl of Redcliffe

Basics ~ Character Generation ~ Classes ~ The Party ~ Companions ~ Supporting Cast ~ Equipment ~ Bestiary ~ **Walkthroughs** ~ Side Quests ~ Random Encounters ~ Achievements/Trophies

Redcliffe Castle (Courtyard)

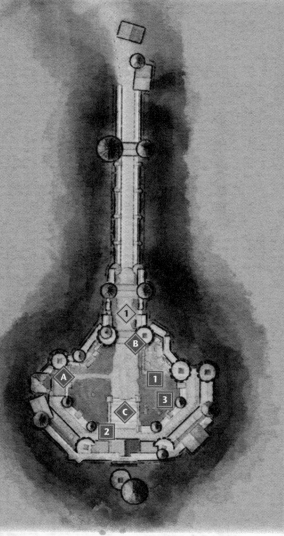

Legend

- ① Ser Perth & His Men
- ❶ Shambling Corpses
- ❷ Skeleton Archers
- ❸ Revenant

Runthrough
(Redcliffe Castle: Courtyard)

Summary: Fight through the courtyard and pull the gate lever to let Ser Perth and his men into the castle.

A. Enter the courtyard.

B. Pull the gate lever.

C. Discuss with Ser Perth the situation and reenter the first floor.

Redcliffe Castle
(Courtyard) Cheatsheet

Main Plot Quests
- The Trouble with Castle Redcliffe

Important NPCs
- Ser Perth

Key Items
- None

Monsters
- Revenant
- Shambling Corpses
- Skeleton Archers

Side Quests
- None

B The gate lever opens the main gates and allows Ser Perth and his men to charge in and fight with you. Together you have a better chance of surviving the sheer numbers of undead. Shortly after the battle begins, a ranked revenant enters the fray. The revenant hits hard, so make sure your healer is aware of who the revenant is attacking and keep a healthy dose of healing on that target. Once the revenant and its lesser shambling corpses wither to the ground, charge up the stairs and deal with any remaining skeleton archers (who may already be dead with the help of Ser Perth's men).

A It may seem like a serene courtyard scene when you emerge out of the cellar, but it's not. Plenty of monsters surround you. If you wander too far out in the middle, skeleton archers will rain arrows down from the upper level and shambling corpses will seek to swarm your party. Instead, make a beeline for the gate lever to the northeast.

C Assuming Ser Perth survived the battle, speak with him before reentering the first floor through the courtyard door. You can ask Ser Perth to enter the main hall with your party. If so, he will assist you in the upcoming battle against demonic forces.

Redcliffe Castle (Return to the First Floor)

Summary: Return to the first floor and find Bann Teagan, Lady Isolde, and Connor.

A. Reenter the main hall.

B. You may choose to sacrifice Isolde and cast a blood ritual to save Connor.

C. You may choose to kill Connor. Locate the stairs to the second floor here.

Legend

1. Bann Teagan
2. Guards
3. Guards
4. Suits of Armor
5. Chamberlain & Shambling Corpses

1. Desk & Book
2. Chest (locked)
3. Cabinet (locked)
4. Vanity

Redcliffe Castle (Return to the First Floor) Cheatsheet

Main Plot Quests
- The Possessed Child

Important NPCs
- Bann Teagan
- Connor
- Lady Isolde

Key Items
- Alistair's Mother's Necklace
- Vault Key

Monsters
- Bann Teagan
- Chamberlain
- Guards
- Shambling Corpses
- Suits of Armor

Side Quests
- None

A When you enter the main hall, you see a bizarre scene. Arl Eamon's son, Connor, is possessed by a demon and controls the minds of Bann Teagan and his men. They are Connor's puppets, and after your dialogue with the demon, Connor commands Bann Teagan and the guards to attack you, then flees. Don't hold back—you won't kill Bann Teagan in battle. Defeat him and his men to save your own lives and advance to the next stage of the quest.

B If you released Jowan and allowed him to stay in the castle, you can opt to save Connor through a blood ritual. Isolde volunteers to sacrifice her life energy to the ritual, which will cast a mage into the Fade to hunt the demon (either the PC mage, Morrigan, or Wynne). Proceed to the last section in this chapter: The Fade.

TIP

If you have completed the "Broken Circle" quest line, or do so now, you can recruit the Circle of Magi to initiate the Fade encounter without sacrificing Isolde.

NOTE

If you don't have a mage in your party, you can exit the castle, return to camp, and swap either Morrigan or Wynne into the active party.

C If you killed Jowan or exiled him from the castle, and you haven't completed the "Broken Circle" quest line yet, you have no choice but to slay Connor to slay the demon inside him. Step in the room on the west and prepare your party for a trap. As soon as you near the stairs, the suits of armor in the hall animate and attack. They hit hard and can surround you quickly, so backtrack into the main hall and bottleneck them at the doorway so they can't flank.

The far room down the hall is Arl Eamon's study, and if you search the desk you'll find one of Alistair's gifts: his mother's necklace. The southern room holds a chamberlain and more corpses. Defeat them and you gain the vault key, which unlocks the second floor vault door for more treasure. When you are finished with the first level, proceed up the stairs up to the second floor and chase after Connor.

Redcliffe Castle (Second Floor)

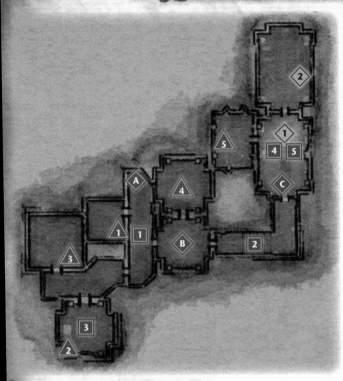

Runthrough (Redcliffe Castle: Second Floor)

Summary: Find Arl Eamon's bedroom and kill the demon.

A. You arrive on the second floor here.

B. Open the vault for extra treasure if you have the key from the first floor.

C. Talk to Connor and battle the desire demon.

Redcliffe Castle (Second Floor) Cheatsheet

Main Plot Quests
- The Possessed Child

Important NPCs
- Arl Eamon
- Connor

Key Items
- None

Monsters
- Desire Demon
- Devouring Corpses
- Lesser Rage Demons
- Shambling Corpses

Side Quests
- None

Legend

①	Connor	⑤	Shambling Corpses
②	Arl Eamon	Ⓐ	Vanity
❶	Shambling Corpses	Ⓑ	Chest
❷	Devouring Corpses & Shambling Corpses	Ⓒ	Chest (locked)
❸	Devouring Corpses	Ⓓ	The Vault
❹	Desire Demon	Ⓔ	Book

B In this hallway, you may open the vault door to the north if you hold the chamberlain's key from the first floor. Clean out the weapon stands, armor stands, and chests for some quality loot. Continue east when your party is healed up and ready to go.

A You arrive on the second floor at the top of a long hallway. All the dead bodies on the ground are actually shambling corpses that will rise as soon as you pass the halfway point in the hall. Stay close together and have the tank pull as much threat as possible; the corpses will be easier to handle on one target instead of the entire party. Heal when necessary and watch your AoE attacks; there isn't a lot of room in the hallway.

C In the hallway outside the bedchamber, you encounter Connor again. Speak with Connor until he transforms into the demon. Your tank should jump on the desire demon immediately and hold her attention. The healer concentrates healing on the tank. Anyone else alive in your party chips in with damage. When you have her down about one quarter of her health, the desire demon will vanish and corpses will animate around you. If they are across the hall, you can try an AoE spell such as Fireball to maximize damage, but be very careful not to catch your own party in the blast.

primagames.com

When you defeat the corpses, the desire demon reappears. The tank should once again grab threat and keep her maintained. When the demon drops about three quarters of her health, she disappears again, replaced with lesser rage demons. After dispatching the lesser rage demons, you have the final battle against the desire demon. It's a long, long fight, so restore whatever mana you can with lyrium potions; Rejuvenate also helps to pump up everyone's stamina.

After you slay the desire demon, Lady Isolde runs into the room to plead for Connor's life. You can either knock her out and kill Connor yourself, or convince Isolde that her whole family will be trapped in this nightmare unless she concedes to Connor's death. She will ask you to let her kill Connor herself.

Redcliffe Castle (The Fade)

Runthrough
(Redcliffe Castle: The Fade)

Summary: Navigate Connor's dream in the Fade and defeat the demon.

A. Find Connor and battle his demon incarnation.

B. Find Connor and battle his demon incarnation.

C. Find Connor and battle his demon incarnation.

D. Find Connor and battle his demon incarnation.

E. Slay the desire demon.

Redcliffe Castle
(The Fade) Cheatsheet

Main Plot Quests	Key Items
• The Possessed Child	• None
Important NPCs	**Monsters**
• Arl Eamon	• Desire Demon
• Connor	**Side Quests**
	• None

Legend

① Arl Eamon	① Fade Portal
▫ Desire Demon	② Fade Portal
② Desire Demon & Lesser Rage Demon	③ Fade Portal
③ Desire Demon & Lesser Rage Demons	④ Fade Portal
④ Desire Demon	⑤ Fade Portal

A You begin the northeast corner of Connor's dream in the Fade. Wander to the west and find Arl Eamon. He's confused and doesn't want to believe his son is possessed by a demon, but it's

reassuring to talk to him and know he's still alive. Take the first portal to the second portal.

Arl of Redcliffe

NOTE

Portals in the Fade glow purple when they are active. The portal automatically takes you to the next location, even if it's the portal you just stepped through.

B Find Connor near his bed. Speak with him and goad the desire demon into attacking you. Defeat the demon to open the portal to the next location (it's the same portal you stepped through to get here).

C Find Connor again. This time the desire demon attacks with a lesser rage demon at her side. Hit the desire demon with a stunning spell such as Mind Blast or root spell such as Crushing Prison, then focus on the lesser rage demon. Cold spells work great. The lesser demon falls quickly, so hopefully you can switch back to the desire demon before she regains her senses and attacks. Defeat her a second time to open the portal to the next area.

D After speaking with Connor, prepare for two lesser rage demons to appear with the desire demon. Heal often in this fight, whether with spells or health poultices. If your mana runs low, sip a lyrium potion and continue to pour on the damage, first on the lesser rage demons and then the desire demon.

E The final demon incarnation hides here. You can either kill the desire demon outright, or bargain with her. When you confront the desire demon, she offers you a choice: a reward for Connor's soul at a later date. She agrees to free him for now and let you finish your duties against the Blight, but in some future time, you agree to let her return and claim Connor's soul. It won't affect your game play, only your conscience.

The reward can be one of the following: blood magic specialization, an approval increase with any companion except Oghren, a special tome that grants one talent point, or you can ask for pleasure from the desire demon. If you choose not to accept the reward, you battle to the death. Slaying the demon in the Fade frees Connor and returns you to Redcliffe Castle.

NOTE

Accepting the desire demon's offer is the only way to earn the blood mage specialization.

To Save Arl Eamon

Whether you kill Connor, let Isolde sacrifice herself for her son, or save both with the Circle of Magi, you eventually free Redcliffe from the desire demon's influence. Alas, Arl Eamon does not wake, and may be taking a turn for the worse. Natural remedies, and even standard magic healing, will not rescue him. You need the aid of an ancient artifact: the Urn of Sacred Ashes. Only then can you return Eamon to life and ask him to join the Grey Wardens against the coming Blight.

Urn of Sacred Ashes

NOTE

The main quest lines—"Broken Circle" (mage), "Arl of Redcliffe/Urn of Sacred Ashes" (human), "Paragon of Her Kind" (dwarf), and "Nature of the Beast" (elf)—can be completed in any order. However, because this is the second part of the Arl of Redcliffe quest, it's probably best to finish this after Redcliffe because the quest sends you to Denerim looking for Brother Genitivi, and you definitely want to visit Denerim early in your adventures.

Denerim Market District

Chantry   Open Market   Wade's Emporium

Wonders of Thedas   Gnawed Noble Tavern   Brother Gentivi's   Elven Alienage

Legend

1 Wooden Crate	B Sergeant Kylon
2 Wooden Crate	C "Honor Bound" Duel
A Chanter's Board	D Friends of Red Jenny

Runthrough (Denerim Market District)

Summary: Visit the market and seek out Brother Genitivi at his home.

A. Wander the market for vendors and side quests if you like.

B. Stop by Brother Genitivi with questions about the Urn of Sacred Ashes. Unlock the Village of Haven on the world map by finding Genitivi's research in his bedroom chest.

Denerim Market District Cheatsheet

Main Plot Quests
- The Urn of Sacred Ashes

Important NPCs
- Weylon

Key Items
- Genitivi's Research

Monsters
- None

Side Quests
- Chanter's Board
- Sergeant Kylon's quests
- Honor Bound
- Friends of Red Jenny
- Gnawed Noble Tavern quests

Your first destination on the quest for the Urn of Sacred Ashes lies in the opposite direction from the urn: Denerim. You're looking for the famous researcher Brother Genitivi, a scholar who has searched for the urn most of his life. If anyone has knowledge of its existence, it would be Brother Genitivi. You can wander the marketplace in Denerim all you like, and there plenty of events to keep you busy, from spending money at vendors to collecting loads of side quests in and around Denerim. When you are ready to continue on the "Urn of Sacred Ashes" quest, head to Brother Genitivi's home in the Market District's southeast section.

Urn of Sacred Ashes

Basics ~ Character Generation ~ Classes ~ The Party ~ Companions ~ Supporting Cast ~ Equipment ~ Bestiary ~ **Walkthroughs** ~ Side Quests ~ Random Encounters ~ Achievements/Trophies

NOTE

You can complete many side quests in Denerim. If you would like to earn more experience or rewards, or whenever you don't feel like setting out into the world map on a big adventure, accept any quests that you fancy. See the Side Quests chapter for complete details.

CAUTION

If you don't reveal Weylon as a traitor and listen to his lies, he will direct you to the Spoiled Princess tavern in Lake Calenhad. You can question the innkeeper there about Brother Genitivi, and when you exit you'll be ambushed by some weird cultists. Weylon has set you up for execution. Return to Genitivi's house angry and you'll trigger an attack by Weylon then.

B Enter Brother Genitivi's home. Genitivi's assistant tells you that the explorer has been missing for a while and was last seen in Lake Calenhad. You shouldn't trust Weylon, however. If you have a high enough cunning score, you can reveal that he's lying and he'll attack you. If you can't trick him with dialogue, go to open the door into Brother Genitivi's bedroom and Weylon will interpose. If you insist on opening the door, Weylon will attack.

~ Brother Gentivi's Home ~

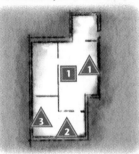

Four on one is good odds, and despite Weylon's formidable Lightning spells, he should go down if you stun him once or twice or counteract his damage with healing. Search the chest in Genitivi's bedroom and you'll find some of Genitivi's research. This unlocks the Village of Haven on your world map. It's your next destination.

Legend

1	Weylon	**2**	Book
1	Book	**3**	Chest

Village of Haven

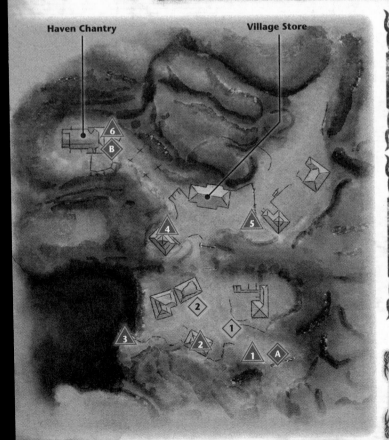

Haven Chantry

Village Store

Runthrough (Village of Haven)

Summary: You are strangers in the Village of Haven. Journey to the Haven Chantry and fight the guards to free Brother Genitivi.

A. Survey Haven. You will not be welcome.

B. Talk to Father Eirik in the Haven Chantry. Free the captive Brother Genitivi.

Village of Haven Cheatsheet

Main Plot Quests
- The Urn of Sacred Ashes

Important NPCs
- Boy
- Father Genitivi
- Guard

Key Items
- Cultist Medallion

Monsters
- Father Eirik
- Guards

Side Quests
- None

Legend

①	Guard	③	Chest (locked)
②	Child	④	Sack
🔺	Deathroot	⑤	Deathroot
🔺	Chests (locked)	⑥	Deathroot

primagames.com

A Haven is not a welcoming place, and its citizens will do anything to keep their secrets. The villagers treat you coldly, and if you snoop around enough, they become hostile and cultists attack you. You can investigate a bloodied altar in the empty home or discover the corpse of a missing Redcliffe knight in the shop. If you want to play it inconspicuously, simply head up the hill to the Haven Chantry and speak with Father Eirik inside the church.

B Inside the Haven Chantry, Father Eirik tries to politely shoo you away, but if you pursue your questioning regarding Brother Genitivi, Eirik orders the guards to attack. You start out surrounded; to avoid penalties, move your party to a corner and eliminate flanking. The tank should take Brother Eirik while an off-tank warrior or rogue takes on the guards. Healers will have to be quick to spread the healing around.

~ Haven Chantry ~

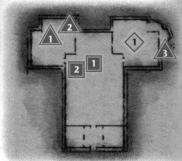

After you slay Father Eirik, you recover the Cultist Medallion from his body. This is your key into the Ruined Temple, so make sure you have it with you when you leave the Chantry. Slide open a secret passage in the Chantry's northeast corner. Inside the small room lies Brother Genitivi. He's hurt, but he can manage to limp and show you the entrance to the Ruined Temple, where the hunt for the Urn of Sacred Ashes continues.

Legend

- ◇1 Brother Genitivi
- □1 Father Eirik
- □2 Guards
- ◁1 Inscribed Chest
- ◁2 Chest (locked)
- ◁3 Chest (locked)

Ruined Temple

~ See map on next page ~

Runthrough (Ruined Temple)

Summary: Navigate the treacherous temple to discover the Wyrmling Lair.

A. Let Brother Genitivi open the temple door and guide you in.

B. Take the stairs as you battle a handful of mad cultists.

C. Use the south eastern chamber key to get the main door key.

D. Open the main doors with the special key.

E. Light the brazier to continue forward.

F. Survive the trap with an ash wraith and ambushing cultists.

G. Find the stairs to the Wyrmling Lair.

Ruined Temple Cheatsheet

Main Plot Quests
- The Urn of Sacred Ashes

Important NPCs
- Brother Genitivi

Key Items
- South Eastern Chamber Key
- Main Door Key

Monsters
- Ash Wraiths
- Bronto
- Cultist Archers
- Cultist Mages
- Cultist Reavers

Side Quests
- None

A With the help of the Cultist Medallion, Brother Genitivi guides you into the Ruined Temple. He waits for you at the entrance, which is a safe zone, so you can always go back and talk to him if you like. If you are careful not to stray too close to the large stairs directly in front of you at the chamber's far end, you can explore both side passages. Cultists guard some loot on the west side, while you can uncover some interesting texts on the east side. A locked door on the east side leads into the southeastern chambers. You'll come back later with the key.

B Cultists reaver and archers man the stairs. You have to battle through them to progress farther into the dungeon. Inch up slowly, and when the first cultist comes into range, strike him with an AoE attack

Urn of Sacred Ashes

Basics ~ Character Generation ~ Classes ~ The Party ~ Companions ~ Supporting Cast ~ Equipment ~ Bestiary ~ **Walkthroughs** ~ Side Quests ~ Random Encounters ~ Achievements/Trophies

Legend

- ① Brother Genitivi
- 1 Cultists
- 2 Cultist Reavers & Cultist Archers
- 3 Cultist Reavers & Cultist Archers
- 4 Bronto
- 5 Cultist Archers
- 6 Cultists
- 7 Cultist Mage
- 8 Cultist Mage
- 9 Cultists
- 10 Cultists & Ash Wraiths
- 11 Cultists Archers
- 12 Ash Wraith
- 13 Cultists
- 14 Cultist Mage & Ash Wraiths
- 15 Cultists
- 16 Cultists

- 17 Cultist Mage & Ash Wraiths
- 18 Cultists
- △1 Cabinet & Bookshelf
- △2 Adventurer
- △3 Ancient Texts
- △4 Chest (locked)
- △5 Ancient Texts
- △6 Wooden Crates
- △7 Chest (locked)
- △8 Dusty Scrolls
- △9 Ornate Chest
- △10 Chests
- △11 Fallen Knight
- △12 Ornate Chest
- △13 Chests
- △14 Vase
- Ⓐ Scrolls for "Forgotten Verses"
- Ⓧ Trap

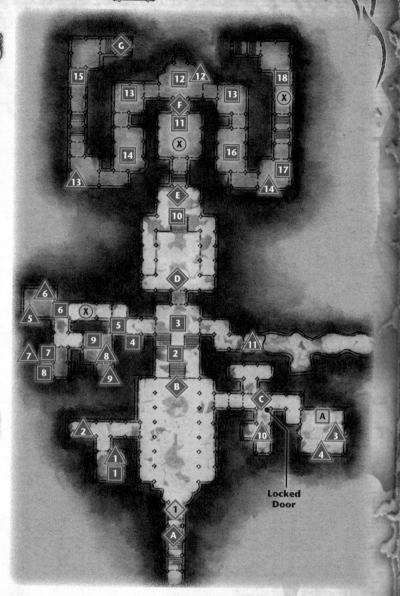

Locked Door

(say, Fireball) or a long-range arrow. Pull cultists to you, so you don't get caught in a crossfire. After you thin out a few, send your tank up to engage the remaining cultists and work as a team to wipe them out. After the stairs, begin on the western chambers. Take it slowly; there are a lot of cultists. AoE attacks work great as long as you can keep your own party out of them. Grab the south eastern chamber key from the ornate chest (marked triangle 9 on the map).

C When you leave the western chambers, watch out for another cultist ambush from below the steps, guarding the doorway to the southeastern chamber (which was empty earlier). Keep the high ground and rain down ranged attacks on the ambush below. Let them come to you and pick them off as they charge up the stairs. Your tank can meet and greet them if they make it to your party. Once the ambush is dispersed, use the south eastern chamber key to enter the small area. Open all the chests that you can, and make sure you pocket the main door key to open the doors at the top of the stairs.

D Use the main door key to open the door leading to the temple's northern section. A cultist mage stands at the top of the stairs at the chamber's far end. Cultist archers flank you along the top ledge on either side. To make matters worse, ash wraiths appear as soon as you try to get in range of the cultists. Your number-one priority is the cultist mage. He can wreck you if left unharassed up on the stairs. Lock him down with a spell such as Crushing Prison, send a rogue to stun him with Dirty Fighting, or have the tank haul his armored butt up there as quickly as possible. The off-tank should grab the threat on the ash wraiths. Healers have to scan the entire battlefield and heal whenever the health bars drop low.

E Ignite the magic brazier to pass through the door into the next section of the dungeon. (This step isn't necessary in the console version.)

F When you reach the top chamber, it appears empty. It's not. An ash wraith materializes in the center as soon as you step in, and once it has your attention, the doors on either side of the chamber spring open and cultists charge in. The tank should take the ash wraith, and your ranged DPSers should concentrate fire on the cultist mage who loves to toss Fireballs. If you have Wynne, use her Group Heal often, as soon as the majority of your party is below one third health. Once the ash wraith dies, focus on a new target, and keep out of the way of the ranged cultists down the halls.

TIP

You can close the chamber doors for a few seconds of breathing space and to force the ranged cultists to draw closer and open them.

G Take the west fork to the stairs leading out of the temple; it's a slightly easier battle. Fight through all the cultists and forget the chest loot on the way, except for the locked chest. The other chests hold no treasure and summon ash wraiths. The stairs at the end lead into the Wyrmling Lair.

CAUTION

Ash wraiths appear when you open the normal chests at triangle 13 on the map. The only safe chest to open is the locked one (if you have a competent rogue).

Wyrmling Lair

~ See map on next page ~

Runthrough (Wyrmling Lair)

Summary: Wipe out everything in the lair on your way to the exit.

A. Slay the cultist overseer and cultist reavers near the entrance and enter the dungeon.

B. Choose the left passage at the fork after you battle cultists and dragonlings.

C. A major battle occurs here between a powerful cultist overseer and drakes.

D. Speak with Kolgrim. Choose to cooperate or kill him, then seek out the mountaintop.

Wyrmling Lair Cheatsheet

Main Plot Quests
- The Urn of Sacred Ashes

Important NPCs
- Kolgrim

Key Items
- Drake Scales
- Kolgrim's Horn

Monsters
- Cultist Archers

- Cultist Assassins
- Cultist Mages
- Cultist Overseer
- Cultist Reavers
- Drakes
- Dragonlings

Side Quests
- Drake Scale Armor

A The first main chamber in the Wyrmling Lair hosts a cultist overseer and a bunch of his men. A large rock shields you from them as you enter; use that to your advantage and spread your party out into attack formation, with the tank near the rock to grab the closest threat and ranged attackers and healers near the doorway. A ranged attacker can slip to the side and launch a shot into the enemy's midst to pull them toward you. The tank jumps out and surprises them as they near.

B Where the intersection splits in two, cultists congregate on the chamber's left side and dragonlings lurk on the right. Sneak up on the room and pull the closest cultists with the strongest

Urn of Sacred Ashes

Basics ~ Character Generation ~ Classes ~ The Party ~ Companions ~ Supporting Cast ~ Equipment ~ Bestiary ~ **Walkthroughs** ~ Side Quests ~ Random Encounters ~ Achievements/Trophies

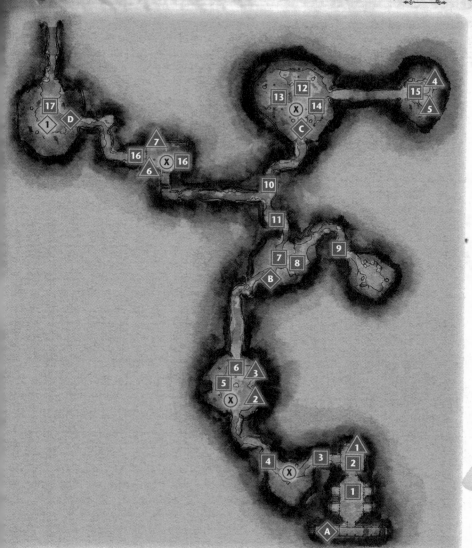

Legend

① Kolgrim
1 Cultist Overseer & Cultist Reavers
2 Cultist Mages
3 Cultists
4 Dragonlings
5 Cultists
6 Cultists
7 Cultists
8 Dragonlings
9 Drakes
10 Cultist Mage
11 Cultist Assassins
12 Cultist Reavers
13 Cultist Overseer
14 Drakes & Dragonlings
15 Drake & Cultists
16 Cultists
17 Cultists
△1 Wooden Crate
△2 Chest (locked)
△3 Chest (locked)
△4 Dragon Egg
△5 Book
△6 Chest (locked)
△7 Wooden Crates
Ⓧ Trap

ranged attack that you have (Fireball works excellently). Set up a strong defensive position in the corridor just before the chamber and hold there. You can't be flanked, and enemies have to attack at most side by side. If you pull correctly, only the cultists attack. Then you can pull the dragonlings and fight two smaller battles rather than one large melee.

CAUTION

Don't go to the right passage unless you hope to gain a drake scale or two. There's no loot down there, and it's a dead end. On top of that, the three drakes appear behind you in an ambush. The drakes are very difficult, as they can knock you off your feet and have a devastating overrun attack that pins you to the ground and deals massive damage.

When you take the left passage, watch out for an immediate ambush. A lone cultist mage up the passage draws your attention while invisible cultist assassins appear behind you and try for brutal backstabs. Fire off a few ranged attacks at the mage to stop him, while your tank grabs the threat on the assassins. Their blades are coated with poison to stop you from healing so it'll be a race to out-damage them.

NOTE

The two northeast chambers in the Wyrmling Lair are optional. You fight tough opposition; however, the rewards are worth it if you have an experienced team.

Ⓒ As you approach this chamber—stop! Hold your party in the passage where you can just see into the room. Now take your best long-ranged attacker and inch up until you can target the cultist reavers

straight ahead. Hit the reavers with your best attack and run back to the group. Fight the cultist reavers in the passage, otherwise you will trigger more creatures to spawn and soon be overwhelmed.

primagames.com

Next, inch into the room and, if you have a rogue, try to disarm the bear traps to your left. Dragonlings will spawn all around you, including one behind you in the passage. Retreat to your original location and fight through all the dragonlings.

A cultist overseer stands on the dais at the top of the stairs to your left. He has an anti-magic shield around him, so a warrior or rogue should charge up the stairs and engage as soon as possible. Stun him often so he can't counterattack with his spells.

Unfortunately, it's not just the overseer to deal with. Two drakes spawn when you attack the overseer. Watch out that the one nearest the passage doesn't catch someone unawares (like your healer!). If you can get everyone up on the overseer's dais and kill him off quickly, your tank can hold the stairs against the drakes as long as they don't overrun quickly. Throw your best spells and talents the drakes' way. It will be a long fight; hang in there and pop a lot of potions and poultices to survive.

NOTE

If a drake drops a drake scale, collect it to start the "Drake Scale Armor" quest. Return to Denerim to Wade's Emporium in the Market District and ask him to make you a fine piece of armor.

D In the final chamber, you meet another crazed father, Kolgrim. He believes that the prophet Andraste has been resurrected in dragon form and asks you to destroy Andraste's ashes to empower the dragon.

Defile the Urn

Kolgrim, the leader of the cult responsible for keeping the Urn of Sacred Ashes' location a secret for so long, will teach the player the Reaver specialization in exchange for defiling the Urn of Sacred Ashes with Dragon's Blood.

Defile the Urn (continued)

Step 1: The player must speak with Kolgrim in the Caverns beyond the Ruined Temple. If you accept Kolgrim's offer to taint the urn, you receive a vial of Dragon's Blood, which is to be poured over Andraste's ashes.

Step 2: The urn is at the end of the Gauntlet, which is across the mountaintop and outside the Wyrmling Lair. Kolgrim will placate the dragon waiting to devour the party on the mountaintop and stay there until the party returns. Once you have the ashes, pouring the Dragon's Blood on the ashes will cause the Guardian to attack, along with Wynne and Leliana if they are present.

Step 3: Return to Kolgrim on the mountaintop. If the ashes have been defiled, he rewards the player with the Reaver specialization; otherwise, he's a bit upset that the PC hasn't done what he wanted just yet.

At any point after first encountering Kolgrim the player can provoke him into fighting and kill him. This gives the player access to Kolgrim's Horn (or a gong in the console version), which can be used to call the high dragon down from the mountaintop to fight the party.

Assuming you don't want to defile the urn, simply annoy Kolgrim with one of your dialogue choices and he'll fly off the handle and attack. This is a difficult battle that will require all your tactics to survive. First, Kolgrim hits very, very hard, so root him with one of your spells or talents (it's even better if you can cycle through different party member's talents to hold him in place, or at least delay his attacks). Next, fire off ranged attacks to destroy the two cultist mages that flank your position. If you don't, AoE spell damage will destroy you over the course of the battle. Third, have the tank draw the threat from the attacking reavers, unless the tank has to lock onto Kolgrim. Wipe out the reavers and turn all your damage onto Kolgrim. His swings can be lethal, so use heal spells and health poultices to top off health whenever possible.

Eventually, Kolgrim and his lunatic men fall. Take the northern passage out of the lair and up to the mountaintop to continue your search for the urn.

Urn of Sacred Ashes

Basics ~ Character Generation ~ Classes ~ The Party ~ Companions ~ Supporting Cast ~ Equipment ~ Bestiary ~ **Walkthroughs** ~ Side Quests ~ Random Encounters ~ Achievements/Trophies

Mountaintop

Exiting the Wyrmling Lair brings you atop the mountain. The high dragon swoops down and rests on one of the nearby peaks. To continue your search for the urn, run across the mountaintop area and to the Gauntlet entranceway on the far side. Nothing will threaten you.

If you'd rather have some pain before continuing the "Urn of Sacred Ashes" quest, blow Kolgrim's Horn (or use the gong on the console version) to summon the high dragon. Unless your party is geared out to defend against the dragon, you stand little chance. You need lots of fire resistance to compete with the high dragon's fire breathing. It's possible to try to continuously root/stun the dragon with all the spells and talents in your group, but you still need to put a serious amount of damage on the beast to bring it down. It's better to avoid the dragon fight unless you have a veteran group.

The Gauntlet

Secret Mountain Path

To Mountaintop

Secret Mountain Path

Runthrough (The Gauntlet)

Summary: Beat the four challenges of the Gauntlet to claim Andraste's ashes.

A. Speak with the Guardian to enter the Gauntlet.

B. Solve the eight riddles to pass the locked door.

C. Visit a ghost from the past.

D. Doppelgangers of your party attack and you must defeat yourself in deadly combat.

E. Figure out the bridge puzzle to pass.

F. Step through the fires to finally reach the Urn of Sacred Ashes.

The Gauntlet Cheatsheet

Main Plot Quests
- The Urn of Sacred Ashes

Important NPCs
- Archon Hessarian
- Brona
- Disciple Cathaire
- Disciple Havard
- Ealisay
- General Maferath

- Ghost of the Past
- Lady Vasilia
- Thane Shartan
- The Guardian

Key Items
- Urn of Sacred Ashes

Monsters
- Party Doppelgangers

Side Quests
- None

Legend

① The Guardian	⑤ Disciple Cathaire	⑨ Archon Hessarian	△ Vase
② Ealisay	⑥ Brona	⑩ Ghost of the Past	△ Urn of Sacred Ashes
③ Lady Vasilia	⑦ Thane Shartan	☐ Party Doppelgangers	Ⓐ Altar
④ Disciple Havard	⑧ General Maferath	△ Rubble	

A Inside the Gauntlet, proceed to the first chamber and speak with the Guardian. He safeguards the urn and tells you that you must pass four challenges of faith to be judged worthy of approaching the urn. Treat him kindly and he will let you pass.

B The far door in the next large chamber is locked. If you figure out the eight riddles, the spirit of each ghost will enter the locked door and it will click open. Beginning on the right side and working around the room, the riddle answers are:

Ealisay: A tune

Lady Vasilia: Vengeance

Disciple Havard: The mountains

Disciple Cathaire: Hunger

Brona: Dreams

Thane Shartan: Home

General Maferath: Jealousy

Archon Hessarian: Mercy

◆◆◆ TIP ◆◆◆

You don't have to know the answer to all eight riddles. For each riddle that you miss, the NPC transforms into an ash wraith. Slay the ash wraith and its spirit enters the door lock as if you had answered the riddle correctly.

C Next you speak with a ghost from your past. The ghost depends on your origin story, so Jowan for mages, a family member of House Cousland for human noble, etc. Answer according to your conscience; the ghost allows you to pass no matter your dialogue choice.

D The second challenge pits your party against doppelgangers. The duplicate party has all your talents, spells, equipment, and levels, but doesn't have your smarts. It will be a grueling battle

(and fun to see how you fare against your own abilities!); however, your tactics will win the day. Each party makeup will be different. If your party has a healer, such as Wynne, target her first. Just as it's difficult to kill your party with a healer replenishing health, the same goes for the enemy. If you get the doppelganger healer out of the way and you still maintain your healer, you'll come out on top.

◆◆◆ TIP ◆◆◆

You should know your party well. Try to anticipate how each character will react and counter appropriately. For instance, if a mage begins to channel, it's going to be something deadly such as Inferno, so stun him immediately with a rogue's Dirty Fighting or a warrior's Shield Bash.

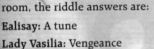

E The third challenge looks impossible at first. A bottomless pit separates you from the chamber with Andraste's ashes. No bridge physically exists, but you can create a ghost bridge by standing on the correct combination of stones. There are six stones on the left side and six stones on the right side (facing the urn chamber ahead). You need a full group to do this one. Send your three companions to stand on the stones while your PC crosses the ghost bridge.

◆◆◆ CAUTION ◆◆◆

You can stand on the ghost bridge only when it becomes solid, which takes overlapping ghostly images.

The first time a bridge piece appears, it looks faint. It's still insubstantial and can't be stepped on. If two insubstantial pieces overlap, which happens as different stones are touched by companions along the sides, then the ghost bridge becomes solid where the images overlap. To cross, follow this pattern:

Step 1: Right one, right two, left three.

Step 2: PC steps on first section of ghost bridge.

Step 3: Right two, left three, left six.

Step 4: PC steps on second section of ghost bridge.

Step 5: Right two, right four, left six.

Step 6: Right four, left one, left six.

Step 7: PC steps on third section of ghost bridge.

Step 8: Right four, right five, left one.

Step 9: Right five, left one, left five.

Step 10: PC crosses successfully.

◆◆◆ NOTE ◆◆◆

On the console version of the game, as each bridge piece becomes solid, it remains solid permanently.

Urn of Sacred Ashes

Basics ~ Character Generation ~ Classes ~ The Party ~ Companions ~ Supporting Cast ~ Equipment ~ Bestiary ~ **Walkthroughs** ~ Side Quests ~ Random Encounters ~ Achievements/Trophies

Approach the altar without entering the fire yet. Click on the altar and remove all your equipment. This is the final test of faith: walk through the fire naked without any protection. The flames will not harm you, and your party finally reaches the Urn of Sacred Ashes. Take a pinch of the ashes to cure Arl Eamon and leave the urn for the future faithful. When you are ready, exit via the secret mountain path exit. Return to Brother Genitivi (you can take the shortcut Ruined Temple entrance on the mountaintop). Allow Brother Genitivi to spread the word about the urn or else you have to kill him. If you let him live and visit him again in Denerim, he will give you a reward for his rescue.

Saving Arl Eamon

With the ashes from the urn safely secured, return to Bann Teagon at Redcliffe Castle (main chamber on the first floor). The ashes will heal Arl Eamon. Ask for his help against the Blight. He also gives you a reward if you allow him: an item and the Champion specialization for warriors. Eamon explains that a Landsmeet is needed so that the lords of the land can decide who should be the new king: the traitor Loghain or the last of the blood line, Alistair. When you are ready to proceed to the endgame, after you have completed all of the treaty quest lines, speak with Arl Eamon at Redcliffe Castle and start the Landsmeet quests.

Champion Specialization

At the conclusion of the "Urn of Sacred Ashes" quest, decide to be a little bit greedy. Arl Eamon offers you a reward, and part of that reward is the Champion specialization for warriors. After all that you've been through to recover the most cherished artifact in the land, you deserve a reward like this. Even if your main PC isn't a warrior, it helps beef up Alistair and Sten if you choose to specialize in the art of inspiring comrades.

Soldiers of Redcliffe Army

If you saved Arl Eamon with Andraste's ashes, then the human soldiers of Redcliffe join the Grey Warden army for the final battle against the archdemon. The soldiers of Redcliffe are hardy infantry troops. They're useful against armored targets but have no ranged weapons.

primagames.com

Paragon of Her Kind

NOTE

The main quest lines—"Broken Circle" (mage), "Arl of Redcliffe/Urn of Sacred Ashes" (human), "Paragon of Her Kind" (dwarf), and "Nature of the Beast" (elf)—can be completed in any order. Because Oghren joins your party in Orzammar, if you need a tank or extra melee DPS companion for your party, you should complete the dwarf quest line earlier.

NOTE

"The Stone Prisoner" is an optional quest line available via download. Shale, a golem companion, must be freed from a darkspawn horde that has destroyed an entire village. See the "Stone Prisoner" section of the Walkthrough chapter for the complete rundown.

Frostback Mountains

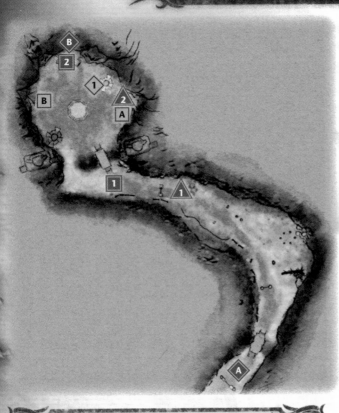

Runthrough (Frostback Mountains)

Summary: You head to Orzammar to get help from the dwarves.

A. Arrive at the pass through Frostback Mountains.

B. Enter Orzammar after dealing with Loghain's messenger.

Legend

①	Faryn (vendor)	Ⓐ (2)	Barrel
1	Bounty Hunters	A	Tomas the Deserter for "Dereliction of Duty"
2	Imrek & Bodyguards	B	Starrick for "Notice of Termination"
△1	Deathroot		

A Enter the Frostback Mountains. Up ahead you'll run into the group of bounty hunters if it's your first time in the area. If you've been fighting for a while now, you'll wipe them up without much problem. Past them is a small vendor area outside the main gates to Orzammar.

Frostback Mountains Cheatsheet

Main Plot Quests
- Paragon of Her Kind

Important NPCs
- Faryn

Key Items
- None

Monsters
- Bodyguards

- Bounty Hunters
- Imrek

Side Quests
- Cammen's Lament
- Dereliction of Duty
- Notice of Termination

B Imrek, a messenger from Loghain, tries to get into Orzammar without success. You show the gatekeeper the Grey Warden treaty and he agrees to allow you entry. Imrek, Loghain's messenger, takes offense to this and attacks you with his two bodyguards (one a mage), unless you can persuade or intimidate him out of his rash decision.

Paragon of Her Kind

Basics ~ Character Generation ~ Classes ~ The Party ~ Companions ~ Supporting Cast ~ Equipment ~ Bestiary ~ **Walkthroughs** ~ Side Quests ~ Random Encounters ~ Achievements/Trophies

Orzammar Commons

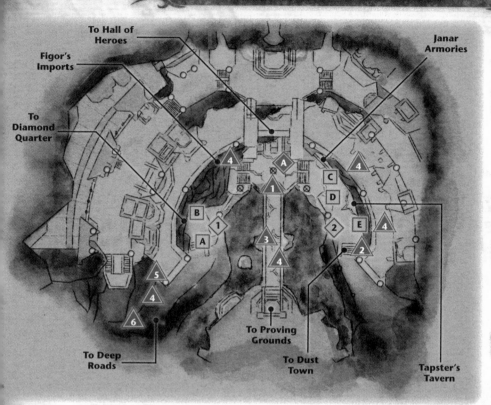

To Hall of Heroes

Figor's Imports

Janar Armories

To Diamond Quarter

To Deep Roads

To Proving Grounds

To Dust Town

Tapster's Tavern

Legend

1. Garin (vendor)
2. Legnar (vendor)
1. Floor Carving (codex)
2. Wall Carving (codex)
3. Document (codex)
4. Nug
5. Runestone (codex)
6. Rune Plate (codex)
A. "A Mother's Hope"
B. Nug Wrangler
C. "An Unlikely Scholar"
D. "Political Attacks"
E. "Chant in the Deeps"

Runthrough
(Orzammar Commons)

Summary: Explore Orzammar to get help from the dwarves.

A. Speak with the Captain of the Guard to discover the political scene in Orzammar.

Orzammar Commons Cheatsheet

Main Plot Quests
- Paragon of Her Kind

Important NPCs
- Brother Burkel
- Captain of the Guard
- Dagna
- Filda
- Nug Wrangler Boermor

Key Items
- None

Monsters
- Fanatics (either for Bhelen or Harrowmont)

Side Quests
- A Mother's Hope
- An Unlikely Scholar
- A Lost Nug
- Political Attacks
- The Chant in the Deeps
- The Key to the City

A After passing through the Hall of Heroes (don't forget to collect some codex entries by clicking on the statues), you enter the Orzammar Commons with its many vendors and access ways. The Captain of the Guard informs you that two dwarves are fighting for the crown, Prince Bhelen and Lord Harrowmont. He also tells you that due to all the fighting, they keep themselves secured and have their seconds-in-command handle their business. You get a quest to speak to each of them (either at the Royal Palace for Bhelen or Lord Harrowmont's Estate for Harrowmont).

✦◦⬦── NOTE ──⬦◦✦

You need side with one of the dwarven politicians, either Prince Bhelen or Lord Harrowmont, before adventuring into the Deep Roads on the main quest. It really doesn't matter which politician you choose; they're both corrupt to some degree. However, they offer slightly different quests to reach the "Paragon of Her Kind" quests so select one and stick with him.

Siding with Lord Harrowmont

Harrowmont's Estate

You meet Dulin here, but he won't let you talk to Harrowmont until you've proven yourselves trustworthy. Your first task will be representing Harrowmont in the Proving Grounds, as several of his best fighters have dropped out due to intimidation by Bhelen.

Proving Grounds

One of the fighters who withdrew, Baizyl, is in the waiting pen prior to speaking with the Proving Master. If you can succeed in persuading or intimidating him, he will rejoin the fight. In order to convince him, you must pass a medium Intimidation check. Baizyl will reveal that he is being blackmailed and you must obtain love letters for him from Myaja, one of Bhelen's fighters. If you can retrieve the love letters, Baizyl will agree to fight for Harrowmont again. They are inside a chest in Myaja's quarters, which may be accessed in one of two ways: lockpick the door to Myaja's quarters by passing a medium lockpicking check, or pickpocket Myaja to steal the key to her quarters (requires a rogue). If you can't retrieve the love letters, then you won't get Baizyl's help. The other fighter who withdrew is Gwiddon. Again, you can try to persuade or intimidate him into joining you.

TIP

The Proving Armsman can set up team battles for you with small rewards for winning.

Speak to the Proving Master when you are ready to begin. The first battle is a one-on-one fight against a warrior named Seweryn. In the second round, you have

to fight two warriors, Myaja and Lucjan. In the third round you go back to one versus one against the silent sister Hanashan. In the fourth round you fight against the warrior Wojech and his rogue follower Velanz. Before the fight starts, you get to choose one of your companions to join you in the fight. In the last round, your party battles a full squad. Your opponent is Piotin, his two henchmen, and Piotin's Right Hand. Make it through all that to prove yourself a champion and continue with Harrowmont's quests.

Tapster's Tavern

After winning the tournament, you meet Dulin in the back of Tapster's Tavern. He now takes you back to Harrowmont's Estate to meet with Lord Harrowmont.

Harrowmont's Estate

You finally meet with Lord Harrowmont and he gives you another task. You are to head to Dust Town and infiltrate the house of crime boss Jarvia and take her out. Once you seek Jarvia, your quest line is the same as a Bhelen supporter.

Paragon of Her Kind

Basics ~ Character Generation ~ Classes ~ The Party ~ Companions ~ Supporting Cast ~ Equipment ~ Bestiary ~ **Walkthroughs** ~ Side Quests ~ Random Encounters ~ Achievements/Trophies

Siding with Prince Bhelen

NOTE

This section details Prince Bhelen's quests. If you sided with Harrowmont, see the previous section.

Chamber of the Assembly

You meet with Prince Bhelen's second-in-command, Vartag Govorn. He won't let you meet the prince until you prove you are trustworthy by completing several tasks. He asks you to deliver two notes, one to Lord Helmi and one to Lady Dace.

For your first task, deliver a note to Lady Dace, but she doesn't have the authority to vote. She tells you to find her father, who is on an expedition in the Deep Roads. She gives you a map to the Deep Roads to help you find him.

Tapster's Tavern

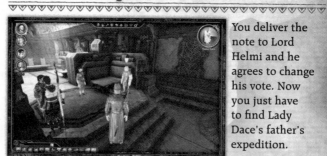

You deliver the note to Lord Helmi and he agrees to change his vote. Now you just have to find Lady Dace's father's expedition.

Deep Roads: Aeducan Thaig

~ See map on next page ~

Runthrough (Aeducan Thaig)

Summary: Find Lord Dace in the darkspawn-infested caverns.

A. Enter the Aeducan Thaig.

B. Ask Lord Dace for his help in the coming dwarven elections.

Aeducan Thaig Cheatsheet

Main Plot Quests
• Paragon of Her Kind

Important NPCs
• Lord Dace

Key Items
• None

Monsters
• Deepstalkers

• Deepstalker Leader
• Genlocks
• Genlock Alpha
• Genlock Emissary
• Hurlocks
• Hurlock Emissary

Side Quests
• Asunder

Diamond Quarter

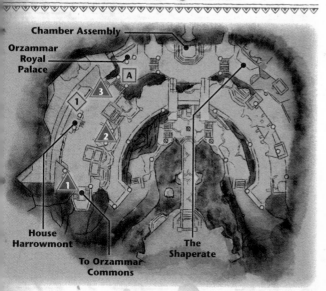

Chamber Assembly

Orzammar Royal Palace

House Harrowmont

To Orzammar Commons

The Shaperate

Legend

① Lady Dace
⚠ Council Writ (codex)
② Weapon Rack
③ Wall Carving (codex)
Ⓐ "Political Attacks"

primagames.com

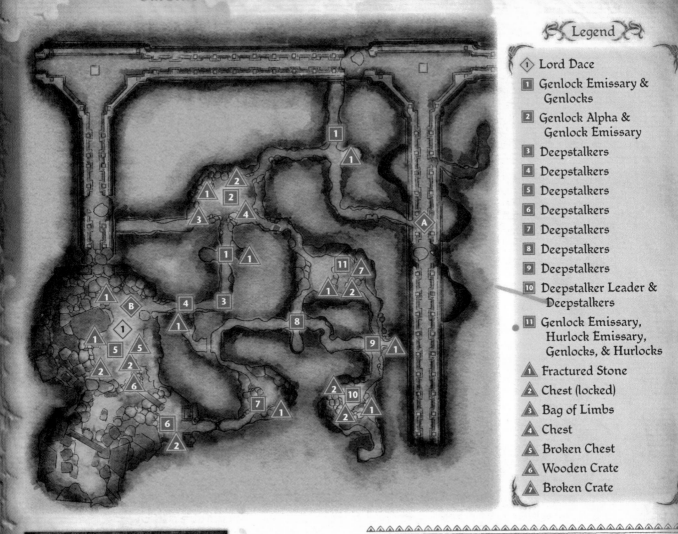

Legend

- ◇1 Lord Dace
- ☐1 Genlock Emissary & Genlocks
- ☐2 Genlock Alpha & Genlock Emissary
- ☐3 Deepstalkers
- ☐4 Deepstalkers
- ☐5 Deepstalkers
- ☐6 Deepstalkers
- ☐7 Deepstalkers
- ☐8 Deepstalkers
- ☐9 Deepstalkers
- ☐10 Deepstalker Leader & Deepstalkers
- ☐11 Genlock Emissary, Hurlock Emissary, Genlocks, & Hurlocks
- △1 Fractured Stone
- △2 Chest (locked)
- △3 Bag of Limbs
- △4 Chest
- △5 Broken Chest
- △6 Wooden Crate
- △7 Broken Crate

Ⓐ Enter in the cavern at the hole in the wall and prepare to battle lots of darkspawn and deepstalkers as you seek out Lord Dace.

Ⓑ Lord Dace and his mercenaries are here, being overrun by deepstalkers. After you kill the first wave of deepstalkers, more pop up (nine plus a deepstalker leader). If you save Lord Dace and show him the papers, he will return to the city and change his vote. You can go with him as well if you want to take a shortcut.

Chamber of the Assembly

You return to Vartag after delivering the notes. Now that you have been proven trustworthy, he takes you to see Prince Bhelen.

Royal Estate

Vartag brings you to meet Prince Bhelen at his estate. The prince has another task for you; he wants you to eliminate the crime boss Jarvia. Once you seek Jarvia, your quest line is the same as a Harrowmont supporter.

Paragon of Her Kind

Basics ~ Character Generation ~ Classes ~ The Party ~ Companions ~ Supporting Cast ~ Equipment ~ Bestiary ~ **Walkthroughs** ~ Side Quests ~ Random Encounters ~ Achievements/Trophies

Dust Town

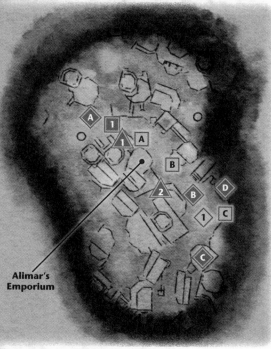

Alimar's
Emporium

Legend

① Nadezda
1 Ruffians
⚠ Rubble (codex)
② Assembly Directive (codex)

Ⓐ Rogek
Ⓑ Shady Corbeit
Ⓒ Zerlinda

Runthrough (Dust Town)

Summary: Search Dust Town for clues on how to enter Jarvia's secret hideout.

A. Enter Dust Town and survive the ambush.

B. Talk to Nadezda for information about Jarvia's hideout.

C. Beat up Jarvia's thugs for the finger bone token.

D. Use the finger bone token on the suspicious door to enter the hideout.

Dust Town Cheatsheet

Main Plot Quests
• Paragon of Her Kind

Important NPCs
• Nadezda
• Rogek
• Zerlinda

Key Items
• Finger Bone Token

Monsters
• Dust Town Thug Leader
• Dust Town Thugs

• Shady Corebit
• Thug Leader
• Thugs

Side Quests
• A Thief in the House of Learning
• Casteless Ambush
• Precious Metals
• The Key to the City
• Zerlinda's Woe

on the suspicious door in Dust Town. You can also gain the Jarvia information from the shady-looking dwarf named Rogek by bribing him with a lot of gold, or from Alimar, who is in Alimar's Emporium.

Ⓒ You enter the Slums Household here and get ambushed by some of Jarvia's men: a ranked thug leader and six thugs. When the leader gets low on health, he will surrender, and you can attempt to intimidate or persuade him into telling you how to get to Jarvia's base. If you don't succeed, he will attack again and when you finish him off, he has the finger bone token on his body.

Ⓐ When you enter Dust Town for the first time, you will be ambushed by some ruffians (part of the "Casteless Ambush" side quest). Dispatch hem and look around for information on the location of arvia's hideout. (If you are a Dwarf Commoner you will un into Leske, who gives you some misinformation before unning off to hide from Jarvia.)

Ⓓ Once you have the finger bone token, you can go to the suspicious door and use the token to unlock the door.

Ⓑ Speak with Nadezda near the fire. After some prompting, she tells you that you need to find a token from one of Jarvia's men and then you can use the token

Dragon Age
ORIGINS
PRIMA Official Game Guide

Carta Hideout

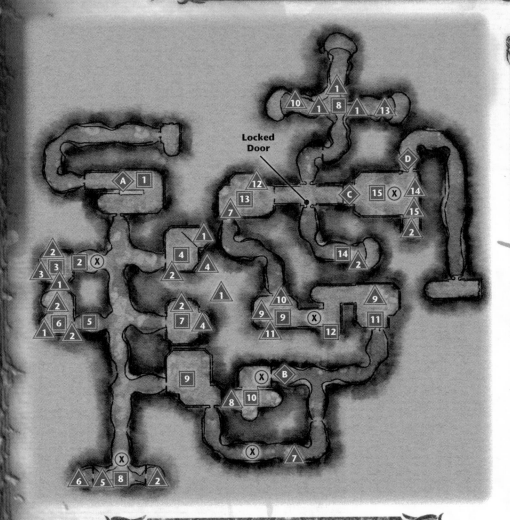

Locked Door

Legend

1. Carta Doorman & Carta Thugs
2. Carta Thugs
3. Carta Thugs
4. Quanari Mercenary & Carta Thugs
5. Carta Thugs
6. Carta Thugs
7. Carta Assassin, Elven Merc, & Quanari Merc
8. Carta Thugs
9. Carta Thugs
10. Carta Assassin, Carta Jailor, & Carta Thugs
11. Carta Assassins
12. Quanari Mercs
13. Carta Assassin, Elven Merc, & Carta Thugs
14. Giant Spiders
15. Jarvia, Carta Assassins, & Carta Thugs

△1. Wooden Crate
△2. Chest (locked)
△3. Jammer's Journal (codex)
△4. Kanky's Common Box (take silver ring only)
△5. Weapon Stand
△6. Armor Stand
△7. Barrels
△8. Dwarf Corpse
△9. Barrels
△10. Crate
△11. Jammer's Common Box (take iron letter opener only)
△12. Pique's Common Box (take garnet trinket only)
△13. Jammer's Stash Box
△14. Chest
△15. Weapon Rack

Ⓧ Trap

Runthrough (Carta Hideout)

Summary: Enter the Carta Hideout to finish off Jarvia.

A. Defeat the carta doorman and his henchmen near the entrance.

B. Free Leske with the key from the jailor.

C. Take down Jarvia in her quarters.

D. Access the secret passage up to Janar's armor shop.

Carta Hideout Cheatsheet

Main Plot Quests
- Paragon of Her Kind

Important NPCs
- Leske

Key Items
- Finger Bone Token

Monsters
- Carta Assassins
- Carta Doorman

- Carta Jailor
- Carta Thugs
- Elven Mercenaries
- Giant Spiders
- Jarvia
- Qunari Mercenaries

Side Quests
- Jammer's Stash

A Shortly after entering the hideout, you run into the ranked carta doorman and four thugs. He asks for the password, which you don't know, so you're forced to fight them. Hit them with a big AoE attack right away if you can, then tank and spank each in turn.

B Retrieve the cell key from the nearby carta jailor and free the prisoner Leske. (If you played through the Dwarf Commoner origin, Leske won't be in the cell. Instead, you'll encounter him shortly as one of Jarvia's right hand assassins.)

C Here you finally find Jarvia. She isn't interested in talking, so you're forced to fight her and her bodyguards: eight carta thugs and three ranked carta assassins. Keep the fight in the doorway leading into the chamber. Any step past the halfway point in the room will trigger any of a series of exploding traps that inflict serious damage. Try to root Jarvia and concentrate on thinning the weaker targets such as the carta thugs or an assassin if you can deal enough damage to knock him out of commission before he disappears again. Don't expose your back to any of them, and keep healing everyone to peak health to avoid Jarvia's sudden and damaging slashes.

D After killing Jarvia, you get a key that opens a door in the northeast corner. The passage behind it leads to a secret exit that comes out in Janar's armor shop. Return to your candidate and he will tell you that a vote for the throne is coming up in a couple of days. To win the Assembly, he wants you to go find the missing paragon, Branka, somewhere in Caridin's Cross.

✦❖✦ NOTE ✦❖✦
While passing through the Commons, the dwarf Oghren joins you in your search for Branka. You now have a berserker warrior in your party.

Caridin's Cross

~ See map on next page ~

Runthrough (Caridin's Cross)
Summary: Search for signs of Branka in Caridin's Cross.
A. Take the shortcut through the caverns.
B. Destroy the genlock camp to continue.
C. Follow the trail to Ortan Thaig.

A There are two main routes through Caridin's Cross. The first turn to the right leads through caverns that are infested with darkspawn. A little farther ahead and to the left is another route with mostly weak deepstalkers, which ends with a genlock camp. This second route is slightly easier, so follow the main road until you reach a cave in, and take the left there.

Caridin's Cross Cheatsheet

Main Plot Quests
• Paragon of Her Kind

Important NPCs
• None

Key Items
• None

Monsters
• Bronto
• Deepstalkers
• Deepstalker Leader
• Elven Mercenary
• Genlocks
• Genlock Emissaries

• Hired Goons
• Hurlocks
• Hurlock Alpha
• Hurlock Emissary
• Ogre
• Ogre Alpha
• Shriek

Side Quests
• Asunder
• The Drifter's Cache
• The Shaper's Life
• Topsider's Honor

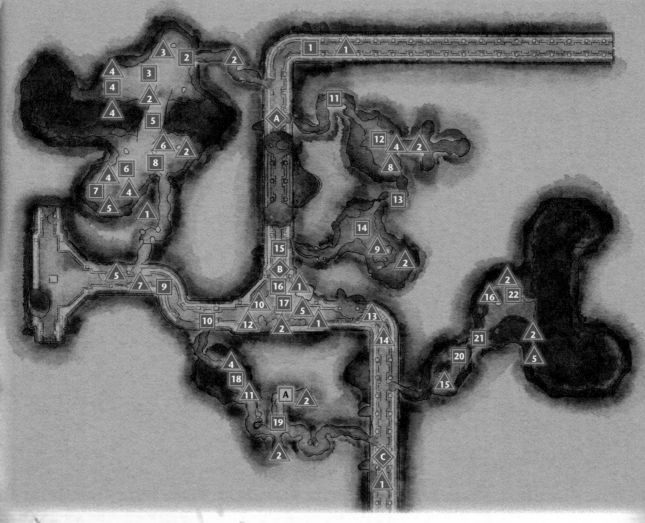

Legend

1. Elven Merc & Hired Goons
2. Genlocks & Hurlocks
3. Hurlocks
4. Hurlock Emissary & Genlocks
5. Hurlock Alpha & Genlocks
6. Genlocks
7. Ogre
8. Shrieks
9. Bronto & Genlocks
10. Genlock Runners
11. Deepstalkers
12. Deepstalkers
13. Deepstalkers
14. Deepstalkers
15. Bronto & Genlocks
16. Genlocks with Ballista
17. Genlock Emissary & Genlocks
18. Genlock Emissary, Hurlocks, & Shrieks
19. Ogre Alpha & Shrieks
20. Genlocks
21. Deepstalkers
22. Deepstalker Matriarch & Deepstalkers

1. Road Marker
2. Fractured Stone
3. Firepit (codex)
4. Chest (locked)
5. Rubble (codex)
6. Rubble
7. Statue (codex)
8. Small Bloody Sack
9. Runestone (codex)
10. Chest
11. Broken Chest
12. Barrel
13. Broken Crate
14. Glass Phylactery
15. Small Bloody Sack
16. Sarcophagus

A. Drifter's Cache

Paragon of Her Kind

Basics ~ Character Generation ~ Classes ~ The Party ~ Companions ~ Supporting Cast ~ Equipment ~ Bestiary ~ **Walkthroughs** ~ Side Quests ~ Random Encounters ~ Achievements/Trophies

B After passing through some caves, you get to a genlock camp. There are two groups of three genlocks on each side, and one genlock with a ballista.

You can pull each group separately, though one genlock may stay behind with the ballista. If this is the case, deal with the others, then just charge in and finish the last one off. Inside the camp is a genlock emissary. Be sure to stun it immediately to avoid nasty AoE damage.

C The clues lead you to the next section of the Deep Roads. Follow the highway here to Ortan Thaig.

Ortan Thaig

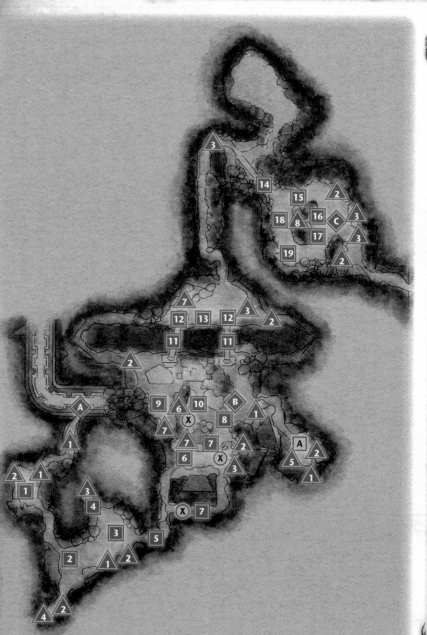

Legend

1. Giants Spiders & Thaig Crawlers
2. Ogre, Poisonous Spider, Thaig Crawler & Giant Spiders
3. Genlock Alpha, Hurlocks, Poisonous Spiders, & Thaig Crawlers
4. Shriek Alpha
5. Giant Poisonous Spiders
6. Forgotten Spirits, Indignant Spirits, & Stone Golem
7. Giants Spiders & Thaig Crawlers
8. Giant Spiders, Poisonous Spiders, & Thaig Crawlers
9. Enraged Spirit, Forgotten Spirits, Indignant Spirits, & Stone Golem
10. Thaig Crawlers & Giant Poisonous Spider
11. Stone Golem
12. Indignant Spirits
13. Enraged Spirit & Forgotten Spirits
14. Corrupted Spiders
15. Genlock Emissary
16. Corrupted Spider Queen & Corrupted Spiders
17. Corrupted Spiders
18. Corrupted Spiders
19. Corrupted Spiders & Genlock Emissary

△1. Darkspawn Corpse
△2. Fractured Stone
△3. Chest (locked)
△4. Warrior's Grave (codex)
△5. Vase
△6. Book (codex)
△7. Broken Chest
△8. Cocoon
Ⓐ "A Mother's Hope"
Ⓧ Trap

primagames.com

Runthrough (Ortan Thaig)

Summary: Search for signs of Branka in Ortan Thaig.

A. Enter Ortan Thaig.

B. Ruck warns you to stay away and then runs off.

C. Battle the corrupted spider queen to gain Branka's journal.

Ortan Thaig Cheatsheet

Main Plot Quests
- Paragon of Her Kind

Important NPCs
- Ruck

Key Items
- None

Monsters
- Corrupted Spiders
- Corrupted Spider Queen
- Enraged Spirits
- Forgotten Spirits
- Genlocks
- Genlock Alphas
- Genlock Emissary
- Giant Poisonous Spiders
- Giant Spiders
- Hurlocks
- Indignant Spirits
- Ogre
- Poisonous Spiders
- Shriek Alpha
- Stone Golems
- Thaig Crawlers

Side Quests
- Asunder
- Topsider's Honor

A Mother's Hope

B A crazy dwarf named Ruck warns you to stay away from his "claim," then runs off. You are then ambushed by some spiders (square 8 on the map). You can find Ruck to the east to complete "A Mother's Hope" side quest, and you can trade with him as well.

C As you approach Branka's journal, a corrupted spider queen appears nearby. The queen is a pretty difficult fight if you just stand and fight where she spawns. Soon after she appears, two corrupted spiders appear to help. During the fight she stays back and spits at random party members. The spit splashes to nearby allies, so you should spread out. Also, as she takes damage (at 75, 50, and 25 percent increments) she will web-wrap the whole team and vanish before returning to her original spawn point.

When you finally manage to kill her, eight more corrupted spiders spawn and can overwhelm you after the difficult boss fight. To make this fight easier, clear out the other side of the large rock in the middle of the room (near square 18 on the map) and send one person to pull her and drag her back to that side. This way you fight her alone, and when she weakens and web-wraps the team, her vanish will take you out of combat and allow you to regen for a few seconds before she returns on her own. Fighting this way allows you to avoid immediately engaging the eight extra corrupted spiders once you kill the queen. You can pull them afterward when you are ready. When the battle is over, you find Branka's journal and read that they left Ortan Thaig to go to the Dead Trenches. Follow the passage to the east to reach the next area.

A Enter Ortan Thaig. You have but one choice: head south through the crumbled wall and navigate the twisting cavern passages.

The Dead Trenches

~ See map on next page ~

Runthrough (The Dead Trenches)

Summary: Catch up to Branka in the Dead Trenches.

A. Help the legionnaires fight off wave after wave of darkspawn.

B. Listen to Hespith's mad ramblings.

C. Search the Legionnaire Altar for a key.

D. Use the legionnaire key on the locked door.

E. Destroy the broodmother.

Paragon of Her Kind

Basics ~ Character Generation ~ Classes ~ The Party ~ Companions ~ Supporting Cast ~ Equipment ~ Bestiary ~ **Walkthroughs** ~ Side Quests ~ Random Encounters ~ Achievements/Trophies

The Dead Trenches Cheatsheet

Main Plot Quests
- Paragon of Her Kind

Important NPCs
- Hespith
- Kardol

Key Items
- Legionnaire Key

Monsters
- Ancient Darkspawn
- Bronto
- Broodmother
- Devouring Skeletons
- Genlocks
- Genlock Alpha
- Genlock Emissary
- Genlock Forge Master
- Hurlock Alpha
- Legion Spirit
- Ogre
- Shrieks

Side Quests
- The Dead Caste
- The Gangue Shade
- The Shaper's Life
- Stalata Negat
- Topsider's Honor

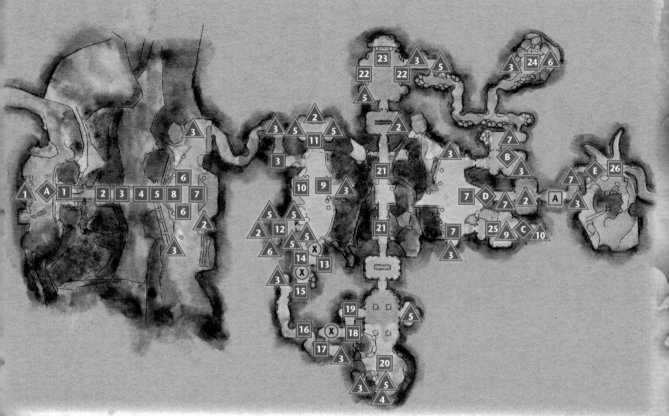

Legend

1 Hurlock Alpha, Genlock Alpha, & Genlocks

2 Genlock Alpha, Genlocks, & Hurlocks

3 Genlocks & Hurlocks

4 Genlocks & Hurlocks

5 Hurlock Alpha & Shrieks

6 Genlocks

7 Ogre

8 Shrieks

9 Hurlocks & Bronto

10 Genlock Emissary & Genlocks

11 Genlocks & Shrieks

12 Corrupted Spiders, Genlock Emissary, Genlocks, & Hurlocks

13 Genlock

14 Genlocks

15 Genlocks

16 Corrupted Spiders, Genlock Emissary, & Hurlocks

17 Ancient Darkspawn

18 Genlocks, Hurlocks, & Shrieks

19 Hurlocks

20 Genlock Forge Master & Hurlock Alpha

21 Shrieks

22 Devouring Skeletons

23 Hurlock Emissary & Devouring Skeletons

24 Corrupted Spiders & Hurlock Emissary

25 Legion Spirits

26 Broodmother

△1 Statue (codex)

△2 Runestone (codex)

△3 Fractured Stone

△4 Broken Chest

△5 Sarcophagus

△6 Chest (locked)

△7 Fleshy Sack

△8 Rubble

△9 Legion of the Dead (codex)

△10 Legionnaire Altar

A Sarcophagus for "The Dead Caste"

X Trap

A You arrive in the Dead Trenches just in time to aid a small band of dwarves against an army of darkspawn. Help Kardol and his legionnaires fight off the swarm of darkspawn as they charge down the stone bridge in wave after wave. Take the brunt of the charges early to shield the damage from Kardol's legionnaires, and let them assist you to keep the numbers on your side for the smaller battles. If you find yourself weakening or running low on mana for healing, drop back and let the legionnaires take a wave so you can recover. Push slowly down the bridge until you clear out the other side and let Kardol's men set up defense there.

Kardol and the Legion of the Dead Army

You meet Kardol in the Deep Roads and help him repel the darkspawn horde. Later on, after you complete the "Paragon of Her Kind" quest line, you run into him in the Noble Quarter in Orzammar and if you're a dwarf (or an extremely persuasive Grey Warden), you can convince the legionnaires to join your army for the final battle against the archdemon.

B Meet a corrupted dwarf named Hespith here. She rambles on about Branka having done something unspeakable and then runs off without giving any clear answers.

C Seek out the Legionnaire Altar. It has another piece of legionnaire armor if you want to work on "The Dead Caste" side quest, and it holds a key. Bring the

key back up to the locked door to the north.

D The legionnaire key opens this locked door so you can proceed.

E Enter the lair of the broodmother. The broodmother stays in the same place the whole fight, so you can use large AoE spells on her. She spits at party members and uses her tentacles, which pop out of the ground and attack. The tentacles deal the most damage, so any party members with weak armor should move away whenever a tentacle appears near them. During the fight, the brood-mother summons extra help periodically (genlocks, hurlocks, and shrieks). Down these enemies quickly or else they can pile up on you, along with the tentacles continuously dealing damage. When the tentacles drop down into the earth, charge the broodmother and deal each companion's maximum damage. You can even get in here and hit her with melee damage.

It's a long fight, but you should beat her if you can withstand her tentacle assault. Exit via the back passage and you have but one more area to overcome: the Anvil of the Void.

NOTE

Make sure to stock up before moving on to the Anvil of the Void, as you're locked into the area once you enter.

Paragon of Her Kind

Basics ~ Character Generation ~ Classes ~ The Party ~ Companions ~ Supporting Cast ~ Equipment ~ Bestiary ~ **Walkthroughs** ~ Side Quests ~ Random Encounters ~ Achievements/Trophies

Anvil of the Void

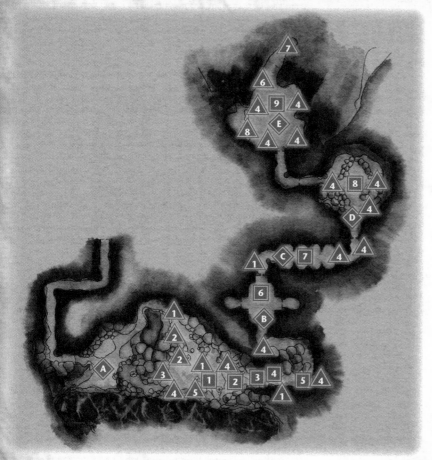

Legend

1. Genlock Alpha, Genlocks, & Hurlocks
2. Genlock Emissary, Genlocks, & Hurlocks
3. Ogre
4. Genlocks
5. Genlocks & Hurlocks
6. Stone Golems
7. Stone Golems
8. Spirit Apparatus
9. Branka or Caridin & Stone Golems
1. Dwarf Corpse
2. Darkspawn Corpse
3. Broken Crate
4. Lyrium Vein
5. Barrel
6. Chest
7. Anvil of the Void
8. Golem Registry

Runthrough (Anvil of the Void)

Summary: Choose to side with Branka or Caridin as the ultimate fate of the Anvil of the Void is decided.

A. Meet Branka.

B. Escape the poison gas trap.

C. Navigate the golem room.

D. Destroy the Spirit Apparatus.

E. Beat Branka or Caridin in the battle for the Anvil of the Void.

Anvil of the Void Cheatsheet

Main Plot Quests
- Paragon of Her Kind

Important NPCs
- Branka
- Caridin

Key Items
- Anvil of the Void

Monsters
- Enraged Spirits

- Forgotten Spirits
- Genlocks
- Genlock Alpha
- Genlock Emissary
- Hurlocks
- Ogre
- Spirit Apparatus
- Stone Golems

Side Quests
- None

A You finally meet Branka and learn that the Anvil of the Void is nearby. Branka locks you in the Anvil of the Void area, so it's time to help Branka get past the traps guarding the anvil. At this point, Oghren must join our party.

B Four stone golems guard this room, which floods with poison gas. When you enter, one of the golems activates and attacks you. To get rid of the poison gas, you need to flip all four gas valve switches. When you fight the golem, go back down the hallway. That way, when the golem dies, the next one won't activate until you approach again and you get a moment to breathe. Kill all four golems to proceed.

C The next room has golems that activate in pairs. You get an initial break: the first pair does not activate. As you approach the next pair, they do activate. Also, beware of blade traps near the activation points. The third pair of statues will also activate, but not until after you pass.

D In the center of this room is a giant Spirit Apparatus that activates when you enter. It summons four forgotten spirits to defend it. When one of the spirits dies, the corresponding Spirit Anvil is activated. Click it to shoot energy back at the Spirit Apparatus. After all four spirits die, four enraged spirits will be summoned. Again, killing a spirit will activate a Spirit Anvil, which you can use to shoot the Spirit Apparatus. Once you shoot it on all four sides, twice, it is destroyed and the door opens to the final chamber.

NOTE

In the battle for the Anvil of the Void, you must choose to side with Branka or Caridin. If you side with Branka, you gain the use of golems in the final battle against the archdemon, though companions with higher morality will take offense and you'll lose their approval. If you side with Caridin, the Anvil of the Void will be destroyed after the battle, but only Oghren will suffer an approval drop.

E You finally reach the Anvil of the Void chamber where you meet Caridin. He is the creator of the anvil and says that it requires souls of the living to create the golems. He wants to destroy it and you must choose to help him or Branka. It's a huge battle royale among your party, many golems, and either Branka or Caridin (who battle each other too). AoE whenever you can, and keep the bosses away from you until you can reduce the head count against you and deal with them singularly. Spells such as Earthquake and Grease will give you necessary breathing room. Ranged DPS should circle the perimeter, out of the reach of the golem attacks, and plink away with continuous damage. Tanks and melee DPS have a difficult time, surrounded by massive bodies and booming attacks. Your healer has to be in top form to keep everyone standing.

TIP

Make use of the many lyrium veins in the chamber, both to keep your healer's mana up, and to keep Branka from using them.

If you defeat Caridin, Branka finally has the Anvil of the Void. She will forge you a Paragon Crown to take back to the Assembly. She also agrees to send golem reinforcements to the Blight battle. If you defeat Branka, Caridin makes the crown for you and then asks that you destroy the anvil forever before he too takes his life by jumping in the lava river coursing below.

A King Is Crowned

With the paragon found, you return to the Chamber of the Assembly to crown the new king. Give the crown to your chosen candidate and the kingdom of Orzammar has a new king. After you select Bhelen or Harrowmont, the other refuses to accept the decision and his men attack. It takes one last battle to bring unity to the dwarves. After the battle the new king thanks you for your help and promises to send a dwarven army to aid with the Blight.

Dwarf Army

If you complete the "Paragon of Her Kind" quest line, the new king pledges a dwarven army for the final battle against the archdemon. The dwarves of Orzammar are battle-hardened infantry troops. They make for strong defensive units, but lack ranged weapons.

Golem Army

If you sided with Branka against Caridin in the fight for the Anvil of the Void, Branka will promise a golem army for the final battle against the archdemon. The golems are extremely powerful in melee combat and have some ranged powers. They are very difficult to bring down.

Paragon of Her Kind - Nature of the Beast

Basics ~ Character Generation ~ Classes ~ The Party ~ Companions ~ Supporting Cast ~ Equipment ~ Bestiary ~ **Walkthroughs** ~ Side Quests ~ Random Encounters ~ Achievements/Trophies

Nature of the Beast

◄► NOTE ◄►

The main quest lines—"Broken Circle" (mage), "Arl of Redcliffe/Urn of Sacred Ashes" (human), "Paragon of Her Kind" (dwarf), and "Nature of the Beast" (elf)—can be completed in any order. If you are a mage and would like the arcane warrior specialization, complete the Dalish elf quest line earlier, probably after "Broken Circle."

Dalish Camp

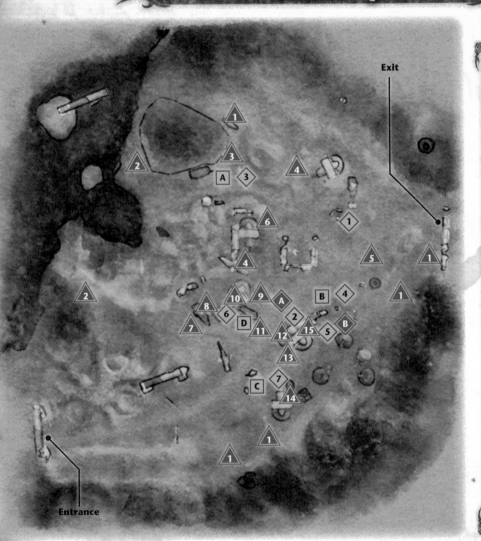

Legend

1. Gheyna
2. Lanaya
3. Elora
4. Cammen
5. Sarel
6. Varathorn
7. Athras

△1. Elfroot
△2. Deathroot
△3. Ghilan'nain (codex)
△4. Chest (locked)
△5. Fen'Harel (codex)
△6. Pile of Sacks
△7. Eldest of the Sun (codex)
△8. Barrel & Chest
△9. Wooden Crate
△10. Pile of Scrolls
△11. Andruil (codex)
△12. Sylaise (codex)
△13. God of the Craft (codex)
△14. Colored Ink (codex)
△15. Chest

A. "Elora's Halla"
B. "Cammen's Lament"
C. "Lost to the Curse"
D. "Rare Ironbark"

Runthrough (Dalish Camp)

Summary: You visit the Dalish camp in the Brecilian Forest to see if the elves will uphold their promise in the treaty with the Grey Wardens. When you arrive, you find that they have been fighting with werewolves and need your help.

A. Accept Zathrian's quest to kill Witherfang.

B. Hear some history on the werewolves from Sarel.

Dalish Camp Cheatsheet

Main Plot Quests
- Nature of the Beast

Important NPCs
- Athras
- Cammen
- Elora
- Gheyna
- Lanaya
- Sarel
- Varathorn
- Zathrian

Key Items
- None

Monsters
- None

Side Quests
- Cammen's Lament
- Elora's Halla
- Lost to the Curse
- Rare Ironbark

A Keeper Zathrian says they have been at war with werewolves, and many of their warriors have been slain or cursed and will die soon without help. He asks you to find the great wolf Witherfang and bring back its heart. Hopefully this will lift the curse.

B If you want a little history and background on the werewolves, visit Sarel and listen to the elven tales. After you've explored all of camp and are ready to head deeper into the forest, leave the campsite via the eastern exit.

West Brecilian Forest

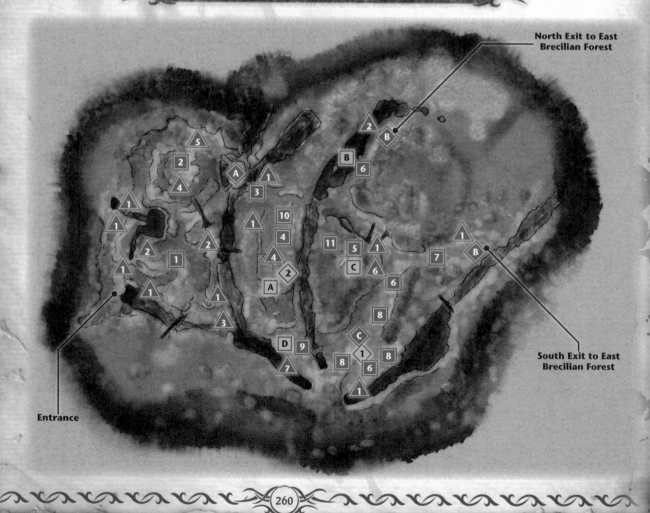

North Exit to East Brecilian Forest

South Exit to East Brecilian Forest

Entrance

Nature of the Beast

Basics ~ Character Generation ~ Classes ~ The Party ~ Companions ~ Supporting Cast ~ Equipment ~ Bestiary ~ **Walkthroughs** ~ Side Quests ~ Random Encounters ~ Achievements/Trophies

Runthrough
(West Brecilian Forest)

Summary: You head into the forest in search of Witherfang.

A. Swiftrunner warns you to turn back.

B. Exit to the East Brecilian Forest.

C. Return acorn to Grand Oak (or slay Grand Oak).

West Brecilian
Forest Cheatsheet

Main Plot Quests
- Nature of the Beast

Important NPCs
- Grand Oak

Key Items
- None

Monsters
- Blight Wolves
- Fanged Skeleton
- Great Bear
- Greater Shade
- Hurlocks
- Ogre
- Rabid Werewolves

- Revenant
- Shade
- Skeleton Archers
- Skeleton Mages
- Swiftrunner
- Werewolves
- Wild Sylvan
- Wolves

Side Quests
- Mage's Treasure
- Rare Ironbark
- Shade Campsite
- Wounded in the Forest

Legend

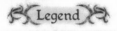

① Grand Oak
② Deygan
1 Wolves, Blighted Wolf, & Werewolves
2 Great Bear
3 Swiftrunner & Werewolves
4 Rabid Werewolves
5 Hurlocks & Ogre
6 Wild Sylvan
7 Werewolves
8 Wild Sylvan
9 Greater Shade
10 Werewolves & Wolves

11 Revenant & Skeletons
Ⓐ Elfroot
Ⓐ Deathroot
Ⓐ Skeleton
Ⓐ Corpse
Ⓐ Andraste's Grace
Ⓐ Rubble
Ⓐ Piles of Bones & Chest
A "Wounded in the Forest"
B Rare Ironbark
C "Mage's Treasure"
D Shade Campsite

A A werewolf named Swiftrunner warns you to turn back and tell the elves you failed your mission. If you refuse, Swiftrunner and his two werewolf bodyguards attack you. Once Swiftrunner is wounded (at half health), he stops the fight and says the forest has "eyes" that will be watching you. The werewolves then run off.

B After encountering Swiftrunner, you can either visit the Grand Oak (to side with it on the quest to disable the barrier) or exit to East Brecilian Forest via one of the two exit points.

NOTE

To pass the magical barrier in the East Brecilian Forest to reach the Brecilian Ruins, you must side with either the Grand Oak or the Mad Hermit and complete your given task. It doesn't matter which one you choose, but it will make you the sworn enemy of the other.

C If you visit the Grand Oak and side with it over the Mad Hermit, the talking tree will ask you to retrieve a stolen acorn (in the possession of the Mad Hermit).

You will find the thief in the East Brecilian Forest. Return here with the acorn and the Grand Oak will give you a branch (magic staff) that allows you to pass through all of the forest safely.

If you decide to side with the Mad Hermit, return to this spot to defeat Grand Oak. DPS it quickly, otherwise it will send up roots through the ground to literally root the party in place and deal moderate damage. If you have access to fire weapons or fire spells, ignite the Grand Oak and its wild sylvan bodyguards with as many fire attacks as possible for maximum damage.

primagames.com

East Brecilian Forest

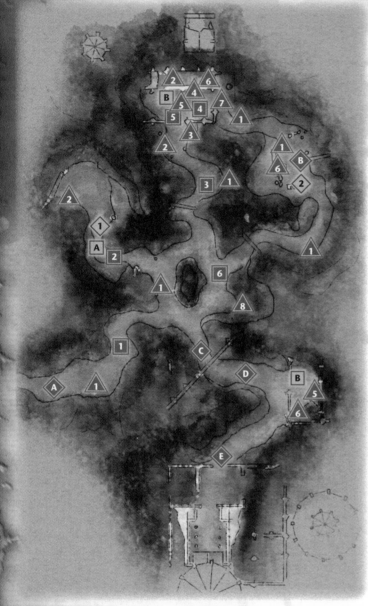

Runthrough (East Brecilian Forest)

Summary: You head into the forest in search of Witherfang.

A. Enter the East Brecilian Forest.

B. Seek out the Mad Hermit (for the Grand Oak's acorn or to side with him).

C. Bypass the magic barrier by completing tasks for either Grand Oak or the Mad Hermit.

D. Swiftrunner attacks again and escapes.

E. Meet the Werewolf Gatekeeper.

East Brecilian Forest Cheatsheet

Main Plot Quests
- Nature of the Beast

Important NPCs
- Danyla
- Mad Hermit

Key Items
- Grand Acorn
- Red Scarf

Monsters
- Black Bear
- Devouring Skeletons
- Fanged Skeleton

- Great Bear
- Greater Rage Demon
- Ogre
- Rabid Werewolves
- Revenant
- Skeleton Archers
- Swiftrunner
- Werewolves
- Wild Sylvan

Side Quests
- Lost to the Curse
- Mage's Treasure

Legend

- ① Danyla
- ② Mad Hermit
- 1 Wild Sylvan
- 2 Werewolves
- 3 Black Bears & Great Bear
- 4 Ogre
- 5 Revenant & Skeletons
- 6 Wild Sylvan
- ⚠ Elfroot
- ② Deathroot
- ③ Rubble
- ④ Rubble & Pile of Bones
- ⑤ Pile of Bones
- ⑥ Chest (locked)
- ⑦ Charred Corpse
- ⑧ Skeleton
- A "Lost to the Curse"
- B "A Mage's Treasure"

A Enter the East Brecilian Forest here. Just to the north, you find Danyla ("Lost to the Curse"), and she has been turned into a werewolf. She wants you to go back to her husband and tell him she is dead. She begs you to finish her off, and if you don't, will attack you to force you to kill her. The red scarf you gain from Danyla can serve as barter item when you speak with the Mad Hermit.

Nature of the Beast

Basics ~ Character Generation ~ Classes ~ The Party ~ Companions ~ Supporting Cast ~ Equipment ~ Bestiary ~ **Walkthroughs** ~ Side Quests ~ Random Encounters ~ Achievements/Trophies

NOTE

To pass the magical barrier in the East Brecilian Forest and reach the Brecilian Ruins, you must side with either the Grand Oak or the Mad Hermit and complete your given task. It doesn't matter which one you choose, but it will make you the sworn enemy of the other.

C Without either the enchanted branch from the Grand Oak or the werewolf disguise from the Mad Hermit, you will be blocked from approaching the werewolf lair in the heart of the forest by a strange mist cloud. Once you have either of these items, you can pass through the barrier freely.

B The Grand Oak tells you that the Mad Hermit has stolen his acorn and he wants it back. You can poke around in the tree stump here and grab the acorn out of it.

The hermit will then attack you. He's a mage, so defend with all your anti-mage abilities, such as templar talents, stuns, constant damage to disrupt his casting, etc.

You can also speak with the hermit and try to barter for the acorn. He will accept any of the following: the pendant you can get for doing Athras's quest, the book that Cammen will reward the player with if he's reunited with Gheyna, the scarf you can obtain from the werewolf Danyla, the boots the player can loot from Deygan, the halla amulet that Varathorn can make with the halla's antlers, the ironbark bracer that Varathorn can make if he obtains some ironbark, or Lanaya's songbook.

If you don't want to trade with him, the Mad Hermit will task you with killing the Grand Oak, who "torments" him. Return to the Grand Oak, slay the elder tree, and head back to the Mad Hermit. He needs a werewolf pelt, which you can obtain by killing a nearby rabid werewolf. He'll then enchant the pelt, allowing you to slip deeper into the forest without notice.

D Swiftrunner is here again and, no matter what you say, he attacks you with three rabid werewolf bodyguards. Focus fire on Swiftrunner, until combat ends and Swiftrunner escapes again.

E You spot the Werewolf Gatekeeper here. He retreats ahead of you to warn the others. It's time to enter the Elven Ruins and descend into the den of the werewolves.

Elven Ruins: Upper Level

~ See map on next page ~

Runthrough
(Elven Ruins: Upper Level)

Summary: Continue your search for the elusive Witherfang.

A. Enter the Elven Ruins.

B. Slay the dragon to access the exit.

C. Speak with Zathrian after meeting the Lady of the Forest in the Lair of the Werewolves.

Elven Ruins:
Top Level Cheatsheet

Main Plot Quests
• Nature of the Beast

Important NPCs
• Zathrian

Key Items
• None

Monsters
• Dragon

• Fanged Skeletons
• Giant Spiders
• Poisonous Spiders
• Shambling Skeletons
• Skeleton Archers
• Werewolves

Side Quests
• None

primagames.com

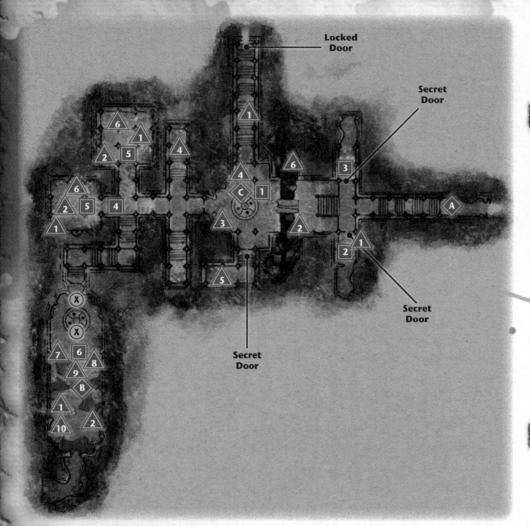

Legend

1. Werewolves
2. Skeletons
3. Skeletons
4. Giant Spider
5. Spiders
6. Dragon
1. Chest (locked)
2. Pile of Bones
3. Pile of Filth
4. Rubble
5. Pile of Bones
6. Cocoon
7. Soldier Corpse
8. Knight Corpse
9. Dwarf Corpse
10. Dragon Hoard
X. Trap

Locked Door

Secret Door

Secret Door

Secret Door

A Enter the Elven Ruins here. Up ahead in the first room lies a secret door. When you open the secret door to the left, another door on the opposite wall behind you also opens. Both doors have a couple undead behind them. You can skip the encounters, but you'll miss out on a locked chest with a love letter in it.

B Tread into this large chamber with extreme caution. Traps line the floor, and they cannot be disarmed. You can sprint across the floor to avoid most of the trap damage; however, a dragon will drop from the ceiling and attack. Alternately, you can have one party member

run out to trigger the dragon, then retreat to the smaller entrance to fight. If you have it, don your fire resistance gear against the dragon's flame breath. A mage's Force Field on the tank (after he's dealt damage and built up threat) or constant healing can keep the dragon focused on your tank while the rest of the team takes potshots. If you prefer space to move around and want to spread out so the companions won't all get hit by the fire breath at once, you must sprint across the trap zone and fight the dragon on the chamber's far side. Don't forget to loot the dragon hoard after combat.

After you meet with the Lady of the Forest and return here

C (through the locked door in the north), Zathrian waits to speak with you about your final intentions. You can convince him to return with you and speak with the Lady.

Nature of the Beast

Basics ~ Character Generation ~ Classes ~ The Party ~ Companions ~ Supporting Cast ~ Equipment ~ Bestiary ~ **Walkthroughs** ~ Side Quests ~ Random Encounters ~ Achievements/Trophies

Elven Ruins: Lower Level

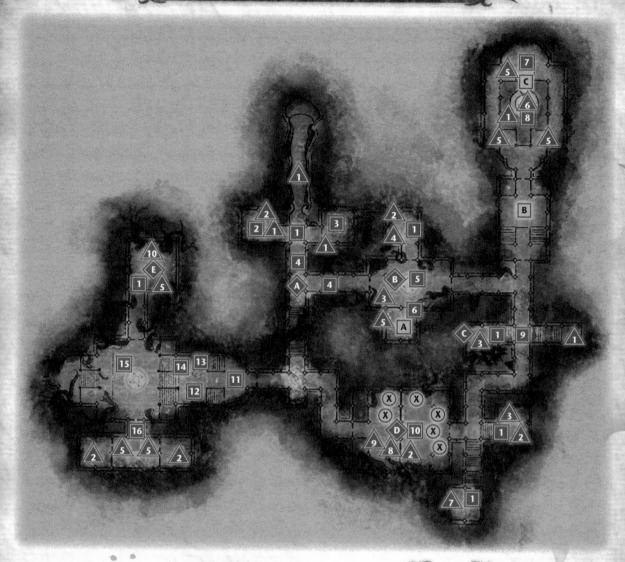

Runthrough
(Elven Ruins: Lower Level)

Summary: Continue your search for the elusive Witherfang.

A. Spider ambush after entering level.

B. Ghost boy and skeleton ambush.

C. Arcane warrior specialization.

D. Skeleton battle and traps.

E. Pool exit leads into the Lair of the Werewolves.

Legend

1	Skeletons		16	Skeletons
2	Skeletons		1	Pile of Bones
3	Skeletons		2	Chest (locked)
4	Poisonous Spider		3	Broken Crate
5	Skeletons		4	Charred Corpse
6	Fanged Skeleton		5	Sarcophagus
7	Skeleton Archers		6	Elven Burial Chamber
8	Shade & Greater Shade		7	Pile of Sacks
9	Skeletons		8	Knight Corpse
10	Skeleton Archers		9	Adventurer's Corpse
11	Skeleton Archer		10	Soldier Corpse
12	Shambling Skeletons		A	"Elven Ritual" Tablet
13	Devouring Skeletons		B	Perform Ritual
14	Skeletons		C	"Elven Ritual" Battle
15	Arcane Horror		X	Trap

Elven Ruins: Lower Level Cheatsheet

Main Plot Quests
- Nature of the Beast

Important NPCs
- None

Key Items
- Arcane Warrior Specialization

Monsters
- Arcane Horror
- Devouring Skeletons
- Fanged Skeletons
- Greater Shade
- Poisonous Spiders
- Shades
- Shambling Skeletons
- Skeletons
- Skeleton Archers

Side Quests
- Elven Ritual

enough to cast an AoE spell, Blizzard or Inferno, or even Fireball if you're lower level, can severely injure the undead and give you much better positioning.

C Find the mage's arcane warrior specialization here. You come across a spirit in a phylactery that is seeking freedom. Examine the phylactery to start a dialogue with the spirit. Touching the gem starts a conversation with the presence inside. Agree to help the presence, and you can "approach the stone altar with the gem."

At this point, the presence offers to share its memories with you. If you accept, this unlocks the arcane warrior specialization for the player's profile. Once you have the specialization, you can either place the artifact on the altar to release it or toss it aside to betray the presence.

A Enter the lower level and be on your toes for a spider ambush in the first intersection. Two packs of poisonous spiders attack from different sides, and as long as you don't get caught in a crossfire of webs that stick you in place and leave you defenseless, your party's combat expertise should cut through the beasts fairly easily.

B A ghost boy here is in a panic, looking for his mother. He won't respond to anything you say and when he vanishes, you are ambushed by undead. Look for a pack of skeletons, a nearby fanged skeleton, and a pack of fanged, devouring, and shambling skeletons. Try not to get surrounded. You can defend in a corner, or pull skeletons out into the nearby corridor. If you can mass stun the skeletons (Mind Blast works great), beat feet out of the chamber far

D Watch out for the traps in this room, and the skeleton archers that pelt you from all sides. To make things easier, pull the skeletons to the previous corridor, and you won't have to worry about the fire traps. When you have time, send a rogue in to disarm the traps and continue.

E At the end of the level, look for a pool that leads into the Lair of the Werewolves. You have one more dungeon level to finish off the main quest.

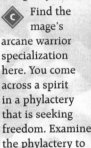

Lair of the Werewolves

~ See map on next page ~

Runthrough (Lair of the Werewolves)

Summary: Choose to ally with Zathrian or the Lady of the Forest and end the werewolf curse.

A. Encounter the Gatekeeper.

B. Speak with the Lady of the Forest.

C. Side with Zathrian or the werewolves and fight.

Lair of the Werewolves Cheatsheet

Main Plot Quests
- Nature of the Beast

Important NPCs
- Zathrian
- Lady of the Forest

Key Items
- None

Monsters
- Gatekeeper
- Rabid Wolves
- Revenant
- Shadow Wolves
- Swiftrunner
- Werewolves
- Witherfang

Side Quests
- The Scrolls of Banastor

Nature of the Beast

Basics ~ Character Generation ~ Classes ~ The Party ~ Companions ~ Supporting Cast ~ Equipment ~ Bestiary ~ **Walkthroughs** ~ Side Quests ~ Random Encounters ~ Achievements/Trophies

Legend

1	Werewolves & Shadow Wolves	**2**	Corpse
2	Werewolves & Shadow Wolves	**3**	Rubble
3	Revenant	**4**	Pile of Filth
4	Gatekeeper & Werewolves	**5**	Chest (locked)
5	Werewolves & Shadow Wolves	**6**	Pile of Junk
6	Witherfang, Swiftrunner, & Werewolves	**7**	Sack
7	Zathrian, Wild Sylvans, & Greater Shades	**8**	Sarcophagus
		9	Glass Phylactery
△1	Corpse	**10**	Scroll of Banastor
		11	Pile of Rags
		12	Treasure Pile
		X	Trap

A The Gatekeeper here tells you the werewolves are ready to parley. He brings you to the "Lady" to discuss things if you want to skip a fight. You can also fight here and then proceed, if you prefer to get the extra experience and loot in this area.

B You meet with the Lady of the Forest and learn that it was Zathrian who originally created the werewolf curse to get revenge against some humans a long time ago. The Lady asks you to seek out Zathrian and bring him back here so she can convince him to end the curse. You can refuse this offer and fight, in which case the Lady turns into Witherfang and you can kill her to retrieve the heart. It's not going to be an easy fight, so break out your crowd control to help reduce the number of werewolves attacking you at once. If you can, stun or root Witherfang to avoid the pounding you'll take if she's left unchecked to attack one of your party members. Focus party fire on the weakest target and work your way through them until you can manage what's left.

If you agree to return with Zathrian, the Lady opens a door to the east that returns you to the upper level of the ruins where Zathrian waits.

C You return with Zathrian and he argues with the Lady. Zathrian refuses to lift the curse and you must choose to side with him and slay Witherfang or help the werewolves and kill Zathrian instead. If you help the werewolves, Zathrian summons three wild sylvans and two greater shades to assist him. Zathrian also puts a Mass Paralysis spell on Witherfang and all the werewolves, so they cannot assist you. Zathrian's first action against you will be a huge Blizzard spell. The entire party should run toward him to escape the AoE radius. Once in tight, you can limit the spells Zathrian casts because of the proximity, and stun him whenever he loads up for big damage or tries to escape.

If you defeat Zathrian, he surrenders before dying and finally agrees to remove the curse, killing him and the Lady. You can then speak with the cured werewolves. If you want, you can demand a reward from the werewolves for curing them (a shield) and then return to camp to speak with Lanaya who will promise the elves' help against the Blight. Or, when first speaking with the Lady, if your Persuade skill is high enough, you gain a new option: "I have another plan. Kill the elves. Kill Zathrian." If you persuaded her successfully, you and werewolves will jump to the Dalish camp and be met by Zathrian. After a conversation, you and werewolves can set upon the elves. After killing the elves, the Lady and Swift-runner promise you that the werewolves will fight alongside you against the Blight.

primagames.com

Elf Army

If you sided with Zathrian or killed Zathrian but spared the Dalish camp, then the elves join the Grey Warden army for the final battle against the archdemon. The Dalish elves are powerful ranged combatants, but will not stand as long as other units in melee combat.

Werewolf Army

If you ambush Zathrian at the Dalish camp with the Lady and the werewolves, then the werewolves join the Grey Warden army for the final battle against the archdemon. The werewolves of the Brecilian Forest are lethal offensive attackers, but are weak defensively.

The Landsmeet

◄—◆—► NOTE ◄—◆—►

You must complete all of the main quest lines—"Broken Circle," "Arl of Redcliffe/Urn of Sacred Ashes," "Paragon of Her Kind," and "Nature of the Beast"—before calling for the Landsmeet. Once you do, you are on the final quest line to battle the archdemon.

Calling for the Landsmeet

After completing all your main quests, go see Arl Eamon in Redcliffe Castle. Speak to him and he'll ask if you're ready to travel to Denerim and begin the Landsmeet. You can still visit the Circle Tower, Redcliffe, Orzammar, and the Brecilian Forest, but you will officially begin the quest chain leading to a new ruler of Ferelden and the final battle against the archdemon.

Arl Eamon takes you to his estate in Denerim. Seek him out on the first floor of the estate. Queen Anora's maid, Erlina, has asked for your assistance. Queen Anora has been taken prisoner in Arl Howe's estate, and it's up to you to free her before she's executed and the blame put on Arl Eamon. When you are ready to begin the "Rescue the Queen" quest, set out for the new city map location in Denerim, the Arl of Denerim's Estate.

On the way to the Arl of Denerim's Estate (or another Denerim city map location, if you choose to visit there first), a "random" encounter will occur. The Antivan Crows have returned for Zevran, which triggers Zevran's "crisis moment." Depending on your approval rating with Zevran, he will either fight with you against the Crows, turn against you and fight with the Crows, or stay neutral and let you slug it out with the Crows. For more details, see Zevran's section in the Companions chapter.

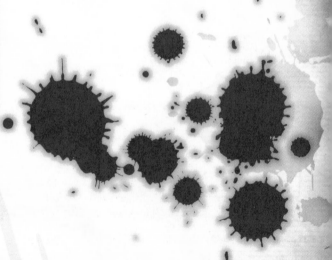

Nature of the Beast - The Landsmeet

Basics ~ Character Generation ~ Classes ~ The Party ~ Companions ~ Supporting Cast ~ Equipment ~ Bestiary ~ **Walkthroughs** ~ Side Quests ~ Random Encounters ~ Achievements/Trophies

Arl of Denerim's Estate: Exterior

Runthrough
(Arl of Denerim's Estate: Exterior)

Summary: Infiltrate the Arl of Denerim's estate.

A. Enter the estate grounds.

B. Meet Erlina at the front doors.

C. Reach the rear entrance.

Arl of Denerim's Estate: Exterior Cheatsheet

Main Plot Quests	Key Items
• Rescue the Queen	• None
Important NPCs	**Monsters**
• Erlina	• Soldiers
	Side Quests
	• None

Legend

◇1	Erlina	△2	Elfroot
☐1	Soldiers	△3	Elfroot
☐2	Soldiers	△4	Deathroot
△1	Elfroot	△5	Sack

A Enter Arl Howe's estate from the courtyard in the south. Make sure you are properly equipped for a long quest; you won't be visiting the Market District any time soon.

B An angry mob riots at the estate's front doors. Erlina meets you here and tells you that you must sneak into the estate through the rear entrance to avoid detection. Wagons block the path to the east. You must go west. Hug the interior wall of the estate (or stealth if a rogue) to avoid the guards. If you played through the City Elf origin, just around the first corner is a pile of rocks where you can hide Vaughan's bribe. If you do alert any guards, slay them and continue to the rear entrance. Even if you engage the exterior guards, you can still slip into the estate without alerting the interior guards.

C Travel to the rear entrance. Erlina tells you she intends to distract the guards. You can follow her suggestion and hide in the bushes, or approach the guards and attack them. If Erlina distracts the guards, you can enter the rear entrance without a fight; otherwise, slay the guards and enter after the battle.

Arl of Denerim's Estate: Interior

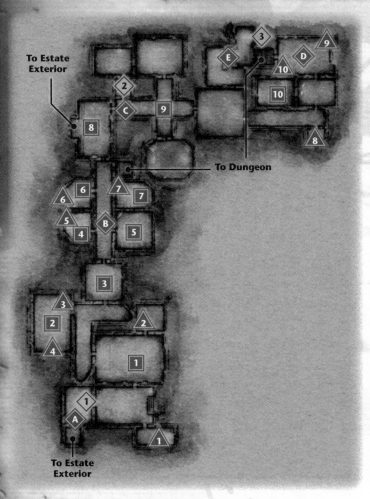

To Estate Exterior

To Dungeon

To Estate Exterior

Runthrough
(Arl of Denerim's Estate: Interior)

Summary: Attempt to rescue Anora and get to the dungeon.

A. Enter the estate and put on the disguise (optional) if you want to avoid combat.

B. A large battle may ensue in this hallway if you don't fool the guards with your disguises.

C. Speak with Queen Anora.

D. Go to Howe's bedroom and find the key to the dungeon.

E. Rescue Riordan.

Arl of Denerim's Estate: Interior Cheatsheet

Main Plot Quests
- Rescue the Queen

Important NPCs
- Erlina
- Queen Anora
- Riordan

Key Items
- Grey Warden Documents

Monsters
- Guards
- Mabari
- Soldiers

Side Quests
- None

Legend

①	Erlina	⑩	Guard
②	Queen Anora	△1	Wooden Crates
③	Riordan	△2	Wooden Crate
1	Soldiers	△3	Armor Stand
2	Soldiers	△4	Weapon Stand
3	Soldiers	△5	Chest (locked)
4	Guard Captain	△6	Chest (locked)
5	Mabari	△7	Chest (locked)
6	Soldiers	△8	Treasure Room
7	Soldiers	△9	Book
8	Guards	△10	Grey Warden Documents
9	Patrolling Guard		

❧ NOTE ❧

If you want to avoid combat inside the estate, put on the disguises Erlina gives you. Without the guards' disguises, you will alert every guard you pass by. You can start with the disguises on and take them off at any time by speaking with Erlina (who follows safely behind you).

A Enter the estate and put on the disguise if you want to avoid lots of combat. If you don't have a disguise on, when you walk into the kitchen, the cooking staff will think you're brigands and call for the guards. The soldiers from the room to the north will pile i and the fight is on.

B This hallway is surrounded by guards. If you have the disguise on, you can slip through here quickly, but watch that you don't interact with the guard captain or he will blow your cover. If you don't have your disguise on, you will alert all the guards when you step in this hallway. Soldiers pour out of the northern rooms, Mabari war dogs attack from your right, and the guard captain attacks from your left. It will be a massive battle. Hit the bulk of the soldiers with heavy AoE damage and retreat to the southern room from which you entered the hallway. Set your tank to hold the door and inflict heavy damage on whatever guard tries to enter. Paralysis and root spells can give you a big edge if you separate guards so that they don't attack all at once.

C Find Queen Anora locked in her cell. You can't let her out yet; a magical barrier seals the door shut. The only way to remove the barrier is to find Howe's mage, who travels alongside Howe. Erlina suggests looking in Howe's bedchambers next, so head down the hall to the east.

D There's not much opposition left as you head to Howe's bedroom. If you investigate the bedroom along the way with the guard (marked square 10 on the map), he will expose your disguises and you lose them. The small room south of Howe's bedroom is a formidable treasure vault. If someone in your party has a high enough lockpick skill, open the door and score big riches (or get the key from Howe later). In Howe's bedroom, pick up the Grey Warden documents. They allow you to access the Grey Warden Cache in the Denerim Market District (the warehouse door in the back alley behind the Gnawed Noble Tavern), which holds some of the best weapons and armor in the game. To unlock the cache, speak with Riordan back at Arl Eamon's estate, then venture into the warehouse's back room for the cache.

E Rescue the captured Grey Warden Riordan. Mention the documents you got from Howe's room and ask him about the Grey Warden Cache when Riordan mentions it. At this point, it's time to head into the dungeon through the door next to Riordan's cell and hunt down Howe.

Arl of Denerim's Estate: Dungeon

~ See map on next page ~

Runthrough
(Arl of Denerim's Estate: Dungeon)

Summary: Kill Arl Howe and his mages to free Queen Anora.

A. Enter the dungeon.
B. Avoid the fire trap.
C. Slay Howe's men and grab the jailor's key.
D. Kill Arl Howe and his men.
E. Deal with the prisoner Vaughan.

Arl of Denerim's Estate: Dungeon Cheatsheet

Main Plot Quests
- Rescue the Queen

Important NPCs
- Rexel
- Soris (City Elf origin only)

Key Items
- Key to Lower Prison
- Howe's Key

Monsters
- Arl Howe
- Howe Guards
- Jailor
- Mabari
- Mages

Side Quests
- Lost Templar
- Missing in Action
- Tortured Noble

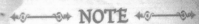

To Main Level

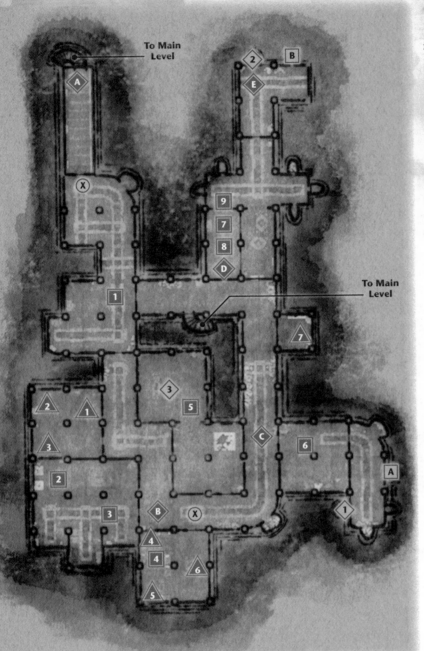

To Main Level

✦ NOTE ✦

The disguise will only help you on the main level. Inside the dungeon it's useless; Howe's men will spot you right away.

A Enter the dungeon through the door near Riordan's cell. At the bottom of the stairs, switch to your rogue and search for traps. You'll find one as soon as you open the door (a tripwire between two exploding barrels). Disarm the trap and then take on Howe's men on the other side of the room. They shoot at you with bows. It's tough going early on for your tank to lock on, but your ranged casters and DPSers will have fun blasting at them from afar. Once Howe's guards are down, continue to head south. There's a locked door on the east wall, but you don't need to access it until after you beat Arl Howe.

B Beware of the fire trap at this spot that engulfs the whole corridor in flames. If you hug the south wall, you can avoid the trap and duck inside the room with the guards and mage. Stun or root the mage so he can't unleash any brutal spells on you, then fight through the Howe guards to slaughter the mage as soon as he's in blade range.

✦ Legend ✦

◇1 Soren	▢6 Howe Guards & Jailor	△A Chest (locked)
◇2 Vaughan	▢7 Arl Howe	△B Chest (locked)
◇3 Oswyn	▢8 Guards	△7 Chest (locked)
▢1 Howe Guards	▢9 Mages	▣A Rexel from "Missing in Action"
▢2 Howe Guards	△1 Barrels	▣B Irminric from "Lost Templar"
▢3 Mabari	△2 Wooden Crate	ⓧ Trap
▢4 Howe Guards & Mage	△3 Pile of Sacks	
▢5 Torturers	△4 Chest (locked)	

The Landsmeet

Basics ~ Character Generation ~ Classes ~ The Party ~ Companions ~ Supporting Cast ~ Equipment ~ Bestiary ~ **Walkthroughs** ~ Side Quests ~ Random Encounters ~ Achievements/Trophies

C Around the corner from the fire trap, several of Howe's guards and the jailor secure a room next to a cell block. Dispatch Howe's men and grab the key from the jailor. Open all the cells and release the prisoners. The first cell holds Rexel from the "Missing in Action" side quest (see the "Denerim" section in the Side Quests chapter). You can free or put him out of his misery to finish off that quest. The second cell holds Soris from the City Elf origin quests, unless the PC took full responsibility for the events in the Arl of Denerim's estate the first time around. If freed, Soris can be found at the PC's home in the Elven Alienage.

D Near the end of the dungeon, Arl Howe and his guards and mages wait in another cellblock area. As soon as you enter, Howe will taunt you in dialogue and then they attack. Your tank should hold the threat on Howe, while the rest of the group takes out the mages first. If you can mass root or stun, do so at the battle's start so you can get into proper position. Whittle away at the enemies one by one until only Howe is left. Pour on the damage and give him the death he so justly deserves.

Don't forget to loot Howe's corpse for some rewards and his key. The key lets you open the first locked door that you passed in the dungeon, which is a shortcut back to the queen's room and opens the treasure vault.

E The northern cell holds Vaughan from the City Elf origin (unless he was killed by the PC). You can choose to kill Vaughan or let him rot, convince him to vote for you in the Landsmeet if you free him, force Vaughan to give you money in exchange for his freedom (the money is in a chest in an upstairs bedroom), or, if you have a high enough Persuade skill, you can convince Vaughan to give the key to his money without releasing him.

Next to Vaughan's cell lies Irminric, who gives you the "Lost Templar" quest (and another potential Landsmeet vote). If you used the disguise, go back through Howe's room to avoid fighting guards in the barracks. If you rescue Anora without killing any unnecessary guards, you gain extra experience points.

The Rescue

Return to Anora and free her. She accompanies you to the estate exit. At the doors, Ser Cauthrien intercepts you, and you can do any of the following:

- Surrender so that Anora can escape. This leads directly to the "Captured!" quest.
- Try to explain that Anora was captured. Unfortunately, Anora betrays you and Cauthrien attacks.
- Choose to attack Ser Cauthrien.

If you surrender or are defeated, the "Captured!" quest begins. If you defeat Ser Cauthrien and her men, you skip the "Captured!" event and gain Ser Cauthrien's Summer Sword. It may be a very good upgrade for any party member who uses a two-handed weapon. Don't feel too bad if you lose; there are more than a dozen tough enemies to battle through.

Fort Drakon

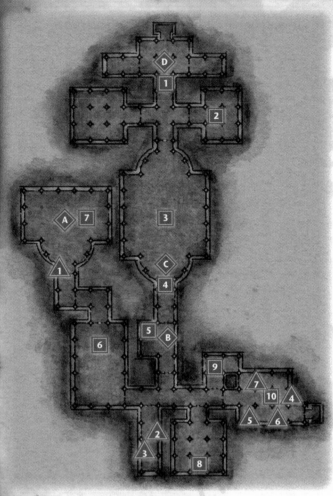

Runthrough (Fort Drakon)

Summary: Escape from Fort Drakon.

A. Escape cell (or companions rescue PC).

B. Fight through Fort Drakon guards.

C. Engage off-duty guards (or companions talk past sergeant).

D. Escape Fort Drakon (or companions talk past guards and captain to enter).

Fort Drakon Cheatsheet

Main Plot Quests	• Colonel
• Captured!	• Guards
Important NPCs	• Mabari
• None	• Off-Duty Guards
Key Items	• Sergeant Tanna
• None	• Soldiers
Monsters	**Side Quests**
• Captain	• None

A If you choose to break out of Fort Drakon yourself, it will be the PC alone or with Alistair if he was also in the party at the time of capture. Several methods can break you out:

- Call the guard over by clicking on him or on the door.
- A player with very high lockpick skill can unlock the cell door.
- A female player with any Persuade score or a male player with very high Persuade can seduce the guard.
- A player with high dexterity can slip past the guard and out of the cell.
- A player with moderate or better strength can knock the guard out.
- A player with moderate Persuade skill can convince the guard to remove his armor.
- The player can also just choose to attack the guard.
- A player with any significant Persuade skill can convince the guard that there are darkspawn nearby.
- The player can pretend to be ill.

Once out of the cell, click on the chest by the door to get your equipment back. If you don't get your equipment now, it will be returned to you when you leave the fort, but why battle guards with such a handicap?

Legend

1	Guards	**10**	Guards
2	Captain	**1**	Your Equipment
3	Off-Duty Guards	**2**	Weapon Stand
4	Sergeant Tanna	**3**	Guard Uniforms
5	Guards	**4**	List of Passwords
6	Guard & Mabari	**5**	Wooden Crates
7	Guard	**6**	Barrel
8	Guard	**7**	Wooden Crates
9	Colonel & Soldiers		

NOTE

You can escape from Fort Drakon two ways: rely on yourself to get free from the cell or let your companions sneak in from the outside. If you break out yourself, progress through the fort from diamonds A to D. If you break in with companions, you will start at diamond D and end up at diamond A before retracing your steps out of the prison.

The Landsmeet

Basics ~ Character Generation ~ Classes ~ The Party ~ Companions ~ Supporting Cast ~ Equipment ~ Bestiary ~ **Walkthroughs** ~ Side Quests ~ Random Encounters ~ Achievements/Trophies

If you enter as companions, you rescue the PC (and Alistair if he was in the party) at this location. From here on out you fight as a party again.

From this point on, the companions entering the fort can no longer bluff and must fight to free the PC. There are only two of you, so take your time and don't pull more enemies than you can handle.

B Attack the guard and his Mabari war dogs in the kennel and then look for a storage room to the right after you leave the kennel. Inside the storage room, look for an armor stand that has guard uniforms. Put on the uniforms to blend in with the guards and avoid unnecessary combat. Remove the uniform by returning to the armor stand or choosing to attack when talking to guards.

Head east to the storage room where two guards are working to clean things up. Slay them, or pickpocket one of them if your Stealing skill is high enough, and loot the password list.

You can also speak with the colonel in his room. Enter in disguise and he will assume you are a new recruit. Pretend to be a guard and attempt the following:

- Talk to the guard (assistant quartermaster) in the armory. Kill him or convince him you are there to relieve him.
- Collect the guards in the storage room. (You need to pass a Persuade or Intimidate check to convince them to come. Otherwise they will attack.)
- Get the regulation swords from the armory.
- A player with the Poison-Making skill can give the guard an acidic coating (giving an acid flask will cause the player to fail.)
- A player with high Intimidation skill can convince the guard to give the swords.
- A player with high Persuade skill can bribe the guard or convince him that going out on patrol might get the storage guards hurt or killed.

If the player has already persuaded the assistant quartermaster to leave, just click on the weapon rack to get the swords.

Report to the colonel for inspection.

Perusade the colonel you are ready for inspection and can follow orders.

If you pass inspection, proceed to the guarded checkpoint (the doors at diamond B on the map) and the guards will let you pass. If you haven't passed inspection, choose the correct password listed on the password list ("Rabbit"). Otherwise, you'll be forced to fight your way out.

C If you have a high Persuade score and the uniform on, you can convince the sergeant that you are off duty. If you've passed inspection, you can walk right by. Otherwise, you must fight your way out.

At the second guard post convince the sergeant to leave her post. You can try this through dialogue, or you can create a distraction. If you talk to the off-duty guards, you can get them to fight each other, or you can start a skirmish with one of the ballistas in the room. When the distraction happens, the sergeant will leave the door and you can enter.

D If you've passed inspection, you can walk out the front door. If you have a fight on your hands, any party member who likes the main PC will show up to help with the battle. Before the fight, if you enter the captain's room and kill him solo, it makes for an easier end battle to escape.

If your PC decides to wait for help, your companions start outside the fort at the front gates (this option occurs only if you have companions with high enough approval that they want to help). Different party members will have different cover stories to enter: Oghren with either Zevran or Sten will pretend they are circus performers; Leliana, Morrigan, and Wynne (any two) will enter as Chantry priests; anyone with Dog will be delivering a war dog; and any other companion combination will be making a delivery of bones for the kennel.

You can bluff the guards at the gate if your Persuade score is high enough. Some characters are better at bluffing than others (Dog is always a good choice). If the bluff succeeds, the guards will fetch the captain. If the bluff fails, you must fight the guards and loot the key from one of the corpses. Next, you must bluff the captain. If the bluff succeeds, the captain will let you into the main hall. If not, kill the captain and take his key.

Back at the Estate

No matter how you finally escape Fort Drakon, return to Arl Eamon in his Denerim estate. You must now discuss with Eamon and Anora how to upset Loghain in the Landsmeet. You must start making choices about who you want on the Ferelden throne. After talking with Eamon, seek out Anora and speak with her. The queen asks for your support for the throne. You can offer your support unconditionally, ask Anora to marry Alistair, or ask her to marry you (if you are a human noble male). Next, you need to talk to Alistair. He never wanted to be king, though he's more willing to consider it if he's been hardened due to the experience with his sister (see Alistair's section in the Companions chapter for his personal quest information). Alistair can be convinced to support Anora unconditionally, you can ask him to marry Anora, you can convince him to take the throne himself, or you can ask him to marry you (if you are a human noble female).

Landsmeet Support

Heading into the Landsmeet vote, you need a lot of support to crown your candidate. Here are the best ways to drum up support, and some actions that will sink your support, as you vie for Ferelden's throne.

Positive Influence:

- Talk to Anora before the Landsmeet! Tell her you'll support her, even if this is a total lie. You gain a very large positive.
- You get a heavy positive if you rescued Oswyn (Bann Sighard's son) from Howe's torturers during the "Rescue the Queen" quest and you select any option mentioning Arl Howe's crimes.
- You get a heavy positive if you rescued Irminric in Howe's dungeon, gave his ring to Alfstanna in the tavern, and then mention Loghain hiring a blood mage to poison Eamon.
- While you're rescuing people from Howe's dungeon, find Vaughan (yes, the jerk from the City Elf origin). Tell him you want his vote in the Landsmeet, and let him out of his cell.

  There's also an assassin quest in the market that gets you one vote in the Landsmeet.

- Once you confront Loghain at the Landsmeet, talk about the Blight. You need to perform a Persuade check, but bringing this subject up will always win over Arl Wulff, guaranteed.
- Alternately, if you have high Persuade, pick the dialogue choice, "I'm not the one who betrayed Ferelden!" in the first dialogue round. You'll get a small positive.

- You get a small positive for bringing up the slave trade in the Alienage.

Negative Influence:

- Never bring up leaving Cailan to die. After the first dialogue round, this is never a Persuade and it is always a small negative.
- Do not talk about Alistair in the first dialogue round. This is a small negative. If you really must bring him up, do it later, and you need high Persuade.
- When you talk to Anora before the Landsmeet, do not tell her that you think Loghain should die for his crimes. Alternately, never talk to her. Either way, she stabs you in the back.
- You get a heavy negative if you rescued Irminric in Howe's dungeon, refused to give his ring to Alfstanna in the tavern, and then mention Loghain allowing Rendon Howe to imprison and torture innocents.
- Mentioning Arl Eamon is always a negative if you didn't give Irminric's ring to Alfstanna (not just if you teased her with it).

The Landsmeet

Basics ~ Character Generation ~ Classes ~ The Party ~ Companions ~ Supporting Cast ~ Equipment ~ Bestiary ~ **Walkthroughs** ~ Side Quests ~ Random Encounters ~ Achievements/Trophies

Elven Alienage

Apartments
Hospice
Alarith's Store
To City Map
D
2
C
3
1
1
A
E
1
1
B
Valendrian's House
Cyrion's House
A
Slaver Compound

Runthrough (Elven Alienage)

Summary: Find proof that implicates Loghain to undermine him at the Landsmeet.

A. Enter the Elven Alienage.

B. Speak with Shianni.

C. Slip into the Tevinter Hospice through the back door.

D. Navigate through the Run-Down Apartments.

Elven Alienage Cheatsheet

Main Plot Quests
- Unrest in the Alienage

Important NPCs
- Shianni

Key Items
- None

Monsters
- Elf Guard
- Healer Saritor
- Healer Veras
- Tevinter Guards
- Tevinter Supervisor

Side Quests
- Fazzil's Request
- Something Wicked

Legend

- ① Shianni
- ▣ Healer Veras, Healer Saritor, & Tevinter Guards
- ▣ Lone Guard
- ③ Tevinter Guards
- ⒜ Barrel
- Ⓐ Ser Otto for "Something Wicked"

A Anora tells you that there is unrest in the Elven Alienage, and she suspects her father is behind it. You can explore around the Alienage a while if you like before finishing off the main quest. If Soris was freed in the "Rescue the Queen" quest, or if the PC took sole responsibility for the events at the Arl of Denerim's estate in the City Elf origin story, Soris is in the PC's home. He has some information about the unrest in the Alienage. Alarith can be found in his store on the periphery of the crowd gathered in the center of the Alienage. He also has some information about the unrest in the Alienage.

Well... there is another entrance in the alley. There's no crowd snatching, no mages, and only one guard.

B In the center of the Alienage, speak with Shianni. She believes the Tevinters are up to no good inside the hospice, even as they claim they are healing the elves and protecting them from a plague. Among the missing are the hahren, Valendrian, and Cyrion (the city elf's father).

primagames.com

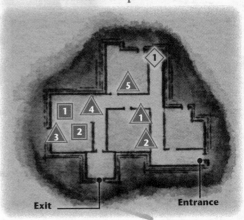

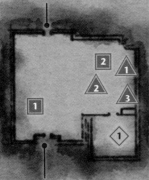

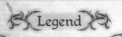

Slip around to the rear entrance of the hospice. A lone guard defends it, and this fight is much easier than trying to go through the front door. If you don't feel like fighting, you can also bribe the guard at the rear entrance. Loot the key from his corpse if you don't bribe your way in.

You can also enter the hospice by pretending to have the plague (elf only). The healers out front will insist that you be taken into the hospice alone. Enter, then resist and fight the healers. Of course, you can always fight through the front door if you want a larger battle to ensue. Loot the key from the healer's corpse to gain entrance through the front door.

~ Tevinter Hospice ~

Front Entrance

Rear Entrance

Enter the hospice and eliminate the guards and supervisor. Loot the room of its valuables, including the note on the table (which also holds a key to unlock the apartments' main door). You can release the imprisoned elves if you like. When you leave, the front door enemies will attack, so be prepared for another big fight out in the streets (civilians even join in!). Once combat is over, return to Shianni and let her know what you've found. She'll direct you to the Run-Down Apartments next.

~ Legend ~

- ① Elven Prisoners
- 1 Guards
- 2 Supervisor
- △ Note & Pile of Coins
- △ Wooden Crate
- △ Chest (locked)

Inside the Run-Down Apartments, turn the corner and speak to the elf at the end of the hallway. He knows what's going on in here, and he will tell you that they march elves through here to the landlord's

office and you never see them again (including Valendrian). Around the next corner, the room to the north holds the sextant that completes the "Fazzil's Request" side quest. The southern room opposite it contains some minor loot.

~ Rundown Apartments ~

Exit   **Entrance**

~ Legend ~

- ① Elf
- 1 Tevinter Guards
- 2 Elf Guard
- △ Wooden Crate
- △ Chest (locked)
- △ Chests (locked)
- △ Pile of Book
- △ Free Sailor Sextant for "Fazzil's Request"

The westernmost room is the landlord's office. You can pick the lock with a high enough lockpicking skill and battle a few Tevinter guards here, plus claim some more loot in locked chests. The last door opens with the key you gained from the hospice. Exit through the back door and prepare for a battle against more Tevinter guards in the hidden alley behind the building.

A half a dozen Tevinter guards secure the hidden alley (accessible only through the back door of the Run-Down Apartments). You can try to talk your way through them, but they won't buy it and the fight is on. Half the guards will charge you and half will sit back and fire arrows at range. Stun or root the near group, or blow away the far group with massive AoE damage, so you don't have to deal with both groups at once. Once you have the guards down and you're healed back up to full, enter the warehouse door into the Slaver Compound.

The Landsmeet

Basics ~ Character Generation ~ Classes ~ The Party ~ Companions ~ Supporting Cast ~ Equipment ~ Bestiary ~ **Walkthroughs** ~ Side Quests ~ Random Encounters ~ Achievements/Trophies

~ Slaver Compound ~

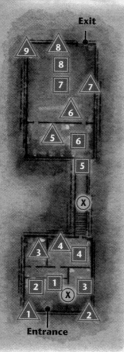

Legend

- 1 Devera
- 2 Tevinter Guards
- 3 Tevinter Guards
- 4 Tevinter Guards
- 5 Tevinter Guards
- 6 Tevinter Guards
- 7 Tevinter Guards
- 8 Caladrius
- 1 Weapon Stand
- 2 Barrel
- 3 Chest
- 4 Wooden Crate
- 5 Chest (locked)
- 6 Vase
- 7 Cabinet
- 8 Chest (locked)
- 9 Wooden Crate
- X Trap

As soon as you enter the compound, Devera and her men challenge you. Devera reveals that the Tevinter Hospice is a front for a slave trade, sanctioned by Loghain. With a high enough Persuade or Intimidate score, you can convince Devera to avoid a fight and take you straight to the slave trade leader, Caladrius. Otherwise, you must defeat Devera and her men. It's a difficult fight. The guards near the entrance will charge and surround you in the tight quarters. Devera will retreat to the side room, behind a line of claw traps on the floor. There she and her fellow archers will drill you with multiple arrow volleys. If your warrior invested in the Weapon and Shield tree, make sure Shield Cover is up. Your ranged mages and DPSers have to shut down the ranged enemies or the continuous stuns from those attacks will cripple you. A Cone of Cold or Fireball followed by Inferno distracts them nicely. The tank, with the help of stuns such as Mind Blast or a bard's Captivating Song, can keep them off the whole party as you dismantle them one by one.

Three more guard groups stand in your way of the final room with Caladrius. Move slowly and take them out one group at a time (watch for the poison trap in front of the second group). When you enter the final room, Caladrius greets you with multiple options to avoid combat.

You can:

- Bribe Caladrius to give you evidence against Loghain and leave. Caladrius takes your bribe, his profits, and all the slaves.
- A player with very high Intimidation can convince Caladrius to leave his profits and the evidence against Loghain. Caladrius leaves with the slaves.
- A player with very high Persuade skill can convince Caladrius to give the evidence for free. Caladrius leaves with his profits and the slaves.

- Otherwise, defeat Caladrius in combat. If defeated, Caladrius surrenders and offers to use the life force of the slaves to boost your constitution. If you accept the offer, all the slaves are killed, you get the profits, evidence, and a stat boost.

After the battle, you can let Caladrius go or continue the battle and kill him. The slaves are freed, you gain the profits and the evidence against Loghain either way. Make sure you loot the slaver documents from Caladrius's corpse should you run him through.

Alienage Aftermath

After gaining the evidence on Loghain from the slavers, head to Valendrian's home to wrap things up and receive a dagger that belonged to Duncan. Alternately, if you are a city elf, head to your father's home to receive a dagger that once belonged to your mother. When you've finished with the Alienage, return to Arl Eamon in his estate and he will leave for the actual Landsmeet.

primagames.com

Once you decide it's time for the Landsmeet, journey to the Royal Palace on the Denerim city map. If you didn't kill Ser Cauthrien, now's your chance for some revenge. She intercepts you as you enter the palace, and she wants to keep you from the Landsmeet assembly. Defeat Ser Cauthrien and her men to enter the Landsmeet and present your case against Loghain, or you can convince her to stand down if your Persuade skill is high enough (you won't get any loot if you persuade her, though).

Who wins the Landsmeet challenge depends on how much support you have drummed up leading up to the event. You can gain favor with the other nobles through dialogue (Queen Anora) or completing side quests ("Lost Templar," for example). If you win the challenge, Loghain rebels and you choose a large battle or a duel versus Loghain. If Loghain wins, you rebel and trigger a battle and then a duel.

The battle will be your party and allies versus Loghain's supporters. It's a massive battle. Stay near the outskirts early on and pick off enemy targets; avoid getting caught in the middle and surrounded. Use AoE as much as you can to hit large enemy pockets, and not strike your allies. Eventually, Loghain will come for you. Try to stun or root him and deal with his entourage first. When Loghain falls the battle ends, but he is not going to drop quickly.

When you all but knock Loghain out, the nobles call a halt to the battle and a duel of honor is announced. Any one of your party can fight Loghain one on one. Generally, your PC will be the best choice, but if you want one of the others, the option is there. Use your best tricks of the trade to defeat Loghain a second time.

After you defeat Loghain in the duel, you have a choice: kill him or force him to undergo the Joining and become a Grey Warden. If you let Loghain live, Alistair will disown you and leave the group. However, Anora will be pleased. Loghain will then join you as a warrior companion (see the Companions chapter for details). If you kill Loghain, Alistair will be pleased; Anora will not.

Who ends up on the throne depends on many factors. Is Loghain alive? Who killed Loghain? Was Alistair changed by his experience with his sister? Is your PC male or female? Here are the various scenarios:

- **Alistair rules alone:** Easiest to do if Alistair has been changed and Loghain has been killed.

- **Alistair rules with Anora:** This will take some convincing, particularly if Alistair is in a relationship with you. Keeping the relationship after the betrothal is even harder. If Loghain lives, Alistair will only get the throne if he is changed. Otherwise, he will try to kill Loghain or leave. Anora won't marry Alistair, however, if Alistair killed or executed Loghain; you will have to do it in that case. Anora will not marry her father's murderer.

- **If Alistair is changed:** If Alistair has a hostile approval rating, Alistair will not marry you, but will rule alone. If Alistair is neutral or interested in you, he will require a very high Persuade check to rule with you. If Alistair is warm or cares about you, he will require a medium Persuade check, depending on the tactic you take. If Alistair is friendly or in love with you, he will require a low Persuade check.

- **If Alistair is not changed:** If Alistair has a hostile approval rating, Alistair will not marry you, but will rule alone. If Alistair is neutral or interested in you, he will require a very high Persuade check to rule with you. If Alistair is warm or cares about you, he will require a high Persuade check, depending on the tactic you take. If Alistair is friendly or in love with you, he will require a medium Persuade check.

- **Alistair rules with a human noble female PC:** Easiest to do if Alistair has been changed and is in a relationship with you. If you let Loghain live, Alistair will not marry you—and he will leave the party. If Alistair is changed and killed Loghain, and not in an active romance with a human noble female player, and not willing to marry Anora (you convinced him to marry her and she didn't betray you at the Landsmeet), then Alistair will assume the throne and the subject of marriage will never come up.

- **Anora rules alone:** Not that difficult; Alistair doesn't want the kingship. Loghain may or may not be dead.

- **Anora rules with human noble male PC:** Only if you let Loghain live, or Alistair kills or executes Loghain. Anora will not marry her father's murderer.

The complicated political weavings will all become clear by the finish of the Landsmeet. Alistair or Anora will be on the throne, and Arl Eamon will return to Redcliffe for the final preparations against the full strength of the Blight. When you are ready to hunt down the archdemon, your next step leads Redcliffe once again.

The Landsmeet ~ The Final Onslaught

Basics ~ Character Generation ~ Classes ~ The Party ~ Companions ~ Supporting Cast ~ Equipment ~ Bestiary ~ **Walkthroughs** ~ Side Quests ~ Random Encounters ~ Achievements/Trophies

The Final Onslaught

── NOTE ──

You must complete the Landsmeet before continuing to the last quest:
"The Final Onslaught." It's your party versus the archdemon to the death.

Redcliffe Village (Destroyed)

Runthrough
(Redcliffe Village: Destroyed)

Summary: Head off the darkspawn horde that has invaded Redcliffe.

A. Speak with the Redcliffe survivor and fight the nearby darkspawn.

B. Rescue the village from rampaging darkspawn.

C. Exit to Redcliffe Castle.

Redcliffe Village:
Destroyed Cheatsheet

Main Plot Quests	Monsters
• The Final Onslaught	• Hurlock Alpha
Important NPCs	• Hurlock Emissary
• Redcliffe Survivor	• Hurlocks
Key Items	• Ogres
• None	**Side Quests**
	• None

── NOTE ──

Throughout the course of "The Final Onslaught" leading up to the fight with the archdemon, you will be swarmed with the throng of the darkspawn invasion. Get used to fighting lots and lots of enemies at once. The good news is that they are generally weaker than your average foe and, individually, will go down quickly.

── Legend ──

1. Redcliffe Survivor
1. Hurlocks & Hurlock Emissary
2. Hurlocks & Blight Wolves
3. Hurlocks & Hurlock Alpha
4. Ogres & Hurlocks

A After entering Redcliffe, meet the Redcliffe survivor on the far side of the bridge. He tells you that the village and castle have been besieged by the darkspawn horde. Ultimately, you must journey to Redcliffe

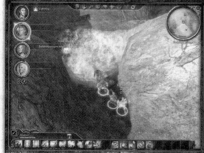

Castle via the nearby exit point; however, as soon as the survivor leaves, you enter combat against the hurlocks, blight wolves, and the hurlock emissary to the south down the hill. After you defeat them, you can enter the Redcliffe Castle exit point.

primagames.com

B It's optional to continue down to the village and wipe out the darkspawn, but hey, if you saved the town from walking corpses before, how can you leave it to darkspawn now? If you continue down, a group of hurlocks led by a hurlock alpha guards the lower bridge near the waterfall. Down in the town square, two ogres and a bunch of hurlocks cause havoc. Lay down AoE as soon as you spot the enemy, then sweep in and clean up the half-dead stragglers.

C Take the exit to Redcliffe Castle. It's also under attack, so be ready to enter battle as soon as you get on the other side.

Redcliffe Castle Courtyard

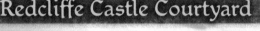

Runthrough (Redcliffe Castle Courtyard)

Summary: Defeat the darkspawn horde on the steps of Redcliffe Castle.

A. Battle the darkspawn in the courtyard.

B. Slay the ogre alpha to enter the castle.

Redcliffe Castle Courtyard Cheatsheet

Main Plot Quests
- The Final Onslaught

Important NPCs
- Redcliffe Soldiers

Key Items
- None

Monsters
- Hurlock Alpha
- Hurlock Emissary
- Hurlock Grunts
- Ogre Alpha

Side Quests
- None

Legend

1 Hurlock Grunts
2 Hurlock Emissary
3 Hurlock Grunts
4 Hurlock Grunts
5 Hurlock Emissary
6 Hurlock Grunts
7 Hurlock Alpha
8 Ogre Alpha (after other darkspawn die)

The Final Onslaught

Basics ~ Character Generation ~ Classes ~ The Party ~ Companions ~ Supporting Cast ~ Equipment ~ Bestiary ~ **Walkthroughs** ~ Side Quests ~ Random Encounters ~ Achievements/Trophies

A When you enter the courtyard, darkspawn have assaulted the castle steps. Dozens of hurlock grunts jam the courtyard, with a hurlock emissary flanked on either side. A hurlock alpha guides a group of hurlocks fighting the Redcliffe soldiers on the main steps. From your starting position, rain down whatever AoE damage you have into the center of the enemy mass. Don't charge in; draw darkspawn to you and eliminate them in small groups. As soon as you can get close enough to target the hurlock emissaries, concentrate all damage on them to avoid the magic counterattack. Methodically inch down the courtyard and up the stairs till you meet the Redcliffe soldiers. Waves of new hurlocks appear until you defeat the two hurlock emissaries and the hurlock alpha.

B As soon as the last of the hurlocks fall, an ogre alpha appears back near the portcullis. Attempt to root it quickly or else it will charge and smash through anyone in its way with an AoE sweep attack. The tank should get the ogre's attention and hold the threat as long as possible. The healer should throw constant heal spells to keep the tank's health nearly full. If the ogre alpha grabs and throttles the tank (or anyone else, for that matter), the victim's health total will drop in huge chunks. You must either out-heal the damage or stun the ogre to make it let go. With enough damage, the ogre alpha will slump. Speak with the Redcliffe soldiers and they'll let you in the castle proper.

CAUTION

At this point all previous game plots become locked. You will not be able to travel on the world map once you enter the castle.

Redcliffe Battle Plans

Inside Redcliffe Castle, Riordan and Arl Eamon fill you in on what's happened. The darkspawn invasion, led by the archdemon, is on the move to wipe out Denerim. You have to stop it. In the morning you leave for the city, but first Riordan wants to speak to you in private. Go up to Riordan's room on the second floor and speak with Riordan again. He tells you that for the archdemon to die, one of the Grey Wardens must sacrifice himself with the killing blow, or the archdemon will survive. It looks like you're not all going to make it through the final battle.

TIP

Bodahn and Sandal follow you to Castle Redcliffe. Seek them out on the first floor if you have any vendor needs.

Morrigan's Ritual

However, there is a way to avoid one of the Grey Wardens dying. Morrigan waits for you back in your room. She offers you an alternative to sacrificing yourself when you kill the archdemon. She asks you to lie with her and conceive a child; when the archdemon is slain, its spirit will travel into the child, destroying the archdemon, and creating a child with the soul of an Old God.

NOTE

The ritual involves sleeping with Morrigan to impregnate her; therefore, this route is available only for male players.

If you agree and sleep with Morrigan, you will not die at the end of the climax when the archdemon perishes. If you are female, or if you are male and refuse to conduct the ritual with Morrigan, she will present another option: She will perform the ritual with another Grey Warden (either Alistair or Loghain, depending on which one is with you after the Landsmeet). If you agree to this, you must talk to Alistair or Loghain and convince them to have the ritual with Morrigan. No one will die at the end of the climax.

Should you decide not to agree to the ritual at all, Morrigan will not offer again, she will not be available for the final battle, and she will leave the party forever.

City Gates

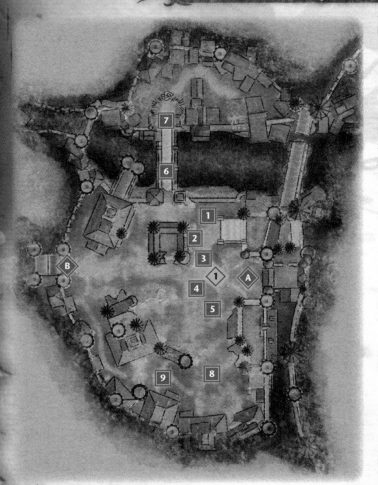

Runthrough (City Gates)

Summary: Breach the darkspawn army and gain a foothold inside the city walls.

A. Enter the City Gates area and battle the darkspawn.

B. After speaking with Riordan, exit the City Gates.

City Gates Cheatsheet

Main Plot Quests
- The Final Onslaught

Important NPCs
- All Your Companions
- Riordan

Key Items
- None

Monsters
- Genlocks
- Genlock Alphas
- Hurlocks

Side Quests
- None

Legend

① Riordan		⑤ Genlocks	
1 Genlocks		6 Genlocks	
2 Genlock Alpha		7 Hurlocks	
3 Genlocks & Hurlocks		8 Genlocks & Hurlocks	
4 Genlock Alpha		9 Genlocks & Hurlocks	

NOTE

You control only your PC in the City Gates. The rest of your companions join you in the battle, but as allies not under your direct control.

A. In this race against the darkspawn destruction of Denerim you want to take it slowly. You control only your PC here; your companions will join you as allies, but you can't control their actions, so there is no guarantee that they will always aid you in every skirmish. Other allies, such as Riordan and Denerim soldiers, will fight with you as well. Pick battles wisely, and, of course, come to aid of any companion you see in trouble. You have two genlock alpha enemies and a whole mess of genlocks and hurlocks to wade through to reach the exit point on the far side.

B. Clear out the entire area of darkspawn. After you defeat all the darkspawn, you can speak with Riordan and he will gather everyone and expla[in] his plan. Riordan hopes to track the archdemon and attract it to Fort Drakon where it can be cornered and slain. Yo[ur] task will be to move through the city toward Fort Drakon and reach its roof where the archdemon awaits. Riordan also warn[s] that two of the archdemon's generals are in the city. Before reaching the fort, you should slay these generals or else they will aid the archdemon in the final battle (and the archdemon doesn't need any more help!). You also choose one of your companions to lead a task force to defend the City Gates after you leave (composed of your remaining non-party companion[s]

NOTE

When leaving the City Gates, you can choose to go to either t[he] Market District or the Elven Alienage. The order does not mat[ter]

Denerim Market District (Destroyed)

Runthrough (Denerim Market District: Destroyed)

Summary: Slay darkspawn and eliminate the archdemon's general.

A. Enter the Market District.

B. Battle through the ogres and genlock emissaries.

C. Slay the hurlock general before exiting.

Denerim Market District: Destroyed Cheatsheet

Main Plot Quests
- The Final Onslaught

Important NPCs
- Ancient Treaties' Armies

Key Items
- None

Monsters
- Genlock Emissaries
- Hurlock General
- Ogres
- Hurlocks

Side Quests
- None

Player Army Tips

After you leave the City Gates, you have access to the armies you gathered by completing the Ancient Treaties quests. Deploy them as needed, but remember that only a single army can be active in one area. Once an army has been defeated in an area, you can deploy another army. An army does not replenish its lost soldiers. Here's what you have to aid you:

- You will always have the Redcliffe soldiers available. The Redcliffe soldiers are average melee combatants.

- Depending on the outcome of the "Nature of the Beast" quest, you have elves or werewolves on your side. Elves are good archers and deal excellent damage at range. Werewolves are brutal melee combatants, but lack defense.

- You have templars or mages fighting with you, depending on the outcome of the "Broken Circle" quest. Mages have a devastating ranged damage output but can die quickly if attacked in melee. Templars are tough all-around: good defenders, good melee, and minimal ranged weapons ability.

- You always have the dwarves as an army, but if the player convinced Kardol (leader of the Legion of the Dead) to help, then occasionally a legionnaire will spawn along with the normal dwarves armies. The regular dwarves are melee defenders. The Legion of the Dead soldiers are elite combatants: they are very good defenders and are capable of unleashing great amounts of damage.

- If you sided with Branka in the "Paragon of Her Kind" quest then you will have a small contingent of golems at your disposal. Golems are the most powerful combatants available. They can withstand huge amounts of damage and inflict even more, including ranged attacks (throwing rocks).

Legend

1	Genlock Emissaries	**5**	Ogre
2	Ogre	**6**	Hurlock General
3	Ogre	**7**	Ogres
4	Ogres	**A**	Rubble

A Enter the destroyed Market District through the back (opposite the way you would normally enter). Around the first corner wait several ogres and two genlock emissaries. Summon your army troops if you want assistance in the coming battle.

TIP

Deploy an army of dwarves, golems, Redcliffe soldiers, or werewolves in the Denerim Market District if you want assistance.

B Hit the ogres out in the open with long-range AoE attacks. Stand your ground and pull them to you, unleashing either heavy damage through single-target abilities or stun/root abilities to hold them in place. By the time they reach you, each ogre should be knocked down by half or completely eliminated. More ogres and the hurlock emissaries join the battle. Nullify the emissaries as quickly as you can with templar abilities, Mana Drain, stuns, etc. If you keep your healer back near the entrance and heal appropriately, it will be a difficult fight, but you'll come out on top.

C To reach the exit point, you must first defeat the hurlock general and its ogre bodyguards. When you spot them, hit the nearest target with AoE or a big damage spell. Draw the ogres toward you while rooting the general if you can. The ogres are ranked normal, so take the initial ogres down first before concentrating efforts on the general. More ogres spawn as the battle continues. Bring down the general before too many reinforcements wear you down. You definitely want the general dead so it doesn't join the archdemon later in the battle.

Elven Alienage (Destroyed)

Runthrough (Elven Alienage: Destroyed)

Summary: Slay darkspawn and eliminate the archdemon's general.

A. Enter the Elven Alienage.

B. Talk to the elven survivors.

C. Slay the invading darkspawn at the gates to the Elven Alienage.

Elven Alienage Cheatsheet

Main Plot Quests
- The Final Onslaught

Important NPCs
- Ancient Treaties' Armies

Key Items
- None

Monsters
- Genlock Alpha
- Hurlock General
- Hurlock Grunts
- Ogres

Side Quests
- None

Legend

- ① Shianni
- 1 Hurlock Grunts
- 2 Ogre
- 3 Genlock Alpha
- 4 Hurlock Grunts
- 5 Hurlock Grunts
- 6 Hurlock General
- 7 Hurlock Alpha & Hurlocks

The Final Onslaught

Basics ~ Character Generation ~ Classes ~ The Party ~ Companions ~ Supporting Cast ~ Equipment ~ Bestiary ~ **Walkthroughs** ~ Side Quests ~ Random Encounters ~ Achievements/Trophies

A You enter the Alienage on the northern side. The darkspawn haven't invaded yet, so all is quiet throughout most of the Alienage.

C Use the gate as a choke point to prevent too many darkspawn from swarming you at once. First slay the rampaging ogre that breaks down the gate. Let your allied army handle most of the grunts and seek out the hurlock general in the back. Concentrate your heavy damage and special talents on him just as you did with the hurlock general battle at the Denerim Market. After some prolonged fighting, the general will fall and you just need to clean up the remaining darkspawn to finish off the area. Speak with Shianni back near the Alienage Tree and she gives you the Dawn Ring (+4 strength, -1 cunning) as a reward for saving the Alienage.

TIP

Deploy an army of dwarves, golems, Redcliffe soldiers, or werewolves in the Elven Alienage if you want assistance.

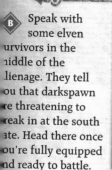

B Speak with some elven survivors in the middle of the Alienage. They tell you that darkspawn are threatening to break in at the south gate. Head there once you're fully equipped and ready to battle. Summon your army troops to assist you at the south gate battle.

Hold the Gates

During your travel to the Palace District, the story shifts back into the City Gates where your secondary party was left to defend the area. You take control of this party and have to defend the area against a force of darkspawn who are trying to retake the area from outside the city. Once the fight is over, a messenger appears. Talk to the messenger to switch control back to your main party.

Palace District

~ See map on next page ~

Runthrough (Palace District)

Summary: Cross the Palace District to reach Fort Drakon.

A. Enter the Palace District.

B. Battle darkspawn on the tiers.

C. Fight through to the Fort Drakon entrance.

Palace District Cheatsheet

Main Plot Quests
- The Final Onslaught

Important NPCs
- Ancient Treaties' Armies

Key Items
- None

Monsters
- Genlock Alphas
- Genlock Emissary
- Genlocks
- Hurlock Grunts
- Ogres
- Shrieks

Side Quests
- None

primagames.com

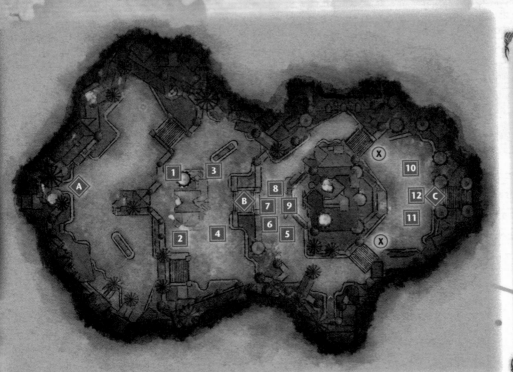

A Back at the Palace District, Riordan ambushes the archdemon by jumping on its back off one of the high towers. He manages to cut a deep wound into one of the archdemon's wings and forces it to land on the roof of Fort Drakon. Riordan, however, loses his grip and falls to his death. You are down to two Grey Wardens. Enter the Palace District and begin to ascend its tiers.

TIP

Deploy an army of dwarves, golems, Redcliffe soldiers, or werewolves in the Palace District if you want assistance.

B Darkspawn archers guard the first tier. Pick them off at range so you can mount the first set of stairs safely. Head to the north stairs or the south stairs; it really doesn't matter because the

darkspawn shift positions and pile after you anyway. The second tier stairs are a choke point, with the main darkspaw force sitting at the top. You have to go through them. Either summon your army to help take the stairs, or toss lots of ranged AoE attacks at the top of those stairs first to soften up the targets. Then move in and finish off whatever is still standing.

C The final tier hosts two hurlock emissaries surrounded by hurlocks and shrieks. Each staircase leading up to the tier has a tripwire at the top that triggers a poison trap to slow your movement. If you have army help, let them take the brunt of the melee, while you aim ranged damage on the emissaries. If you can root or stun the emissaries and prevent them from counterattacking with Fireballs and the like, the battle will go much smoother When you wipe out all the darkspawn, you can enter Fort Drakon for the final climb up to the archdemon.

Fort Drakon

~ Exterior ~

Runthrough (Fork Drakon)

Summary: Climb to the Fort Drakon roof to destroy the archdemon once and for all.

A. Enter Fort Drakon.

B. Battle darkspawn to reach the first floor.

C. Enter the main floor.

D. Survive the ambush by the genlock conjurer.

E. Find Sandal by the stairs to the second floor.

Fort Drakon Cheatsheet

Main Plot Quests
- The Final Onslaught

Important NPCs
- Ancient Treaties' Armies

Key Items
- None

Monsters
- Archdemon
- Dragon Thralls
- Genlock Alphas
- Hurlock Emissaries
- Hurlock Grunts

Side Quests
- None

Legend

1 Hurlock Grunts	**5** Hurlock Emissaries & Genlock Alpha
2 Hurlock Grunts	**6** Genlock Alpha & Hurlocks
3 Hurlock Grunts	
4 Dragon Thrall	

TIP

Deploy an army of elves or mages in the Fort Drakon exterior if you want assistance.

A As soon as you enter the Fort Drakon exterior, you get ambushed. Two hurlock groups on your right and one on your left catch you in a crossfire of arrows. At the same time, a dragon thrall lands in front the second right group. Hit all three hurlock groups with E damage immediately. The faster you kill them, the better ance you have of getting out of the shooting gallery alive. Try root the dragon thrall to deal with in a minute. If you don't ve a full arsenal, pull out your own bows and fire back until e hurlocks are dead and let the tank hold the dragon thrall th healing backup. A second dragon thrall arrives soon, so ximize damage as best you can.

B The second wave of enemies stands on the stairs leading up to the first floor doors. Alphas and emissaries can rain down lots of damage on you from long distance. If you have access to either the elf army or the mage army, summon them after you clear out the initial enemies. The ranged firepower of the extra army will out-match the genlocks and hurlocks on the stairs. If you rely on your own party, stay at range and hit them with disruptive AoE spells, such as Fireball or Earthquake. You can't cover the ground to them quickly enough unless you have serious missile defense. Stand your ground and let the damage fly. Once all enemies are dead you can open the first floor doors.

~ Main Floor ~

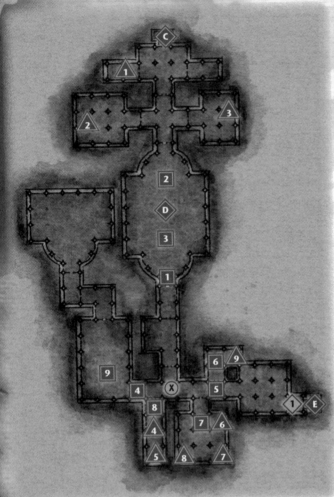

C Enter Fort Drakon and take a look around. You can claim some minor loot in the first few rooms.

D When you cross the middle of the central chamber, a genlock conjurer summons in a greater shade and lesser shades to surround you. A few seconds later the conjurer enters from the door to the south to try to surprise you. Root or continuously stun the greater shade and concentrate ranged fire on the conjurer to take him out before he can do more damage. One by one pick off the lesser shades then finish off the greater shade last.

E Through the door and down the hall you come to a three-way intersection. Tread carefully. There's a trap in the intersection, and you're surrounded by enraged, devouring, and shambling corpses that attack as soon as you enter the intersection. You also have a hurlock emissary and genlock shapechanger flanking you. Have your rogue disarm the trap while a mage hits the hurlock emissary's side of the corridor with massive AoE. Try to burn down the emissary quickly. The shapechanger will transform and attack; the tank should pick up the shapechanger and go toe-to-toe until all other enemies are down. Then combine forces and finish off the shapechanger.

If you want a little more loot, there's plenty in the side room. Exit via the warehouse door to the east, where you'll find Sandal surrounded by a pile of dead bodies. He won't tell you what happened here, but at least you get one last run at enchanting and your main vendor before heading into the final battle.

Legend

①	Sandal	②	Pile of Books
1	Genlock Conjurer	③	Pile of Books
2	Greater Shade & Lesser Shades	△	Weapon Stands
		⑤	Wooden Crate
3	Lesser Shades	⑥	Chest (locked) & Armor Stands
4	Hurlock Emissary		
5	Genlock Shapechanger	△	Chest (locked) & Armor Stands
6	Corpses	△	Wooden Crates
7	Corpses	△	Chest (locked) & Armoires
8	Corpses		
9	Corpses	ⓧ	Trap
△	Chest (locked)		

The Final Onslaught

Basics ~ Character Generation ~ Classes ~ The Party ~ Companions ~ Supporting Cast ~ Equipment ~ Bestiary ~ **Walkthroughs** ~ Side Quests ~ Random Encounters ~ Achievements/Trophies

~ Second Floor ~

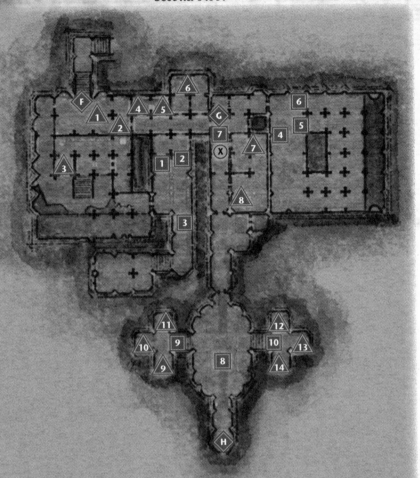

Legend

1. Hurlock Alpha
2. Genlock Alpha
3. Hurlock Alpha
4. Genlocks
5. Genlock Alphas & Genlocks
6. Genlocks
7. Genlock Master Assassin & Genlock Assassin Acolytes
8. Hurlock Emissary
9. Ogre
10. Ogre
1. Wooden Crate & Barrel
2. Sack
3. Chest (locked)
4. Chest (locked)
5. Chest (locked)
6. Chests
7. Wooden Crates
8. Wooden Crate
9. Wooden Crate
10. Chests
11. Chest (locked)
12. Chest (locked)
13. Chest (locked)
14. Chest
X. Trap

F You enter the second floor in the northwest corner. You can pick up some loot in the first two rooms, and when you're ready, take the west door and circle around the corridor until you come to the door that leads into

the banquet hall. A genlock alpha and two hurlock alphas wait in ambush strategically around the room. Three companions should charge into the room and around the corner to the right to take on the hurlock alpha there. One companion (mage with AoE damage and root spells, or tank) should go after the other two. Once the first hurlock alpha drops, everyone converges on the most wounded alpha, and then moves to the last one.

G When you get to the door heading south at diamond G, prepare for a serious ambush. A genlock master assassin and his two acolytes appear out of thin air and attack. If you rush into the room, they

appear behind you and immediately backstab. Plus, there's a line leghold trap straight ahead that may stick someone if it's not deactivated by a rogue. Send your rogue through the door toward the trap to deactivate it. The assassins appear in front of the main group, and the rogue can turn around and backstab them. If you can root the master assassin, don't wait. He can kill in seconds. Lock the master assassin up with your tank and heal the tank like crazy. Whatever you do, don't expose your back to any of the three or you could be in for pain.

primagames.com

H To get to the roof, you need to pass through the final room on the second floor. A hurlock emissary appears to stand alone, except two ogres hide in the side passages. As soon as you engage the emissary, the ogres charge out to confront the party. When you enter the room, fire the best ranged attacks you have at the emissary. Root or stun him, and don't let him regain much time or he'll heal back up to full and bombard you with spells. It's better to take out the emissary, even if you take a little pounding from the ogres. You may want the tank to head off at least one of the ogres and keep the healer on the tank, while the other two companions remove the emissary. When you have the emissary down, train your offense on one ogre then the other.

Be sure to scavenge the side passages for loot. If you have a competent rogue, you'll be rewarded with even more health poultices and lyrium potions for your battle. The door in the south takes you up to the roof and the archdemon. Don't step through until you are 100 percent prepared.

~ Roof ~

Partially Collapsed Area

Legend

1. Archdemon (Elite Boss)
2. Shrieks
3. Hurlock Grunts
4. Shrieks
5. Hurlock Grunts
B. Ballista

I This is it: the final battle against the archdemon, and it's going to be glorious and long! You had better be stocked up on health poultices and lyrium potions (at least 20 or more of each; the higher the potency, the better). Because the archdemon's powers are all Spirit-based, don whatever Spirit resistance gear you have, and use whatever spirit shards and spirit balms you may have. Everyone should have a ranged weapon to damage the archdemon from afar. No one can stand toe-to-claw with the archdemon for long.

Archdemon Powers

- At 100 percent health, the archdemon comes at you full force. It will use any and all of the following: massive attack (big AoE damage), sweep (AoE knockback), roar (mass stun), flame breath (AoE frontal damage), bite (massive DPS), and flight (breaks targeting and repositions archdemon for surprise attacks).

- At 75 percent health the archdemon jumps away to its second stage and starts using a new power: Vortex. This power spawns a persistent vortex that inflicts damage over time and incurs major debuffs to attack and defense. Darkspawn are not affected while inside it.

- At 50 percent health the archdemon jumps to its third stage: a partially collapsed section of the area that is inaccessible. The archdemon can still use ranged abilities while there and you can attack it using ranged attacks of your own (including ballistas). During this time many darkspawn pour into the area to challenge the party. The archdemon now starts using a new power: Smite. This is a long-range ability in which the archdemon sends blasts of energy from the skies.

- At 25 percent health the archdemon jumps to its final stage. More darkspawn appear here to join the fight. The archdemon starts using its last power: Detonate Darkspawn. Essentially, it uses the darkspawn as cannon fodder. Once one of the darkspawn nears a party member or army members the archdemon may choose to detonate that darkspawn, inflicting damage to anyone nearby.

The Final Onslaught

Basics ~ Character Generation ~ Classes ~ The Party ~ Companions ~ Supporting Cast ~ Equipment ~ Bestiary ~ **Walkthroughs** ~ Side Quests ~ Random Encounters ~ Achievements/Trophies

You begin in the middle of the battle, after the archdemon has wrecked some of Denerim's loyal soldiers. Before you can target the archdemon, it takes flight and repositions itself. Get used to that maneuver. The archdemon never stays in one spot too long, especially if you have it pinned down with damage. It will fly straight up in the air, disappear from view (canceling any targeting you may have on it), then reappear and drop down behind someone. Employ constant vigilance! If you fail to see the demon drop behind one of your companions, that companion may be dead before you can bring help.

At the start of the fight, spread out your party. You want to be close enough that the healer can still target everyone, and close enough that everyone can hit the archdemon with a ranged weapon, but not close enough that it can attack more than one companion at a time, even with its sweep or flame breath. If the archdemon starts hitting more than one companion at a time with damage, your healing won't be able to keep up.

When you're in range, watch out for the archdemon's attacks. From the rear with its tail or from the front with its taloned feet, the archdemon can sweep multiple opponents aside with a huge knockback attack. Otherwise, it can roast anyone in front of it with a wide AoE flame breath attack. Its massive attack will damage everyone in close proximity, and the archdemon's roar stuns all targets in a medium radius around it.

Learn to recognize each attack so you can defend against it. Moving out from in front of it, unless you can throw up a Force Field to block the damage, will save you a lot of damage over the course of the fight. Stay away from its frontal attacks, except if you're the tank charging in to dish out some damage, and even then, you want to strike from the side or rear if possible.

Archdemon Battle Tips

- Across the area are massive ballistas used to defend the fortress. You can rotate them inside and use them to attack the archdemon. There is a chance on every shot fired that the ballistas will get jammed. Only a rogue can attempt to repair and reload them, and he may do so up to three times per ballista.

- The archdemon's breath weapon inflicts Spirit damage (as all of his other special powers). Stock up on your Spirit resistance gear.

- Against the archdemon's Vortex power, move out of the AoE radius and fire off a Group Heal if you have one to offset the constant drop in the party's health.

- After the archdemon loses half of its life, it retreats to a partially collapsed section accessible only by ranged fire. Switch to your second weapon set and fire with the best damage items that you have. Archers should load up on special arrows to inflict more damage. Spellcasters should hit it with potent AoE (you won't have to worry about it affecting your team) and any spell that can deal damage over time.

- Once the archdemon is near death, it will begin to detonate darkspawn, which causes darkspawn to explode and damage anyone nearby. One or two ranged companions should concentrate on picking off any darkspawn that approach, so that none get close enough to explode into the party.

- The best time to attack the archdemon in melee is when it is in the middle of other time-consuming attacks, such as its breath weapon or grabbing an enemy with its mouth.

Fortunately, you are not alone in your fight to end the darkspawn threat forever. Allies that you've met in the past, such as First Enchanter Irving or Arl Eamon, will join you during the battle and lend their skills. You also have all the remaining armies to summon for one last call. Early on, summon any armies with only a few allies left. You might as well use them up and chip away at the archdemon's health.

TIP

At the start of the final battle, summon whatever partial armies you have to hassle the archdemon. However, you should save one ranged force to hit the archdemon when it flees to the collapsed area (below 50 percent of its health) and one melee force to deal with the last darkspawn horde (when the archdemon drops below 25 percent health).

Your healer should Group Heal whenever the archdemon catches more than one companion in a damage burst. The healer will be busy with Group Heal once the archdemon drops below 75 percent health and starts using its Vortex power to suck the life out of everyone in the area. Keep on the move and out of the way of archdemon damage so you're always free to spot heal as the circumstances dictate.

Keep the damage going on the archdemon. It takes time, but you will see a steady decline in its health bar if you can nail it with continuous ranged attacks and get some army allies attacking it. Powerful damage spells such as Blizzard, Inferno, and Tempest work well. The archdemon will fly out of them if it can, but it also may be forced to fly back in on a return trip.

You can also rack up damage with the ballista. Send your weakest ranged companion to man a ballista (or even two companions if you don't have the natural firepower to compete with the archdemon). Rotate the ballista to point at the

archdemon and fire each time it reloads. If you run out of mana at any time, make a beeline for a ballista and keep the pressure on.

Once it drops below half of its life, it retreats to the collapsed area. You won't be able to reach it on foot. Forget melee, and have everyone switch to ranged weapons. Summon your best ranged army to aid with zapping the archdemon in its new hiding place.

TIP

The elves and mages lend the best support against the archdemon when it retreats to the partially collapsed section.

Darkspawn swarm the rooftop now. If your ranged troops have a steady stream of damage going against the archdemon, head off the darkspawn and prevent them from hindering your ranged army. If all you have left are melee

troops, let them deal with the darkspawn and you continue to hit the archdemon with your ranged attacks. Don't forget the ballista shots too.

When the archdemon falls below 25 percent health, even more darkspawn assault you. Pull out all the stops here. Dance around so the darkspawn can't get close to you, and call in your best remaining army to take on the darkspawn

charge. Keep popping those potions and hitting the archdemon with everything you've got. Think defense first, don't get careless, and you should bring the elite boss down to within seconds of death.

TIP

Summon your best melee army to finish out the battle and deal with detonating darkspawn.

A Grey Warden must launch the final blow against the archdemon to kill it. If you or a fellow Grey Warden had a child with Morrigan, no Grey Warden will die with the final blow. If you refused Morrigan's ritual, you must choose to slay the

archdemon yourself (in which case, you sacrifice yourself) or allow your fellow Grey Warden (Alistair or Loghain) to slay the archdemon and perish in the process.

With that one final act, the archdemon is forever destroyed. The Blight disperses, and though darkspawn still trouble the darker edges of civilization, peace and prosperity fill the lives of generations. The Grey Wardens are once again a

brotherhood loved and respected throughout the land.

The Final Onslaught - Warden's Keep

Basics ~ Character Generation ~ Classes ~ The Party ~ Companions ~ Supporting Cast ~ Equipment ~ Bestiary ~ **Walkthroughs** ~ Side Quests ~ Random Encounters ~ Achievements/Trophies

Warden's Keep

NOTE

The "Warden's Keep" quest is available only as downloadable content. "Warden's Keep" takes you to the new world map location Soldier's Peak, and you can complete it anytime after you leave Lothering. If you find your party inventory filling up frequently, complete "Warden's Keep" to gain the additional inventory space from the new party storage chest.

Soldier's Peak

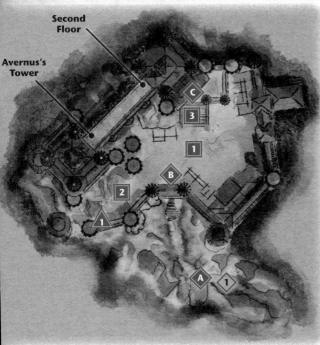

Second Floor

Avernus's Tower

Runthrough (Soldier's Peak)

Summary: Venture into Soldier's Peak to find the ancient Grey Warden fortress.

A. Levi guides you to Soldier's Peak.

B. Prepare for an ambush by skeletons.

C. Fight through the undead to reach the keep entrance.

Soldier's Peak Cheatsheet

Main Plot Quests
- Soldier's Peak

Important NPCs
- Levi Dryden

Key Items
- None

Monsters
- Arland Corpses
- Arland Skeletons
- Warden Master Skeleton
- Warden Skeletons

Side Quests
- Ancient History

Legend

- ① Levi Dryden
- 1 Arland Skeletons & Arland Corpses
- 2 Warden Skeletons
- 3 Warden Master Scout & Warden Skeletons
- ⚠ Statue (codex)

A Once you have downloaded "Warden's Keep," you will find Levi Dryden at party camp. Visit him there and accept the quest to Soldier's Peak. The new location will appear on your world map, and Levi will take you to the snowy hills outside the fortress.

B As you enter the main compound, ghosts appear at the gate and reenact the first part of the tale of what befell the Grey Wardens at Soldier's Peak. If you travel a little farther toward the steps leading up to the keep entrance, an ambush springs. Arland undead rise from the ground to the northeast in the courtyard before the stairs, while a second set of Warden skeletons appears to the west near the codex statue. Tackle the Arland undead first, then swing around and battle the Warden skeletons. If you're quick, you can launch ranged attacks and whittle down the numbers before they overwhelm your party.

primagames.com

C More dead Wardens hold the staircase leading up to the keep entrance. A Warden master scout and its skeleton followers attack with deadly accuracy as they pelt you with arrows. Return fire with ranged AoE spells, such as a Fireball or Tempest, and once the smoke clears, send your melee DPSers up to clean up the survivors. When you are healed back up, enter the keep through the main doors.

First Floor

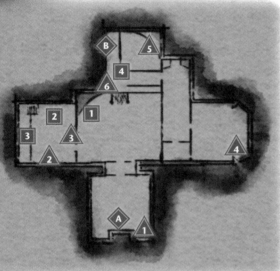

Runthrough (First Floor)
Summary: Find the Archivist's Book on the first floor.
A. Enter the first floor and battle through the horrors within.
B. Slay the Archivist and read his book.

First Floor Cheatsheet

Main Plot Quests
• Soldier's Peak

Important NPCs
• None

Key Items
• Archivist's Book

Monsters
• Arcane Horror

• Archivist
• Commander Athlar
• Demons
• Lesser Rage Demons
• Warden Skeletons

Side Quests
• Ancient History

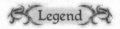
Legend

1 Arcane Horror & Lesser Rage Demons
2 Commander Athlar
3 Warden Skeletons
4 Archivist & Demons

1 Statement of Defiance
2 Weapon Stand
3 Chest (locked)
4 Chest
5 Archivist's Book
6 Book (codex)

A On the first floor, the second room holds an arcane horror and lesser rage demons. Nail the arcane horror with stuns and root talents/spells and rip through the lesser rage demons. Once the lesser foes have fallen, concentrate the party's power on the arcane horror to bring it down. If you want a little more battle experience and extra loot, open the door to the west and fight Commander Athlar and a bunch of Warden skeletal archers.

B Head to the east and then north to the back room. The Archivist and its demonic lackeys appear and attack. Take the same tactics as you did with the arcane horror in the prior room. Once you finish off all foes, read the Archivist's Book for more of the keep's tale.

Warden's Keep

Basics ~ Character Generation ~ Classes ~ The Party ~ Companions ~ Supporting Cast ~ Equipment ~ Bestiary ~ **Walkthroughs** ~ Side Quests ~ Random Encounters ~ Achievements/Trophies

Second Floor

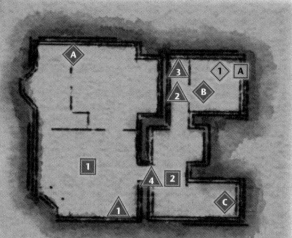

Runthrough (Second Floor)

Summary: Speak with Sophia on the second floor.

A. Enter the second floor and fight the rage demon and its minions.

B. Speak with Sophia.

C. Exit through the magic barrier.

Second Floor Cheatsheet

Main Plot Quests
- Soldier's Peak

Important NPCs
- Sophia

Key Items
- None

Monsters
- Dead Wardens
- Rage Demon
- Shambling Skeletons

Side Quests
- Ancient History

Legend

- ◇1 Sophia
- ▢1 Rage Demon & Dead Wardens
- ▢2 Shambling Skeletons
- △1 Vase
- △2 Chest
- △3 Chest (locked)
- △4 Raspberry Jam (codex)
- Ⓐ Asturian's Portrait for "Ancient History"

A In the large open chamber near the second floor stairs several magic circles glow on the floor. As you approach, the rage demon and dead Wardens from out of the keep's past materialize. Though the rage demon can abuse your party, you must defeat the dead Wardens on the magic circles first. The Wardens power up the rage demon, and it's nearly impossible to deal enough damage to kill the rage demon while the dead Wardens continuously heal it. With the magic circles empty, you can focus your party's firepower and eliminate the rage demon with your tank taking the lion's share of the combat damage.

B Unfortunately when you reach the northeast chamber, you find Levi's ancestor, Sophia, possessed by a demon. If you have a very high Persuade skill, you can convince Sophia to seal the tear in the Veil that is letting all these demons through to the keep. If you don't have a very high Persuade score, or you want to head to Avernus's Tower anyway (recommended if you want two new talents for your class), agree to help Sophia against Avernus in the tower. You can always change your mind later on. Leave via the exit door to the tower.

C A magical barrier blocks exit from the second floor. A few shambling skeletons bar your way too. You must first speak with Sophia to remove the barrier and pass through to Avernus's Tower.

primagames.com

Avernus's Tower

Runthrough (Avernus's Tower)

Summary: Speak with Sophia on the second floor.

A. Enter the tower and examine Avernus's experiments.

B. Speak with Avernus.

Avernus's Tower Cheatsheet

Main Plot Quests
- Infernal Dealings

Important NPCs
- Avernus

Key Items
- Ability Notes

- Alchemical Concoction

Monsters
- Warden Corpses

Side Quests
- Ancient History

Legend

1. Avernus
1. Warden Corpses
1. Ability Notes
2. Alchemical Concoction & Book
3. Corpse (codex)
4. Chest (locked)

Avernus's New Abilities

Avernus has discovered two new talents/spells for each class. If you drink the Alchemical Concoction on the table before Avernus's chamber, you gain two of the following Power of Blood talents based on your appropriate class:

Warrior

Blood Thirst: The warrior's own tainted blood spills in sacrifice, increasing movement speed, attack speed, and critical hit chance. For as long as the mode is active, however, the warrior suffers greater damage and continuously diminishing health.

Blood Fury: The warrior sprays tainted blood to knock back nearby enemies, which they may resist by passing a physical resistance check. The gush of blood, however, results in a loss of personal health.

Mage

Dark Sustenance: A self-inflicted wound lets the mage draw from the power of tainted blood, rapidly regenerating a significant amount of mana but taking a small hit to health.

Bloody Grasp: The mage's own tainted blood becomes a weapon, sapping the caster's health slightly but inflicting Spirit damage on the target. Darkspawn targets suffer additional damage for a short period.

Rogue

Dark Passage: Tapping the power of tainted blood makes the rogue more nimble, able to move more quickly while using Stealth, and more likely to dodge a physical attack.

The Tainted Blade: The rogue's blood gushes forth, coating the edges of weapons with a deadly taint. The character gains a bonus to damage determined by the cunning attribute, but suffers continuously depleting health in return.

A Warden skeletons and traps guard the bridge leading to Avernus's Tower. Don't charge across the bridge. Hold your ground and take down the skeletons with ranged attacks. If you have a rogue, disarm the set of leghold traps that litter the bridge just in front of the second floor entrance.

Inside the tower, Warden corpses defend the second room. Defeat them and then study Avernus's ability notes (northeast corner near the door) and book (on the table). Avernus has conducted some horrific experiments, but his perserverance has paid off with new advances for all three classes. If your conscience can handle it, drink the Alchemical Concoction to gain two new talents/spells. (See the Avernus's New Abilities sidebar for more info.)

B Enter Avernus's chamber and hear his side of the story. You have a choice to make: side with Sophia or Avernus. Both are corrupt, but which one do you want to champion?

Warden's Keep

Basics ~ Character Generation ~ Classes ~ The Party ~ Companions ~ Supporting Cast ~ Equipment ~ Bestiary ~ **Walkthroughs** ~ Side Quests ~ Random Encounters ~ Achievements/Trophies

Avernus vs. Sophia

After speaking with Avernus, return to Sophia. If you side with Sophia, slay Avernus with Sophia's help. If you side with Avernus, slay Sophia with Avernus's assistance. It doesn't matter who you side with to complete the quest. As with most boss fights, have your tank grab Avernus's or Sophia's attention and try to disrupt your foe from getting off any big attacks. Rotate through your party stuns to keep your foe off-balance. Watch AoEs in the chamber's tight quarters, but unleash as much DPS as you can in a short amount of time to avoid major counterattacks.

TIP

You can get a special piece of Grey Warden armor if you kill Sophia Dryden and loot her body. However, if you choose to let Sophia leave you will not get her armor.

New "Warden's Keep" Items

Want some new gear to deck out your character? There are 10 new pieces in the "Warden's Keep" quest line, each of which can be found from random loot drops or some story/sidequest events:

- Antique Warden Crossbow (Warden Master Scout's body in Soldier's Peak)
- Asturian's Might (reward for "Ancient History" side quest)
- Robes of Avernus (Avernus in the Avernus's Tower area)
- Shadow Belt (reward for "Ancient History" side quest)
- Starfang (greatsword; Mikhael in the Grey Warden base, part of the "Super Metal" random encounter)
- Starfang (longsword; Mikhael in the Grey Warden base, part of the "Super Metal" random encounter)
- Warden Commander Armor (Sophia in Soldier's Peak)
- Warden Commander Boots (Sophia in Soldier's Peak)
- Warden Commander Gloves (Sophia in Soldier's Peak)
- Winter's Breath (rage demon in abomination form on the second floor of the keep in Soldier's Peak)

Closing the Veil

After the final battle, your ally will attempt to seal the Veil in the chamber with the magic circles. Battle through a series of increasingly more difficult enemies that appear out of these circles: lesser rage demons, greater shades, ash wraiths, and a powerful desire demon. Speak with your ally and Levi one last time and the keep is in Grey Warden hands once again.

Warden's Keep

With the end of the quest, Levi and his family establish a new Warden's Keep which you can visit throughout the rest of the game. Levi and his brother, Mikhael, become new vendors for you: Levi sells accessories and crafting supplies; Mikhael is a blacksmith and sells weapons and armor. If you have the meteorite material from the "Super Metal" random encounter (see the Random Encountes chapter), Mikhael will fasten the metal into a fine blade. Perhaps the greatest resource at the keep is the super-useful party storage chest. Load up whatever you don't want to lug around into the chest and return when you need the extra supplies. Its capacity is huge, so you won't be stuck destroying items again.

primagames.com

The Stone Prisoner

NOTE

"The Stone Prisoner" quest is available only as downloadable content. "The Stone Prisoner" starts at the new world map location Sulcher's Pass, and you can complete it any time after you leave Lothering. However, it's highly recommended that you complete the quest and unlock the golem Shale as your companion before heading to Orzammar and attempting the "Paragon of Her Kind" quest line.

Village of Honnleath

Runthrough (Village of Honnleath)

Summary: Clear the darkspawn out of the village to reach Shale.

A. Enter the village outskirts and prepare to meet the darkspawn.

B. Battle the first wave of genlocks and hurlocks.

C. Battle the second wave of genlocks and hurlocks.

D. Discover Wilhelm's Cellar.

Village of Honnleath Cheatsheet

Main Plot Quests
- The Golem in Honnleath

Important NPCs
- Shale

Key Items
- Bloodied Bronze Key

Monsters
- Genlocks
- Hurlock Alpha
- Hurlocks

Side Quests
- None

Legend

- ① Shale
- ☐1 Genlocks
- ☐2 Genlocks & Hurlocks
- ☐3 Genlocks & Hurlocks
- ☐4 Hurlock Alpha, Genlocks, & Hurlocks
- ☐5 Genlocks & Hurlocks

- ⚠1 Barrel
- ⚠2 Broken Chest
- ⚠3 Chest
- ⚠4 Villager
- ⚠5 Olaf's Chest (locked)
- ⚠6 Note
- ⚠7 Basket of Birdseed

golem control rod. A new location appears on your world map, and you can enter the village. Be careful, for darkspawn lurk at almost every turn.

A Once you have downloaded "The Stone Prisoner," you will find Felix at Sulcher's Pass on the western side of your world map. Visit him there and accept the quest to the Village of Honnleath after he gives you the special

B The first darkspawn wave meets you at the village gate and the first clearing inside the village. Pull the genlocks at the gate toward you with a ranged attack and dispatch them easily with AoE damage and melee attacks once they close. In the clearing near the well, engage the first group and watch for a second darkspawn group to assault you from the hill to the north. Don't take too long with the first group; the second group will stay clear and strike you with arrows. The damage will pile up the longer the encounter goes on.

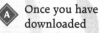

The Stone Prisoner

Basics ~ Character Generation ~ Classes ~ The Party ~ Companions ~ Supporting Cast ~ Equipment ~ Bestiary ~ **Walkthroughs** ~ Side Quests ~ Random Encounters ~ Achievements/Trophies

New "Stone Prisoner" Items

Want some new gear to deck out your character? There are eight new pieces in "The Stone Prisoner" quest line, each of which can be found on a creature or at specific location:

- Blood Gorged Amulet (Hurlock emissary in Cadash Thaig)
- Cadash Stompers (Cadash Thaig ogre)
- Cord of Shattered Dreams (Kitty)
- Dead Thaig Shanker (Cadash Thaig chest)
- Harvest Festival Ring (Dust wraith leader in Wilhelm's Cellar)
- Helm of Honnleath (Kitty)
- Oalf's Prized Cheese Knife (Locked chest in village)
- Wilhelm's Magus Staff (Kitty, if you ask for a reward in return for freeing her)

New items appear at vendors as well. The following items can now be purchased as gifts for Shale.

- Remarkable Amethyst (Alimar's Emporium, Orzammar's Dust Town)
- Remarkable Diamond (Garin's Gem Store, Orzammar Commons, console version only)
- Remarkable Emerald (Figor's Store, Orzammar Commons)
- Remarkable Garnet (Wonders of Thedas Store, Denerim Market District)
- Remarkable Greenstone (Cellars, Village of Honnleath)
- Remarkable Malachite (Shaperate Store, Circle Tower)
- Remarkable Ruby (Alarith's Store, Denerim's Elven Alienage)
- Remarkable Sapphire (Legnar's Store, Orzammar Commons)
- Remarkable Topaz (Faryn's Store, Frostback Mountains)

C Genlocks and hurlocks led by a hurlock alpha comprise the second darkspawn wave in the town square around the immobilized golem, Shale. The group on the eastern side will likely engage first. Watch for the second group to loop around and flank your party. The tank should line up with the hurlock alpha, while a mage with AoE damage or multiple melee DPSers handle the rest of the throng. The tank can join the rest once the hurlock alpha falls.

D Interact with Shale after the battle. The golem's still stuck in a frozen stance, even after you try your control rod. You need a new activation phrase, so you'll have to find the rest of the villagers who are holed up in Wilhelm's Cellar under the village. Grab the bloodied bronze key from the dead villager corpse by Shale and use it to loot Olaf's chest, located back near the village gate, and then head through the cellar door.

Wilhelm's Cellar

Exit to Village of Honnleath

Legend

① Matthias	② Chest
② Amalia & Kitty	③ Charred Corpse
1 Genlocks & Hurlocks	④ Chest
2 Genlocks & Hurlocks	⑤ Wilhelm's Special Brew
3 Genlock Emissary, Genlocks, & Hurlocks	⑥ Glowing Crystal
4 Dust Wraith & Lesser Shades	⑦ Deathroot & Elfroot
5 Lesser Shades	⑧ Fractured Stone
6 Lesser Shades	⑨ Chest
① Strange Crystal Cluster	⑩ Book
	⑪ Strange Crystals
	⑫ A Decades-Old Letter

primagames.com

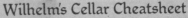

Runthrough (Wilhelm's Cellar)

Summary: Navigate through Wilhelm's Cellar to uncover Shale's activation phrase.

A. Enter the mage laboratory.

B. Free Matthias and the villagers from the darkspawn.

C. Use the door behind the force field to reach the second half of the dungeon.

D. Speak with Amalia and Kitty.

Wilhelm's Cellar Cheatsheet

Main Plot Quests
- The Golem in Honnleath

Important NPCs
- Amalia
- Kitty
- Matthias

Key Items
- None

Monsters
- Dust Wraith
- Genlock Emissary
- Genlocks
- Hurlocks
- Lesser Shades

Side Quests
- None

A Enter Wilhelm's Cellar and cut through the darkspawn in the research library. Two enemy groups of genlocks and hurlocks will try to swarm you. Hit them with ranged attacks and finish off the stragglers when they near melee range. If you get thirsty, you can stop for Wilhelm's Special Brew (a gift Oghren will particularly enjoy) before the next encounter.

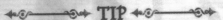

> **TIP**
>
> Pick up any strange crystals you see. These are the special golem crystals that give Shale different offensive and defensive abilities.

B In the next room a whole lot of darkspawn, led by a genlock emissary, threaten the remaining villagers. Matthias has the villagers safely behind a force field, but you must destroy all the darkspawn to talk to Matthias. A big AoE attack from the doorway can reduce the numbers, while more ranged fire concentrates on the emissary to drop it before a counterattack. After your AoE flurry, race in and sweep through the half-dead darkspawn that remain.

C Interact with the protective field to begin a conversation with Matthias. He asks that you help find his daughter Amalia who is lost deeper in the mage laboratory. In return, Matthias will give you the golem activation phrase for Shale. In the next room, a dust wraith and lesser shades materialize and attack. The tank should grab the dust wraith while the party cuts down the lesser shades. Once the dust wraith dies, it's clear till the final encounter.

> **CAUTION**
>
> The lesser shade encounters, marked square 5 and square 6 or the map, trigger on the return trip to Matthias. You only face them after you speak with Amalia and Kitty.

D In the final cellar chamber, you meet up with Amalia and her cat Kitty. Turns out that Kitty is a demon who has Amalia completely enthralled. If you want to take the shortest path to completing the quest, then refuse to help the demon. Kitty will possess Amalia (no matter what you try) and you must defeat the demoness. She summons lesser rage demons to distract you. Ignore them as best as possible and fix all damage on Kitty. She will fall eventually, and then the lesser rage demons next. Return to Matthias and tell him that his beloved Amalia didn't make it. Matthias will thank you for trying and give you the golem activation phrase.

The Stone Prisoner

Basics ~ Character Generation ~ Classes ~ The Party ~ Companions ~ Supporting Cast ~ Equipment ~ Bestiary ~ **Walkthroughs** ~ Side Quests ~ Random Encounters ~ Achievements/Trophies

Siding with the Demon

You don't have to fight Kitty immediately. You can also side with her or try to trick her. If you agree to help the demoness, you have two main choices: complete the chamber puzzle to free Kitty or return to Matthias and tell him what happened.

If you attempt the puzzle, you must connect the flaming torch on the initial corner with the one on the opposite corner (see screenshot). Slide the tiles so that the arrows flow the fire in the proper direction. Tile arrows pointing into each other will extinguish the blaze. Keep working the arrows and slowly move in the direction of the opposite corner.

With the puzzle beaten, the field holding Kitty in the room drops. The demoness will possess Amalia (though you can demand a reward to let her do so), and the new "Amalia" returns to her father's side. Matthias is fooled and gives you the golem activation phrase.

In the puzzle room, it's also possible to lie to Kitty about completing the puzzle. Refuse to let Kitty possess Amalia and the girl actually runs away and escapes. You then have to fight Kitty.

If you agreed to help the demoness, but leave the room and tell Matthias about the events, he rushes to save his daughter and gets possessed himself. At that point, you can either let the demoness go or not. If you do, Matthias and Amalia leave after giving you the activation phrase for Shale. If you refuse to let the demoness go, Amalia runs away and you're forced to battle the Kitty-possessed Matthias.

Head back up to the surface and speak with Shale. The new activation phrase works, and Shale joins your party after a little bit of convincing. The golem can either take the role of main tank or melee DPSer; Shale's new golem talents work incredibly well in either role. You can continue with your main quests, or, if you've already met the dwarven paragon Caridin in the Deep Roads beneath Orzammar, speak with Shale back at party camp and venture forth on the golem's personal quest into Cadash Thaig.

NOTE

See the "Shale" section in the Companions chapter for complete details on how to integrate Shale into your party.

NOTE

Completing the Village of Honnleath and Wilhelm's Cellar maps frees Shale as a golem companion for your party. Cadash Thaig is a hidden location in Orzammar's Deep Roads. It unlocks after you meet Caridin in the "Paragon of Her Kind" quest line. Undertaking Shale's personal quest to Cadash Thaig will greatly improve your standing with the golem.

Cadash Thaig

~ See map on next page ~

Runthrough (Cadash Thaig)

Summary: Help Shale find meaning and a secret past in the darkspawn-infested ruins of an ancient Thaig.

A. Enter Cadash Thaig.

B. Prepare for a series of darkspawn ambushes.

C. Defeat the ogre alpha and access the monolith with Shale's history.

Cadash Thaig Cheatsheet

Main Plot Quests
- A Golem's Memories

Important NPCs
- None

Key Items
- None

Monsters
- Bronto
- Deepstalkers
- Genlock Alpha
- Genlock Rogues
- Genlocks
- Hurlock Emissary
- Hurlocks
- Ogre Alpha
- Shrieks

Side Quests
- None

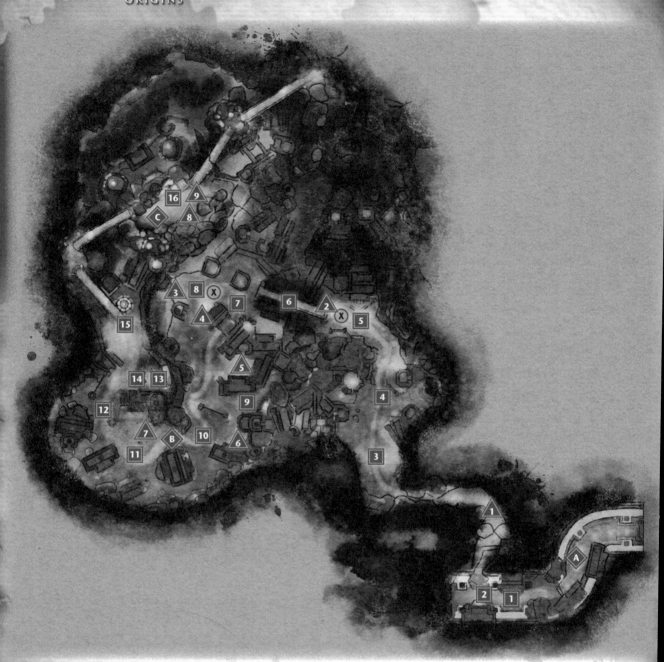

Legend

The Stone Prisoner

Basics ~ Character Generation ~ Classes ~ The Party ~ Companions ~ Supporting Cast ~ Equipment ~ Bestiary ~ **Walkthroughs** ~ Side Quests ~ Random Encounters ~ Achievements/Trophies

A You can unlock Shale's personal quest only after completing "Paragon of Her Kind." If you side with Caridin, or side with Branka and Persuade Shale to stay after the battle, then Shale tells you about Cadash Thaig either at the Anvil of the Void (if Shale is in your party) or back at party camp.

CAUTION

If you journey to the Altar of the Void with Shale in your party, and you side with Branka, Shale will turn against you and fight you to the death.

After Shale tells you about Cadash Thaig in party camp, seek out the Deep Roads in Orzammar. Shale will comment on Cadash Thaig and add it to your Deep Roads map when you enter Caridin's Cross (following Branka's defeat). Once you enter the Thaig, however, genlocks, hurlocks, and shrieks will harass you near the entrance.

B Watch out for traps before the first bridge and near the ancient structures where the deepstalkers spawn. Once the deepstalkers thin out, a series of darkspawn ambushes will try to end your adventuring career. First, past the rubble pile, genlock rogues appear around you and look for backstab attacks. A group of genlocks and hurlocks will join in from the buildings to the north. After them, more hurlocks stream out in front of a hurlock alpha who takes aim on the party from afar. The alpha will stay in its protected alcove and deal critical hit after critical hit. When you close on him, genlock rogues appear to defend him. You may also get genlocks from the bridge to the north. Finally, after all those enemies lie still, you can proceed to the final encounter.

C An ogre alpha guards some treasure and a monolith that holds some answers about Shale's past. Send the tank at the ogre and prepare for a swarm of shrieks to appear when you engage. Battle off the shrieks; the healer should concentrate heals on the tank and watch for health drops in the rest of the party while they fight the shrieks. Unload whatever big damage attacks you have; this is the last fight. When the ogre and shrieks are down, let the golem uncover its ancient origins and then partake of the treasure from the broken chest. Continue speaking with Shale after Cadash Thaig and your approval should keep rising with the formidable golem.

primagames.com

Side Quests

Blackstone Irregulars

A Change in Leadership

Type: Combat

Start: Blackstone Irregulars

Destination: Random encounter at Taoran's Camp

Task: Kill Raelnor or Taoran

Quest Tips: This quest is only active once all the other Blackstone Irregulars quests have been completed. Kill Raelnor in Denerim Market District or agree to kill Taoran; talk to or kill Taoran in the Taoran's Camp random encounter.

Dereliction of Duty

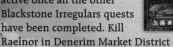

Type: Combat

Start: Blackstone Irregulars in Gnawed Noble Tavern

Destination: Three different locations in Denerim, Lake Calenhad Docks, and Frostback Mountains

Task: Confront three deserters and demand justice for the Irregulars

Quest Tips: Track down the following deserters, speak to them, and slay them and their bodyguards:

- Layson the Deserter (Denerim's Run-down Back Street in a Dirty Hovel)
- Sammael the Deserter (Lake Calenhad Docks)
- Tornas the Deserter (Frostback Mountains)

Grease the Wheels

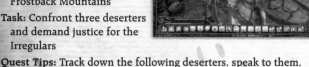

Type: Messenger

Start: Blackstone Irregulars in Redcliffe Village

Destination: Five different locations in Denerim

Task: Deliver notices of appreciation to five hooded couriers

Quest Tips: Track down the five hooded couriers in Denerim located in the Market District, Dark Alley, Alienage, Pearl, and Run-down Back Street.

Notices of Death

Type: Messenger

Start: Blackstone Irregulars in Gnawed Noble Tavern

Destination: Deliver four notes to four different locations

Task: Hand out four death notifications

Quest Tips: Deliver four death notifications to the following people:

- Irenia (Redcliffe Chantry)
- Larana (Spoiled Princess in Lake Calenhad Docks)
- Sara (Denerim Market District)
- Tania (Dirty Back Alley in Denerim)

Restocking the Guild

Type: Crafting

Start: Blackstone Irregulars in Gnawed Noble Tavern

Destination: Various

Task: Collect 20 health poultices for the Irregulars

Quest Tips: Collect 20 health poultices from whatever sources you can find, whether dropped from creatures or crafted yourself. They will accept lesser health poultices, so gain as many of those as possible before trading in others of higher value.

Scraping the Barrel

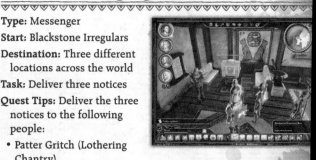

Type: Messenger

Start: Blackstone Irregulars

Destination: Three different locations across the world

Task: Deliver three notices

Quest Tips: Deliver the three notices to the following people:

- Patter Gritch (Lothering Chantry)
- Varel Baern (Elven Alienage)
- Dernal Garrison (Redcliffe, generic cottage)

Blackstone Irregluars - Brecilian Forest

Basics ~ Character Generation ~ Classes ~ The Party ~ Companions ~ Supporting Cast ~ Equipment ~ Bestiary ~ Walkthroughs ~ Side Quests ~ Random Encounters ~ Achievements/Trophies

Brecilian Forest

NOTE

See the "Nature of the Beast" walkthrough for the various Brecilian maps that show you all the side quest locations.

Cammen's Lament

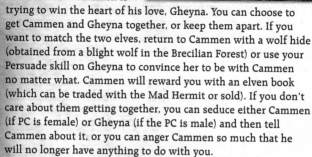

Type: Messenger

Start: Cammen in Dalish Camp

Destination: Gheyna in Dalish Camp

Task: Reconcile Cammen and Gheyna (or not)

Quest Tips: A young elven hunter named Cammen is trying to win the heart of his love, Gheyna. You can choose to get Cammen and Gheyna together, or keep them apart. If you want to match the two elves, return to Cammen with a wolf hide (obtained from a blight wolf in the Brecilian Forest) or use your Persuade skill on Gheyna to convince her to be with Cammen no matter what. Cammen will reward you with an elven book (which can be traded with the Mad Hermit or sold). If you don't care about them getting together, you can seduce either Cammen (if PC is female) or Gheyna (if the PC is male) and then tell Cammen about it, or you can anger Cammen so much that he will no longer have anything to do with you.

Elora's Halla

Type: Messenger

Start: Elora in Dalish Camp

Destination: Halla next to Elora

Task: Determine the nature of the halla's illness (or not)

Quest Tips: Elora tends her animals on the north side of camp. You can offer to help her with her sick halla and choose one of the following actions:

- Use your Survival skill to try to calm the halla

- Use your Persuade skill to only pretend to examine the halla

After examining or pretending to examine the halla, you can lie to Elora. If your Persuade is high enough, she will kill the halla and reward the PC with a set of antlers (which the PC can turn over to Varathorn the armorer to make into an item for him). If Elora catches you in a lie, she will get angry and no longer speak with you. If you successfully use your Survival skill, Elora will find the source of the halla's distress and you will earn her goodwill (and some experience points).

Elven Ritual

Type: Messenger

Start: Sarcophagus table in Brecilian Ruins

Destination: Elven altar in Brecilian Ruins

Task: Peform a multiple-step ritual to reveal a secret cache

Quest Tips: In the Brecilian Ruins, you discover an elven altar that looks like it was home to an ancient ritual. To succeed at the ritual, you must recover the tablet that explains what actions to take. The tablet can be found in a sarcophagus in one of the side rooms near where you encounter a ghostly boy near the start of this level. Follow the steps written in the tablet codex. If you perform the ritual steps in the wrong order, shades will appear and attack the party. The steps for the ritual are:

- Examine the fountain to start its dialog
- Fill the earthen jug with water
- Leave the pool alone
- Examine the altar to start its dialogue
- Place the filled earthen jug on top of the altar
- Kneel before the altar and pray
- Examine the earthen jug on the altar
- Take a single sip from the water in the jug
- Take the earthen jug
- Leave the altar alone
- Examine the fountain to start its dialog
- Dump the water in the jug back into the pool

If you perform the ritual steps in the right order, the large doors in this room will open, revealing an elven burial chamber. Inside, a shade guarding a sarcophagus awaits. The rewards for this and the "Mage's Treasure" side quest are all pieces of the Juggernaut armor, one of the better armor sets in the game.

Lost to the Curse

Type: Exploration

Start: Athras in Dalish Camp

Destination: Danyla in the East Brecilian Forest

Task: Slay some werewolves and speak with Danyla

Quest Tips: A hunter named Athras in the Dalish Camp is searching for any clues as to the whereabouts of his wife, Danyla. (You can stumble upon Danyla without speaking with Athras first.) After Athras tells you about his missing wife, locate Danyla in the East Brecilian Forest. Defeat the werewolves with her, and then talk to Danyla. She wants you to kill her and will attack you if you refuse. She gives the player a scarf to bring to Athras. Return to Athras and inform him of Danyla's passing. He will reward you with an amulet for this information, unless you toy with his emotions and joke around about Danyla's death, in which case you get no reward at all.

Mage's Treasure

Type: Combat

Start: North grove in the East Brecilian Forest

Destination: Several locations around the Brecilian Forest

Task: Defeat revenants and skeletons to claim special items

Quest Tips: This quest is activated at the clearing in the East Brecilian Forest where the player will come across two ogres. Among the ruined buildings is a tombstone. If you disturb the tomb, a revenant and several skeletons spawn. The revenant guards a piece of the Juggernaut armor. You can find other pieces of the armor at:

- A tombstone in West Brecilian Forest (near where you first fought with some darkspawn and an ogre).

- A tombstone in the East Brecilian Forest, past the misty barrier, among some ruins.

- A sarcophagus in the Brecilian Ruins. You must solve the "Elven Ritual" quest to get access to this room and then fight a shade to get access to the sarcophagus.

The rewards for this and the "Elven Ritual" side quest are all pieces of the Juggernaut armor, one of the better armor sets in the game.

Panowen

Type: Combat

Start: Panowen in West Brecilian Forest

Destination: Panowen

Task: Defeat Panowen or avoid conflict

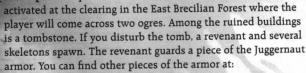

Quest Tips: In the forest, after resolving the main "Nature of the Beast" quest, you run into a group of elven hunters led by Panowen. If you anger Panowen, she will attack your party, but if you offer Panowen a reasonable explanation for your actions, she will reward you with a magic ring.

Rare Ironbark

Type: Exploration

Start: Varathorn in Dalish Camp

Destination: West Brecilian Forest

Task: Retrieve ironbark for Varathorn

Quest Tips: Varathorn, the Dalish armorsmith, seeks a

rare commodity, ironbark. There is an ironbark tree in the Brecilian Forest (on a fallen tree near a stream in the easte half of the map). Return to Varathorn with the ironbark. He make either a Dalish longbow or a breastplate. If you are gr you can demand both, but if the clan's attitude toward you not high enough, you will get nothing. (The clan's attitude improved by successfully doing quests or listening to storie from the various elves in the camp).

Shade Campsite

Type: Combat

Start: Campsite in West Brecilian Forest

Destination: Campsite

Task: Defeat the shade with a single party member

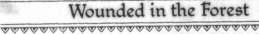

Quest Tips: You spot a tranquil campsite that looks peaceful enough. If you investigate the camp, your entire party will be overcor the powers of a shade. Only the party member with the hi willpower can resist the shade's influence and must fight alone.

Wounded in the Forest

Type: Exploration

Start: Deygan in Dalish Camp

Destination: West Brecilian Forest

Task: Heal Deygan in the forest

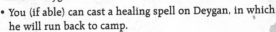

Quest Tips: In the West Brecilian Forest you come across a wounded Dalish elf named Deygan. You can take several actions:

- You (if able) can cast a healing spell on Deygan, in which he will run back to camp.

- You can loot Deygan's equipment. He has some good stu it will hurt your approval with the camp.

- You can bring the unconscious Deygan back to Mithra at camp where he will be saved. The next time you are in c. you can speak with Deygan and collect a reward (a gem y sell or trade with the Mad Hermit). If you looted his equ first, you have the option of returning an heirloom to De avoid losing favor with the clan.

- You can leave Deygan where he is or kill him.

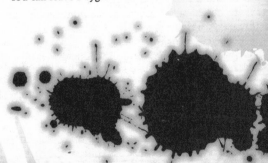

Brecilian Forest – Chanter's Board

Basics ~ Character Generation ~ Classes ~ The Party ~ Companions ~ Supporting Cast ~ Equipment ~ Bestiary ~ Walkthroughs ~ **Side Quests** ~ Random Encounters ~ Achievements/Trophies

Chanter's Board

Back Alley Justice

Type: Combat

Start: Chanter's Board in Denerim Market District

Destination: Dark Alley

Task: Defeat the gang of thugs in three Denerim areas: Dark Alley, Dirty Back Alley, and Run-Down Back Street

Quest Tips: When you arrive at each alley, a large band of thugs will block your way in the main part of the street. It would be a challenge if this was all of them, but there are smaller thug groups down the side alleys and up the stairs. The safest position is to retreat to the entrance location and battle there. Mages should heave long-range bombs on the larger groups, and your tank may want to employ Shield Cover to defend against the constant arrow volleys. If you get overwhelmed near the entrance, move to an alley, defeat the smaller thug group holed up there and form a new line of defense until all the thugs lie lifeless. Once all three areas are cleaned up, you can return to the Chanter's Board for your reward.

Brothers and Sons

Type: Combat

Start: Chanter's Board in Redcliffe Village

Destination: Battlefield location marked on world map

Task: Slay all the wolves and loot the soldier's diary from the bloody corpse

Quest Tips: Pick up the soldier's diary from the nearest corpse on the "deserted" battlefield and watch for a wolf ambush after you pass the first barricade. Stay near the entrance and defeat the first wolf pack. Proceed toward the exit only after the first wave is dead so you don't pull all groups to you at once. Go slowly; there are many, many wolves.

Caravan Down

Type: Combat

Start: Chanter's Board in Redcliffe Village

Destination: Caravan location marked on world map

Task: Kill all the darkspawn at the caravan

Quest Tips: You can set up a nice ambush point from the entrance hill that overlooks the destroyed caravan. Without attracting attention, slide along to the right and launch a long-range attack at the nearest genlock emissary (Fireball works wonders). Aim your archers or other ranged attacks on the second genlock emissary, who will cross the field to get into spell range. After the two emissaries

are down, finish off the genlock alpha. Report back to the Chanter's Board that the caravan was wiped out and claim your reward.

Desperate Haven

Type: Combat

Start: Chanter's Board in Denerim and Redcliffe Village

Destination: Refugees location marked on world map

Task: Kill all the darkspawn around the refugees

Quest Tips: You can launch some long-ranged attacks before the fighting gets hot and heavy. Stay close to the remaining refugees and protect them if you can (they will help you for the rest of the battle if you keep them alive). Watch for the hurlock emissary in the rear. The emissary can seriously hurt you with AoE spells so the quicker you get to him, the better. Stun or root him and close with your tank to prevent the big AoEs from damaging you too much.

Fazzil's Request

Type: Collection

Start: Chanter's Board in Denerim

Destination: Apartments in Denerim's Elven Alienage

Task: Retrieve Fazzil's sextant

Quest Tips: The Landsmeet must have begun and you must complete the "Rescue the Queen" quest to enter the Elven Alienage and retrieve Fazzil's sextant. Enter the apartments in the Elven Alienage and pick up the sextant from a chest in the apartment building.

◄◄► — NOTE ◄►►

See the Alienage maps in the "Landsmeet" walkthrough for the location of Fazzil's sextant.

Jowan's Intentions

Type: Combat

Start: Chanter's Board

Destination: Random encounter

Task: After battling darkspawn, kill or release Jowan

Quest Tips: This quest is available only after the "Arl of Redcliffe" and "Urn of Sacred Ashes" quest lines are complete, and if Jowan is still alive. After you dispatch the darkspawn surrounding Jowan, you must make one last decision on Jowan: Does he deserve to live or pay for his crimes?

Loghain's Push

Type: Combat

Start: Chanter's Board in Denerim Market District

Destination: Civil War location marked on world map

Task: Defeat all of Loghain's men at the location

Quest Tips: Side with the soldiers fighting Loghain's men and lend some aid. Concentrate your party efforts on one of Loghain's men at a time. Slowly, your allies will gain numbers and the battle will go in your favor.

Missing in Action

Type: Exploration

Start: Chanter's Board after Landsmeet begins

Destination: Arl Howe's Estate in Denerim

Task: Rescue Rexel from the estate dungeon

Quest Tips: You cannot begin open this quest until after the Landsmeet begins. A missing veteran, Rexel, has been locked up in the dungeon of Arl Howe's Denerim estate. During the "Rescue the Queen" quest, you can free Rexel with the key to his cell door, found on the jailor in the same room. Kill the jailor, unlock the cell, and tell Rexel that he's free to go.

> ### NOTE
> See the estate maps in the "Landsmeet" walkthrough for Rexel's cell location.

Skin Deep

Type: Collection

Start: Chanter's Board

Destination: Redcliffe Village and Redcliffe Castle

Task: Collect nine corpse galls to complete the quest

Quest Tips: Slay walking corpses and collect corpse gall drops as you defeat the undead. It doesn't matter where you get them from, though if you have this quest before you venture into Redcliffe for the first time, it won't be hard to accumulate the gruesome gall. When you have nine corpse gall drops, you can turn them in to complete the quest. If you collect 18 galls, you gain bonus gold.

Unintended Consequences

Type: Combat

Start: Chanter's Board

Destination: Random encounter along a roadside stop

Task: Slay Trickster Whim

Quest Tips: This quest opens up only after you complete the "Summoning Sciences Lesson 2" quest from the Circle Tower. When the random encounter occurs, defeat Trickster Whim and report back to the closest Chanter's Board.

The Circle of Magi

> ### NOTE
> See the "Broken Circle" walkthrough for detailed maps with the locations of all your side quest points of interest.

Circles Within Circles

Type: Exploration

Start: Senior Mage Quarters, Irving's Room

Destination: Irving's Bookshelf

Task: Find codex on Irving's bookshelf

Quest Tips: This is about as straightforward as it gets: Find the hidden codex on Irving's bookshelf.

Desire and Need

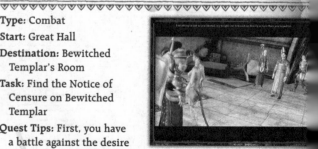

Type: Combat

Start: Great Hall

Destination: Bewitched Templar's Room

Task: Find the Notice of Censure on Bewitched Templar

Quest Tips: First, you have a battle against the desire demon and the bewitched templar. After the battle, recover the notice of censure from the downed templar. If you don't care

Chanter's Board - The Circle of Magi

Basics ~ Character Generation ~ Classes ~ The Party ~ Companions ~ Supporting Cast ~ Equipment ~ Bestiary ~ Walkthroughs ~ **Side Quests** ~ Random Encounters ~ Achievements/Trophies

about the censure, you have the option of letting the templar and the demon escape together, and the discussion usually triggers some interesting party dialogue and moral questions on the nature of truth and happiness.

Extracurricular Studies

Type: Exploration

Start: Templar Quarters

Destination: Piles of Filth and Piles of Books

Task: Find three codex entries

Quest Tips: Search the Templar Quarters for three codex entries hidden in piles of filth and piles of books.

Five Pages, Four Mages

Type: Exploration

Start: Great Hall

Destination: Random encounter

Task: Find five torn pages and defeat Beyha Joam

Quest Tips: First, search the Great Hall for five torn pages. Once you have them all, journey across the world map and trigger a random encounter. Slay Beyha Joam and claim your reward.

Friends of Red Jenny

Type: Exploration

Start: The Long Road (random encounter where you meet Zevran)

Destination: Mysterious Door in Denerim Market District

Task: Return the painted box to the mysterious Friends of Red Jenny

Quest Tips: After defeating Zevran's rogue band in the Long Road random encounter, loot a note from one of the travelers. Next, retrieve the painted box in Irving's room. Finally, travel to Denerim Market District and present the box at the mysterious door in the alley behind the Gnawed Noble Tavern. No one will talk to you, but they will hand you a nice reward.

Irving's Mistake

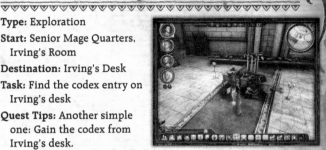

Type: Exploration

Start: Senior Mage Quarters, Irving's Room

Destination: Irving's Desk

Task: Find the codex entry on Irving's desk

Quest Tips: Another simple one: Gain the codex from Irving's desk.

Maleficarum Regrets

Type: Exploration

Start: Blood Mage near Lothering exit

Destination: Senior Mage Quarters

Task: Find Bel's Cache in the Circle Tower

Quest Tips: Note that this quest begins in Lothering, so be sure to pick it up before the darkspawn destroy the town. Loot the sealed letter on the blood mage near the northern Lothering exit. Follow the letter to the Circle Tower, and recover Bel's Cache on the tower's second floor.

Promises of Pride

Type: Exploration

Start: A scrap of paper

Destination: Various points in the tower

Task: Find six scraps of paper

Quest Tips: Find the six scraps of paper that make up the "Promises of Pride" on these levels of the tower:

- Apprentice Quarters (first floor): Find one scrap of paper
- Senior Mage Quarters (second floor): Find two scraps of paper
- Great Hall (third floor): Find two scraps of paper
- Templar Quarters (fourth floor): Find one scrap of paper

The Spot

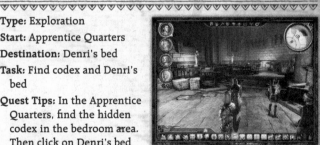

Type: Exploration

Start: Apprentice Quarters

Destination: Denri's bed

Task: Find codex and Denri's bed

Quest Tips: In the Apprentice Quarters, find the hidden codex in the bedroom area. Then click on Denri's bed for your reward.

Summoning Sciences

Type: Puzzle

Start: Apprentice Quarters

Destination: Various places on the first floor

Task: Find the book, click the correct summoning flames for each lesson

Quest Tips: Retrieve one or both halves of a book in the library, then click the summoning font. Summoning flames appear. Click them in the correct order for each lesson:

- Lesson 1: Spirit Hog
- Lesson 2: Trickster Whim

After successfully completing the first three lessons, click the summoning font and go through the procedure for all three exercises (minus the summoning flame step) and click "Summoning the Fourth" behind the shelves in the circular study. The second summoning exercise is needed to trigger the Trickster Whim quest. Going through the procedure for all three exercises after all three creatures are summoned actually triggers an easter egg, making Arl Foreshadow appear. You then have the opportunity to steal a note from him before he disappears, which adds a codex entry to your journal.

Watchguard of the Reaching

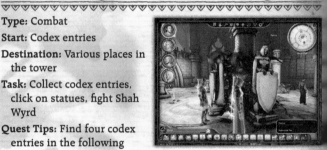

Type: Combat

Start: Codex entries

Destination: Various places in the tower

Task: Collect codex entries, click on statues, fight Shah Wyrd

Quest Tips: Find four codex entries in the following areas:

- Apprentice Quarters: Find two codex entries in footlockers, one in library.
- Senior Mage: Find one codex entry in the study by Owain, one codex entry on the opposite end of the study by the blood mages.
- Great Hall: Find one codex entry near the back wall of the main room.

After you find all the codex entries, activate the Great Hall statues in the correct order: vessel in hand, sword raised, sword lowered, spear raised in central area. (The statues will burn you for damage if you interact with them without activating the other items from the side quest.) Then open the door to the Basement and fight Shah Wyrd.

Denerim

~ Denerim Market District ~

Open Market · Chantry · Wade's Emporium · Elven Alienage

A · F · G · B · C · H · E · D

Wonders of Thedas · Gnawed Noble Tavern · Brother Gentivi's

→ NOTE ←

Many of the Denerim side quests can be performed in any order, whenever you have down time between your main quests. However, certain series, such as the combat ones given out by Sergeant Kylon or the stealth and stealing quests given out by Slim Couldry, must be carried out in sequence.

Legend

- A Chantry Board
- B Sergeant Kylon
- C Messenger for "Antivan Crows" Quests
- D "Honor Bound" Duel
- E Friends of Red Jenny
- F Mages' Collective
- G Slim Couldry
- H Warehouse

The Circle of Magi - Denerim

Basics ~ Character Generation ~ Classes ~ The Party ~ Companions ~ Supporting Cast ~ Equipment ~ Bestiary ~ Walkthroughs ~ **Side Quests** ~ Random Encounters ~ Achievements/Trophies

Slim Couldry's Quests

*** Crime Wave ***

Type: Messenger

Start: Slim Couldry

Destination: Denerim Market District

Task: Speak to Slim Couldry about a series of Stealth and Stealing quests

Quest Tips: This is the first in the series of Slim Couldry quests. If you are a rogue and have the Stealth talent, Couldry will assign you the following quests: "The Absent Mistress," "A Fistful of Silver," "The Private Collection," and "The Tears of Andraste." If you have the Stealing skill, Couldry will assign you the following quests: "Lady in Waiting," "A Stolen Blade," "Market Day," and "The Traitor's Crown." If you have both Stealth and Stealing, you can complete all eight quests. You will have to pay Couldry up front for the quest information, but the rewards are worth it when you return to him after a successful mission.

*** The Absent Mistress ***

Type: Stealth

Start: Slim Couldry

Destination: Gnawed Noble Tavern

Task: Slip into Lady Sophie's room and steal her valuables

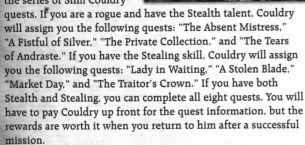

Quest Tips: This is the first in the Stealth chain of Slim Couldry quests. Speak with Slim Couldry and pay him the gold for the quest information. Enter the Gnawed Noble Tavern and unlock the door to Lady Sophie's room (Deft Hands talent necessary). Open the chest and remove the contents. Return to Slim for your reward.

*** A Fistful of Silver ***

Type: Stealth

Start: Slim Couldry

Destination: Warehouse in Denerim Market District

Task: Enter the warehouse, slay the guards, and take the silver

Quest Tips: This is the second in the Stealth chain of Slim Couldry quests. Speak with Slim Couldry and pay him the gold for the quest information. Break into the warehouse in the marketplace (in the same alley as the Wonders of Thedas). Remove the silver bars from the chest after beating all the guards in the small room.

*** The Private Collection ***

Type: Stealth

Start: Slim Couldry

Destination: Bann Franderel's Estate

Task: Fight your way out of the estate after a trap is sprung

Quest Tips: This is the third in the Stealth chain of Slim Couldry quests. Speak with Slim Couldry and pay him the gold for the quest information. Enter Bann Franderel's Estate in search of the valuables. When you reach the designated chest, it has nothing to speak of in it and the estate guards surround you. Battle out of the estate and return to Slim. You get nothing out of this quest, but Slim is so distraught, he's willing to give you the next quest for free. Note that this quest can only be started after the Landsmeet has begun.

*** Tears of Andraste ***

Type: Stealth

Start: Slim Couldry

Destination: Bann Franderel's Estate

Task: Make it to the vault without alerting the guards and steal the Tears of Andraste

Quest Tips: This is the fourth in the Stealth chain of Slim Couldry quests. Leave the Market District and return; Slim will return from his trip. Speak with Slim Couldry and he'll send you back to Bann Franderel's Estate. Slip past all the guards unseen and find the vault. Once in the treasure room, steal the Tears of Andraste and return them to Slim for a big reward.

*** Lady in Waiting ***

Type: Stealing

Start: Slim Couldry

Destination: Denerim Market District

Task: Pickpocket the servant girl in the market

Quest Tips: This is the first in the Stealing chain of Slim Couldry quests. Speak with Slim Couldry and pay him the gold for the quest information. Head to the center of the marketplace and look for the lady's maid shopping. With the Stealing skill, you can pickpocket her easily. Return to Slim for your reward.

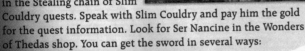

*** A Stolen Blade ***

Type: Stealing

Start: Slim Couldry

Destination: Wonders of Thedas in Denerim Market District

Task: Pickpocket a patron of the Wonders of Thedas

Quest Tips: This is the second in the Stealing chain of Slim Couldry quests. Speak with Slim Couldry and pay him the gold for the quest information. Look for Ser Nancine in the Wonders of Thedas shop. You can get the sword in several ways:

- If you have a high enough Persuade skill, you can convince Ser Nancine she is dying and get her out of her armor, taking the sword for yourself.
- You can pickpocket the sword right off of her.
- Again, with a high enough Persuade skill, you can pretend to be store help and sell Nancine a dress. This will remove her armor, and you can take the sword.

*** Market Day ***

Type: Stealing

Start: Slim Couldry

Destination: Denerim Market District

Task: Steal loot from the two chests in the center of the Denerim Market District

Quest Tips: This is the third in the Stealing chain of Slim Couldry quests. Speak with Slim Couldry and pay him the gold for the quest information. You must acquire a key that Master Tilver has to open two chests in the center of the marketplace. Of course, Tilver has two guards with him at all times. You can get past the guards in a number of ways:

- A character with a high enough Stealth skill (Combat Stealth or higher) can sneak past them and pickpocket the key from Master Tilver.
- Through dialogue, a player with a high enough Persuade skill can convince the guards to let him pass.
- Pay a messenger boy to distract the guards.

Once you've stolen the key, unlock the two chests under the center tent of the marketplace and remove their inventory. Return to Slim for your reward.

*** The Traitor's Crown ***

Type: Stealing

Start: Slim Couldry

Destination: Gnawed Noble Tavern

Task: Outwit or stealth past the guards and steal the crown

Quest Tips: This is the fourth in the Stealing chain of Slim Couldry quests. Speak with Slim Couldry and pay him the gold for the quest information. Enter the Gnawed Noble Tavern and bypass the guards. You can accomplish this in many different fashions:

- A character with a high enough Stealth skill (Master Stealth) can sneak past them and pickpocket the crown from the seneschal.
- The PC can get by the many guards a couple of ways via the waitresses. The PC can convince the waitresses either with Persuade (at level 1 or higher) or a bribe (3 gold) to go over and keep the guards happy and entertained. If the guards are suspicious, then they turn the waitresses away. If they aren't, you can walk by them. They initiate conversation, but are highly distracted.
- The PC can buy a round of potent dwarven spirits for the guards (for 5 gold). When they drink it, the guards are very out of it. You can walk right by at that point.
- A PC with Poison (at level 1 or higher) can spike some drinks with sleeping poison. That will KO all of the guards and the seneshal. Then the PC can just grab the crown.
- The waitresses can catch on to the player trying to pull a fast one, in which case the conversation game ends.
- Talking with the guards is another possibility. The PC can pretend to have an urgent message for the seneschal or just be looking for a quiet table to drink. This might have had a chance of working, but the guards recognize the PC. They then play along, but should be acting suspicious enough for the PC to be tipped off.
- You can go inside the room, but then all the guards attack.
- You can just attack the guards. In this case, cue a fun but bloody combat. A couple of lieutenant guards plus numbers should be enough.
- The PC can use Intimidate to convince the guards to run. Intimidate (at level 2 or higher) is necessary to succeed (otherwise cue combat). If this works, all the guards leave. The seneschal will either give the PC the crown or be attacked.

Once the PC maneuvers near the seneshal, he still needs to steal the crown with Expert Stealing. Return to Couldry and inform him of the success.

Drake Scale Armor

Type: Crafting

Start: Once you've collected a drake scale

Destination: Wade's Emporium in Denerim Market District

Task: Collect three drake scales to turn into drake scale armor

Quest Tips: Once you have three drake scales (collected from any drake, mainly found in the Wyrmling Lair), return to Wade's Emporium and Master Wade will craft a unique set of drake scale armor for you. During the transaction, you will have the option to pay Master Wade for the armor. While this will not affect the quality of the drake scale armor, it will influence what type of dragon scale armor (regular or superior) will be made in the "Dragon Scale Armor" quest. If the player pays, a superior suit of armor can be made. The armor will take some time to make. Once you leave the Denerim Market District, and then return, the armor will be ready. Wade will be displeased with his creation and will inform you that if he can get more scales he can make another set of armor. Collect three more drake scales, ask Wade to make a second suit and offer to pay. Once you pick up the second set, the quest is complete.

Denerim

Basics ~ Character Generation ~ Classes ~ The Party ~ Companions ~ Supporting Cast ~ Equipment ~ Bestiary ~ Walkthroughs ~ **Side Quests** ~ Random Encounters ~ Achievements/Trophies

Dragon Scale Armor

Type: Crafting

Start: Once you've collected a dragon scale

Destination: Wade's Emporium in Denerim Market District

Task: Collect one dragon scale to turn into dragon scale armor

Quest Tips: You must complete the "Drake Scale Armor" quest first to gain dragon scale armor. Master Wade can make you a set of dragon scale armor from the scale of the high dragon in the "Urn of Sacred Ashes" quest. Wade can make one of three different types of armor: medium, heavy, or massive. He might make a superior version of the type requested if you've paid for drake scale armor both times.

Forgotten Verses

Type: Collection

Start: Ruined Temple in the "Urn of Sacred Ashes" quest

Destination: Sister Justine in Denerim Market District

Task: Collect some ancient scrolls and return them to the Denerim Chantry

Quest Tips: Pick up the scrolls in the Ruined Temple and head to the Denerim Market District. Speak with Sister Justine for your reward.

❦ NOTE ❦

See the Ruined Temple map in the "Urn of Sacred Ashes" walkthrough for the locations of the hidden scrolls.

Hearing Voices

Type: Collection

Start: Abandoned Orphanage

Destination: Deranged Beggar in the Elven Alienage

Task: Collect an amulet and return it to the Deranged Beggar

Quest Tips: Pick up the amulet in the last room in the Abandoned Orphanage in the Elven Alienage. This will start the quest, and all you have to do is return it to the Deranged Beggar in the Alienage.

Honor Bound

Type: Combat

Start: Outside the Gnawed Noble Tavern.

Destination: The alley behind the Gnawed Noble Tavern

Task: Duel Ser Landry (or persuade him not to duel)

Quest Tips: You meet Ser Landry just outside the Gnawed Noble Tavern in the Denerim Market District. Ser Landry was at Ostagar and challenges you to a duel. You can accept and fight one on one, or as a group, or refuse. If the player refuses, Landry will leave but later confront the player in a random encounter on the Denerim city map. Also, if you have a high enough Persuade skill, you can convince Ser Landry not to duel at all. If the fight is on, follow Ser Landry to the duel spot around the corner in the alley behind the Gnawed Noble Tavern. Beat him to finish the quest.

The Last Request

Type: Combat

Start: Ser Friden's corpse in Denerim's Run-down Back Street

Destination: Elven Alienage

Task: Destroy the blood mages in the Alienage

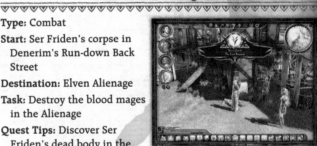
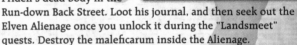

Quest Tips: Discover Ser Friden's dead body in the Run-down Back Street. Loot his journal, and then seek out the Elven Alienage once you unlock it during the "Landsmeet" quests. Destroy the maleficarum inside the Alienage.

Lost Templar

Type: Exploration

Start: Arl of Denerim's Estate

Destination: Gnawed Noble Tavern

Task: Free Irminric from a Denerim Estate cell

Quest Tips: During your run through the Arl of Denerim's Estate for the Landsmeet quest line, free Irminric from his dungeon cell (he's near Vaughan in the northern part of the dungeon). After speaking with Irminric, return his signet ring to his sister, Bann Alfstanna, in the Gnawed Noble Tavern in Denerim. This will gain you favor in the Landsmeet vote.

Sergeant Kylon's Quests

*** Pearls Before Swine ***

Type: Combat

Start: Sergeant Kylon in the market district

Destination: White Falcon Veteran in the Pearl

Task: Defeat the mercenaries in the Pearl to leave (or persuade them without a fight)

Quest Tips: This is the first quest in the Sergeant Kylon quest sequence. You need to clear out the mercenaries in the Pearl. This can be achieved several ways:

- If the Landsmeet plot is complete, the mercenaries will leave voluntarily.
- In dialogue, a character with a high enough Persuade skill can convince the group to leave peacefully.
- In dialogue, a character with a high enough Intimidate skill can force the group to leave peacefully.
- You can attack the group of mercenaries.

Once the mercenaries are nearly dead, the leader will surrender. You can then tell the mercs to leave, or you could also demand that they pay you first before they leave. En route to the market, you will be stopped by Sergeant Kylon who wishes to thank you. The sergeant is interrupted by Cristof, leader of the mercenaries, who attacks. Now you're free to kill off the mercenaries and end the problem for good.

*** The Crimson Oars ***

Type: Combat

Start: Sergeant Kylon

Destination: Gnawed Noble Tavern

Task: Break up the Crimson Oars mercenaries who are congregated unlawfully

Quest Tips: This is the second in the Sergeant Kylon quest line. Head to the Gnawed Noble Tavern. You can either beat down the Crimson Oars mercenaries or persuade them to leave with a few drinks. In a fight, if you take down their leader first, the rest will give up.

Something Wicked

Type: Exploration

Start: Ser Otto in the Elven Alienage

Destination: Abandoned Orphanage

Task: Discover the clues that lead you to the Abandoned Orphanage and dispatch the demon

Quest Tips: Seek out Ser Otto in the Elven Alienage. He asks you to help him track down some unusual activity. You must collect a couple of clues to enter the Abandoned Orphanage. Any two of the following around the Alienage will do:

- A pool of fresh blood.
- A feral dog.
- A dead dog.
- An insane beggar.

Follow Otto to the orphanage and keep him alive while he cleanses the area. At the end, you must defeat the demon to complete the quest.

— NOTE —

See the Elven Alienage map in the "Landsmeet" walkthrough for the location the clues and the Abandoned Orphanage.

Tortured Noble

Type: Exploration

Start: Arl of Denerim's Estate

Destination: Gnawed Noble Tavern

Task: Free Oswyn from a Denerim Estate cell

Quest Tips: During your run through the Arl of Denerim's Estate for the Landsmeet quest line, free Oswyn from his dungeon cell. After speaking with Oswyn, seek out his father Sighard in the Gnawed Noble Tavern in Denerim. This will gain you favor in the Landsmeet vote.

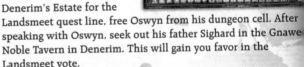

Antivan Crows Quests

❧ NOTE ❧

Unlike other side quests that can be completed in any order, the Antivan Crows' quest line must be performed in the following order, beginning with "The Trial of Crows."

*** The Trial of Crows ***

Type: Messenger

Start: Speak with the messenger boy in Denerim Market District or Master Ignacio directly

Destination: Master Ignacio in the Gnawed Noble Tavern

Task: Speak with the messenger, then Ignacio and accept his first assassination quest

Quest Tips: This is a series of assassination quests offered by Master Ignacio on behalf of the Antivan Crows. To initiate the quest, just talk with Master Ignacio in the Market District, then try to leave (or talk to the messenger boy in the market). The messenger boy quickly delivers a message indicating that you should go to one of the back rooms of the Gnawed Noble Tavern. Once there you can talk with Master Ignacio who will offer some assassination contracts, or you can choose to kill Master Ignacio. After you complete all the other assassination quests, return to Master Ignacio one last time to complete "The Trial of Crows" quest. His assistant, Cesar, will open a special store for you in the marketplace.

❧ CAUTION ❧

Because you are on assassination missions for the Antivan Crows, your approval rating will suffer a small amount with the moral companions in the group, such as Wynne.

*** The First Test ***

Type: Combat

Start: Master Ignacio

Destination: Paedan in the Pearl

Task: Assassinate Paedan in the Pearl

Quest Tips: After Master Ignacio hands you the "First Test" scroll, return to the market and examine the wall near the Elven Alienage for a Grey Warden poster. It's part of a scam to lure Grey Wardens into an ambush at the Pearl, and it holds the password to enter the trap. The man behind the trap, Paeden, waits behind a locked door in the back of the Pearl. Slay Paeden and his lackeys. Note that you can do this quest without having talked to Ignacio. All you need to do is click on the poster. If Arl Howe is dead at this point, the guys in the Pearl will no longer attack you, as their boss is too dead to pay.

*** Mercenary Hunt ***

Type: Combat

Start: Master Ignacio

Destination: Kadan-Fe Hideout on the world map

Task: Assassinate Kadan-Fe and his gang at their hideout

Quest Tips: After completing "The First Test," obtain the contract from the chest behind Master Ignacio. Travel to the Kadan-Fe Hideout location on the world map. Slaughter everyone there and return to Master Ignacio.

*** An Audience with the Ambassador ***

Type: Combat

Start: Master Ignacio

Destination: The Orzammar Royal Palace

Task: Assassinate Ambassador Gainley

Quest Tips: After completing "The First Test," obtain the contract from the chest behind Master Ignacio. You must have completed the "A Paragon of Her Kind" quest line or sided with Prince Bhelen during the political struggles in Orzammar to get to the ambassador. Slay Gainley and return to Master Ignacio in the Gnawed Noble when the deed is done.

*** The Ransom ***

Type: Combat

Start: Master Ignacio

Destination: Ransom Drop Location

Task: Assassinate Captain Chase and his men

Quest Tips: You must have completed all the other Antivan Crows' quests before you can undertake this one. Head to the Ransom Drop Location on the Denerim city map. Captain Chase and his men are holding a child hostage, and you're showing up with other Crows to take them out. As soon as you approach Captain Chase, the other Crows attack and it's a giant free-for-all. Don't get caught in the middle or you get flanked easily. Stay near the entrance and pull enemies to you. Don't worry so much about the Crows; the guild has more.

Favors for Certain Interested Parties

NOTE

The following Rogues' Guild quests can be obtained in Denerim from the bartender in the Gnawed Noble Tavern. The "D" quests begin with "Solving Problems" and must be completed in order. The "K" quests begin with "Negotiation Aids" and must be completed in order.

Correspondence Interruptus

Type: Collection

Start: Bartender in Gnawed Noble Tavern

Destination: Various locations

Task: Collect 12 love letters from chests

Quest Tips: Find all 12 love letters in the following locations:

- Brecilian Ruins (south, secret hallway just inside entrance)
- Circle Tower (Senior Mage Quarters, behind wall in east bedroom)

- Dalish Camp (just north of Varathorn)
- Denerim (Pearl, one of the back rooms)
- Denerim (Wade's Emporium)
- Denerim (Arl Eamon's Estate, Arl's bedroom upstairs)
- Haven (Villager House, along the wall)
- Lake Calenhad Docks (Spoiled Princess, northeast corner of the inn)
- Orzammar (Carta Hideout, southeast corner room of Jarvia encounter)
- Orzammar (Royal Palace, small room on east side of palace)
- Redcliffe Basement (northwest alcove)
- Redcliffe Village (Windmill, east side)

"K" Quests

*** Negotiation Aids ***

Type: Collection

Start: Bartender in Gnawed Noble Tavern

Destination: Various vendors

Task: Collect 15 toxin extracts

Quest Tips: This is the first in the series of "K" quests. During your travels, it's easy enough to collect 15 toxin extracts. Visit local vendors and collect a handful at a time. The best vendor is Varathorn in the Dalish camp (who can give you all the toxin extracts in one shot), or you can visit Cesar in the Denerim Market District, Faryn in Frostback Mountains, Alimar's in Orzammar, Olinda's in Orzammar.

*** Untraceable ***

Type: Collection

Start: Bartender in Gnawed Noble Tavern

Destination: Various vendors

Task: Collect 10 garnets

Quest Tips: This is the second in the series of "K" quests. Save up all your garnet drops from adventuring. If you've already sold some of them off, retrace your steps and buy them back from the various vendors. Turn in 10 garnets to complete the quest.

*** Dead Drops ***

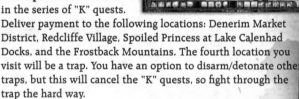

Type: Messenger

Start: Bartender in Gnawed Noble Tavern

Destination: Four different locations

Task: Make three drops and escape from a trap

Quest Tips: This is the third in the series of "K" quests. Deliver payment to the following locations: Denerim Market District, Redcliffe Village, Spoiled Princess at Lake Calenhad Docks, and the Frostback Mountains. The fourth location you visit will be a trap. You have an option to disarm/detonate other traps, but this will cancel the "K" quests, so fight through the trap the hard way.

*** New Ground ***

Type: Combat

Start: Bartender in Gnawed Noble Tavern

Destination: Denerim and random encounter

Task: Signal three people with K's wink and nod, signal guard contact, kill D's lieutenant, kill D

Quest Tips: Note this is the fourth in the series of "K" quests. Finishing this quest will remove the end of the "D" line of quests. First, signal three people with K's special wink and nod. Second, signal the guard contact. Third, kill D's lieutenant in a random city encounter and take the directions from the lieutenant's corpse to find D's location on the Denerim city map. Finally, kill D himself in the indoor area.

Favors for Certain Interested Parties - Korcari Wilds

Basics ~ Character Generation ~ Classes ~ The Party ~ Companions ~ Supporting Cast ~ Equipment ~ Bestiary ~ Walkthroughs ~ **Side Quests** ~ Random Encounters ~ Achievements/Trophies

"D" Quests

*** Solving Problems ***

Type: Messenger

Start: Bartender in Gnawed Noble Tavern

Destination: Three places in Denerim

Task: Dispose of three bodies for the rogues' guild

Quest Tips: This is the first in the series of "D" quests. Collect three bodies and dispose of them at the marked "dumped site" inside the Chantry walls. Find the bodies in the following locations: Market District (alley beside the Chantry), the Warehouse in the Wonders of Thedas alley (in the back room), and the Pearl (one of the back rooms).

*** Sign of Safe Passage ***

Type: Combat

Start: Bartender in Gnawed Noble Tavern

Destination: Brecilian West Forest

Task: Fire a messenger arrow from a location in the Brecilian West Forest

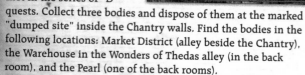

Quest Tips: This is the second in the series of "D" quests. Fire an arrow from a firing point just east of the south entrance of the Brecilian West Forest (you must equip a bow on your main PC to do this). Fight the mercenaries that arrive, and loot the folded missive from one of the corpses when you're finished with them.

*** False Witness ***

Type: Combat

Start: Bartender in Gnawed Noble Tavern

Destination: Three different locations across the map

Task: Kill Cam of Redside, Skinny Frank, and Brian

Quest Tips: This is the third in the series of "D" quests. You must hunt down three unfortunates who have stolen from the guild: Cam of Redside in the Wonders of Thedas, Skinny Frank at the Lake Calenhad Docks, and Brian in the Frostback Mountains. Cam and Skinny Frank have bodyguards to worry about too; poor Brian is, well, a pushover.

*** Harsh Decisions ***

Type: Combat

Start: Bartender in Gnawed Noble Tavern

Destination: Denerim and random encounter

Task: Kill K's lieutenant, kill K

Quest Tips: This is the fourth in the series of "D" quests. Finishing this quest will remove the end of the "K" line of quests. First, travel on the Denerim city map and you'll trigger a random encounter with K's lieutenant. Slay him and his guards and pick up the hideout directions from the lieutenant's corpse. Next, travel to K's hideout on the Denerim city map. Slay K and his men. Return to the Gnawed Noble bartender for your reward.

Korcari Wilds

~ See map on next page ~

NOTE

The Korcari Wilds side quests can be performed in any order, whenever you have down time during your main prelude quest to become a Grey Warden.

A Pinch of Ashes

Type: Combat

Start: Ashes from dead soldier corpse at bridge fight

Destination: Summoning point north of corpse

Task: Loot the ashes and summon the ash wraith Gazarath

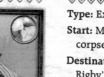

Quest Tips: Loot pouch of ashes from dead soldier corpse at the bridge fight. Head north and click on pile of rocks overlooking a sunken rotunda. Use the ash and fight the ash wraith Gazarath.

Last Will and Testament

Type: Exploration

Start: Missionary Rigby's corpse

Destination: The chest near Rigby's corpse

Task: Find the hidden treasure chest in the Wilds

Quest Tips: Find Missionary Rigby's corpse in the Wilds gazebo. Loot the bow and money from lockbox. Keep the item or deliver it to Jetta in Redcliffe Chantry for some extra experience.

primagames.com

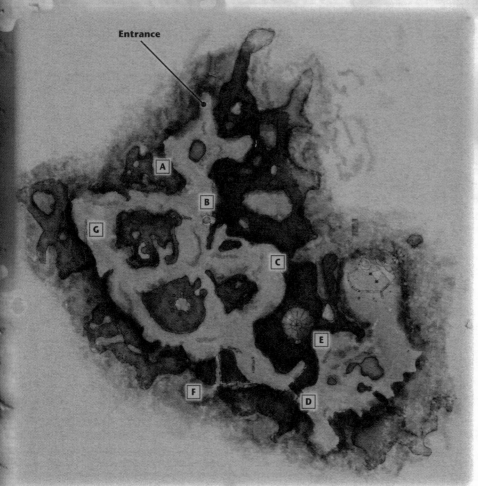

Entrance

Legend

- **A** Missionary Jogby's Body
- **B** Wilds Flower for "Mabari Hound"
- **C** Missionary Rigby's Body
- **D** Dead Soldier for "A Pinch of Ash"
- **E** Summon Point for Gazarath
- **F** Hidden Chest for "The Missionary"
- **G** Missionary Rigby's Field Journal

The Missionary

Type: Exploration

Start: Missionary Jogby's corpse

Destination: The chest between two trees

Task: Find the hidden treasure chest in the Wilds

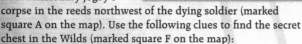

Quest Tips: Loot the letter from Missionary Jogby's corpse in the reeds northwest of the dying soldier (marked square A on the map). Use the following clues to find the secret chest in the Wilds (marked square F on the map):

- Look for a tree leaning on a ruined building
- Pass under a fallen tree bridge
- Pass a submerged tower on the right
- Look between a high, ruined arch and a mossy standing stone
- Walk along a path of roots and stones
- Look for two large statues with a chest between them

Signs of the Chasind

Type: Exploration

Start: Missionary Rigby's Field Journal

Destination: Hidden cache

Task: Find a hidden cache in the Wilds

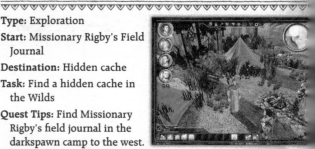

Quest Tips: Find Missionary Rigby's field journal in the darkspawn camp to the west. Follow Chasind trail signs (map notes) throughout the Wilds to a hidden cache in a darkspawn camp south of the bridge fight.

Korcari Wilds ~ The Mage's Collective

Basics ~ Character Generation ~ Classes ~ The Party ~ Companions ~ Supporting Cast ~ Equipment ~ Bestiary ~ Walkthroughs ~ **Side Quests** ~ Random Encounters ~ Achievements/Trophies

The Mages' Collective

A Gift of Silence (or Justice Must be Served)

Type: Crafting

Start: Mages' Collective at Denerim Market District

Destination: Knight-Commander Harrith in Redcliffe Village or Knight-Commander Tavish in Denerim Market District

Task: Bring 10 lyrium potions to either of the Knight-Commanders

Quest Tips: Note that this quest is only active after the attack on Redcliffe by the undead. First, create or buy 10 lyrium potions. You then have a choice to bring the 10 lyrium potions to the knight-commander in Redcliffe Village (Harrith up by the windmill) or in Denerim Market District (Tavish by the estate gate). This sets up whose side you'll be on in the "Defending the Collective" final Mages' Collective quest.

Blood of Warning

Type: Exploration

Start: Mages' Collective at Denerim Market District

Destination: Four doors around Denerim

Task: Mark four blood mage relatives' doors

Quest Tips: As you leave the Mages' Collective in Denerim, open up your map and note the two nearby doors you have to mark. Click on those, then head to the Dirty Back Alley and mark the single door there. The last door is in the Dark Alley, and there may be a large group of thugs waiting to ambush you if you haven't cleared them out already. Dispatch the enemy group and mark the final door for your reward.

Careless Accusations

Type: Exploration

Start: Mages' Collective at Lake Calenhad Docks

Destination: Random encounter in Wooded Glen

Task: Prevent an adventuring group from delivering false testimony

Quest Tips: Shortly after you pick up this side quest, while traveling across the world map, you will trigger a "random" encounter in the Wooded Glen. You can either persuade or intimidate the adventuring party there into not giving false testimony in Denerim, or you can just battle it out for extra experience and loot. It's a relatively simple quest once you find them.

Defending the Collective

Type: Messenger

Start: Mages' Collective at Redcliffe Village

Destination: Knight-Commander Harrith at Redcliffe Village

Task: Deliver the bundled testimony to Knight-Commander Harrith

Quest Tips: If you choose Harrith in the "A Gift of Silence" quest, you will deliver your bundled testimony to him in Redcliffe Village. Otherwise, seek out Knight-Commander Tavish in the Denerim Market District. Pick up your big reward for completing all the Mages' Collective quests.

Have You Seen Me?

Type: Combat

Start: Mages' Collective at Denerim Market District

Destination: Random encounter

Task: Defeat the abomination in the random encounter

Quest Tips: Shortly after you pick up this side quest, while traveling across the world map, you will trigger a "random" encounter in the Out of the Way map. Stun the abomination often and don't give it much chance to counter-attack. After it dies, return to Mages' Collective operative for your reward.

Herbal Magic

Type: Exploration

Start: Mages' Collective at Lake Calenhad Docks

Destination: Various places

Task: Present 10 deep mushrooms to the Mages' Collective

Quest Tips: As you adventure, save the deep mushrooms you find until you have 10 and hand them in. If you don't feel like waiting, you can visit the following shops to pick up the deep mushrooms immediately: Lloyd's Tavern in Redcliffe, Olinda's in the Orzammar Commons, Gnawed Noble Tavern in Denerim, and the biggest mushroom stockpile in Alimar's in Orzammar's Dust Town (or Figor's in Orzammar if you've unlocked the door).

Notice of Termination

Type: Messenger

Start: Mages' Collective at Lake Calenhad Docks

Destination: Three separate locations across Ferelden: two in the Denerim Market District and one in the Frostback Mountains

Task: Deliver three termination notes to apprentices across Ferelden

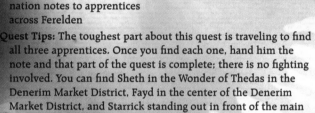

Quest Tips: The toughest part about this quest is traveling to find all three apprentices. Once you find each one, hand him the note and that part of the quest is complete; there is no fighting involved. You can find Sheth in the Wonder of Thedas in the Denerim Market District, Fayd in the center of the Denerim Market District, and Starrick standing out in front of the main doors to Orzammar, by the row of market goods in the Frostback Mountains.

Places of Power

Type: Exploration

Start: Mages' Collective at Denerim Market District

Destination: Four separate locations across Ferelden

Task: Unlock four hidden locations

Quest Tips: The four hidden places of power are: East Brecilian Forest (gravestone in the northern ogre grove), Ortan Thaig (Altar of Sundering), The Alienage (Alienage Tree), and Apprentice Quarters in the Circle Tower (activate the middle of the floor). Because these are in difficult-to-reach places, this will likely be the last Mages' Collective quest you complete before the final "Defending the Collective" quest.

The Scrolls of Banastor

Type: Collection

Start: Mages' Collective at Denerim Market District

Destination: Various places

Task: Collect five scrolls hidden around the world.

Quest Tips: The scrolls are in ancient texts treasure piles in the following locations: Circle Tower (Senior Mage Quarters level, southeast ruined room), Circle Tower (Great Hall level, northwest large room), Wyrmling Lair on the "Urn of Sacred Ashes" quest (southeast library), Wyrmling Lair on the "Urn of Sacred Ashes" quest (middle west barracks), and Werewolf Lair in the Brecilian Ruins (southeast werewolf bedroom). Once you have them all, return for your reward.

See the Circle Tower maps in the "Broken Circle" walkthrough, Wyrmling Lair map in the "Urn of Sacred Ashes" walkthrough, and Lair of the Werewolf map in the "Nature of the Beast" walkthrough for the Scrolls of Banastor ancient texts locations.

Thy Brother's Killer

Type: Combat

Start: Mages' Collective at Lake Calenhad Docks

Destination: Northern grove in the East Brecilian Forest

Task: Slay the dark Maleficarum Cabal

Quest Tips: To discover the Maleficarum Cabal's hidden ritual, you must first clear the northern grove in the East Brecilian Forest of the ogres that normally inhabit the area. Leave the East Brecilian Forest, then reenter and return to the northern grove. Four dark mages will be chanting in a circle. Speak with them and then the fight is on. If you have Alistair, use his templar abilities to great effect against the mages, especially if you have Holy Smite to drain the mages of mana and deal Spirit damage. A rogue's Dirty Fighting or mage's Crushing Prison can nullify a single target, or Earthquake can knock most or all of them off their feet. If you have distance, and the mages do like to keep their range, return deadly AoE of your own with spells such as Fireball or Inferno. Anti-Magic Ward on your tank will usually mean lights out for at least one of the mages.

Origin Stories

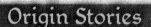

NOTE

See the individual Origins walkthroughs for more details on side quests relevant to the main quests.

The Mage's Collective - Orzammar

Basics ~ Character Generation ~ Classes ~ The Party ~ Companions ~ Supporting Cast ~ Equipment ~ Bestiary ~ Walkthroughs ~ **Side Quests** ~ Random Encounters ~ Achievements/Trophies

The Mabari Hound

Type: Exploration

Start: Human Noble Origin

Destination: Castle Cousland Pantry

Task: Meet up with Dog in the pantry

Quest Tips: In the Human Noble origin story, you can gain Dog as a companion

by going to the kitchen, speaking with Nan, and then entering the pantry. Dog will become a member of your party. If you aren't of Human Noble origin, speak with the Kennel Master in Ostagar and complete "The Mabari Hound" quest. Return the wild flower from the Wilds to the Kennel Master to heal Dog, then he'll join you in a random encounter after Flemeth rescues you from the Tower of Ishal.

Orzammar

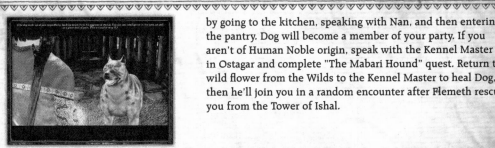

⟡ NOTE ⟡

See the "Paragon of Her Kind" walkthrough for detailed maps with the locations of all your Orzammar side quest points of interest.

A Lost Nug

Type: Exploration

Start: Nug Wrangler Boermor in Orzammar Commons

Destination: Any nug in Orzammar

Task: Return a nug to Boermor

Quest Tips: Nug Wrangler Boermor has lost his nugs and needs you to round them up for him. Once you activate the quest, nugs will be hidden throughout Orzammar. Return a nug to Boermor for a reward. Even after the quest is complete, you can return nugs to Boermor for a reward, and if you return more than 10 to him, he grants a big reward.

An Unlikely Scholar

Type: Messenger

Start: Dagna in Orzammar Commons

Destination: Circle Tower

Task: Ask the Circle Tower to allow Dagna to study there

Quest Tips: Find Dagna in the Orzammar Commons. Agree to help her and set out for the Circle Tower. You must complete the "Broken Circle" quest line if you haven't already done so. If First Enchanter Irving is alive and in charge, he will allow Dagna to come study at the tower. If Greagoir is in charge, he will deny her the opportunity.

A Mother's Hope

Type: Exploration

Start: Orzammar Commons

Destination: Deep Roads

Task: Find Filda's missing son, Ruck

Quest Tips: Journey into the Deep Roads to find Filda's missing son, Ruck. He's in Ortan Thaig. When you first spot him, he runs away from you, but you can track him down slightly north of his original position.

Asunder

Type: Exploration

Start: A small bloody sack

Destination: Altar of Sundering in Ortan Thaig

Task: Find the three small bloody sacks and place them on Altar of Sundering

Quest Tips: Find the bag of limbs in the first darkspawn clearing in Aeducan Thaig. Find the torso in a bag in the southeast cavern of Caridin's Cross. Find the head in a bag in the deepstalker clearing in Caridin's Cross. Once you have all three components, seek out the Altar of Sundering in Ortan Thaig. Place the three bloody items on the altar. You can then choose to fight the Fade beast that arrives for XP or let it go and get a substantial amount of gold as reward.

primagames.com

Caged in Stone

Type: Combat **Start:** Royal Palace Throne

Destination: Royal Palace Throne

Task: Find codex on throne, solve puzzle, fight dragon

Quest Tips: In the Royal Throne Room, click on the throne to gain a codex entry. Next, you need to solve

the puzzle. Leave your PC standing next to the throne. Send two companions to stand on the pressure points that look like arrows in the southwest corner (you will hear sliding stone if you stand on each one correctly). Send your last companion out into the main hall to stand on the central square pressure point. With all three companions in the correct position, access the throne again. A dragon will appear. Defeat the dragon for your reward (the Ageless two-handed sword is part of your reward).

Casteless Ambush

Type: Combat

Start: Dust Town

Destination: Dust Town

Task: Survive a Dust Town ambush

Quest Tips: As soon as you enter Dust Town for the first time, you get jumped by a band of thugs. Beat them down.

The Chant in the Deeps

Type: Messenger

Start: Orzammar Commons

Destination: The Shaperate

Task: Speak to the Shaper of Memories on Brother Burkel's behalf

Quest Tips: Speak with Brother Burkel in the Orzammar Commons and
proceed to the Shaperate in the Diamond Quarter. You need to get the Shaper's permission to open the Chantry by either:

• Telling the Shaper that the Chantry's charities could aid Orzammar and passing a medium Persuasion check.

• Asking the Shaper what harm it would do to let Burkel preach and passing a high Persuasion check.

• Threatening the Shaper with forced conversion by a human army and passing a high Intimidation check.

If you succeed, return to Brother Burkel with the good news.

The Dead Caste

Type: Exploration

Start: The Dead Trenches

Destination: The Dead Trenches

Task: Find the four pieces of the Legion of the Dead armor

Quest Tips: Discover four codex entries pertaining to the Legion of the Dead

armor throughout the Dead Trenches. Look for them in the following places:

• The boots are in a sarcophagus in the room immediately to the left of the tunnel exit from the first bridge area where the legionnaires are fighting the darkspawn.

• The gloves are in a sarcophagus in the room directly opposite the first containing a fire-breathing dwarven statue trap.

• The breastplate is in a sarcophagus in the room with the hurlock emissary who summons skeletons.

• The helmet is resting on the legion altar within the Legionnaire Shrine.

After you locate all four pieces, find the grave revealed by completing the codex located in the tunnel leading up to the broodmother and obtain the insignia. Return the insignia to the Shaperate in Orzammar.

The Drifter's Cache

Type: Exploration

Start: Caridin's Cross

Destination: Caridin's Cross

Task: Find four piles of rubble with codex entries

Quest Tips: There are four piles of rubble with codex entries to unlock the Drifter's Cache: a pile at the

west exit, southwest of the bridge, in the central triangle, and east of the deepstalker cave. Once you've tagged all four, a new pile of rubble reveals itself in the south cave corridor where you can claim your reward.

Exotic Methods

Type: Crafting

Start: Herbalist Widron in Royal Palace

Destination: Herbalist Widron

Task: Craft a Dwarven Regicide Antidote

Quest Tips: You can only get access to this quest if you side with Bhelen early on.

In the western chamber in the Royal Palace, speak with Herbalist Widron. He needs help making a special antidote, which requires a Master Herbalism skill and the following ingredients: elfroot (x4), lifestone (x2), flask, and concentrator agent (x2).

Orzammar

Basics ~ Character Generation ~ Classes ~ The Party ~ Companions ~ Supporting Cast ~ Equipment ~ Bestiary ~ Walkthroughs ~ **Side Quests** ~ Random Encounters ~ Achievements/Trophies

The Gangue Shade

Type: Combat

Start: Legion of the Dead Relic

Destination: Legion of the Dead Relic

Task: Defeat the Gangue Shade

Quest Tips: For this quest to be active, a party member must wear the complete Legion of the Dead armor set (requires 42 strength). Find the Legion of the Dead Relic and click on it. Defeat the Gangue Shade and claim your reward.

The Golem Registry

Type: Messenger

Start: Near the Anvil of the Void

Destination: The Shaperate

Task: Deliver a tracking to the Shaper

Quest Tips: Near the Anvil of the Void, you can make a tracing of the golem registry. Bring the tracing back to the Shaper and he will reward you.

Jammer's Stash

Type: Exploration

Start: Jammer's Journal in Carta Hideout

Destination: Carta Hideout

Task: Find Jammer's stash box

Quest Tips: Find Jammer's Journal early in the Carta Hideout. Then find three common boxes and take only the cheapest item out of each box:

- Jammer's Common Box: Iron Letter Opener
- Kanky's Common Box: Silver Ring
- Pique's Common Box: Garnet Trinket

Discover Jammer's stash box near the tame brontos and open for your reward.

The Key to the City

Type: Exploration

Start: Any of the locations around Orzammar

Destination: Diplomatic cache in the Assembly

Task: Unlock the diplomatic cache in the Assembly

Quest Tips: To unlock the diplomatic cache in the Assembly, access the following locations around Orzammar:

- Hall of Heroes (find commission report)
- Commons (find document on bridge to Proving)
- Proving Grounds (find writ of censure in fighter's area)
- Diamond Quarter (find council writ behind doors to Commons)
- Dust Town (find Assembly directive in niche)

Lost to the Memories

Type: Messenger

Start: Orta in the Shaperate

Destination: Ortan Thaig

Task: Recover Ortan records

Quest Tips: Orta asks you to search for the long-lost House Ortan records in Ortan Thaig. Venture into Ortan Thaig and recover the records from a chest located in the main Thaig area. Even if you don't speak with Orta first, you can recover these records. Return the documents to Orta. You must leave Orzammar (and the Frostback Mountains) and return later to claim a reward from Orta in the Assembly.

Of Noble Birth

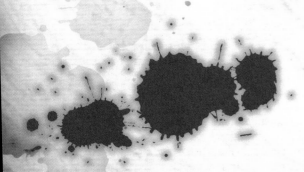

Type: Messenger

Start: Mardy

Destination: Bhelen or Harrowmont

Task: Gain a birthright for your illegitimate son

Quest Tips: This quest only becomes active if you are a dwarven noble player who indulged in the company of Mardy during the origin story. You encounter Mardy again when you return to Orzammar. Because you were exiled, your illegitimate son with Mardy is considered casteless. She wants you to restore the boy's birthright. You can get Bhelen or Harrowmont to accept the child into their house if you help them become king (or do so immediately after they have helped them acquire the crown). If you leave Orzammar without having Bhelen or Harrowmont grant the child status, the boy is doomed to life as a casteless dwarf.

Dragon Age ORIGINS

PRIMA Official Game Guide

Political Attacks

Type: Combat

Start: Faction Supporters

Destination: Three locations in Orzammar

Task: Defeat the faction supporters who want you dead

Quest Tips: There are three bands of faction supporters (for Lord Harrowmont if you support Bhelen, and for Bhelen if you support Harrowmont) in three different Orzammar locations: Commons, Diamond Quarter, and Proving Grounds. Defeat all three groups to finish the quest.

Precious Metals

Type: Messenger

Start: Dust Town

Destination: Godwin in the Circle Tower

Task: Deliver a shipment of expensive lyrium to Rogek's contact, Godwin

Quest Tips: Speak with the smuggler Rogek in Dust Town. You must buy a shipment of lyrium from Rogek to deliver to his contact, Godwin, in the Circle Tower. The shipment costs a whopping 50 gold (40 gold if you pass a medium Persuade check), and you must have the money or else Rogek walks away from you and the quest is dead. Travel to Godwin in the Senior Mage Quarters of the Circle Tower. Godwin will pay 50 gold for the lyrium shipment, or 60 gold, or 65 gold and a dagger (depending on how high your Persuade is). After the delivery, return to Rogek and he will reward you with 10 gold (or as much as 20 or 25 gold depending on your Persuade score). If Rogek or Godwin are dead, the transaction cannot be completed. If you get stuck with the lyrium, you can always sell it to any merchant to recover some of your cost.

Proving After Dark

Type: Combat

Start: Proving Armsman in Proving Grounds

Destination: Proving Grounds

Task: Defeat a team of four Proving Grounds experts

Quest Tips: Talk to the Proving Armsman in the Proving Grounds fighter area. Accept his proposal to fight on the side and defeat four ranked opponents each match. The first match features three warriors and a blood mage. The second match features two warriors, a Dust Town thug, and a champion. Earn some respect and tiny bit of cash.

The Shaper's Life

Type: Exploration

Start: Wall of Memories in Shaperate

Destination: Three locations around Orzammar

Task: Consult three rune stones and return to the Wall of Memories

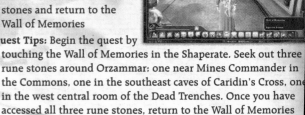

Quest Tips: Begin the quest by touching the Wall of Memories in the Shaperate. Seek out three rune stones around Orzammar: one near Mines Commander in the Commons, one in the southeast caves of Caridin's Cross, one in the west central room of the Dead Trenches. Once you have accessed all three rune stones, return to the Wall of Memories and receive XP as your reward.

Stalata Negat

Type: Exploration

Start: Dead Trenches

Destination: Four locations in the Dead Trenches

Task: Find four rune stones

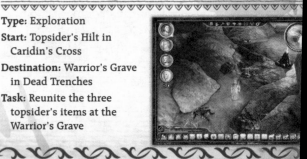

Quest Tips: Find the four rune stones in the Dead Trenches at the following places: by the Gates of Bownammar, in the northeast room, near the north genlock emissary/ghost encounter, in the corridor before the broodmother cave.

Thief in the House of Learning

Type: Messenger

Start: Shaper Assistant Milldrate

Destination: Proving Grounds

Task: Track down the Shaperate stolen goods

Quest Tips: Talk to Shaper Assistant Milldrate to start the quest. Next, get a proving receipt from Shady Corebit in Dust Town. Then head to the Proving Grounds and demand "A Volume of Shaper History" book from Fixer Gredin. You can either return the book to Milldrate or sell it to Go-To Jertrin in the Proving Grounds.

Topsider's Honor

Type: Exploration

Start: Topsider's Hilt in Caridin's Cross

Destination: Warrior's Grave in Dead Trenches

Task: Reunite the three topsider's items at the Warrior's Grave

Orzammar - Redcliffe

Basics ~ Character Generation ~ Classes ~ The Party ~ Companions ~ Supporting Cast ~ Equipment ~ Bestiary ~ Walkthroughs ~ **Side Quests** ~ Random Encounters ~ Achievements/Trophies

Quest Tips: Find Topsider's Hilt on the genlock emissary in south cave corridor of Caridin's Cross. Find the Topsider's Pommel in a vase in Ruck's cave. Examine the Warrior's Grave in the beginning of Ortan Thaig. Find the Topsider's Blade on an ancient darkspawn in southcentral Dead Trenches. Once you have all three items, return to the Warrior's Grave in Ortan Thaig and collect your reward.

Unintended Breakthrough

Type: Combat

Start: Side room in Royal Palace

Destination: Side room in Royal Palace

Task: Defeat the tunneling thieves

Quest Tips: When you first enter the area to the east in the Royal Palace, tunneling thieves will burrow up through the floor in the room with the brown cross on the floor. Defeat the tunneling thieves for some extra experience and thanks from the palace guards.

Zerlinda's Woe

Type: Messenger

Start: Dust Town

Destination: Tapster's Tavern

Task: Convince Zerlinda's father to take her back

Quest Tips: Speak with Zerlinda in Dust Town; she has been disowned for having a child with a casteless man. Seek out Zerlinda's father, Ordel, in Tapster's Tavern. If you tell Ordel that Zerlinda will die unless he takes her back, and you make a medium Persuade check, Ordel will agree to bring Zerlinda back into the family. If your Persuade score isn't high enough, you can tell Zerlinda to go to the surface where no one cares about castes, speak to Brother Burkel (if you've completed "The Chant in the Deeps" quest and set up a Chantry in Orzammar) and he will agree to take Zerlinda and her son in, or convince Zerlinda to leave the child in the Deep Roads with a medium Persuade check.

Party Camp

Restocking the Camp

Type: Collection

Start: Party camp emissaries

Destination: Various locations

Task: Trade in certain goods for experience at the party camp emissaries

Quest Tips: Each time you complete a major quest line, an emissary for that army will appear at party camp. For example, Emissary Pether appears in camp to represent the mages after you complete the "Broken Circle" quest line. You can trade in the following goods for experience points:

- Elven Emissary: Deathroot, deep mushrooms, elfroot, metal shards
- Werewolf Emissary: Nugs
- Dwarven Emissary: Amethyst, malachite, sapphires, topaz
- Arl Eamon's Emissary: 10 gold, 1 gold, 50 silver, 1 silver
- Mage Emissary: Novice runes, Journeyman runes, Expert runes, Master runes

Redcliffe

❖ NOTE ❖

See the "Arl of Redcliffe" walkthrough for detailed maps that will help with side quest locations.

The Dwarven Veteran

Type: Messenger

Start: Murdock in the village square

Destination: Dwyn's home in Redcliffe

Task: Persuade Dwyn to fight with the Redcliffe militia

Quest Tips: Dwyn, an experienced warrior, refuses to help defend the village. After speaking with Murdock, head to Dwyn's home in the village. Gain entrance by picking his lock or simply breaking the door down. Once you talk to Dwyn, convince him to help by using persuasion, intimidation, or a bribe. If you do not convince Dwyn to help before the battle starts, Dwyn will not participate. If you kill Dwyn and tell Murdock, the militia's morale will suffer.

primagames.com

Every Little Bit Helps

Type: Exploration

Start: Redcliffe General Store

Destination: Ser Perth

Task: Click on oil barrels and talk to Ser Perth

Quest Tips: Add fire to the village defenses with another defensive weapon. Go to the general store, click on the oil barrels there, then talk to Ser Perth and he'll agree to set up a flame trap for the undead on the upper-level path.

Lost in the Castle

Type: Exploration

Start: Owen in the Smithy

Destination: Valena in Redcliffe Castle

Task: Rescue Valena from the creatures in the castle

Quest Tips: To get Owen to aid the militia, you promise to look for his daughter lost in Redcliffe Castle. After "A Village Under Siege" is completed, enter the castle and look for Valena in a small storage room on the main floor (see the "Arl of Redcliffe" walkthrough maps for her exact location). Return to Owen for a reward. If Valena is not found before "The Possessed Child" is completed, Valena is lost forever. Even if you don't recover Valena, you can speak with Owen to receive a reward for your efforts. If you tell Owen the truth, he will kill himself. If you lie, he will not.

The Maker's Shield

Type: Messenger

Start: Ser Perth

Destination: Mother Hannah in the Chantry

Task: Speak with Mother Hannah to receive holy amulets for the militia

Quest Tips: Ser Perth wants Mother Hannah to provide holy protection for the coming battle. Even though Hannah insists no such thing exists, you can use your Persuade or Intimidate skill to convince her to provide the amulets. Return to Ser Perth with the amulets and his knights get a morale boost. If you do not convince Hannah to provide the amulets or do not inform Ser Perth that the amulets are available before the battle starts, the knights will fight without the amulets.

A Missing Child

Type: Exploration

Start: Redcliffe Chantry

Destination: Kaitlyn's House

Task: Find Kaitlyn's brother Bevin

Quest Tips: Speak with Kaitlyn in the Redcliffe Chantry and she gives you the "A Missing Child" side quest to find her brother Bevin. Find the boy hiding in the dresser at Kaitlyn's home. You can persuade/intimidate Bevin into giving you the key to a locked chest on the house's second floor that contains the magic family sword: The Green Blade. There is also a book in the house for another codex entry: The Legend of Calenhad: Chapter 1.

Spy!

Type: Exploration

Start: Bella or Lloyd in the tavern

Destination: Berwick in the tavern

Task: Reveal Berwick as a spy for Loghain

Quest Tips: Berwick, an elf in the tavern, is a spy sent by Loghain to keep an eye on Redcliffe Castle. Before you confront him, talk to Bella or Lloyd to learn Berwick's name. Knowing Berwick's name makes it easier to convince Berwick to reveal himself. You can also steal a letter from Berwick. Confronting Berwick with this evidence convinces him to reveal himself. After you've done one of those two things, speak with Berwick and uncover him as a spy. Berwick will initially deflect your questions, but there are several ways to break past his defenses:

- Calling Berwick by his name.
- Asking about the letter you pickpocketed.
- Having Zevran in your party.
- Having Leliana in your party.

Don't allow Berwick to leave for "the Chantry" or he will be gone permanently. Instead, you can tell him to defend the village or attack and kill him.

Stiff Drink to Dull the Pain

Type: Messenger

Start: Militia in the tavern

Destination: Lloyd in the tavern

Task: Convince Lloyd to give out free drinks

Quest Tips: The bartender, Lloyd, has been charging the militia for ale. They believe they should drink for free. You can convince Lloyd to give out free drinks through your Persuade skill or Intimidate skill, or by paying for the drinks yourself. If Lloyd is killed or sent outside to fight, Bella will give the militia free ale. After the big battle, if you return to Lloyd, he will give you an item for helping out the town.

Redcliffe - Wide Open World

Basics ~ Character Generation ~ Classes ~ The Party ~ Companions ~ Supporting Cast ~ Equipment ~ Bestiary ~ Walkthroughs ~ **Side Quests** ~ Random Encounters ~ Achievements/Trophies

Warden's Keep (DLC Only)

Ancient History

Type: Exploration

Start: Soldier's Peak

Destination: Warden's Keep

Task: Find four codex entries

Quest Tips: Collect any of the four codex entries around the Warden's Keep area. They are found at the statue, codex book,

raspberry jam, and corpse (see the "Warden's Keep" walkthrough maps for exact locations). Once you have all four codex entries, examine Asturian's Portrait on the second floor of the keep. Recite the Grey Warden oath and reveal a secret chest labeled Asturian's Stash. The chest contains the sword Asturian's Might and the Shadow Belt.

Wide Open World

The Black Vials

Type: Combat

Start: Find a glass phylactery associated with the quest

Destination: Civil War location marked on world map

Task: Find six secret locations and defeat a revenant at each location

Quest Tips: Find the black vials located in the following six locations and slay the revenants guarding them:

- Circle Tower (Senior Mage Quarters, statue room)
- Denerim (Back Alley)
- Orzammar Palace (back room)
- Deep Roads (Caridin's Cross near exit)
- Brecilian Ruins (Lower Ruins, small southeast room)
- Brecilian Ruins (Lair of the Werewolf, northwest werewolf bedroom)

Dominance

Type: Exploration

Start: Any of the 10 locations

Destination: Various places

Task: Take control of Dog and mark 10 landmarks

Quest Tips: While in control of Dog, click on the following 12 locations:

- King's Camp in Ostagar (Landmark Woodpile)
- Lothering (Landmark Tree northeast of Lothering)
- Dalish Camp (Landmark Tent—Zathrian's)

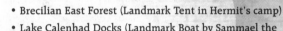

- Brecilian West Forest (Landmark Tree beside Grand Oak)
- Brecilian East Forest (Landmark Tent in Hermit's camp)
- Lake Calenhad Docks (Landmark Boat by Sammael the Destroyer)
- Redcliffe Village (Landmark Tree beside windmill)
- Redcliffe Castle Courtyard (Landmark Tree in castle courtyard)
- Denerim Alienage (Landmark Tree in center)
- Denerim Market District (Landmark Wagon)

Once you mark a location, Dog receives a buff whenever he's in the area that's been marked, making him more effective in combat.

Unbound

Type: Combat

Start: Find an adventurer's corpse associated with the quest

Destination: Four various locations

Task: Find three adventurers and then confront Gaxkang in Denerim

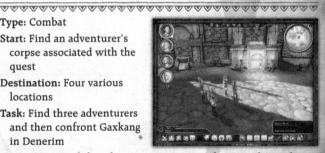

Quest Tips: Find the adventurer's corpse in the Ruined Temple on the "Urn of Sacred Ashes" quest (southwest corridor). Find the adventurer's corpse in the Brecilian Ruins' Lower Ruins (south fire trap room). In Orzammar, head to Tapster's Tavern and speak to the adventurer within. Travel back to Denerim and head to the Dirty Back Alley. Open the house door on your left and kill Gaxkang for your reward, one of the best one-hand sword/shield combos in the game.

primagames.com

Random Encounters

Bandits love your gold, and hurlocks won't pass up a chance to disrupt your stroll through the countryside. Welcome to the wide open world that is Ferelden, full of fantastic locales from the Frostback Mountains to the marshes around Flemeth's Hut, and all the random encounters in between. Except in *Dragon Age: Online*, even the "random" encounters have a story.

Random encounters are divided into three main categories: world encounters, plot encounters, and random encounters. World encounters appear as actual map locations when a certain set of circumstances happen. Plot encounters trigger when circumstances around companions occur. Random encounters play out exactly as they sound: they spring on you randomly as you travel from main location to main location.

Each time you leave a location and journey across the world map, you run the risk of a random encounter. It's the wilds of Ferelden, after all. Most long journeys will trigger an encounter, though you can only run into a single random

encounter on the same trip. Certain storyline-driven encounters occur at set points during your adventure, and you will only see them once. Other, more common, encounters may happen more than once, though it's rare to run into repeats unless you spend more time on the road than a gold-lusting trader.

NOTE

When you head to your party camp, you will almost never trigger a random encounter. However, when you leave your party camp, you may very well find yourself walking into another ambush.

Most encounters involve enemy numbers much greater than your party's size. Don't forget your standard battle tactics: warrior tanking the toughest foes, rogue dishing out damage wisely, mage lending AoE damage or timely healing. Use the terrain to your advantage. Cover can shield you from ranged fire, and obstacles such as fences and rocks can minimize flanking attempts. In the encounters where it's not a pure hack-and-slash battle royale, think about consequences of your actions and what appeals most to your style of play and character's personality.

Remember, the Blight doesn't just seep up from the Deep Roads or engulf Lothering; it's everywhere. Always prepare for a fight on the road, and your party will live to see their veteran days.

World Encounters

When these areas become accessible they can be found on the world map. Look for signs of civil war, darkspawn feeding, and refugees fleeing the carnage of their homelands.

Brothers and Sons

Trigger: Chanter's Board

Map: Battlefield

Description: You come upon the remains of a battlefield.

Actions: Before looting the bodies on a battlefield you have to battle wolves scavenging the corpses. A bear arrives later.

Caravan Down

Trigger: Chanter's Board

Map: Forest Meadow

Description: Coming around the bend, you can see darkspawn looking over their recent kills. It's not until you approach that they notice you and attack.

Actions: Defeat the darkspawn. Bodies to loot at the end.

Desperate Haven

Trigger: Accept the quest from the Chanter's Board in the Denerim Market District.

Map: Abandoned Meadow

Description: You arrive just in time to see some refugees about to be assaulted by a sizable darkspawn force. You must protect the refugees from the darkspawn.

Actions: Saving all or some of the refugees just nets you their thanks.

Jowan's Intention

Trigger: Chanter's Board

Map: Hillside Path

Description: A short reunion with Jowan is interrupted by an attack from Blight-ridden beasts.

Actions: Jowan is trying to protect some refugees; you can work with him to save the innocents. When talking to Jowan, you can choose to put him to death for his crimes; however, the refugees with him won't understand and you will have to beat Jowan and the refugees. Alternately, you don't have to save Jowan or the refugees. The beasts will be fixated on Jowan and the refugees. Let them finish each other off and pick off any remaining beasts.

Loghain's Push

Trigger: Accept the quest from the Chanter's Board in the Denerim Market District.

Map: Forest Outcropping

Description: Loghain's troops are fighting the Bannorn. It's your job to help the Bannorn and kill Loghain's troops.

Actions: Defeat all of Loghain's troops to save the Bannorn troops and complete the quest. You can watch the two sides kill each other completely off as well. The quest is still completed in either case.

Plot Encounters

Plot encounters are triggered by a certain set of circumstances, and always take precedence over other kinds of random encounters.

Darkspawn Ambush!

Trigger: Player has to become warm with Wynne, make sure she is in your party, and talk to Wynne about abominations. One of the next major random encounters should be this one.

Map: Hillside Path

Description: It starts out as a very typical darkspawn encounter, but it ends with Wynne collapsing and showing something else is wrong.

Actions: Fight and defeat the darkspawn. On the way out of the area (to the north) Wynne will stumble and collapse. She says it's nothing and she'll talk about it later. To follow up with her, talk to her again at the camp, and push the topic.

The Dog

Trigger: If the player is not a Human Noble and saved the Mabari Hound in Ostagar, this occurs as a random encounter just prior to Lothering.

Map: Plains/Highway Road

Description: If the player has not obtained Dog as a companion from the Human Noble origin and has cured Dog in Ostagar, the party will encounter Dog being chased by darkspawn on the way to Lothering.

Actions: Simply fight the darkspawn and rescue Dog. If you would like to invite Dog to accompany you, you can do so in the conversation with him after the fight. This is the only opportunity to get Dog in your party if you are not a Human Noble.

Harassed from the Past

Trigger: This is part of Leliana's personal quest. After she talks about Marjolaine, the next major random encounter should be this one as long as Leliana is in the party.

Map: Forest Stream

Description: After discussing Marjolaine, the player is ambushed by assassins.

Actions: Defeat the assassins. The leader will surrender and give you the next lead to search for Marjolaine in Denerim. You have the option to kill him. Aside from Leliana being displeased with you, ending his life won't do anything else.

The Long Road

Trigger: This occurs as a random encounter shortly after Lothering and should happen within the first few trips.

Map: Plains/Highway Road

Description: Caught in an ambush, the player turns the tables and gets the unique chance to have one of the assassins join his cause.

Actions: You meet a traveler on the road who says she was attacked by bandits. She'll ask you to follow her and run off. When you catch up, it becomes clear it was a setup. Kill all the bandits, and you'll find one survivor: their leader, Zevran. You can let him join you as a companion or leave him to die.

Low Road

Trigger: Have the "Darkspawn Ambush!" encounter as above and talk to Wynne back at camp about the ordeal. She will tell you she died in the tower and was revived and now sustained by a good spirit from the Fade that she believes to be a spirit of faith. The next major encounter should be this one.

Map: Plains/Highway Road

Description: In a planned darkspawn ambush, the party is defeated, only to have Wynne revive and bring them back from the brink of death. She discovers the spirit within herself.

Actions: While Wynne is enveloped by the spirit she will be a much more powerful spellcaster. Use her magic against the superior darkspawn numbers. The darkspawn omega is the greatest threat on top of the cliff. Once this is over, she will have unlocked her ability to summon the spirit of faith. Use it as any other talent.

Random Encounters

Most of your traveling encounters will be random from this list. Prepare to battle through more enemies. A few encounters will test your wits, and one will test your pocketbook.

Axe in the Stump

Trigger: Insanely low chance of triggering.

Map: Strange Wood

Description: An old axe is lodged in a stump. Peasants are convinced that whoever pulls it out will be in line to be the next ruler of Ferelden.

Actions: There is no combat in this encounter. Simply pull the axe from the stump. It may not make you the next ruler of Ferelden, but at least you'll get a nice axe from the deal.

Bandits

Trigger: Low chance during travels to any forest location.

Map: River Crossing

Description: Party is caught in a bandit ambush by a stream.

Actions: Defeat the bandits.

Demons

Trigger: After the mage tower has fallen, during a plains visit.

Map: Steep Path

Description: A little off the beaten path where the Veil has thinned since the fall of the mages' tower, a group of fire demons are being created from living fire.

Actions: Defeat the flaming demons.

Demons 2

Trigger: After the "Broken Circle," and only if the tower has fallen.

Map: Lakeside Road

Description: After the tower has fallen, the templars are still cleaning up the remnants. Now they're over their heads in demons, and you must help them.

Actions: Defeat all the demons. Rescue as many templars as possible.

Dwarven Army

Trigger: After "Paragon" plot is completed.

Map: Winding Road

Description: A group of dwarves from Orzammar fight the darkspawn.

Actions: Defeat the darkspawn and save the dwarves.

Elven Army

Trigger: After "Nature of the Beast." You must have allied with the elves.

Map: Rocky Road

Description: Group of elves from your army fight the darkspawn.

Actions: Defeat the darkspawn and save the elves.

Elves and Werewolves

Trigger: After completing "Nature of the Beast" if you did not free the elves from the curse. Small chance traveling to forest locations.

Map: Forest Path

Description: The elves and werewolves are fighting each other. Help your ally.

Actions: Help the side you allied with.

Mages

Trigger: After the "Broken Circle," assuming you saved the mages.

Map: Roadside

Description: A group of mages is beset by darkspawn.

Actions: Protect the mages and kill the darkspawn.

One Ring

Trigger: Very small chance at any time while traveling to a forest location.

Map: Treacherous Path

Description: Get ambushed by some shades, including a greater shade, after seeing a pair of elves.

Actions: Defeat the shades and claim the treasure, including the ring on the bodies.

Orzammar Rebels

Trigger: Finish "Paragon."

Map: Forest Incline

Description: Dwarven rebels from the opposing faction track you down and lay an ambush.

Actions: The dwarven clan that didn't get the throne will ambush your party. Defe them.

Redcliffe Army

Trigger: After Arl Eamon awakens.

Map: Roadside Field

Description: Soldiers from Redcliffe fight unit of darkspawn.

Actions: Defeat the darkspawn and rescu the soliders.

Spiders

Trigger: Chance any time while traveling a forest location.

Map: Dark Forest

Description: Combat in a spider-infested forest.

Actions: Through this snake-like forest, spiders will drop from the trees to atta Defeat them all. Then defeat the spide queen. Watch out for the web traps.

Stealing Payback

Trigger: If you pickpocketed or stole fro the Dalish elves, this will trigger trave to some forest location afterward.

Map: Wooded Hills

Description: An elf hunter named Melo will track you down if you've stolen f the Dalish elves.

Actions: Defeat Melora and her hunters

Random Encounters

Basics ~ Character Generation ~ Classes ~ The Party ~ Companions ~ Supporting Cast ~ Equipment ~ Bestiary ~ Walkthroughs ~ Side Quests ~ **Random Encounters** ~ Achievements/Trophies

Super Metal (DLC Only)

Trigger: Very small chance of occurring during travels to the plains locations.

Map: The Crater

Description: Encounter a couple who visited a recent meteor crash site. They leave, but some ore is left behind.

Actions: Watch the cutscene, go into the crater. You can get a hunk of "star metal" in this random encounter, and if you bring that to a blacksmith named Mikhael in the Grey Warden base at Soldier's Peak (downloadable content), he'll craft it into a weapon for you. Mikhael shows up only once you've completed that plot (made the fortress secure). The choice of weapon is: Starfang (Longsword, dexterity +3, damage +3, armor penetration +5) or Starfang (Greatsword, strength +3, armor penetration +5, attack +8).

Surprising the Bandits

Trigger: Traveling to a forest location, small chance.

Map: Twisted Path

Description: You get to ambush bandits this time around if you like.

Actions: Choose to either attack the bandits, or try to sneak past them. If you wait, you will be discovered and have to fight them anyway. To sneak past them, back up from your listening point, turn left and follow the path down. Skirt the outside of the camp and you can avoid them entirely.

Templars

Trigger: After stealing (pickpocketing) in the "Broken Circle" tower, and finishing the "Broken Circle" plot.

Map: Narrow Road

Description: You've been caught stealing from the templars. Either pay up or face justice.

Actions: The templars stop you on the road and accuse you of stealing. They charge you a fee based on your character's level, in compensation. If you pay, they will leave. If you don't pay, you will have a rather difficult fight.

Traveling Merchant

Trigger: Low chance of happening any time while traveling to a non-forest location.

Map: Gentle Path

Description: There is no battle here, only a merchant selling his wares.

Actions: This encounter is repeatable. The merchant here sells various odds and ends, and he will pop up now and then. You can buy some gifts for the companions here. You may want to wait on weapons and armor: if you come back later they will be more powerful, but if you bought the items earlier, he will be out of stock.

Twisted Beasts

Trigger: Medium chance at any time when traveling to plains locations.

Map: The Low Road

Description: Blighted creatures attack the party.

Actions: Defeat the Blighted creatures.

Werewolf Army

Trigger: After "Nature of the Beast," assuming the elves' curse wasn't lifted. You must have allied with the werewolves.

Map: Wooded Highway

Description: The werewolves fight darkspawn on the road. They need your help.

Actions: Defeat the darkspawn and save the werewolves.

Werewolves

Trigger: After "Nature of the Beast" is completed and if the curse wasn't lifted from the elves. Traveling to a forest region.

Map: Forest Clearing

Description: A group of werewolves ambush the player.

Actions: A group of werewolves surround and ambush the party.

Wild Sylvans

Trigger: After "Nature of the Beast," traveling to any forest location.

Map: Twisted Forest

Description: Attacked by the forest itself.

Actions: The sylvans surround the party from all sides. Defeat them.

Wolves

Trigger: Medium chance at any time.

Map: Desolate Highway

Description: Attacked by a group of wolves on the highway.

Actions: Defeat the wolves. Try to avoid the traps.

Achievements and Trophies

There are so many accomplishments in *Dragon Age: Origins* that it will take you several game lifetimes to achieve them all. You could max out the perfect warrior at level 20 and still not be anywhere close to fulfilling all the Achievements; it will take several full game plays with all three classes to fill your Achievements tab with all those fabulous medallions. So where do you start and how do you know how much you've done?

Who doesn't have fun collecting all these titles? Sure, you've got your standard storyline ones—Hero of Redcliffe for completing "The Arl of Redcliffe" quest line or Annulment Invoker for siding with the templars in the "Broken Circle" quest line—but you also have Achievements for combat (inflict 250 damage in a single hit, yet?), romancing companions, crafting, mastering spell blocks, setting traps, using a tome, and even setting foot in every area of the game. Achievement difficulty ranges from the supremely difficult (Dragonslayer) to the relatively painless (Last of the Wardens). Of course, the aptly named Perfectionist is awarded to the player who really has explored the game thoroughly and discovered all possible endings.

The following charts show all the Achievements for both the PC and console versions. Each Achievement lists the requirements, as well as whether it's a secret or not. The console chart also gives you all the Gamerscore points for the Xbox 360® and Trophy awards for the PLAYSTATION®3. Combat Achievements lean toward the hack-and-slash player. Companions deal with romance and the final battle, while Origins reward you for completing the early introduction quests. Personal Achievements can be accomplished by your own actions, such as crafting items, disabling traps, hitting the level 20 cap, learning specializations and all of one spell/talent school, persuading and intimidating, and more. Finally, questing Achievements revolve around the storyline and its effect on your PC.

So, if you want your player profile looking more like a Trophy wall than a bare cupboard, get back into the game and kill your 1,000 darkspawn already.

PC Achievements

Title	Descripiton	Type	Secret?
A Dark Promise	Defeated the archdemon and, through a dark ritual with Morrigan, spared your own life	Companions	Secret
Accomplished Rogue	Main character learned all Rogue talents	Personal	No
Accomplished Warrior	Main character learned all Warrior talents	Personal	No
Annulment Invoker	Sided with the templars in "Broken Circle"	Questing	Secret
Archery Master	Main character learned all Archery talents	Personal	No
Archmage	Main character achieved level 20 as a mage	Personal	No
Battery	Killed 50 enemies using the Assault talent	Combat	No
Bhelen's Ally	Sided with Bhelen in "A Paragon of Her Kind"	Questing	Secret
Blackstone Auxillary	Completed a job-board quest for the Blackstone Irregulars	Questing	No
Blight Queller	Killed 1,000 darkspawn	Combat	No
Bloodied	Completed an origin story without the main character ever falling in battle	Origin	No
Bully	Succeeded at 5 difficult Intimidate attempts	Personal	No
Casteless	Completed the Dwarf Commoner origin story	Origin	Secret
Ceremonialist	Defied the Cult of Andraste in "The Urn of Sacred Ashes"	Questing	Secret
Clever	Set a trap or inscribed a glyph	Personal	No
Conjurer	Main character learned all Creation spells	Personal	No
Conscripted	Completed the City Elf origin story	Origin	Secret
Corrupted	Completed the Dalish Elf origin story	Origin	Secret
Crafty	Crafted 25 items	Personal	No
Crusher	Killed 50 enemies using the Mighty Blow talent	Combat	No
Defender	Preserved the lives of half the troops at Denerim's Gates in "The Final Battle"	Questing	Secret
Diabolist	Took advantage of Avernus's research	Downloadable Content	Secret
Dragonslayer	Defeated the dragon guarding the Urn of Sacred Ashes	Combat	Secret
Dual Weaponry Master	Main character learned all Dual Weapon talents	Personal	No
Easily Sidetracked	Completed 75% of all side-quests	Questing	No
Easy Lover	Experienced the thrill of romance with Zevran	Companions	Secret
Educated	Used a tome to improve the main character's attributes, talents, spells, or skills	Personal	No
Elementalist	Main character learned all Primal spells	Personal	No
Elite	Main character learned two specializations	Personal	No
First Knight	Experienced the thrill of romance with Alistair	Companions	Secret
Grey Warden	Killed 100 darkspawn	Combat	No

PC Achievements

Basics ~ Character Generation ~ Classes ~ The Party ~ Companions ~ Supporting Cast ~ Equipment ~ Bestiary ~ Walkthroughs ~ Side Quests ~ Random Encounters ~ **Achievements/Trophies**

Title	Descripiton	Type	Secret?
Harrowed	Completed the Magi origin story	Origin	Secret
Harrowmont's Ally	Sided with Harrowmont in "A Paragon of Her Kind"	Questing	Secret
Heavy Hitter	Main character inflicted 250 damage with a single hit	Combat	No
Hero of Redcliffe	Completed "The Arl of Redcliffe"	Questing	Secret
Hexer	Main character learned all Entropy spells	Personal	No
Hopelessly Romantic	Across all playthroughs, experienced all possible romances	Companions	No
I'm Kind of a Big Deal	Completed the entire game without the main character ever falling in battle	Questing	Secret
Indestructible	Completed "The Landsmeet" without the main character ever falling in battle	Questing	Secret
Insidious	Set 25 traps or glyphs	Personal	No
Kinslayer	Completed the Dwarf Noble origin story	Origin	Secret
Last of the Wardens	Completed Ostagar	Origin	Secret
Last of Your Line	Completed the Human Noble origin story	Origin	Secret
Liberator	Destroyed the Anvil of the Void	Questing	Secret
Lightning Reflexes	Disabled 25 traps	Personal	No
Lockpicker	Picked the lock on a chest or door	Personal	No
Magic Sympathizer	Sided with the mages in "Broken Circle"	Questing	Secret
Master Lockpicker	Picked the locks on 50 chests or doors	Personal	No
Master of Arms	Main character achieved level 20 as a warrior	Personal	No
Master of the Peak	Completed Soldier's Peak	Downloadable Content	No
Master Warden	Killed 500 darkspawn	Combat	No
Menacing	Succeeded at 10 difficult Intimidate attempts	Personal	No
Mercenary	Complete 15 job-board quests	Questing	No
Nimble	Disabled a trap	Personal	No
Perfectionist	Discovered all possible endings (Sacrifice Yourself, Sacrifice Alistair, Sacrifice Loghain, and Morrigan's Ritual)	Questing	No
Persuasive	Succeeded at 5 difficult Persuasion attempts	Personal	No
Pickpocket	Successfully picked someone's pocket	Personal	No
Pilgrim	Completed a Chanter's Board quest	Questing	No
Poacher	Sided with the elves in "Nature of the Beast"	Questing	Secret
Pragmatist	Preserved the Anvil of the Void	Questing	Secret
Rabble-Rouser	Completed "The Landsmeet"	Questing	Secret
Recruiter	Across all playthroughs, recruited all party members	Companions	No
Redeemer	Allowed Loghain to make a great sacrifice in defense of Ferelden	Companions	Secret
Resilient	Completed Ostagar without the main character ever falling in battle	Origin	Secret
Rock and a Hard Place	Completed "A Golem in Honnleath"	Downloadable Content	No
Sacrilegious	Sided with the Cult of Andraste in "The Urn of Sacred Ashes"	Questing	Secret
Shadow	Main character achieved level 20 as a rogue	Personal	No
Sharpshooter	Killed 50 enemies using the Arrow of Slaying talent	Combat	No
Shield Master	Main character learned all Weapon and Shield talents	Personal	No
Silver Tongued	Succeeded at 25 difficult Persuasion attempts	Personal	No
Slayer	Sided with the werewolves in "Nature of the Beast"	Questing	Secret
Standard-Bearer	Used the Grey Warden treaties to recruit all possible allies	Questing	Secret
Stone's Lament	Completed "A Golem's Memories"	Downloadable Content	Secret
Streetwise	Completed a job-board quest for the elusive "K," "D," or "R"	Questing	No
Tactician	Main character killed 250 enemies without them inflicting damage	Combat	No
Thaumaturgist	Main character learned all Spirit spells	Personal	No
The Collective Friend	Completed a job-board quest for the Mages' Collective	Questing	No
The Punisher	Killed 50 enemies using the Punisher talent	Combat	No
The Ultimate Sacrifice	Made the ultimate sacrifice in defense of Ferelden	Personal	Secret
Tinkerer	Crafted an item	Personal	No
Traveler	Set foot in every area in the game	Questing	No
Two-Handed Weapon Master	Main character learned all Two-Handed talents	Personal	No
Veteran	Main character learned a specialization	Personal	No
Warden-Commander	Commanded Alistair to make a great sacrifice in defense of Ferelden	Companions	Secret
Whirling Dervish	Killed 50 enemies using the Whirlwind talent	Combat	No
Wine, Woman, and Song	Experienced the thrill of romance with Leliana	Companions	Secret
Witch Gone Wild	Experienced the thrill of romance with Morrigan	Companions	Secret

Console Achievements

Title	Method of Achievement	Xbox Gamerscore Points Awarded	PS3 Trophy Awarded	Secret?
A Dark Promise	Defeated the archdemon and, through a dark ritual with Morrigan, spared your own life	50	Gold	Secret
Annulment Invoker	Sided with the templars in "Broken Circle"	20	Bronze	Secret
Archmage	Main character achieved level 20 as a mage	25	Silver	No
Bhelen's Ally	Sided with Bhelen in "A Paragon of Her Kind"	20	Bronze	Secret
Blight Queller	Killed 1,000 darkspawn (multiple playthroughs possible)	25	Gold	No
Bloodied	Completed an origin story without the main character ever falling in battle	10	Bronze	No
Bully	Succeeded at five difficult Intimidate attempts	10	Bronze	No
Casteless	Completed the Dwarf Commoner origin story	10	Bronze	Secret
Ceremonialist	Defied the Cult of Andraste in "The Urn of Sacred Ashes"	20	Bronze	Secret
Conscripted	Completed the City Elf origin story	10	Bronze	Secret
Corrupted	Completed the Dalish Elf origin story	10	Bronze	Secret
Defender	Preserved the lives of half the troops at Denerim's Gates in "The Final Battle"	20	Bronze	Secret
Diabolist	Took advantage of Avernus' research (DLC only)	25	Bronze	Secret
Dragonslayer	Defeated the dragon guarding the Urn of Sacred Ashes	30	Silver	Secret
Easy Lover	Experienced the thrill of romance with Zevran	10	Bronze	Secret
Educated	Used a tome to improve the main character's attributes, talents, spells, or skills	15	Bronze	No
Elite	Main character learned two specializations	30	Bronze	No
First Knight	Experienced the thrill of romance with Alistair	10	Bronze	Secret
Grey Warden	Killed 100 darkspawn (multiple playthroughs possible)	20	Bronze	No
Harrowed	Completed the Magi origin story	10	Bronze	Secret
Harrowmont's Ally	Sided with Harrowmont in "A Paragon of Her Kind"	20	Bronze	Secret
Heavy Hitter	Main character inflicted 250 damage with a single hit	10	Bronze	No
Hero of Redcliffe	Completed "The Arl of Redcliffe"	20	Bronze	Secret
Hopelessly Romantic	Across all playthroughs, experienced all possible romances	25	Bronze	No
Kinslayer	Completed the Dwarf Noble origin story	10	Bronze	Secret
Last of the Wardens	Completed Ostagar	20	Bronze	Secret
Last of Your Line	Completed the Human Noble origin story	10	Bronze	Secret
Liberator	Destroyed the Anvil of the Void	20	Bronze	Secret
Magic Sympathizer	Sided with the mages in "Broken Circle"	20	Bronze	Secret
Master of Arms	Main character achieved level 20 as a warrior	25	Silver	No
Master of the Peak	Completed Soldier's Peak (DLC only)	25	Bronze	No
Master Warden	Killed 500 darkspawn (multiple playthroughs possible)	25	Silver	No
Menacing	Succeeded at 10 difficult Intimidate attempts	20	Bronze	No
Mercenary	Complete 15 job-board quests	20	Bronze	No
Perfectionist	Discovered all possible endings (Sacrifice Yourself, Sacrifice Alistair, Sacrifice Loghain, and Morrigan's Ritual)	50	Bronze	No
Persuasive	Succeeded at five difficult Persuasion attempts	10	Bronze	No
Pilgrim	Completed a Chanter's Board quest	10	Bronze	No
Poacher	Sided with the elves in "Nature of the Beast"	20	Bronze	Secret
Pragmatist	Preserved the Anvil of the Void	20	Bronze	Secret
Rabble-Rouser	Completed "The Landsmeet"	20	Bronze	Secret
Recruiter	Across all playthroughs, recruited all party members	25	Bronze	No
Rock and a Hard Place	Completed "A Golem in Honnleath" (DLC only)	25	Bronze	No
Sacrilegious	Sided with the Cult of Andraste in "The Urn of Sacred Ashes"	20	Bronze	Secret
Shadow	Main character achieved level 20 as a rogue	25	Silver	No
Silver Tongued	Succeeded at 25 difficult Persuasion attempts	20	Bronze	No
Slayer	Sided with the werewolves in "Nature of the Beast"	20	Bronze	Secret
Standard-Bearer	Used the Grey Warden treaties to recruit all possible allies	20	Bronze	Secret
Stone's Lament	Completed "A Golem's Memories" (DLC only)	25	Bronze	Secret
The Ultimate Reward	Completed all Trophies (PS3 only)	—	Platinum	No
The Ultimate Sacrifice	Made the ultimate sacrifice in defense of Ferelden	50	Gold	Secret
Tinkerer	Crafted an item	10	Bronze	No
Traveler	Set foot in every area in the game	35	Bronze	No
Veteran	Main character learned a specialization	25	Bronze	No
Wine, Woman, and Song	Experienced the thrill of romance with Leliana	10	Bronze	Secret
Witch Gone Wild	Experienced the thrill of romance with Morrigan	10	Bronze	Secret